The World and Its Wonders

The World and Its Wonders

Peter Lafferty

STANDARD EDUCATIONAL CORPORATION

Copyright © 1996 Standard Educational Corporation
Chicago, Illinois, U.S.A

ISBN 0-87392-309-9
Library of Congress Catalog Card Number 96-68267

All rights reserved.

Printed and manufactured in
the United States of America.

Contents

Looking Into Space

The Sky at Night 11
The Sun and Its Family 15
Planet Earth and Its Moon 17
The Inner Planets 21
The Outer Planets 24
Space Debris 30
Life of a Star 34
How the Earth is Formed 44
The Violent Earth 49
Rocks and the Story They Tell 58
Shaping the Landscape 67
The Watery World 72

Weather Watching

Weather, Climate, and Seasons 78
Air on the Move 83

Water's Endless Cycle 92
Stormy Weather 101

Matter and Energy

Elements and Compounds 108

Forces and Energy 118

Heat and Cold 129

Electricity 137

Magnetism 146

Light 156

Sound 169

Glossary 178
Index 190

Looking Into Space

The Sky at Night

On a clear night, you can see around 2,500 stars in the sky. With binoculars or a small telescope, one can see many thousands more.

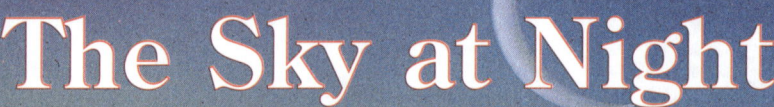

The Sky at Night

If you look at the sky on a clear night, you will see a beautiful sight: thousands of stars scattered across the blackness of space. Across the sky, you will see a broad band of stars called the Milky Way. These stars are relatively close to us. Like the sun, they belong to a group of stars called the Milky Way galaxy. A galaxy is a group of as many as 100,000 million stars collected together. If your eyes are sharp, you might be able to see other, more distant galaxies as indistinct blurs. You might also see a faint nebula, a distant cloud of glowing gas in the space between the stars. Perhaps you will see a "falling star," a flash of light streaking across the sky. Or perhaps you will spot a planet, a bright object that does not twinkle like a star.

The Milky Way is a band of stars that stretches across the night sky. The stars are part of our home galaxy, the Milky Way galaxy. This picture was taken with a camera that turns at the same slow speed as the stars appear to move in the night sky. An artificial satellite appears as a long, curving trail.

Looking Into Space

Gazing at the stars, you will see that groups of them seem to form patterns. These groups of stars are called constellations. The constellations sometimes look like people or animals. Long ago, the constellations were thought to be shaped like gods or great heroes. For instance, the constellation Orion, easily seen in the winter sky of the Northern Hemisphere, is named for a gigantic hunter of Greek mythology.

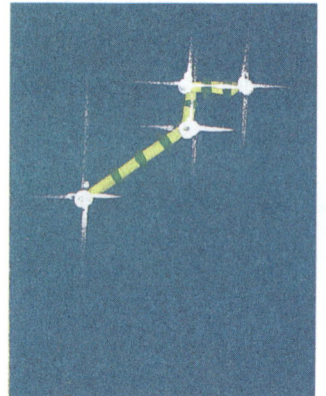

The Little Dog

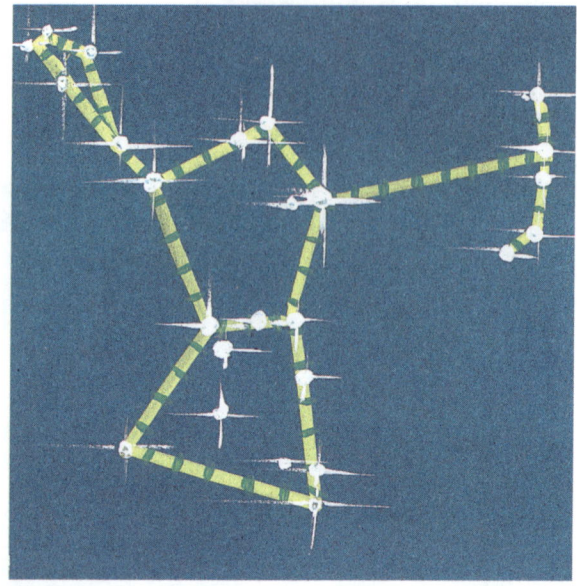

Orion

The Great Dog

Some well-known constellations. In the Northern Hemisphere, Orion can be seen in the south during winter. In the Southern Hemisphere, Orion can be seen in the north during summer.

The Sky at Night

In the Northern Hemisphere, the Big Dipper and the Little Dipper can be seen in the north throughout the year. The Big Dipper is part of a constellation called the Great Bear (Ursa Major). The Little Dipper is part of a constellation called the Little Bear (Ursa Minor).

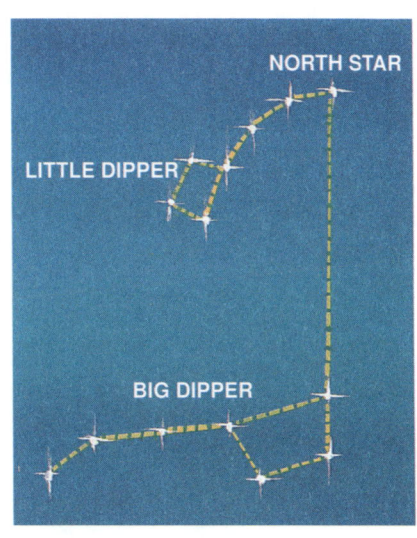

There are many stories and legends about the people and creatures outlined by the constellations. For example, Orion was said to be very proud of his hunting skills. He boasted that he could kill any creature on Earth. However, he forgot the tiny scorpion. One day the scorpion stung Orion and he died. The powerful god Jupiter placed him in the sky. The scorpion was also placed in the sky, as the constellation Scorpio. To make sure that Orion would not be stung again, the scorpion was placed on the opposite side of the sky, so that they are always a long way apart.

Of course, none of these stories are true. However, they make it easier to remember the names and shapes of the constellations, and they turn the night sky into a huge story book.

Left: From the top, Orion the mighty hunter; Leo the lion; and the Little Bear and Great Bear, which contain the group of stars making up the Little Dipper and the Big Dipper.

Looking Into Space

A good way to learn about stars is to learn to find the major constellations. These constellations can be signposts to find your way about the night sky. For instance, the two end stars of the Big Dipper point to the North Star (also called Polaris). The North Star is part of the Little Dipper. The constellation of Orion can also be used to locate nearby stars and constellations. For instance, the brightest star in the sky, Sirius, is in line with the three stars forming Orion's belt.

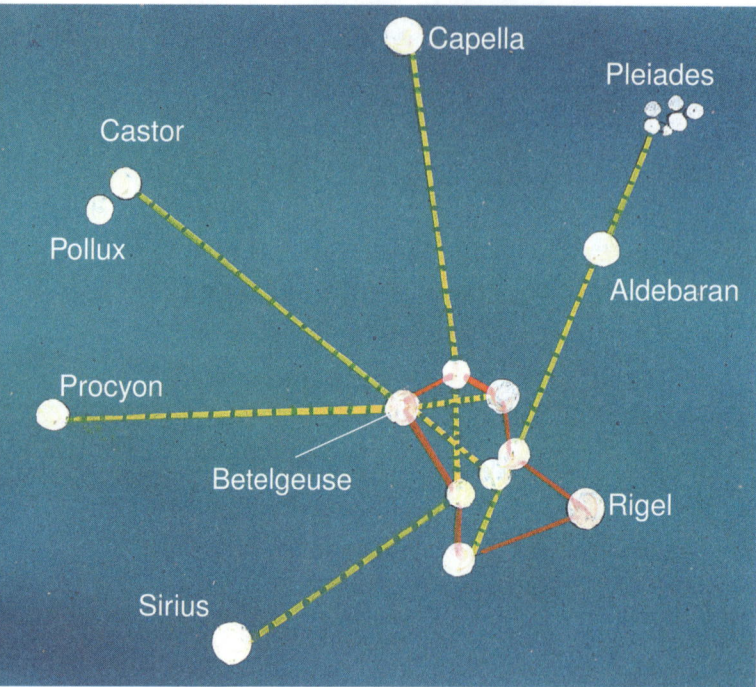

The constellation of Orion is a signpost in the sky. It can be used to locate many bright stars.

The stars are an enormous distance away from Earth. The closest star to the Earth is, of course, the sun. The next closest stars belong to a group called Alpha Centauri. The three stars of Alpha Centauri lie in the southern skies, near the constellation of Crux, or the Southern Cross. Alpha Centauri is 25,000,000,000,000 (25 million, million) miles (40,000,000,000,000 km) away.

Distances in space are so great that astronomers – scientists who study planets, stars, galaxies, and the other objects found in space – measure distances in special units called light-years.

A light-year is the distance a beam of light travels in one year – 5.9 million, million miles (9.46 million, million km). Alpha Centauri is 4.3 light-years from Earth. This means that light from Alpha Centauri takes 4.3 years to reach Earth.

14

The Sun and Its Family

The Sun and Its Family

The sun is a star, a very hot ball of gas that gives out light and heat. At the center of the sun, the temperature is 27 million degrees Fahrenheit (15 million degrees Celsius). The sun's great heat keeps it in constant turmoil. Giant flames called prominences shoot out from the sun's surface up to a distance of 310,000 miles (500,000 km), more than the distance from the Earth to the moon. Bright patches, called flares, erupt on the surface. The surface of the sun also contains dark, cooler patches called sunspots.

Nine planets and countless smaller bodies orbit the sun. These smaller bodies include asteroids, comets, and tiny pieces of rock. The family of objects orbiting the sun is called the Solar System. The Solar System is held together by the force of the sun's gravity, which attracts the planets, asteroids, and comets toward the sun.

The visible surface of the sun is called the photosphere. Above the photosphere is a layer of gas called the chromosphere. The corona is the sun's outer layer. The arrows represent heat, light, and radiation.

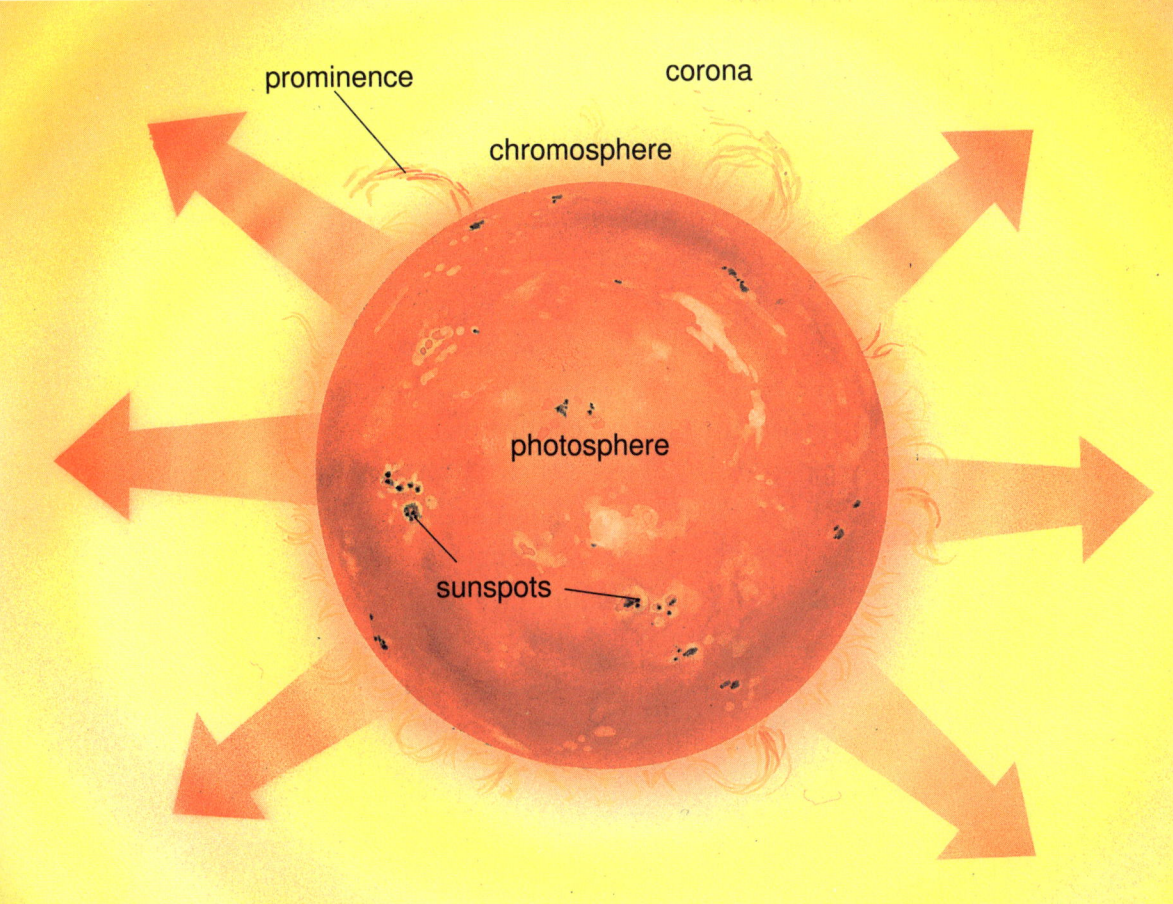

The planets vary in size from tiny Pluto to the giant Jupiter. Saturn has several beautiful rings around it. This diagram does not show the distances between the planets to scale.

The sun is very large. It would take 109 of our Earths in a row to extend across the diameter of the sun. It would take 1,300,000 globes the size of the Earth to fill the globe of the sun. It is the great distance from us that makes the sun look as small as it does. It is 93 million miles (149 million km) from Earth. The black dot shows the size of Earth compared to the sun.

The planets move around the sun in slightly oval orbits. The speed of the planets and other bodies as they race along their orbits keeps them from being pulled into the sun. In order out from the sun, the planets are Mercury, Venus, Earth, Mars, Jupiter, Saturn, Uranus, Neptune, and Pluto. All the planets move around the sun in the same direction and in almost the same plane (their orbits lie on a level with one another). Between the orbits of Mars and Jupiter, there are many millions of small rocky bodies called asteroids.

It is difficult to grasp the size of the Solar System. If we made a scale model of the Solar System with the sun the size of a beach ball 3 feet (90 cm) across, then the innermost planet, Mercury, would be the size of a peppercorn, 120 feet (37 m) away. Venus would be the size of a pea, 231 feet (70 m) away. The Earth would be the size of a pea, 321 feet (98 m) away. Mars would be the size of a peppercorn, 488 feet (149 m) away. Jupiter would be the size of an apple, 1,666 feet (508 m) away. Saturn would be the size of a tangerine, 3,060 feet (933 m) away. Uranus would be the size of a Ping-Pong ball, 1.1 miles (1.8 km) away. Neptune would also be the size of a Ping-Pong ball, 1.8 miles (2.9 km) away. Finally, Pluto would be the size of a pinhead, 2.4 miles (3.8 km) away.

Planet Earth and Its Moon

Did you know that even while sitting quietly in a chair, you are traveling at high speed? This is because the Earth and everything on it moves 18 miles (30 km) every second in its orbit around the sun. It takes the Earth 365.25 days, or one year, to complete an orbit around the sun. The distance traveled by the Earth during a single orbit of the sun is 584 million miles (940 million km). On average, the Earth is 93 million miles (149 million km) from the sun during its journey. Viewed from the moon, the Earth is seen to be a tiny blue planet against the blackness of space. It is the spaceship in which we travel around the sun.

The Earth's axis is tipped to one side relative to the line of its orbit. This means that when the earth's north pole is tipped toward the sun, the south pole is tipped away from the sun.

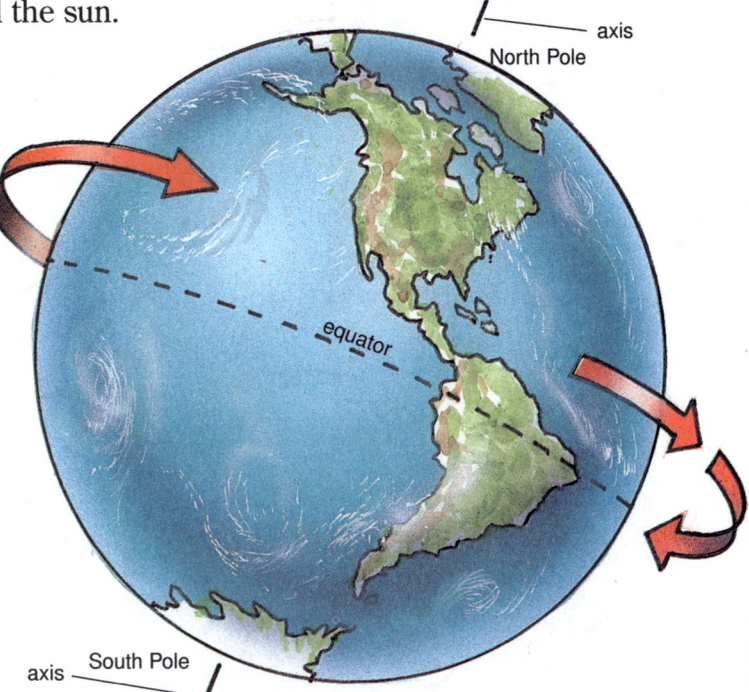

While the Earth is moving around the sun, it is also spinning from west to east. It spins once in just under 24 hours. The axis, or imaginary line around which the Earth spins, runs through the North and South Poles. When we are on the side of the Earth facing the sun, it is daytime. When we are on the side of the Earth facing away from the sun, it is night time.

The Earth has a neighbor in space – the moon. The moon circles the Earth, taking just over 27 days for a round trip. It is much closer to the Earth than any other heavenly body. The moon is about 234,000 miles (376,000 km) from the Earth. This is the distance you

Looking Into Space

would travel if you went around the world ten times, but is small compared to the distances between the planets and the sun. The sun is about 400 times as far from the Earth.

The moon is a dead and lifeless place, with no water or atmosphere. Its surface is covered with craters. A crater is a hole with a ridge around it. Some craters are over 90 miles (144 km) across. With a powerful telescope, about 500,000 craters can be seen on the face of the moon that is turned toward the Earth. It is thought that the craters were caused by objects that collided with the moon long ago. Because the moon has no atmosphere, it is very hot during the day and very cold during the night. The temperature reaches 220°F (105°C) at midday and falls to −240°F (−151°C) during the night.

The diameter of the moon is only 2,160 miles (3,475 km), about one quarter that of the Earth, but it would take about 50 moons to fill a globe the size of the Earth. The force of gravity on the moon's surface is only one sixth of gravity on the Earth, so a person weighing 180 lb (81.6 kg) on Earth would only weigh 30 lb (13.6 kg) on the moon.

The moon is much smaller than the Earth. Here it is drawn on the same scale as the United States.

Like the Earth, the moon is spinning as it travels around the Earth. The moon makes just one turn on its axis during the time that it takes to go around the Earth. Therefore, it always keeps the same side toward the Earth, and from Earth we always see the same side of the moon.

Planet Earth and Its Moon

As the moon circles around the Earth each month, its appearance changes through a regular cycle of shapes called phases. These phases occur because different parts of the moon are lit by the sun at different times. When only the edge of the moon is lit, it appears to have a crescent shape. When all the moon is lit, it appears as a round full moon.

Once in a while, for a few minutes, the moon comes exactly between us and the sun so that it blots out our view of the sun. When this happens, a part of the Earth gets as dark as it does on a cloudy day. This chain of events is called an eclipse of the sun.

A total eclipse of the sun. During a total eclipse, scientists are able to study the outer layer of the sun, the corona.

Sometimes, on a night when we would normally see a full moon, the moon gets on the opposite side of the Earth from the sun so that the Earth blocks the sun's rays to the moon. That is, the moon gets in the Earth's shadow. We call this an eclipse of the moon and it may last for several hours.

The phases of the moon. Seen from Earth, the moon's appearance changes throughout each month as different areas of the surface are lit by sunlight.

Looking Into Space

On July 20, 1969, Neil Armstrong, an American astronaut, became the first human to set foot on the moon. As he stepped from his space vehicle, he said: "That's one small step for a man, one giant leap for mankind." In all, twelve astronauts visited the moon during the Apollo project of the late 1960s and early 1970s. They collected samples of moon rock and did many experiments. They also placed instruments on the moon that sent information back to Earth about conditions there.

One of the lunar surface samples collected on the Apollo 12 mission. It is a fine-grained rock with needles of the mineral feldspar.

Scientists know more about the moon than any other heavenly body because astronauts have traveled to the moon and explored it.

The Inner Planets

Mercury is a small planet, just a little larger than our moon. It is also the planet nearest to the sun. Being the nearest, Mercury has the shortest journey around the sun; also its speed is greatest. And, of course, it is the hottest – at least, it has the hottest day. During the day, the temperature can reach 800°F (427°C). At night the temperature can drop to –260°F (–162°C). As compared with our year of 365 days, it takes Mercury only 88 days to make one complete trip around the sun, so its year is 88 Earth days long. However, Mercury turns only once on its axis every 59 days, meaning that its day is two thirds as long as its year. Photographs of Mercury taken from the unmanned Mariner spacecraft in 1974 show that the planet is covered with many craters, much like the Earth's moon.

In addition to photographing Mercury's surface, Mariner 10 measured temperatures ranging from a night low of –260°F (–162°C) to a noon high of around 800°F (427°C).

Venus is the next planet out from the sun. It is about twice as far from the sun as Mercury. It is almost as large as the Earth, and its orbit is closer to the Earth's than any other planet's. For this reason, Venus was the first planet to which unmanned spacecraft were sent. Several of these craft actually landed on the surface of

Looking Into Space

Venus, where they recorded temperatures as high as 900°F (482°C), hot enough to melt lead. The reason for the high temperatures is that Venus is covered by a dense layer of clouds. The clouds consist mainly of carbon dioxide. The carbon dioxide acts like a one-way glass around the planet, allowing heat from the sun to reach the planet but not to escape back into space. This is called the greenhouse effect. A greenhouse effect also operates on Earth, slowly raising the temperature of Earth's atmosphere. On Venus, however, the greenhouse effect has gone wild.

Venus and Earth formed at the same time in the history of the solar system. The two planets have some similarities. This artist's impression shows the three Venusian continental masses, and also reveals a major difference between Venus and Earth – Venus has no oceans.

In 1990 the U.S. space probe Magellan arrived at Venus after a 15-month journey from the Earth. It went into orbit and mapped the surface of Venus using radar. It revealed that under the cloud layer the surface consists mainly of plains pitted with craters.

The Magellan Venus probe was launched in May 1989 to add detail to the maps made of Venus by large radio-telescopes on Earth.

The Inner Planets

One of the Viking probe's jobs was to take soil samples, using an extendable arm. Some of the samples were tested for signs of life, but no traces were found.

The next planet out from the sun is the Earth. Then comes Mars, which is often called the red planet because of its reddish color when seen in the night sky. Mars takes almost twice as long to go around the sun as the Earth takes. The day on Mars is about the same length as ours. Mars has white polar caps made of ice and frozen carbon dioxide. There are four enormous volcanoes, of which the largest is called Olympus Mons. It is 15 miles (24 km) high. Mars has two tiny moons, about 6 to 20 miles (10 to 32 km) in diameter, which travel around the planet much as our moon circles the Earth.

In 1976 two U.S. space probes Viking 1 and 2 landed on the Martian surface. Color television pictures transmitted to Earth revealed that the surface was reddish brown and the sky was pink, colored by iron oxide dust blowing in the atmosphere. Instruments on the Viking craft revealed that the atmosphere was thin and consisted mainly of carbon dioxide. Because the atmosphere is thin, there is no greenhouse effect on Mars. The temperature can rise as high as 70°F (21°C) during the day and drop as low as −80°F (−62°C) at night. The temperature at the poles of Mars are constant at −180°F (−118°C) all the time.

Looking Into Space

The Outer Planets

The outer planets Jupiter, Saturn, Uranus, and Neptune, are giant balls of gas with small solid cores. They differ from the inner planets, which are smaller rocky bodies. Pluto, the outermost planet, is a small rocky body like the inner planets.

Jupiter is the planet next out from the sun after Mars. It is more than three times as far from the sun as Mars. Jupiter is truly the giant of the planets, containing twice as much matter as the other eight planets put together. It is more than 11 times larger in diameter than the Earth. It could contain 1,323 Earths inside its globe.

Jupiter spins very rapidly on its axis, making a complete rotation in less than 10 hours. A point on the equator of Jupiter moves around the center of the planet at a speed of 28,273 mph (45,500 km/h). The speed is so great that it makes the planet bulge slightly at its equator.

The relative sizes of the sun, Earth, and Jupiter. Even though Jupiter is larger than all the other planets put together, it is dwarfed by the sun.

The Outer Planets

Four of the sixteen known satellites of Jupiter, the Galilean moons, orbit close to the planet's equatorial plane.

Seen through a telescope, Jupiter shows a surface marked with many colored bands, which are actually the tops of dense clouds. Also visible through a telescope is a giant spot, called the Great Red Spot. This is an enormous revolving storm that has been going on for at least 300 years. Beneath the atmosphere, Jupiter is largely made of hydrogen and helium, compressed into a liquid by the immense pressure of the atmosphere. There is a solid core at the center probably larger than the Earth.

The giant planet has at least 16 moons, of which four are about as large as our moon. Three small moons were discovered in 1979

Looking Into Space

Our own planet shrinks into insignificance compared to the Great Red Spot on Jupiter.

by the Voyager space probes that visited the planet. The probes also discovered a faint ring of dust around Jupiter's equator. In late 1995, the U.S. space probe Galileo arrived at Jupiter. While the main probe went into orbit around Jupiter, a smaller probe was dropped toward Jupiter to study the planet's atmosphere.

The next planet out from the sun, Saturn, is nearly as large as Jupiter and almost twice as far from the sun. In some ways, Saturn is like a smaller

Saturn and seven of its moons. The rings of Saturn are very thin compared to their width. They are only 300 feet (100 m) thick but 171,000 miles (275,000 km) in diameter.

26

The Outer Planets

The ice particles that make up Saturn's rings range from tiny gravel-like fragments to hunks as large as houses. Seen edge-on, the rings may be no thicker than 300 feet (90 meters).

version of Jupiter. It has a small solid core, surrounded by a layer of liquid hydrogen and a hydrogen-rich atmosphere. However, Saturn has two special features: it is the planet with the most moons, and it has a series of bright rings around it. Saturn has 21 to 23 moons; the exact number is uncertain because of difficulty in identifying

The rings of Saturn dwarf our planet shown to the same scale. Yet if they are viewed edge-on, it is difficult to see them from Earth-bound telescopes.

Looking Into Space

the individual moons. The largest moon, called Titan, is about the size of the planet Mercury and has an atmosphere. The rings around Saturn are made from small chunks of ice and rock, about 3 feet (1 m) across.

Next comes Uranus, the farthest planet that can be seen without a telescope. It is nearly twice as far from the sun as Saturn and about 19 times further from the sun than the Earth. If a supersonic airliner flew to Uranus at its usual cruising speed, the journey from Earth to Uranus would take 150 years.

Uranus shows blue-green in this Voyager 2 image, because the small amount of methane gas in the planet's atmosphere absorbs light in the red part of the spectrum.

The peculiar thing about Uranus is that its axis of spin is tilted much more than the axis of any other planet. While the other planets spin in an almost upright position, like a top, Uranus spins on its side. This means that the polar regions are warmer than the equator. At the poles, a day lasts for 42 Earth years, followed by an equally long night. Through a telescope, Uranus looks like a featureless bluish green disc. The color is due to the gas methane in the atmosphere. There is thought to be a solid core at the center of the planet, surrounded by a layer of hot water and ammonia. Uranus has 15 moons and at least 10 thin rings around its equator.

Still further away is Neptune. It is about 30 times further from the sun than the Earth is. Neptune is very similar to Uranus; both planets are roughly the same size and mass. Like Uranus, Neptune has a blue color due to methane in the atmosphere. Neptune has eight moons, two of which are visible from Earth. The coldest known place in the Solar System is the surface of Neptune's largest moon, Triton, which has a temperature of −391°F (−235°C).

The Outer Planets

Neptune has a faint set of rings around it. Like Jupiter, Saturn, and Uranus, Neptune is a ball of gas surrounding a solid core. The Voyager 2 space probe flew past Neptune in 1989, revealing features in the cloudy atmosphere. A great storm, the size of the Earth, was seen and named the Great Dark Spot.

Pluto is so small and far away that no one even suspected it existed until the early 1900s, and it was not actually sighted until 1930. Not much is known about it except that it takes nearly 248 years to make one trip around the sun. It is smaller than our moon, only 1,400 miles (2,300 km) across. Perhaps it was once a moon of Neptune that escaped the pull of Neptune's gravity. Pluto has one claim to fame, however. Its orbit is more oval shaped than the orbits of the other planets.

FACTS ABOUT THE PLANETS

Planet	Diameter	Distance from sun
Mercury	3,032 miles (4,878 km)	36.0 million miles (57.9 million km)
Venus	7,521 miles (12,104 km)	67.2 million miles (108.1 million km)
Earth	7,926 miles (12,756 km)	92.9 million miles (159.6 million km)
Mars	4,217 miles (6,787 km)	141.6 million miles (227.9 million km)
Jupiter	88,850 miles (142,980 km)	483.6 million miles (778.3 million km)
Saturn	74,900 miles (120,540 km)	886.7 million miles (1,427 million km)
Uranus	31,760 miles (51,120 km)	1,783.1 million miles (2,869.6 million km)
Neptune	30,780 miles (49,530 km)	2,794.1 million miles (4,496.6 million km)
Pluto	1,400 miles (2,300 km)	3,666.0 million miles (5,899.9 million km)

Planet	Length of day* (time taken to rotate once) D H M	Length of year (time in Earth years and days to revolve around sun)
Mercury	58　15　30	87.97 days
Venus	243　　　24	224.70 days
Earth	23　56	365.25 days
Mars	24　37	1.88 yrs
Jupiter	9　50	11.86 yrs
Saturn	10　39	29.45 yrs
Uranus	17　14	84.01 yrs
Neptune	16　 7	164.79 yrs
Pluto	6　 9　17	247.69 yrs

*Figures given in Earth days, hours, and minutes

Looking Into Space

Space Debris

What some people call "falling stars" or "shooting stars" are not stars at all. They are meteors or meteorites. A meteor is a small particle of dust that falls from space and burns in the upper atmosphere. As it burns, we see a streak of light flashing across the night sky. Most meteors are no bigger than a grain of sand. On most nights, you should be able to see two or three meteors every hour. Sometimes, it is possible to see many more. This happens during a meteor shower. One of the most spectacular showers, called the Perseid shower, takes place in August each year.

A meteorite is a larger piece of space debris that survives its journey through the atmosphere and hits the ground. Some meteorites are stony rocks, but some are metallic and made up of a mixture of iron and nickel. It is estimated that about 150 meteorites fall each year onto the land surface of the Earth. The largest known

Small pieces of space debris burn up completely as they enter the atmosphere. Large pieces may survive to reach the ground as meteorites. Others may "bounce" off the atmosphere and disappear back into space.

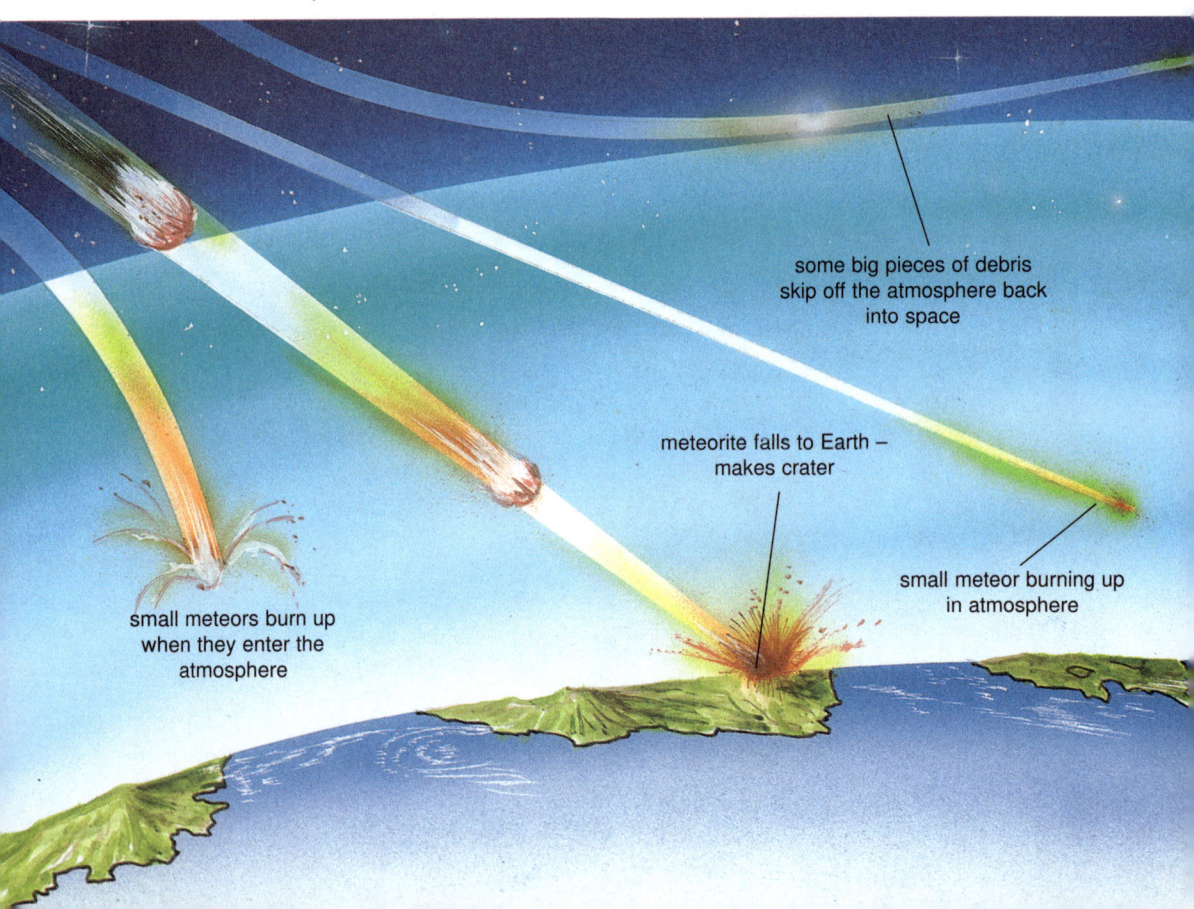

some big pieces of debris skip off the atmosphere back into space

meteorite falls to Earth – makes crater

small meteor burning up in atmosphere

small meteors burn up when they enter the atmosphere

Space Debris

Most asteroids orbit between Mars and Jupiter, held in position by Jupiter's gravity.

meteorite was found near Hoba West, Grootfontein, Namibia, in 1920. It weighed 54 tons and was 9 feet (2.75 m) long. Near Winslow, Arizona, is a giant crater caused by a meteorite which hit the Earth about 30,000 years ago. The crater is about 575 feet (175 m) deep and 3,940 feet (1,200 m) across. The meteorite which caused the crater must have been the size of a jumbo jet.

The largest collection of space debris in the Solar System is the asteroid belt. Asteroids are pieces of rock which were left over from

A meteorite created the Barringer Crater in Arizona when it crashed to Earth. The crater is from 100 to 150 feet (30 to 45 meters) deep.

Looking Into Space

the time when the Solar System formed 4,600 million years ago. Most asteroids travel around the sun in orbits between Mars and Jupiter. A few asteroids pass beyond the orbit of Jupiter, and a few pass close to the Earth.

There are probably over a million asteroids larger than 3,300 feet (1 km) in the asteroid belt. The largest asteroid is called Ceres. It has a diameter of 637 miles (1,025 km), large enough to cover most of the state of Texas. In 1991 the U.S. space probe Galileo flew to within 10,000 miles (16,200 km) of the asteroid Gaspra. Galileo then went on to fly by the asteroid Ida in 1993.

Comets are also space debris. They appear in the night sky as fuzzy patches of light, sometimes with long tails. Some comets, called periodics, return at regular intervals. Halley's comet, for example, appears every 76 years. Most comets, however, appear only once and then disappear from sight. Perhaps they will return in thousands of years. More than 700 comets have been observed. About six new ones are discovered each year.

Bennett's comet, photographed in 1970, and was named after the South African amateur astronomer who discovered it. Many amateurs specialize in searching for comets, and they discover more comets than the professionals.

Space Debris

Comets are in orbit around the sun, like the planets. However, their orbits are even more elongated than those of the planets, shaped more like an oval than a circle. Comets are probably balls of icy material and have been called "dirty snowballs." When a comet comes close to the sun, some of the ice is vaporized to form a long tail, sometimes stretching for millions of miles through space. The tail always points away from the sun. It is blown away from the sun by the pressure of the solar wind, a stream of particles given out by the sun.

When Halley's comet last returned, in 1986, it was visited by six spacecraft. The closest approach was made by the European Space Agency's craft Giotto. It flew to within 335 miles (540 km) of the comet's nucleus or core. The nucleus was revealed to be a peanut-shaped object about 9 miles (15 km) long and 5 miles (8 km) across.

A comet follows an oval-shaped orbit around the sun. This shape is called an ellipse. A comet's tail always points away from the sun.

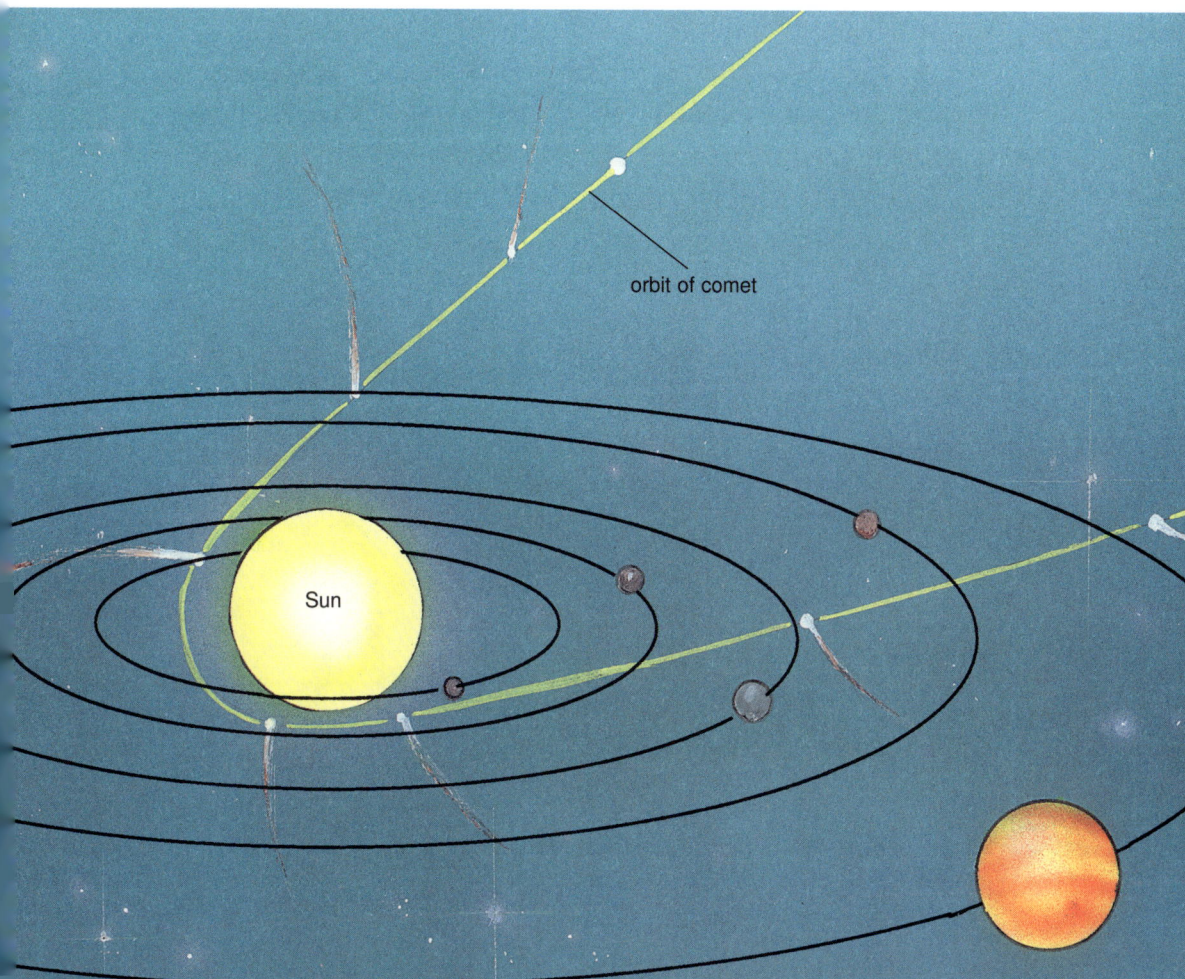

Life of a Star

Stars are born deep inside the gas clouds, called nebulae, that are found in space. Gravity pulls the thin gas of the nebula into balls of denser gas, called protostars. Then the protostars shrink, pulled inward by their own gravity. Inside the shrinking protostars, the pressure and temperature increases. Eventually the temperature at the center of the protostar rises to around 18 million°F (10 million°C). At this temperature, the hydrogen gas that makes up the protostar starts to change into helium. In the process, heat and light are released. The star starts to shine.

The process of changing hydrogen into helium is a nuclear reaction. During the reaction, the center parts (called the nuclei) of hydrogen atoms are joined together. Four hydrogen nuclei come together to form a helium nucleus. This process is called nuclear fusion because hydrogen nuclei fuse, or join. Nuclear fusion produces the heat and light energy that makes a star shine. It is also the process that makes a hydrogen bomb explode, so stars are like giant hydrogen bombs.

Once nuclear fusion starts inside a star, the star will keep on shining until it starts to run out of hydrogen. Then other types of nuclei take part in nuclear fusion reactions and produce heat and light. Eventually, the star consumes all its nuclear fuel. Then it dies. Stars, however, do not just flicker and go out like a candle. Exactly what happens depends on the mass of the star.

Life of a Star

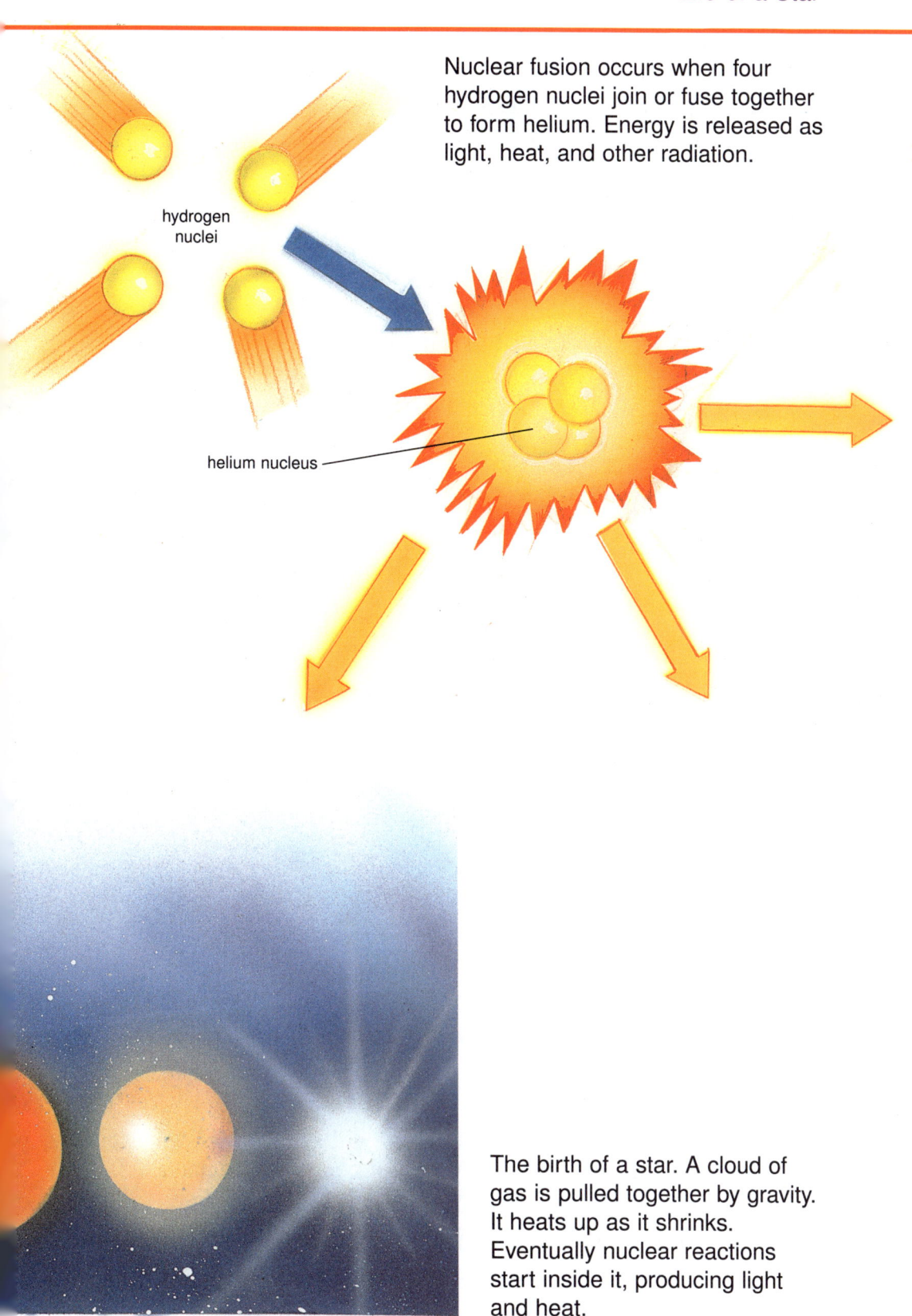

Nuclear fusion occurs when four hydrogen nuclei join or fuse together to form helium. Energy is released as light, heat, and other radiation.

hydrogen nuclei

helium nucleus

The birth of a star. A cloud of gas is pulled together by gravity. It heats up as it shrinks. Eventually nuclear reactions start inside it, producing light and heat.

Looking Into Space

An average star, such as the sun, shines steadily for about 10,000 million years. Then, as its fuel starts to run out, it expands greatly in size and begins to glow red. It is then called a red giant. Eventually when all its fuel is exhausted, the red giant collapses into a small dense star called a white dwarf. A white dwarf is made up of the parts of atoms – electrons and nuclei – squeezed together very tightly by gravity. The material is very dense, about 100,000 times as dense as water. A piece of white dwarf material the size of a sugar cube weighs about 2,200 pounds (1 metric ton).

For a star with a much greater mass than the sun, the red giant stage is reached after a few million years. The star continues to expand, becoming a supergiant. Then it blasts itself apart in an enormous explosion called a supernova. The exploding star suddenly becomes brighter than 1,000 million suns. After the explosion, the remains of the star collapse to form a very dense object called a neutron star, made up of nuclear particles called

The way a star dies depends upon how massive it is. A star like the sun gradually expands into a red giant, then gradually shrinks again until it becomes a white dwarf.

red giant

neutrons. Neutron stars are only about 12 miles (20 km) across. However, the mass of a neutron star is about the same as the mass of the sun. That means that the density of neutron star material is 100,000,000,000,000 times that of water. All neutron stars are spinning rapidly, sending out very short and rapid pulses of light, radio waves, and X-rays. For this reason, neutron stars are also called pulsars.

Life of a Star

When a very massive star explodes, a black hole may form. A black hole forms when the gravity of the exploding star is so strong that it squeezes the remains of the explosion completely out of existence. It is as if there was a hole in space into which the remains had vanished. In fact, anything falling into a black hole will never be seen again. The gravity of a black hole is so strong that it prevents anything from escaping from the hole. Not even light can escape from a black hole; this is why it is black.

supergiant

A much larger star dies a more dramatic death. It expands until it becomes an enormous supergiant. Then it explodes spectacularly, ending up as a neutron star, or black hole.

white dwarf

Looking Into Space

Nebulae and Galaxies

The space between the stars is not empty. It contains much gas and dust. Some of the dust and gas can be seen as faint glowing clouds called nebulae. A nebula can be seen in the constellation of Orion, near the stars that outline Orion's club. The Coal Sack, in the southern skies near the Southern Cross constellation, is a dark nebula. It is a cloud of gas and dust that does not glow. Instead it blocks light from distant stars and forms a dark patch in the sky.

Most nebulae are lit up by the stars within the dust cloud. The stars form out of the dust and gas of the nebula. This is the Great Nebula in Orion. It can be seen with the naked eye, but to appreciate its great beauty you need to view it through a telescope.

Nebulae should not be confused with galaxies, which also appear as faint blurs in the night sky. With a telescope, galaxies are seen to be made up of thousands of millions of stars. A typical galaxy contains 100,000 million stars. The stars in a galaxy are spread through an enormous volume of space. If stars were the size of a rice grain, a typical galaxy would measure 236,000 miles (380,000 km) across, the distance between the Earth and the moon. The

Nebulae and Galaxies

stars are spread as thinly throughout a galaxy as a handful of rice scattered across an area twice the size of Texas.

Most galaxies are spiral-shaped. They each have a central region, called the nucleus, containing many stars. Surrounding this nucleus is a flat disc in which spiral lines of stars can be seen. Other galaxies are shaped like eggs, and others are irregular and have no distinct shape.

We live in a spiral galaxy. The band of stars called the Milky Way, which runs across the night sky, is made up of stars belonging to our galaxy. For this reason, our galaxy is called the Milky Way galaxy. Our galaxy is slightly larger than the average galaxy. The sun lies in one of the spiral arms of the Milky Way galaxy, about two-thirds of the way out from the center.

The most distant galaxies can be seen only through very powerful telescopes. These galaxies are around 12,000 million light-years away. By examining the light from these distant

eliptical galaxies

spiral galaxy

barred spiral galaxy

Some galaxies are spherical or oval shaped. Many galaxies are beautiful spirals, sometimes with a bar running through the central bulge.

39

galaxies, astronomers have discovered a strange thing about them. They are all moving away from us at high speed. The reason for this seems to be that the Universe is expanding. Imagine a balloon with dots drawn on its surface to represent the galaxies. As the balloon is inflated, it expands and the dots move apart, just as the galaxies are doing. Most scientists think that the Universe is expanding like a balloon being blown up.

If the Universe is expanding now, then it must have been smaller in the past. We can deduce that, long ago, all the material in the Universe must have been squashed close together in a small ball of matter. This ball, called the cosmic egg, began to expand about 15,000 million years ago. A giant explosion called the Big Bang started the Universe expanding.

This is one of the most distinctive galaxies in the heavens. It is called the Whirlpool. It is actually two galaxies connected together.

Nebulae and Galaxies

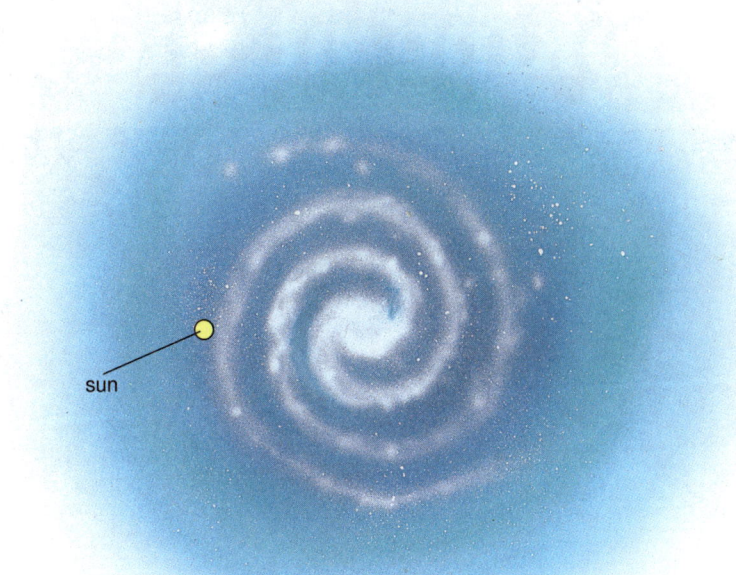

Our galaxy. It is about 100,000 light-years across. The sun lies in one arm about 60,000 light-years from the center of the galaxy.

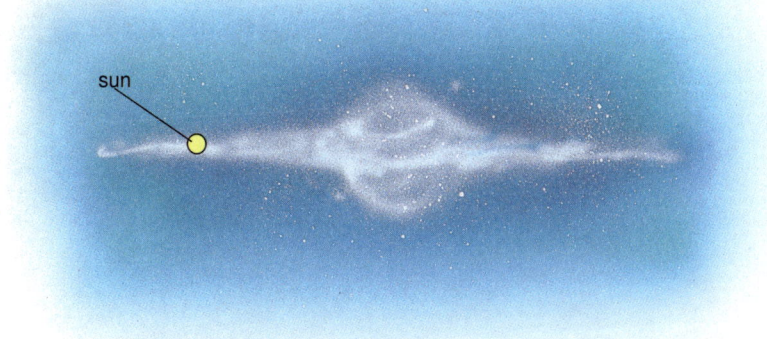

The temperature inside the Big Bang was enormous. One hundredth of a second after the Big Bang, the Universe was the size of the sun and the temperature was 180,000,000,000,000°F (100,000,000,000,000°C). As time passed and the Universe expanded, its temperature dropped. When the Universe was about 300,000 years old, hydrogen and helium atoms formed. After 500 million years, galaxies began to form from the hydrogen and helium. After 2,000 million years, the Milky Way galaxy was formed. Then, 10,000 million years after the Big Bang, our sun was formed.

Looking at the Earth

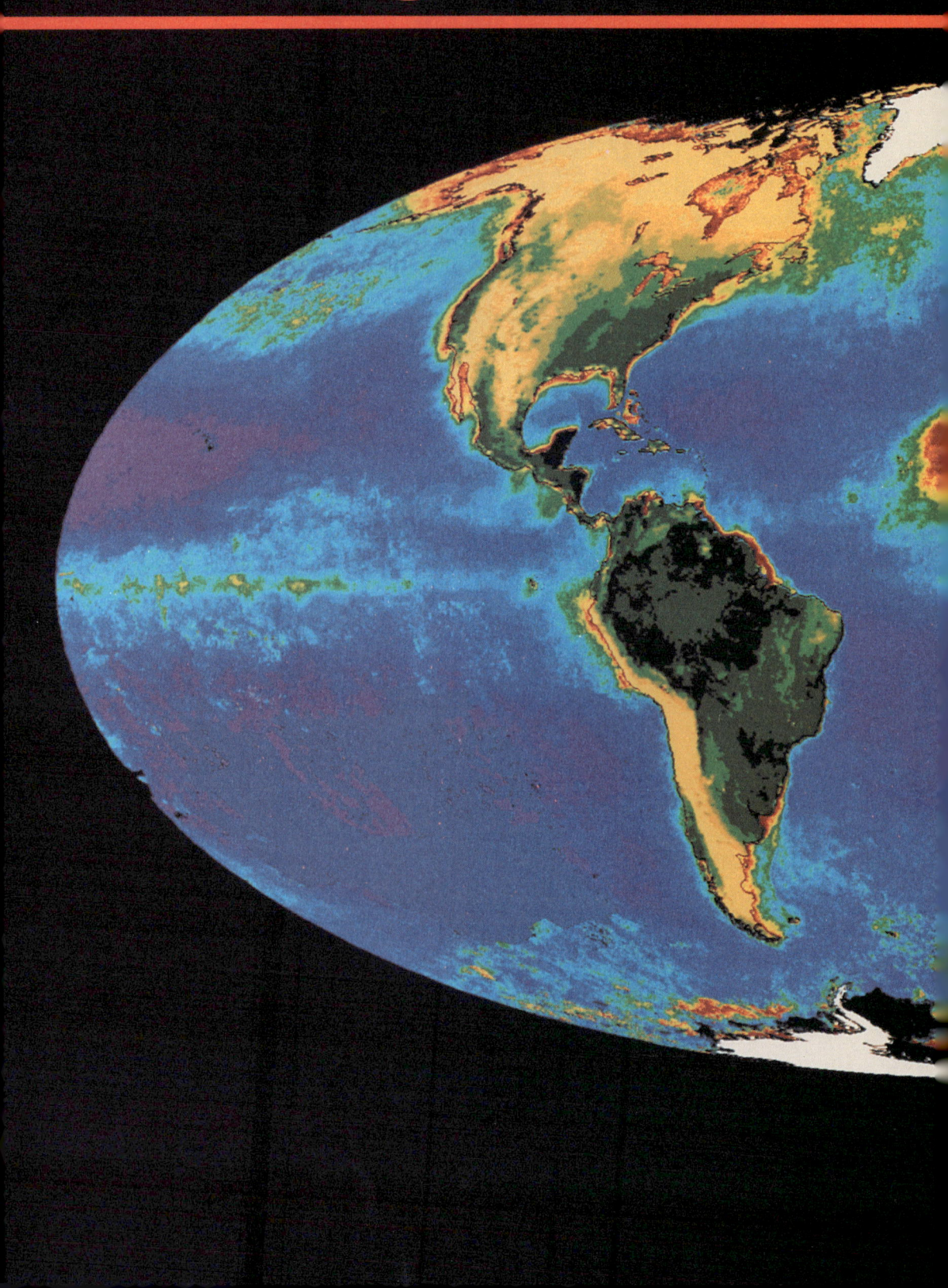

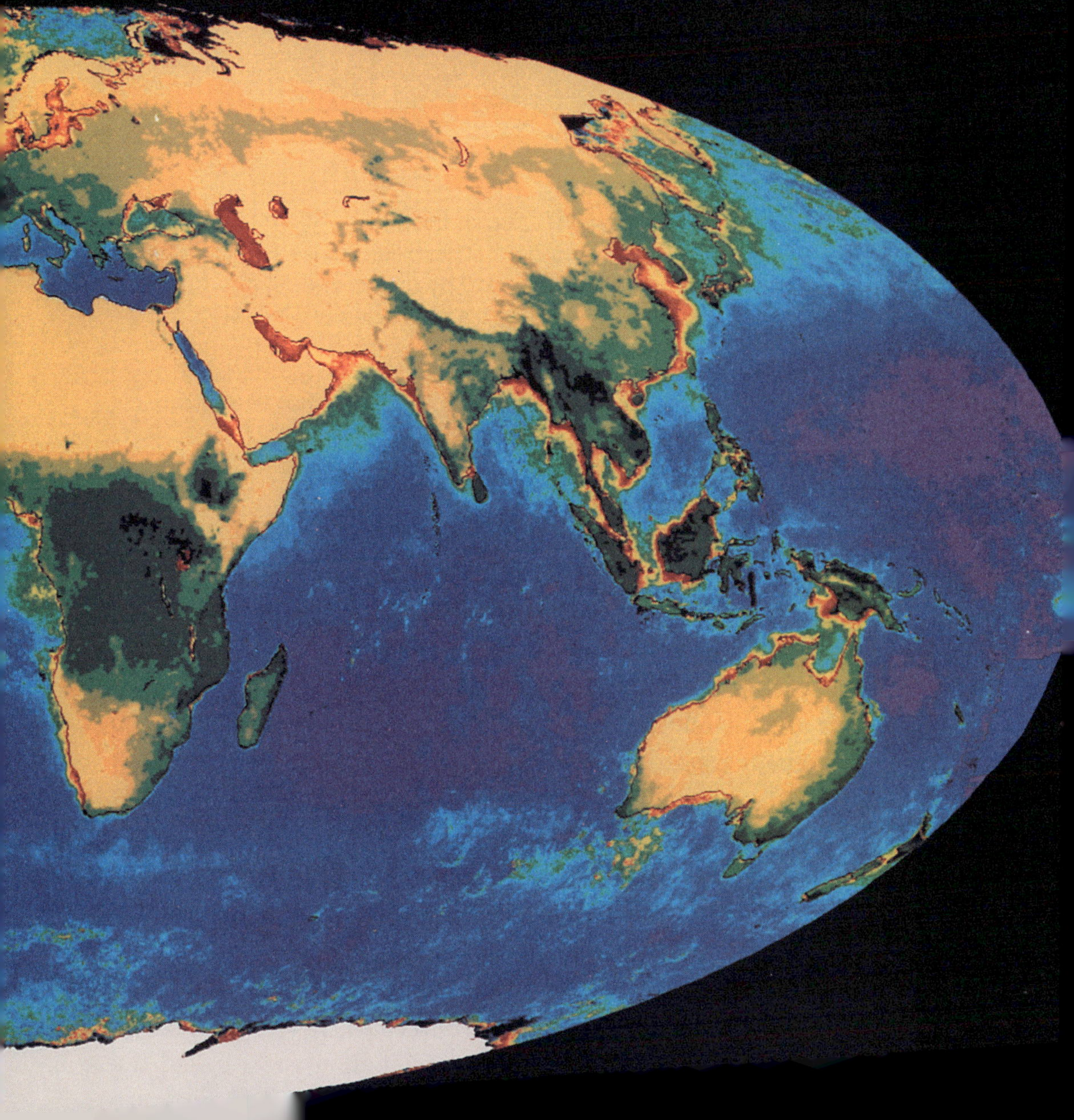

Looking at the Earth

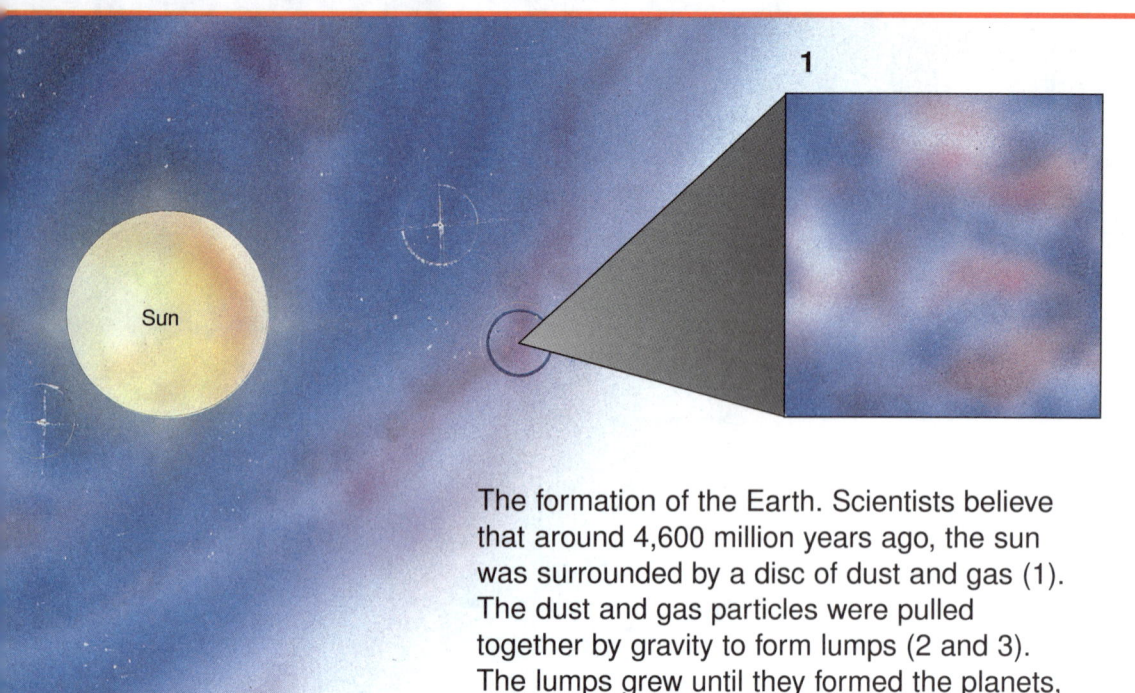

The formation of the Earth. Scientists believe that around 4,600 million years ago, the sun was surrounded by a disc of dust and gas (1). The dust and gas particles were pulled together by gravity to form lumps (2 and 3). The lumps grew until they formed the planets, including the Earth (4).

How the Earth Is Formed

Scientists believe that the sun and planets formed about 4,600 million years ago. The sun and planets formed from a nebula, a huge cloud of gas and dust in space. According to scientific theory, this cloud began to collapse. The force of gravity pulled the particles of gas and dust inward. As the cloud collapsed, it formed a disc with a bulge at the center. The disc spun around the central bulge. The force of gravity caused the matter at the center to become hotter and hotter until it started to shine like a star – the sun was born. The gas and dust in the disc were pulled together by gravity into lumps. These lumps formed the planets, including the Earth.

When the Earth first formed, it was red hot and molten. Heavy materials, such as liquid iron and nickel, sank to the center. Rocks, which were lighter than the molten metals, were left on the surface. Eventually, the Earth cooled and the outer layer, or crust, became solid. Beneath the crust, a layer of semi-molten rock, called the mantle, formed. At the center of the Earth, immense pressure turned the iron and nickel into a solid mass, called the inner core. A layer of liquid iron and nickel, called the outer core, formed between the inner core and the mantle.

How the Earth is Formed

2

3

4

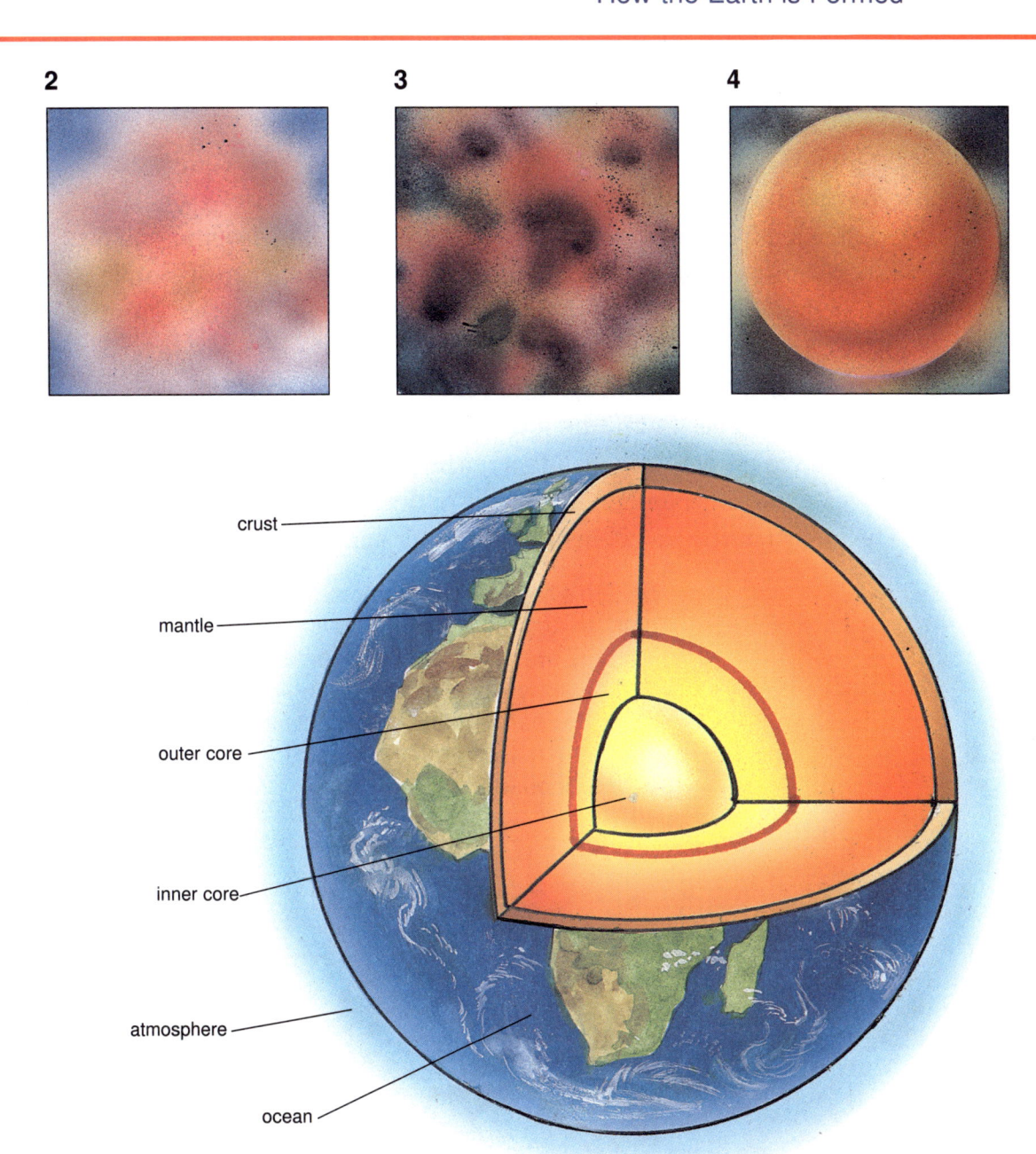

- crust
- mantle
- outer core
- inner core
- atmosphere
- ocean

The Earth is built of several different layers. At the center is a solid ball, called the inner core, of iron and nickel. The outer core is liquid iron and nickel. Between the outer core and the crust, the mantle is made of semi-molten rock. The outer layer is the crust.

The Earth's crust is about 6 miles (10 km) thick under the sea and 25 miles (40 km) thick elsewhere. The mantle extends from the crust to a depth of about 1,800 miles (2,900 km). The solid inner core has a radius of about 795 miles (1,275 km). The

45

Looking at the Earth

temperature in the inner core may be as high as 6,700°F (3,700°C).

When the Earth was young, a layer of gas, called the atmosphere, formed around it. At first the atmosphere was hot. It was made up of gases such as methane, nitrogen, hydrogen, water vapor, and carbon dioxide. About 2,000 million years ago, simple living things called algae began to appear on the Earth. These plants produced oxygen. Gradually the plants added more and more oxygen to the atmosphere. Today the Earth's atmosphere is made up of about four-fifths nitrogen and one-fifth oxygen. There are also small amounts of other gases, such as carbon dioxide, neon, helium, krypton, methane, and hydrogen, in the atmosphere. The atmosphere also contains water vapor and dust.

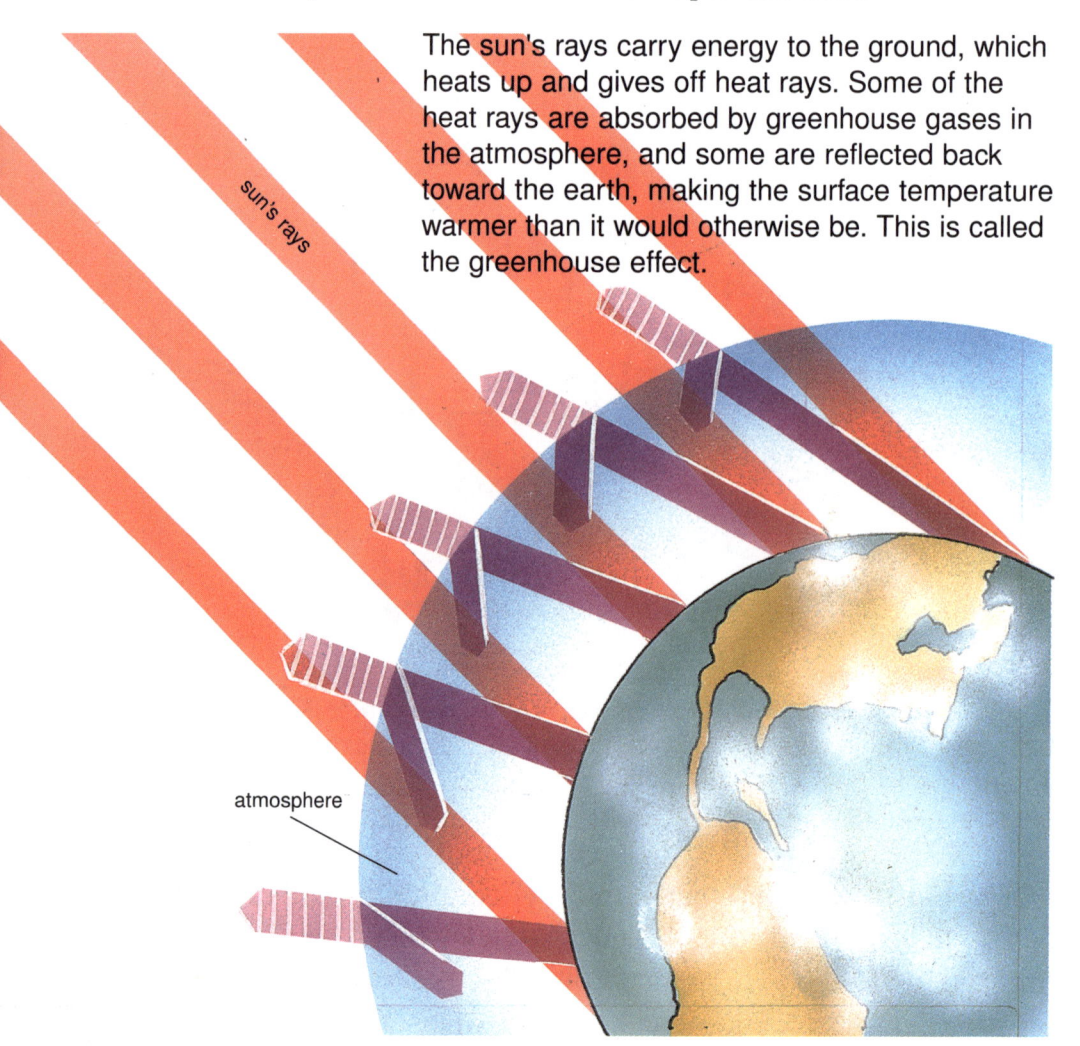

The sun's rays carry energy to the ground, which heats up and gives off heat rays. Some of the heat rays are absorbed by greenhouse gases in the atmosphere, and some are reflected back toward the earth, making the surface temperature warmer than it would otherwise be. This is called the greenhouse effect.

How the Earth is Formed

The weight of the air in the atmosphere presses down on us and on everything on Earth. It exerts a force we call the atmospheric pressure. The average atmospheric pressure at sea level is about 14.7 pounds per square inch (1 kg per square cm). As you climb above sea level, there is less weight of air above, and the atmospheric pressure falls. So does the density of the air – we say the air gets thinner.

The air is thickest, then, in the lower part of the atmosphere. We call this part the troposphere. It forms the first of several layers of atmosphere, each of which has its own special properties. The layers are shown and described at right.

The atmosphere is only a thin layer around the Earth. If the Earth were the size of an apple, the atmosphere would be no thicker than the skin of the apple. Although only a thin layer, the atmosphere is a warm blanket that keeps our planet at a comfortable temperature. The atmosphere traps the sun's heat. It lets the sun's rays penetrate to the ground, but stops most of the outgoing heat from escaping

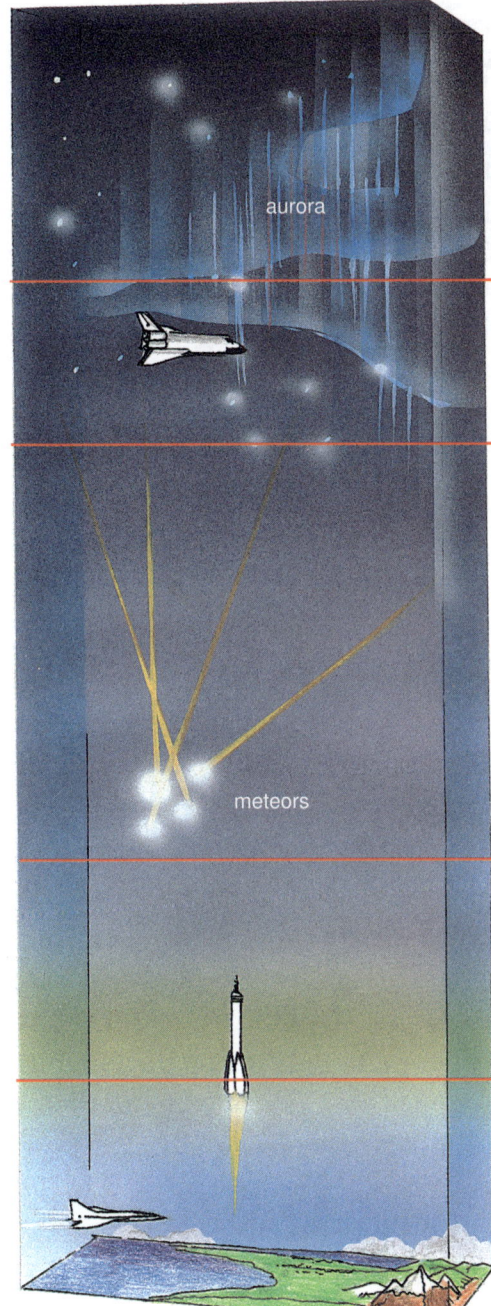

The exosphere is the last layer of atmosphere, which begins at a height of about 300 miles (480 km) and gradually merges into space.

The ionosphere starts where the mesosphere ends.

The mesosphere begins where the stratosphere ends and continues up to a height of about 50 miles (80 km).

The stratosphere extends from the troposphere up to a height of about 30 miles (48 km). It contains the ozone layer.

The troposhere extends up to a height of about seven miles (11 km) on average, but reaches higher above the equator and lower over the poles.

Looking at the Earth

Pictures taken from space show how thin the layer of air around the Earth is. It can be seen here as the dark blue band on the horizon.

into space. This is sometimes called the greenhouse effect, because a green-house also traps heat. Without the atmosphere, temp-eratures on Earth would drop to −220°F (−140°C) at night.

Carbon dioxide and methane are sometimes called "greenhouse gases." They are the gases in the atmosphere that stop heat from escaping into space. The amount of carbon dioxide in the atmosphere has been increasing since the 1880s. This has happened because people have been burning oil and coal. Carbon dioxide is produced when these fuels (called fossil fuels) are burned. The average temperature of the Earth may be gradually rising as a result. Scientists call such a rise in temperature global warming. If global warming is really occurring, world climates can be expected to change in the future. Low-lying cities may be flooded as polar ice melts and the seas rise.

Scientists have identified different zones, or layers, in the atmosphere. The lowest layer is called the troposphere. The troposphere produces the weather. Above the troposphere lies the stratosphere. At the top of the stratosphere is the ozone layer, which contains a form of oxygen called ozone. The ozone protects life on Earth by absorbing ultraviolet rays from the sun. Above the ozone layer are the mesosphere, which merges into space.

Scientists have discovered that a "hole" occurs in the ozone layer over Antarctica. The amount of ozone in the atmosphere here is much lower than normal. The hole may be caused by chemicals called chlorofluorocarbons, or CFC's, which were used in aerosols and refrigerators. If these chemicals escape into the atmosphere, they destroy ozone. To prevent further damage to the ozone layer, most industries have replaced CFC's with other substances. CFC's are also greenhouse gases. They trap even more heat than carbon dioxide can trap.

The Violent Earth

On a map, it appears that the coast of South America fits neatly into the coast of Africa. It is as if the South American and African continents were pieces of a jigsaw puzzle that fitted together. In fact, about 200 million years ago, the two continents were joined together. Since that time they have slowly moved apart. They are still moving apart. Each year they move about 2 inches (5 cm) further from each other. The slow movement of the continents is called continental drift.

The idea of continental drift was first suggested in 1915 by a German geologist, Alfred Wegener. (A geologist is a scientist who studies the Earth and its rocks.) To support his theory, Wegener did not only rely on the way continents fitted together. He also showed that there are similarities between the rocks and fossils in areas where the continents were

About 200 million years ago, there was just one continent called Pangaea. Gradually it split into separate smaller continents.

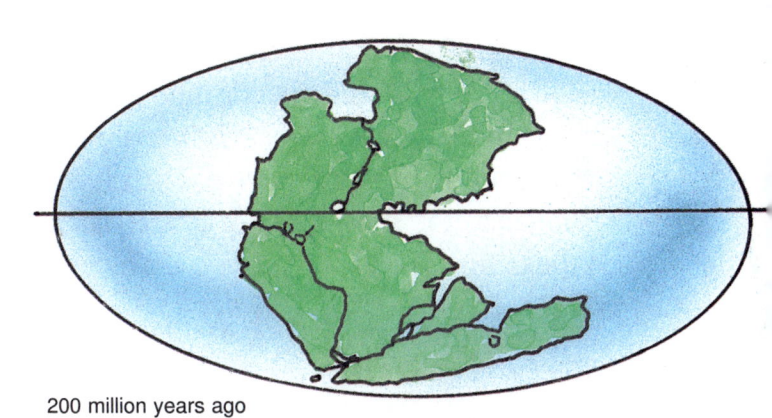

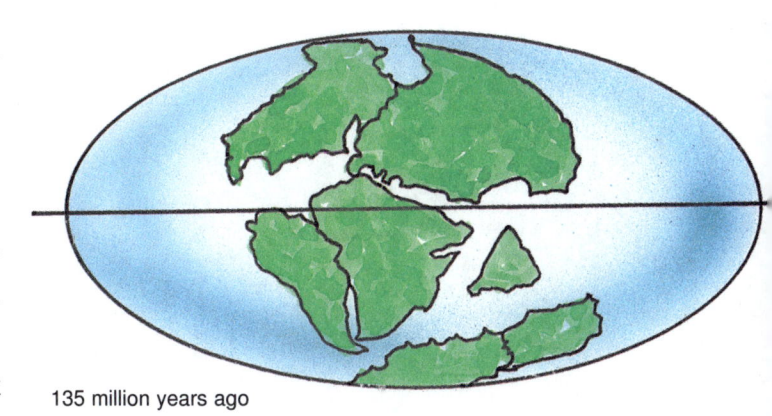

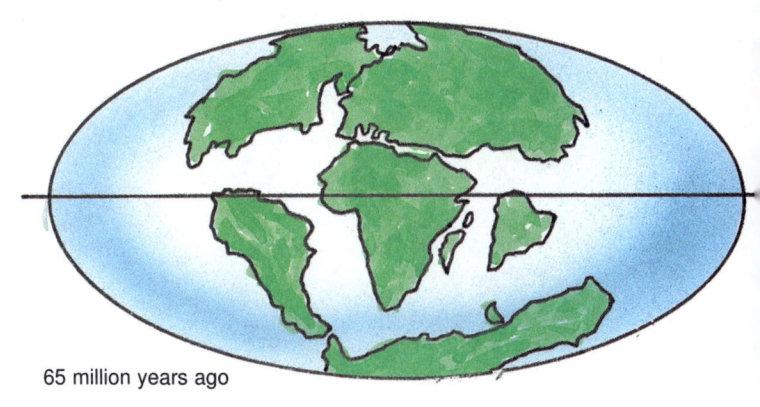

200 million years ago

135 million years ago

65 million years ago

Looking at the Earth

once joined. Fossils are the rock-like remains of long-dead animals and plants. Wegener concluded that, in the distant past, all the continents were joined together into one huge continent. This supercontinent split into smaller parts, which slowly drifted apart.

In the 1960s, scientists gained a better understanding of how the continents move. It was found that the Earth's crust is not one solid piece. It is broken into seven large pieces and several smaller pieces, called plates. The plates fit together like the pieces of a jigsaw to form the complete crust. The plates float on the semi-molten rock of the mantle and are carried along as the rocks beneath them move. Heat rising from deep inside the Earth makes the rocks of the mantle move. The movement of the heated rocks is similar to the movement of heated air above a room heater. This type of flow is called a convection current.

The Earth's crust is divided into several huge sections, or plates, as shown in this map. The plates move slowly, carrying the continents with them.

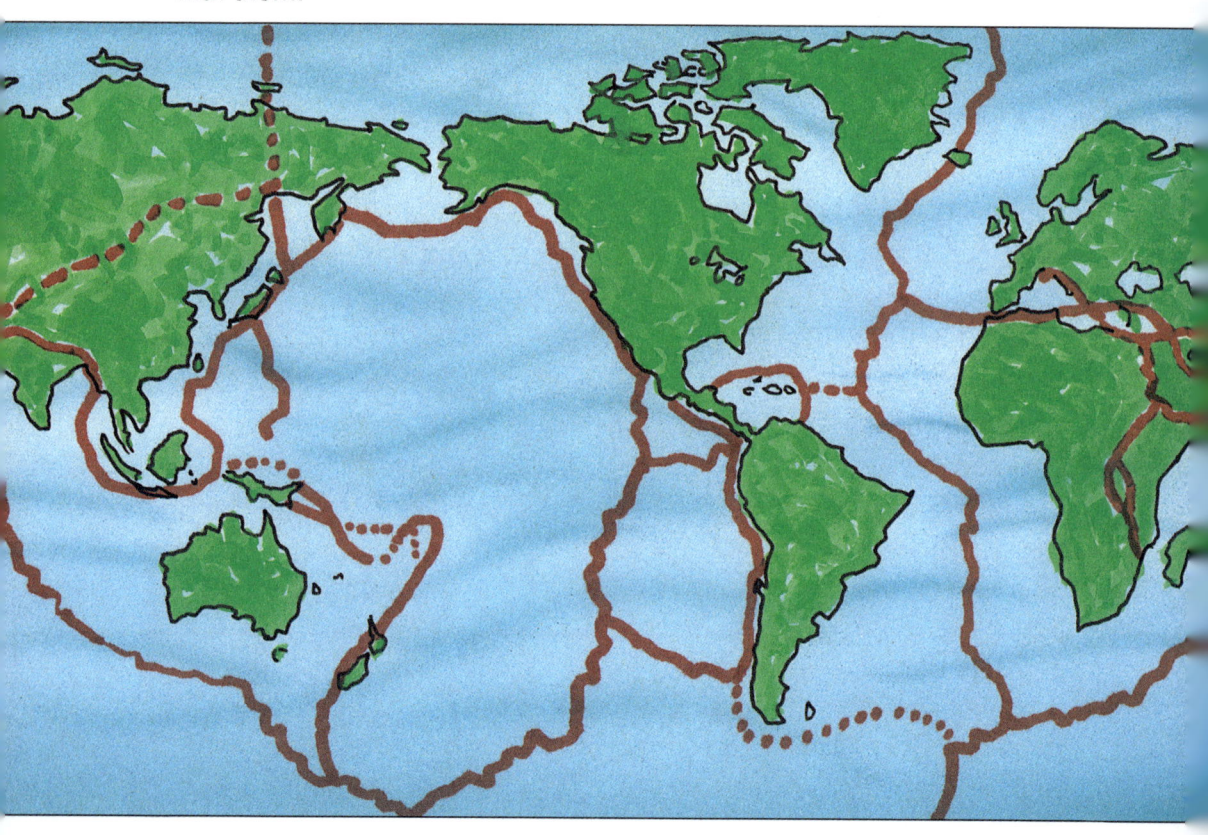

The Violent Earth

Each of the continents is on a separate plate. The plates carry the continents along as they move slowly around the surface of the Earth. Each plate moves between 0.5 to 6 inches (1 to 15 cm) each year. Since the Earth's plates formed 2,000 million years ago, the continents have traveled around the globe at least four times.

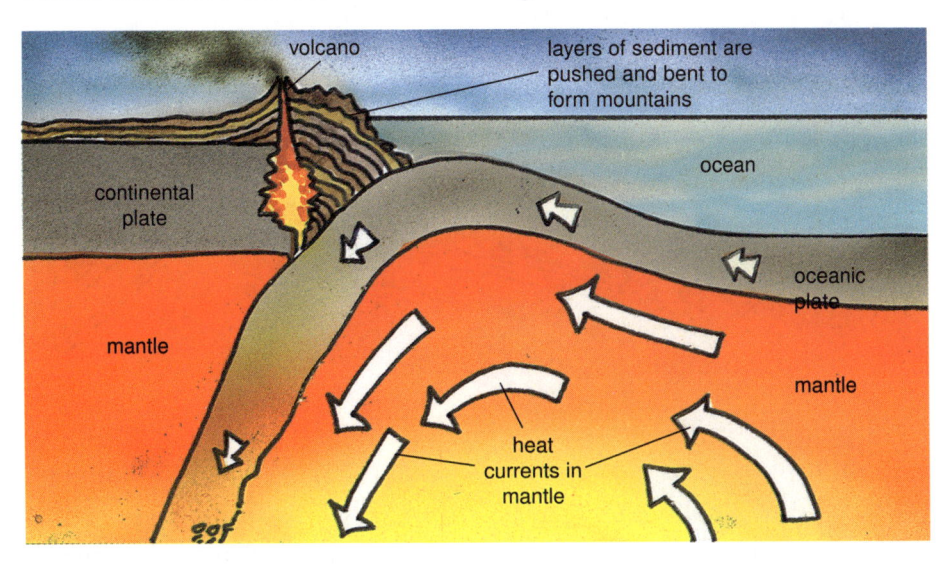

Heat currents in the mantle push the plates against one another. Usually one plate is forced underneath the other, and the lower plate melts and is absorbed by the mantle.

The San Andreas fault in California is a great crack in the crust that marks the edge of the North American plate and another, smaller plate. It stretches north from the Gulf of California for about 600 miles (965 km). Over 15 million years, as the plates have drifted, California has moved 186 miles (300 km) northward.

Some continents, such as South America and Africa, are moving apart, but this does not mean that a gap develops between the plates carrying them. There is no gap in the middle of the Atlantic Ocean, for example. Instead, there is an underwater ridge, called the Mid-Atlantic Ridge, running down the center of the Atlantic Ocean. The ridge is caused by semi-molten rock rising into the crack between the South American plate and the African plate. When the rock reaches the surface of the ocean floor, some of it moves east and some moves west, helping to push the plates apart. This sort of plate boundary is called a constructive margin. The action of a constructive margin creates new rock to fill the gap between the moving plates.

Looking at the Earth

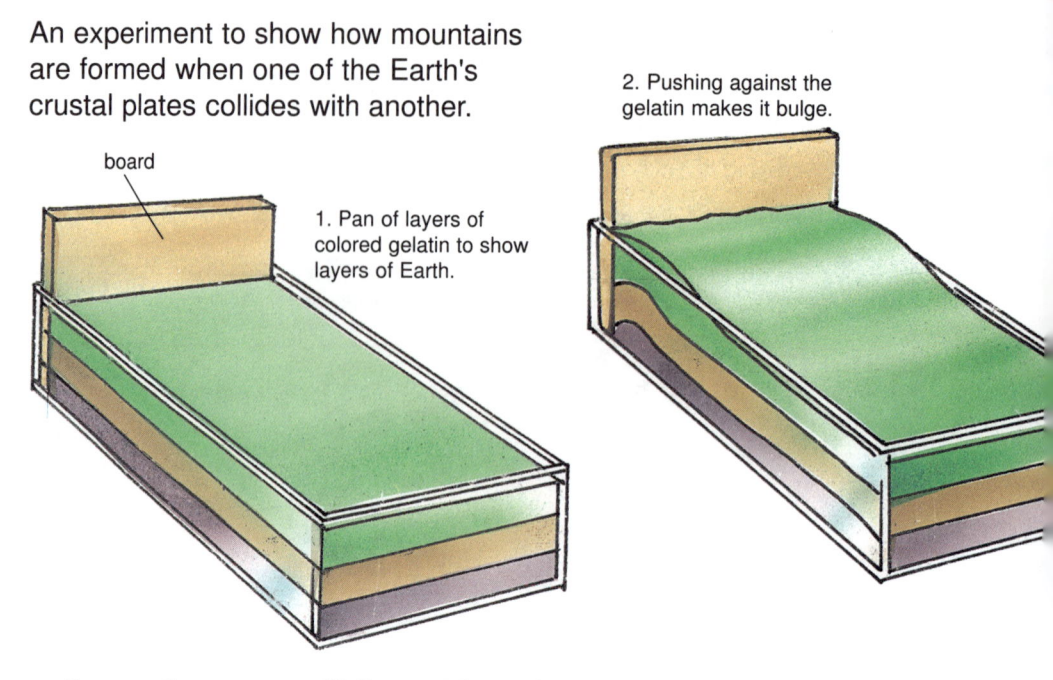

An experiment to show how mountains are formed when one of the Earth's crustal plates collides with another.

board

1. Pan of layers of colored gelatin to show layers of Earth.

2. Pushing against the gelatin makes it bulge.

Some plates are colliding with each other. When this happens, one plate is pushed under the other. The upper plate is forced upward, and the lower plate is forced downward into the mantle where it eventually melts and is destroyed. A plate boundary where one plate is destroyed is called a destructive margin. Destructive margins run along the west coast of South America. Here the plate under the Pacific Ocean is moving eastward and colliding with the plate carrying South America westward. The Andes Mountains were formed as the plates buckled under the force of the collision.

The Rocky Mountains were formed when the Pacific crustal plate collided with the North American plate.

The Violent Earth

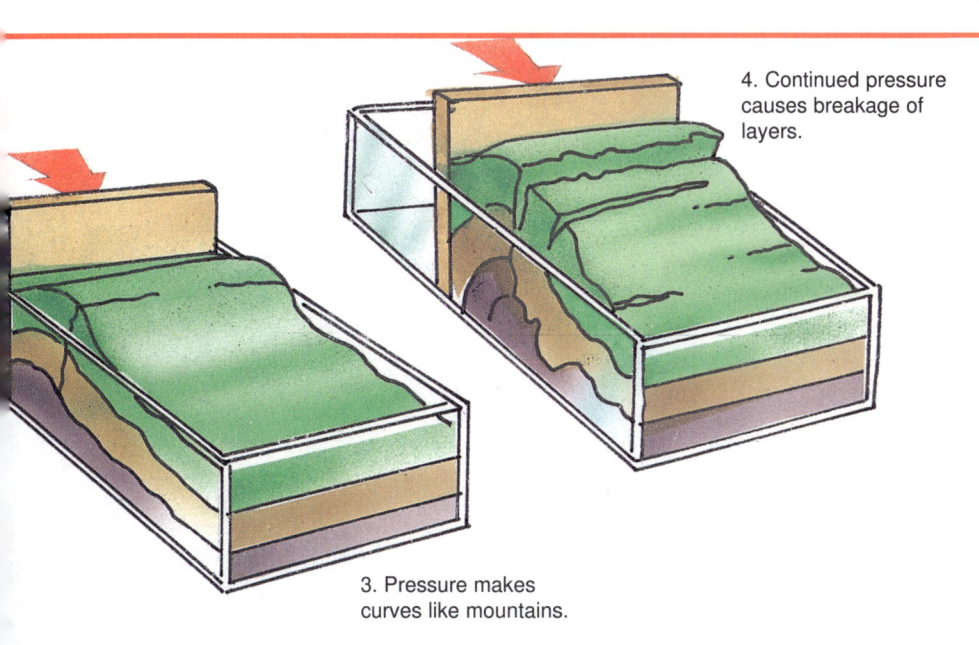

3. Pressure makes curves like mountains.

4. Continued pressure causes breakage of layers.

The Rocky Mountains were formed in the same way, when the Pacific plate collided with the North American plate. The world's highest mountains, the Himalayas, were formed when the Indian plate collided with the Eurasian plate.

Some Prominent Mountains of the World

Name	Location	Height
Mt. Everest	Nepal-Tibet	29,028 feet (8,848 m)
K2	Kashmir	28,250 feet (8,611 m)
Mt. Kanchenjunga	Nepal-India	28,208 feet (8,598 m)
Mt. Makalu	Nepal-Tibet	27,824 feet (8,481 m)
Annapurna	Nepal	26,504 feet (8,078 m)
Aconcagua	Argentina	22,831 feet (6,959 m)
Mt. McKinley	Alaska	20,320 feet (6,194 m)
Mt. Logan	Canada	19,524 feet (5,951 m)
Mt. Kilimanjaro	Tanzania	19,340 feet (5,895 m)
Mt. Elbrus	Russia	18,510 feet (5,642 m)
Popocatépetl	Mexico	17,887 feet (5,452 m)
Vinson Massif	Antarctica	16,864 feet (5,140 m)
Mont Blanc	France	15,771 feet (4,807 m)
Matterhorn	Switzerland-Italy	14,692 feet (4,478 m)
Mt Whitney	California	14,491 feet (4,417 m)
Mt. Elbert	Colorado	14,433 feet (3,350 m)
Mt. Shasta	California	14,162 feet (4,317 m)
Pikes Peak	Colorado	14,110 feet (4,301 m)
Mauna Kea	Hawaii	13,796 feet (4,205 m)
Mauna Loa	Hawaii	13,667 feet (4,169 m)
Fujiyama	Japan	12,388 feet (3,776 m)
Mt. Cook	New Zealand	12,316 feet (3,754 m)

Looking at the Earth

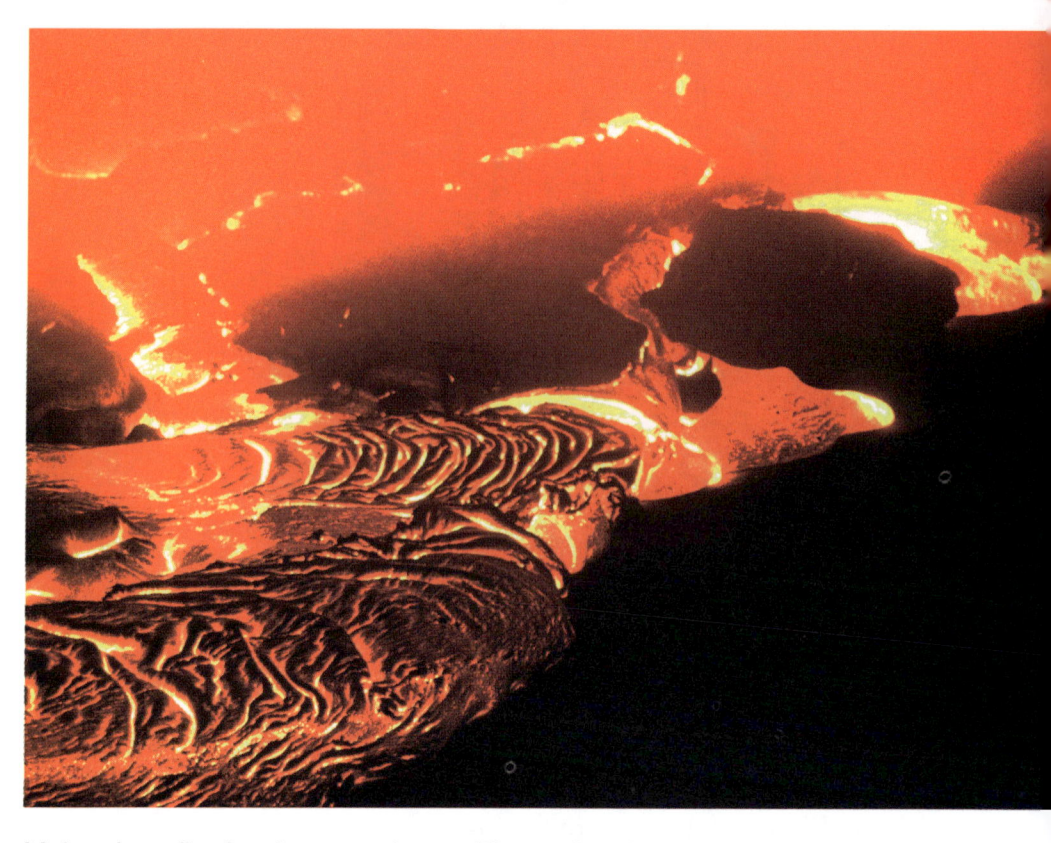

Molten lava flowing from a volcano. The molten lava can be as hot as 2,190°F (1,200°C) and can flow a long distance from the volcano.

Most volcanoes occur at the edge of colliding plates. Scientists know of about 600 active volcanoes. About half of these are in a "ring of fire," which circles the Pacific Ocean. The ring of fire marks the edge of the plate under the Pacific Ocean. Indonesia alone has about 160 active volcanoes. The largest active volcano on Earth is Mauna Loa in Hawaii. It is 13,677 feet (4,168 m) high.

Volcanoes erupt when hot liquid rock deep underground, called magma, forces its way to the surface. As the magma nears the surface, gases dissolved in it bubble up and escape. The magma that reaches the Earth's surface is called lava. If the magma is prevented from reaching the surface by a layer of rock, pressure builds up. If the pressure is great enough, there is a huge explosion, which sends ash, rock, and lava high into the air. Once the lava has escaped into the cooler air, it solidifies to form rock. The solidified lava builds up around the vent or mouth of the volcano to form a cone-shaped hill. Often molten lava pours down the side of the cone for a while after

The Violent Earth

the explosion. Sometimes the lava may solidify in the vent and block it. If this happens, the volcano may explode a second time when the pressure has built up again.

Some volcanoes erupt constantly. The volcano on the island of Stromboli, Italy, shoots glowing ash into the air every 20 minutes. Other volcanoes are dormant, or "sleeping." These volcanoes may not erupt for many years. Mount Etna, in Sicily, has erupted as often as 150 times in the last 3,500 years. In 1980 Mount St. Helens

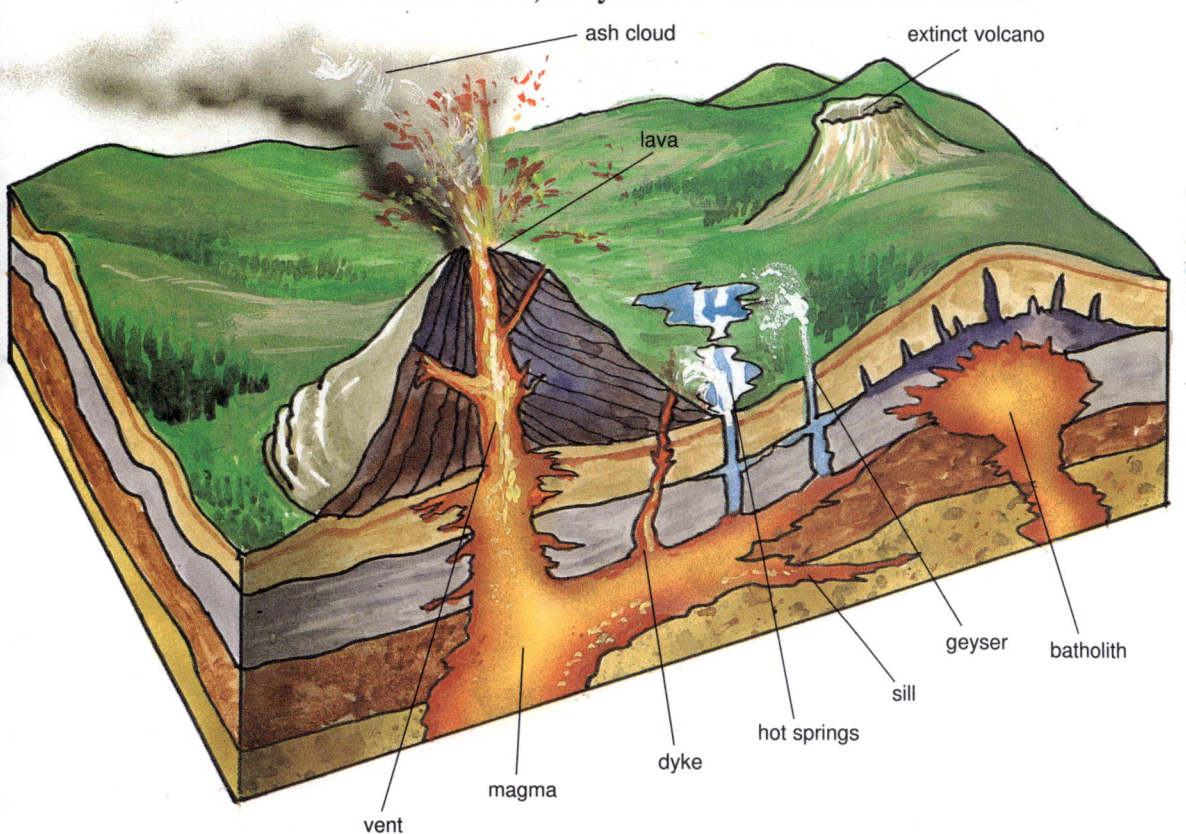

Inside a volcano. Most of the lava flows from the main vent at the summit of the volcano. Underneath the volcano is a mass of molten rock in the magma chamber. A batholith may form where magma moves toward the surface but does not break out.

in Washington State erupted for the first time in nearly 150 years. Ash from the eruption circled the world in 17 days, at a height of more than 30,000 feet (9,100 m).

The loudest sound ever heard was the explosion of Krakatoa, an island between Java and Sumatra in the Pacific Ocean, in 1883. The

Looking at the Earth

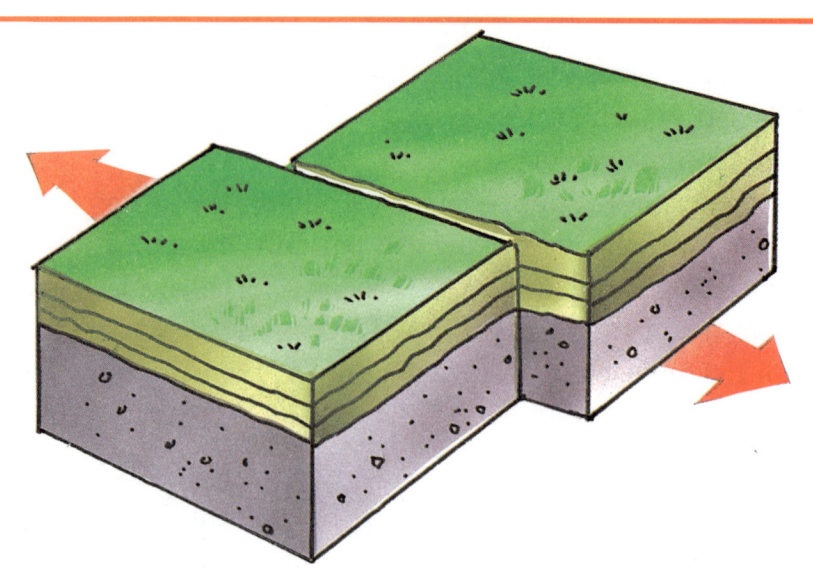

Layers of rock can slip sideways and cause an earthquake.

noise of the explosion was heard in Australia 3,000 miles (4,800 km) away and the shock was felt in California 9,000 miles (14,500 km) away. The dense cloud of dust produced by the explosion traveled around the world, causing blazing red sunsets as far away as England.

About 90 percent of the world's earthquakes, or shakings of the ground, also occur in the "ring of fire" around the Pacific Ocean. Many others occur in a belt that stretches from Spain to Turkey, and on through the Himalayas to Southeast Asia.

About a million earthquakes occur every year. Most are small, but a large earthquake happens about every two weeks, usually under the sea. Earthquakes ordinarily last for less than a minute, but in 1966 a series of earthquakes in Tashkent, Kazakhstan, continued for 38 days. Earthquakes occur when forces build up in the Earth's crust. These forces compress or stretch the rocks. When the forces become too great, the rocks suddenly crack or slip along what is called a fault line. This makes the ground shake and vibrate for several miles around. In the United States, earthquakes are most common around California's San Andreas fault, which marks the edge of the North American plate. These quakes are often felt in Los Angeles and San Francisco.

The power, or magnitude, of an earthquake is measured on the Richter scale. On the scale, each number signifies an earthquake ten times more powerful than the number below. An earthquake of magnitude seven on the Richter scale is as powerful as one million tons of explosive being detonated. The strongest earthquake of all occurred off the coast of Colombia on January 31, 1906. The quake measured 8.9 on the Richter scale.

One of the world's strongest earthquakes was in Prince William Sound, Alaska, in 1964. The worst recorded earthquake in history was on January 23, 1556 when 830,000 people died in the Chinese province of Shaanxi. The highest death toll from an earthquake in modern times was in Tangshan, China, in 1976. The earthquake, which some observers recorded at 8.2 on the Richter scale, may have killed nearly 750,000 people.

The principle of the seismograph. The waves produced by the earthquake, called seismic waves, cause the instrument to shake. A heavy weight hanging on a spring tends to stay still. The pen attached to the weight makes a trace on the paper on a revolving drum.

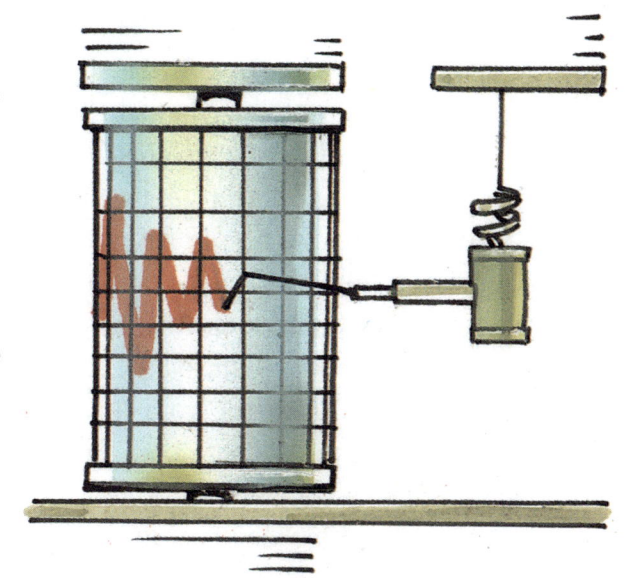

Scientists measure the vibrations of earthquakes using an instrument called a seismograph. The vibrations of the earthquake are recorded by a pen on a revolving drum of paper. A sensitive seismograph can record vibrations from an earthquake on the other side of the Earth.

Vibrations from distant earthquakes are used to study the interior of the Earth. There are different types of vibrations or waves produced by an earthquake. Some waves travel along the surface of the Earth. Some waves travel through the Earth's crust and mantle. Other waves travel right through the molten core of the Earth. By observing how long the different waves take to travel from the earthquake center, scientists can calculate what sort of rocks they have passed through.

Looking at the Earth

Rocks and the Story They Tell

The Earth's solid surface is made up mostly of rocks. There are many different kinds of rocks: black volcanic rocks, red sandstones, and white chalk, for example. Most rocks are composed of minerals. A mineral is an inorganic, solid, natural substance. Some rocks consist of only one mineral. An example is quartz. The millions of shiny glass-like grains in sand are also quartz. It is a very abundant mineral. Many everyday things, such as glass and sandpaper, are made from quartz.

Most rocks are composed of more than one mineral. Granite is this type of rock. Granite is made of three minerals: quartz, feldspar, and mica. The minerals in granite fit together very tightly, and do not crumble apart easily. It is hard for wind and weather to wear away granite. Because of this, people use granite for buildings that they want to last for a long time.

Metals and valuable stones such as diamonds are found in ore deposits. Ore is any rocky material that people can treat in some way to get a valuable material out of it. Hematite is an example of a mineral ore: it contains iron. This ore must be heated in a hot furnace to get the iron from it. Pitchblende is a mineral ore that contains uranium. The metal, uranium, is valuable because it is used in nuclear power plants.

If you examine various minerals, you will find that some of them are very hard and some are quite soft. Surprising as it may seem, graphite, of which the "lead" in your pencil is made, and coal are both composed of the same substance as diamonds. A diamond is the hardest substance known, while graphite is very soft and greasy, so much so that it is used for making slippery surfaces. There is nothing in their appearance to suggest that diamond and

Some precious stones in their natural and polished forms.

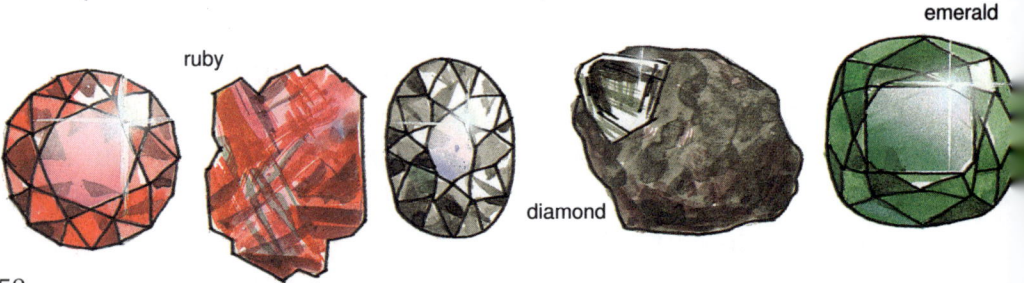

ruby

diamond

emerald

Rocks and the Story They Tell

Granite is one of the most common igneous rocks. It contains specks of mica that sparkle in the sunlight.

graphite are both made of the same substance, carbon. The differences between diamond and graphite occur because the carbon in them has gone through different natural processes. The diamond came from bits of carbon that were crystallized by the tremendous heat and pressure under the Earth. Graphite did not receive this treatment.

Rocks are formed in three main ways. Millions of years ago, when the Earth was very hot, much of the matter from which rocks are made was molten and liquid. When the liquid rock cooled and became solid, a certain kind of rock formed. This kind of rock is called igneous rock, meaning "formed by fire."

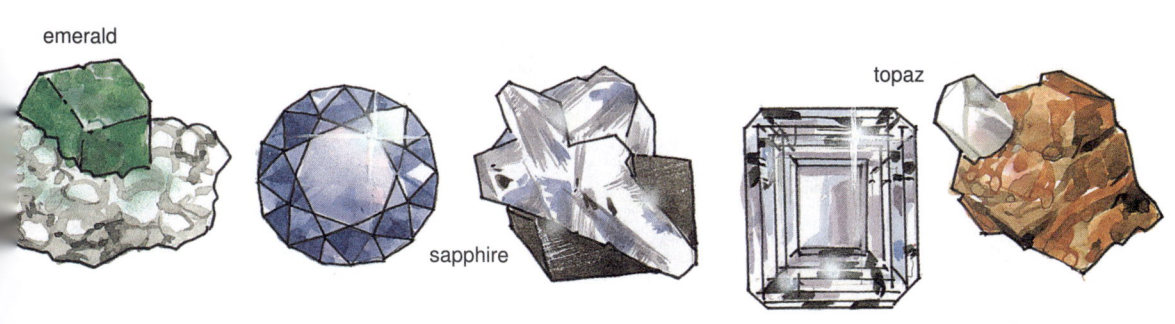

emerald

sapphire

topaz

59

Looking at the Earth

When sand and sea shells and other particles settle at the bottom of a sea or stream, a layer of rock is gradually formed. At the bottom of the ocean, sea shells continually collect and, after many thousands of years, deep layers of rocks form. These rocks are called "sedimentary rocks," because the particles that settle at the bottom of bodies of water are known as "sediment." As parts of the Earth's surface have shifted, many sedimentary rocks that were once at the bottom of the sea are now found on land.

Both igneous and sedimentary rocks are sometimes changed by great pressure or heat into another type of rock. In the pushing and sliding of parts of the Earth's surface that makes mountains and causes earthquakes, some rocks get enormous pressure put on them. This pressure causes rocks to undergo major changes. The new type of rock formed by such pressure is given a name that means "changed." It is called "metamorphic rock."

So we have three types of rock: igneous, sedimentary, and metamorphic. Granite is one of the most common igneous rocks. Limestone is a common type of sedimentary rock. It is a fairly soft rock and is quite easy to cut and shape.

Sandstone is also sedimentary. It is formed by small grains of sand becoming firmly cemented together. This often happens to sand that settles to the bottom of a stream and remains there over a long period. Another sedimentary rock is shale, which is formed by clays and mud settling on the water bed and gradually hardening.

When granite is changed by heat and pressure, the minerals in it become arranged in streaks or bands and the rock is then called gneiss. When shale is changed by heat and pressure, it forms slate. Slate is harder than shale, and because it

Slate has a pronounced layered structure. This allows the rock to be split easily into thin sheets.

Rocks and the Story They Tell

breaks into thin sheets, it is used for roofing shingles. When limestone is changed by heat and pressure, it becomes marble. Gneiss, slate, and marble are examples of metamorphic rocks.

Scientists who study the rocks and from them piece together the story of the Earth are called geologists. It is difficult for geologists to discover the whole story of the Earth. The layers of rock formed at different periods each contain records of what was happening on Earth at that time. However, the rocks have been warped and shifted so much over the years that to read them is like reading a book that has been torn and battered, with some of the pages missing.

Sedimentary rocks hold the most information about the Earth's history. Sea animals died and their bodies sank to the bottom of the ocean. Rivers and floods washed huge loads of sediment into the ocean and lakes, carrying with it the bodies or skeletons of land animals. As the layers of limestone, shale, and sandstone were

A "family" of ammonites, partly cut out of the rock in which they are embedded.

Looking at the Earth

formed, they held embedded in them the remains of the animals. Over the years, the remains were turned into stone copies of the skeletons and bodies called fossils. Scientists study the fossil remains to discover the animals and plants that lived millions of years ago.

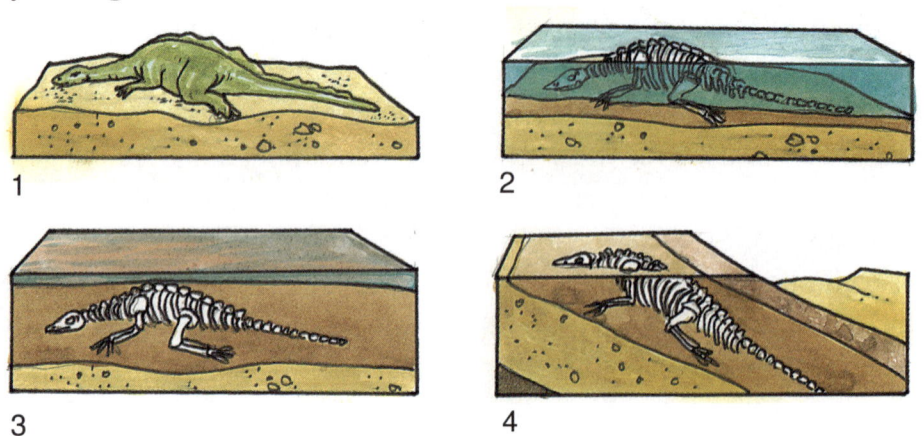

How a fossil forms. 1. A dead animal falls to the sea bed. 2. Its skeleton becomes covered with sand and mud. 3. Minerals seep into the bones and harden them. 4. Millions of years later, the rock-like skeleton is exposed as the mud wears away.

The evolution of life on Earth. The first life forms were simple organisms in the sea. These gradually evolved into more complex forms of life.

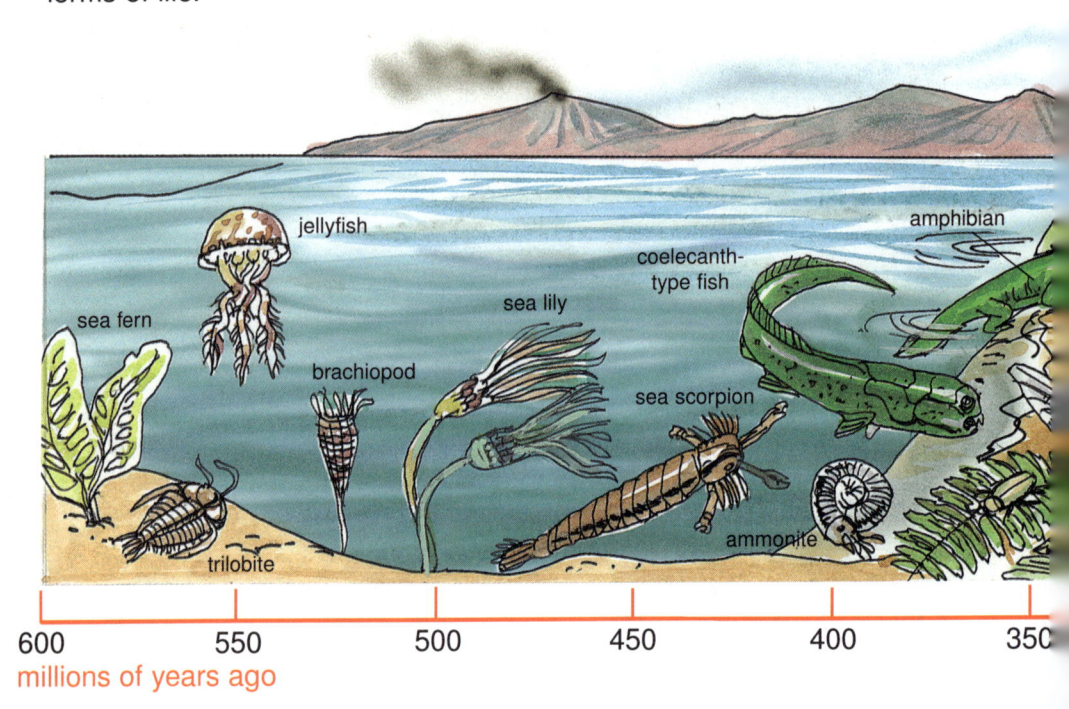

600　550　500　450　400　350
millions of years ago

Rocks and the Story They Tell

The earliest known fossils are of single celled organisms similar to modern bacteria. They date from about 3,400 million years ago. Since then life has developed into many different forms. The process by which all living things have developed from primitive organisms over billions of years is called evolution.

More than 500 million years ago, there was a great increase of life in the Earth's oceans. During this time, many different creatures with hard skeletons developed, and they left numerous fossil remains. Their descendants, called lampshells, still exist today. Primitive fish appeared around 500 million years ago. Plants began to establish on the land around the same time.

The first animals ventured out of the seas and onto land around 350 million years ago. They were called amphibians because they could live both in water and on land. At this time, too, huge forests of tall ferns and horsetails grew up in the swamps around the oceans. The remains of these plants eventually formed into coal. As the plants died, they fell to the ground and rotted away to form a layer of soft matted material called peat. As mud and sand built up over the peat, and millions of years went by, the peat was compressed into coal.

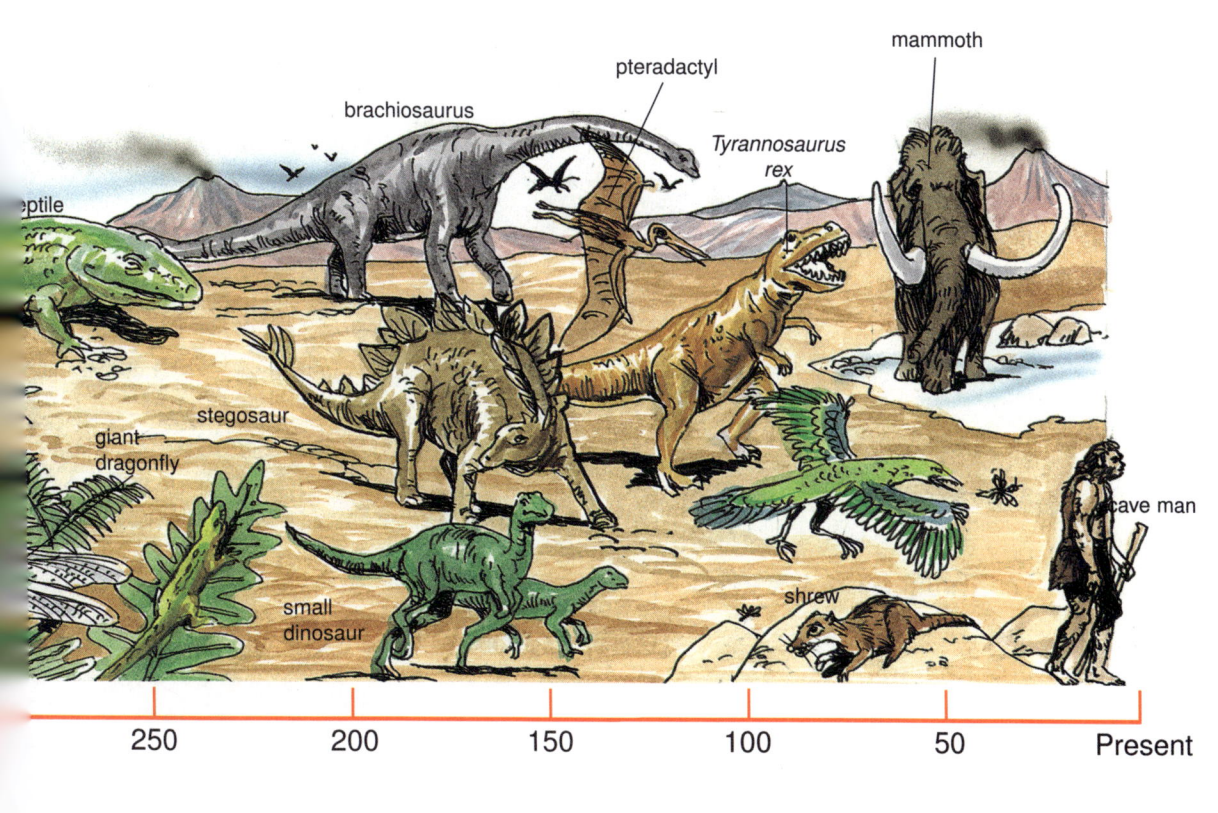

Looking at the Earth

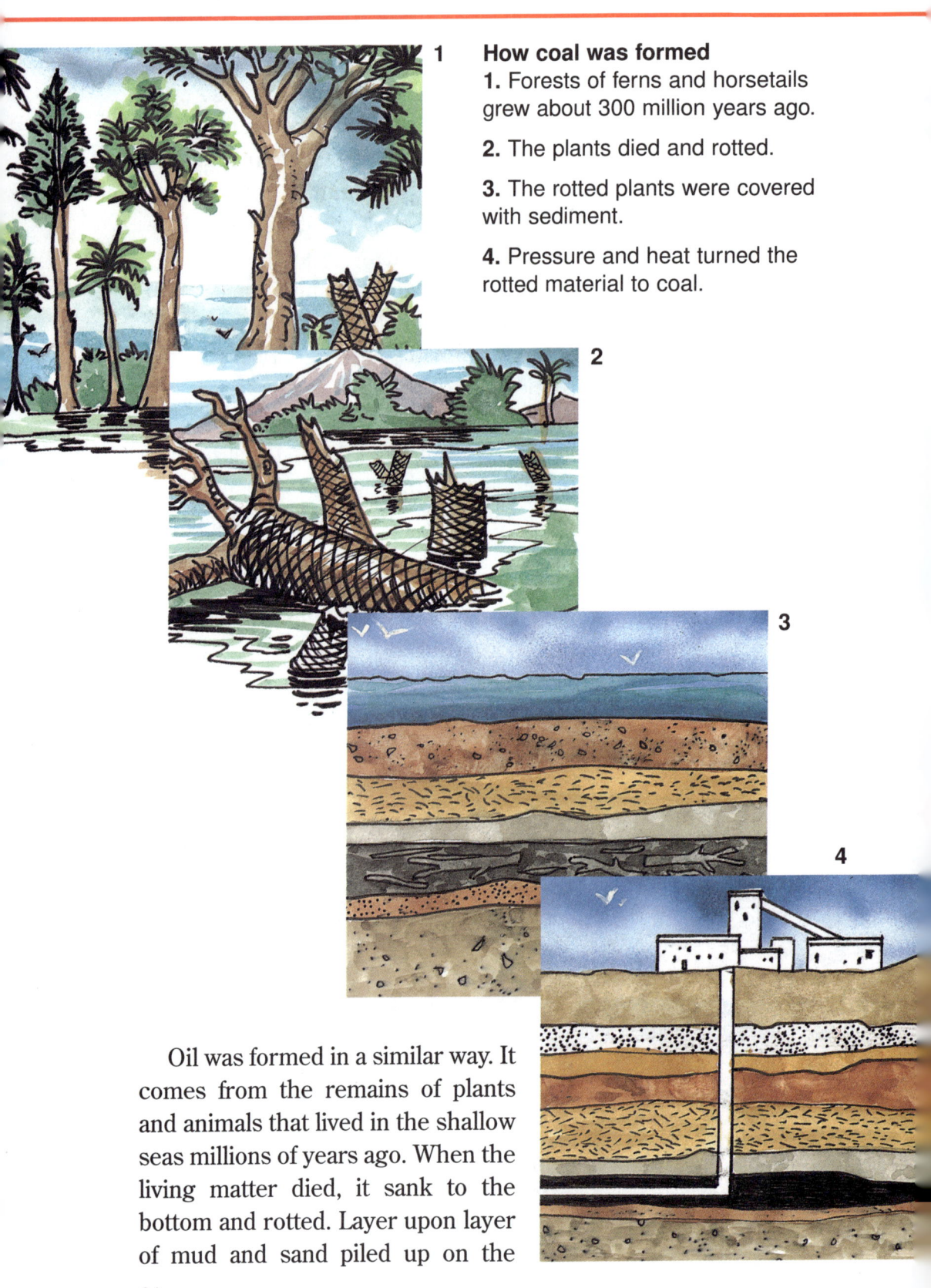

How coal was formed

1. Forests of ferns and horsetails grew about 300 million years ago.

2. The plants died and rotted.

3. The rotted plants were covered with sediment.

4. Pressure and heat turned the rotted material to coal.

Oil was formed in a similar way. It comes from the remains of plants and animals that lived in the shallow seas millions of years ago. When the living matter died, it sank to the bottom and rotted. Layer upon layer of mud and sand piled up on the rotting remains and compressed them. Gradually the remains turned into oil. The oil seeped through the layers of soft rock until it became trapped under a bowl-shaped layer of hard rock.

The first reptiles appeared in the forests, and gradually became the dominant life form. They included crocodiles, lizards, and dinosaurs. About 65 million years ago, the dinosaurs disappeared from the Earth. No one knows why this happened. One theory is that huge meteorites bombarded the Earth from space, causing so much dust that the sun's heat and light were blotted out for months.

The extinction of the dinosaurs provided a chance for small warm-blooded creatures called mammals to develop. The first mammals were about the size of a mouse, and ate insects. The mammals became the dominant life form. Many mammals grew to enormous size; for example, an early rhinoceros was 20 feet (6 m) tall. These giant mammals died out about 10,000 years ago, leaving life much as it is today.

A swampy forest during the Carboniferous Period. Giant dragonflies darted through the trees.

Looking at the Earth

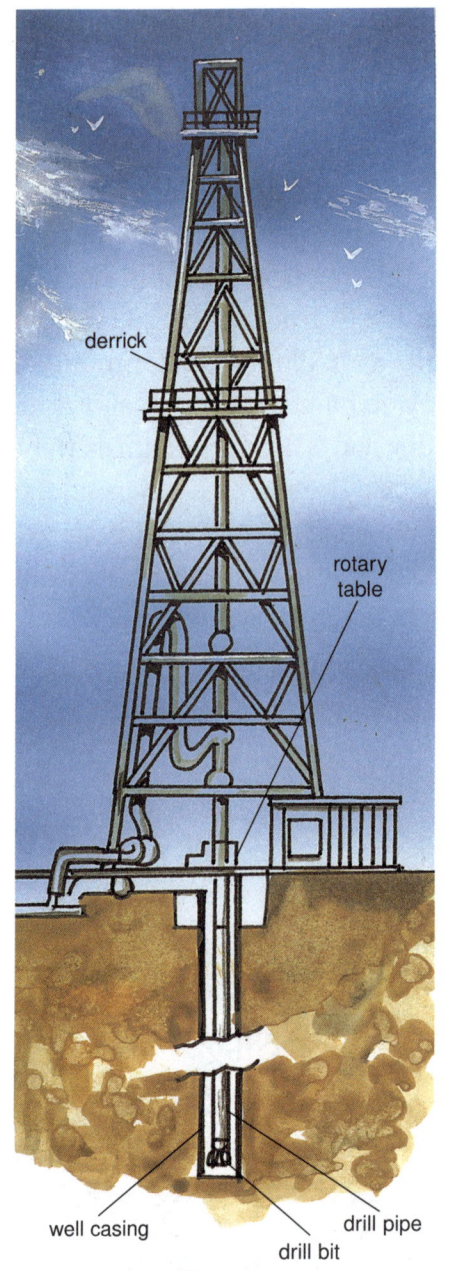

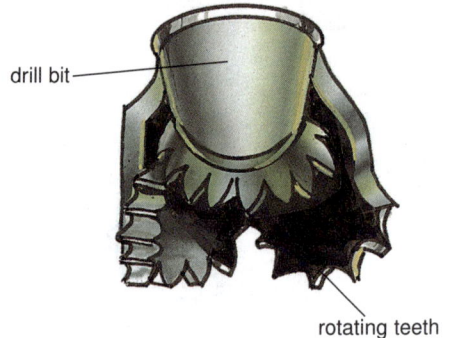

(Diagram labels: derrick, rotary table, well casing, drill pipe, drill bit, rotating teeth)

It is difficult to comprehend the long periods of time needed for life to evolve. It was a process that started slowly and then speeded up. Imagine that one year represents the entire span of life on Earth, and that one day represents 10 million years. Algae-like organisms appeared in August. The first soft-bodied animals appeared toward the end of September. The first fish appeared in the middle of November, along with the first land plants. Amphibians and insects appeared at the end of November. Reptiles appeared in early December. The first dinosaur appeared in the middle of December. A week later, the first birds appeared. The dinosaurs became extinct at the beginning of the last week of the year. The earliest apes appeared halfway through the last week. Humans did not appear until the evening of December 31.

A rig is used to drill for oil. The main structure of the rig is the tower, or derrick. This has lifting tackle to lift the long lengths of pipes used for drilling. At the end of the bottom pipe is the drill bit, which cuts through the rock. The bit has rotating teeth that cut as the drill pipes are rotated by the driving mechanism on the rotary table.

Shaping the Landscape

The surface of the Earth is always changing. Rocks are constantly being worn down, broken into pieces, and carried away. Even high mountain ranges can eventually wear down. The process of breaking down and wearing away the rocks is called erosion. Erosion caused by the sun, wind, and frost is called weathering. Erosion can also be caused by flowing rivers, moving glaciers, and by the sea pounding on a coast.

The weather can break down rocks in different ways. The heat of the sun can shatter rocks. The sun heats the rocks' outer layers, which expand. The cold rock underneath the surface does not expand. This unequal expansion weakens the rock. At night, the surface layer of the rock cools more than the layer inside. Once again, unequal expansion weakens the rock. Eventually, the surface layers flake off.

In sandy deserts, the wind plays an important part in weathering. It blows sand grains against the rocks, blasting them with a powerful force. The wind can carry sand and dust for vast

Monument Valley, Arizona. Once the whole area was covered by sandstone. The sandstone gradually eroded away to leave columns of harder rocks, called mesas and buttes.

Looking at the Earth

distances. Scientists have calculated that a strong windstorm can carry a million tons of sand for more than 1,800 miles (2,900 km). Sand blown by the wind can strike rocks and wear them away. Softer rocks wear away more quickly than harder rocks, and the rocks in windy desert areas are often carved into strange shapes.

Ice can crack rocks because water expands when it freezes to form ice or frost. When water in a crack in a rock freezes, the expansion forces the rock apart, perhaps splitting it. The expansion

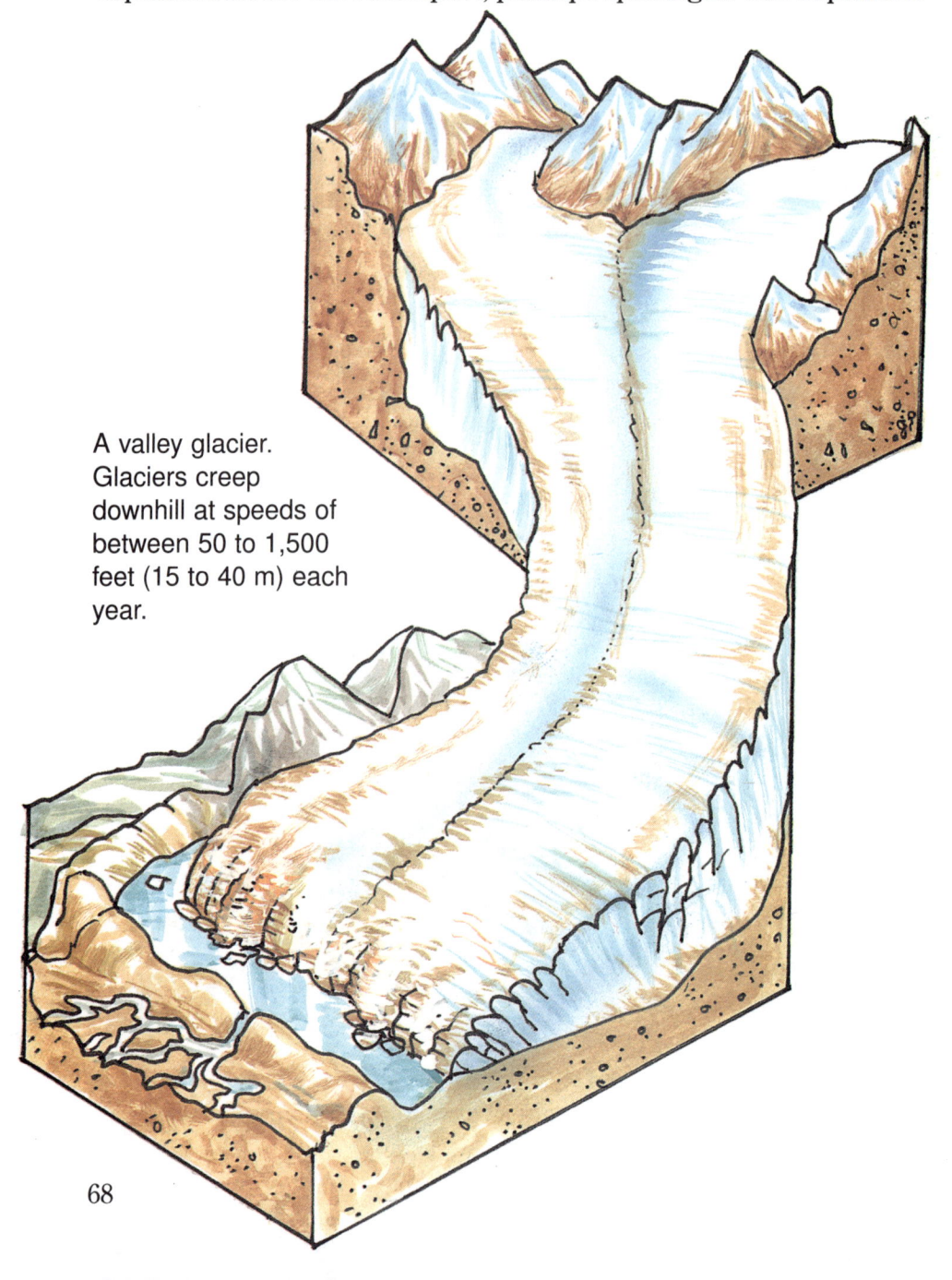

A valley glacier. Glaciers creep downhill at speeds of between 50 to 1,500 feet (15 to 40 m) each year.

Shaping the Landscape

can create enormous forces, equivalent to the force of several locomotives pulling at the rock. The force eventually cracks the rock, breaking it down into smaller pieces.

Glaciers are rivers of ice found in cold and mountainous regions. A glacier forms when snow builds up in a mountain valley and changes to ice. When the glacier gets heavy enough, it begins to move downhill. Rocks embedded in the sides and bottom of the glacier scrape away the surrounding rocks. The glacier gouges out a U-shaped valley.

There are many glaciers in North America, especially along the mountainous coasts of southern Alaska and northern British Columbia. Other North American glaciers are found in Montana and on such high western peaks as Mount Rainier in Washington State and Mount Shasta in California. A section of Montana has been set aside as Glacier National Park.

The effect of water is very noticeable in areas that have a large amount of limestone under the soil. Limestone is made of a chemical called calcium carbonate. It is easily dissolved by acids in rainwater. As the acid rainwater runs over limestone rocks, the rock

Traleika glacier is one of the many "rivers of ice" in Alaska.

Looking at the Earth

slowly dissolves. This process is called chemical weathering. Acid rainwater often trickles down vertical cracks in limestone. The rainwater dissolves limestone as it goes, gradually widening the crack in the stone until a deep hole, called a sink hole, is formed.

In some places, caves may be formed underground. In many caves, the water drips from the roof to the floor. As it does so, it evaporates, leaving behind the limestone that was dissolved in it. This causes formations of limestone called stalactites to grow down from the roof like stone icicles. On the floor, formations of limestone called stalagmites build up where the water drips. Eventually, stalactites and stalagmites join to form columns from floor to ceiling.

Water flowing in rivers has an important effect on the landscape. Fast-flowing rivers cut into the rocks they flow over, forming valleys and canyons. Many rivers have carved deep canyons. The Snake River, which empties into the Columbia, has cut the deepest canyon in the United States where it flows between the boundaries of Idaho and Oregon. The canyon averages 5,500 feet (1,676 m) in depth for a distance of 40 miles (64 km). The Yellowstone River in Wyoming and the Yakima River in Washington State also have deep canyons.

The most wonderful canyon of all is the Grand Canyon, cut by the Colorado River in northwestern Arizona. The Grand Canyon is

How erosion by a river can alter the landscape. At first, the river cuts a deep canyon. Later, the canyons widen to produce valleys and hills.

Shaping the Landscape

about 217 miles (349 km) long, 4 to 18 miles (6 to 29 km) wide, and more than 1 mile (1.6 km) deep.

Soil is produced when rocks are broken down. At first, only a loose mass of rock fragments, stones, and sand exist. After a while, however, plants take root and help bind the particles together. When the plants die, their rotting remains sink into the mass, turning into soil. Bacteria and fungi in the soil help break the plants down even more, producing a brown substance called humus. Earthworms and other animals, digging in the soil, help mix the humus with the rock particles. When they die, their remains mix with the soil and enrich it. Eventually, a fertile soil is produced.

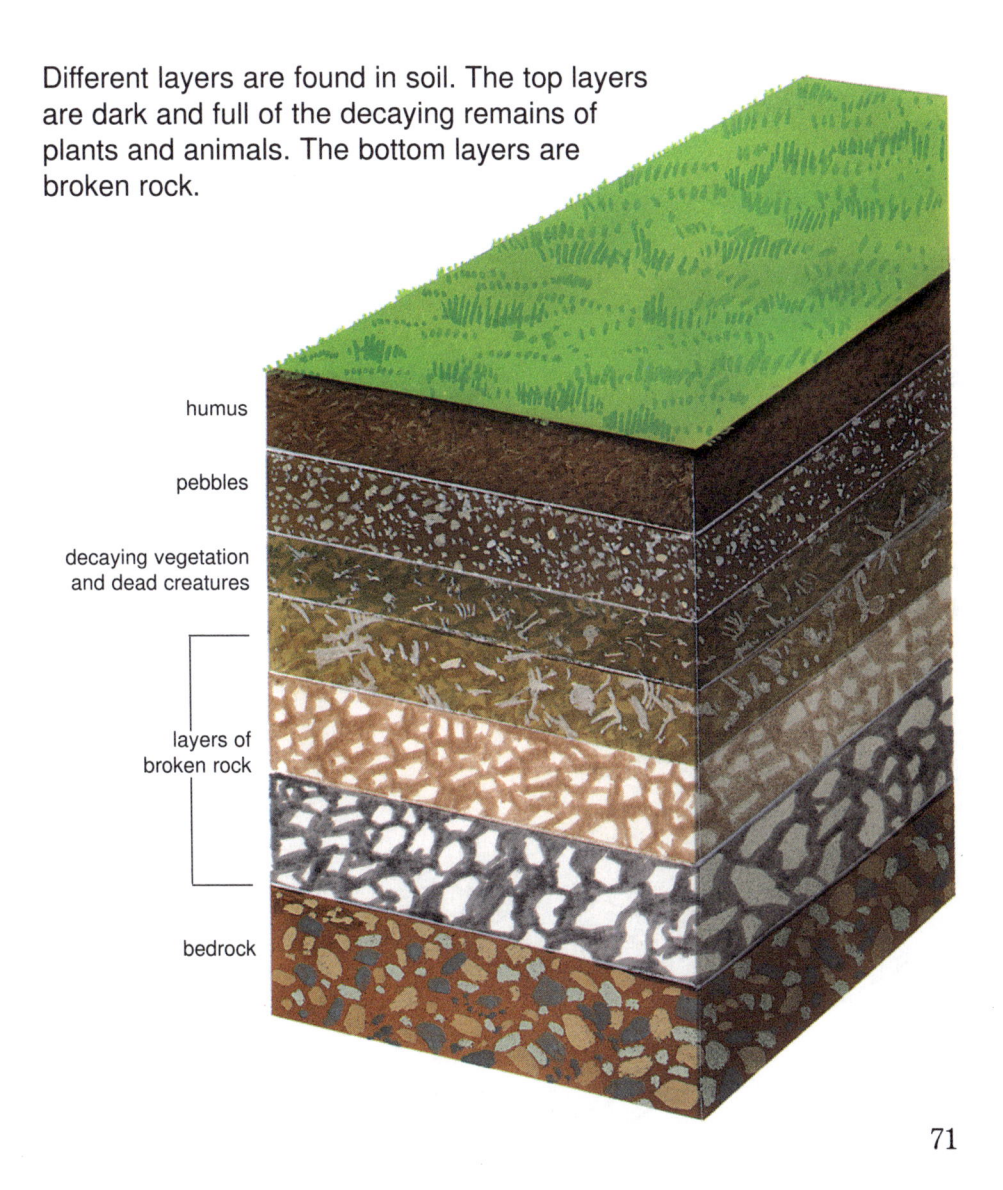

Different layers are found in soil. The top layers are dark and full of the decaying remains of plants and animals. The bottom layers are broken rock.

humus

pebbles

decaying vegetation and dead creatures

layers of broken rock

bedrock

Looking at the Earth

The Watery World

When rain falls onto the ground, it may soak in or it may run off. If it runs off, it will run toward lower ground, forming a little stream. Other streams arise from springs bubbling out of the earth. Small streams join together to form creeks; creeks empty into rivers. Rivers flow into lakes or into the ocean.

Rivers may be youthful, mature, or old, like people. When a river is youthful, its flowing waters form steep V-shaped valleys. Young streams are swift-flowing and usually have very crooked courses. There are deep canyons and steep ridges in a region that has many youthful streams.

After millions of years of stream erosion, a youthful river valley becomes wider and smoother, turning into a mature river valley. Tributaries cut through the ridges and high crests of land. The land becomes less rugged. The river curves less sharply and the water does not flow as fast.

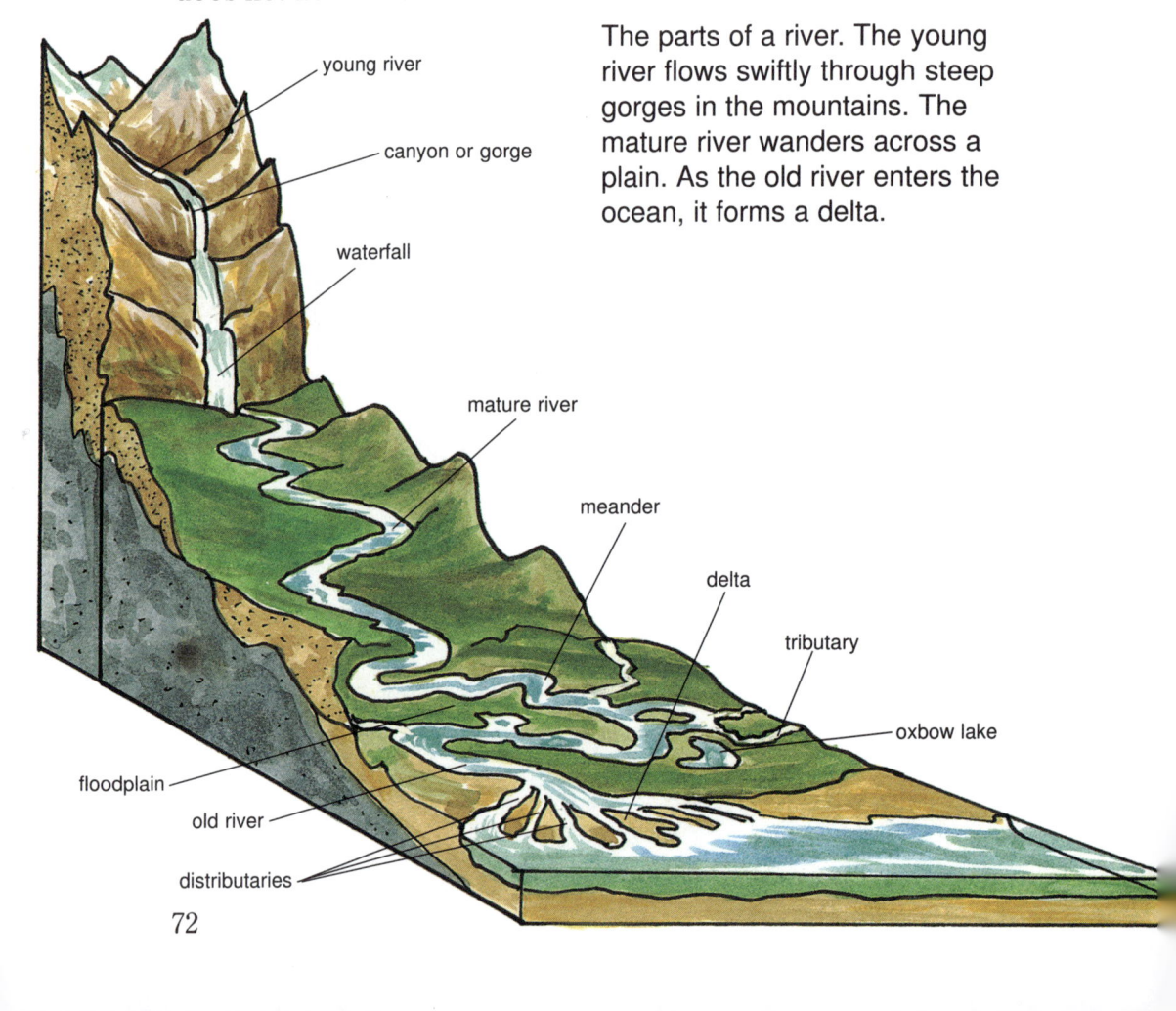

The parts of a river. The young river flows swiftly through steep gorges in the mountains. The mature river wanders across a plain. As the old river enters the ocean, it forms a delta.

The Watery World

If stream erosion continues for more millions of years, the countryside will change again. The water will wear away the land until the river winds slowly across a nearly level plain. The water of the river will cut into the banks and widen the stream bed. Finally the river valley becomes broad and quiet. A river like this is called an old river.

Sometimes part of an old winding river cuts across one of its own curves, leaving a curved portion of water behind. The curved portion of water may become permanently separated from the river and form a lake. We call a lake formed in this way an oxbow lake because of its shape.

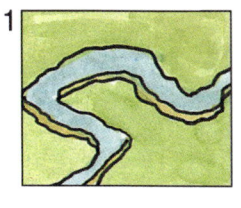

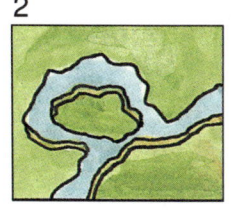

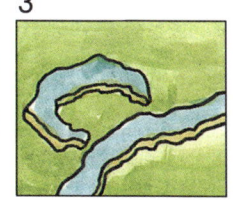

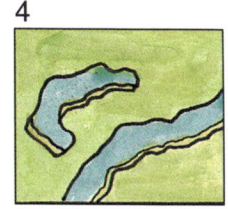

The formation of an oxbow lake.

Lakes can form wherever there is a cup or basin in the Earth's surface to catch and hold water. There are several ways these basins can form. Most of the lakes in Minnesota, Wisconsin,

Some Prominent Rivers of the World

Name	Location	Flows into	Length
Nile	Africa	Mediterranean Sea	4,100 miles (6,600 km)
Amazon	South America	Atlantic Ocean	4,000 miles (6,400 km)
Mississippi-Missouri	North America	Gulf of Mexico	3,741 miles (6,021 km)
Ob-Irtysh	Asia	Gulf of Ob	3,460 miles (5,570 km)
Yangtze	Asia	East China Sea	3,400 miles (5,500 km)
Congo	Africa	Atlantic Ocean	2,900 miles (4,700 km)
Murray-Darling	Australia	Great Australian Bight	2,310 miles (3,718 km)
Volga	Europe	Caspian Sea	2,290 miles (3,685 km)
La Plata	South America	Atlantic Ocean	2,100 miles (3,400 km)
Rio Grande	North America	Gulf of Mexico	1,885 miles (3,034 km)
Yukon	North America	Bering Sea	1,875 miles (2,989 km)
Danube	Europe	Black Sea	1,750 miles (2,816 km)

Looking at the Earth

Michigan, and New York were formed by glaciers gouging out basins. The best-known lakes made in this way are the Great Lakes – Lakes Superior, Michigan, Huron, Erie, and Ontario. Lake Superior is the world's largest freshwater lake. The largest saltwater lake is the Caspian Sea.

Some Prominent Lakes of the World

Name	Location	Area	Greatest depth
Caspian Sea	Russia-Iran	143,200 sq mi (371,000 sq km)	3,363 feet (1,025 m)
Superior	U.S.A.-Canada	31,700 sq mi (82,100 sq km)	1,332 feet (406 m)
Victoria	Africa	26,800 sq mi (69,500 sq km)	269 feet (82 m)
Huron	U.S.A.-Canada	23,000 sq mi (59,600 sq km)	750 feet (229 m)
Michigan	U.S.A.	22,300 sq mi (57,800 sq km)	922 feet (281 m)
Large Aral	Russia	12,950 sq mi (33,500 sq km)	100 feet (30 m)
Tanganyika	Africa	12,700 sq mi (32,900 sq km)	4,823 feet (1,470 m)
Great Bear Lake	Canada	12,100 sq mi (31,500 sq km)	1,463 feet (446 m)
Baykal	Russia	12,200 sq mi (31,500 sq km)	5,315 feet (1,620 m)
Erie	U.S.A.-Canada	9,900 sq mi (25,700 sq km)	210 feet (64 m)
Ontario	U.S.A.-Canada	7,300 sq mi (19,000 sq km)	800 feet (244 m)

In Kentucky, there are hundreds of small lakes that were made by water collecting in "sinks" in the limestone rock of this region. In Oregon the Warner Lakes were formed by the breaking and slipping of a part of the Earth's crust, the same sort of event that causes earthquakes. The ground sank enough in some places to form basins that filled with water.

As the waters of rivers spread out upon entering the ocean, their rate of flow slows down, and they deposit the soil and other sediment they carry. Sometimes the sediment forms a delta, a promontory of land at the river mouth. River water also carries traces of salt and other minerals with it. In this way the ocean continues to get more and more salty. If all the salt in the ocean were separated from the water and spread out in a layer, it would make a blanket 150 feet (46 m) deep covering the entire surface of the Earth.

About 70 percent of the Earth's surface is covered by water. There are four oceans: the Pacific, Atlantic, Indian, and Arctic. The largest ocean, the Pacific, covers nearly one-third of the Earth's surface. At its widest point, between Panama and Malaysia, it stretches nearly halfway around the world.

The Watery World

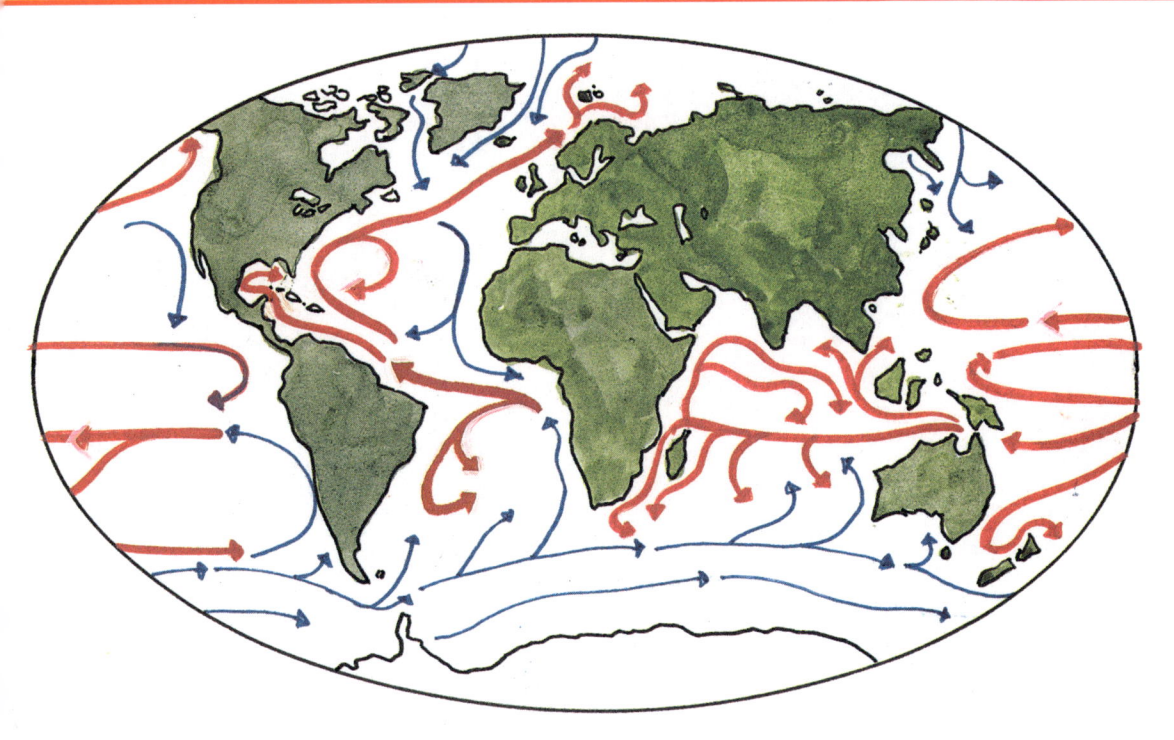

The main cool (blue) and warm (red) ocean currents. The currents circulate in the same directions as the winds.

Within the oceans, mighty currents of water circulate, like rivers within the seas. There are two clockwise circulations in the northern hemisphere – in the North Atlantic and the North Pacific. In the southern oceans, there are three counter-clockwise circular currents – in the southern Pacific, the southern Atlantic, and the southern Indian Ocean. Although the ocean currents are slow-moving, they carry enormous amounts of water. The Gulf Stream carries 1,050 million cubic feet (30 million cubic m) of water northward along the Florida coast every second, for example.

The tides are caused by the pull of the moon's gravity on the waters of the oceans. The pull of the moon makes the ocean water bulge toward the moon, and a high tide occurs at the places directly beneath the moon. At the same time, places on the opposite side of the Earth also have a high tide. The sun also pulls the ocean water, but not so strongly. Once a month, when the sun and moon are in line, the sun's pull adds to the moon's pull, creating a very high tide called a spring tide. At other times, the sun's pull acts against the moon's pull, and the tide is lower than usual.

Weather Watching

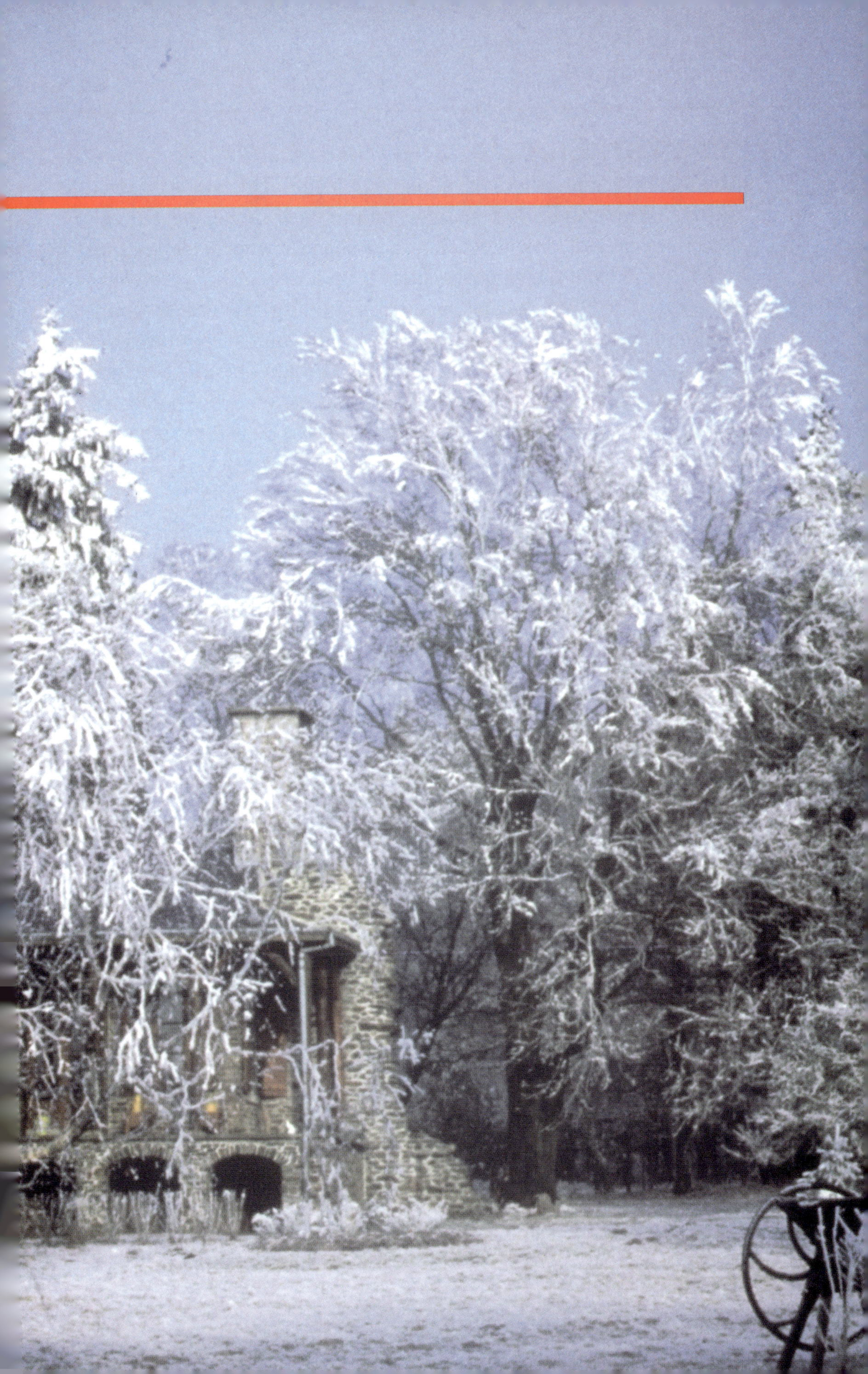

Weather Watching

Weather, Climate, and Seasons

The Earth's atmosphere is a restless place. The air is always moving. Winds and breezes are air on the move. When air moves, it carries water vapor with it. The water vapor may form clouds and rain may fall from the clouds. Violent thunderstorms may develop. You can see that strong winds, pounding rain, and loud thunderclaps are full of energy. This energy comes from the sun, the source of almost all energy on Earth. The sun's energy reaches the Earth as radiation – heat, light, and other forms such as ultraviolet rays. The radiation travels across the empty space between the sun and the Earth.

The radiation travels through the Earth's atmosphere to the ground. The ground heats up and then warms the air just above the ground. The warm air rises, carrying some heat away from the ground. Warm air rises because it is less dense than cold air. Perhaps the sun's energy reaches a lake, sea, or pool of water. If the water becomes hot enough, it evaporates (changes into a gas), forming warm water vapor. The water vapor rises into the air, carrying heat away from the lake, sea, or pool.

The total weight of the air pressing down on a book is about 2,000 pounds, or one ton (907 kg).

At places where the air is rising, the atmospheric pressure is falling. As the air rises, it does not press so heavily on the ground. Atmospheric pressure is caused by the tremendous weight of air in the atmosphere pressing down on the Earth. At sea level, this pressure is 14.7 pounds on each square inch of surface area

78

Weather, Climate, and Seasons

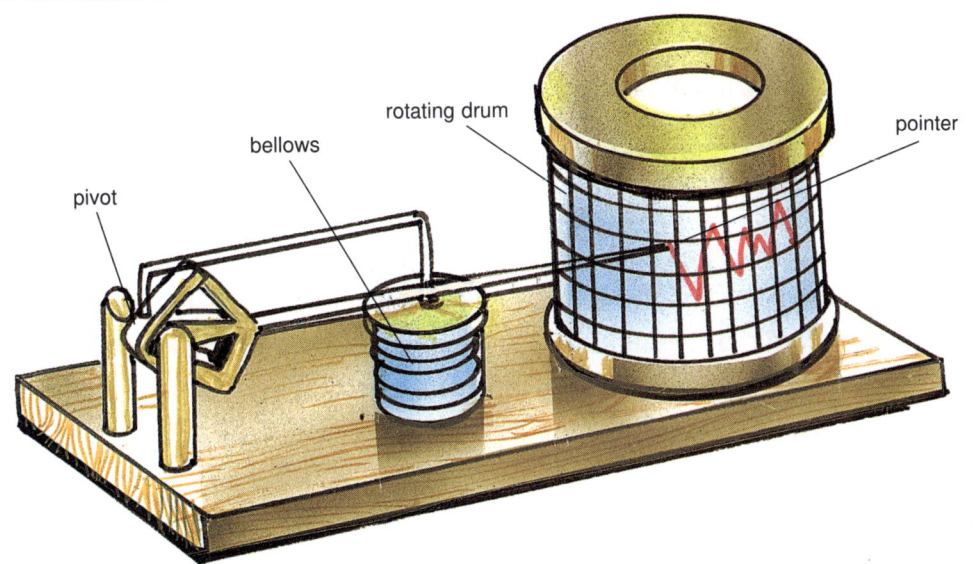

The barograph, a type of barometer, is a common weather instrument. It records atmospheric pressure as a tracing on paper wrapped around a slowly moving drum. The bellows is an evacuated (airless) chamber which rises and falls as the atmospheric pressure changes. The movement of the bellows makes the pen or pointer move up and down.

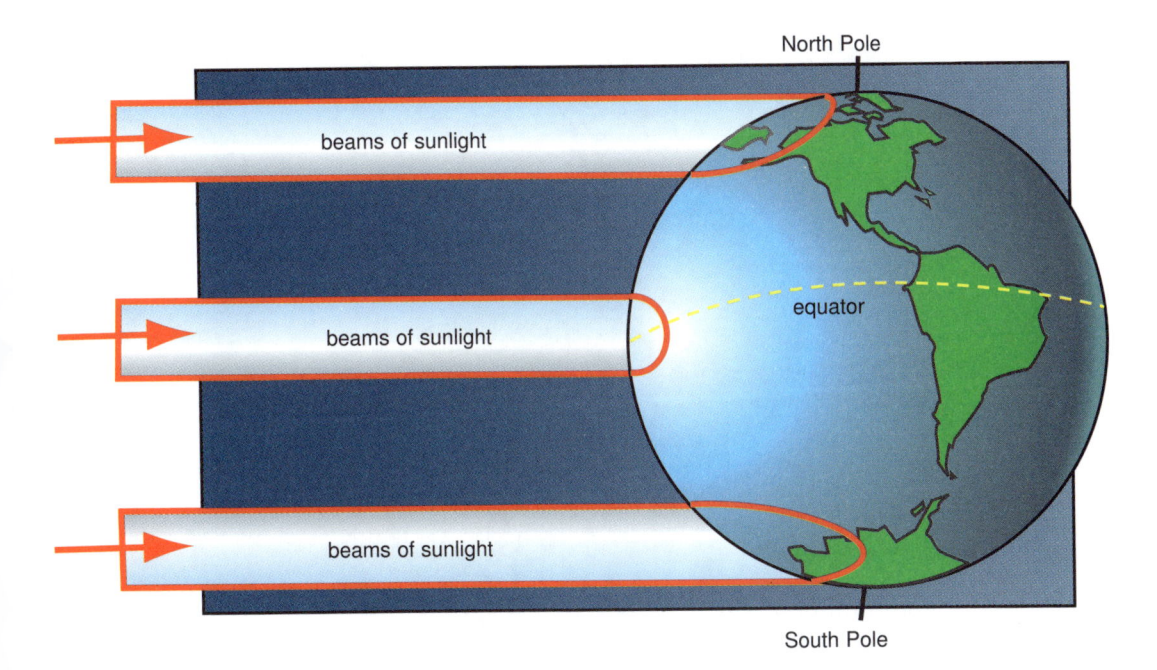

The heat from the sun is most concentrated when it strikes the ground at right angles. This means that the sun's heat is most concentrated at the equator, and more spread out at the poles.

Weather Watching

(101,030 newtons per square meter). Atmospheric pressure is measured with an instrument called a barometer. Because changing pressure is a sign that the weather is about to change, meteorologists (scientists who study the weather) use barometers to help forecast the weather.

Winds blow from areas of high pressure to areas of low pressure and carry heat from one place to another. The winds play an important role in regulating the climate because the sun's energy does not fall evenly on all parts of the Earth. The sun's energy is more concentrated in the tropics than at the poles. At any time, the

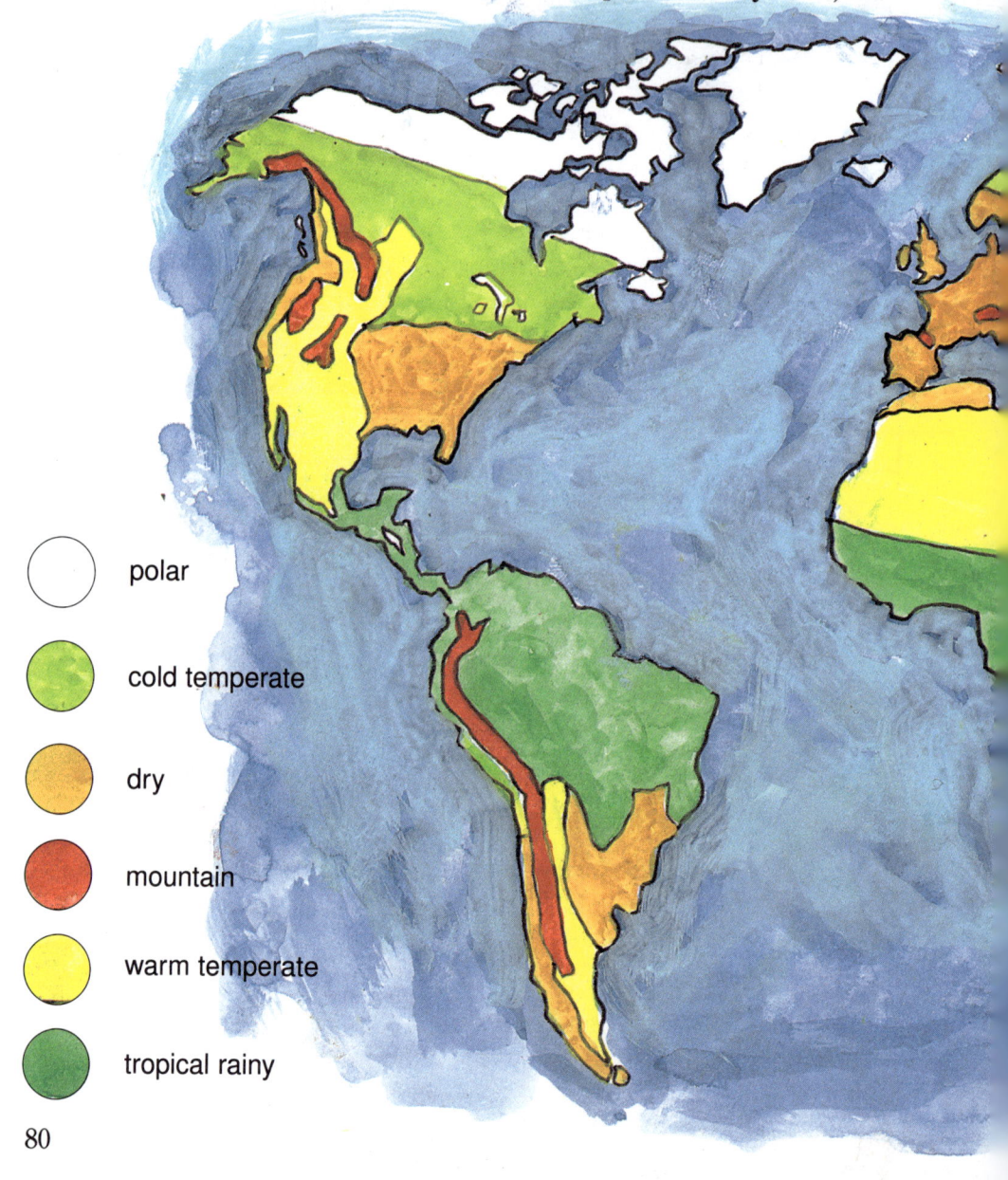

polar

cold temperate

dry

mountain

warm temperate

tropical rainy

Weather, Climate, and Seasons

temperature at the equator can be as much as 180°F (82°C) hotter than the temperature in the Arctic. There are two reasons why temperatures are high near the equator. First, because the Earth's surface is curved, the sun's rays reach the equator more directly than they reach the poles. Second, the sun's rays are weakened by the time they reach the poles because they pass through a greater amount of atmosphere before reaching the ground.

The uneven distribution of the sun's energy across the globe produces different climates in different places. Some places are cold, some are hot, and some have moderate temperatures. How

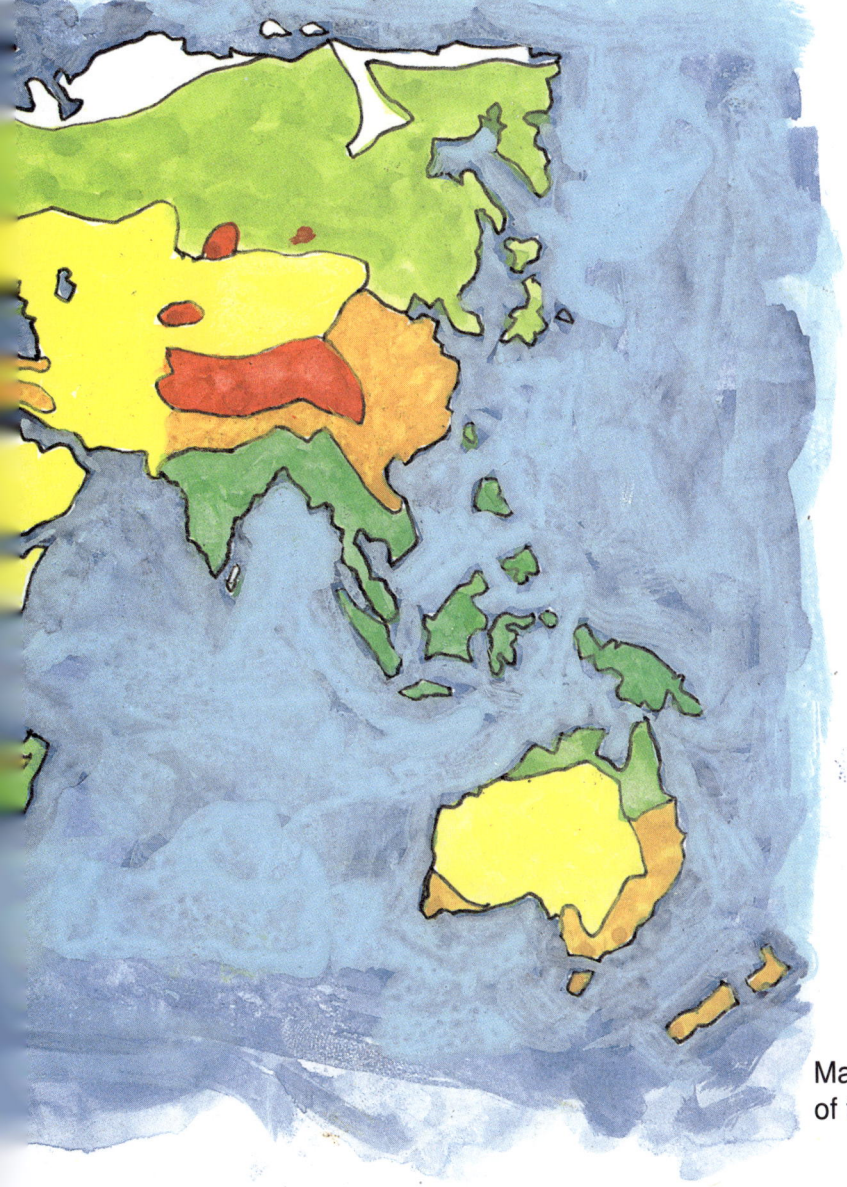

Major climatic regions of the world.

81

Weather Watching

hot a place is depends mainly on how far it is from the equator. It is generally hotter near the equator than in other parts of the world. But climate, or average weather conditions, also depends upon local circumstances. The higher up a place is, the colder its climate will be. If a warm ocean flows along a coast, the coast will have a warmer climate than a coast that has no warm current.

The seasons occur because the Earth is tilted as it travels around the sun. The Earth's axis of rotation – the imaginary line around which the Earth spins – is tilted at an angle of 23½ degrees in relation to the plane of its orbit. This means that, at certain times of the year, some areas of the Earth are tilted away from the sun and other areas are tilted toward the sun. The Northern Hemisphere is tilted toward the sun during the middle of the year, so June and July are warm summer months in the Northern Hemisphere. The Southern Hemisphere is tilted away from the sun at this time, so it is winter in southern lands in June and July. Six months later the situation is reversed: it is summer in the Southern Hemisphere and winter in the Northern Hemisphere.

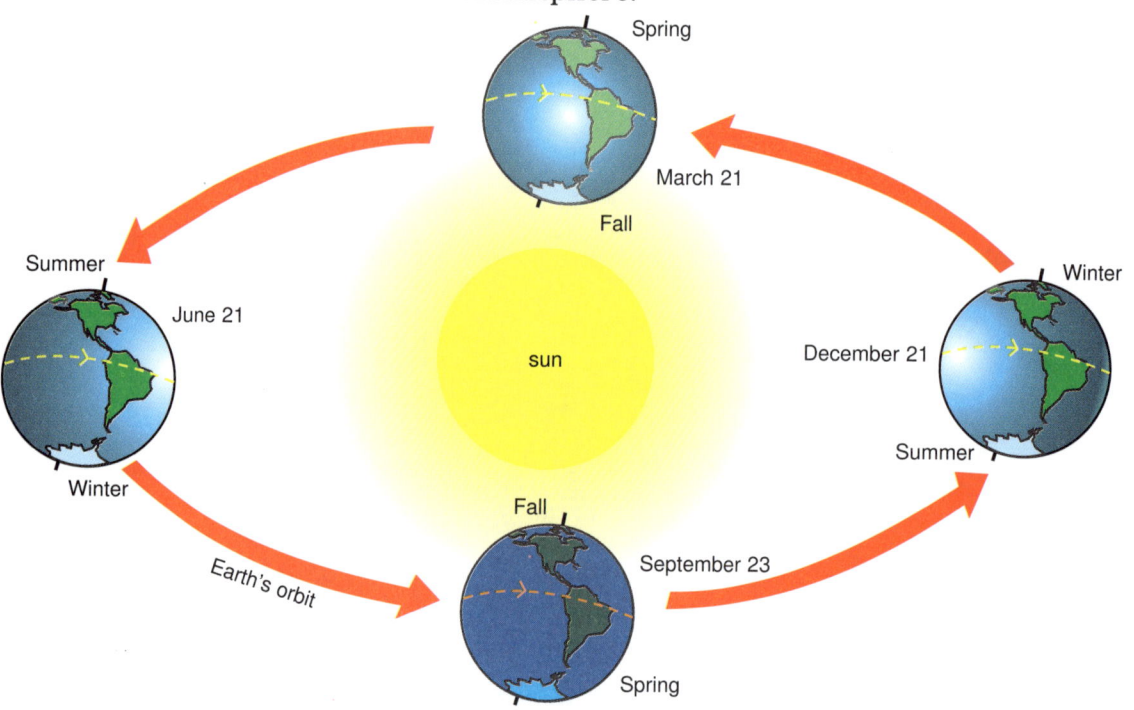

The positions of the Earth and the sun during the year. On June 21, the Northern Hemisphere is tilted toward the sun and it is summer. On December 21, the Northern Hemisphere is tilted away from the sun and it is winter.

82

Air on the Move

Currents of hot air are continually rising over hot areas, such as hillsides that catch the sunlight or cities that generate heat. Cool air moves in to take the place of the hot air that has risen. In turn, this air is heated and rises. A continuous current of air results. Such currents are called convection currents.

Convection currents do not just occur in the atmosphere. They are found wherever liquids or gases are heated – in coffee cups, saucepans, and oceans, for example. In the atmosphere, convection currents are called winds or breezes. They can be large currents that move air over great distances, or small local breezes. Land and sea breezes are convection currents on a small scale. On a hot sunny day, air above the land heats up more quickly than the air above the sea. This causes air to rise over the land and cooler air to

In coastal regions, a light breeze blows in from the sea during the day. This breeze is called a sea breeze. During the night, the breeze blows in the opposite direction.

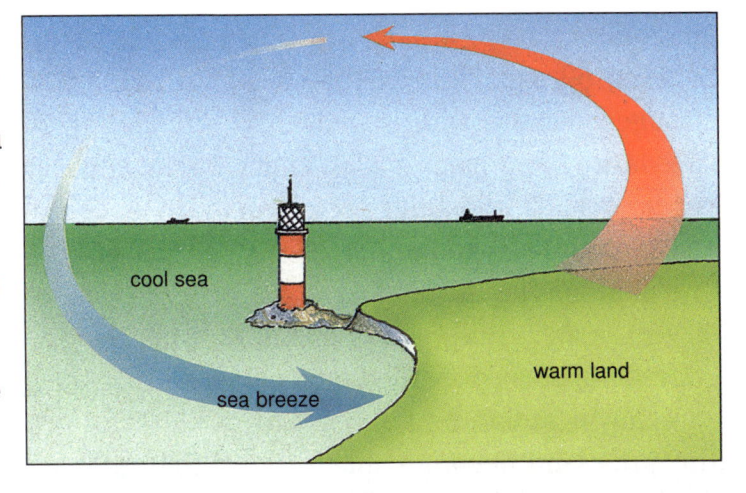

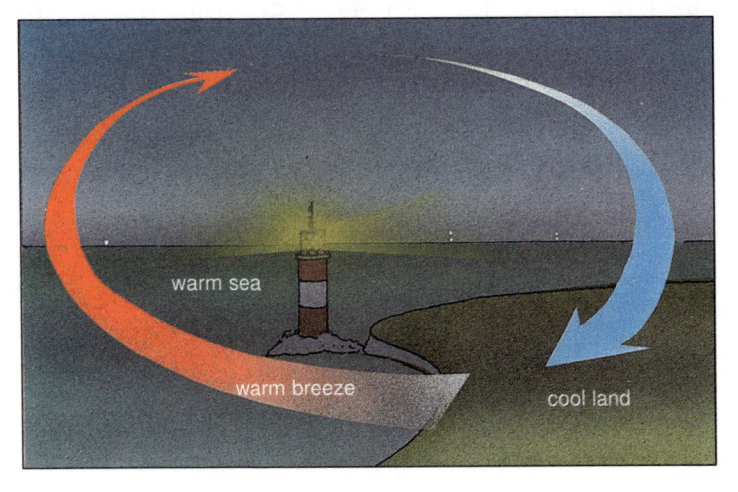

cool sea

warm land

sea breeze

warm sea

warm breeze

cool land

Weather Watching

flow inland from the sea. A cool breeze blowing from the sea is called a sea breeze. At night, the land cools more rapidly than the sea and the situation is reversed: the breeze blows from the land to the sea. This breeze is called a land breeze.

We could have explained land and sea breezes in terms of atmospheric pressure differences. Where where hot air rises, the pressure is low. Where cold air falls, the pressure is greater. Thus temperature differences exist, so do pressure differences. During the day, pressure over the sea is higher than pressure over the land, for example. Air flows from areas of high pressure to areas of low pressure. Therefore the air moves from the sea to the land during the day. During the night, the land breeze flows from the area of high pressure on the land to the area of low pressure over the sea.

We use the term "breeze" for a light wind, up to a speed of about 30 miles per hour (50 kilometers per hour). Winds blowing at up to about 60 mph (96 km/h) are called gales. A storm has winds of between 60 and 75 mph (96-120 km/h). Hurricanes possess the strongest winds, with speeds over 75 mph (120 km/h). Wind speeds are often measured in knots. 1 knot equals about 1.15 miles per hour (1.85 kilometers per hour). The speed of ships at sea is also measured in knots.

Winds similar to land and sea breezes can blow on a much larger scale. India, for example, has large and powerful convection currents called monsoons. During the spring and early summer in India, the temperature of the land gradually rises. In June, the land becomes much hotter than the sea. The air above the land grows hot and rises. Air from the sea flows toward the land and the monsoon wind begins to blow inland from the sea.

Calm
wind speed
less than 1 mph

Gentle Breeze
wind speed
8-12 mph

Moderate Breeze
wind speed
13-18 mph

Fresh Breeze
wind speed
19-24 mph

Air on the Move

Because it blows from the sea, the summer monsoon is full of moisture and causes torrential rain. As much as 30 feet (9 m) of rain can fall in a month.

During the fall and winter, the land cools down until it is cooler than the sea. Now, the monsoon wind reverses and blows from the land to the sea. The winter monsoon is a dry wind because it comes from the parched country areas in the north of India.

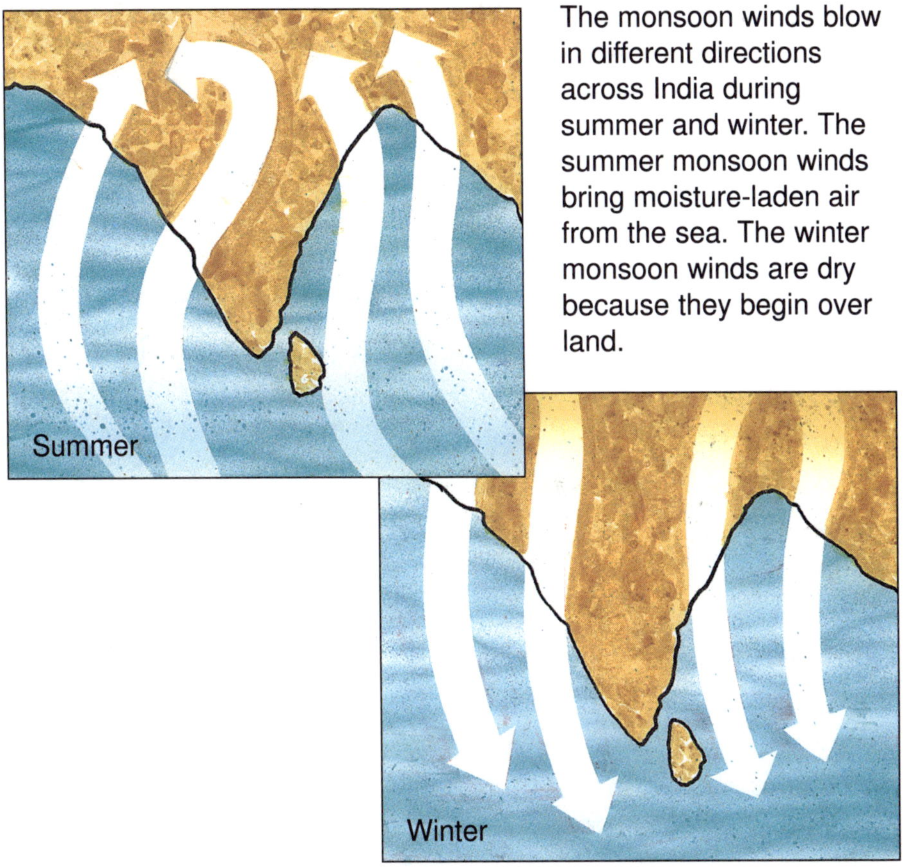

The monsoon winds blow in different directions across India during summer and winter. The summer monsoon winds bring moisture-laden air from the sea. The winter monsoon winds are dry because they begin over land.

Summer

Winter

Strong Breeze
wind speed
25-31 mph

Near Gale
wind speed
32-38 mph

Gale
wind speed
39-46 mph

Strong Gale
wind speed
47-54 mph

Storm
wind speed
55-63 mph

85

Weather Watching

The trade winds that blow toward the equator over the oceans of the tropics are also large-scale convection currents. At the equator, hot air rises and, high above the ground, moves toward the poles. Eventually the air cools and drops to the ground. The cool air then flows back to the equator. This ground-level flow creates the trade winds, blowing toward the equator. However, the flow of air is affected by the west-to-east rotation of the Earth. The rotation deflects the trade winds from a strict north-south direction and, as a result, the trade winds north of the equator blow from the northeast, while the trade winds in the Southern Hemisphere blow from the southeast.

In polar regions, convection currents cause winds called the polar easterlies to blow toward the equator, away from the high pressure areas at the poles. In middle latitudes – about halfway between the equator and the poles – the westerly winds blow. In these regions, cold air from the poles meets and mixes with warm tropical air. The result is turbulent air, with areas of low and high pressure forming and being carried along by the westerly winds.

The jet streams follow a zigzag course around the globe. They can form large loops with high pressure at the center. A balloon released into the jet stream would take two weeks to travel around the globe.

Air on the Move

The low pressure areas form when warm air from the tropics pushes poleward into the cold air. The warm air rises over the cold air, creating the area of low pressure. The low pressure area, called a depression, is blown eastward by the wind. The warm air that rises eventually cools and sinks toward the ground. A high pressure area develops where the air descends. The high pressure area is called an anticyclone. The anticyclone is blown eastward along with the depressions. The weather in these regions is influenced by a series of depressions and anticyclones blown in from the west.

Fast-blowing winds occur high in the atmosphere at middle latitudes. These eastward-blowing winds are called jet streams. They are found 6 miles (10 km) up and blow at speeds up to 400 mph (645 km/h). When high-flying aircraft first entered service, pilots found that flying to Europe from America across the Atlantic Ocean was much faster than flying to America from Europe. The aircraft were being blown eastward by the jet streams when traveling to Europe and had to battle against the jet streams when returning.

The jet streams follow a zigzag path as they blow around the world. They have an important effect on the weather. Depressions often form where the jet stream veers to the north, and anticyclones form where the jet stream veers to the south. Sometimes the jet stream veers so much that a circular loop of wind is formed. These loops are called blocking highs because the air inside them is at high pressure. When a blocking high forms, the normal flow of depressions and anticyclones from the west stops. The weather becomes hot and dry for a long time.

In some parts of the world, such as over the oceans or over large continents, huge masses of air develop. Inside these air masses, the temperature and moisture content is the same over a large area. The air mass may be warm or cold, dry or moist, depending on the temperature of the land or sea area under it. The two main air masses are the warm tropical air mass, formed near the equator, and the cold polar air mass, formed near the poles. These air masses drift over the Earth's surface, bringing changes of weather as they move to new locations. During winter over North America, the cold polar air mass moves south from the Arctic and meets the warm air

Weather Watching

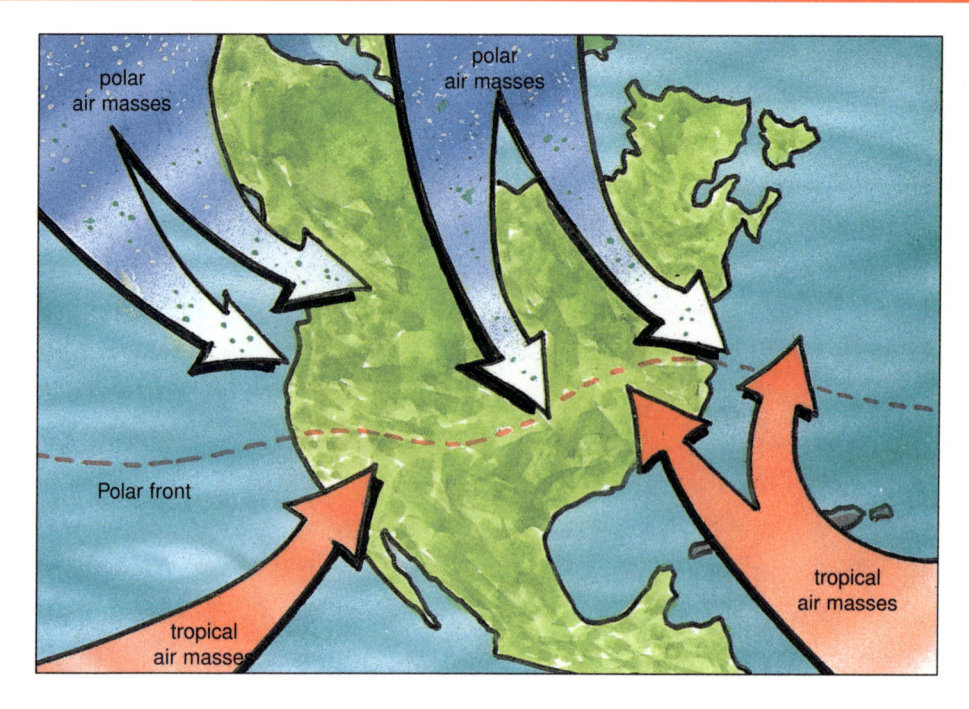

The cold polar air mass moves south over North America during the winter. A warm air mass moves north from the tropics in summer.

mass moving north from the tropics. Where they meet, the weather is unsettled and changeable, with clouds, rain, and storms.

The boundaries between air masses are called fronts. The three types of fronts are warm, cold, and occluded. In a warm front, warm air moves into an area occupied by cold air. Because warm air is less dense than cold air, it flows over and above the cold air. Often steady rain falls ahead of a warm front. In a cold front, cold air moves into an area occupied by warm air. The denser cold air slides under the warm air. Clouds and rain are produced as the warm air is forced upward. A period of heavy rain, followed by showers alternating with periods of sunshine, often occurs when a cold front moves into an area. An occluded front occurs when a moving cold front overtakes a warm front. The cold front lifts the warm front off the ground and carries it along. Steady rain is produced, followed by brighter weather.

The state of the weather at any time is shown on a weather chart. A weather chart is a map that shows the air pressure, winds, temperature, cloud cover, rainfall, and humidity at each place on the map. Sometimes a weather chart is called a synoptic

Air on the Move

Cold Front

warm air

warm air

cold air

Warm Front

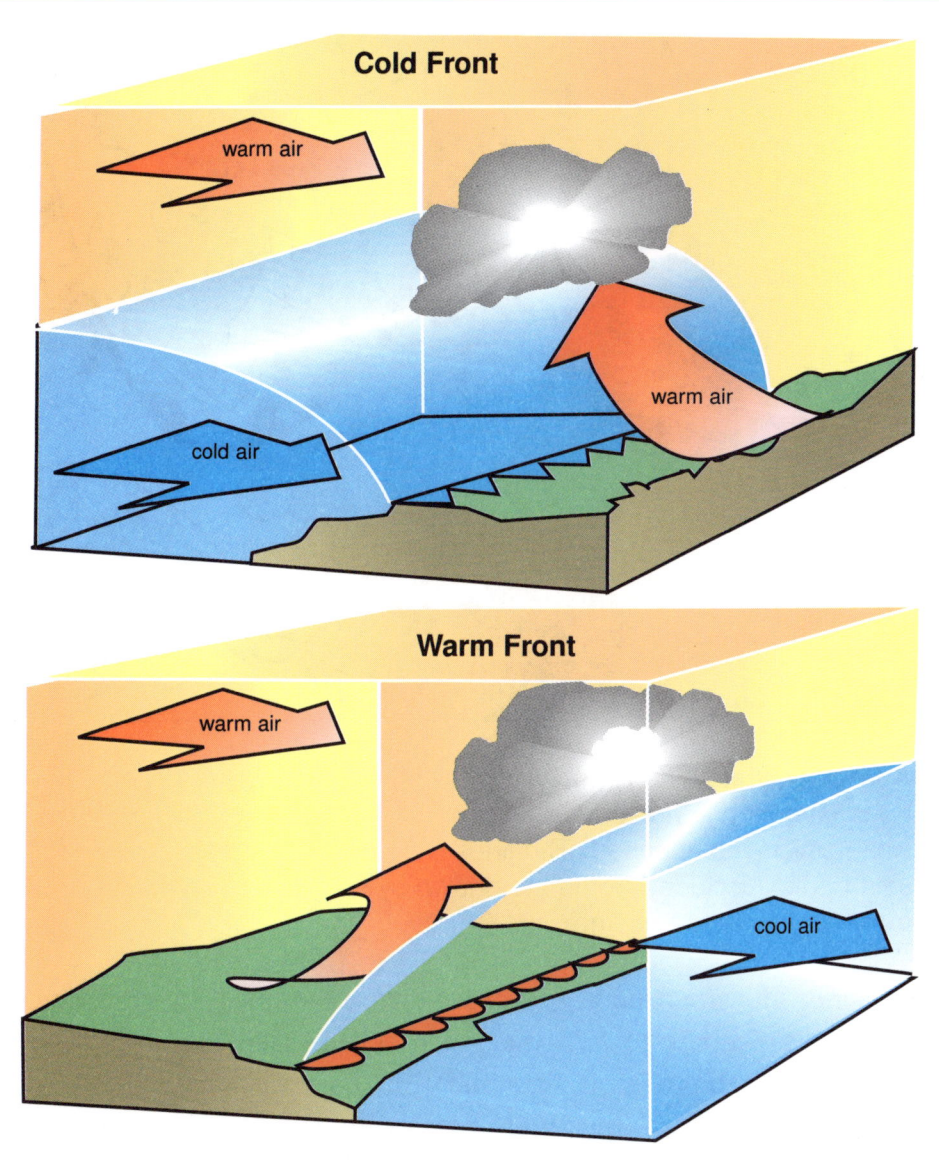

warm air

cool air

In a cold front, a wedge of cold air pushes under a mass of stationary warm air. In a warm front, a moving mass of warm air rises over a stationary mass of cold air. In both cases, the warm air cools as it rises, producing clouds.

chart because it presents a synopsis, or summary, of the weather at a certain time.

Lines called isobars are drawn on a weather chart to join places of equal sea level pressure. Anticyclones or areas of high pressure are marked with an H for "high." Depressions or areas of low pressure are marked with an L for "low." Wind speed and direction are indicated by arrow-like symbols.

89

Weather Watching

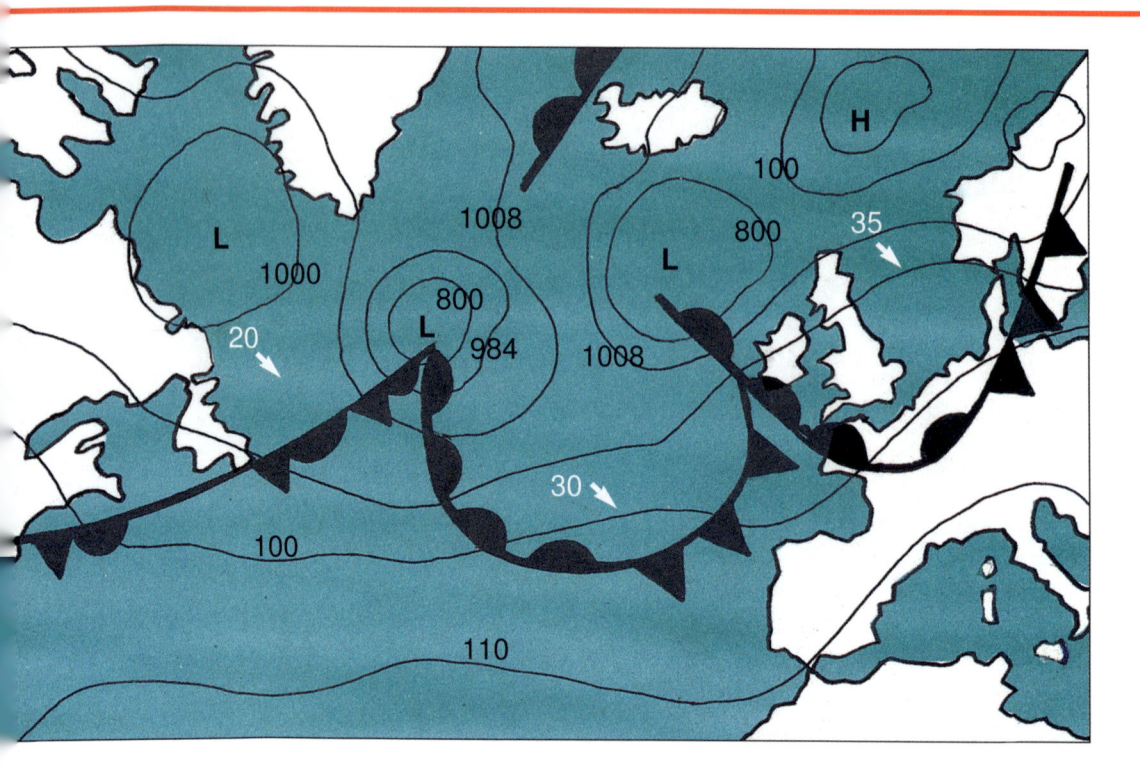

A weather chart. The lines, called isobars, join places of equal sea-level atmospheric pressure. Warm fronts are represented by lines with semicircles attached. The lines with triangles attached represent cold fronts. Occluded fronts are shown by semicircles and triangles drawn along the same line.

Winds blowing around a low-pressure area blow a short distance across the isobars toward the low pressure area. Winds blowing around a high-pressure area blow a short distance across the isobars away from the high pressure area. In the Northern Hemisphere, the winds blow clockwise around a high-pressure area, and counter-clockwise around a low-pressure area. In the Southern Hemisphere, the winds blow in the opposite direction.

A cold front is represented on a weather chart by a line with triangles attached. A warm front is represented by a line with small semicircles attached. An occluded front is indicated by a line with alternating triangles and semicircles. Other symbols indicate cloud cover, rain, snow, fog, thunderstorms, and other details of the weather.

Weather charts are drawn by meteorologists at the weather center. They use information received from weather stations around the country, from ships at sea, and from satellites in orbit above Earth.

Air on the Move

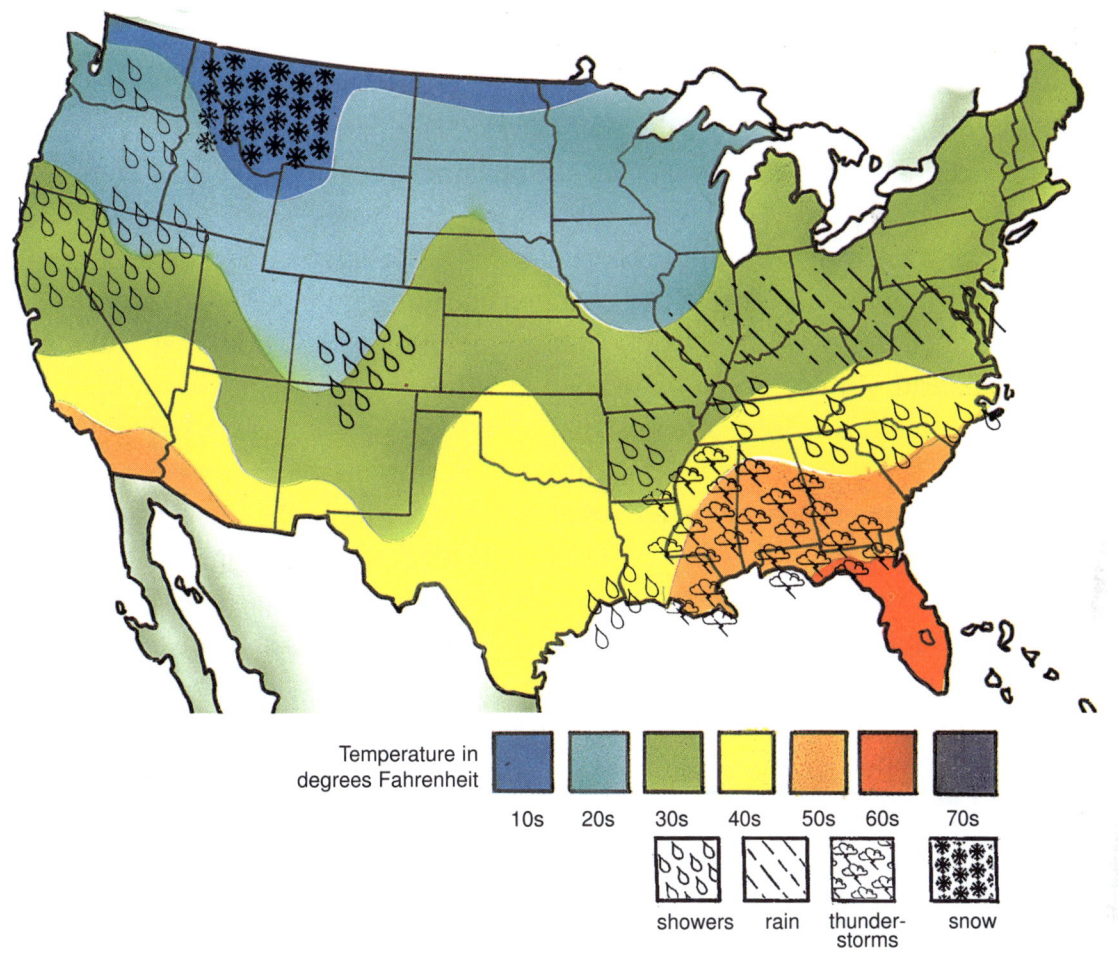

A map showing the predicted weather conditions over the United States.

Powerful computers calculate the way the weather is likely to develop. Using the laws of physics and mathematics, the computer calculates how the pressure, wind, temperature, and humidity will change at many different places across the country in the near future. For an accurate forecast, the computers do weather calculations every 60 miles (100 km) across the map, from east to west and north to south. The computer must also calculate the weather at 20 different heights above the ground. About 1,500 million calculations are needed to produce a daily global weather forecast. No wonder powerful computers are needed! The two largest weather computers are in Washington, D.C., and Bracknell, England. They can do about 3,000 million calculations each second and produce a forecast in about 7 minutes.

Weather Watching

Water's Endless Cycle

In nature, water is constantly being recycled. It is taking part in an endless process called the water cycle. The first stage of the cycle occurs when the sun heats the sea or some other body of water. The water evaporates and water vapor rises into the air. The wind blows the water vapor inland. Perhaps it is blown up a mountain slope. As the vapor rises, it cools and changes back into water, or condenses. The water falls as rain. In cold climates, hail or snow may fall instead of rain. The rain, or melted snow and hail, runs down the mountainside into streams and rivers. The streams and rivers return the water to the sea. The cycle is now complete.

In tropical coastal areas, water can run through the entire water cycle in an hour. In other places, the cycle takes much longer. In the Arctic, it can take tens of thousands of years to complete one cycle. In tropical coastal areas, rain may fall close to the sea from which the water evaporated. In other areas, a drop of water may travel thousands of miles between the time it evaporates and the time it falls to the ground again.

The water cycle combines convection currents – flows of heated air – with the evaporation and condensation of water. This combination

The sun is the driving force of the water cycle. It evaporates water from the sea, forming clouds.

Water's Endless Cycle

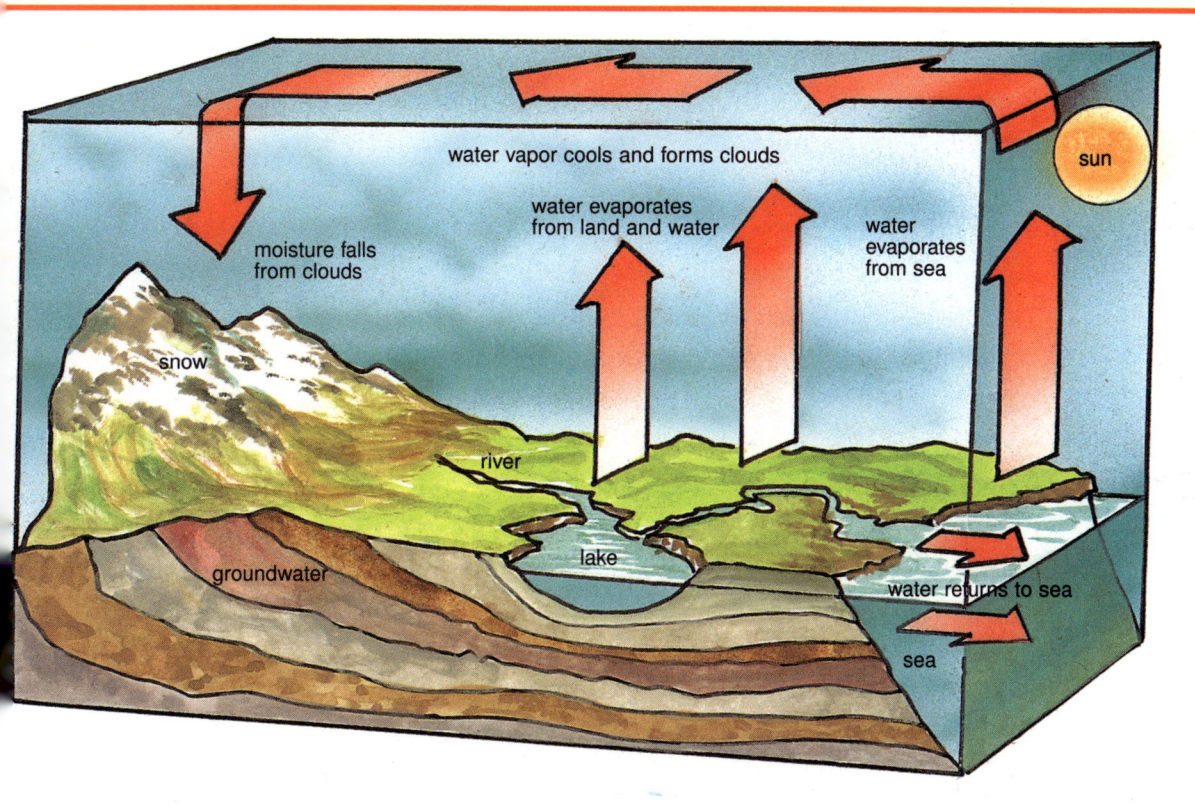

Water is being constantly recycled in the water cycle. Water evaporates from the sea, lakes, soil, and plants, and returns to the sea in rivers or by seeping through the ground.

is a very efficient way of transferring heat from one place to another. Heat is carried along not only by the hot air but also by the water vapor. Water gains heat when it turns into vapor and the vapor loses heat when it condenses. Thus the water cycle carries heat from the place where water evaporates to the place where the water vapor condenses.

A similar process takes place in a refrigerator. Inside a refrigerator, a liquid called the refrigerant evaporates to form a gas, absorbing heat as it does so. The gas is pumped to pipes at the back of the refrigerator where it condenses back into a liquid. As it condenses, the gas releases into the outside air the heat it absorbed inside the refrigerator. This process transfers heat from inside the refrigerator to the air outside the refrigerator.

When air contains a lot of water vapor on a warm day, the weather feels uncomfortable and "muggy." The cause of the discomfort is that air can hold only a limited amount of water

Weather Watching

vapor. On a hot and humid day, our sweat is not able to evaporate from our skins and thus cool us, because the air already has all the moisture it can hold.

The water vapor content of the air is called its humidity. When humidity is expressed as a percentage of the maximum possible, it is called relative humidity. The relative humidity in clouds and fog is 100 percent, since the air in clouds and fog contains the maximum amount of water vapor possible. In desert areas, where there is little water vapor in the air, the relative humidity is low, perhaps 10 percent or less.

Warm air can hold more water vapor than cold air. This is why dew, fog, and clouds form. Dew forms during the night when the temperature drops until the air can no longer hold its load of water vapor. The vapor condenses as tiny drops of water on cold surfaces, such as grass and spider webs.

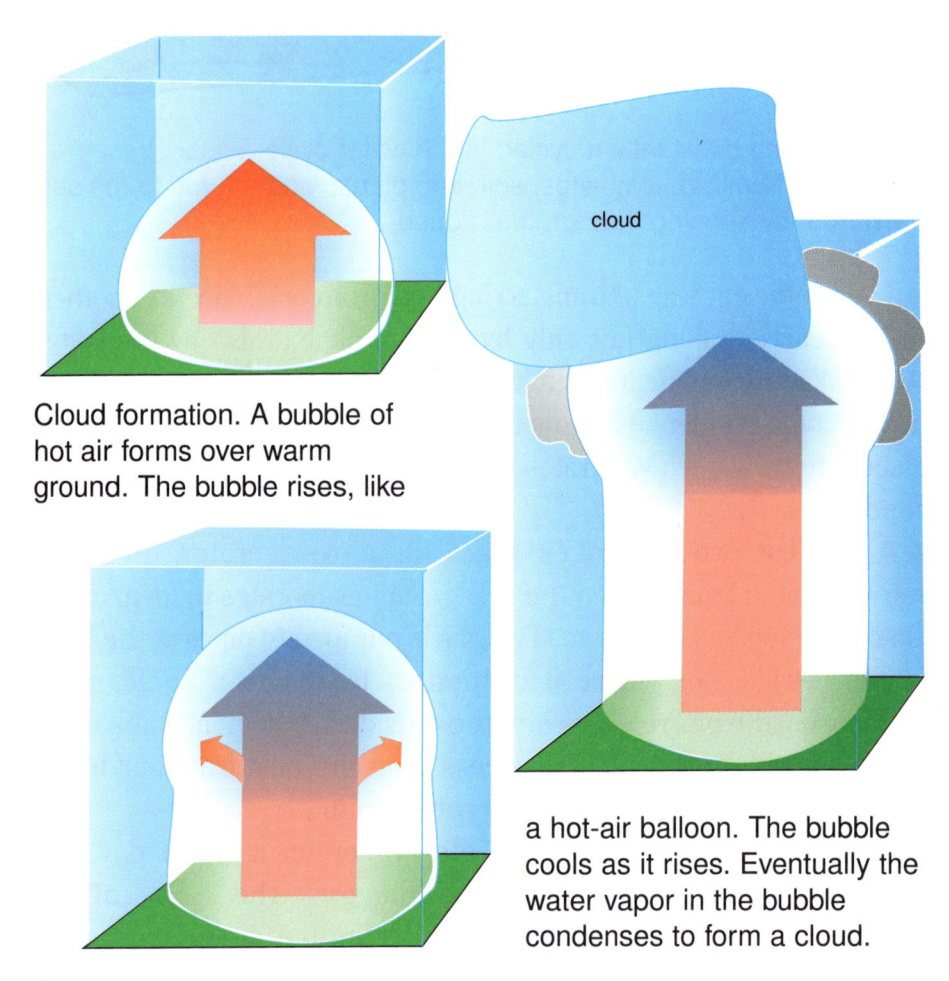

Cloud formation. A bubble of hot air forms over warm ground. The bubble rises, like a hot-air balloon. The bubble cools as it rises. Eventually the water vapor in the bubble condenses to form a cloud.

Water's Endless Cycle

In the fall, dew on a spider web is a familiar sight after a cold night.

You can make dew drops at home. Fill a jar with ice cubes and put a cover on it. Be sure that the outside of the jar is dry. Watch this dry surface closely. Soon you will see tiny drops of water form on the surface. The drops form when water vapor in the air condenses on the cold surface of the jar.

Fog and mist form when the air temperature lowers and tiny droplets of water condense on dust or other tiny particles in the air. Smog is a mixture of smoke and fog. It forms when vapor condenses on particles of soot in smoke or other airborne pollution.

Clouds form when warm air rises and cools. If the air cools enough, water vapor in the air will condense. Tiny droplets of liquid water or ice crystals form on particles in the air. The water droplets or crystals form a cloud. On summer days, fluffy "cotton ball" type clouds form over plowed fields or other warm areas. The air over the field forms a bubble of warm air that rises like a hot-air balloon. A small fluffy cloud may hold 100 to 1,000 tons (90 to 900 metric tons) of moisture. Looked at in another way, the cloud is carrying water weighing as much as 20 to 200 African elephants.

Weather Watching

Clouds also form along weather fronts. Along a front, warm air is forced to rise by the slow movement of large air masses. Clouds also form on the windward side of mountains and on mountain tops. Here the winds are forced to rise as they blow across the mountains.

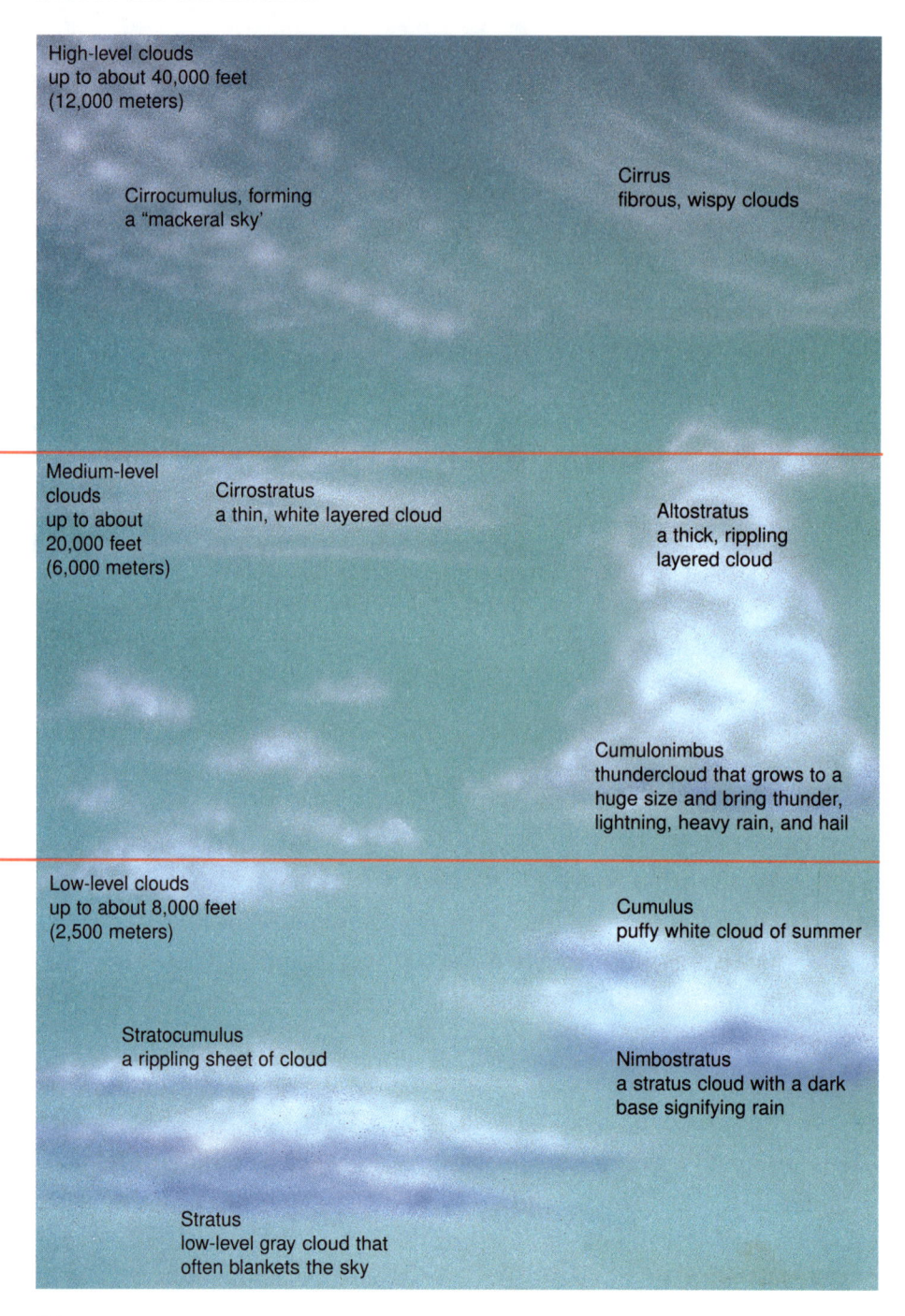

High-level clouds
up to about 40,000 feet
(12,000 meters)

Cirrocumulus, forming a "mackeral sky"

Cirrus
fibrous, wispy clouds

Medium-level clouds
up to about 20,000 feet
(6,000 meters)

Cirrostratus
a thin, white layered cloud

Altostratus
a thick, rippling layered cloud

Cumulonimbus
thundercloud that grows to a huge size and bring thunder, lightning, heavy rain, and hail

Low-level clouds
up to about 8,000 feet
(2,500 meters)

Cumulus
puffy white cloud of summer

Stratocumulus
a rippling sheet of cloud

Nimbostratus
a stratus cloud with a dark base signifying rain

Stratus
low-level gray cloud that often blankets the sky

Water's Endless Cycle

Clouds seem to come in all shapes and sizes. However there are really three basic cloud types. First, there are fluffy, "cotton ball" shaped clouds, called cumulus clouds. Next are layered clouds called stratus clouds. They are low, shapeless clouds that often cover small hills and valleys. Finally, there are thin, wispy clouds, called cirrus clouds. They appear high in the sky.

All clouds are variations or combinations of the three basic types. A low layer of fluffy clouds is called stratocumulus. It is a combination of stratus and cumulus clouds. Cirrocumulus clouds are fluffy clouds found high in the sky.

If a cloud is rain-bearing, its name begins or ends with "nimbo" or "nimbus." For example, a cumulonimbus cloud is a fluffy rain-bearing cloud. A nimbostratus cloud is a low layer of rain-bearing cloud.

The names given to clouds tell us the height at which the clouds are found. Cirrus clouds are all found high in the sky, and so are cirrocumulus and cirronimbus clouds. Clouds found at middle heights have names beginning with "alto." Altostratus clouds are layered clouds found at middle heights. Nimbostratus, stratocumulus and stratus clouds are all found at low heights. Cumulus and cumulonimbus clouds are found at a range of heights. A cumulonimbus cloud can be enormous. It can reach as high as 11 miles (18 km), twice as high as Mount Everest, and be 6 miles (10 km) across.

As clouds travel up over a mountain, they cool and lose their moisture. This means that rain falls on one side, and not on the other side of the mountain.

Weather Watching

Most cloud droplets are small and light. They float in the air like mist. Some droplets, however, are heavier and start to fall. As they fall, the droplets collide and join together to form rain drops. Each rain drop is made up of several million cloud droplets. In cold regions, where the tops of clouds often contain ice crystals, rain forms by another process. Here, the ice crystals combine until they fall through the cloud. In the lower parts of the clouds, the ice crystals melt to make rain drops.

Air pollution can make rain into a dangerous mixture of chemicals called acid rain. The chief culprit is sulfur dioxide, a chemical produced when coal or oil is burned. Another culprit is nitrogen dioxide, which is given off by car exhausts. These gases combine with water droplets in clouds to form an acid. When the acid droplets fall as rain, the rain is acid enough to slowly kill forests and fish in lakes. Rain in New York State is often ten times more acidic than unpolluted rain. Trees in the Appalachian Mountains have been killed by acid rain.

Hailstones develop when small droplets of frozen rain form high

Trees damaged by acid rain. Large areas of forest in the northeastern United States, Canada, and northern Europe are now dying from the effects of acid rain.

in a thundercloud. The small particles of ice start to fall, but updrafts in the turbulent storm cloud catch them. The droplets are carried back to the freezing upper part of the cloud and more ice freezes around them. Again they drop and the process is repeated. Each time the ice particle is carried to the freezing upper regions, it adds a layer of ice. Eventually, it becomes heavy enough to fall to the ground. Hailstones can grow as big as tennis balls.

Snow forms inside very cold clouds. Ice crystals form on tiny dust particles. One crystal fastens to another and, when many of them are joined together, they become a snowflake. Eventually a flake becomes heavy enough to fall to the ground. Large snowflakes can measure 2 inches (51 mm) across. The largest snowflake ever measured was 8 inches by 12 inches (200 mm by 305 mm). It fell at Bratsk, Siberia, in 1971.

Ice crystals have six sides and form beautiful star shapes and flower designs. One must look at snowflakes through a magnifying glass in order to see the delicate crystal patterns clearly. No two snowflakes are exactly alike. However, most snowflakes have a six-sided shape which echoes the shape of the crystals from which they are built.

Weather Watching

In North America, the high Rocky, Sierra Nevada, and Cascade mountain ranges in the west have the heaviest snowfalls. For example, Mount Rainier, in the Cascade Range of Washington State, had a record-breaking snowfall of 1,224 inches (31,090 mm) in the period between February 1971 and February 1972.

No two snowflakes are identical because each is formed under different conditions. Temperature, humidity, and air currents all affect the size and shape of snowfalkes.

Stormy Weather

The weather can be very destructive. A tropical storm that occurred in Bangladesh in 1970 killed about a million people. In 1925 a tornado, or "twister," tore through the town of Annapolis, Missouri, leaving a trail of destruction 900 feet (300 m) wide. A powerful hurricane called Andrew hit southern Florida on August 24, 1992. Its winds reached speeds of 200 mph (320 km/h). The hurricane destroyed tens of thousands of homes, making more than 150,000 people homeless. More than 50 people died. Hurricane Andrew laid waste an area the size of the city of Chicago.

Thunderstorms are common. Every year more than 16 million thunderstorms occur around the world. At any one time, 2,000 thunderstorms are in progress. The electric power in a typical lightning return stroke can measure more than 100 million volts.

Inside a thundercloud, currents of air carry water droplets and hailstones upward. The droplets and hailstones rub against one another as they travel. The rubbing gives them an electric charge in the same way that a plastic comb becomes charged with

Lightning flashes light up the sky. The brightest strokes travel from the cloud to the ground at speeds of more than 62,000 miles (100,000 km) a second.

Weather Watching

The build-up of electric charge on a thundercloud. Air currents carry electrically charged water droplets and hailstones up through the cloud.

electricity when you quickly pull it through your hair. After a while, a large electric charge builds up in the cloud. The charge concentrates at the top of the cloud, carried there by light water droplets and hailstones lifted upward by currents of air. The bottom of the cloud also becomes charged because heavier droplets and hailstones tend to drop to the lower levels of the cloud. After a while there may be a giant spark – a flash of lightning – as electricity jumps between the top and bottom of the cloud.

Lightning that jumps from cloud to cloud or from one part of a cloud to another part is called sheet lightning. Sheet lightning is

Stormy Weather

often hidden from direct view and appears to be a flickering light within the cloud. Sometimes lightning will jump from the bottom of a cloud to the ground. This is called forked lightning. The lightning follows a jagged, forked path as it travels between the cloud and the ground. The lightning heats the air along its path to a very high temperature, around 54,000°F (30,000°C). The heat causes the air around the spark to expand outward at great speed, and we hear a clap of thunder.

You can estimate how far from you the lightning is by measuring the time between when you see the flash and when you hear the thunder. Sound travels about 1 mile in 5 seconds (1 km in 3 seconds), so the distance to the lightning is found by dividing the time in seconds between the flash and the thunder by 5 (to obtain the distance in miles) or by 3 (to obtain the distance in kilometers).

The tornado, or twister, is a spinning storm. The storm begins when an updraft in a thundercloud is started spinning by winds in the upper part of the cloud. A column of rising air starts spinning.

A tornado is seen here spinning its destructive way through open countryside.

Air is sucked into the spinning column at the bottom. The air speeds up as it spirals toward the center of the column. You may have noticed that when water flows down a whirlpool or a bathtub drain, it speeds up as it spirals inward. In a tornado, the winds in the central column can reach speeds of 280 mph (450 km/h). The column grows downward from the cloud bottom until it touches the ground. The violent updraft inside the column acts like a giant vacuum cleaner that can tear the roofs off buildings and lift cars and people into the air.

In 1981 a tornado lifted a baby from its carriage in the Italian city of Ancona. The baby was carried 50 feet (15 m) into the air and set down safely 300 feet (90 m) away. During a tornado in Ponca City, Oklahoma, a man and his wife were carried aloft in their house. The walls and roof of the house were blown away, but the floor remained intact. The floor eventually glided down to the ground and the couple survived their ordeal.

A tornado column speeds across the land, leaving behind a narrow trail of destruction. Inside the column of a tornado, the air pressure is very low. When the column passes over a house, the air inside the house expands outward, tearing the house to bits. In 1950 a tornado lifted some chickens from their run in Bedfordshire, England. The chickens' feathers exploded because the air pressure inside the quills was much higher than the low pressure in the tornado.

The most destructive of all storms are tropical cyclones. These storms begin over the warm tropical seas and sometimes move onto the land. When the storms begin over the Atlantic Ocean or the Caribbean Sea, they are called hurricanes. When they begin over the Pacific Ocean, they are called typhoons. When they begin over the Indian Ocean, they are known as tropical cyclones.

Hurricanes are large spinning storms. Very strong winds circle around a region of low pressure. Surprisingly, there is a small quiet area called the "eye" at the center of a hurricane. In the eye, the air is still and the sky is clear. However, just outside the eye, the full power of the hurricane is felt. Wind speeds may reach 220 mph (360 km/h). Torrential rains pour down and the wind whips up giant waves.

Stormy Weather

A satellite view of a hurricane. The quiet eye of the storm can be seen at the center of the spiral cloud patterns.

In 1921, a hurricane deposited 23 inches (584 mm) of rain on Texas in a single day. Hurricanes, typhoons, and tropical cyclones may be as much as 480 miles (800 km) across. They can take 18 hours to pass over a coastal town as they move inland. Every second, a hurricane releases as much energy as the explosion of over 100 million tons of dynamite. The energy released in a day by a hurricane would, if converted into electricity, keep the entire United States supplied with electrical power for three years. This energy comes from the heat the hurricane draws up from the warm tropical sea.

A hurricane begins when winds from opposite directions meet and cause an upward-moving spiral of air. Water vapor, drawn from the warm sea, is sucked upward. The vapor carries the heat it absorbed from the sea. As the water vapor rises, it cools and condenses. The heat carried by the vapor is released, warming the air. As the air is warmed, it rises even faster. The updraft begins to act like a chimney, sucking in air at the bottom and blowing it out at the top. As the air is sucked in at the bottom, it spirals inward toward the rising air column. The air speeds up as it spirals inward, just as the winds in a tornado speed up as they spiral inward. As the winds speed up, greater and greater amounts of water vapor are drawn upward. More and more heat is released at the top of the hurricane. Nothing can now stop the hurricane. It will go on increasing in size and ferocity until it moves over the land and runs out of its vital fuel, water vapor.

Matter and Energy

A highly magnified microscope image of oxalic acid needles. Oxalic acid is found in the tissues of many plants such as spinach, chard, and rhubarb.

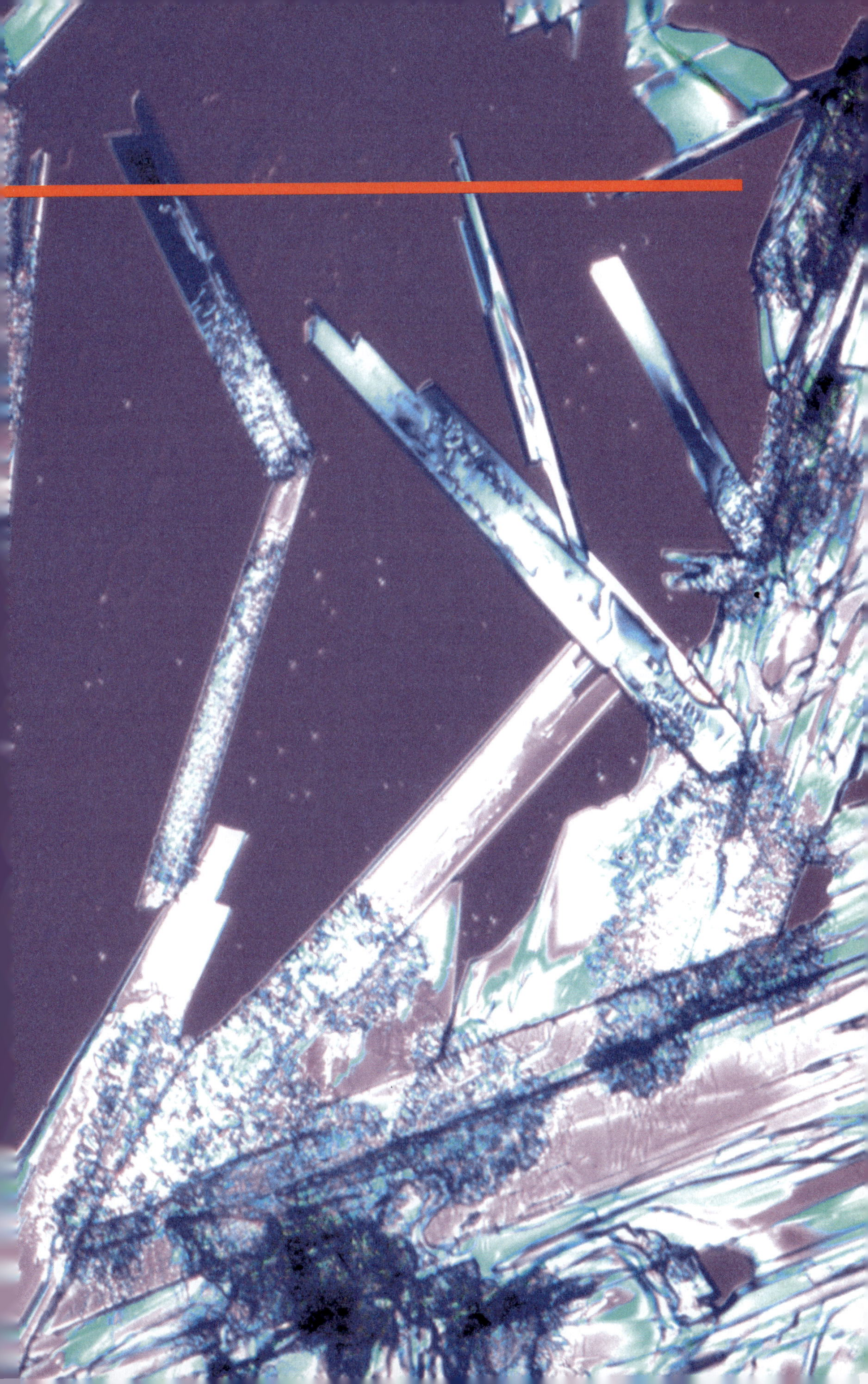

Elements and Compounds

Elements and Compounds

Everything we see in the world around us is made up of matter. Matter is anything that has mass and occupies space. The water we drink, the ground we walk on, the air we breathe – all these things are made up of matter.

We find many different substances, or forms of matter, in the world. Some substances are solids, some are liquids, and some are gases. Scientists believe that all these different substances are built up from more than 100 basic "building blocks" called the chemical elements.

Matter can occur in three states: liquid, solid, and gas. For example, water is a liquid in the sea, a solid in the iceberg, and vapor in the air.

Oxygen, copper, and mercury are examples of elements. There is nothing in oxygen but oxygen, nothing in copper but copper, and nothing in mercury but mercury. All elements follow this rule. They are the substances that have not been formed from simpler substances. These elements combine in many ways to make the great variety of things we find all around us.

Names have been given to all the elements. Scientists do not always use the whole word when they write the name. They use an abbreviation, which they call the symbol for the element. O is the symbol for oxygen. H is the symbol for hydrogen.

Some Important Chemical Elements

	Symbol	Form of matter	Atomic no.	Atomic weight
Hydrogen	H	G	1	1
Helium	He	G	2	4
Lithium	Li	S	3	7
Carbon	C	S	6	12
Nitrogen	N	G	7	14
Oxygen	O	G	8	16
Fluorine	F	G	9	19
Neon	Ne	G	10	20
Sodium	Na	S	11	23
Magnesium	Mg	S	12	24
Aluminum	Al	S	13	27
Silicon	Si	S	14	28
Phosphorus	P	S	15	31
Sulfur	S	S	16	32
Chlorine	Cl	G	17	35
Argon	Ar	G	18	40
Potassium	K	S	19	39
Calcium	Ca	S	20	40
Chromium	Cr	S	24	52
Manganese	Mn	S	25	55
Iron	Fe	S	26	56
Cobalt	Co	S	27	59
Nickel	Ni	S	28	59
Copper	Cu	S	29	66
Zinc	Zn	S	30	65
Arsenic	As	S	33	75
Bromine	Br	L	35	80
Silver	Ag	S	47	108
Cadmium	Cd	S	48	112
Tin	Sn	S	50	119
Iodine	I	S	53	127
Barium	Ba	S	56	137
Tungsten	W	S	74	184
Platinum	Pt	S	78	195
Gold	Au	S	79	197
Mercury	Hg	L	80	201
Lead	Pb	S	82	207
Bismuth	Bi	S	83	209
Radium	Ra	S	88	226
Uranium	U	S	92	238

Elements and Compounds

The smallest part of an element that is still like the element is called an atom. An atom is so small that it can only be seen under the most powerful type of microscope: 100 million atoms in a row would take up less than an inch (2.54 cm). A one-inch cube of iron contains about 1 1/2 billion billion atoms.

If each person were the size of an atom, the entire population of the United States could sit on the head of a pin.

Atoms themselves are composed of still smaller particles called protons, neutrons, and electrons. The electrons have one kind of electrical charge that is called a negative charge. The protons have another kind of electrical charge, which is called a positive charge. The neutron has no electric charge.

Most of an atom's mass is concentrated in its nucleus, or central core. The nucleus consists of protons and neutrons. Each proton and neutron is about 2,000 times heavier than an electron. The electrons move around the nucleus. There are as many electrons circling an atomic nucleus as there are protons in the nucleus. Atoms are mostly empty space. If the nucleus was the size of a tennis ball, the nearest electron would be over half a mile (1 km) away.

Matter and Energy

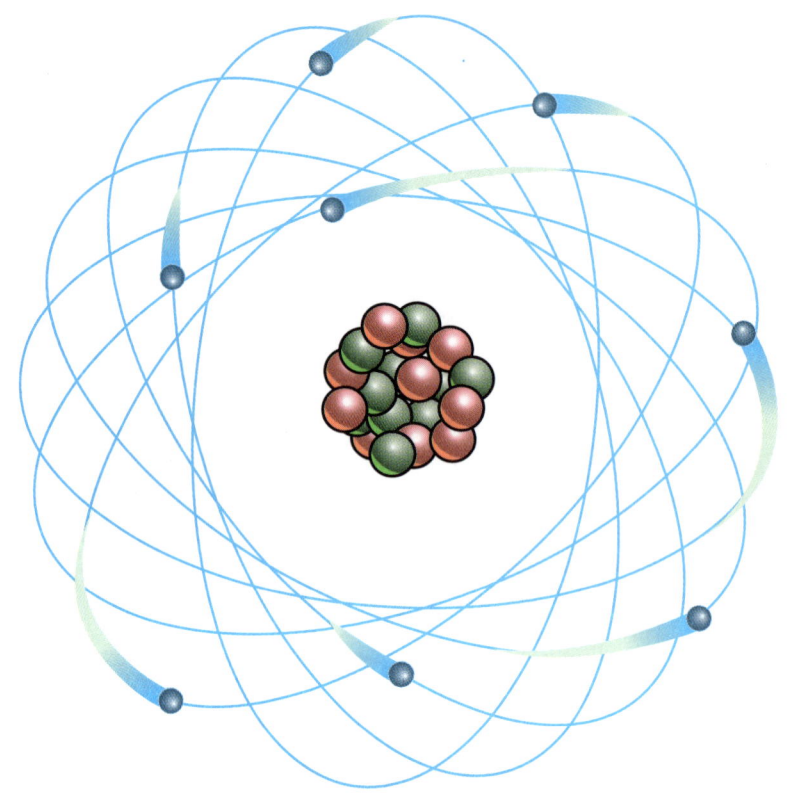

Inside the atom. Electrons move around a central nucleus consisting of protons and neutrons.

Even though protons and neutrons are smaller than atoms, they are not the smallest particles that exist. Inside protons and neutrons are even smaller particles called quarks. There are six different types of quarks – the up, down, charm, strange, top, and bottom quarks. The proton and neutron each contain three quarks.

There are many different subatomic particles (particles smaller than an atom). There are heavy particles, such as the pion and the kaon. Like the proton and neutron, these particles are made up of quarks. There are also light particles, such as the neutrino. Neutrinos are not made up of quarks, nor are electrons and the particles called the tau and the muon.

Electrons and protons attract each other because opposite electrical charges attract. As the electrons move around the nucleus of an atom, they are always attracted toward the center by the protons in the nucleus. The attractive force of the electrons and protons for each other holds the atom together.

Elements and Compounds

The smallest and simplest atom is that of hydrogen. It consists of a single electron moving around a single proton. All other atoms have both neutrons and protons in their nuclei. The nucleus of oxygen, for example, consists of 8 protons and 8 neutrons. Oxygen has 8 electrons.

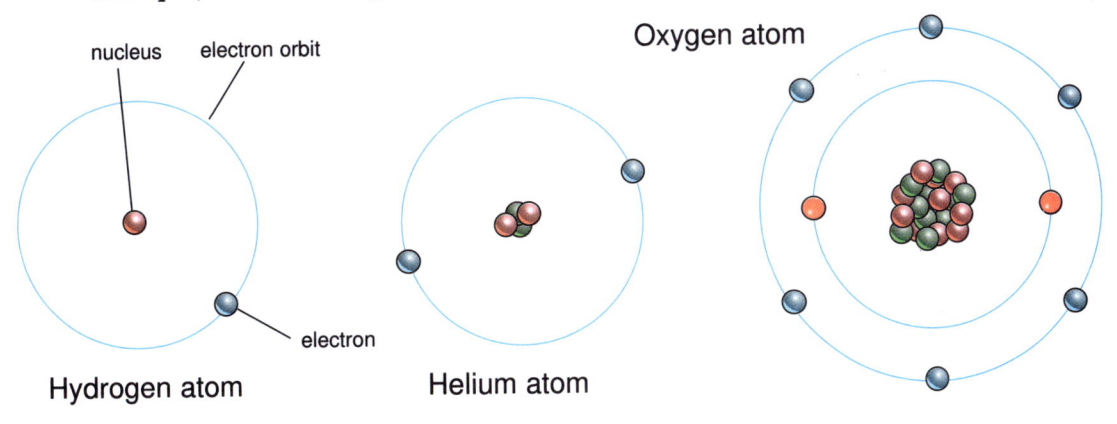

Hydrogen atom — nucleus, electron orbit, electron

Helium atom

Oxygen atom

Each element has a different number of protons and electrons in its atoms. The electrons of heavy atoms are arranged around the nucleus in layers called shells. The diagrams above are not to scale.

Each element has a different number of protons. The "atomic number" of an element tells us the number of protons in the nucleus of the element, and the number of electrons moving around the nucleus. Thus the element with atomic number 1 (hydrogen) has one proton and one electron. The element with atomic number 2 (helium) has two protons and two electrons.

The atoms of an element all have the same number of protons, but they may have differing numbers of neutrons. The total number of protons and neutrons in the nucleus of an atom is called the "mass number." Since hydrogen atoms have only one proton and no neutrons, hydrogen has a mass number of 1.

Atoms of an element with differing numbers of neutrons are called isotopes. Many elements occur naturally as a mixture of isotopes. Chlorine, for example, has two isotopes. Each isotope has 17 protons, but one of the isotopes has 18 neutrons, and the other 20 neutrons. The different isotopes are called chlorine-35 and chlorine-37, or Cl-35 and Cl-37.

Although there are fewer than 125 chemical elements, more than 1,700 isotopes exist. Many of these isotopes are unstable. Their

Matter and Energy

nucleus breaks down, or decays, and they emit radiation. These isotopes are called radioactive isotopes. Radioactive isotopes give out three types of radiation when they decay: alpha rays, beta rays, and gamma rays. Alpha rays consist of a stream of tiny particles called alpha particles, each made up of two protons and two neutrons. Beta rays consist of high-energy electrons.

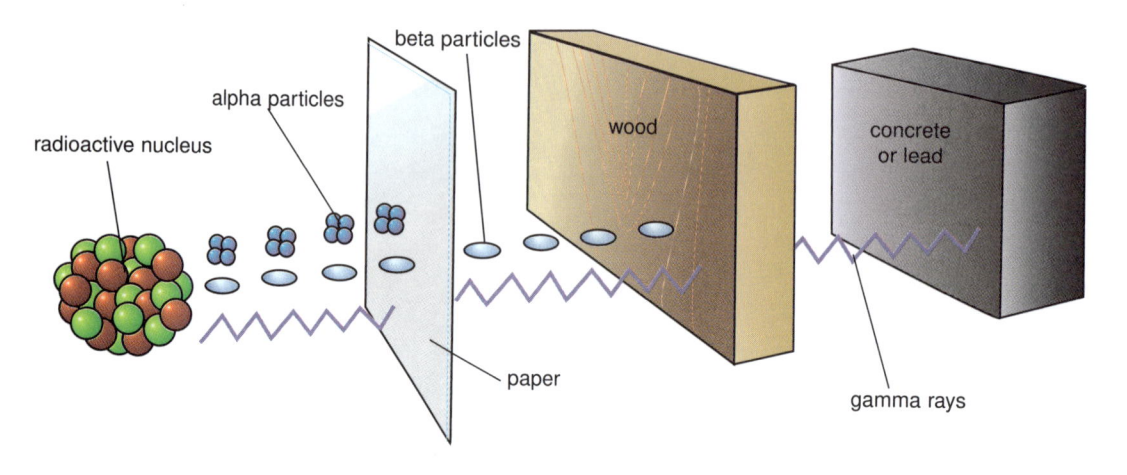

The three kinds of radiation given off by radioactive atoms each have different penetrating power. A sheet of paper will stop alpha particles. A block of wood will stop beta particles. A thick concrete block or lead is needed to stop gamma rays.

Another number used to describe elements is the "atomic weight," or "relative atomic mass." This number gives the weight of an atom compared to the weight of the carbon atom. A carbon atom has an atomic weight of 12. Hydrogen has an atomic weight of 1, so a hydrogen atom is one-twelfth the weight of a carbon atom. A magnesium atom is twice the weight of a carbon atom, and so magnesium has an atomic weight of 24.

The atoms of elements combine in many different ways to make the great variety of substances we have around us. Sometimes atoms of the same element cling together to form larger particles. This occurs in some gases, such as hydrogen and oxygen. For example, one atom of hydrogen unites with another atom of hydrogen. This results in a molecule of hydrogen. A molecule is a group of atoms joined together. A chemist uses a kind of shorthand called an equation to show how hydrogen atoms join together:

Elements and Compounds

$H + H = H_2$. In the equation, an atom of hydrogen is represented by H and a molecule of hydrogen (consisting of two hydrogen atoms joined) is represented by H_2.

Often atoms of an element combine with atoms of one or more other elements to form molecules of different kinds of substances called compounds. For example, hydrogen unites with oxygen to form a substance that is entirely different from either one of them. The compound formed is water. Thus hydrogen (an element) + oxygen (an element) = water (a compound) or $2H_2 + O_2 = 2H_2O$. To a chemist this equation means that 2 molecules of hydrogen (H_2) unite with 1 molecule of oxygen (O_2) to make 2 molecules of water (H_2O). A molecule is very, very small. A drop of water contains about a million billion billion molecules.

H_2O is called the formula for water. Chemists usually write the names of compounds by using such formulas. A formula shows how many atoms of each element are in a molecule of the compound.

Compounds usually do not look or act like the elements from which they are made. Water is a good example. Water is a liquid. Hydrogen and oxygen, which combine to make water, are gases. Oxygen helps things to burn, hydrogen burns rapidly, but water neither helps things to burn nor does it burn itself.

When sodium is placed in water it reacts violently with the water and gives off a great deal of heat. Chlorine is a green, poisonous gas. When chlorine and sodium unite to make a compound, what do you suppose is formed? Everyday table salt, or sodium chloride. This is another example of a compound that is different from the elements of which it is composed. The formula of table salt is NaCl.

Compounds can unite with each other to form new compounds. For example, compounds called acids unite with other compounds called bases. Lemon juice, grapefruit juice, and vinegar are acids. Hydrochloric acid is a well-known acid with a formula HCl. Lye is an example of a base. Its chemical name is sodium hydroxide and its formula is NaOH. When hydrochloric acid is added to sodium hydroxide, two new substances, salt and water, are formed, $HCl + NaOH = NaCl + H_2O$.

Matter and Energy

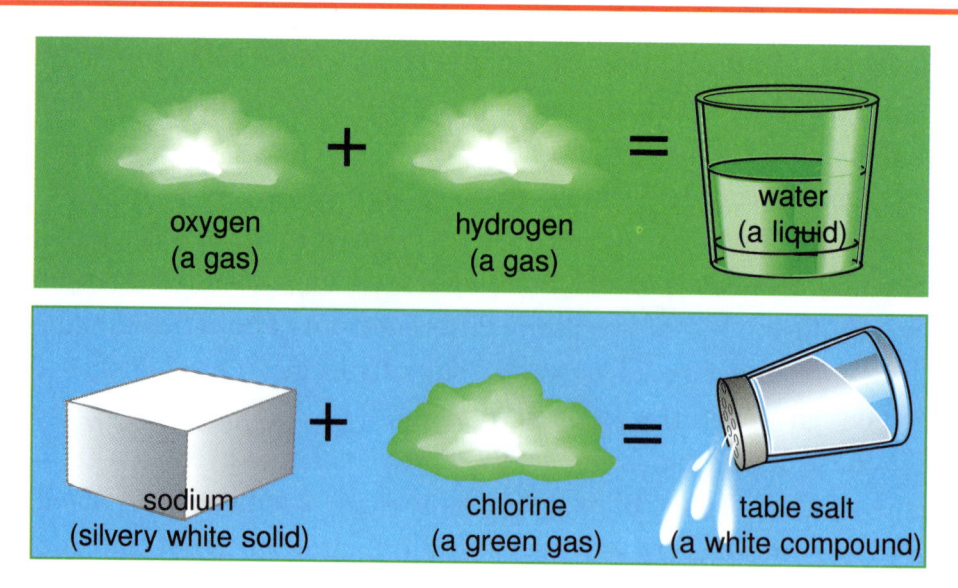

See how these elements combine to make new substances.

Compounds can be broken down to the elements that make them up. For instance, when an electric current is passed between two wires dipping into water, hydrogen bubbles off one wire and oxygen bubbles off the other wire. This process is called electrolysis. Electrolysis breaks the compound water into its elements, hydrogen and oxygen. The equation representing this process is $2H_2O = 2H_2 + O_2$.

When elements unite, or compounds react together to form new compounds, or compounds are broken down into elements, we say a chemical change or a chemical reaction has taken place. Chemical

Burning is a chemical reaction in which the element carbon (in the wood) combines with oxygen (in the air) to make carbon dioxide.

Elements and Compounds

reactions often release energy. This happens, for example, when wood burns. Even more energy is released when a nuclear reaction takes place. A nuclear reaction is a change that involves the nucleus of an atom. There are two nuclear reactions: fission and fusion. During fission, a large nucleus splits into smaller parts. Fission is the process that takes place in a nuclear reactor. An isotope of uranium, called uranium-235, splits into two roughly equal parts, releasing large amounts of energy. In fusion, light nuclei, such as hydrogen nuclei, join together to make heavier nuclei. In the process, much energy is released. Fusion is the process that produces energy inside the sun and stars.

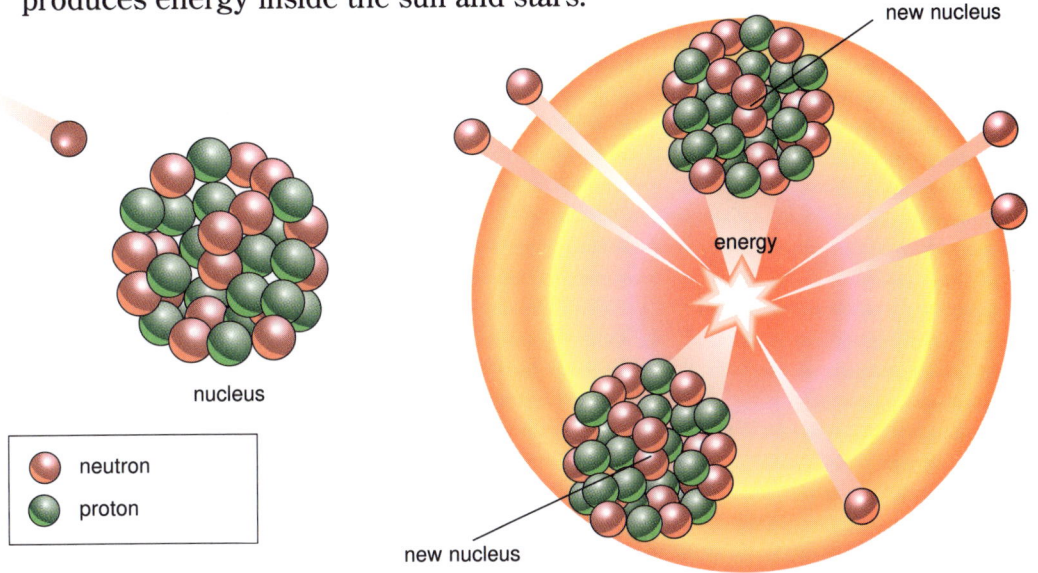

When a neutron collides with the nucleus of an atom of uranium-235, the nucleus splits in half, releasing energy. This reaction is called nuclear fission.

Many of the materials in our world are mixtures. Air is one of the most common mixtures. It is made up of several elements and compounds mixed together. They are oxygen, nitrogen, argon, water vapor, carbon dioxide, and a few other substances. In a mixture, the substances are not chemically united with each other. This means that they can be present in varying amounts. In air, for example, the amount of oxygen can change. In a compound, the amount by weight of each element is always exactly the same. Sea water is a mixture of water, salt, and other minerals. Milk is a mixture of water, butterfat, minerals, and protein. Ink is a mixture of water and dyes.

117

Forces and Energy

Forces and Energy

We live in a constantly changing world. Around us, things are always on the move: cars speed down the street, clouds race across the sky, waves crash on the seashore. None of these things could happen without forces and energy.

A force is a push or a pull. When you push on your bicycle pedal, you exert a force on it. The effect of the force is to start the bicycle moving. Once the bicycle is moving, it is acted on by another force –

A climber relies on the force of friction. The friction between his feet and the rocks keeps him from falling.

Matter and Energy

friction. Friction is a force that occurs whenever rough surfaces rub together. It slows down moving objects that rub against other objects.

Some forces act only when two objects are in contact. These forces are called contact forces. You need to have your foot on the bicycle pedal to make it move; this is because your foot exerts a contact force. The force of friction is a contact force; it only operates between touching objects.

Other forces are non-contact forces. They act without touching the object they are pulling or pushing. The force that a magnet exerts on a piece of iron or steel is a non-contact force. The force of the magnet attracts iron and steel even when the magnet is not in contact with them. Gravity is another non-contact force. Gravity is the force that causes pieces of matter to attract each other. The Earth's gravity attracts all objects near it, pulling them toward the center of the Earth. The pull of the Earth's gravity gives objects their weight.

The Earth's gravitational force attracts all objects on the Earth toward its center. It is not just the Earth that has gravity. There is gravitational attraction between any two objects.

The strongest natural force is found inside the atomic nucleus. The two types of nuclear force are called the strong and the weak

Forces and Energy

force. The strong nuclear force is the strongest force of all. It is 10,000 billion billion billion billion times stronger than gravity. The other nuclear force is called the weak force. Despite its name, this force is much stronger than gravity, but weaker than electric and magnetic forces.

About 300 years ago, the English scientist Isaac Newton (1642-1727) discovered how objects behave when forces act on them. He put forward three laws of motion that summed up his ideas.

Newton's first law states that if an object is not being pushed or pulled by a force, it will either stay still or keep moving in a straight line at a steady speed. The tendency of an object to stay still, or continue moving at the same speed in a straight line, is called inertia.

If a horse stops suddenly, the rider is thrown forward over the horse's neck. This happens because of the rider's inertia. The rider continues moving forward when the horse stops.

Matter and Energy

It may seem obvious that no object can start moving unless it is given a push or a pull. It is less obvious that a moving object will continue moving unless it is acted on by a force. This is because the force of friction slows down most of the moving objects we see around us. It is only in situations where there is no or little friction that we see inertia at work. When an ice hockey puck is hit, it travels over the ice at great speed. Because there is little friction between the puck and the ice, the puck does not slow down until it has traveled a great distance over the ice.

Newton's second law describes what happens when a force acts on an object – the object speeds up, slows down, or changes its direction of motion. When a rocket is launched into space, its engines provide a force that lifts it from the launch pad. We can see the rocket speeding up, or accelerating, as the engine force acts on it. When a baseball player catches the ball, the force of the glove decelerates, or slows, the ball. When a ball bounces off a wall, it changes the direction of its motion because the wall exerts a force on the ball.

It takes more force to throw a baseball than a tennis ball because the baseball has more mass. The mass of an object is the amount of matter it contains. Newton's second law states that the greater the mass of an object, the greater the force needed to accelerate it. This is why a heavily loaded truck needs a more powerful engine than a small car. The second law also states that the bigger the force, the more acceleration produced. So the harder an ice hockey player hits the puck, the greater the acceleration of the puck.

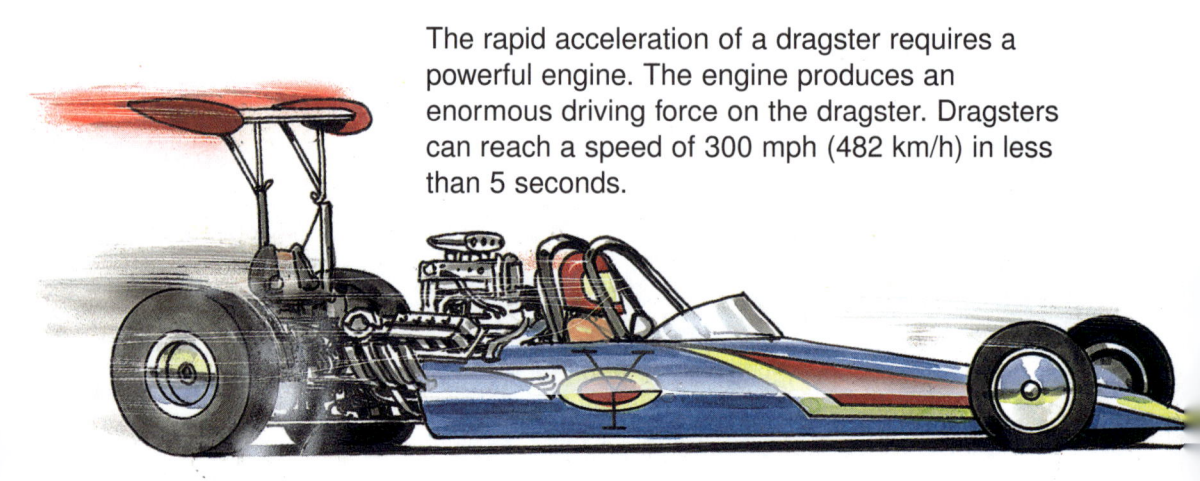

The rapid acceleration of a dragster requires a powerful engine. The engine produces an enormous driving force on the dragster. Dragsters can reach a speed of 300 mph (482 km/h) in less than 5 seconds.

Forces and Energy

Isaac Newton made another discovery about forces: they always work in pairs. He expressed this by saying that to every action there is an equal and opposite reaction. He called this his third law of motion. If you push hard on a wall, you are exerting a force on the wall. The wall is also pushing on you with an equal force in the opposite direction. Your push is the action force; the push exerted by the wall is called the reaction.

Rowers make use of Newton's third law. When they pull on the oars, they push water backward. The backward force on the water is accompanied by an equal reaction force pushing the boat forward. An inflated balloon flies through the air when it is released. The stretched rubber of the balloon squeezes the air in the balloon, exerting a force that blows the air backward out of the balloon. The reaction force acts to push the balloon forward.

A balloon flies around the room when air escapes from it. The force of the escaping air produces an equal and opposite force, pushing the balloon forward.

Matter and Energy

Machines can magnify or increase forces. For example, a rope passed around several pulley wheels can magnify a force; the rope need only be pulled gently to produce a large force. Machines can also magnify movements. For example, the levers inside a piano magnify the small movements of the pianist's fingers to produce larger movements of the instrument hammers.

There are six simple machines: the slope, or inclined plane, the screw, the lever, the pulley, the wheel and axle, and the wedge. Complicated machines are made up of simple machines. Even the most complex machine is made up of levers, wedges, pulleys, wheel and axles, and screws. These simple machines are connected together in many ingenious ways to make cars, sewing machines, aircraft, or photocopiers.

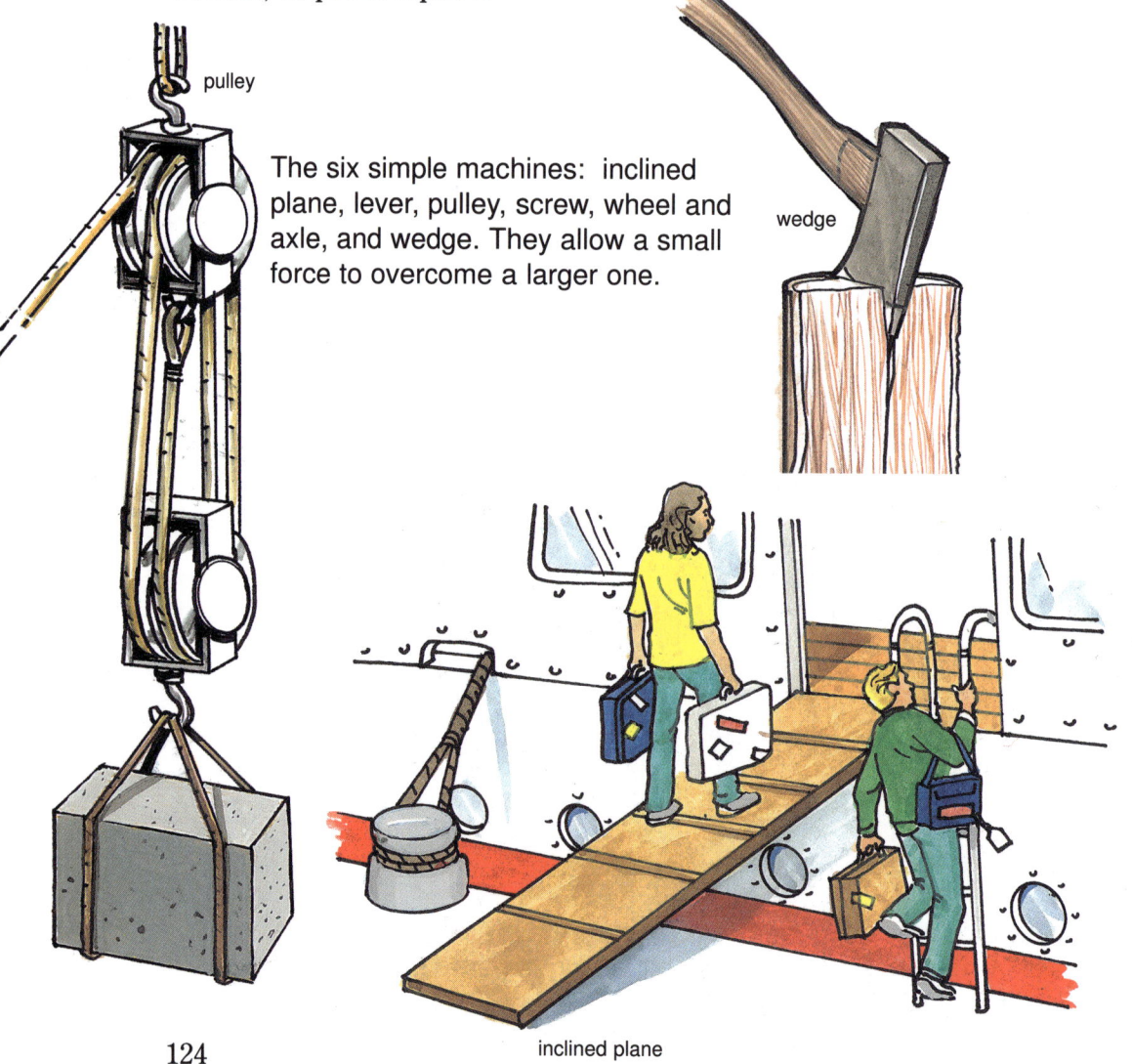

pulley

The six simple machines: inclined plane, lever, pulley, screw, wheel and axle, and wedge. They allow a small force to overcome a larger one.

wedge

inclined plane

Forces and Energy

No machine can work without energy. But what is energy? We easily recognize its presence but we cannot see it, hold it or smell it. Energy can be thought of as the ability to do work. Work is done whenever a force moves an object. For example, if you lift a weight, you are doing work. This cannot happen unless energy is converted from one form to another.

Work is done when a force moves something. When a weight is lifted, work is done. The amount of work done is found by multiplying the amount of force used by the distance the force moves.

Energy occurs in many different forms. Almost all of the energy on Earth comes from the sun. Originally, this energy was nuclear energy, produced by nuclear fusion reactions deep inside the sun. The heat and light produced in the sun traveled across the vastness of space to the Earth.

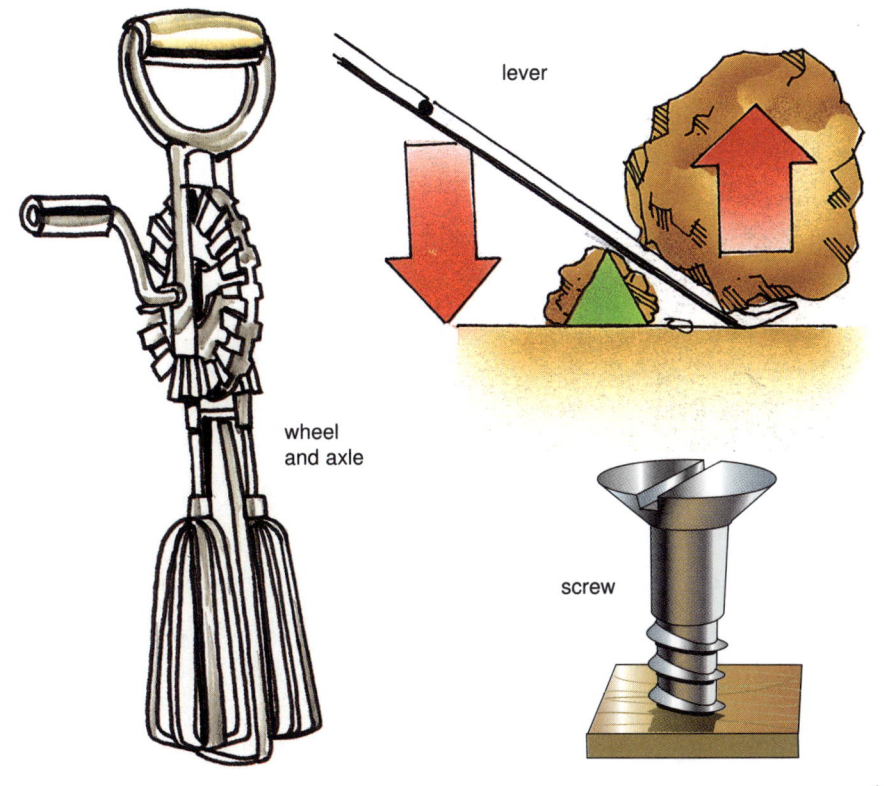

lever

wheel and axle

screw

Matter and Energy

The sun is the ultimate source of almost all our energy. The energy arrives on Earth in the sun's rays, as heat and light.

Energy that can travel across empty space is called radiation, or radiant energy. Heat and light are radiant energy. They are made up of electromagnetic waves – ripples of magnetic and electric forces that travel across space like waves travel across the surface of a pond.

On Earth, the sun's radiation is rapidly converted into other forms of energy. Some light energy is absorbed by the leaves of plants and converted to chemical energy. Energy-packed chemicals called carbohydrates are produced in the leaves. Animals, including humans, eat plants to extract the chemical energy.

Energy from the sun heats the atmosphere and causes winds. The energy of motion, seen in the winds, is called kinetic energy. Some of the sun's energy evaporates water from the sea. The water vapor may later produce rain over a high mountain range. The water produced has energy, called potential energy, because of its elevated position. The water will run downhill if allowed.

A weight held above the ground has potential energy because of its elevated position; if released, the object falls. As it falls, its potential energy is converted to energy of motion (kinetic energy). In the same way, water rushing down a stream bed converts its

Forces and Energy

potential energy to kinetic energy. If the water passes through the turbine of a hydroelectric power plant, another form of energy is produced – electricity.

In a hydroelectric power plant, the kinetic energy of water flowing rapidly through the pen stocks into the turbines is converted into electrical energy.

Electricity is the most useful form of energy. It can easily be converted into other forms of energy. An electric motor converts electrical energy to kinetic energy; an electric heater produces heat and light energy from electricity; a light bulb converts electrical energy to light energy; a radio or stereo speaker converts electricity into sound, another form of energy.

Energy is continually changing form. When a fireworks rocket is on the ground, it has a large amount of chemical energy in its gunpowder fuel. It has no kinetic energy since it is not moving. Also, it has no potential energy since it is not above the ground.

When the rocket shoots skyward, it gradually loses chemical energy as its fuel burns away, but it gains potential energy as it rises. It also has kinetic energy while it moves upward. At its

Matter and Energy

A burst of energy as a firework explodes. The chemical energy of the firework is converted into heat, light, sound, and potential and kinetic energy.

highest point, the rocket is motionless. Its kinetic energy is zero, but its potential energy is great.

Energy can neither be created nor destroyed, but only converted from one form to another. This statement is one of the most important principles in science. It is called the law of conservation of energy. When a rubber ball drops from a height, it gains kinetic energy as it falls. At the same time, it loses potential energy. The law of conservation of energy tells us that the two energy changes are balanced: the gain in kinetic energy equals the loss of potential energy. In this way, the total energy of the ball remains the same.

Heat and Cold

Matter and Energy

Heat and Cold

A summer day is usually hotter than a winter day, but how much hotter? To answer this question, we must have a precise way of measuring heat, or temperature. We need to divide a temperature range into parts called degrees. This produces a temperature scale that can be attached to a thermometer. Then we can describe a temperature accurately by saying how many degrees it is.

To make a temperature scale, two standard temperatures (called fixed points) must be used. These are temperatures that can easily be obtained by anyone making a thermometer. The upper standard temperature is usually the temperature of boiling water, called the boiling point; the lower standard temperature is the temperature of water when it freezes, called the freezing point.

In the Celsius, or centigrade, scale, the difference between these temperatures is divided into 100 equal degrees. The temperature of freezing water is 0°C, and the temperature of boiling water is 100°C.

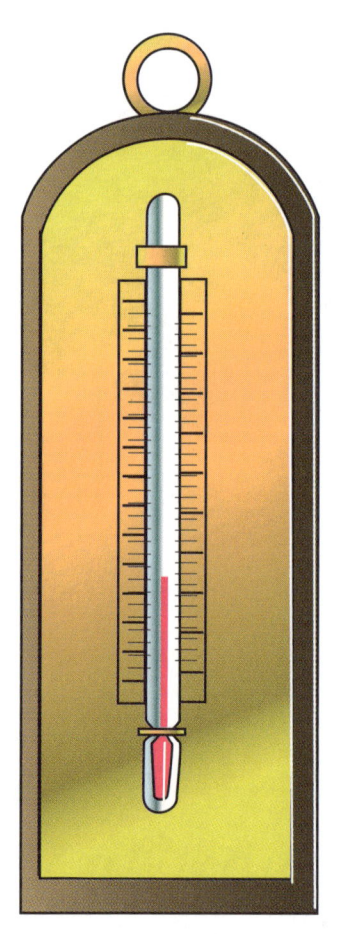

In the Fahrenheit scale, the temperature of freezing water is 32°F and the temperature of boiling water is 212°F.

A household thermometer (left) and a medical thermometer (right). A medical thermometer contains mercury. A household thermometer may contain mercury or colored alcohol.

Heat and Cold

Another temperature scale is called the absolute scale. In this scale, the lowest possible temperature (called absolute zero, − 459°F or −273°C) is called 0K (or Kelvin). The freezing point of water is 273K and the boiling point is 373K.

There are many different types of thermometers. The common ones utilize the fact that liquids expand when they get hotter. By watching how much a liquid expands as it is heated, we can measure a rise in temperature. Common household thermometers are filled with either mercury or alcohol. The mercury or alcohol expands up a thin glass tube as the temperature rises. The temperature is read off a scale attached the thermometer tube.

When you use a thermometer to measure the temperature of an object, you are really measuring the speed of movement of the object's molecules. The molecules move at all temperatures except at absolute zero. They move rapidly at high temperatures and more slowly at low temperatures. The energy due to the motion of the molecules is called heat energy.

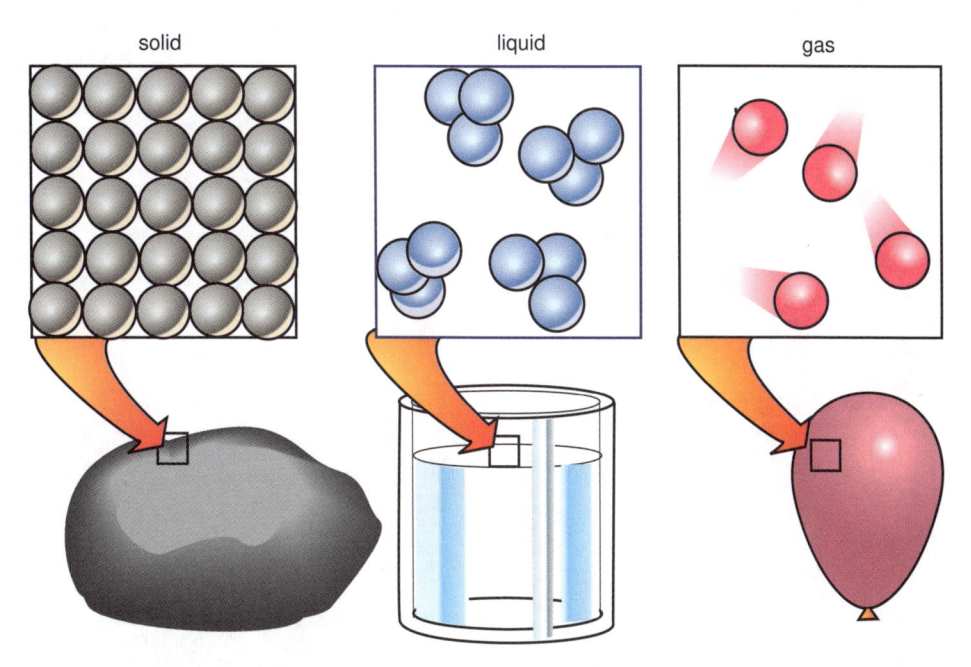

In a solid, the molecules are packed close together and do not move about. In a liquid, molecules have small spaces between them and can move about slightly. In a gas, the molecules are far apart and move at great speeds. The molecules in air move ten times faster than the winds in a hurricane.

Matter and Energy

In a solid, each molecule cannot move away from its position, but can only vibrate (move back and forth). Also, the molecules in a solid are packed quite closely together. In a liquid, molecules are not so firmly fixed in position. They can move around. There is space between the liquid molecules which allows them to move. In a gas, molecules are much further apart and they move freely around at great speed.

As a solid is heated, its atoms and molecules vibrate faster and faster. The higher the temperature, the faster the atoms and molecules vibrate. The vibrating molecules take up more space as they vibrate faster, so the solid expands (gets bigger). The same thing happens when a liquid or gas is heated. The space between the molecules increases and the liquid or gas expands.

At high temperatures, the molecules of a solid are vibrating so fast that they break away from their normal positions. The molecules become free to move around, and the solid melts. When a liquid is heated to a high temperature, its molecules move so fast

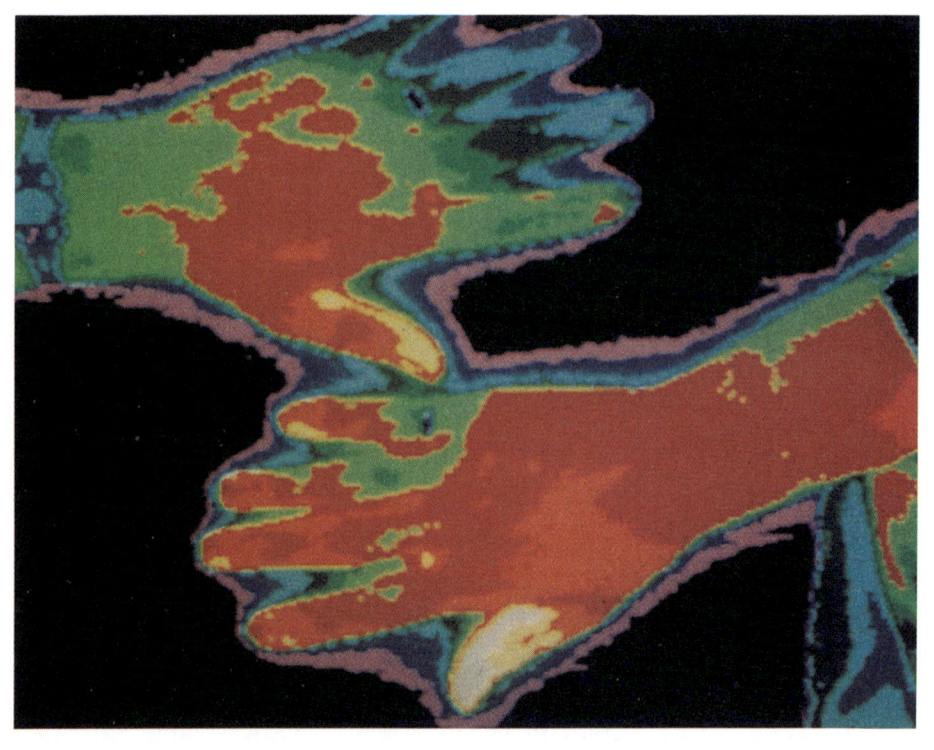

All warm objects give off heat or infrared rays. The rays are invisible but can be recorded on heat-sensitive film. Infrared photographs can reveal the presence of diseases, such as cancer.

that they break through the surface of the liquid. This is what happens when a liquid evaporates or boils.

Substances expand when they are heated. The fraction by which a substance expands when its temperature rises by one degree is called its coefficient of expansion. Silver, for example, has a Celsius coefficient of expansion of 0.000,019, so a silver rod expands by 19 millionths of its length when it is heated by 1°C.

Liquids and gases expand much more than solids when they are heated. Liquids can expand between 10 and 100 times more than solids. Gases expand about 1,000 times more than solids.

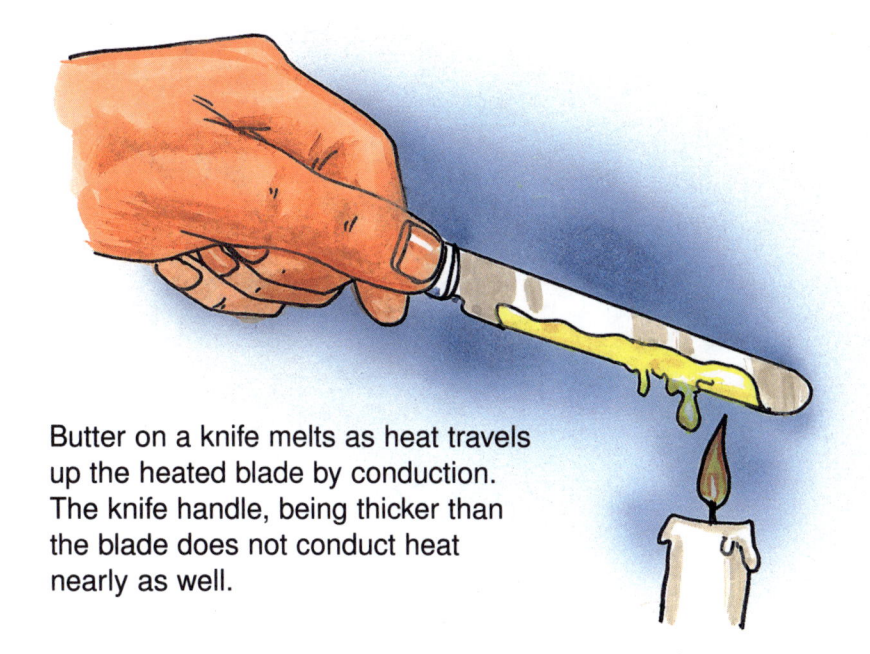

Butter on a knife melts as heat travels up the heated blade by conduction. The knife handle, being thicker than the blade does not conduct heat nearly as well.

You can see many examples of expansion in everyday life. On hot days, power lines sag because they have expanded. In winter, they contract (become shorter) and they sag less. Bridges with steel girders expand during the summer. The bridge span has to be placed on rollers to allow for the expansion. Railway lines are laid with small gaps between lengths of rail. The gaps become smaller as the rails expand.

Heat energy can travel great distances. The heat of the sun travels 93 million miles (150 million km) through empty space to the Earth. Energy that can travel through empty space is called

Matter and Energy

Heating the air in a hot-air balloon makes it rise. This is because the hot air is less dense than the air around it.

radiation. Heat rays are called infrared rays.

Heat can also travel through solids, such as metals. When one end of a metal rod is heated, the other end soon grows warm as heat travels along the rod. This method of heat transport is called conduction.

A hot-air balloon rises because the hot air inside it is less dense than the cool air outside. The hot air expands when it is heated and becomes less dense. Hot air rises even when it is not in a balloon.

Heat and Cold

The hot air above a heater, for example, rises and spreads around the room. The air eventually cools and falls as it cools. Thus, a circular current of air is set up, with hot air rising and cool air falling. These movements of air are called convection currents.

Heat energy is put to use by engines. Engines come in many different shapes and sizes but they all do the same thing: convert heat energy into movement. They work because a hot gas expands.

Some engines, such as car engines, have pistons that move back and forth inside chambers called cylinders. They are called reciprocating engines. Other engines do not have pistons. Gas turbines, for example, have blades like a windmill that turn as hot gas flows against them.

A steam engine converts heat energy into movement. Coal is burned to heat water and produce steam. The pressure of the steam drives pistons, which turn the wheels.

Engines that burn fuel inside the engine are called internal-combustion engines. Car engines and rocket engines are both internal-combustion engines. The steam engine, on the other hand, is not an internal-combustion engine. It burns its fuel in a furnace that is separate from the engine itself.

Most cars have a four-stroke engine. This means that the engine

135

Matter and Energy

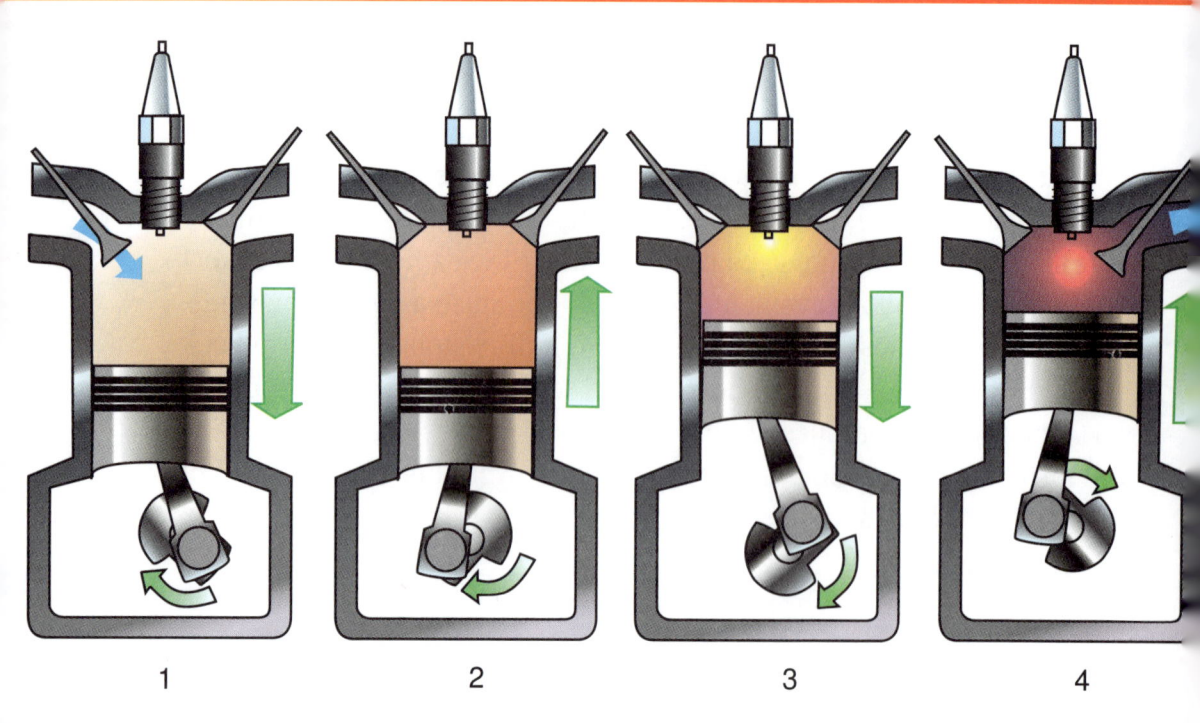

The four-stroke engine cycle. (1) Gasoline and air are sucked into the cylinder, and then (2) compressed as the piston moves up. The mixture is ignited (3) and the expanding gases force the piston down. The burnt gases are pushed out of the cylinder on the next upward stroke (4).

produces its power with four movements, or strokes, of the piston. One stroke sucks a mixture of fuel and air into the cylinder. The next stroke compresses the mixture. Then the mixture is exploded by a spark plug. The hot gases produced by the explosion expand, forcing the piston down. The next stroke pushes the burnt gases from the cylinder.

Some diesel engines also operate with four strokes. However, in a diesel engine, fuel oil is squirted into the cylinder after the air has been compressed. The compressed air is so hot that a spark plug is not needed to explode the fuel and air mixture.

Many motorcycles have a simpler type of engine called the two-stroke engine. This produces its power with two movements of the piston. The first stroke sucks the fuel and air mixture into the engine and compresses the mixture in the cylinder. During the second stroke, the burnt fuel escapes from the cylinder and new fuel/air mixture flows into the cylinder.

Electricity

Electricity arcs across a 400 kilovolt insulator under test for wet conditions.

Matter and Energy

Electricity

When a blown-up balloon is rubbed with cloth, electrons are detached from the atoms in the cloth and stick to the balloon. Because the electrons have an electrical charge, the cloth and the balloon become electrically charged. The cloth becomes positively charged because it has fewer electrons than normal. The balloon becomes negatively charged because it has more electrons than normal. The cloth and balloon will then attract each other. Rub a balloon against your sweater and the balloon will stick to the sweater as if it were glued. This experiment shows that opposite electrical charges attract.

A balloon will stick to your sweater if you rub the balloon on the sweater first. The sweater and balloon become electrically charged.

Two balloons, rubbed with cloth, will repel each other because they both have a negative charge. This experiment shows that like electrical charges repel each other. For instance, two electrons repel each other because they both have a negative electric charge.

Electricity

The electricity produced by rubbing is called static electricity because it does not move. A charged balloon stays charged for a long time. The extra electrons on the balloon leak away into the air very slowly.

In a metal wire, electrons move about quite easily. Normally the electrons move in all directions – some move to the left and some move to the right. However, if we connect a battery to the ends of the wire, the electrons behave very differently. They all move in the same direction along the wire, toward the positive terminal of the battery.

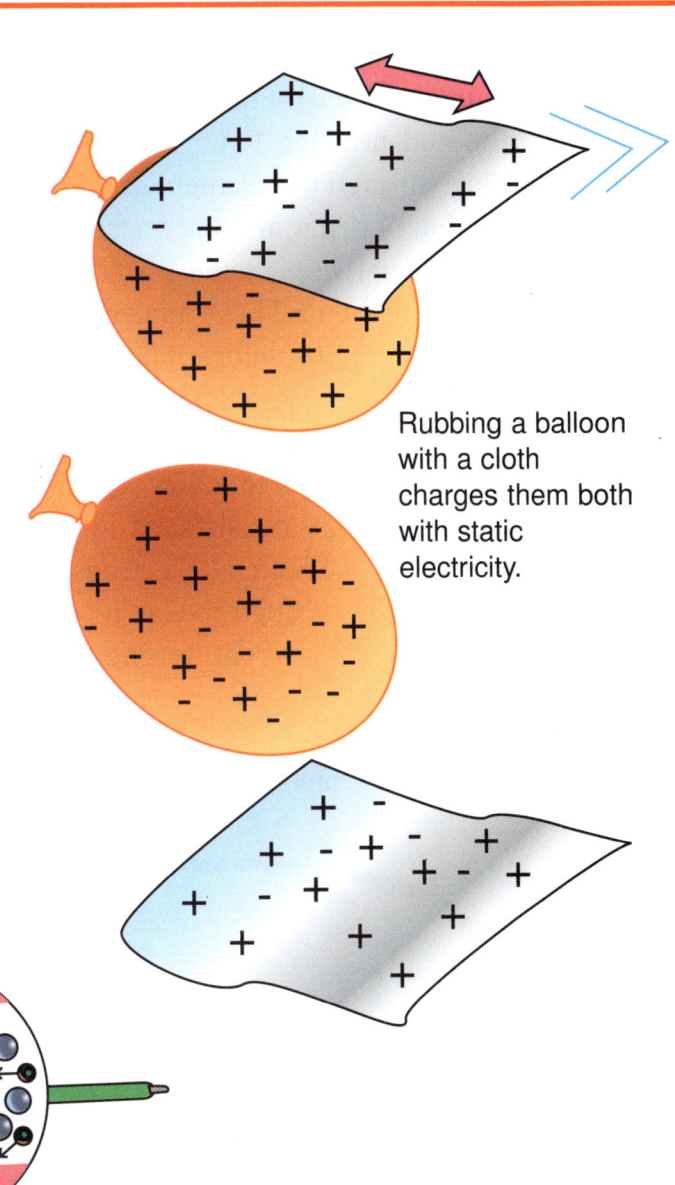

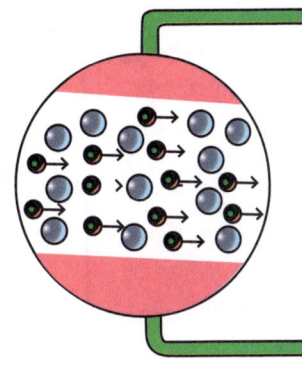

Rubbing a balloon with a cloth charges them both with static electricity.

Electrons in a metal wire wander among the atoms at random if no battery is connected. With a battery connected to the ends of the wire, the electrons all move toward the positive terminal of the battery.

Matter and Energy

The movement of electrons along a wire is called an electric current. In a light bulb, the electric current makes the filament heat up and produce light. About 3,000,000,000,000,000,000 electrons flow through the filament of the light bulb every second.

Not all materials carry, or conduct, an electric current as easily as a metal wire. Some materials do not allow electrons to move through them. These materials are called insulators. Glass and plastics are insulators. Materials that allow electrons to flow are called conductors. Metals are good conductors.

For an electric current to flow, there must be a complete pathway for the electrons to follow. The pathway is called a circuit. A very simple circuit consists of a lamp connected by wires to the terminals of a battery. Electrons flow from the negative terminal of the battery, through the lamp, to the positive terminal.

An electric current flowing through a wire can be compared to water flowing through a pipe. A pump is needed to make water flow in a pipe. The pump provides the pressure that drives water through the pipe. In an electric circuit, a battery acts as an "electron

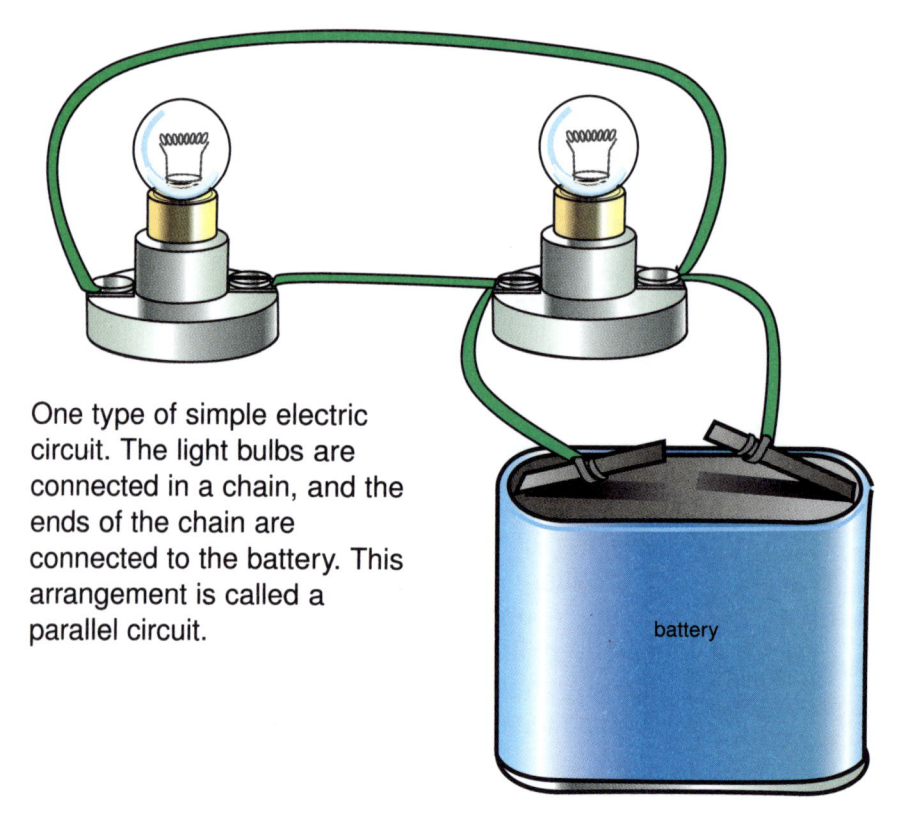

One type of simple electric circuit. The light bulbs are connected in a chain, and the ends of the chain are connected to the battery. This arrangement is called a parallel circuit.

battery

140

Electricity

pump" and drives electrons around the circuit. The electrical pressure is called the "electromotive force" and is measured in volts. The volt is named after the Italian scientist Alessandro Volta (1745-1827).

Measuring the size of an electric current is the same as counting the number of electrons passing through the circuit. A special instrument, called an ammeter, must be used for this task since billions of electrons may pass each second. The ammeter measures a current in units called amperes, named after the French scientist André Ampère (1775-1836).

In an electric circuit, the electron flow is never completely smooth. The electrons collide with atoms in the circuit wire. This creates resistance to the electron flow. Some wires have more resistance than others. Copper has low resistance – electrons flow easily through it. On the other hand, nichrome wire, which is used for heating elements in stoves, has a high resistance. Electrical resistance is measured in units called ohms, after the German scientist Georg Ohm (1787-1854).

Current electricity can be produced using a battery or a generator. The most common battery today is the dry cell battery. Other batteries, called secondary cells, can be used more than once. If they stop producing electricity, they can be recharged with electricity. These batteries are sometimes called storage batteries or accumulators. Automobiles use storage batteries.

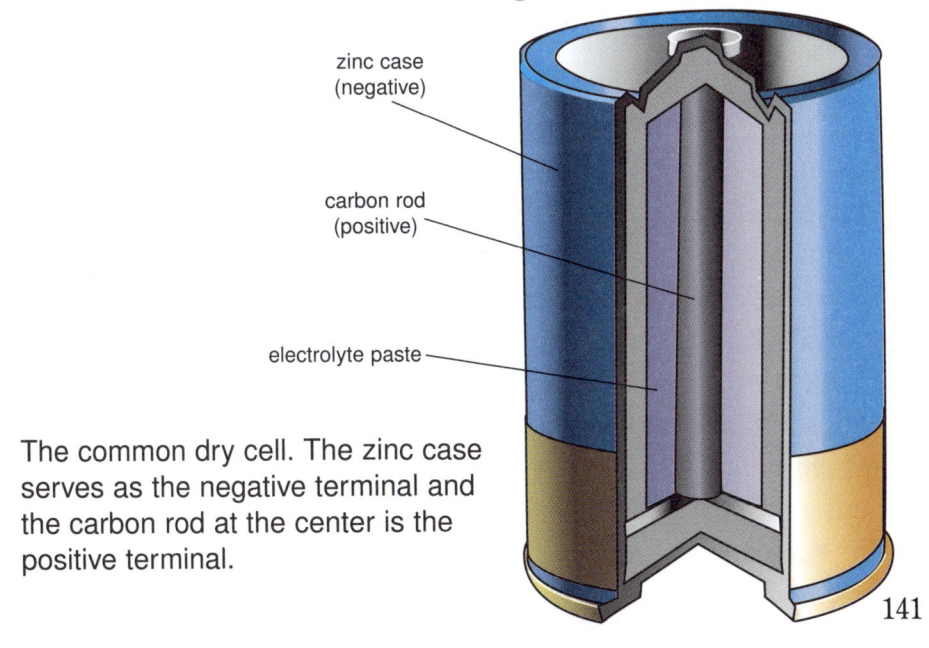

zinc case (negative)

carbon rod (positive)

electrolyte paste

The common dry cell. The zinc case serves as the negative terminal and the carbon rod at the center is the positive terminal.

Matter and Energy

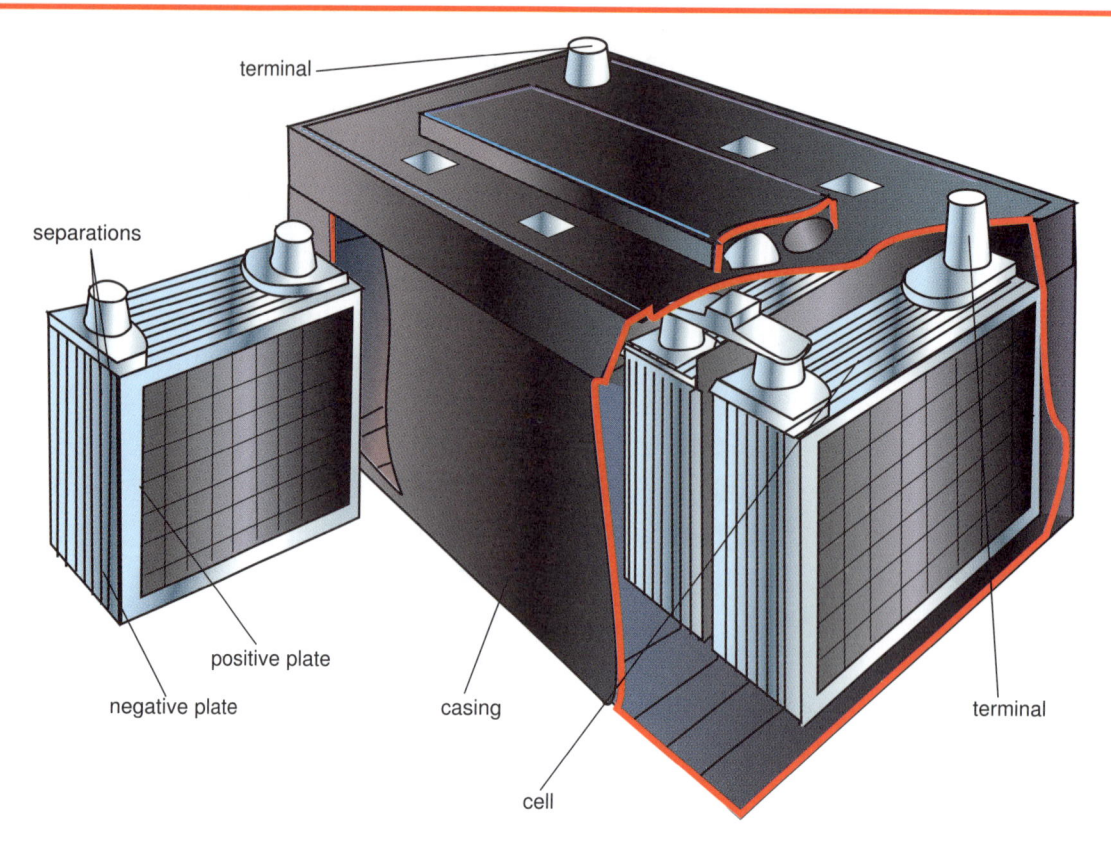

An automobile battery. The negative terminal consists of lead plates. The positive terminal is made of lead oxide plates. The plates dip into sulfuric acid.

A simple generator consists of a coil of wire that is rotated between the poles of a permanent magnet. As the coil rotates, a current is produced in it.

The current in the coil can be drawn off and fed to an external circuit in one of two ways. One way is to attach semi-circular metal pieces to the ends of the coil, forming a device called a commutator. Pieces of carbon (called brushes) press against the commutator and draw off the current. The commutator ensures that the current produced always flows in the same direction. This type of current is called direct current, or DC.

A second method of drawing off the current is to have a circular metal piece attached to each end of the coil. The metal pieces are called slip rings. Carbon brushes press against the rings to draw off the current. This type of generator is often called an alternator.

The current produced by an alternator reverses direction as the coil rotates. The current flows first in one direction, rising to a maximum and then falling to nothing. The current then reverses direction and flows in the opposite direction before falling off to zero again. This type of current is called alternating current, or AC. Power plants produce alternating current and transmit it to our homes.

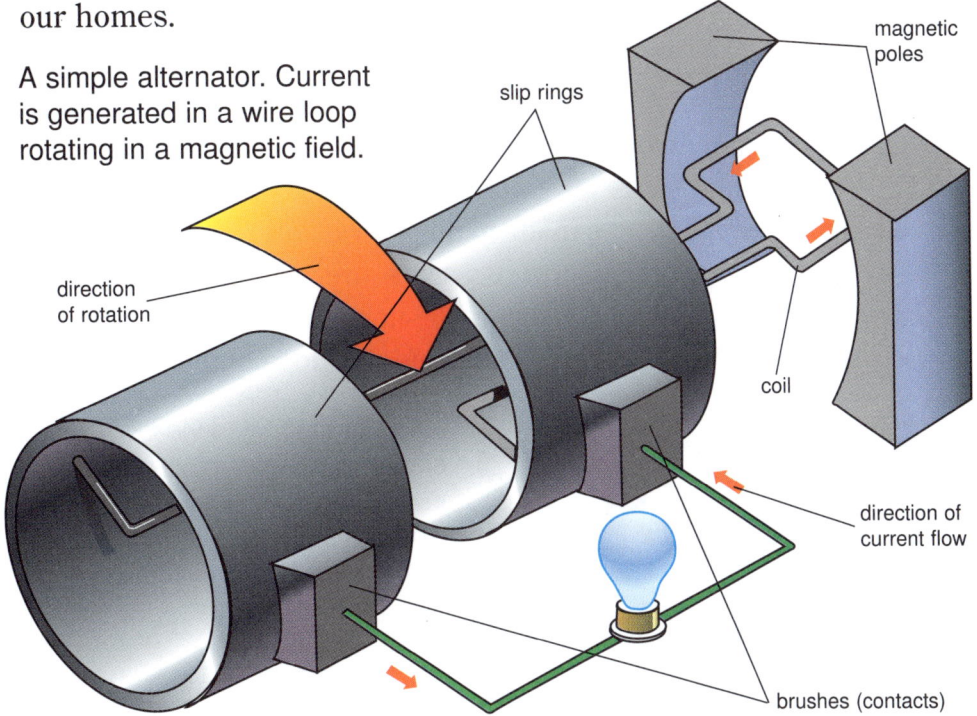

A simple alternator. Current is generated in a wire loop rotating in a magnetic field.

magnetic poles
slip rings
direction of rotation
coil
direction of current flow
brushes (contacts)

Inside the power plants, fuel is burned to turn water to steam. Coal, oil, and natural gas are the most common fuels. In a nuclear power plant, uranium fuel is used to turn the water to steam. The steam drives turbines, which turn the electricity generators. In hydroelectric systems, the immense power of flowing water drives the turbines. The electricity generated is boosted to a high voltage by devices called transformers. The high-voltage electricity is then transmitted across the country through a system of underground cables and overhead wires, called transmission lines. When the electricity reaches its destination, a transformer reduces the voltage to 120 volts, and the electricity flows into our homes.

Many of the electrical appliances in our homes rely on integrated circuits, or ICs, to work. Integrated circuits are complicated electronic circuits built on small pieces of silicon. A silicon chip may have millions of components, along with the connecting links, on it.

Matter and Energy

There are many types of integrated circuit. Some integrated circuits are built to do a particular job. For instance, the chips used in calculators are made specially for calculator work. Radios, too, have most of their main components on a single chip. Other chips are built to link together parts of computers.

The most important, and complicated, IC is called the microprocessor. The microprocessor is sometimes called the "computer on a chip" because it can do almost everything that a full-size computer can. It can remember instructions, do arithmetic, and make decisions. By changing the instructions to a microprocessor, it can be made to do many different tasks. Because they are so flexible, microprocessors are now found in many household and industrial devices, such as washing machines, sewing machines, cameras, robots, and desktop computers.

A highly magnified view of the electrical pathways on a microprocessor. The complicated circuit is built up in a number of stages during manufacture.

Your brain is like a computer. It can do calculations, make decisions, and remember information. An electronic computer can do these things, too, and is sometimes called an "electronic brain." But a computer is not as smart as you. It cannot do even the simplest task without a detailed set of instructions, called a program.

A computer has four main components. The first is the input module, where the instructions, or program, and other information can be fed into the computer. The most common input device is a keyboard, like a typewriter keyboard.

The second component of a computer is the central processing unit. This contains the microprocessor, which receives the program

Electricity

instructions, does the calculations, and tells the output device what the results are.

The third part is the computer memory. This memory is where the computer stores the program and other information needed for its work. A computer system has several types of memory, on memory chips inside the computer. Some of these chips contain the read-only memory (or ROM), which holds information that can be used at any time but cannot be deleted or changed. The second kind of memory chips contain the random access memory (or RAM). These chips are used to store information that is only temporarily needed.

Most computers also have disk memory. There are two types of disk: floppy disks and hard disks. These disks hold information as a magnetic pattern on their surface. Floppy disks are like small flexible music recordings. Hard disks are rigid and made of metal. They can hold much more information than a floppy disk.

The final part of a computer is the output device. This is where the computer shows the results of its work. A common output device is a visual display unit (or VDU) similar to a television screen. Printers are also output devices.

Students working at a computer terminal. Using different programs, they can use the computer for a variety of purposes, for example, word processing and desktop publishing.

145

Magnetism

Magnetic compasses have been used since the early fifteenth century. Most compasses in ships, planes, and cars are usually filled with liquid. The liquid stops the magnetic needle from swinging around too wildly, and allows it to give a constant accurate reading.

Magnetism

Long ago, an unusual kind of black iron ore was discovered. The ore attracted iron objects. When a long, slender piece of the ore was hung by a string, it always came to rest in a north-south position. The stone was used to guide travelers, so it was named the "leading-stone" or "lodestone." The lodestone on a string was the first compass.

We now know that the lodestone is a natural magnet. Today we are not dependent on pieces of lodestone – a magnet may be purchased for a few cents, and many children have them for playthings. Many home appliances use magnets – television sets, record players, electric motors, and tape recorders, for example.

Small magnets are usually made of a bar of iron or steel. Some, called horseshoe magnets, are U-shaped. If one end of a magnet is touched to a small object made of iron, such as a tack or small nail, the magnet will pick it up. Other substances, such as copper, gold, paper, rubber, or wood are not attracted by a magnet. Iron, cobalt, and nickel are the only substances that are highly magnetic. The most powerful magnets are made out of alloys (mixtures) of iron, cobalt, and nickel. Some substances exist, mainly antimony and bismuth, that are weakly repelled or pushed away by a magnet.

Iron filings scattered over glass or paper placed on a magnet can show lines of force. The lines indicate the direction and strength of the magnetic field. The field is strongest where the lines are close together.

Matter and Energy

Every magnet has two poles, or areas where its magnetic force is strongest. The poles of a bar magnet are usually at the ends. One end is called a north pole and the other end a south pole. Sometimes the poles of a magnet are marked N and S. Both poles will attract iron, yet they are different, as a simple experiment will show.

Tie a string around the center of a bar magnet so that the magnet hangs level. Then let the magnet swing freely. First, notice that the magnet lines itself up in a north-south direction, with the N (north) pole pointing north and the S (south) pole pointing south. Next, hold the N pole of a second bar magnet near the N pole of the first magnet. You will see the N pole of the suspended magnet pushed away by the N pole of the other magnet.

Now hold the S pole of the second magnet near the S pole of the first magnet. They, too, repel each other. Hold the S pole near the N pole. These poles are attracted to each other. So you see there is something different about the N and S poles of magnets. The north and south poles attract each other, while one N pole repels another N pole, and one S pole repels another S pole. The rule is "Unlike poles attract, like poles repel." This is true of all magnets.

The space around a magnet in which it can affect a piece of iron is called the "magnetic field." Even though the magnetic force

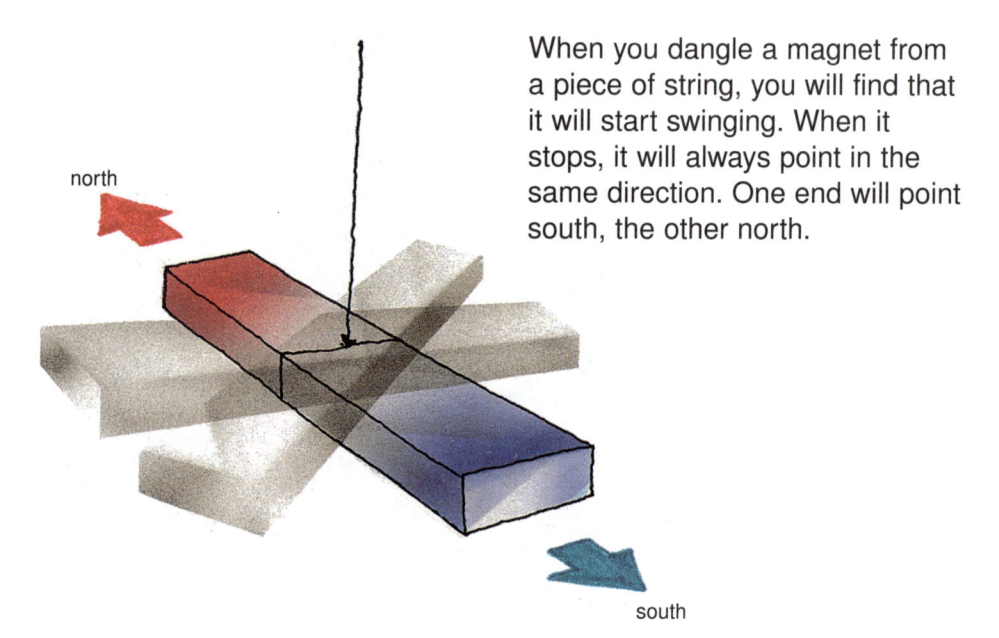

When you dangle a magnet from a piece of string, you will find that it will start swinging. When it stops, it will always point in the same direction. One end will point south, the other north.

north

south

Magnetism

cannot be seen, it is possible to get a picture of the magnetic field. If a piece of glass or paper is placed over a magnet and iron filings are sprinkled on it, the filings will arrange themselves in curved lines that seem to come out of the north pole and pass in a curve around to the south pole. These lines are called "lines of force."

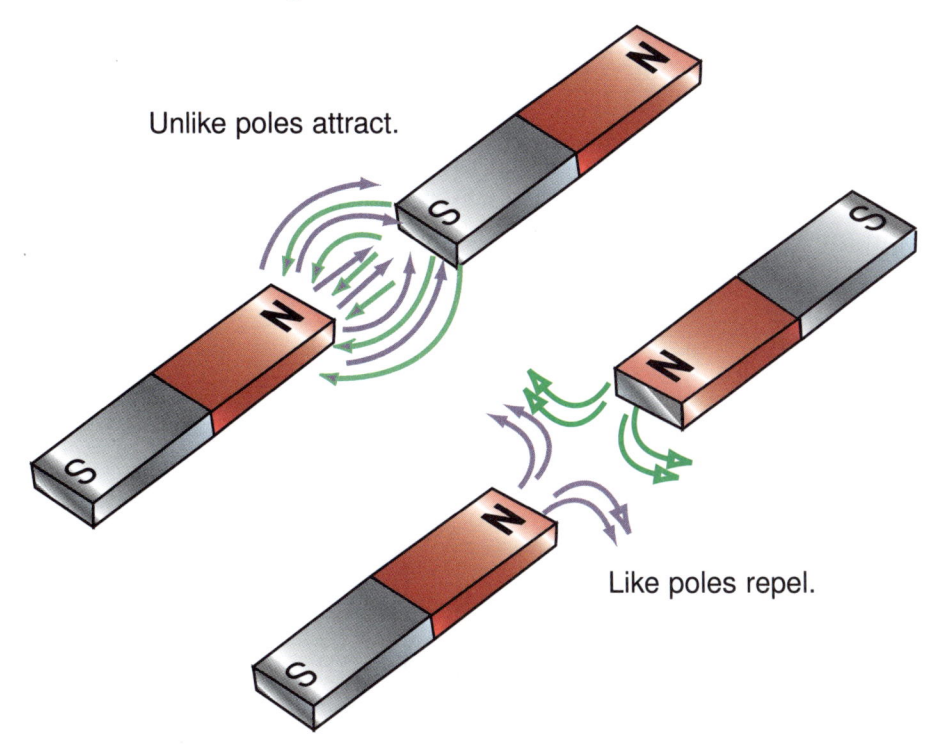

Unlike poles attract.

Like poles repel.

If two north poles or two south poles are placed near each other, their lines of force are seen to push against each other and crowd away from the magnets. This suggests why like poles repel each other. If a N pole is placed near a S pole, the lines of force run from the N pole directly to the S pole. The arrangement of the iron filings suggests that the lines of force are pulling the opposite poles together.

Every piece of magnetized iron has a north pole and a south pole. If this iron is cut in two pieces, each piece becomes a magnet with a north and south pole. These pieces in turn may be cut in halves, and they too would have north and south poles. This fact gives us a clue to what happens when iron is magnetized.

Remember that all materials are made up of small particles called atoms or molecules. Iron is made of molecules. Each molecule of iron is a magnet. When the molecules of a piece of iron are

Matter and Energy

disorganized, with their poles pointing in every possible direction, then the iron is not magnetized. When the molecules get lined up so that their south poles point in one direction and their north poles point in the other direction, then the iron is magnetized.

There are several ways to magnetize a piece of unmagnetized iron. Each method arranges the molecules so that their north poles point in one direction. An easy way to make a magnet is by stroking an iron nail with a magnet. The magnet pulls the molecules until they are all in line. Another way of making a magnet is to hammer an iron bar while it is pointing north. The hammering jostles the molecules and the Earth's magnetism pulls them into line. A magnet made in this way is weak, and its magnetism can easily be lost.

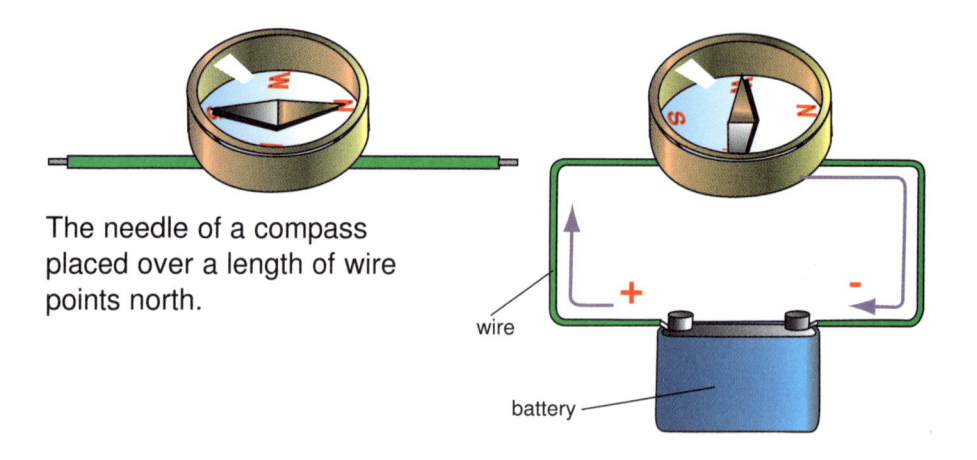

The needle of a compass placed over a length of wire points north.

The magnetic effect of an electric current can be demonstrated by this simple experiment. When a current flows through the wire, the wire acts like a magnet, attracting one end of the compass needle.

Usually a magnet loses its magnetism if it is hammered. The hammering disturbs the molecules and they become disarranged. Heating a magnet also makes it lose its magnetism. So, be careful. Do not hit, drop, or heat a magnet.

Iron will keep its magnetism for a long time, but will lose it more easily than a piece of hard steel. For this reason, most bar and horseshoe magnets are made from steel. Because such magnets keep their magnetism so long, they are often referred to as permanent magnets. Magnets of soft iron, which can be

Magnetism

magnetized easily but lose their magnetism easily, are called temporary magnets.

The most useful kind of temporary magnet is the electromagnet. It is made by passing an electric current through a covered wire that has been coiled around an iron bolt or bar. The strength of an electromagnet can be increased by wrapping more turns of wire around the iron, or by increasing the amount of current passing through the coiled wire.

One of the most important advantages of the electromagnet is that it has its magnetism only while the electric current is turned on. Electromagnets are an important part of many electrical devices. They are used in electric door bells and huge lifting cranes that load and unload scrap iron or heavy iron bars.

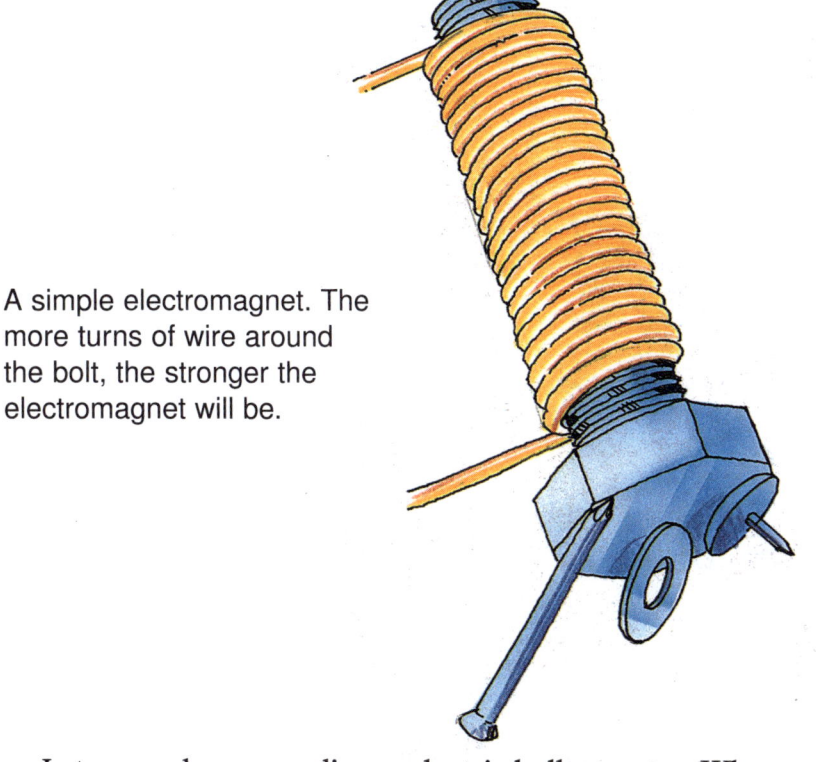

A simple electromagnet. The more turns of wire around the bolt, the stronger the electromagnet will be.

Let us see how an ordinary electric bell operates. When you push the button, it closes the circuit, and electricity flows through the coils of wire in the electromagnet. The magnet pulls the arm to which the clapper is attached, making the clapper strike the bell. As it does so, the path of the electric current is broken so that the magnet loses its strength, and a spring in the arm causes the arm

Matter and Energy

to snap back. But when the arm snaps back, the path of the electric current is completed again and the magnet, regaining its force, pulls the clapper arm toward it once more, again causing it to strike the bell. Of course, this action takes place very rapidly, giving the bell a nearly steady ring. It will continue to ring as long as you push the button.

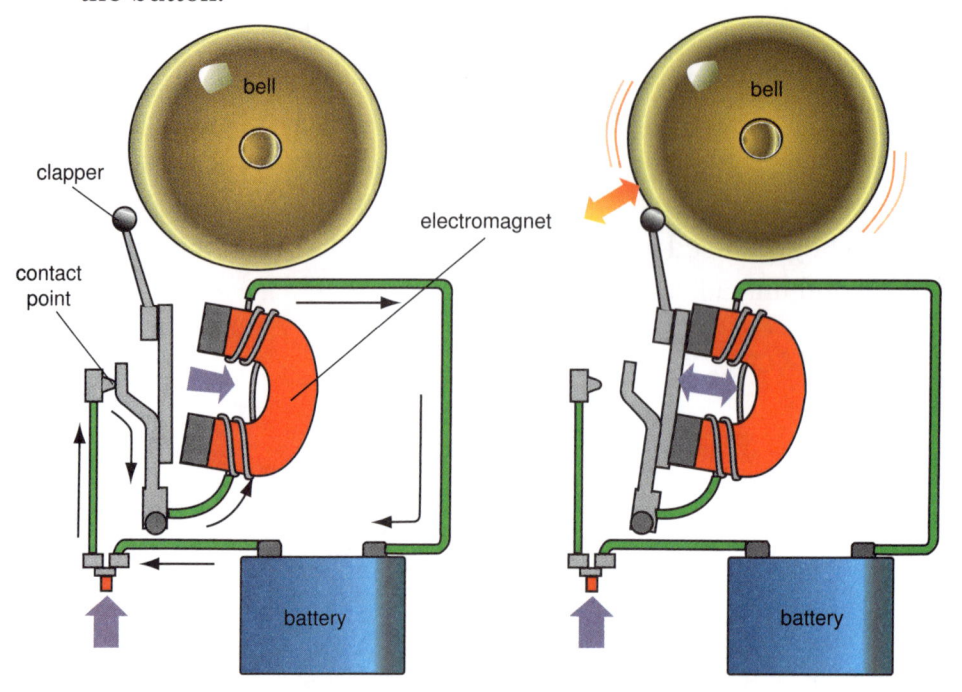

The electromagnet pulls the clapper arm toward the bell when the current flows. The clapper strikes the bell and breaks the current at the contact point, stopping the current. The clapper arm springs away from the bell, allowing the current to flow. The electromagnet again pulls the arm to the bell, and the process repeats itself.

Electromagnets are a necessary part of every electric motor and electric generator. In an electric motor, a coil of wire is positioned between the poles of a permanent magnet or an electromagnet. When an electric current flows through the coil, the coil becomes an electromagnet. The attraction between the coil and the permanent or electromagnet causes the coil to turn.

In a generator, a coil of wire is turned between the poles of a permanent or electromagnet. An electric current is generated in the coil as long as the coil turns. Electromagnets are also used in

Magnetism

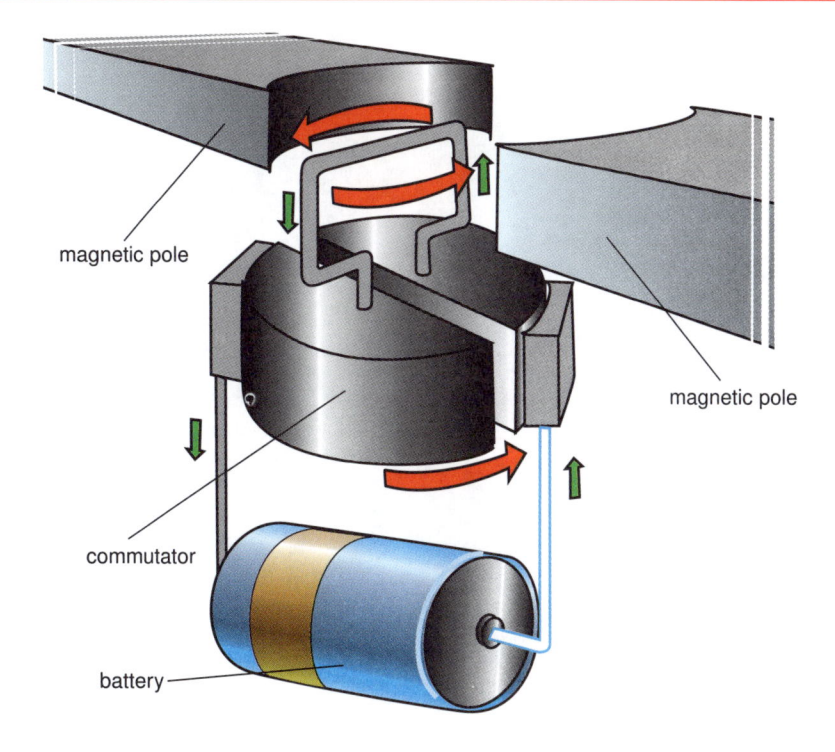

A simple electric motor. The electric current from the battery flows to the coil through the commutator. This device reverses the direction of the current every half-turn, ensuring that the coil keeps turning in the same direction.

telephone receivers, loudspeakers, computer memories, and many other devices.

The Earth itself is a huge magnet. Most of this magnetism is probably caused by electric currents deep inside the Earth's core. Like any other magnet, the Earth has two magnetic poles. One of these poles is in northern Canada near the North Pole. The other magnetic pole is in Antarctica near the South Pole. A magnetic field exists around the Earth just as it does around an ordinary bar magnet.

The magnetic field of the Earth is only one-tenth as strong as an ordinary bar magnet. This field affects a compass needle and makes the N pole of the needle turn toward the magnetic pole in the north. Since the northern magnetic pole is not exactly at the North Pole, the compass needle in most parts of the Earth does not point to true north. The compass needle is a useful direction finder, however, even though it is not perfectly accurate.

Matter and Energy

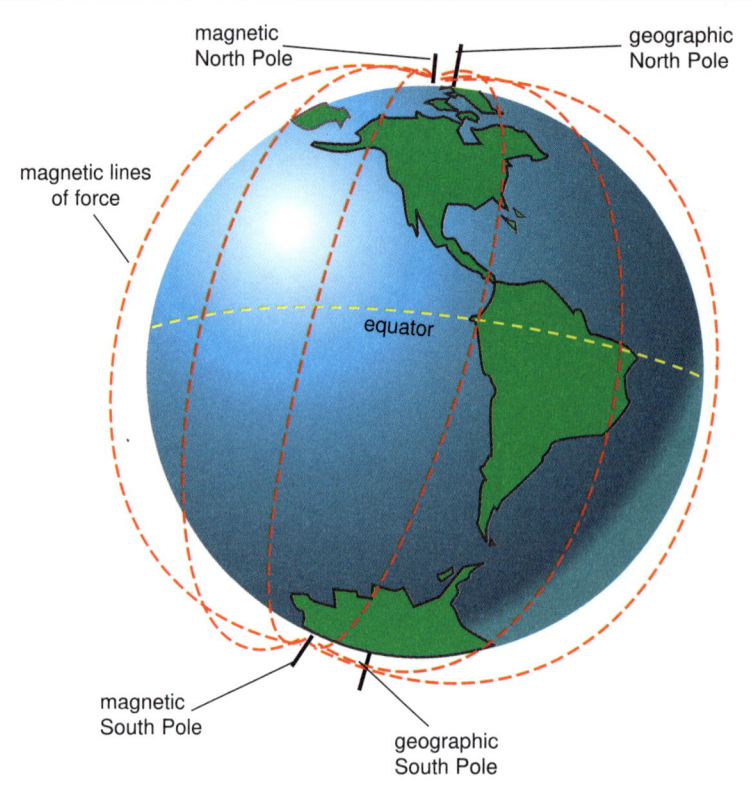

labels on diagram: magnetic North Pole, geographic North Pole, magnetic lines of force, equator, magnetic South Pole, geographic South Pole

The Earth's magnetic field is the same as that of a huge bar magnet buried inside the Earth. The poles of this imaginary magnet are located near the Earth's North and South Poles.

The energy we get from the sun is carried across space by waves called electromagnetic waves. These waves are like ripples of electric and magnetic force that spread out from any magnet or electric charge. All electromagnetic waves travel at the same speed, 186,000 miles (300,000 km) per second. They can travel around the Earth seven times in one second, and take just eight minutes to reach the Earth from the sun.

As an electromagnetic wave moves through space, it has a similar shape to the ripples on a pond. There is always the same distance between each crest of the electromagnetic wave as it moves along. This distance is called the wavelength.

The height of a wave crest or the depth of a trough is called the amplitude of the wave. The greater the amplitude of the wave, the more energy it is carrying.

The number of wave crests passing a point in one second is called the frequency of the wave. Frequency is measured in units called

Magnetism

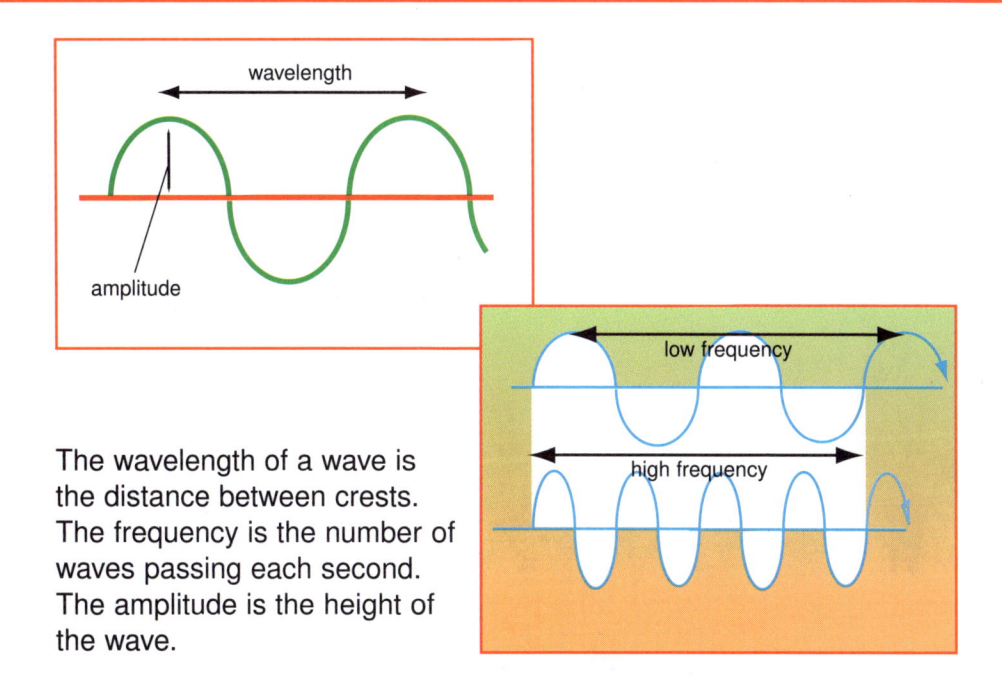

The wavelength of a wave is the distance between crests. The frequency is the number of waves passing each second. The amplitude is the height of the wave.

hertz, after the German physicist Heinrich Hertz (1857-1894), who proved the existence of electromagnetic waves. One hertz is one wave per second.

There is a whole family of electromagnetic waves, each with a different wavelength. The family is called the electromagnetic spectrum. Our senses can detect some of these waves. For example, visible light consists of electromagnetic waves we can see. We can feel other electromagnetic waves as heat rays, called infrared radiation. However, most electromagnetic waves are invisible. These include radio waves, microwaves, ultraviolet rays, X-rays, gamma rays, and cosmic rays.

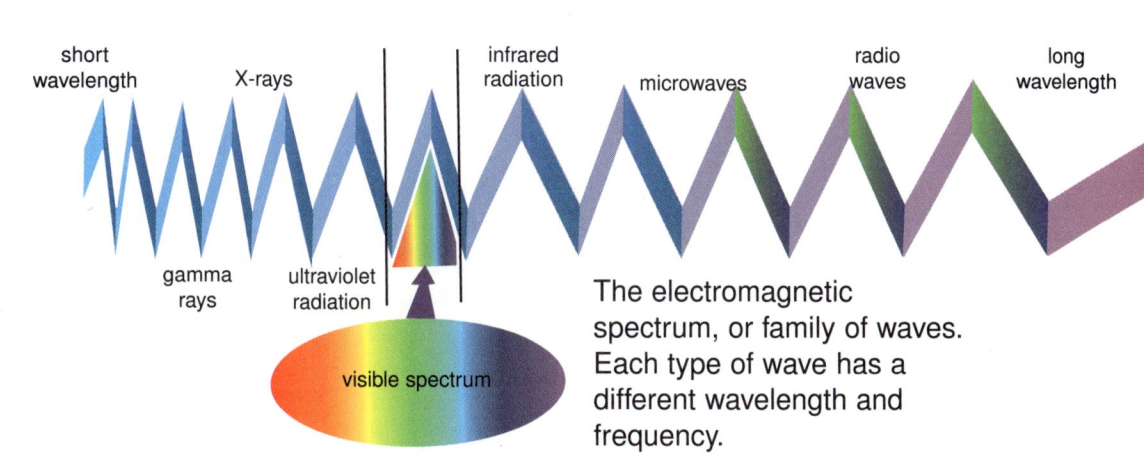

The electromagnetic spectrum, or family of waves. Each type of wave has a different wavelength and frequency.

155

Light

Light

Light consists of electromagnetic waves. The waves travel through empty space at a speed of 186,000 miles (300,000 km) per second. Light takes about 8 minutes to travel to the Earth from the sun, 93 million miles (150 million km) away.

Some objects, such as the sun, electric light bulbs, or fireflies, produce light. They are said to be "luminous." We can see most objects only because they reflect light into our eyes. You see this book or the house next door because of reflected light. These objects, which do not produce light, are called "non-luminous."

The shadows in a forest form because the trees block out the sunlight. Light travels in straight lines and so it cannot curve around the tree trunks.

Matter and Energy

Normally, light travels in straight lines. It does not curve around buildings or around corners. If it did, you would be able to see around objects.

Light can pass through some materials, such as glass and water, and these materials are said to be "transparent." You can see through transparent materials. Other materials permit a little light to pass through them, but not enough to see through them clearly. Frosted glass, ice, and wax paper are examples. These materials are called "translucent." Solid objects that permit no light at all to pass through them are said to be "opaque." Such objects cast a shadow when light shines upon one side of them.

The light we see coming directly from a source of light, such as an electric light bulb, is known as "direct" light. If this light is reflected or bounced off a surface, the light is known as "indirect" or "reflected" light. The light we see from the moon or planets is an example of indirect light. It is the light from the sun that has been reflected by the surface of the moon that reaches our eyes and lets us see the moon.

If a surface is rough, the light that strikes it will be reflected in many directions. Light reflected by such a surface is "diffused," like

When light is reflected from a mirror, the angle of incidence equals the angle of reflection.

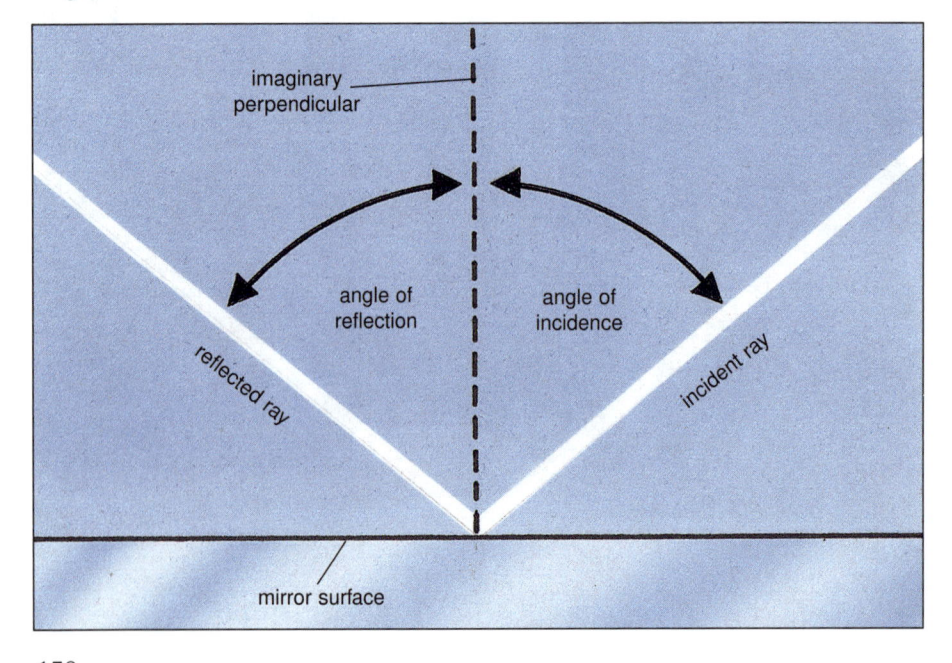

Light

the light from a frosted light bulb or a frosted window. A smooth surface reflects light evenly. This happens when light falls on a mirror or a piece of brightly polished metal.

When a light beam is reflected off a mirror, it is possible to calculate the angle at which the beam will "bounce off" the mirror. The light beam that strikes the mirror is known as the incident ray. The angle between the incident ray and an imaginary line perpendicular to the mirror surface is known as the angle of incidence. The light ray that has bounced off the mirror is called the reflected ray, and the angle between this ray and the imaginary perpendicular line is known as the angle of reflection. In every case, the angle of incidence is equal to the angle of reflection. This is called the "Law of Reflection."

We usually use flat mirrors, but curved mirrors also exist. In a fairground, curved mirrors are used in the "Hall of Mirrors" to produce amusing images. If you look into a polished spoon, it acts as a curved mirror. You will see an upside-down image (picture) in the bowl of the spoon. A mirror that curves inward like the bowl of a spoon is called a concave mirror.

If you turn the spoon over, the surface will form a mirror that bulges outward. This is called a convex mirror. Your image will

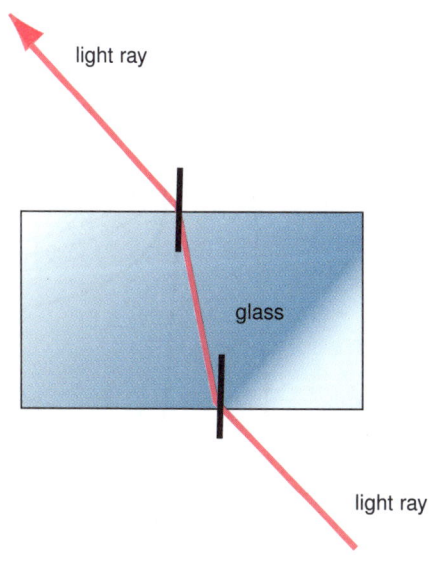

light ray

glass

light ray

If a ray of light passes from a less dense material (such as air) to a more dense material (such as glass), it is bent toward an imaginary line drawn perpendicular to the glass surface. When the ray passes from glass to air, it is bent in the opposite direction.

Matter and Energy

no longer be upside down. You might notice that you can see almost all of the room around you; a convex mirror produces a wide-angle image.

The shiny metal in the back part of an automobile headlight is a concave mirror. It reflects the light from the headlight bulb into a small area on the road ahead. Some large telescopes that astronomers use to study the stars have huge concave mirrors to collect light from the stars and direct it to the eye of the astronomer or to a camera.

Convex mirrors are used where a wide-angle view is needed. A car's rear-view and side-view mirrors are convex mirrors because the driver needs to see a wide area of the road behind the car. Store employees use convex mirrors to watch for shoplifters in supermarkets.

Put a spoon in a glass of water and notice how the spoon seems to be bent. If you move the spoon over to the other side of the glass, it will appear to bend in the other direction. Actually, it is not the spoon that is bent; it is the light reflected from it that is bent, when

A spoon appears bent or broken in a glass of water because the light from it is bent, or refracted, as it leaves the water.

it leaves the water. This bending of light rays as they pass from one material to another is called "refraction."

Refraction often plays tricks on our eyes. If you see a fish from the edge of a pond, the fish is not actually where your eyes tell you it is. Light from the fish bends as it leaves the water. This makes the fish appear to be above the spot that it actually is. For the same reason, a coin in a glass of water appears much closer to the surface than it really is.

To a fisherman on the river bank, the fish appears to be higher in the water than it really is. This effect is due to refraction of light.

Desert travelers have often been confused by seeing what looks like an oasis a short distance away, only to be disappointed when they approach it. What happens is that certain conditions in the atmosphere cause refraction so that an object seems relatively close when it is really far away. Such a vision is called a "mirage." Some mirages occur when light from the sky is bent upward by a hot air layer near the ground. The light appears to come from the ground; it looks like a pool of blue water on the ground.

Pieces of glass or other transparent material with curved

Matter and Energy

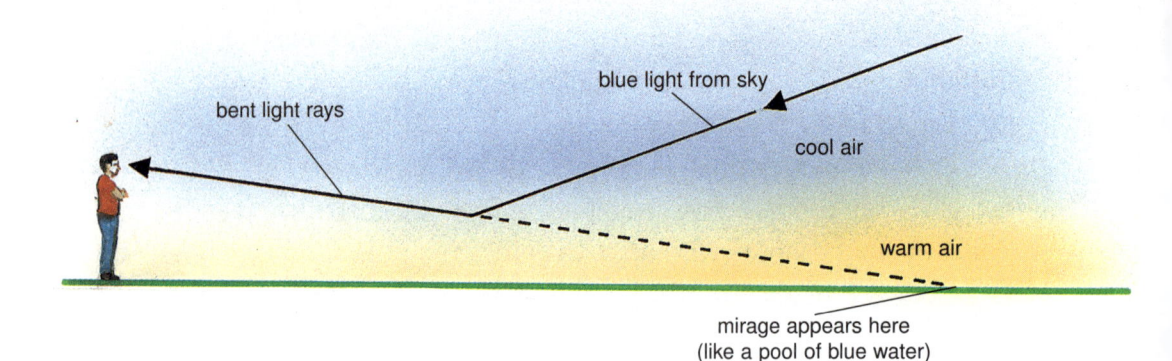

blue light from sky
bent light rays
cool air
warm air
mirage appears here
(like a pool of blue water)

When light bends, we can see things in the wrong place. A mirage occurs when light from the sky is bent by a layer of warm air near the ground. As a result, we see the mirage near the ground.

surfaces are called "lenses." Lenses bend light rays by refraction, and because of this they have many important uses. The most common use is in eyeglasses, but lenses are also used in microscopes, telescopes, and cameras.

There are two kinds of lenses, concave, which curve inward, and convex, which curve outward. Eyeglasses are either concave or convex, depending upon the need of the person who wears them. Concave lenses spread light rays out over a wider area, and convex lenses gather light toward a point, called a "focus."

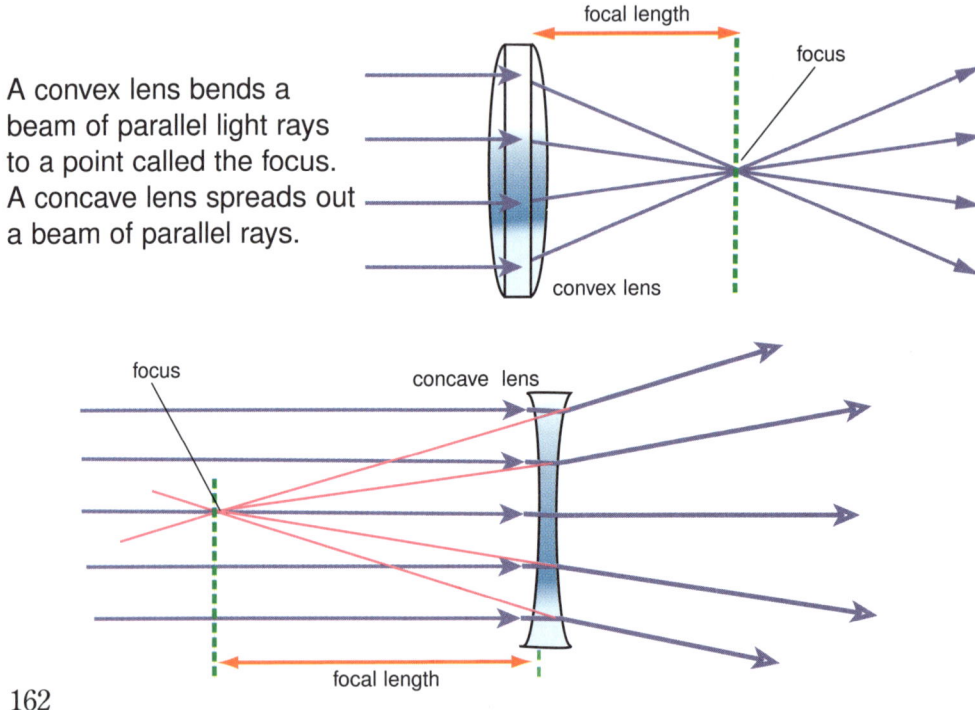

A convex lens bends a beam of parallel light rays to a point called the focus. A concave lens spreads out a beam of parallel rays.

focal length
focus
convex lens

focus
concave lens
focal length

162

Light

A convex lens makes a good magnifying glass. If you place a small object between the focus and the lens, and look at the object through the lens, you will see a magnified image of the object. The magnifying power depends on the thickness of the lens. The thicker the lens, the more it magnifies.

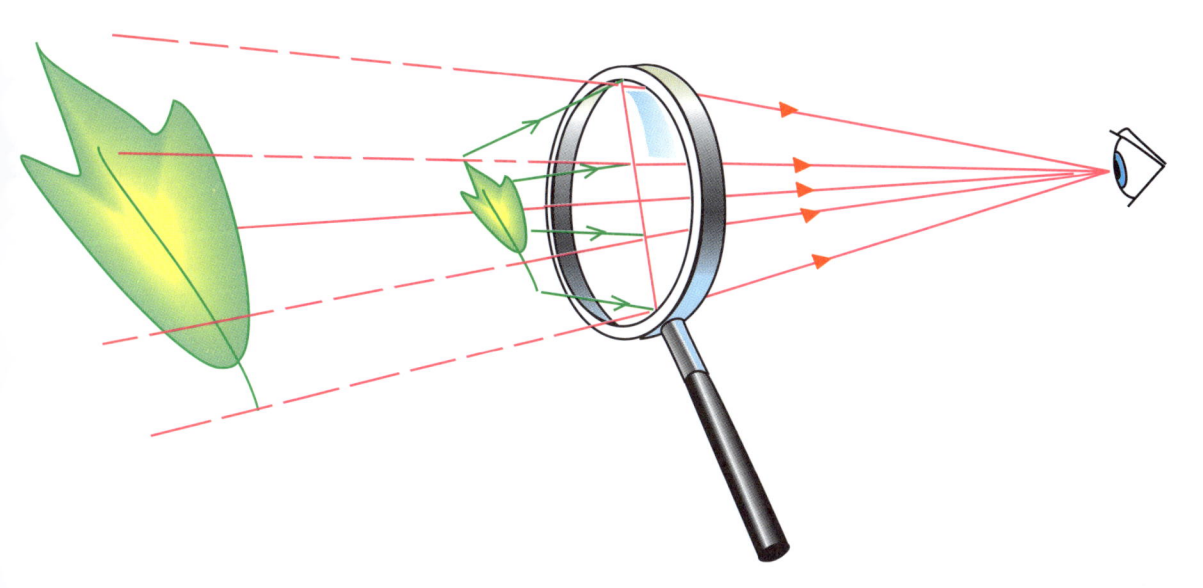

How a magnifying glass forms a magnified image. The glass lens bends light rays from an object so that they appear to come from a larger object.

The most wonderful lenses are those in our eyes. These are not made of glass, of course, but they work in the same way as a glass lens. Light enters the eye through a small opening at the front, called the pupil. The lens, directly behind the pupil, bends the light so that it forms an image on the retina. The retina is a light-sensitive layer at the back of the eyeball. Nerves run from the retina to the brain. If more light is needed on the retina in order to see clearly, the pupil opens wider. The size of the pupil is regulated by the iris, a membrane surrounding the pupil. The iris also gives the eye its color.

When we look at distant objects, the lenses of our eyes become thinner. When we look at close objects, the lenses get thicker. Small muscles in the eye squeeze the lens to make it thicker or thinner. Sometimes, however, the lenses do not change shape

Matter and Energy

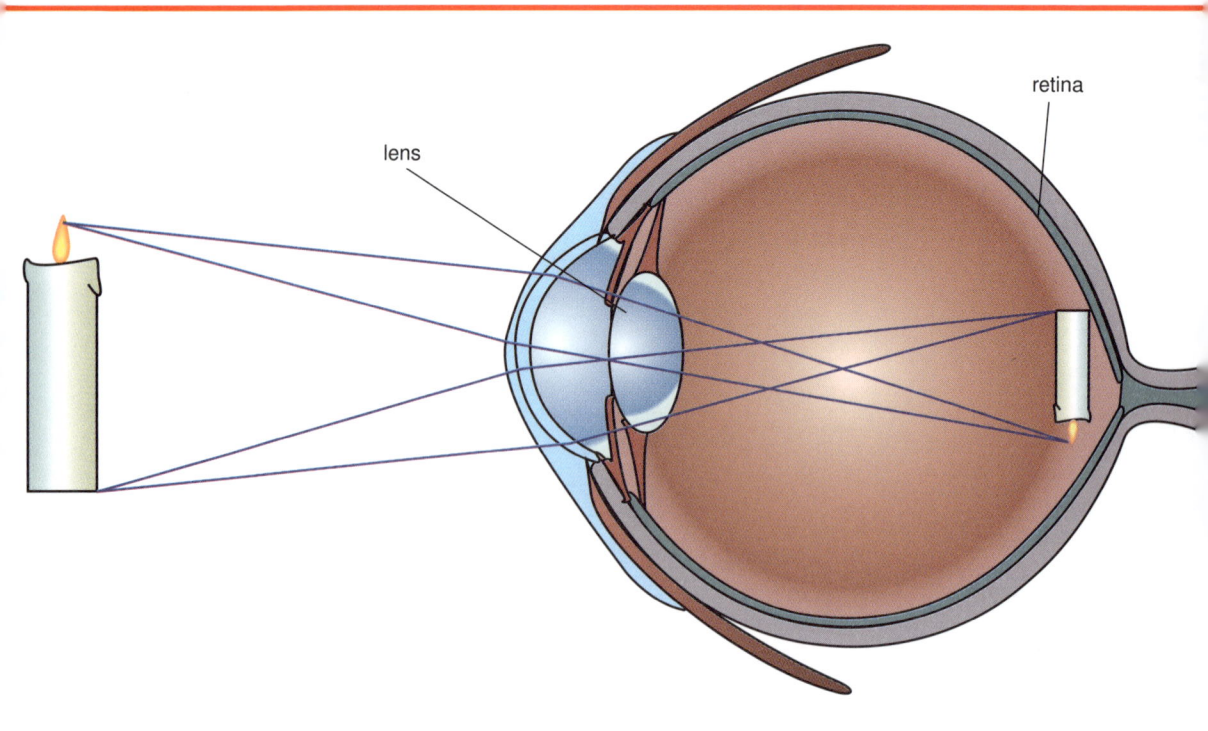

The eye forms an upside-down image of an object on the retina. We see the object right-side-up because the brain correctly interprets the image.

easily, or the shape of the eyeball is such that images do not form properly on the retina. The lenses need help. It is then that people wear glasses or contact lenses. The glasses or contact lenses help direct the light so that it forms clear images on the retina.

White light is really a mixture of several colors of light. When white light passes through a triangular shaped piece of glass called a prism, it splits into a multicolored beam, consisting of violet, indigo, blue, green, yellow, orange, and red. This is the same pattern of color as in a rainbow, which is caused by sunlight shining through a shower of rain.

Each color corresponds to a different wavelength in the spectrum of electromagnetic waves. Orange light has a wavelength of around 600 thousand millionths of a meter, or 600 nanometers. Green light has a wavelength of around 500 nanometers, and violet around 400 nanometers. Light wavelengths are usually measured in nanometers rather than inches.

Objects appear to us the same color as the color of the light they

Light

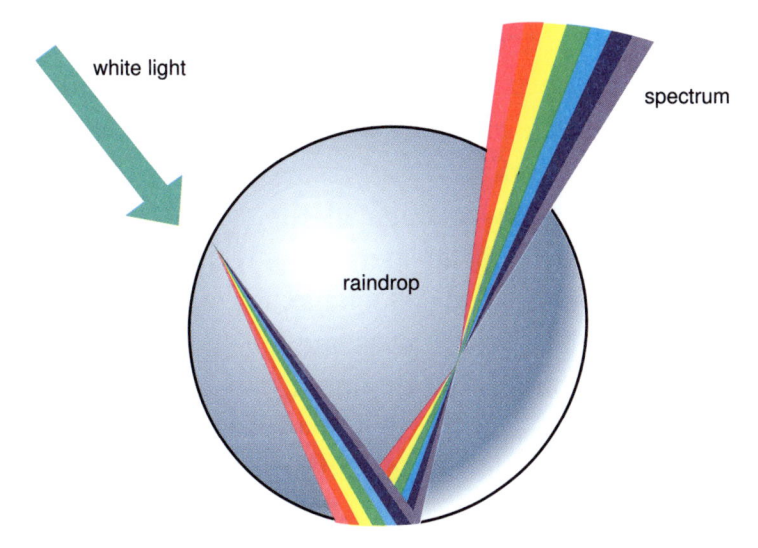

A rainbow forms when white light is split into a spectrum of colors when it passes through raindrops. The light is reflected from the back of the raindrops into our eyes.

A rainbow is seen when light rays from the sun are reflected by raindrops. Sometimes a second bow is seen outside the brighter primary bow. The colors of the secondary bow are reversed, with red on the inside of the bow. This is caused by light being reflected twice inside the raindrops.

Matter and Energy

reflect. A red apple reflects red light and absorbs the other colors. A yellow pencil reflects yellow light and absorbs the other colors. A white object reflects all colors of light equally and a black object does not reflect any light.

Colorless cellophane permits all the colors of light to pass through it. Colored cellophane permits only the light of a particular color to pass through. Blue cellophane, for example, permits only the blue part of white light to pass and blocks the other colors.

You may have noticed that the picture on a television screen is made up of tiny stripes or dots of only three colors: red, green, and blue. Red, green, and blue are called primary colors because they can be mixed to make any color. All the colors on the screen are produced by combining various amounts of light of these three colors. White light is produced by mixing equal amounts of red, green, and blue light.

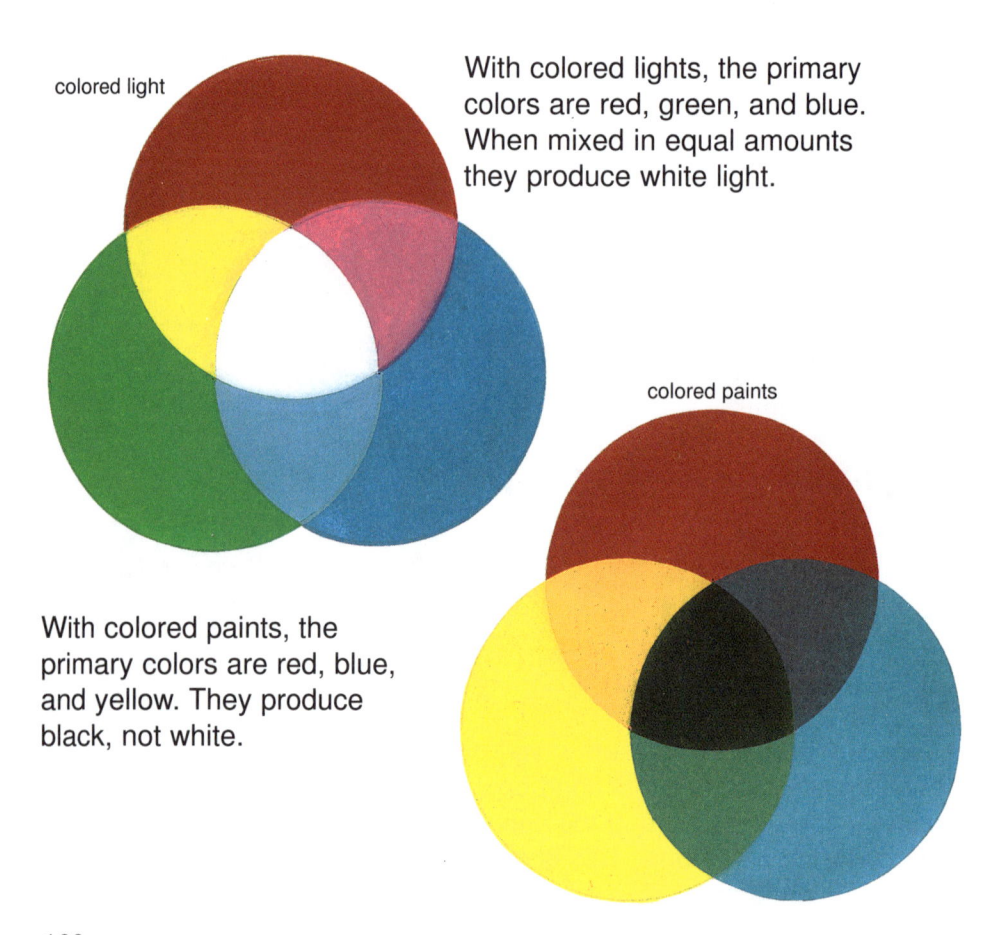

colored light

With colored lights, the primary colors are red, green, and blue. When mixed in equal amounts they produce white light.

colored paints

With colored paints, the primary colors are red, blue, and yellow. They produce black, not white.

Light

Mixing colored paints involves a different color production process from mixing colored lights. Mixing blue and yellow paints makes green. This happens because the pigments in the paints are not pure colors. Yellow paint contains pigment that reflects yellow light. That is why the paint appears yellow. It also contains some green and red pigments, too. In the same way, blue paint reflects a little green and indigo as well as blue. A mixture of the paints appears green because green is the only color reflected by both paints.

A laser is a device that produces a narrow, powerful beam of colored light. Laser light is produced by the atoms inside the laser. When the laser is first turned on, a few atoms give out light. The light bounces back and forth between mirrors at the ends of the laser. As the light travels back and forth, more atoms give out light. The light inside the laser becomes brighter and brighter. Eventually the beam becomes so bright that it bursts out one end of the laser as a narrow, powerful beam.

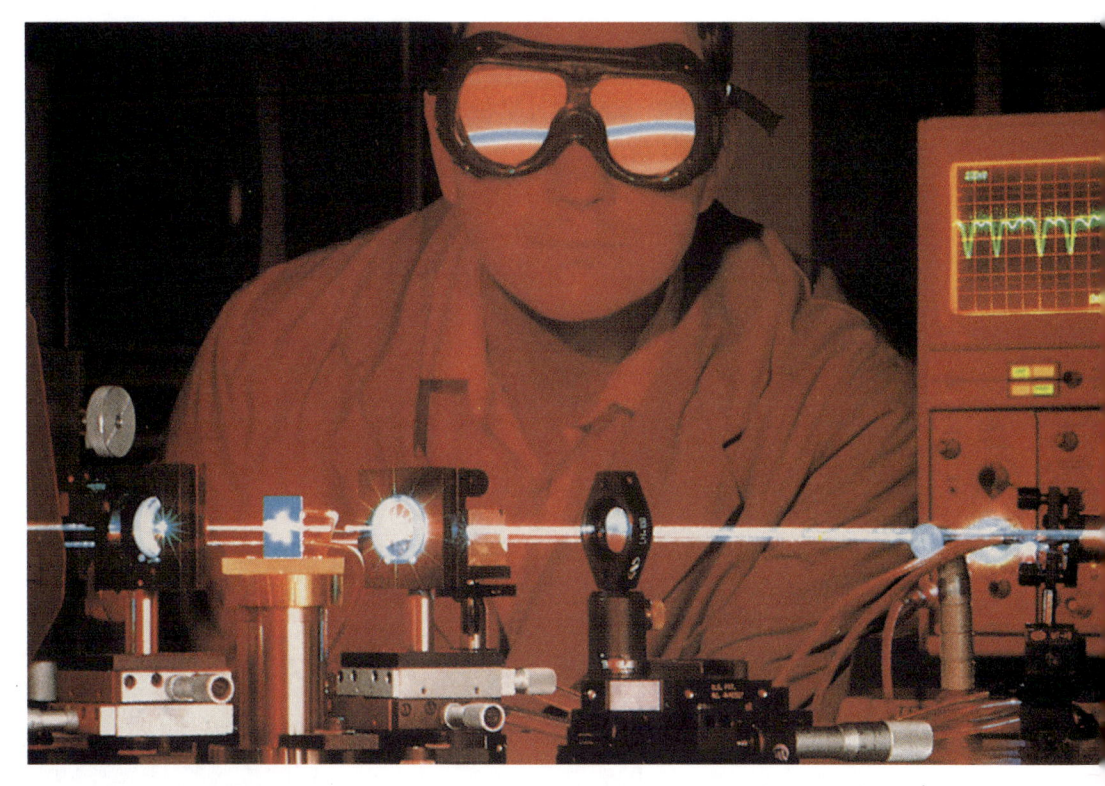

The power and pin-point accuracy of laser beams are used in many applications in industry and medicine.

Matter and Energy

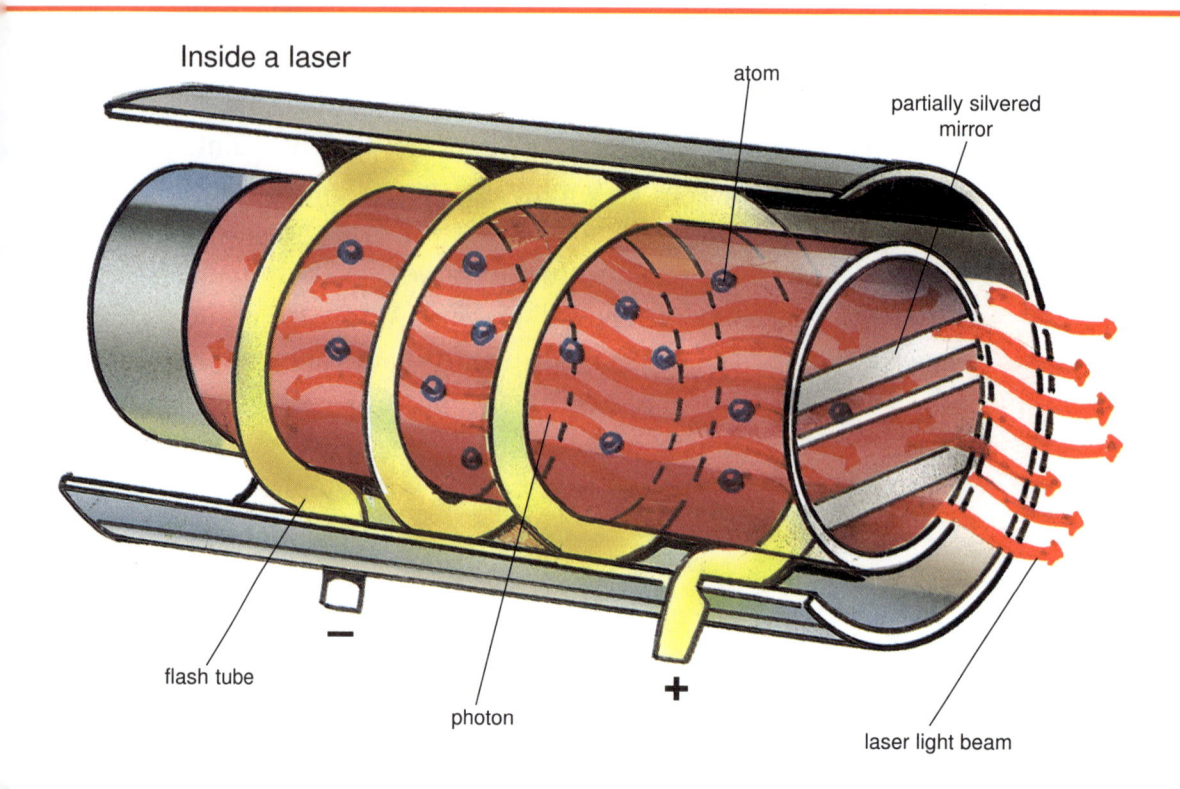

Inside a laser

- atom
- partially silvered mirror
- flash tube
- photon
- laser light beam

A laser beam can be used to drill tiny holes in hard materials such as diamond or to cut through steel. Dentists use lasers to remove decay from teeth. Doctors use lasers to carry out delicate eye and brain operations. At supermarket checkouts, low-power lasers are used to read bar codes. Lasers are found in compact disc players and in some computer printers.

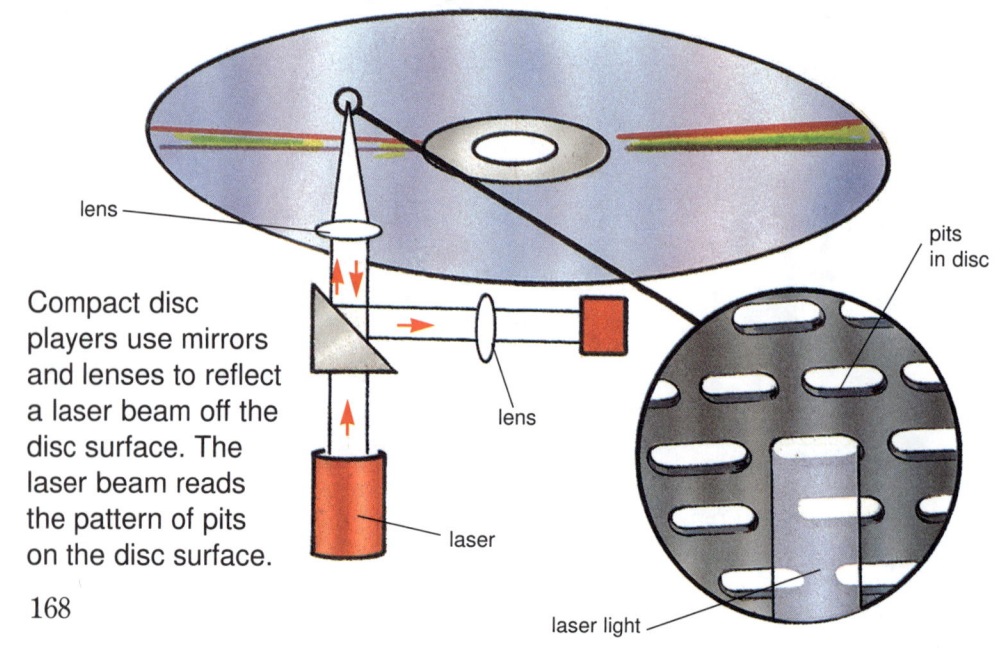

Compact disc players use mirrors and lenses to reflect a laser beam off the disc surface. The laser beam reads the pattern of pits on the disc surface.

- lens
- pits in disc
- lens
- laser
- laser light

Sound

Matter and Energy

Sound

When you sit quietly and listen, you are likely to hear many sounds. Perhaps you have wondered how these sounds occur. Every sound is made by something vibrating, that is, moving very quickly back and forth. When a door slams, we hear it because the bumping of

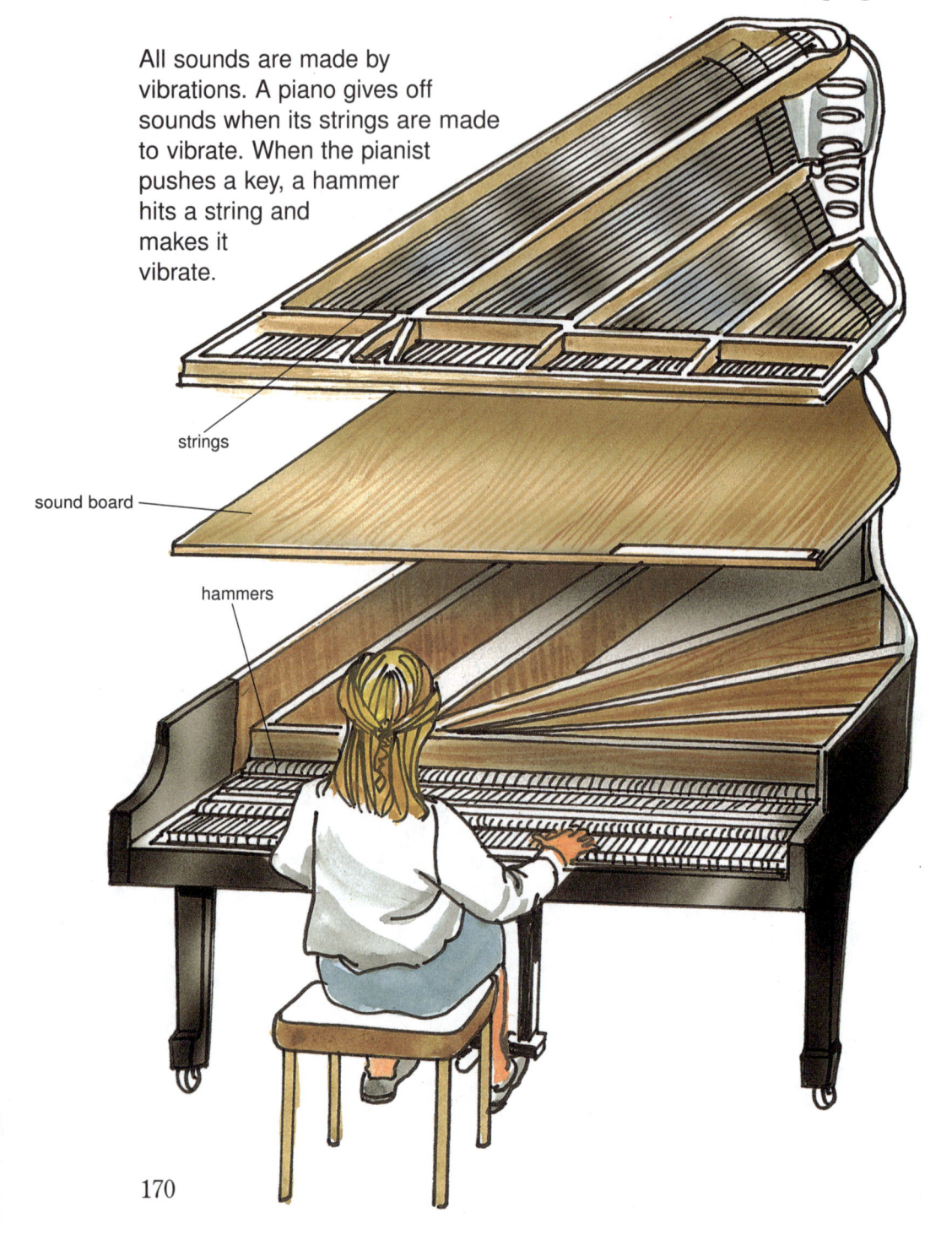

All sounds are made by vibrations. A piano gives off sounds when its strings are made to vibrate. When the pianist pushes a key, a hammer hits a string and makes it vibrate.

strings

sound board

hammers

Sound

the door against its frame causes vibrations in the wood of the door. If you pluck the string of a guitar, you will see the string vibrate and hear the sound produced. You hear your friend's voice because vibrations are set up in his vocal cords as he speaks. Place your fingers at the side of his throat and you will feel the vibrations produced as he speaks.

But how do the sounds reach our ears? They come to us as sound waves in the air. When an object vibrates, it pushes air molecules in front of it, crowding them together. This creates a small area of high pressure where the molecules are packed together. As the vibrating object moves back in the opposite direction, the air molecules can spread out slightly. This creates an area of low pressure. In this way, the object creates areas of high and low pressure in the air as it vibrates. The areas of high and low pressure move outward from the vibrating object as waves in the air – sound waves. When the waves reach our ears, we hear a sound.

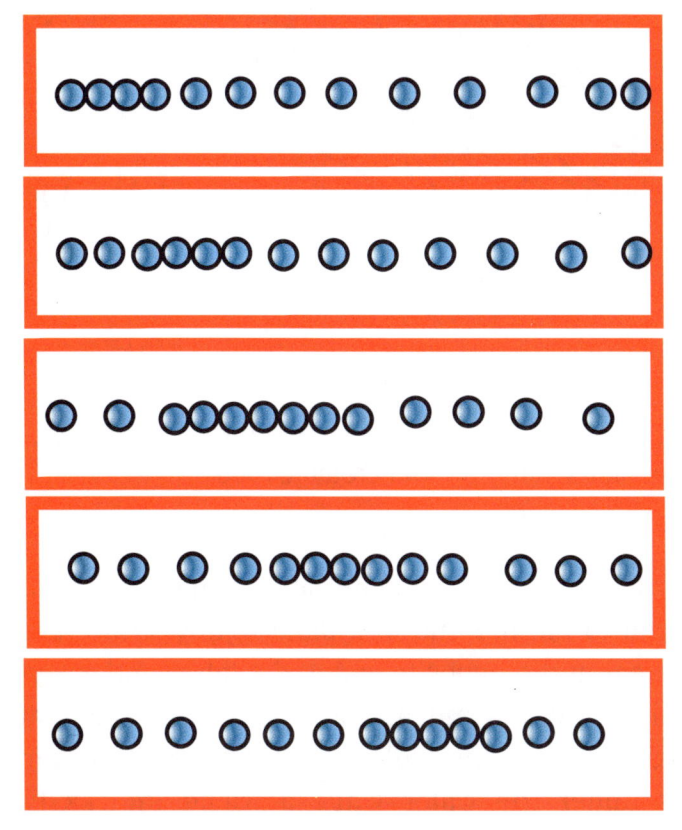

As a sound wave passes through the air, molecules collide with each other, vibrating back and forth in a regular manner.

Matter and Energy

The outer parts of our ears collect the sound waves and direct them to the eardrum. The sound waves strike the eardrum and make it vibrate, causing tiny bones connected to it to vibrate. These carry the sound to the inner ear. Here the vibrations are converted into an electrical signal by a shell-shaped organ called the cochlea. The electrical signal is carried by nerves to the brain. When the signal gets to the brain, you hear the sound.

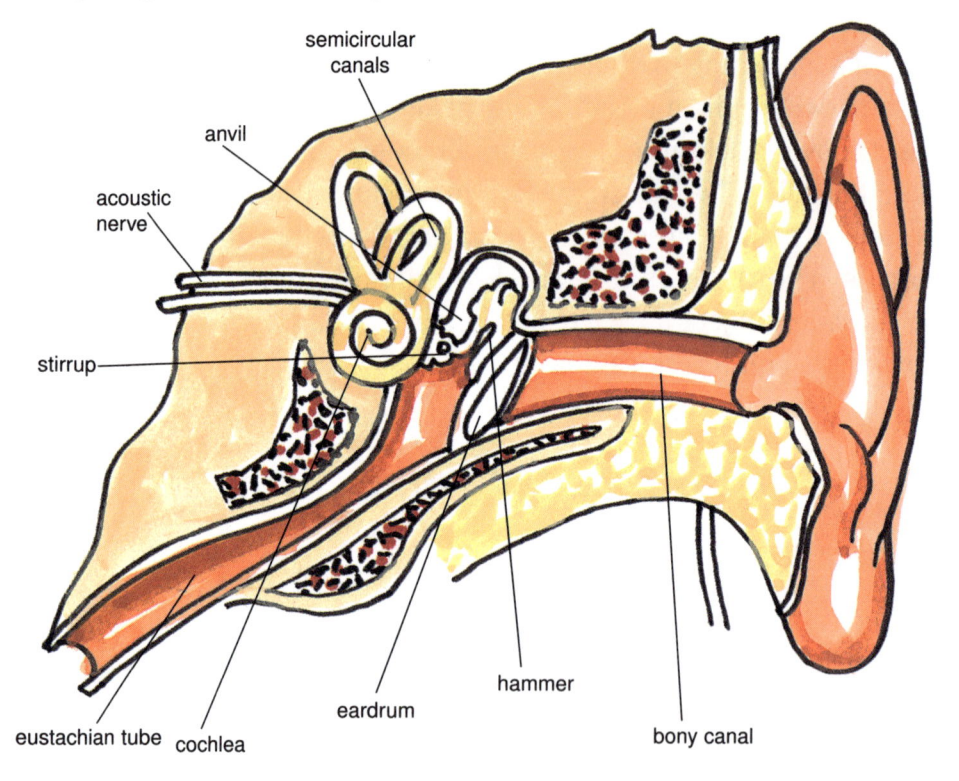

The human ear. The complex structure of the ear enables us to detect the fine vibrations in the air that create sound.

Sound travels through all materials – liquids, solids, and gases. Ask a friend to tap the end of a table lightly with a pencil. Then place your ear at the opposite end of the table, and ask your friend to tap again. Note how much clearer the sound seems when your ear is placed against the table. Some day when swimming, hold your ears under the water while a friend knocks two stones together in the water a short distance away from you. You will hear the sound very distinctly.

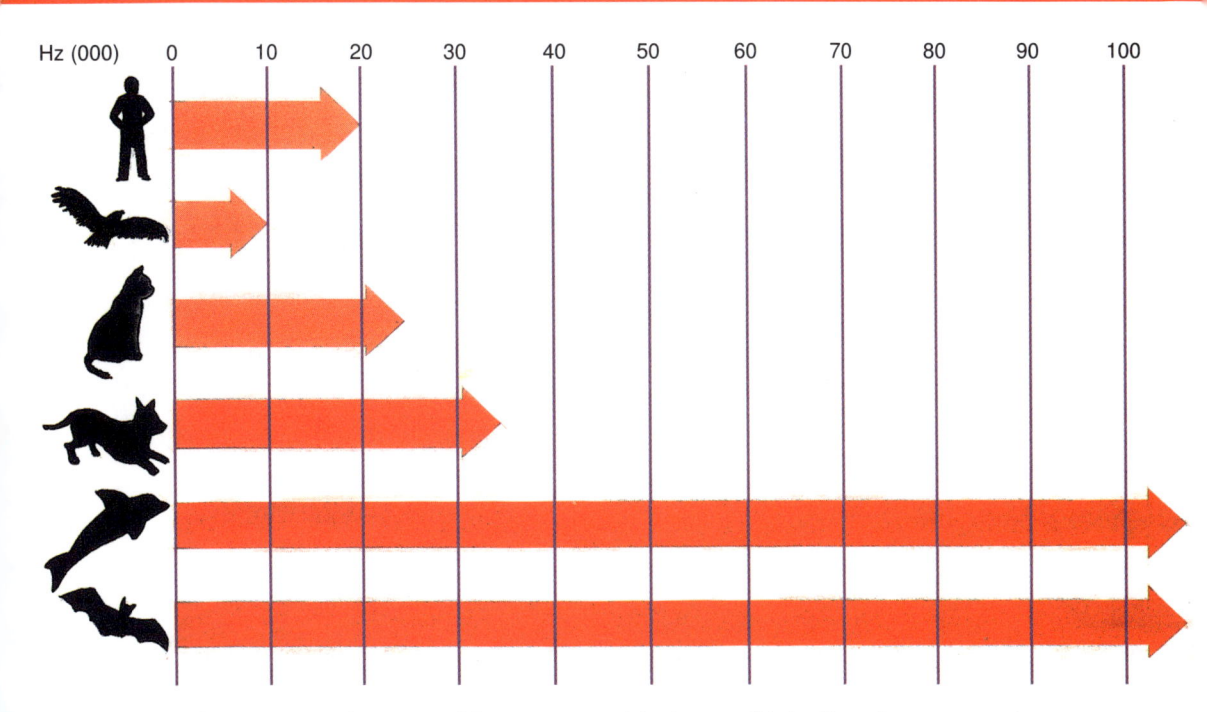

The frequency of a sound is measured in hertz (Hz). One hertz equals one wave per second. The diagram shows the frequency range that can be heard by humans and other animals.

Sound travels through some materials better than others. It will not travel through a vacuum (an empty space from which the air has been removed). If an electric bell is placed inside a sealed jar and the air pumped out, the sound will get fainter as the air inside gets thinner, although the bell can be seen to vibrate just as strongly. This shows that sound waves must have some material to travel through.

Sound waves travel in air at the rate of about 1,100 feet (335 m) each second. This equals about 750 mph (1,200 km/h), or a mile in 5 seconds (a kilometer in 3 seconds). On a warm day sound waves travel a little faster than on a cold day. For each degree Fahrenheit the temperature rises, the speed of sound rises by 1.1 feet (0.33 m) per second. At 32°F, sound travels in air at about 1,090 feet (332 m) per second, and at 68°F it travels at about 1,130 feet (344 m) per second.

The speed of sound waves also depends upon the material they are traveling through. They travel faster in a denser medium, such as glass or water, than in air. For instance, sound waves travel at

Matter and Energy

about 1,128 feet (344 m) per second in air, at about 4,792 feet (1,461 m) per second in water, and in steel at 16,400 feet (5,000 m) per second.

When sounds strike a solid surface, such as a cliff, some distance away, we often hear an echo, or repetition of the sound. The echo occurs because the sound has been reflected off the cliff. When a person shouts into a deep well, a great confusion of sounds results. This is called "reverberation." Reflection of the sound occurs over and over again as the sound waves bounce back and forth from one wall to another. Echoes and reverberation occur in large rooms and concert halls unless the buildings are planned properly to avoid such annoyances.

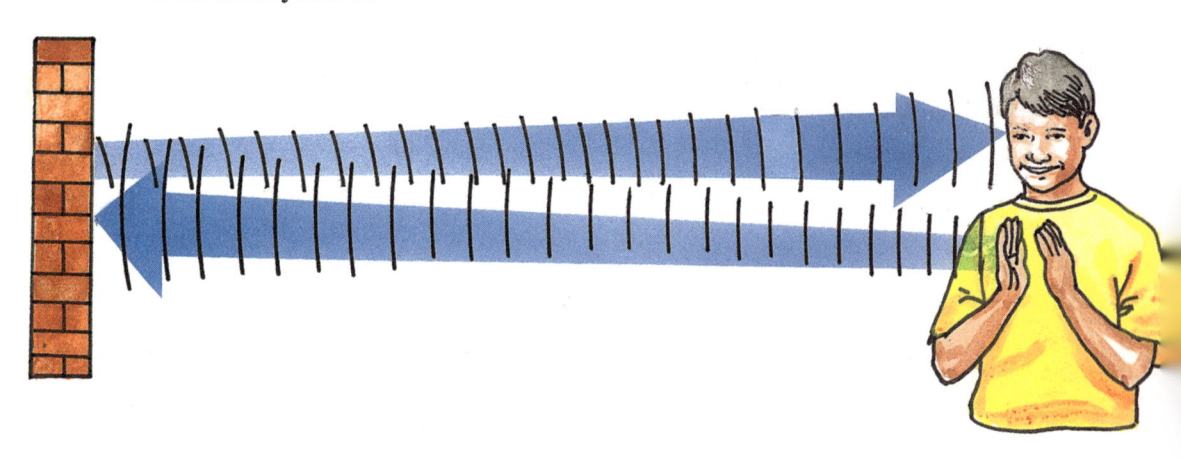

Echoes can be used to find the speed of sound by using a stopwatch to measure the time it takes for the sound of clapping hands to be reflected back from a wall. If the person is 250 feet (76 m) from the wall, the sound has traveled to the wall and back, a distance of 500 feet (152 m), in the time measured.

Some sounds are loud and some are soft. Some are high-pitched whistles and some are low-pitched rumbles. Some are pleasant and musical and some are unpleasant noises. What makes sounds so different? The answer is that sounds have different shaped waves, and that most sounds are combinations of different waves.

Scientists sometimes draw pictures to represent sound waves, even though sound waves themselves cannot be seen. The musical sound produced by a flute, for example, might be shown as a smooth line, moving back and forth in a regular way. The picture showing a noise would be a very irregular and uneven-looking line. A noise is a sound that has irregular sound waves. A musical tone results when a vibrating object gives off regular and uniform sound waves.

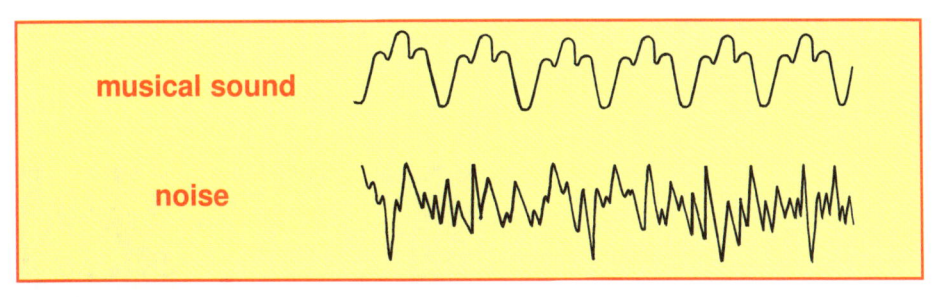

A drawing of a musical sound (top) and a noise (bottom). The musical sound has a regular wave, and the noise an irregular wave.

The distance between two successive areas of high pressure in a sound wave is called the wavelength of the sound wave. The wavelength of a wave is closely related to its frequency, or the number of wave crests that pass a given point in one second. The shorter the wavelength, the greater the frequency of a sound.

The notes played from the right side of the piano keyboard have a higher tone than those played from the left. This "highness" or "lowness" of a musical sound is called its pitch. The pitch of a sound is related to the frequency of the sound. The greater the frequency of a note, the higher the pitch of the sound we hear.

The amplitude of a sound wave is related to the loudness of the sound. The greater the amplitude, the louder the sound. When a guitar string is plucked strongly, the string moves a greater distance as it vibrates back and forth than if it were struck lightly. This means that a louder sound is produced.

The human ear is very sensitive. Yet most people cannot hear sounds that have fewer than 20 vibrations per second or more than about 20,000 vibrations per second.

Some animals, however, can hear these sounds. Dogs and cats can hear high-pitched whistles. Dolphins can hear sounds with frequencies over eight times higher than those heard by human ears. Elephants communicate using very low-frequency sounds. Some birds can hear the low-frequency sounds made by sea waves from great distances away.

Matter and Energy

The loudness of sound waves is measured in decibels. The softest sound that we can hear has a value of 0 decibels. A jet aircraft taking off has a value of around 120 decibels.

aircraft engine 100-120 decibels
painfully loud

thunder 100 decibels
very loud

railroad train 90 decibels
very loud

crowd of people at a rally
70 decibels
loud

normal conversation 40-60 decibels
moderate

rustling leaves 10 decibels
faint

Ships use sonar (sound navigation and ranging) to find the depth of the seabed beneath them and to locate fish or wrecks. Pulses of ultrasound are transmitted into the ocean. The time taken for the echoes to bounce back is measured, and the depth can then be calculated.

Bats home in on their insect prey by emitting ultrasonic waves and listening for their echoes. Doctors use a similar method to look inside the human body. Their ultrasound scanner sends out ultrasonic waves that are reflected from body tissues and organs. From the pattern of reflections, a computer can build up a picture of the inside of the body.

Glossary

ACOUSTICS The science that studies sound and hearing.

ALTERNATING CURRENT (AC) Electric current that flows first one way, then the other. It is this kind of electricity that is supplied to our homes. Compare to DIRECT CURRENT.

ALTERNATOR An electric generator that produces alternating electric current.

AMMETER An instrument that measures electric current.

AMMONITE An animal that lived in ancient seas, something like an octopus in a coiled shell.

AMPERE The unit used to measure electric current, named after the French electrical pioneer André Ampère (1775-1836). Also called Amp.

AMPLITUDE The strength of a wave. It is the distance from the top of a wave crest to the low point of the wave.

ANALOG RECORDING A recording that stores sound as a continuous signal or pattern.

ANEMOMETER An instrument that measures the speed of the wind.

ANGLE OF INCIDENCE The angle at which light hits a mirror or enters a transparent material.

ANGLE OF REFLECTION The angle at which light is reflected from a mirror or smooth surface.

ANTICYCLONE A region of high atmospheric pressure.

ASTEROIDS Small rocky bodies that circle the sun, mainly in a "belt" between the orbits of Mars and Jupiter. They are also called the minor planets.

ASTROLOGY Study of the positions of the heavenly bodies with a view to foretelling future events in people's lives.

ASTRONOMY The scientific study of the heavens and the bodies therein: the sun, the moon, the planets, their moons, the stars, and the galaxies.

ATMOSPHERE The layer of air that surrounds the Earth. More generally, a layer of gases that surrounds a heavenly body, such as a planet or a moon.

ATMOSPHERIC PRESSURE The pressure exerted by the atmosphere. At sea level, the atmospheric pressure is about 14.7 pounds per square inch (1 kg per square cm). The pressure decreases as you climb above sea level.

ATOM A very small particle, the smallest part of a chemical element that takes part in a chemical reaction. Atoms are about a tenth of a millionth of a millimeter across.

Glossary

AURORA A colorful glow seen in far northern and far southern skies, produced when charged particles from the sun collide with particles of dust in the upper atmosphere. See also NORTHERN LIGHTS; SOUTHERN LIGHTS.

BAR The unit with which meteorologists measure atmospheric pressure. They usually quote pressures as so many millibars, or thousandths of a bar.

BAROMETER An instrument that measures the pressure of the atmosphere. A barograph is a barometer that records the pressure as an ink line on paper.

BASALT One of the most common igneous rocks. It forms on the Earth's surface and has only microscopic crystals.

BATTERY A device that produces electric current as a result of a chemical reaction.

BEAUFORT SCALE A scale for estimating wind force (speed) from its effect on the surroundings.

BREEZE A light wind.

CAPACITOR A device that can store electric charge.

CENOZOIC ERA The era of recent life; the period of geological time from about 64 million years ago to the present day.

CHIP A thin slice of semiconductor crystal, usually silicon, containing microscopic electronic circuits.

CHROMOSPHERE The middle layer of the sun's atmosphere, which is pink in color. We can see it during a total eclipse of the sun.

CIRRUS A high-level cloud that has a wispy appearance.

CLIMATE The general pattern of weather over a long period of time.

CLOUD A mass of little water droplets or ice crystals in the sky.

COCHLEA A coiled tube in the inner ear, where vibrations from sound waves are changed into electrical impulses. The impulses are sent to the brain, which interprets them as sounds.

COLD FRONT The boundary formed when a cold air mass pushes away a warm air mass.

COMET A "dirty snowball" of rock, ice, and dust, which starts to shine when it approaches the sun.

COMMUTATOR A split-ring device used in electric motors and generators to change the direction of electric current as the motor or generator turns.

CONCAVE LENS OR MIRROR A lens or mirror whose surface is curved inward, like a small cave.

CONDENSATION A process in which water vapor in the atmosphere changes back into water when it is cooled. It is the opposite of evaporation.

CONDUCTOR A material that passes on, or conducts, electricity.

Glossary

CONSTELLATIONS Imaginary patterns that bright stars make in the heavens.

CONTINENTAL DRIFT The gradual movement of the land masses of the Earth because of movements of the plates of the crust.

CONVECTION A process in which warm air rises because it is lighter (less dense) than the surrounding cold air.

CONVEX LENS OR MIRROR A lens or mirror that is curved outward. The outside of a shiny spoon forms a convex mirror.

CORNEA The transparent front part of the eyeball. It covers the iris and pupil.

CORONA A white halo, or "crown" we can see around the sun during a total solar eclipse. It is the sun's outer atmosphere.

COSMIC RAY High-energy radiation that reaches the Earth from space.

CRATERS Depressions on the surface of a planet or a moon, made by falling meteorites or by erupting volcanoes.

CRUST The hard, rocky outermost part of the Earth.

CRYSTAL The state most minerals take when they form slowly from molten rock.

CUMULUS A cloud that somewhat resembles a pile of cotton.

CYCLONE This has two meanings in meteorology. (1) A region of low pressure. (2) The name for a hurricane that begins in the Indian Ocean; also called a tropical cyclone.

DECIBEL A unit used for measuring the loudness of sounds. A soft whisper is measured close to 0 decibels. The noise of a jet taking off is about 120 decibels.

DEPRESSION A region of low pressure.

DEW Water drops that appear on surfaces when the Earth cools at night.

DEW POINT The temperature at which water vapor in the atmosphere begins to condense into liquid water.

DIRECT CURRENT (DC) Electric current that flows in one direction only. Compare to ALTERNATING CURRENT.

DIRECT LIGHT Light that comes directly from its source, rather than being reflected off a non-luminous object.

DOLDRUMS A region around the equator where the wind is often light or absent.

DRIZZLE A form of very light rain with small drops that fall from low clouds.

DRY CELL The most common kind of battery, found in flashlights, radios, and the like. Its chemicals are sealed inside a casing, hence it is dry.

DYNAMO An electric generator that produces direct current.

ECLIPSE The passing of one heavenly body in front of another, blotting out its light. We see a solar eclipse, or an eclipse of the sun, when the moon passes in

Glossary

front of the sun. We see a lunar eclipse, or an eclipse of the moon, when the moon moves into the Earth's shadow.

ELECTRODE The terminal in electric apparatus that conducts electricity in or out.

ELECTROLYTE A substance that conducts electricity when it is molten or in solution.

ELECTROMAGNET A temporary magnet consisting of a coil, wound on an iron core. The device becomes magnetic when electricity is passed through the coil.

ELECTROMAGNETIC WAVE A wave of electric and magnetic force that can carry energy through empty space. Light, microwaves, ultraviolet rays, infrared rays, and radio waves are all electromagnetic waves with different wavelengths. They all travel through empty space at the same speed, around 186,000 miles (300,000 meters) per second.

ELECTRON A tiny electrically charged particle that circles the nucleus of an atom. An electric current is a flow of electrons.

ELECTROPLATING Coating a material with metal by means of electrolysis.

ELLIPTICAL ORBIT An orbit that has an elliptical, or oval, shape. The planets travel in elliptical orbits around the sun. Moons travel in elliptical orbits around their planets.

EQUINOXES Times of the year when the sun lies directly over the equator and when the hours of daylight and nighttime are equal all over the world.

EROSION The wearing away of the Earth's surface due to the action of the weather, rivers, glaciers, and other forces of nature.

EVAPORATION The process by which liquid water changes into water vapor. It is the opposite of condensation.

FAULT A crack in the Earth's crust, often caused by the movement of the crustal plates.

FIELD The region around a body where a certain influence is felt, such as an electric or magnetic field.

FOCAL LENGTH The distance between the focus and the reflective surface of a mirror or the optical center of a lens.

FOCAL POINT See FOCUS.

FOCUS The point at which light rays meet to form a sharp image after passing through a lens, or being reflected from a curved mirror. It is also called the focal point.

FOG A "cloud" of fine water droplets suspended in the air at ground level.

FOSSIL The remains or impressions in rocks of animals or plants that lived long ago.

FREQUENCY The number of times something is repeated in a set time. In the movement of waves such as radio waves, the frequency of vibrations or peaks in the wave is measured in hertz (the number of cycles per second).

Glossary

FRONT The boundary between two different air masses. See COLD FRONT, WARM FRONT.

FROST An icy coating on the ground that occurs when the temperature is below freezing. Water vapor freezes as it condenses from the air.

GALAXY A large grouping of stars in space. Galaxies are usually elliptical or spiral in shape. The galaxy to which our sun belongs is known as the Milky Way.

GALE A strong wind.

GALVANOMETER A sensitive instrument used to detect electric current, named after the Italian electrical pioneer Luigi Galvani (1737-1798).

GAMMA RAY A powerful type of electromagnetic radiation, given out when certain atoms disintegrate.

GEOLOGY The study of the Earth and its surface, its origins, and the way it has changed through the ages.

GLACIER A mass of ice, formed of compacted snow, that moves slowly along a valley.

GRANITE One of the most common igneous rocks, which formed underground. It is made up mainly of crystals of the minerals quartz, feldspar, and mica.

GRAVITY The force with which the Earth attracts any object near it. The other heavenly bodies exert a similar force. Gravity is one of the great forces of the Universe.

GREENHOUSE EFFECT A process in which the atmosphere acts like a greenhouse and traps some of the heat from the sun.

GROUNDWATER Water that is held in the soil and rocks.

HAIL A form of precipitation consisting of little balls of ice.

HEAVENLY BODY A body we see in the heavens, or the night sky, such as the moon, a planet, or a star.

HUMIDITY The amount of moisture in the atmosphere, in the form of water vapor.

HYDROCARBON A chemical made up of hydrogen and carbon only. Petroleum and natural gas are made up almost entirely of hydrocarbons.

HYDROELECTRIC POWER Electricity produced by harnessing the energy of flowing water.

HYDROGEN The simplest of all the chemical elements and also the most plentiful element in the Universe.

HYGROMETER An instrument that measures the humidity of the air.

ICE AGE A period when the climate was much colder than it is now and when much of the Earth was covered with sheets of ice.

Glossary

IGNEOUS ROCK A "fire-formed" rock; one that formed from molten magma, either on the surface or under the surface.

ILLUMINATION The brightness or intensity of light falling on a surface. It depends upon the brightness, distance, and angle of the light source.

IMAGE A picture or appearance of a real object formed by an optical or electronic device. A camera forms an image on the film; our eyes form an image on the retina.

INCANDESCENT OBJECT An object that gives out light because it is very hot. The filament of a light bulb is incandescent.

INDIRECT LIGHT Light that reaches the eye after being reflected off a non-luminous object.

INFRARED RADIATION A type of electromagnetic radiation with a wavelength slightly longer than that of red light. It can be felt as heat.

INSULATOR A material that does not conduct electricity.

INTEGRATED CIRCUIT A complete electric circuit – connections as well as components – formed in a single semiconductor crystal. Silicon chips contain thousands of integrated circuits.

IONOSPHERE The layer of atmosphere above the stratosphere, where the gases in the air are present as ions, or electrically charged atoms.

IRIS The colored part of the eye between the clear outer layer (the cornea) and the lens. It contains a muscle that opens and closes the pupil to control the amount of light entering the eye.

ISOBAR A line on a weather map connecting places with the same atmospheric pressure.

JET STREAM A fast-moving current of air high in the atmosphere.

LASER A device that produces a powerful beam of light. A laser is a light amplifier that increases an initial weak pulse of light into an intense, narrow beam. Lasers are used in medicine, industry, and the home.

LAVA Molten rock that flows out of a volcano and that cools and solidifies on the surface.

LENS A piece of glass or other transparent material that has curved surfaces. Light passing through a lens is bent and can form an image. Lenses are used in eyeglasses, cameras, microscopes, and telescopes.

LIGHTNING The light given out when electricity "jumps" between clouds or between clouds and the ground.

LITHOSPHERE The solid part of the Earth's surface, the crust and the upper part of the mantle.

LOW A region of low pressure; also called a depression or cyclone.

LUMINOUS OBJECT An object that produces light.

Glossary

LUNAR Relating to the moon.

MAGNETIC FIELD The region around a magnet in which the magnetic forces act.

MAGNETIC TAPE A tape coated with magnetic particles, used for recording sound and pictures.

MANTLE The rocky material that lies between the Earth's core and crust. Most of it is relatively soft.

MARE A large plain on the moon. Mare (plural maria) is the Latin word for "sea." Early astronomers thought that the maria, or dark areas we see on the moon, could be water-filled seas.

MESOZOIC ERA The era of middle life. The period of Earth's history between about 247 million and 65 million years ago.

METAMORPHIC ROCK A changed rock; existing rock that has been changed in form and sometimes in composition by heat and/or pressure inside the Earth's crust.

METEOR A streak of light we see in the night sky. Meteors occur when bits of rock from outer space plunge through the atmosphere and burn up.

METEORITE A piece of rock from outer space big enough to survive its passage through the atmosphere and reach the ground.

METEOROLOGY The science of the atmosphere and weather.

MICROCHIP Another name for a silicon chip, which is made up of thousands of microscopic electronic circuits.

MINERAL A chemical compound found in the Earth's crust. Every mineral has a definite characteristic of chemical and physical composition.

MOLECULE The smallest particle of a chemical compound, consisting of one or more atoms combined.

MONSOON A seasonal wind that blows in different directions at different times of the year.

MORNING STAR The planet Venus when it shines brightly in the eastern sky at dawn.

NATIVE ELEMENT One that is found in its pure state in the Earth's crust.

NIMBUS A rain cloud.

NORTHERN LIGHTS The display of aurora in the Northern Hemisphere; the Aurora Borealis. See also SOUTHERN LIGHTS.

NUCLEAR ENERGY Energy obtained by splitting the nuclei (centers) of atoms, a process known as fission.

NUCLEAR FUSION The process by which the sun produces its energy. It is a process in which the nuclei (centers) of hydrogen atoms combine with each other. When this happens, enormous energy is given out as light, heat, and other radiation.

Glossary

OBJECTIVE LENS The front, largest lens in a telescope or microscope.

OPAQUE OBJECT An object that light cannot pass through.

ORBIT The path in space of one body around another, such as the Earth around the sun and the moon around the Earth.

OXYGEN The gas in the air that all living things must breathe to stay alive.

OZONE LAYER A region in the upper atmosphere that contains the gas ozone and filters out harmful rays from sunlight.

PALEONTOLOGY The study of fossils.

PALEOZOIC ERA The era of ancient life. The period of the Earth's history between about 590 million and 248 million years ago.

PARTICLE ACCELERATOR A machine used for accelerating electrically charged subatomic particles to high speed. Popularly called an atom smasher.

PENUMBRA The half-dark outer region of a shadow. A large source of light produces shadows that have a penumbra surrounding a smaller dark region called the umbra.

PHASES The different shapes of the moon we see in the sky during the month, as more or less of its surface is lit by the sun. Venus shows phases as well.

PHOTOELECTRIC CELL A cell whose electrical properties change when light falls on it. Such cells are used in camera light meters, television camera tubes, and automatic detection devices.

PHOTON A packet of light energy. In some situations, a beam of light behaves as if it were a stream of small particles that scientists call photons

PITCH The highness or lowness of a sound. Pitch depends upon the frequency of the sound. The greater the frequency, the higher the pitch.

PLANETS Large bodies that circle in space around the sun. The Earth is a planet. There are eight others, some much smaller, and some much bigger than the Earth. Some other stars also have planets circling around them.

PLATE TECTONICS The science concerned with the movement of the Earth's crustal plates and its effects, such as sea-floor spreading and mountain-building.

PLATES Sections of the Earth's crust that are slowly moving, being carried along by currents in the upper mantle.

POLARIZED LIGHT Light in which the wave vibrations are at right angles to the direction of travel of the light.

POLES The ends of a magnet, where its magnetism appears to be concentrated.

PRECIPITATION Water that falls from the clouds as rain, snow, or hail.

PREVAILING WIND One that blows from the same general direction for most of the time.

Glossary

PRIMARY COLORS Three colors that, when mixed together, can produce any other color. With colored lights, the primary colors are red, green, and blue. With paints, the primary colors are red, yellow, and blue.

PROBE A spacecraft sent far into space to explore other heavenly bodies, such as the moon, the planets, and comets.

PROGRAM A set of instructions that enables a computer to operate.

PROMINENCE A fountain of gas that shoots high above the surface of the sun. We can see prominences only during a total eclipse of the sun.

PUPIL The hole in the center of the iris in the eye. Light passes through the pupil and falls on the retina at the back of the eye.

QUARTZ The most common mineral on Earth. It is the chemical silicon dioxide.

RADIATION Rays, given off by the sun and the stars: for example, light rays, ultraviolet rays, infrared rays, and radio waves. These are all different kinds of electromagnetic radiation.

RADIOACTIVE The condition of giving out radiation.

RAIN The most common kind of precipitation.

REAL IMAGE An image, produced by a lens or mirror, that can be projected onto a screen. A movie projector produces a real image. An image that cannot be projected onto a screen is called a virtual image. See also VIRTUAL IMAGE.

RECYCLING Processing waste materials so that they can be used again.

RED SHIFT The color change found in light from the distant galaxies that are moving away from us at great speed. Their light waves are stretched out by their motion and appear redder than normal.

REFRACTION The bending of light rays as they pass from one material to another. Refraction causes a straw in a glass of water to appear bent.

RENEWABLE RESOURCES Resources, such as flowing water and wind, that can be used again and again and will not run out.

RESISTANCE, ELECTRICAL The resistance in a substance to the flow of electric current. Devices with a specific resistance, called resistors, are used in electronic circuits.

RETINA The light-sensitive layer at the back of the eyeball.

REVERBERATION The multiple reflections of sounds inside a building that last for a short while before fading away. Reverberations in some buildings can last for a few seconds.

RIFT VALLEY A valley produced when a section of rock sinks between two faults.

ROCK Solid material that makes up the Earth's crust. Rocks are composed of one or more minerals.

Glossary

SATELLITE A small body that circles around a larger one in space. Most of the planets have natural satellites. The Earth has one, the moon. Saturn has more than 20. The Earth also now has thousands of artificial satellites circling around it, launched into orbit by space scientists.

SEASONS Periods of the year marked by noticeable differences in the weather, particularly in temperature. Many parts of the world experience four distinct seasons: spring, summer, fall and winter. Seasonal changes also take place on other planets, especially Mars. See also EQUINOXES; SOLSTICES.

SEDIMENT Loose rocky material that has been deposited on the surface of the land, usually by flowing water.

SEDIMENTARY ROCK Rock formed from layers of sediment that have over millions of years become compacted and hardened by pressure in the Earth's crust.

SEISMOGRAPH An instrument for recording the shock waves produced by an earthquake.

SEMICONDUCTOR A substance whose ability to conduct electricity is between that of a good conductor and an insulator. In comparison to metals, their conductivity is likely to be much more sensitive to applied voltage. This sensitivity means that the performance of transistors and other semiconductor devices can be very precisely controlled. This is an important requirement for creating electronic circuits that are able to process complicated information, as in a computer.

SILICATE One of the most common types of minerals, containing silicon and oxygen combined with certain metals, particularly sodium, potassium, and aluminum.

SILICON CHIP A wafer-thin slice of silicon that contains thousands of microscopic electronic circuits.

SLEET Precipitation consisting of a mixture of rain and snow.

SOFTWARE The instructions fed into a computer.

SOLAR CELL A cell that converts the energy in sunlight into electricity. Properly called photovoltaic cell.

SOLAR ENERGY Energy from the sun.

SOLAR SYSTEM The family of the sun, which travels through space as a unit. It has the sun at its center, and around the sun circle nine planets (including the Earth), the "belt" of asteroids, and many comets.

SOLAR WIND A stream of charged particles given off by the sun.

SOLSTICES Times of the year when the sun reaches its highest and lowest points in the sky at noon. In the Northern Hemisphere, it reaches its highest point on about June 21 (summer solstice), and its lowest on December 21 (winter solstice). The dates are reversed in the Southern Hemisphere.

SONIC BOOM A loud explosion or bang heard on the ground when a supersonic aircraft passes overhead. It is caused by a shock wave produced by the aircraft.

Glossary

SOUTHERN LIGHTS The display of aurora that occurs in the Southern Hemisphere; the Aurora Australis.

SPECTRUM The rainbow-colored band of light produced when white light is passed through a prism. The colors are arranged in order of the wavelength of their waves; red is longest and violet is the shortest.

STAR A gaseous body that produces its own energy by nuclear fusion. It releases this energy as light, heat, and other radiation. The sun is the nearest star.

STATIC ELECTRICITY The electricity associated with electric charges, which tends to stay where it is ("static") rather than flow away.

STRATOSPHERE The layer of the Earth's atmosphere between the troposphere and the ionosphere.

STRATUS A low-level layer cloud.

SUN Our local star, whose enormous gravity holds the Solar System together over distances of billions of miles.

SUNSPOT An area on the sun's surface that is darker and cooler than normal. Sunspots come and go regularly over a period of about 11 years.

SYNOPTIC CHART A weather map showing the state of the weather at a particular time, prepared during weather forecasting.

TEMPERATE REGIONS Part of the Earth's surface between the polar regions and the tropics.

THERMOMETER An instrument that measures temperature.

THUNDER The noise made when a lightning stroke heats the air in its path. When this occurs, the air expands explosively.

TIDES The rise and fall of the oceans, which occur twice a day. They occur because of the pull of the moon's gravity.

TORNADO A very destructive wind storm, consisting of a rapidly spinning column of air.

TOTAL ECLIPSE An eclipse of the sun in which the disc of the moon completely covers the disc of the sun.

TRANSFORMER An electrical device used to alter the voltage of alternating electric current.

TRANSLUCENT MATERIAL A material that allows some light to pass through but is not transparent. Objects cannot be seen clearly through a translucent material.

TROPICS The region spanning the equator between latitude 23!/2 degrees north (the Tropic of Cancer) and latitude 23!/2 degrees south (the Tropic of Capricorn).

TROPOSPHERE The lowest layer in the atmosphere, in which most of our weather takes place.

Glossary

TUNDRA The barren landscape of the far north, in the Arctic.

TWISTER A popular name for a tornado.

TYPHOON The name given to tropical cyclones that take place in the Far East.

ULTRASOUND Sound waves of a frequency too high to be heard by human beings. Ultrasound is used to detect flaws in metals and, in medical scanning, depth finding, cleaning, and mixing liquids.

ULTRAVIOLET RADIATION A type of electromagnetic radiation with a wavelength shorter than violet light. Ultraviolet rays occur in sunlight and cause sunburn.

UMBRA The dark inner region of a shadow. A large source of light produces shadows that have an umbra surrounded by a half-dark region called the penumbra.

UNIVERSE Everything that exists: the Earth, the moon, the sun, the planets, the stars, and even space itself.

VIBRATION A quick back and forth movement.

VIRTUAL IMAGE An image that cannot be projected onto a screen. The image seen through a magnifying glass is a virtual image.

VOLCANO An opening in the Earth's crust through which molten rock, ash, and gases are expelled.

VOLT The unit of electrical voltage, or "pressure," named after the Italian electrical pioneer Alessandro Volta (1745-1827).

VOLTMETER An instrument for measuring the voltage.

WARM FRONT The boundary formed when a warm air mass pushes away a cold air mass.

WATER CYCLE The never-ending interchange of water between the ground and the atmosphere.

WATER VAPOR Water in the form of a gas.

WEATHER VANE An instrument that indicates the direction of the wind.

ZODIAC An imaginary band in the heavens in which the sun, moon and planets are always found. It is occupied by 13 constellations, the constellations of the zodiac.

INDEX

Absolute temperature scale 130
Acceleration 122
Acid rain 98
Acoustics 178
Alpha particle 114
Alternating current (AC) 143, 178
Alternator 142-143, 178
Ammeter 141, 178
Ammonite 61, 178
Ampere 141, 179
Amplitude 154, 178
Analog recording 178
Anemometer 178
Angle of incidence 158, 178
Angle of reflection 158, 178
Anticyclone 87, 178
Armstrong, Neil 20
Asteroid 15, 16, 31-32, 178
Astrology 178
Astronomy 178
Atmosphere 46-48, 178
Atmospheric pressure 47, 78, 178
Atom 111-114, 178
Atomic weight 114
Aurora 179

Bar 179
Barometer 79, 80, 179
Basalt 179
Battery 141, 142, 179
Beaufort scale 179
Beta particle 114
Big Bang 39-40
Black hole 37
Breeze 83, 84, 179

Capacitor 179
Celsius temperature scale 130
Cenozoic era 179
Chemical reaction 116
Chemical weathering 70
Chip 179
Chromosphere 15, 179
Cirrus 96, 179
Climate 80-81, 179
Cloud 94, 95-97, 179
Coal 63-64
Cochlea 172, 179
Cold front 88-89, 179
Color 164-167
Color mixing 166-167
Comet 15, 32-33, 179
Commutator 153, 179
Compact disc 168
Compound 115
Computer 144-145
Concave lens or mirror 159, 162, 179

Condensation 179
Conduction 134, 179
Conductor 140
Constellation 12-14, 180
Continental drift 49, 180
Convection 83, 135, 180
Convex lens or mirror 159, 162, 180
Cornea 180
Corona 15, 180
Cosmic ray 155, 180
Crater 18, 31, 180
Crust 44, 180
Crystal 100, 180
Cumulus cloud 96, 180
Cyclone 104, 180

Decibel 176, 180
Depression 87, 180
Dew 94, 180
Dew point 180
Direct Current (DC) 142, 180
Direct light 158, 180
Doldrums 180
Dry cell 141, 180
Dynamo 180

Ear 172
Earth 16, 17, 44-58
Earthquake 56
Echo 174
Eclipse 19, 180
Electric bell 151-152
Electric circuit 140
Electric current 139-140
Electric motor 153
Electrode 181
Electrolysis 116
Electrolyte 181
Electromagnet 151, 181
Electromagnetic wave 126, 154-155, 181
Electron 36, 111, 140-141, 181
Electroplating 181
Element 109-110
Elliptical orbit 33, 181
Energy 17, 125-128, 135
Engines 135-6
Equinox 181
Erosion 67-71, 181
Evaporation 78, 181
Evolution 62-63, 66
Exosphere 47
Expanding Universe 40
Expansion 133
Eye 163-164

Fahrenheit temperature scale 130
Fault 56, 181
Field 148, 181
Focal length 181
Focal point 181

190

Index

Focus 162, 181
Fog 94, 181
Force 119-124
Fossil 50, 61-62, 181
Four-stroke engine 136
Frequency 154, 173, 181
Friction 119-120
Front 87-88, 182
Frost 182

Galaxy 11, 39-41, 182
Gale 85, 182
Galvanometer 182
Gamma ray 114, 182
Generator 142-143
Geologist 61
Geology 182
Glacier 68-69, 182
Global warming 48
Granite 182
Gravity 15, 34, 120, 182
Greenhouse effect 46, 48, 182
Groundwater 93, 182

Hail 99, 182
Hertz 173
Humidity 94, 182
Hurricane 104-105
Hydrocarbon 182
Hydroelectric power 127, 182
Hydrogen 34, 182
Hygrometer 182

Ice age 182
Igneous rock 59, 183
Illumination 183
Image 163, 183
Incandescent object 183
Indirect light 158, 183
Inertia 121
Infrared radiation 132, 134, 183
Insulator 140, 183
Integrated circuit 143-144, 183
Ionosphere 47, 183
Iris 183
Isobar 89, 183
Isotope 113

Jet stream 86-87, 183
Jupiter 16, 24-25

Lake 74
Laser 167-168, 183
Lava 54-55, 183
Lens 161-163, 183
Light waves 155, 157
Lightning 101-3, 183
Light-year 14
Line of force 149
Lithosphere 183

Lodestone 147
Loudness 175-176
Low pressure area 80, 183
Luminous object 157, 183

Machines 124
Magnet 147
Magnetic pole 148
Magnetic field 148, 184
Magnetic field of Earth 153-154
Mantle 44, 184
Mars 16, 23
Mercury 16, 21
Mesosphere 47
Mesozoic era 184
Metamorphic rock 60, 184
Meteor 30, 184
Meteorite 30-31, 184
Meteorology 184
Microchip 143-144, 184
Microprocessor 144
Milky Way 11, 39, 41
Mineral 58, 184
Mirage 161
Mixture 117
Molecule 114, 130-131, 184
Monsoon 84-85, 184
Moon 17-20
Mountains 52-53

Nebula 11, 34, 38
Neptune 16, 28-29
Neutrino 112
Neutron 36, 111
Neutron star 36
Newton, Isaac 121
Newton's laws 121-123
Nimbus 97, 184
Noise 175
Nuclear energy 117, 184
Nuclear fission 117
Nuclear force 120-121
Nuclear fusion 34-35, 117, 184
Nucleus 111

Objective lens 185
Ocean 74-75
Ocean currents 75
Oil 64-65
Opaque object 158, 185
Orbit 15, 185
Oxbow lake 73
Ozone layer 48, 185

Paleontology 185
Paleozoic era 185
Pangaea 49
Parallel circuit 140
Particle accelerator 185
Penumbra 185
Phases of Moon 19, 185

191

Index

Photoelectric cell 185
Photon 185
Photosphere 15
Pitch 175, 185
Planet 15-16, 29, 185
Plate 50-52, 185
Plate tectonics 50-52, 185
Pluto 16, 29
Polarized light 185
Pole 148, 185
Precipitation 185
Prevailing wind 185
Primary colors 166, 186
Probe 186
Program 144, 186
Prominence 15, 186
Proton 111
Pulsar 36
Pupil 163, 186

Quark 112
Quartz 58, 186

Radiation 78, 114, 126, 133, 186
Radioactivity 114, 186
Rain 98
Rainbow 165
Real image 186
Recycling 186
Red giant 36
Red shift 186
Reflection 158-159
Refraction 159, 160-161, 186
Renewable resources 186
Resistance 141, 186
Retina 163, 186
Reverberation 174, 186
Richter scale 56
Rift valley 186
River 72, 73
Rock 58-61, 186

San Andreas fault 51
Satellite 187
Saturn 16, 26-28
Season 82, 187
Sediment 60, 187
Sedimentary rock 60, 187
Seismograph 57, 187
Semiconductor 187
Silicate 187
Silicon chip 143, 187
Sleet 187
Snow 99-100
Software 187
Soil 71
Solar cell 187
Solar energy 187
Solar system 15-16, 187
Solar wind 33, 187

Solstice 187
Sonar 177
Sonic boom 187
Sound 170-177
Sound waves 171, 174
Spectrum 155, 188
Speed of light 157
Speed of sound 173-174
Star 11, 14, 34-37, 188
States of matter 109
Static electricity 101, 139, 188
Stratosphere 47, 188
Stratus 96, 188
Sun 15, 188
Sunspot 15, 188
Supergiant 37
Supernova 36
Synoptic chart 88-91, 188

Temperate region 80-81, 188
Temperature 130
Thermometer 130-131, 188
Thunder 103, 188
Tides 75, 188
Tornado 103, 188
Total eclipse 188
Trade winds 86
Transformer 143, 188
Translucent material 158, 188
Tropics 188
Troposphere 47, 188
Tundra 189
Twister 101, 103, 189
Two-stroke engine 136
Typhoon 189

Ultrasound 177, 189
Ultraviolet radiation 48, 189
Umbra 189
Universe 189
Uranus 16, 28

Venus 16, 21-22
Vibration 132, 170, 189
Virtual image 189
Volcano 54-55, 189
Volt 141, 189
Voltmeter 189

Warm front 88-89, 189
Water cycle 92-100, 189
Wavelength 154
Weathering 67-70
Weather chart 88-91
Wegener, Alfred 49
White dwarf 36
Wind 84

Zodiac 189

192

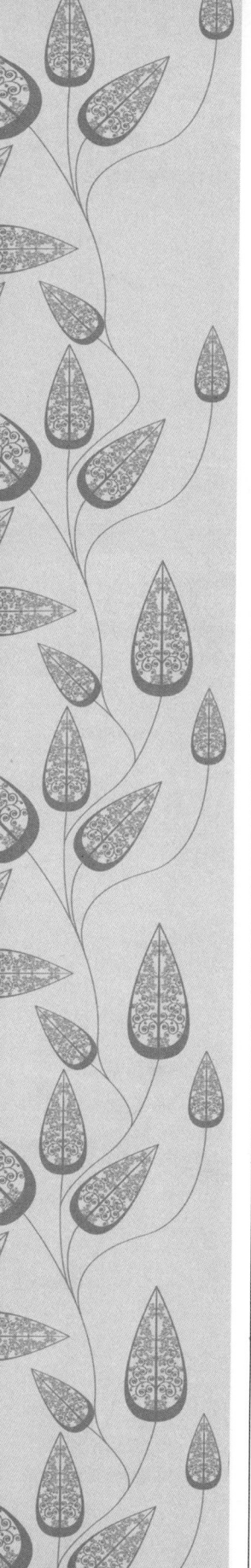

SIXTH EDITION

Instruction

A Models Approach

Thomas H. Estes
University of Virginia

Susan L. Mintz
University of Virginia

Mary Alice Gunter
late of University of Virginia

PEARSON

Boston   Columbus   Indianapolis   New York   San Francisco   Upper Saddle River
Amsterdam   Cape Town   Dubai   London   Madrid   Milan   Munich   Paris   Montreal   Toronto
Delhi   Mexico City   Sao Paulo   Sydney   Hong Kong   Seoul   Singapore   Taipei   Tokyo

Senior Acquisitions Editor: Kelly Villella Canton
Editorial Assistant: Annalea Manalili
Vice President, Director of Marketing: Quinn Perkson
Senior Marketing Manager: Darcy Betts
Production Editor: Annette Joseph
Editorial Production Service: Omegatype Typography, Inc.
Manufacturing Buyer: Megan Cochran
Electronic Composition: Omegatype Typography, Inc.
Interior Design: Omegatype Typography, Inc.

Credits and acknowledgments borrowed from other sources and reproduced, with permission, in this textbook appear on appropriate page within text.

Copyright © 2011, 2007, 2003, 1999, 1995, 1990 Pearson Education, Inc., publishing as Allyn & Bacon, 501 Boylston St., Ste. 900, Boston, MA 02116. All rights reserved. Manufactured in the United States of America. This publication is protected by Copyright, and permission should be obtained from the publisher prior to any prohibited reproduction, storage in a retrieval system, or transmission in any form or by any means, electronic, mechanical, photocopying, recording, or likewise. To obtain permission(s) to use material from this work, please submit a written request to Pearson Education, Inc., Permissions Department, 501 Boylston Street, Boston, MA 02116, or email permissionsus@pearson.com.

Library of Congress Cataloging-in-Publication Data

Estes, Thomas H.
  Instruction : a models approach / Thomas H. Estes, Susan L. Mintz, Mary Alice Gunter.—6th ed.
      p. cm.
  Previous edition cataloged under Gunter, Mary Alice.
  Includes bibliographical references and index.
  ISBN-13: 978-0-13-704673-7 (pbk.)
  ISBN-10: 0-13-704673-1 (pbk.)
 1. Teaching. 2. Curriculum planning. 3. Classroom environment. 4. Group work in education. 5. Teachers—In-service training. I. Mintz, Susan L. II. Gunter, Mary Alice III. Gunter, Mary Alice, Instruction. IV. Title.
  LB1025.3.G86 2011
  371.102—dc22

2010001475

10 9 8 7 6 5 4 3 2   EB   14 13 12 11 10

PEARSON

www.pearsonhighered.com

ISBN 10: 0-13-704673-1
ISBN 13: 978-0-13-704673-7

About the Authors

Thomas H. Estes, professor emeritus of the Curry School of Education at the University of Virginia, is president of Dynamic Literacy, a company specializing in vocabulary development products based in Latin and Greek underpinnings of academic English. He received his Ph.D. in reading education from Syracuse University. Dr. Estes taught in the McGuffey Reading Center of the Curry School of Education and in the Curriculum, Learning, and Teaching program for 31 years.

Susan L. Mintz, associate professor at the Curry School of Education at the University of Virginia, is the program coordinator of Secondary Education. She received her Ph.D. in teacher education from Syracuse University. Dr. Mintz teaches both preservice teachers and graduate students in the Curriculum, Learning, and Teaching program. She is an author of the CLASS-S observation manual, developed at the University of Virginia's Center for the Advanced Study of Teaching and Learning.

Contents

Preface   xxi

Part One   Planning for Instruction   1

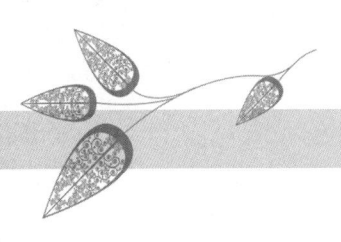

1   Educational Standards   3

Chapter Objectives   3
How Learning Happens   4
Student Characteristics That Affect How Learning Happens   6
The Needs of Learners   9
    Acceptance and Safety   9
    Choice   10
    High Expectations and Appropriate Challenge   10
    Opportunity to Connect the New to the Known   11
    Meaningful Engagement   11
    Clarity   12
    Time to Reflect   12
    Aligned Assessments   13
The Needs of Society   13
    Learning Standards   13
    Moving from Standards to Instruction   15
Summary   17
Extensions   17

2   Organizing Content   18

Chapter Objectives   18
Content   19
    School Curriculum   19
    Analyzing Content   23

Ordering Content   27

Strategy Alert: KWL   28

Instructional Planning   29

    Scope   30
    Focus   30
    Sequence   31
    Chunking Instruction   32

Developing Lesson Plans   33

    Lesson Plan Elements   34
    Deductive and Inductive Organization   35

Summary   35

Extensions   36

3   Instructional Objectives, Assessment, and Instruction   37

Chapter Objectives   37

Purpose of Instructional Objectives   38

Formats for Instructional Objectives   42

    Students Will Know Instructional Objectives   42
    Students Will Understand Instructional Objectives   44
    Students Will Be Able to Instructional Objectives   47

Moving from Standards to Objectives   49

Instructional Alignment   50

Assessing Instructional Objectives   52

    Formative Assessments   53
    Summative Assessments   54

Summary   54

Extensions   55

Summary for Part One   56

Part Two — Matching Objectives to Instruction: A Models Approach 57

4 The Direct Instruction Model: Teaching Skills, Facts, and Knowledge 62

Chapter Objectives 62

In the Elementary Classroom 62

In the Secondary Classroom 63

Basis for the Direct Instruction Model 65

Steps in the Direct Instruction Model 65

　Step 1: Review Previously Learned Material 66

　Step 2: State Objectives for the Lesson 67

Strategy Alert: Advance Organizers 67

　Step 3: Present New Material 68

　Step 4: Guide Practice, Assess Performance, and Provide Corrective Feedback 70

　Step 5: Assign Independent Practice, Assess Performance, and Provide Corrective Feedback 72

Strategy Alert: Scaffolding 73

　Step 6: Review Periodically, Offering Corrective Feedback If Necessary 74

　Summary of Steps in the Direct Instruction Model 74

Evaluating Learning in the Direct Instruction Model 75

　Assessment Alignment 75

　Rubrics 76

Meeting Individual Needs in Direct Instruction 77

　Flexible Grouping 77

　Varying Questions 77

Benefits of the Direct Instruction Model 78

Elementary Grades Lesson
　Direct Instruction: Rhyming with Mother Goose 78

Middle/Secondary Grades Lesson
　Direct Instruction: Writing Haiku 80

Summary 81

Extensions 82

5 The Concept Attainment Model: Defining Concepts Inductively 83

Chapter Objectives 83
In the Elementary Classroom 83
In the Secondary Classroom 84
Basis for the Concept Attainment Model 86
Steps in the Concept Attainment Model 88
   Step 1: Select and Define a Concept through the Concept's Essential Characteristics 88
   Step 2: Develop Positive and Negative Examples 89
   Step 3: Review the Concept Attainment Process with the Class 90
   Step 4: Present the Examples 90
   Step 5: Generate Hypotheses and Continue Example/Hypothesis Cycle 91
Strategy Alert: Generating and Testing Hypotheses 91
   Step 6: Develop a Concept Label and Definition 92
   Step 7: Provide Test Examples to Solidify the Definition 92
   Step 8: Discuss the Process with the Class 92
   Summary of Steps in the Concept Attainment Model 92
Variations on the Concept Attainment Model 93
Evaluating Learning in the Concept Attainment Model 95
Meeting Individual Needs in the Concept Attainment Model 96
Benefits of the Concept Attainment Model 97
Elementary Grades Lesson
   Concept Attainment: Hibernation 97
Middle/Secondary Grades Lesson
   Concept Attainment: Metaphors 99
Summary 100
Extensions 101

6 The Concept Development Model: Analyzing the Relationships between Parts of a Concept 102

Chapter Objectives 102
In the Elementary Classroom 102
In the Secondary Classroom 104

Basis for the Concept Development Model 106
- Conceptual Thinking Is Learned 108
- Concepts Are Creative Ways of Structuring Reality 108
- Concepts Are the Building Blocks of Patterns 109

Steps in the Concept Development Model 110
- Step 1: List as Many Items as Possible That Are Associated with the Subject 110

Strategy Alert: Brainstorming 111

- Step 2: Group the Items Because They Are Alike in Some Way 112
- Step 3: Label the Groups by Defining the Reasons for Grouping 112
- Step 4: Regroup or Subsume Individual Items or Whole Groups under Other Groups 113
- Step 5: Synthesize the Information by Summarizing the Data and Forming Generalizations 113
- Summary of Steps in the Concept Development Model 114

Evaluating Learning in the Concept Development Model 115

Meeting Individual Needs in the Concept Development Model 115

Benefits of Using the Concept Development Model 116

Elementary Grades Lesson
Concept Development: Living and Nonliving Things 117

Middle/Secondary Grades Lesson
Concept Development: Grudge 118

Summary 119

Extensions 119

7 Problem-Centered Inquiry Models: Teaching Problem Solving through Discovery and Questioning 121

Chapter Objectives 121

In the Elementary Classroom 121

In the Secondary Classroom 122

Basis for the Inquiry Approach to Instruction 125

Problem-Centered Model One: The Suchman Inquiry Model 128
- Step 1: Select a Problem and Conduct Research 128
- Step 2: Introduce the Process and Present the Problem 129
- Step 3: Gather Data 130

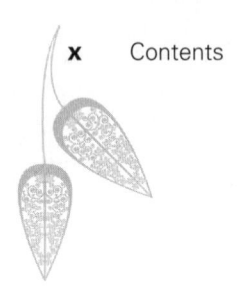

Step 4: Develop a Theory and Verify 130
Step 5: Explain the Theory and State the Rules Associated with It 131
Step 6: Analyze the Process 131
Step 7: Evaluate 131
Summary of Steps in the Suchman Inquiry Model 132

Problem-Centered Model Two: The WebQuest Model of Inquiry 133

Step 1: The Teacher Selects a Problem and Conducts Preliminary Research 133
Step 2: Present the Problem in the WebQuest Template 135
Step 3: Students Gather Data and Information to Solve the Problem 136
Step 4: Students Develop and Verify Their Solutions 136
Summary of Steps in the WebQuest Model of Inquiry 137

Problem-Centered Model Three: Problem-Based Inquiry Model 137

Step 1: Explore the Problem 138

Strategy Alert: Identifying Similarities and Differences 139

Step 2: Use the Inquiry Chart to Map Learning 139
Step 3: Share Different Solutions 141
Step 4: Take Action 141
Summary of Steps in the Problem-Based Inquiry Model 141

Evaluating Learning in the Problem-Centered Inquiry Models 142

Meeting Individual Needs in the Problem-Centered Inquiry Models 143

Benefits of Problem-Centered Inquiry Models 143

Elementary Grades Lesson
Problem-Centered Inquiry: Monarch Butterflies and Stewardship 144

Middle/Secondary Grades Lesson
Problem-Centered Inquiry: Toxins 145

Summary 146

Extensions 146

8 The Synectics Model: Developing Creative Thinking and Problem Solving 148

Chapter Objectives 148

In the Elementary Classroom 148

In the Secondary Classroom 149

Basis for the Synectics Model 152

Version One: Making the Familiar Strange 154
- Step 1: Describe the Topic 154
- Step 2: Create Direct Analogies 155
- Step 3: Describe Personal Analogies 155
- Step 4: Identify Compressed Conflicts 156
- Step 5: Create a New Direct Analogy 157
- Step 6: Reexamine the Original Topic 157
- Summary of Steps in Making the Familiar Strange 157

Version Two: Making the Strange Familiar 158
- Step 1: Provide Information 158
- Step 2: Present the Analogy 158
- Step 3: Use Personal Analogy to Create Compressed Conflicts 159
- Step 4: Compare the Compressed Conflict with the Subject 159
- Step 5: Identify Differences 159
- Step 6: Reexamine the Original Subject 159
- Step 7: Create New Direct Analogies 159
- Summary of Steps in Making the Strange Familiar 160

Version Three: The Synectics Excursion 160
- Step 1: Present the Problem 160
- Step 2: Provide Expert Information 160
- Step 3: Question Obvious Solutions and Purge 161
- Step 4: Generate Individual Problem Statements 161
- Step 5: Choose One Problem Statement for Focus 161
- Step 6: Question through the Use of Analogies 161
- Step 7: Force Analogies to Fit the Problem 162
- Step 8: Determine a Solution from a New Viewpoint 162
- Summary of Steps in the Synectics Excursion 163

Evaluating Learning in the Synectics Model 163

Meeting Individual Needs in the Synectics Model 164

Strategy Alert: Graphic Organizers 165

Benefits of the Synectics Model 166

Elementary Grades Lesson
Synectics Model: The Civil War 166

Middle/Secondary Grades Lesson
Synectics Model: Witches 167

Summary 168

Extensions 169

9 The Cause-and-Effect Model: Influencing Events by Analyzing Causality 170

Chapter Objectives 170
In the Elementary Classroom 170
In the Secondary Classroom 172
Basis for the Cause-and-Effect Model 173
Steps in the Cause-and-Effect Model 175
    Step 1: Choose the Data or Topic, Action, or Problem to Be Analyzed 175
    Step 2: Ask for Causes and Support for Those Causes 176
Strategy Alert: Flow Charts 176
    Step 3: Ask for Effects and Support 177
    Step 4: Ask for Prior Causes and Support 178
    Step 5: Ask for Subsequent Effects and Support 178
    Step 6: Ask for Conclusions 178
    Step 7: Ask for Generalizations 179
    Summary of Steps in the Cause-and-Effect Model 180
Evaluating Learning in the Cause-and-Effect Model 180
Meeting Individual Needs in the Cause-and-Effect Model 181
Benefits of the Cause-and-Effect Model 182
Elementary Grades Lesson
    Cause and Effect: Water Cycle, Blizzards, and *The Long Winter* 183
Secondary Grades Lesson
    Cause and Effect: Hamlet and Claudius 184
Summary 185
Extensions 186

10 The Socratic Seminar Model: Analyzing Text 187

Chapter Objectives 187
In the Elementary Classroom 187
In the Secondary Classroom 189
Basis for the Socratic Seminar Model 190
Versions of the Socratic Seminar 191
Questioning 193

Examples of Question Types 194
    Remembering 194
    Understanding 194
    Applying 194
    Analyzing 195
    Evaluating 195
    Creating 195

Steps in the Socratic Seminar Model 196
    Step 1: Choose the Text—Written, Visual, or Audio 196
    Step 2: Plan and Cluster Several Questions of Varying Cognitive Demand 196
    Step 3: Introduce the Model to the Students 197
    Step 4: Conduct the Discussion 199
    Step 5: Review and Summarize the Discussion 199
    Step 6: Evaluate the Discussion with the Students Based on Previously Stated Criteria 200

Strategy Alert: Reciprocal Teaching 202
    Summary of Steps in the Socratic Seminar Model 203

Evaluating Learning in the Socratic Seminar Model 203

Meeting Individual Needs in the Socratic Seminar Model 204

Benefits of the Socratic Seminar Model 204

Elementary Grades Lesson
    Socratic Seminar: *Old Henry,* by Joan W. Blos 205

Middle/Secondary Grades Lesson
    Socratic Seminar: *The War Prayer* and "Sullivan Ballou's Letter to His Wife" 206

Summary 208

Extensions 208

11 The Vocabulary Acquisition Model: Learning the Spellings and Meanings of Words 209

Chapter Objectives 209

In the Elementary Classroom 209

In the Secondary Classroom 211

Basis for the Vocabulary Acquisition Model 212
    The Spelling–Meaning Connection 212

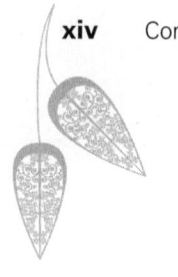

Principles Underlying the Vocabulary Acquisition Model   214
How Vocabulary Is Acquired   217

Steps in the Vocabulary Acquisition Model   217

Step 1: Pretest Knowledge of Words Critical to Content   217
Step 2: Elaborate On and Discuss Invented Spellings and Hypothesized Meanings   218

Strategy Alert: Think–Pair–Share   220

Step 3: Explore Patterns of Meaning   220

Strategy Alert: Link   221

Step 4: Read and Study   224
Step 5: Evaluate and Posttest   224
Summary of Steps in the Vocabulary Acquisition Model   225

Evaluating Learning in the Vocabulary Acquisition Model   226

Meeting Individual Needs in the Vocabulary Acquisition Model   226

Building Vocabulary through Classroom Conversation   227
Using Vocabulary to Tie the Curriculum Together   228
Instruction in the Most Basic Meaningful Parts of Words   228
Model Curiosity   229

Benefits of the Vocabulary Acquisition Model   231

Elementary Grades Lesson
Vocabulary Acquisition: Units of Measurement   231

Middle/Secondary Grades Lesson
Vocabulary Acquisition: The Middle Ages   232

Summary   233

Extensions   234

12 The Integrative Model: Generalizing from Data   235

Chapter Objectives   235

In the Elementary Classroom   235

In the Secondary Classroom   237

Basis for the Integrative Model   241

Steps in the Integrative Model   242

Step 1: Planning for the Integrative Model   242
Step 2: Describe, Compare, and Search for Patterns in a Data Set   245
Step 3: Explain the Identified Similarities and Differences   245

  Step 4: Hypothesize What Would Happen under Different Conditions 246
  Step 5: Make Broad Generalizations about the Topic and the Discussion 246

Strategy Alert: Summarizing 247

 Summary of Steps in the Integrative Model 247

Evaluating Learning in the Integrative Model 249

Meeting Individual Needs in the Integrative Model 250

Strategy Alert: Cubing 251

Benefits of the Integrative Model 251

Elementary Grades Lesson
 Integrative Model: Fractions 252

Middle/Secondary Grades Lesson
 Integrative Model: Societal Changes Affecting Families 253

Summary 254

Extensions 255

13 Cooperative Learning Models: Improving Student Learning Using Small Groups 256

Chapter Objectives 256

In the Elementary Classroom 256

In the Secondary Classroom 257

Basis of Cooperative Learning Models 258

Cooperative Learning Model: The Template 261

 Planning Steps 262
 Implementation Steps 262
 Summary of Cooperative Learning Template Model Steps 263

Specific Cooperative Models 263

The Graffiti Model 263

 Step 1: Prepare the Graffiti Questions and Group Number and Composition 264
 Step 2: Distribute Materials 264
 Step 3: Groups Answer Questions 264
 Step 4: Exchange Questions 265
 Step 5: Return to the Original Question, Summarize, and Make Generalizations 265
 Step 6: Share Information 265

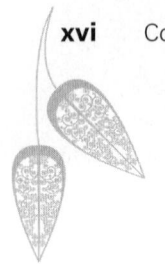

Step 7: Evaluate the Group Process   265
Summary of Graffiti Model Steps   265

The Jigsaw Model   265

Step 1: Introduce the Jigsaw   266
Step 2: Assign Heterogeneously Grouped Students to Expert and Learning Groups   266
Step 3: Explain the Task and Assemble Expert Groups   268
Step 4: Allow Expert Groups to Process Information   268
Step 5: Experts Teach in Their Learning Group   268
Step 6: Hold Individuals Accountable   268
Step 7: Evaluate the Jigsaw Process   269
Summary of Jigsaw Model Steps   269

The Academic Controversy Model   269

Step 1: Students Prepare Their Positions   270
Step 2: Students Present and Advocate Their Positions   270
Step 3: Open Discussion and Rebuttals   271
Step 4: Reverse Positions   271
Step 5: Synthesize and Integrate the Best Evidence into a Joint Position   271
Step 6: Present the Group Synthesis   271
Step 7: Group Processing of the Controversy and Participation of Members   272
Summary of Academic Controversy Steps   272

The Student Teams-Achievement Division (STAD) Model   272

Step 1: Present a New Concept   273
Step 2: Form Teams for Study and Practice   273
Step 3: Test Students on Newly Learned Materials   273
Step 4: Recognize Winning Teams   274
Summary of STAD Steps   274

Evaluating Learning in the Cooperative Learning Models   274

Meeting Individual Needs in the Cooperative Learning Models   275

Benefits of the Cooperative Learning Models   275

Elementary Grades Lesson
Cooperative Learning Jigsaw: Clouds   276

Middle/Secondary Grades Lesson
Cooperative Learning Graffiti: Formal and Informal Speech   277

Summary   278

Extensions   279

Summary for Part Two   279

Part Three — Putting It All Together: Matching Objectives to Instructional Models 281

14 A Kindergarten Case Study 283

Chapter Objectives 283

Miss Abbott's Plan 287

Unit: Lines That Draw Us Together 289

    Opening Activity—Drawing in the Students 290
    Lesson One: Practicing the "Line-Up" 290
    Lesson Two: Defining a Line 291
    Lesson Three: Refining the Concept of Line 292
    Activity: The Line Game 293

Notes on Lessons One, Two, and Three 293

Epilogue 295

Summary 296

Extensions 296

15 A Middle School Case Study 297

Chapter Objectives 297

The Mumford Plan 302

Unit: Perspective—It All Depends on Where You Were When 304

    Lesson One: Toward a Perspective on Point of View 305
    Lesson Two: Perception—It Depends on Where You Are Coming From 306
    Lesson Three: Relating Perception and Perspective 307

Epilogue 308

Summary 309

Extensions 309

16 A High School Case Study 311

Chapter Objectives 311

Mr. Samuels's Plan 313

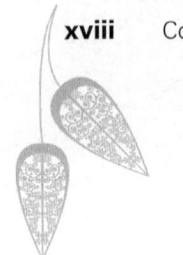

Unit: *Macbeth*—A Study in Ambition Turned to Avarice   318
    Description of Six Lessons on Ambition and the Power of Suggestion   318

Epilogue   321

Summary   323

Extensions   323

17 The Wisdom of Practice: Creating a Positive Learning Environment   325

Chapter Objectives   325

Good Teachers Are the Leaders of Their Classrooms   327

Good Teachers Create a Productive Physical Environment for Learning   328

    Relationship to Student Learning   328
    Furniture Arrangement/Seating   329
    Climate Control   329
    Equipment and Displays   330

Good Teachers Manage Human Relations Effectively   330

Good Teachers Engage Learners in the Process of Their Own Learning   331

Good Teachers Teach Up   332

    They Recognize the Pygmalion Effect   332
    They Capitalize on What Students Know   334
    They Celebrate Differences among Students   334
    They Realize That There is More Than One Right Answer to Important Questions   335
    They Provide Appropriate, Quality Feedback   335

Good Teachers Are Good Learners   335

    They Serve as a Model for Learning   335
    They Recognize the Importance of Professional Knowledge   336
    They Act as Researchers   337

Good Teachers Develop Instructional Objectives with Learners   338

Good Teachers Find Out Why a Plan Is Not Working   338

Good Teachers Strive to Make Their Teaching Engaging   339

Good Teachers Give Learners Access to Information
and Opportunity to Practice   339

Good Teachers Teach for Two Kinds of Knowledge   340

Summary   *341*

Extensions   *341*

Summary for Part Three   *342*

References   343

Index   347

Preface

Teachers today are under pressure from all sides. Everyone, it seems, is an expert on teaching and on what to teach. Advice, mandates, and legislation speak with authority, telling teachers what and how to teach. In a sense, everyone *is* an expert on teaching. After all, didn't everyone go to school for many years and leave with the full knowledge of how school should have been?

Over the last several years, however, schools have changed. The student population is more diverse, the curriculum is more standardized, teacher and school accountability is stressed, and the importance of prior knowledge and experience in learning is more apparent. This sixth edition has responded to these changes by providing **additional examples of each model, current references, strategies** that can be used with all of the models, and **steps for personalizing and evaluating instruction.** Since the first edition of this text, many experienced teachers and teachers in training have found it to be useful. In fact, many teachers have told us that this book has become part of their permanent professional collections. Whenever possible, we have incorporated into this edition the excellent ideas and valuable corrections we have received from classroom teachers who use the models daily. These changes and those detailed in the following list allow more opportunities to construct new concepts and principles of instruction.

New to This Edition

The sixth edition includes a number of noteworthy changes:

- Updated references throughout the text and a comprehensive list of references at the end of the text representing the most relevant new literature and research
- Highlighted objectives for each chapter allowing for metacognition on the part of readers
- Additional graphic organizers including tables, figures, and flow charts
- Strategy Alerts that detail the connections between the strategies and instructional models and show how these specific strategies can be infused in all instruction
- Detailed elementary and middle/secondary grades scenarios that ground each instructional method

- Example lesson plans for elementary and middle school grades that are aligned with the scenarios illustrating lesson plan design presented at the beginning of each chapter
- Extensions at the end of each chapter that include activities and reflective questions to extend or remediate the skills and knowledge presented in the text
- A stronger focus on and directions for moving from standards to classroom objectives
- A major revision of Chapter 5 on concept attainment, including new examples and organization

Instruction

There is a sense in which everyone is a teacher. The root meaning of the word *teach* is "to show, to tell, to point out." Everyone teaches others, and so everyone is a teacher, at least in the amateur sense. This doesn't mean that everyone can be an *effective* teacher, however. If we look at the word *teach* in its professional sense, in relation to the word *instruction,* a more complex picture emerges. The meaning of the word *instruct* derives from the root "to build" or "to structure." Professional teachers not only *teach* in the usual sense of the word, they also instruct. They *structure* classroom environments and *build* experiences for a diverse group of students. Whereas parents, doctors, and others usually teach spontaneously by telling, pointing out, or showing, professional educators must carefully design and plan for their teaching. In fact, in our opinion, you are not teaching unless your instruction is helping students learn. There is a natural analogy between instruction and building based on the process of structuring environments. The teacher, as an instructor, is comparable to the builder in three ways:

1. *Planning for a specific audience.* Both builders and teachers must first figure out the needs of their clients or students. The house required for a single person with a large collection of automobiles should be different from that of a family of six with four dogs, three cats, two hamsters, and a rabbit. Similarly, the instructional design for a freshman conceptual physics class will be different from the design of the AP physics class. The background knowledge of the students and the challenge of the content require different approaches. Both the builder and the teacher must consider their clients, and they need to know how to formulate a plan that will be sound, original, and functional.

A good design for teaching grows out of a clear understanding of the needs of learners and the goals of education. Each design that a professional teacher creates is unique because different groups of learners have individual needs, and different types of learning require specific instructional approaches.

2. *Formulating objectives and evaluation procedures.* Both the builder and the teacher specify the intended outcome of their work as clearly as possible. No builder would think of starting a construction project without having a clear picture of how the final product should look. To get halfway through the project only to realize that what was emerging was not what the client wanted or needed would be professionally embarrassing and costly. The teacher who works without a careful design also leaves too much to chance, not providing appropriate supports that help students learn. As a professional, the teacher must plan how to achieve specific, intended learning outcomes. Otherwise, valuable instructional time can go to waste, and students will not have the appropriate experiences for success on the assessments for which they are accountable.

An essential part of setting objectives is determining effective assessment procedures to make certain that what was intended is taking place. Like the builder who must constantly check on the construction, the teacher must determine whether students are reaching the intended results. It would be foolish to wait until a building has been completed to check on the quality of the work and to determine whether all is proceeding as planned. Likewise, a teacher must use effective formative and summative assessment procedures throughout the teaching process.

Evaluation is continual, forming the basis of all decisions at every step: determining needs, formulating objectives, designing aligned assessments and instructional methods, and selecting materials. Evaluation is the process of continually asking questions: Where are we going? How do we get there? How far along are we? The teacher must continually collect information from students to determine whether the instruction is appropriate and effective. Thus, evaluation showing the intermediate and ultimate effects of instruction (formative and summative assessment) must be used to reform the process of teaching. Continual evaluation makes this possible.

3. *Selecting materials and procedures.* The builder has available a variety of materials and techniques from which to choose and must decide which combination will produce the structure most nearly like the one intended. Each project must be analyzed to determine the appropriate combinations; for instance, not every house is built only of wood or brick. Likewise, each student is an individual with his or her own needs, strengths, and interests. Moreover, each class is unique in terms of the dynamics of a particular group. Therefore, the teacher needs to have at hand a variety of approaches and techniques to accomplish specific instructional objectives and to manage problems as they arise.

Unfortunately, there are classrooms in which there is no instructional variety, leading to monotony and boredom. The teacher who uses the same instructional technique is like the builder who will build only one type of house. The builder may become expert at building that house, but the house will not meet the needs of a wide variety of clients. A repertoire of instructional and management strategies is necessary to meet the varied needs of learners.

A Models Approach

We believe that the process of instruction unites all teachers as professional educators. Our intended audience includes teachers of any subject who teach or plan to teach learners of any age. Teaching is challenging and complex. Models of instruction can help teachers deal with the demanding environment of the classroom.

This text is not a rule or recipe book but an invitation to consider the opportunities for professional educators as instructional decisions are made. Progress toward mastery teaching is a continuous process of learning and adapting, modifying, and changing. With each group of students, teachers must make different instructional decisions, solve different problems, and meet different needs. We offer information that will help teachers make more appropriate and effective choices as they plan and implement instruction.

We have divided this text into three parts. Part One, Planning for Instruction, describes the process of integrating standards into written objectives, assessment, and instruction. A teacher must first decide what is to be learned in the classroom before considering how to present the material through the instruction. A variety of options may be considered in the instructional plan.

Part Two, Matching Objectives to Instruction: A Models Approach, presents a selected group of instructional models along with illustrations of how they can be used in the design process. We are indebted to the many individuals whose research forms the basis for these models. We have also relied on our own experience and the experiences of many classroom teachers in determining what steps make these models most effective.

Part Three, Putting It All Together: Matching Objectives to Instructional Models, contains four chapters. Three are case studies that describe how teachers match objectives, assessments, and instruction in the design process. Part Three concludes with a chapter that suggests ways of creating a positive environment for learning in the classroom.

The content of this book reflects a process of learning by doing. Thus, ample opportunity must be provided for practice and feedback, ideally including peers reviewing videos of practice sequences. No one can learn these models simply from reading about them or memorizing the steps, just as no one can learn to drive a car simply from reading an owner's manual.

We have each had the opportunity to interact with both preservice and experienced teachers who are discovering the possibilities of growing professionally through the use of instructional models. We have seen how the models approach

Retained Features

The following features of previous editions are retained:

- A comprehensive approach to organizing content and skills and developing aligned instruction in planning
- Specific instruction in developing classroom objectives from state standards
- In-depth discussion of the steps and benefits of more than 10 different instructional models
- Attention to how the models can be used to meet individual needs
- Suggestions as to how models can be used to assess student learning

MyEducationLab

"Teacher educators who are developing pedagogies for the analysis of teaching and learning contend that analyzing teaching artifacts has three advantages: it enables new teachers time for reflection while still using the real materials of practice; it provides new teachers with experience thinking about and approaching the complexity of the classroom; and in some cases, it can help new teachers and teacher educators develop a shared understanding and common language about teaching."[1]

As Linda Darling-Hammond and her colleagues point out, grounding teacher education in real classrooms—among real teachers and students and among actual examples of students' and teachers' work—is an important, and perhaps even an essential, part of training teachers for the complexities of teaching in today's classrooms. For this reason, we have created a valuable, time-saving website—MyEducationLab—that provides you with the context of real classrooms and artifacts that research on teacher education tells us is so important. The authentic in-class video footage, interactive skill-building exercises, and other resources available on MyEducationLab offer you a uniquely valuable teacher education tool.

MyEducationLab is easy to use and integrate into both your assignments and your courses. Wherever you see the MyEducationLab logo in the margins or elsewhere in the text, follow the simple instructions to access the videos, strategies, cases, and artifacts associated with these assignments, activities, and learning units on MyEducationLab. MyEducationLab is organized topically to enhance

---

1. Darling-Hammond, L., & Bransford, J. (Eds.). (2005). *Preparing teachers for a changing world.* San Francisco: John Wiley & Sons.

the coverage of the core concepts discussed in the chapters of your book. For each topic on the course you will find most or all of the following resources:

- *Connection to National Standards.* Now it is easier than ever to see how your coursework is connected to national standards. In each topic of MyEducationLab you will find intended learning outcomes connected to the appropriate national standards for your course. All of the Assignments and Activities and all of the Building Teaching Skills and Dispositions in MyEducationLab are mapped to the appropriate national standards and learning outcomes as well.

- *Assignments and Activities.* Designed to save instructors preparation time, these assignable exercises show concepts in action (through videos, cases, or student and teacher artifacts) and then offer thought-provoking questions that probe your understanding of these concepts or strategies. (Feedback for these assignments is available to the instructor.)

- *Building Teaching Skills and Dispositions.* These learning units help you practice and strengthen skills that are essential to quality teaching. First you are presented with the core skill or concept and then given an opportunity to practice your understanding of this concept multiple times by watching video footage (or interacting with other media) and then critically analyzing the strategy or skill presented.

General Resources on Your MyEducationLab Course

The *Resources* section on your MyEducationLab course is designed to help you pass your licensure exam; put together an effective portfolio and lesson plan; prepare for and navigate the first year of your teaching career; and understand key educational standards, policies, and laws. This section includes:

- *Licensure Exams.* Access guidelines for passing the Praxis exam. The Practice Test Exam includes practice questions, Case Histories, and Video Case Studies.
- *Portfolio Builder and Lesson Plan Builder.* Create, update, and share portfolios and lesson plans.
- *Preparing a Portfolio.* Access guidelines for creating a high-quality teaching portfolio that will allow you to practice effective lesson planning.
- *Licensure and Standards.* Link to state licensure standards and national standards.
- *Beginning Your Career.* Educate yourself—access tips, advice, and valuable information on:
  - *Resume Writing and Interviewing.* Expert advice on how to write impressive resumes and prepare for job interviews.
  - *Your First Year of Teaching.* Practical tips to set up your classroom, manage student behavior, and learn to more easily organize for instruction and assessment.

- *Law and Public Policies.* Specific directives and requirements you need to understand under the No Child Left Behind Act and the Individuals with Disabilities Education Improvement Act of 2004.
- *Special Education Interactive Timeline.* Build your own detailed timelines based on different facets of the history and evolution of special education.

Visit www.myeducationlab.com for a demonstration of this exciting new online teaching resource.

Acknowledgments

We wish to thank the many students and teachers who have shared their experiences of instructional models with us to help us understand the challenges and opportunities teaching with instructional models brings. The graduate students in the Curriculum, Teaching, and Learning program at the University of Virginia have been particularly helpful, including Sasha Rehm, Jen Pease, Jeff Carpenter, Emily Davis, Amy Germundson, Todd Brown, Elizabeth Korab, Janine Davis, and Wendy Amato.

Thanks also go to the reviewers who provided guidance for this new edition, including David W. Chobar, Morningside College.

Last but certainly not least in our list, we wish to acknowledge that the manuscript of this edition would not have been completed without the help of Dr. Julie Estes; her knowledge, skills, and good humor have been invaluable.

part 1

Planning for Instruction

An old farmer was asked how his family happened to settle in a remote section of Arkansas. He replied, "Well, we were heading for California when Pap took a wrong turn at the Mississippi River."

Pity these travelers, crossing a continent with no map and only a vague notion of their destination. Likewise, many students and teachers traveling across unfamiliar intellectual terrain experience wrong turns in the classroom. Too often, students and teachers work without a map in the form of specific plans and without clearly defined objectives for their travels. At the end of a poorly planned lesson or unit, students are often let down, not having the support to reach the teacher's intended destination. In the classroom, careful planning is essential if students are to enjoy a successful journey toward knowledge and understanding.

The planning process we describe in the following chapters will guide both teacher and student behavior in ways that will provide students the opportunity to succeed in the classroom. Aligning objectives, assessments, and instruction gives students the chance to process and relate new information and skills to prior knowledge. Aligned instruction also allows teachers to plan a variety of instructional and assessment opportunities. Although there is no exact formula or recipe for good instruction, it is known that good instruction depends on good planning.

Based on what is known about student learning, we recommend the following approach to instructional planning:

1. Study state and national standards.
2. Collect and reflect on individual and collective needs of students.
3. Define and state objectives in the form of what you want students to understand, know, and be able to do.

4. Construct assessments that allow students to demonstrate that they have reached the stated objectives.
5. Create lessons and units that support students as they learn the necessary knowledge and skills to be successful on the assessments.
6. Use a variety of instructional models in lessons to meet a variety of learner needs.

These steps are discussed thoroughly in the next three chapters. We examine broad educational goals, the organization of instruction, and how to align objectives, assessment, and instruction in planning. Planning for instruction is a continual process, and the steps of planning overlap—varying based on the experience and background knowledge of the teacher. Some procedures for instructional design that can help in this process are covered in Part One. It is each reader's responsibility to determine the ways in which he or she will implement these procedures. What is not optional is the incorporation of a serious planning process into every teacher's approach to instruction.

1 Educational Standards

chapter OBJECTIVES

You Will Understand
- Effective teaching is built on what we know about students and student learning
- Schooling is determined by the needs of learners as well as the needs of society

You Will Know
- Eight essential learner needs and how these needs affect standards

You Will Be Able To
- Critically examine specific state standards
- Interpret state standards in relation to learner and classroom needs

What can I do to help my students learn how to construct a sentence, solve an equation, or set up an experiment? "What can I do?" is something a classroom teacher considers on a daily basis. One busy teacher who was asked about educational goals replied, "I have two goals for my teaching. The short-term goal is Friday and the long-term goal is June." Classrooms are complicated places that put a great deal of pressure on teachers to figure out what to do next. Busy teachers may believe they have no time to think about educational goals and standards. The pressure of getting the job done can seem overwhelming. It is common for teachers and prospective teachers to ask for techniques or rules on *how* to teach before acting on *what* to teach. Knowing how begs the question of knowing what to teach. Though both are important, until you know what is to be taught, you cannot accurately determine how it should be taught.

Ideally, teaching is the mission of the school; learning is its product. In reality, no matter how interesting or relevant information may be or how enthusiastic the teacher is about the subject, learners must be willing and able to learn content, skills, and habits of mind. Part of the art of teaching lies in making sure this is true. If teaching does not result in learning, then it fails, and the mission of the school is thwarted. If, however, teaching engages learners in the process of understanding and brings them into appropriate contact with what the teacher and others want them to learn, then learning is likely to occur, and the goals of education can be ensured. This chapter examines several principles of learning on which educational standards and practices should be based. The needs of learners and society and their relationship to educational standards are clarified and explored. Educational standards are investigated and dissected. Students must be the focus of all educational endeavors, including educational standards and how these standards are used.

How Learning Happens

Much is known about how people learn and how the brain works to organize experiences. This information can help teachers make decisions as the learning environment is designed. The following points summarize a few of the principles of how people learn: As you read each principle, think about how it might play out in the classroom.

1. *Learning changes the structure of intelligence.* Academic achievement at any level of schooling by learners at any level of verbal and quantitative ability will have the effect of improving thinking. As they grasp the structures of information to which they are exposed in school, students' thinking will change to accommodate those structures (Jensen, 2005).

2. *The brains of learners are continually being organized and reorganized.* Changes occur in patterns of cognition as new understandings are woven into the fabric of prior knowledge. Developing cognitive structures allow the learner to acquire, retrieve, and use knowledge efficiently. Teachers need to be skilled in helping students gain access to new information that is logically structured and linked to prior knowledge (Donovan & Bransford, 2005).

3. *The typical pattern of brain development is one of starts and stalls.* Different synapses of the brain will work at processing information from a variety of experiences and synaptic connections will develop at diverse rates. So a student may have very rich synaptic connections for literature and more impoverished connections for mathematics. Teaching must reflect that there is not one growth

rate for all parts of students' brains. One part may be more developed than another. The result is that a child may be good at one part of the curriculum while struggling with a different discipline, at least for a time.

4. *Memory has different functions.* Sensory memory is temporary and sends information to working memory. Sensory memory may be fleeting and unconscious; working memory requires constant attention. Learners process information in working memory. If that processing includes repetition, details, and elaboration, the information is more likely to move into permanent memory. Teachers must keep in mind that students need repetition of skills and information and that knowledge and skills must be detailed and related to other, more familiar skills and information (Willingham, 2009).

5. *Learning must be transferred beyond the narrow contexts of initial learning if it is to be useful.* Too often, learners will be able to perform well in the context of instruction, but what they learn fails to evidence itself in their practice. To guard against this, teaching must be explicit, skills must be practiced, and understandings must be applied. Transfer of new learning must occur at a deep level of knowledge—beyond recall. Teachers need to help students see the way new knowledge and skills can be used to solve problems similar to those practiced in the instructional context. It would hardly be an exaggeration to say that what finds no application is soon forgotten by learners (Marzano, 2003).

6. *Conceptual knowledge is based on facts and helps learners transfer information and skills.* To become a competent learner in any discipline, students must have a deep foundation of facts and examples, understand the conceptual framework in which these facts and examples fit, and be able to organize this information so that it can be retrieved (Willingham, 2009).

7. *Students who monitor their own learning are more successful in academic environments.* Learning is enhanced by metacognition—the act of thinking about ourselves as information processors. Metacognitive strategies help students become responsible for their own learning and help them learn beyond recall. Metacognitive strategies are learned and can be explicitly taught in classrooms. To be metacognitive, students need to know the goals toward which they are working, and they must receive feedback on how they are progressing toward these goals. With this information students can become aware, through reflection, of which behaviors lead to success (National Research Council, 2000).

8. *Learning is enhanced by challenge and inhibited by threat.* There is perhaps a subtle distinction to be drawn here; what is a challenge to one learner may be a threat to another. The difference results from how the brain responds, not from what actually occurs. The brain responds to threat with a "fight-or-flight" reaction—resist or remove oneself from the threatening circumstance. Although challenge is always accompanied by risk to one's self-esteem or success, the learner will thrive in what Caine and Caine (1994) call relaxed alertness. The implication for teaching is that students should perceive no risk in what they are

asked to learn. Mistakes are natural in the early stages of learning, and learners need to feel comfortable about making such mistakes. Grades, for example, should be based on the final results of learning, not on intermediate attempts. In fact, the corollary to fear of failing, hope for reward, may be equally inhibiting. Kohn (1999) has termed this "punished by rewards," a concept he discusses in a book of the same name. Being punished by rewards results in a dependence on these rewards, a dependence that can crowd out curiosity and a desire to learn.

9. *Each brain is unique.* As Robert Fulghum (1989), the popular essayist, put it: "The single most powerful statement to come out of brain research in the last twenty-five years is this: We are as different from one another on the inside of our heads as we appear to be from one another on the outside of our heads" (p. 39). The implication for teaching is that teachers need to be completely open to infinite possibilities in learners; that is, they should expect that there will be great diversity in understandings of what they teach. There is serious reason to doubt the notion that everyone will have the same answer or that there is only one answer worth having. Teaching and learning activities should be varied, and learners should have multiple opportunities to learn whatever they are taught. The models in Part Two will provide many teaching options to accomplish these goals.

Taken together, these principles reaffirm that there is no one best way to teach, but there are principles of learning that good teaching must adhere to. Table 1.1 extends what we know about student learning into questions to think about and possible teacher responses. We understand a great deal about learning. Teachers must use this knowledge and adapt instruction to the needs of learners.

Student Characteristics That Affect How Learning Happens

In every classroom there are children with a variety of needs, including students with physical, mental, and emotional challenges; English language learners; students living in poverty; and gifted students. Teachers must respond to each of these students in a respectful and knowledgeable way that provides every child the opportunity for success. Although this text is designed to provide an assortment of general instructional models for classroom use, each can be adapted for students with special characteristics.

Special education services are provided to students with a variety of challenges (see Figure 1.1 on p. 8). Many school districts have excellent special education services and collaborative teachers that can provide support to general education teachers. In addition, there are many websites that offer suggestions and guidance. Special education experts have also identified instructional activities that are effective in working with children who present special challenges.

Table 1.1   Thinking and Responding to What We Know about Learning

Principle	Reflective Question	Possible Teacher Response
Learning changes the structure of intelligence.	How does this principle relate to teacher expectations of student achievement?	We can help students become smarter by providing enriching experiences.
The brains of learners are continually being organized and reorganized.	How can a teacher discover what a student knows about what is being taught?	We need to assess prior knowledge and make explicit connections between what is known and what is to be learned.
The typical pattern of brain development is one of starts and stalls.	How can teachers access supports for struggling learners?	Student achievement grouping must be flexible and students should be assessed frequently and provided with timely interventions.
Memory has different functions.	How can students develop strategies to increase memory and automaticity?	Teachers must provide opportunities for students to practice new skills and receive feedback on their performance.
Learning must be transferred beyond the narrow contexts of initial learning if it is to be useful.	What does transferable knowledge look like?	Students must have an opportunity to apply and analyze knowledge and skills.
Conceptual knowledge is based on facts and helps learners transfer both information and skills.	How do we know what facts and concepts should be taught?	Teachers should provide useful and meaningful facts that support important concepts and generalizations.
Students who monitor their own learning are more successful in academic environments.	How can I model metacognitive behavior in the classroom?	Clear goals and frequent formative assessments are central to instruction.
Learning is enhanced by challenge and inhibited by threat.	How can a safe but challenging classroom environment be developed?	Relationships with students can help determine effective supports and challenges.
Each brain is unique.	How can we meet the needs of all students with whom we work?	Instruction should vary and adapt to student needs.

We are becoming a more diverse nation and the population of English language learners (ELLs) is growing in rural, suburban, and urban areas. Good instructional practice is particularly important for students who have extra burdens in the classroom. English language learners can come from a wide range of ethnic backgrounds and many different background experiences. In all cases, however, we are responsible for teaching both academic content and English language skills. All instruction is improved when there are respectful and caring

Figure 1.1 Categories of Special Education

- Autism
- Deaf-blindness
- Developmental delay
- Emotional disturbance
- Hearing impairments, including deafness
- Mental retardation
- Multiple disabilities
- Orthopedic impairments
- Other health impairments
- Specific learning disabilities
- Speech or language impairments
- Traumatic brain injury
- Visual impairments, including blindness

relationships between students and teachers; when goals and directions are clear; when a variety of instructional strategies and models are used; and when teachers use students' prior experiences, culture, and, in the case of ELL students, language as a basis for presenting new knowledge and skills. English language learners also need clarity in speech, attention to key vocabulary, scaffolding through chunking and unpacking dense text, and attention to their cultural heritage.

Poverty can also affect instruction. Poor children have less academic experience and thus arrive at school with a diminished set of prior experiences to link with new knowledge. The more we learn, the greater our capacity is to learn, so it is important to increase the experiences of children from poverty. Poor neighborhoods are often chaotic and unsafe, so children might arrive at school fearful, which can make learning more difficult. Poor children may also lack sufficient food and health care, increasing the risk of school difficulties. A cooperative, safe classroom community in which good instruction is common can help children stressed by the lack of basic resources.

Even among children who are not identified as having special needs, there are many factors that cause a wide disparity of development in children of the same age. Although there are predictable stages of children's growth and development—physically, intellectually, socially, and morally—one child may be intellectually advanced and physically slow in development, whereas another may have well-developed social skills and yet have problems with physical coordination.

In addition, boys and girls of the same age have different patterns of development. In a sixth grade classroom, most males still look like little boys, while about half of the females look like young women. In their early teens, girls are usually taller, stronger, and more verbal than boys. As teachers set goals for the curriculum, they need to be conscious of the many ways in which children differ from one another.

The Needs of Learners

Knowledge of how learning happens is but the first step toward effective teaching. The next step is to consider in some detail how the needs of learners play into the equation for successful schooling. These are the basic needs that must be met in every classroom, the issues to which the teacher must attend. These needs are the application of the more general principles of learning, and by attending to them, teachers are basing their practice on what is known about how people learn. The following basic needs of all learners are closely related to each other as well as to the general principles of learning:

1. Acceptance and safety
2. Choice
3. High expectations and appropriate challenge
4. Opportunity to connect the new to the known
5. Meaningful engagement
6. Clarity
7. Time to reflect
8. Aligned assessments

Acceptance and Safety

For children to thrive, an accepting and safe environment must surround them. A good learning community is a warm, friendly, and accommodating environment. Within this community, students feel safe, and they are physically and psychologically free to take the risks that deep learning requires. Students learn best in an accepting, positive, and safe environment. Ecological systems theory posits that the connections between family and schools also influence student success so that schools need to provide a caring and accepting environment for both students and their families. Good instruction helps bridge the gaps between school and families. Teachers must know their students—their communities, families, and intellectual preferences (Bronfenbrenner, 1979).

All students need to learn in more than one way to develop their potential. Teachers must accept the unique personalities and skills students bring to the classroom. The more the teacher knows about the students, the more he or she is able to plan a variety of instructional approaches and meet safety and acceptance needs. If a teacher cannot change instruction to meet this variety of needs, many students will be left out of this instructional process. The models presented in Part Two provide a path to this essential variety of instructional approaches and content organization.

As language diversity is part of a student's learning profile, it provides important information about background knowledge and, perhaps, readiness.

America's classrooms are becoming increasingly diverse with the advent of increased immigration from non–English-speaking countries. Non–English-speaking children have a great need for acceptance and safety. Language can isolate students from peers, school norms, and content. Along with good instructional approaches designed to meet student needs, teachers must ensure that English learners feel both physically and emotionally safe in the classroom.

Choice

Even though most people can learn in various ways, they have preferences for how they like to learn and perhaps how they learn best. For instance, some people are reflective and intuitive; others are more impulsive and spontaneous. Some respond to material presented in a logical order; others learn better through unstructured problem solving. Some students learn better through listening; others learn better by reading or viewing films. Some prefer to learn alone; others learn better in groups. Some students prefer to be given the rule and then examples (the deductive approach); others prefer to formulate the rule for themselves after a presentation of examples (the inductive approach).

Despite years of research on the issue, along with literally millions of Internet sites addressing the matter, there is little evidence that teachers have the time or materials to match individual learning styles with instructional approaches. The demands of day-to-day teaching overwhelm the best intentions to teach in ways that actually accommodate all the different ways of learning that might be present in a classroom. Here is what can be said: Teachers who attempt to teach in ways that allow for the same subject matter to be learned in more than one way, and thus who allow choice for their students, do help to balance students' achievement across different learning preferences.

High Expectations and Appropriate Challenge

Expectancy effects have a long history of study. Expectations of their students influence what teachers believe about them and their abilities as learners. In turn, these beliefs affect the instructional decisions in the classroom and the learning opportunities students are provided. The opportunity to learn is a powerful mediator of the experiences of students in the school. Every child deserves the chance to learn from challenging materials and tasks. Students can accomplish more with competent and expert peer and teacher interactions than they can on their own (Weinstein, 2002). Understanding how all people learn and getting to know the gifts as well as the deficits of each student help teachers develop high and realistic expectations for all students.

Intelligence can be defined in different ways. To meet individual student needs, teachers must have a broad view of intelligence that includes the belief that intelligence can be expanded through learning. Changing ideas about intelligence have influenced the views of many teachers and researchers on the role that intelligence preference should play in the classroom. Not only do learners have preferences for how they learn, but research conducted over the past 25 years has affirmed that there are more attributes of intelligence than were previously thought. Howard Gardner (2006), for example, posits distinct aspects to intelligence that are autonomous and malleable. Rather than limiting the concept of intelligence, Gardner and his associates have described several categories of intelligences.

Robert Sternberg (1998) also has developed a theory of intelligence that is more complex than the single IQ score. Sternberg's "triarchic" theory of successful intelligence describes three components of intelligence: analytical intelligence, practical intelligence, and creative intelligence. Sternberg has conducted research on his theory in classrooms at every level. The adaptation of this theory to schools proposes a balance of instruction and assessment across various components of intelligence. The implication of research on intelligence is that what matters most is not how intelligent you are, but how you are intelligent.

Opportunity to Connect the New to the Known

There is nothing more important to new learning than prior knowledge. Successful learning depends on making a connection between what the learner already knows and what he or she is trying to understand, regardless of innate ability or past performance. An informal assessment of the prior knowledge of students in relation to what they are expected to learn is essential to good planning and teaching. The more prior knowledge a student brings to the instructional setting, the more effective and efficient learning will be. Although children and adolescents come to school knowing a lot of information, some of it may be laced with erroneous ideas. It is important to anticipate and identify the misconceptions students bring to school. Misconceptions can concern content, such as an erroneous belief about a scientific principle, or may instead involve the value in what goes on in the classroom. In both cases, explicit instruction aimed at confronting misperceptions is necessary if accurate conceptual and factual information is to be developed.

Often students come to school with background knowledge that is not taken into consideration. Students may have a strong understanding of popular culture, cultural traditions, or social skills that can be tapped for useful examples and analogies as the school curriculum is studied. Teachers can use many methods to determine what students know. Brainstorming, clustering, and concept maps are all techniques that help make student knowledge more explicit, allowing for connections with new information. These techniques are discussed later in the text. Regardless of the technique used, describing individual prior knowledge serves to give learners a part in the preparation for what they are about to undertake.

Meaningful Engagement

Students must be engaged in academic activities to learn. When students are engaged they are answering and asking questions, sharing ideas, working persistently using academic materials, and staying focused on the topic or work that has been assigned. Engagement is enhanced when there are many ways that knowledge and skills can be learned, when scaffolding and feedback are provided so that all students can master the material. Meaningful engagement demonstrates the interdependency of all of the learner needs that have been identified. Teachers can't provide meaningful engagement without knowing their students well, designing appropriately challenging instruction and assessment, and providing a safe and accepting environment in which students can learn (Tomlinson, 2003).

Clarity

Clarity is essential to student understanding (Good & Brophy, 2007). Clarity is related to background knowledge because new information must be integrated with previous knowledge. Students must be familiar with the academic language used in classrooms so that they can follow directions and link new concepts with older information. Information and directions must be clearly organized—the purpose should be evident, and appropriate summaries should be included after chunks of written or oral information have been conveyed. Sequencing is also related to clarity. Content and skills should be presented logically and in a developmentally appropriate manner. A variety of accurate examples and the use of illustrations and analogies help to make new information and directions clear to students. In addition, how the teacher uses volume, pacing, and articulation affects clarity. It is important that teachers organize information so that students can have direct access to knowledge and skills to the greatest possible extent (McCaleb & White, 1980). If students cannot make sense of new knowledge and skills or the tasks of learning, they cannot learn efficiently and effectively.

Time to Reflect

The technical word for reflective activity in the classroom is *metacognition*. It refers to thinking about thinking. It is happening anytime a student is thinking about how to approach a learning task, monitoring progress toward a learning goal, or evaluating the depth of an understanding. It is cognitive reflection, related to how the learner oversees and regulates the effort to learn. Students learn better when they are aware of how they learn and of what they need to learn, how they might best learn it, and why it is worth learning in the first place. Ask a student in a classroom why he or she is doing something (such as reading, writing, or studying) and the likely answer will be "because the teacher said to do it" or "because it will be on the next test." The task of learning is too often the only point being served. Reflective learning, by contrast, implies some sense of the longer-term purpose of learning.

Assessments, both formative and summative, can help students become more metacognitive by providing the information necessary for self-monitoring and self-regulation. Students need time to process new knowledge and skills—something that is often lost in the press to cover content in our classrooms

(National Research Council, 2000). Specific instructional models and strategies provide processing time for learners. Part Two presents several models in which there are discrete steps for guided practice and for providing specific feedback. All of the models link to prior knowledge and provide opportunities for purposefully including processing time.

Aligned Assessments

Assessments can be diagnostic, formative, or summative. Diagnostic assessments are pretests to determine background knowledge prior to instruction. Formative assessments provide students and teachers with information about how students are progressing toward a stated goal. Summative assessments are designed to occur at the end of a chunk of instruction in which students have had the opportunity for formative assessment. Summative assessment provides information about student learning that is frequently translated into a grade. If it is to serve the teacher and the learner well, it must be aligned with teaching, the diagnostic and formative assessments, the objectives, and the instruction provided in the classroom. When objectives, assessments, and instruction are aligned, there is a greater chance for student success. Students have a need and a right to see the connection between what a test asks of them and what they are being asked to show that they know. Recognizing that learners have needs that must be addressed in the classroom, teachers work with unique individuals to help them succeed on common standards. To be successful, the needs of learners must influence teacher decisions regarding planning, assessment, and instruction.

The Needs of Society

An agreed purpose of public schools in the United States is to prepare children to participate in our democracy. How schools do this has been interpreted differently at various periods in history. Since the No Child Left Behind Act (NCLB) was passed by Congress in 2001, the preparation of future citizens has been driven by the idea of holding schools and teachers accountable for teaching basic literacy and computational skills. NCLB builds on the standards movement and purports to hold schools and teachers accountable for helping all students reach state standards.

Learning Standards

The standards movement dominates subject matter content today. It is still possible in some subject areas and in some locales for teachers to make major decisions regarding subject matter to be taught, but testing programs that are aligned with national, state, and local standards make it imperative that teachers keep in mind the criteria against which their students, they, and their school will be judged. No teacher can ignore the fact that accountability is the watchword of the day, and no teacher can afford the risk that the high-stakes test might include what she or he did not teach. Though teachers are not in charge of what gets tested, they must make instructional decisions to insure against surprises for their students.

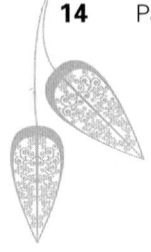

The history of the current standards movement in U.S. schools begins with the 1983 publication of *A Nation at Risk* by the National Commission on Excellence in Education. This short book, like nothing that had come before it, excited both the lay public and professionals in education. Few sentences in the canon of educational literature have been as often repeated as the dire warning it posited with the following words:

> The educational foundations of our society are presently being eroded by a rising tide of mediocrity that threatens our very future as a nation and people. . . . We have, in effect, been committing an act of unthinking, unilateral educational disarmament. (p. 5)

The nation rallied in the cause of excellence to mount a war on mediocrity. States and professional education organizations began immediately developing new content standards and curriculum frameworks. In 1989, 1996, and 1999, major education summits were held at which most state governors, educators, and business leaders came together. At each of these meetings, the major accomplishment was to identify academic standards to combat specific educational problems, including underachievement, the teacher shortage, and the question of accountability for all parties in the educational system. This attention to academic standards has led to several positive effects.

- States have adopted standards for their schools and provided resources for their achievement. Many of the states have extensive and frequently updated resources for teachers on their educational standards websites.
- Most schools in our nation now operate with a more clearly defined mission.
- Children who need special attention to help them reach specific goals are more likely to get that attention.
- A common set of standards provides the basis for a general understanding of what is to be taught and what kind of performance is to be expected.

Despite these positive effects of the standards movement, the overall news to report regarding standards improvements in the nations' schools is mixed. One problem that various articles and reports emphasize is that little if any consensus exists as to what form standards should take or how they should be used. Cross-state comparisons will always put apples and oranges in the same basket. However, whatever judgment one might make of the results presented, it cannot be disputed that many people are engaged in the effort to improve the nation's schools, with the best of intentions and often positive effects.

Not surprisingly, as we are now more than 25 years beyond the National Commission on Excellence in Education's warning of the rising tide of mediocrity, the heralded standards movement has proven more glacial than revolutionary. There are many obstacles to rapid reform of a system as diverse as U.S. education. Although the citizens of our country, on the whole, want schools to adhere to standards, troubling questions will always surround the effort to set those standards: Who shall set the standards? Shall standards be alike for all students, despite differences in cultural and linguistic backgrounds? Shall the accountability for these standards be rigidly applied, or should schools provide alternative educational channels for students with different life goals and academic gifts? These kinds of questions are not easy to answer, but by asking them, educators may confront anew the problems and challenges of their profession.

Moving from Standards to Instruction

Examine your state's standards for the subject areas that you teach. As you read through these standards, ask yourself the following questions:

1. What would each standard look like if I observed the behavior of a student who had accomplished the standard?
2. What are the specific behaviors one might engage in to practice the standard?
3. What specific information and skills does each standard describe?

Look carefully at the verbs that describe the standards of learning for each content area you are teaching. You will probably not see many verbs like *remember* or *recall*. You are very likely to see verbs such as *clarify, explain, use knowledge, question, describe, distinguish, evaluate,* and *compare and contrast*. The tests that assess attainment of standards include questions such as: What would happen if . . . ? What factors were most important? Which statement is best supported by the information given? Because of the information shown, we can conclude that . . . Over and over you will see this kind of thinking demanded on the tests students are given. To ensure students are not surprised by being asked to do such thinking, the instruction they receive needs to demand that kind of thinking.

If your state's department of education provides sample tests or released test items, examine them carefully to see exactly what a student might need to know or be able to do in order to perform well on the test items. Think of these test items as discrete tasks, each of which can be practiced and mastered. With sufficient practice and eventual mastery of the tasks required by the test, directly related to the standards being tested, students can perform well on the tests precisely because they do understand what is being asked of them. That will require only that they be taught in the same way they are to be tested.

This is not an appeal to teach to the tests your students will have to take. It is an appeal to teach what you know will be tested. Educational standards are the goals of teaching, and where those goals are specified *a priori*, teachers are all obligated to design instruction that leads students toward the goals. This is referred to as "instructional design with the end in mind."

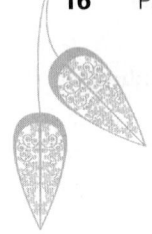

Designing Instruction with the End in Mind

The connections between standards and instructional design may not always be apparent. Try to think of the connection in this way: Standards are measured by incremental tasks that can provide feedback to students and teachers. Each of these items is a discrete task that the learner must perform in order to evidence mastery of the standard. Putting it in the most positive light, one could say each test item is an opportunity for students to show off their knowledge, skill, and logical thinking.

Most high-stakes tests require

1. Inferential comprehension, which is the ability to reason beyond the information given in the item itself
2. Problem to solution thinking, which is the ability to see a problem in terms of its potential solution
3. The ability to read and interpret charts, graphs, and maps
4. Interpretation of cartoons, illustrations, and other textual aids
5. Test-taking skills, particularly the ability to eliminate distracting foils from the choices given
6. A working knowledge of content-related concepts, including vocabulary, phrases, and proper names

Classroom instruction must be aligned with state standards and the associated high-stakes tests in order to provide students the opportunity to be successful. This does not imply, however, that every instructional decision is geared toward drilling students on recalling the content of the test. In fact, the purpose of this text is to design instruction that will help students build conceptual networks that will ensure achievement. These conceptual networks require a strong informational knowledge base to permit the development of rich connections among concepts. Each of the instructional models in this text helps students build these connections. For example, young children need to know the role and responsibilities of community members before they can make the connections regarding these concepts within their communities and with other communities.

Willingham (2009) makes the case that factual knowledge precedes skill and is required for reading and memory development. However, having students memorize lists of unrelated facts in hopes of passing a high-stakes test is not a reasonable strategy. Unrelated facts are difficult to remember. Facts that are related in a rich, meaningful conceptual network will increase student performance. Knowing all of the elements of the periodic table alone will not help in developing rich knowledge of the way that chemicals behave. It is the relationships between the elements that allow for deep understanding, knowledge built on understanding the characteristics of the elements that allows for the description of patterns and trends. All of the instructional models in this text support the development of generalizations—statements of relationships—in all disciplines and with students at all grade levels.

Summary

In determining instructional goals, the teacher should consider (1) the needs of the learners and (2) the needs and demands of the society in which the students are presently living, including the standards for learning that are set for students. The goals of education are subject to continual revision as society's view of what it means to be an educated adult and the needs of learners coming into school redefine the mission and nature of instruction. With these desiderata in mind, the teacher is well equipped to design instruction that will serve students in ways that will make schooling most effective and efficient.

Classroom instruction can meet both learner and societal goals through alignment with both the mandated state standards and the needs of particular students. State standards can provide the outline of classroom objectives that are designed to help a group of students reach specified, clear targets. Designing classroom instruction with what you want students to know, understand, and be able to do in mind provides a roadmap for student accomplishments.

Extensions

ACTIVITIES

1. Many states post standards documents on their department of education websites. Look at the standards on your state's website. Review the standards and the supporting materials available to you.
2. Pay a visit to a website of the professional organization that most closely represents the content area you will teach or are most interested in. What resources are available to help you organize your instruction?
3. If you will be using a textbook in your teaching, compare the text with the state and professional standards which you have examined. What are the similarities and differences?

REFLECTIVE QUESTIONS

1. Did any of the principles of learning discussed in this chapter change your thinking about your own educational experiences? Which of the principles do you believe will be the most difficult to apply to your classroom?
2. What do you believe about how intelligence affects how students learn? What do you still want to know about theories of intelligence?
3. Think about the context in which you are teaching or will teach. What can you do as a teacher to decrease barriers to student learning in this context?
4. How can you organize your classroom to maximize student learning? What would your "ideal" classroom look like?

Organizing Content

You Will Understand
- Good instruction requires teachers to shape standards, benchmarks, and pacing guides into units and lessons that meet the needs of the students with whom they are working

You Will Know
- The principles of organizing content and skills
- How to analyze content in terms of factual, conceptual, procedural, and metacognitive knowledge
- The necessity for aligning content and skills throughout instructional units
- How to identify and develop units and lessons that are instructionally aligned

You Will Be Able To
- Identify and develop units and lessons that are instructionally aligned

Kim is beginning her second year as a sixth grade language arts teacher. Reflecting on her first year, she feels that she has learned a great deal and is thankful for the support of her mentor, as well as the pacing guides provided for each class that she teaches. However, Kim wants to know more about instruction so that she can be in control of instructional decisions rather than only relying on the standards or pacing guides. She wants to feel more comfortable with the content so that she can control events to maximize student success. To this end, Kim is going to focus on how to manipulate both state standards and the pacing guides to meet state goals and the needs of her particular classes. We will follow Kim's journey throughout this chapter as she analyzes and aligns the content and skills in her classes to increase opportunities for student learning.

Content

School Curriculum

The school curriculum includes many subjects, and these subjects or disciplines have a specified set of information and skills that needs to be conveyed to learners. *Webster's Unabridged Dictionary* (2002) defines content in several ways, though for our purposes, this might best capture the idea: "The sum of the attributes or notions comprised in a given conception; the substance or matter of cognition." Thus, the content of mathematics is the sum of what is known and believed about mathematics. A similar definition would apply for other courses of study or content areas that make up the curriculum of the school. In addition, each discipline has a particular way of collecting and organizing information. Information in the language arts has been collected and organized in ways that differ from how information in the sciences has accrued, for example. What is it that distinguishes a particular story as literature and what distinguishes hypothesis from theory in science? Schools must therefore teach students the important knowledge that has accumulated in each subject as well as the skills that are used in the discipline to gather new information and determine its importance.

Content in the school curriculum does not really include everything that comprises a subject. What to include and what to exclude is often controversial—everyone has an opinion about what should be taught in schools, and those highest in the decision-making pecking order often have the strongest voice. Content standards are determined by the U.S. Congress, by legislatures and school boards of the various states, by national professional organizations, and by local school governing agencies, and in the process there are often heated, newsworthy discussions about what should or should not be included. Standards are never easily agreed on and are under constant scrutiny and revision. Open debate surrounding standards is natural and to be expected. Usually, the arguments center on which content should be included in the standards and which information should be left out and on the question of who should be taught what and when it should be taught.

Pressures from both sides of the political spectrum attempt to influence what is taught in schools. State standards reflect some of these pressures, as does the selection of textbooks and supplementary materials. The United States is a large and diverse country, and there is no established national curriculum; states are responsible for education according to the U.S. Constitution, allowing for local emphases. States also choose textbooks, and textbooks frequently influence what is taught in schools. Textbooks are not a curriculum and do not necessarily follow specific state standards. Although notoriously fact-based, textbooks may have several errors in facts or present material in a biased manner. Highly effective teachers will often use texts as one resource among others as they organize content in their classrooms. The textbooks provide support as teachers design units and lesson plans for their classes. In addition, teachers may use district resources, Internet resources, and shared units and plans.

In the final analysis, the crucible of curriculum determination is the classroom teacher. It is she or he who operationalizes the standards and the textbooks. The depth and accuracy of content is determined by the instruction provided to students. However, state content standards can help to normalize what is taught in individual classrooms.

Objectives

Despite the controversies surrounding attempts to establish high expectations for all students through legislated goals, content standards do have great value for educators, helping to keep those concerned with and involved in teaching focused on the main purpose of education: *to provide every child the most appropriate instructional environment and learning opportunity possible.* At different levels of generality or specificity, standards help define the vision of education, the goals of teaching, and the purposes of instruction, also called global, educational, and instructional objectives (Anderson & Krathwohl, 2001), as shown in Table 2.1.

Table 2.1 Types of Educational Objectives

Type of Objective	Purpose	Examples
Global	The goals society has for all students.	All children will be literate, responsible citizens who understand major scientific principles.
Educational	The official curriculum that the state and school system determine.	Students will be able to interpret information presented in a variety of forms. Students will be able to draw logical conclusions from data. Students will understand the role of hypotheses in the sciences.
Instructional	The basis of daily lesson plans and the objectives most important to the classroom teacher because they specify what the student will know, understand, and be able to do at the end of the lesson.	Students will know the difference between a simple and compound sentence. Students will understand that punctuation allows for greater specificity and clarity in writing. Students will be able to write either a compound or simple sentence when asked to do so.

Instructional standards help teachers plan and choose appropriate instructional models for the presentation of content. Without a goal and a plan, the students' experience may be similar to doing a jigsaw puzzle with some missing pieces. Although the act of putting it together is fun, when the pieces have been assembled, it is impossible to tell what the picture was intended to be. Standards allow teachers to choose appropriate and aligned objectives, assessments, and procedures. Specific standards provide cues as to what types of instruction should follow. Where a standard is written in the form "the student will investigate and understand that . . . ," the teacher will want to organize lessons on models that focus on inquiry and information. When a standard is written in the form "the student will describe and determine . . . ," the teacher will want to organize lessons on models that emphasize skills and facts. Standards and high-stakes tests are aligned in almost all states now, and so to ensure satisfactory performance, the teacher is obligated to organize instruction and employ instructional models that are most closely aligned with expectations made available in the statements of standards.

Subject areas of study in U.S. schools are generally organized into sequentially related courses, each subdivided into units and lessons. Standards determine the information and skills that are taught at different grade levels. According to Spillane (2004), "Standards define what students should know and be able to do in core subjects at critical points in their formal schooling" (p. 2).

The sophistication of standards has deepened across the K–12 experience. Knowledge and skills are outlined and states and districts have built on the standards by developing benchmarks (tests that measure progress toward goals), curriculum blueprints, and pacing guides to help teachers implement the standards. Materials outline the knowledge and skills that must be taught at different points. For example, Figure 2.1 shows the progression of skills for pattern recognition in the mathematics curriculum. The articulation of standards has provided classroom teachers with critical information about curriculum scope and sequence. Each of the standards provides indicators for student learning but includes only nonspecific guidelines for classroom instruction. It is up to the teacher, on a day-to-day or week-to-week basis, to determine more immediate and teachable objectives.

Course Design

Standards are certainly the starting points for organizing what students are asked to learn in school. Standards do not, however, provide a precise roadmap for units and lessons. Teachers are responsible for designing the day-to-day procedures used in classrooms. A good instructional design depends on the teacher's ability to organize unit and lesson content in systematic and interesting ways. The main concepts to be considered in the course must be identified and arranged in order of importance. For this to occur, an effective process is needed to plan a unit, organize a lesson, or prepare an instructional strategy.

Figure 2.1   Skill Progression in Pattern Recognition

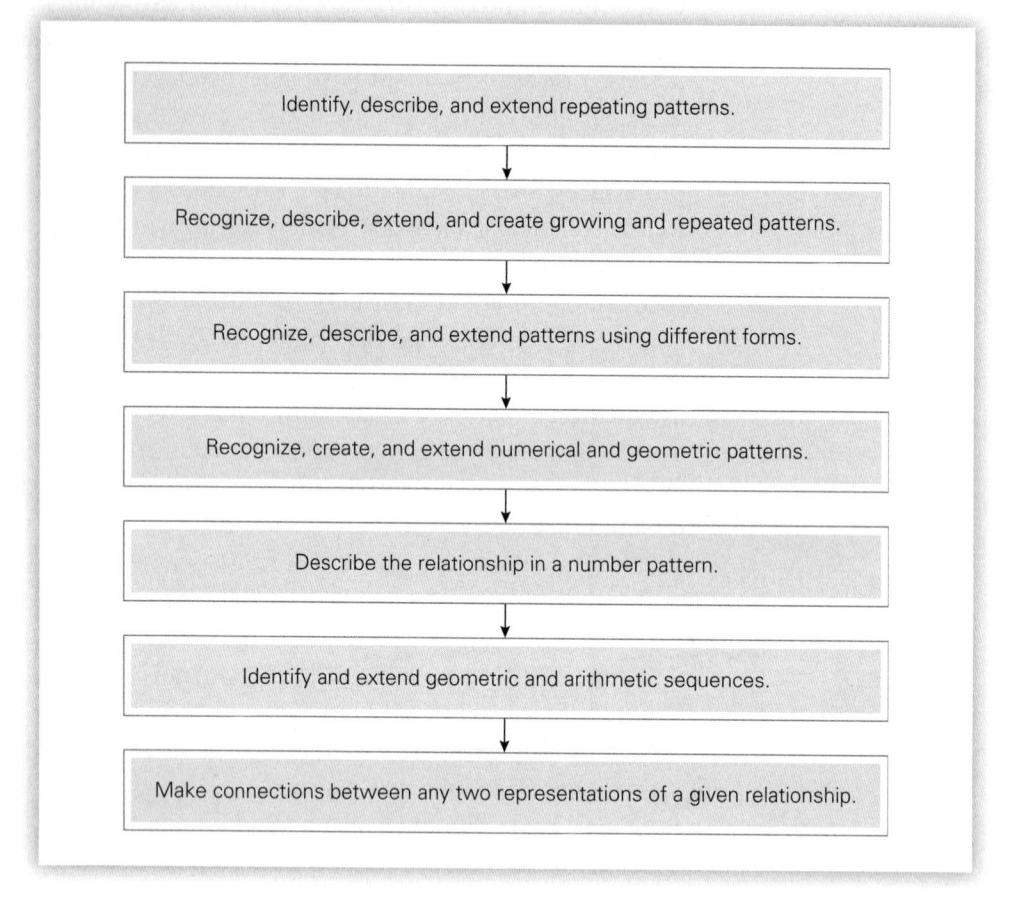

- Identify, describe, and extend repeating patterns.
- Recognize, describe, extend, and create growing and repeated patterns.
- Recognize, describe, and extend patterns using different forms.
- Recognize, create, and extend numerical and geometric patterns.
- Describe the relationship in a number pattern.
- Identify and extend geometric and arithmetic sequences.
- Make connections between any two representations of a given relationship.

In a well-structured course design, the learner will be able to recognize the order behind the plan, to determine how the parts fit into the whole, and to see how each part is related to other parts. Only when teachers carefully consider the organization of the content can they devise clear and concise objectives that are aligned with assessment and instruction. Alignment helps students and teachers understand the goals of learning; it keeps the instructional target in sight.

Public education in the United States today is standards based. Teachers must help students achieve success on standards-based assessments. As the standards movement was developing, cognitive psychology was also providing new understandings of student learning that demand changes in the way teachers teach (see Chapter 1). Standards, along with increased knowledge concerning how people learn, require teachers to look at instruction differently. Schools and classrooms must be tailored to the needs of students through acknowledgment of students as learners; the standards and content that need to be taught; and how information and skills will be communicated, demonstrated, and evaluated. This chapter examines how to arrange standards-based content into lessons and units by exploring the organization of content and instruction.

In summary, teachers do not determine what is taught in classrooms. State and local standards dictate the content of instruction. Teachers make decisions about how the content standards are translated into what students and teachers do in the classroom. These decisions are based not only on the content but on individual student needs, resources, and the teachers' knowledge base. The guiding purpose of this text is to help teachers make the best decisions for a specific classroom. These "best practice" decisions help a teacher choose appropriate objectives, assessment, and instruction for specific classrooms that are congruent with effective instructional decision making.

Analyzing Content

The various skills and bits of knowledge in a content area are not all equal. Some are more inclusive than others; some are more precise but limited in scope. Following the suggestion of Anderson and Krathwohl (2001) that there are different levels of knowledge, we can divide most classroom content into four categories of knowledge: factual, conceptual, procedural, and metacognitive.

Factual Knowledge

Facts are discrete bits of information that provide building blocks for concepts and generalizations. A fact is concrete, verifiable by observation, and applicable to a single example (Anderson & Krathwohl, 2001). Because a fact is based on a real occurrence, it cannot be predictive of future events. Here are some facts that students can determine: On Wednesday of last week we had half an inch of rain. Yesterday, Tuesday, April 24, one and one-half inches of rain was measured. Today the sun is shining brightly, hardly a cloud in the sky, but there is a prediction of more rain by the weekend. Children can collect these factual observations and begin to draw generalizations that can be checked against additional facts, perhaps concluding that "April showers bring May flowers."

Facts can also be defined as the elements that students must know in a discipline to understand concepts or to solve problems. Anderson and Krathwohl (2001) posit that factual knowledge encompasses knowledge of terminology and of specific details and elements. This sense of facts is useful to the classroom teacher because this is the definition of factual knowledge on which we will base our discussion of instructional models. All of the models rely on academic content. The foundation of academic content is facts. Many facts can be linked into an understanding of concepts and many concepts can be described with generalizations.

It is the teacher who chooses the facts that support predetermined concepts and generalizations. This choice comes from the teacher's understanding of the context in which teaching occurs—students, content, resources, and teacher's experiences. There are many facts from which to choose to make the structure of learning meaningful to specific students. In Kim's sixth grade language arts classroom, she teaches many skills that are dependent on factual building blocks. In one case, she wants her students to know that word origins can help them read unfamiliar words by separating prefixes and suffixes. Kim needs to make certain that the words she uses to support this understanding are familiar to her students through either past experiences or previous knowledge.

Conceptual Knowledge

Facts serve as the foundation for higher-level thinking. Concepts are the names given to the categories formed as a result of classifying factual data. To make sense of all the various stimuli in the world, learners of all ages form concepts and give them names. Imagine the cognitive overload if all things in the world were seen as separate and unrelated entities. To form concepts, learners pay attention to likenesses, ignore differences, and place similar objects in the same category. A pussycat asleep by the fire and a tiger in the jungle have many differences, but by attending to similarities and ignoring differences, we form the concept of cat.

Statements that link two or more concepts are generalizations. Unlike facts, generalizations contain more than one element and are predictive. Consider the following: Ten of the 15 students in Ms. McIntyre's fourth grade class brought peanut butter sandwiches for lunch today. Nine students brought peanut butter sandwiches yesterday. Eleven students brought peanut butter sandwiches the day before. These are factual statements formed on the basis of observation. They do not tell us if the sandwiches were eaten by the students or who made the sandwiches but are simply statements of what was observed.

A majority of the students in Ms. McIntyre's class prefer peanut butter sandwiches for lunch. This is a generalization based on the data from observation and from our understanding of concepts such as "peanut butter" and "sandwich." We have inferred from our observation that the students prefer peanut butter sandwiches, and we may predict that a majority of the students will bring peanut butter sandwiches tomorrow.

None of these statements is necessarily true. The students may not prefer the sandwiches; they may simply have no choice in the matter. Peanut butter may have been on sale in the local market this week, and next week cheese may be the main ingredient. From the observed fact of peanut butter sandwiches being brought to school over a period of time, however, we formed a generalization that allowed us to draw inferences and to make predictions. Only data from additional observations would prove the accuracy of the generalization. Principles, on the other hand, are generalizations that are typically accurate.

Anderson and Krathwohl (2001) define conceptual knowledge as "the interrelationships among the basic elements within a larger structure that enable them to function together." They elaborate this as "knowledge of classifications and categories, knowledge of principles and generalizations, and knowledge of theories, models and structures" (p. 27). In Chapters 5 and 6, which focus on

Figure 2.2 Examples of Facts, Concepts, and Generalizations: Impressionism

Facts	• In the middle of the 19th century, photography was becoming more popular and the Romantic movement was ebbing. • Monet, Renoir, Sisley, Bazille, Cezanne, Pissarro, and Guillaumin became friends and often painted together. • They and others used a different approach to painting than was seen at the Salon de Paris. • Their paintings were of outside scenes, used visible short and thick brushstrokes, and had an emphasis on light and the reflection of color while often focusing on movement. • In 1863, the Salon de Paris rejected a painting by Manet. • The artists using these new techniques organized their own art shows.
Concepts	Impressionism Art of spontaneity Collective Art techniques
Generalizations	Impressionism was a reaction to more formal art techniques. Art is influenced by and influences the context in which it is created.

concept attainment and concept development models, we will use this formulation as the basis for going into greater detail about the nature of concepts and how they relate to facts and generalizations. Figure 2.2 shows an example of academic facts, concepts, and generalizations.

As Kim plans her nonfiction unit, she considers the text material she will use, the state standards, and the district pacing guides. She wants to identify the conceptual knowledge students will need for success in the unit. She decides to build some concept maps that contain the essential elements of nonfiction. In her concept map about good arguments, she tries to identify what makes an interesting and notable argument—facts, statistics, examples, expert authority, and logical reasoning come to mind and are confirmed by both the state standards and district guides. Her nonfiction concept map, shown in Figure 2.3, is an example of conceptual knowledge—the relationships among the basic elements of a larger structure.

Procedural Knowledge

Procedural knowledge is the knowledge of how to do something—it is what we need to know in order to perform a task. This type of knowledge is very instruction oriented because it focuses on a specific result. We need to learn how to get to that result. Learning how to do something requires that we know (1) the steps for completing the task (know that), (2) how to complete the steps (know how), and (3) when to implement the procedure (know when). For example, a student learns *that* single-syllable words ending in a silent *e* often have the long sound

Figure 2.3 Good Nonfiction Concept Map

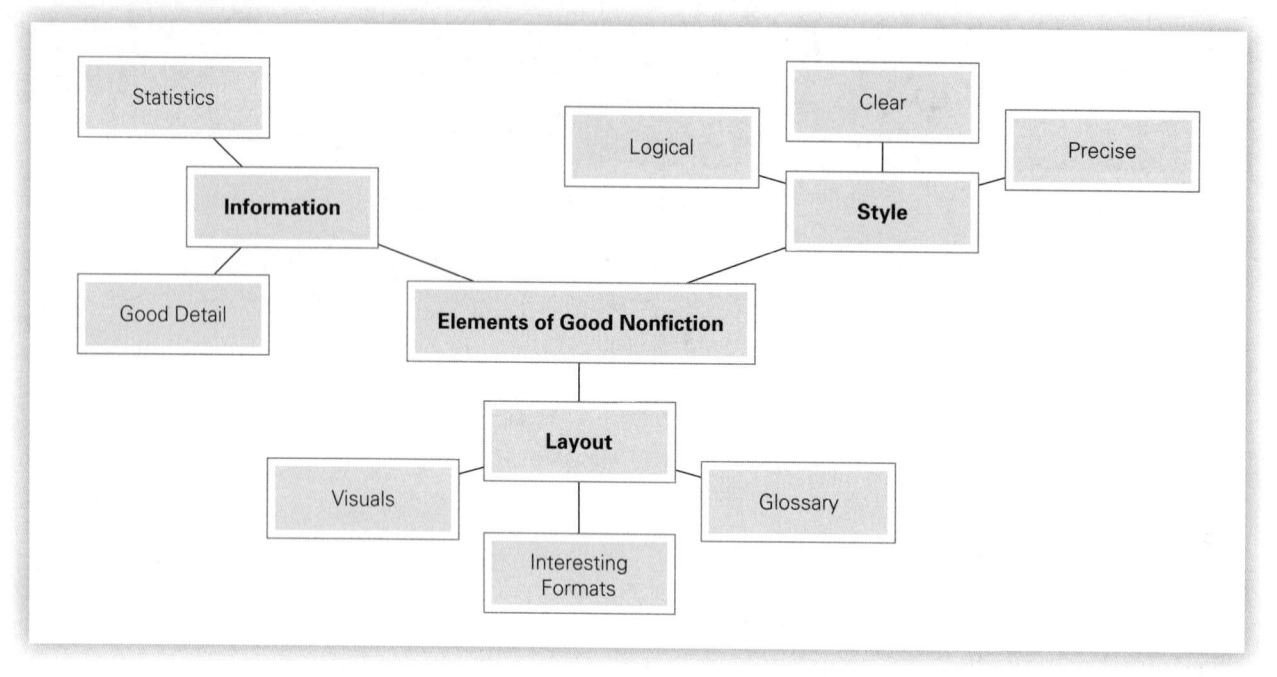

of the vowel. The student learns *how* to make the long vowel sound. To test this with pairs of words, the student can contrast pairs like *hop, hope; rob, robe;* or *rid, ride* to see how the final *e* of these words makes the vowel "say its name." Then, by examining exceptions to the rule in words like *circle, since, house, sure,* and *give,* the student learns *when* the rule does or does not hold.

Procedural knowledge includes methods of inquiry and the criteria for using subject-specific skills that are explicitly taught in classrooms through definition and demonstration. By defining and demonstrating the skill and its importance, students can learn to determine when it is appropriate to implement these skills. Skills such as summarizing, identifying similarities and differences, and brainstorming are just some of the skills that are discussed throughout this text. These strategies represent general procedural knowledge and are supplemented with subject-specific procedures in the classroom. Kim uses procedural knowledge in her sixth grade language arts class when she teaches how to identify word origins by examining prefixes and suffixes.

Metacognitive Knowledge

Metacognitive knowledge refers to the ability of learners to analyze, reflect on, and understand their own cognitive and learning processes. Students who identify appropriate learning strategies in the right context are using metacognition. For example, a student may know that she has trouble picking out the main idea in a reading passage. If she has been taught a simple graphic organizer—such as webbing—to identify the main idea and then chooses on her own to map out the passage in a web, then that student has used metacognition to complete the task. Students who are aware of their own cognitive strengths and weaknesses are more likely to be able to adjust and compensate for them (Fisher & Frey, 2008). Metacognitive knowledge is the most generalizable knowledge the student can possess because it is the basis on which the learner controls the act of learning. One of the global objectives of the educational system is that students become independent learners, able to function and learn beyond the confines of formal schooling. This requires that they be aware of how to learn and what they might best do to learn in any circumstance that requires that they learn. Much success in the workforce has to do with how well and how quickly the employee can learn new information and skills. This success is based in the components of metacognitive knowledge (Dinsmore, Alexander, & Loughlin, 2008).

Metacognitive knowledge is a valuable life skill because it focuses our attention on our own learning and thinking. It allows us to plan for improvement, implement the plan, and evaluate the success of the plan. For a classroom teacher, metacognition is of supreme importance. Reflective teachers use metacognitive knowledge to produce effective strategies that flex according to student needs, content, and context. Kim demonstrates reflective behaviors as she examines her own classroom practices. All of the instructional models and strategies presented in this chapter have elements to support the development of student metacognitive knowledge. Models are blueprints for teacher and student behaviors that focus on academic knowledge and critical thinking skills. The form of instructional models allows both teachers and students to be aware of the learning processes, the conditions that promote learning, and results of the instruction.

In summary, the four knowledge types—factual, conceptual, procedural, and metacognitive—can be found in content standards. Teachers must be able to match best practice instructional strategies with the types of knowledge students are learning.

Ordering Content

All educators owe a great debt to David Ausubel, a founder of cognitive psychology. Ideas about ordering and presenting content are based on his work. Ausubel's approach is rooted in two fundamental principles of the psychology of learning: (1) The single most important factor influencing new learning is what the learner already knows, and (2) any concept is explainable at many different levels of generality, with the highest or most general level most easily understood and the lowest or most specialized level the most difficult (Ausubel, 1968). These principles have had a major impact on both curriculum development and instructional practice (Marzano, 2001; Wiggins & McTighe, 2005).

The implication of Ausubel's first principle is this: New learnings are built on prior learnings. The very young child develops a concept of locomotion by observing the world in motion. He or she then tries to move, at first in a clumsy way, then with increasing coordination, until the idea of full-fledged crawling is mastered. On that foundation walking begins, although for a while crawling is easier. From walking comes running, skipping, dancing, ballet, a limitless repertoire. Notice, though, that each stage of locomotion is a specialized refinement of the one that preceded it.

Prior learning is the foundation for all instruction. Every child comes to school with knowledge and experiences that must be acknowledged and respected as new understandings, information, and skills are taught. All teachers

Strategy Alert

KWL

KWL, designed as a reading comprehension strategy (Ogle, 1986), can be used with a particular text or as a strategy to engage students at the beginning of a unit of instruction. The strategy relies on the students' prior knowledge to organize their thinking about a text or topic. Students are asked to make explicit what they know about the topic or skill, what they want to learn about the topic or skill, and, at the end of the instructional episode, what they learned about the topic or skill. The content may be narrow or broad—a short text excerpt or an entire text. The process may be done individually, in small groups, or in a whole class setting. The elasticity of the strategy belies its power. The KWL strategy is student centered because it encourages engagement and metacognition; students develop a purpose for instruction and a way to monitor instruction. Teachers have information to use in their instructional decision making and can extend the strategy. A column—"How can we find out what we want to learn?"—can be added to allow for the explication of search strategies. And students can be asked to provide a product that demonstrates what they have learned, providing an assessment component of the strategy. What do you notice about the following chart? How might your KWL chart be different? You might want to try a KWL on some of the topics in this text. ■

Topic: KWL Instructional Strategy

What I Know	What I Want to Know	What I Learned
Instruction is a key element in student learning.	What can I do when students are having difficulty sharing what they know?	Being prepared with examples and questions can help students brainstorm what they know.
Some students have difficulty reading text.	How will I know if students have learned something after using this strategy?	Asking students to share why they are articulating specific aspects of prior knowledge can help other students search for their relevant background information.
All new learning is filtered through prior knowledge.	How do I choose text that will work with this strategy?	
All students come to school with valid and interesting information.		KWLs can be used with most texts and topics.
		Teachers can use the information shared about what students know to focus lessons.

must develop procedures for identifying and using the knowledge that students bring with them to the classroom. Sometimes prior knowledge is academic, but sometimes teachers need to make purposeful connections to popular culture and cultural knowledge with which students are intimately familiar. Simply because a student lacks academic knowledge of a concept does not mean he or she has no prior knowledge on which to base new learning.

The implication of Ausubel's second principle is that *any stage of learning and understanding builds on previous, more general levels.* Every concept imaginable subsumes other more complex concepts and is at the same time subsumed by more general concepts. Imagine an analogy here between concepts and the nested boxes young children play with, where each box fits exactly into the next larger one. Think of the boxes as successively inclusive concepts. Each larger concept has the same structure as all the related concepts, whether more or less inclusive, so that a person who understands the structure underlying any one of the concepts can potentially understand any of the other concepts. Here the second principle of learning explains that the easiest concept to learn will always be the one at the next level of generality from a concept already understood. In deciding what to teach, find the "box" that contains the concept you wish to teach and then ask yourself whether the learners already understand the next most inclusive concept. If you determine that they do not understand the concept at that level, move to the next larger "box." It is important to remember that prior learning and general knowledge are the foundation for more sophisticated student learning.

Instructional Planning

Instructional planning can involve different periods of time and different amounts of instructional content, often described as "chunks" of content. Lesson and unit planning are used to describe the chunking process teachers and curriculum developers go through. Chunking is not something you do while you are teaching—it takes place before instruction. There is too much information at any grade level or in any content area to teach. There has to be a way to organize these collected facts and data into manageable pieces. Chunking is a technique to organize large pieces of information into digestible chunks—a smaller number of information-rich items. Small chunks allow for increased comprehension and help learners retrieve information quickly, which facilitates memory. Teachers determine what a meaningful unit of information is for their specific content and classes. The specificity of these decisions is key—how information for lessons is organized and how long to spend on each lesson are important instructional decisions that are dependent on the classroom context.

There are no absolute rules for how long a lesson should take. Although school days are divided into periods, a lesson may occur over any period of time. Some teachers believe that planning constricts the natural give-and-take of teaching and that a lesson plan does not allow teachers to follow through with students' ideas and interests. They see planning as mechanical and lacking the passion that should drive teaching and learning. Other teachers say that they do not have the time to plan—they are too busy thinking of what do to in the classroom for six hours.

However, both research and practice have shown that instructional planning is associated with student achievement. The amount of time for which you plan may vary from short lesson plans to units that include several weeks of daily plans. Wiggins and McTighe (2005) have isolated important decisions about unit and lesson design, represented by the following questions:

- What is worthy of being taught?
- How will students demonstrate that they have learned what has been taught?
- What learning experiences will students need to have so that they can demonstrate this learning?

Scope

What is worthy of being taught helps to determine the scope of what will actually be taught. There is too much information to cover in any single course, so teachers must make decisions about the breadth and depth of the content that will be addressed in the classroom. Some direction for deciding what to teach comes from state and district standards. Additionally, choices will rest on two considerations: (1) the relative importance of factual, conceptual, procedural, and metacognitive knowledge that might be taught in terms of the continuum of the overall curriculum; and (2) the relative importance of the content to be taught with respect to the needs of society and the age, interests, and abilities of the specific learners with whom teachers work.

Wiggins and McTighe (2005) provide guidelines for deciding on what should be taught. They believe that teachers can identify the most significant ideas (enduring understandings) by following four principles:

1. Big ideas must have value outside of the classroom in the real world.
2. The knowledge and skills that are taught must be representative of the content area.
3. The focus should be on common misconceptions that can be addressed instructionally.
4. The content and skills should be engaging for students.

Focus

Units of instruction are chunks of lessons that are related by a concept or a big idea. Often a question or set of questions is the focus of a unit. These questions provide a lens through which all knowledge and activities will be processed. Essential questions are important questions that require open-ended, messy, and divergent responses. What makes the United States great? What would happen if our country ran out of oil? Unit questions may be even more specific. What can be done to help correct the problem of obesity in the United States? What are the differences between jazz and rock? Sometimes units are focused on a concept, like migration, change, or nutrition. The content of the unit is designed to answer the question or explain the concept. The questions or concepts that frame the unit are intended to help students understand that knowledge is made up of answers. Too often, students leave school never realizing that knowledge is made up of answers to someone's prior questions, produced and refined in response to puzzles, inquiry, testing, argument, and revision.

The scope and focus of units are determined, in part, by standards and the standards-based assessments that were discussed in the previous chapter. Teachers must help students achieve success on these assessments. Teachers must be intimately associated with state standards and related assessments. Based on these standards and professional association standards (such as the National Council of Teachers of Mathematics, the National Council of Teachers of English, and the like), units of instruction are developed. Along with analyzing the assessments so that they can design lessons and units to ensure student success, teachers must also recognize what is known about students. During the last two decades there have been changes in our understanding of student learning that also demand changes in teaching. Standards and information about how students learn require teachers to look at unit and lesson planning in a new way. Classrooms must be tailored to the needs of students through acknowledgment of students as learners, the standards and content that need to be taught, and how learning will be communicated, demonstrated, and evaluated—all aspects of unit planning.

Sequence

A third set of decisions to be made concerns the order of subject matter. Subjects may be ordered chronologically or thematically. There is an obvious logic to ordering historical events chronologically, but they might also be ordered thematically, by bringing together topics in areas such as civil unrest, wars, or migrations. The resulting comparisons and contrasts can enrich students' grasp of the material.

Basic skills, such as the fundamentals of reading or arithmetic, usually require that the sequence of skills proceed from the simpler to the more complex. Even in such areas as math and reading, however, it is sometimes appropriate to sequence learning according to interest and variety. For instance, a unit on percent, in which winning percentages of the basketball team are studied, might be undertaken during basketball season, and a unit on consumer spending might be timed to coincide with the December holiday shopping season.

New learning should be based on previous learning. Even when that is assured, it is important to provide connections to help the learner identify how the new learning fits into what is already known. In short, there should be a logical order for the sequence and obvious connections between the parts to be learned and those already known by the students. How the breadth and depth of content is determined and how it is focused and sequenced are significant teacher decisions that directly affect instructional planning.

Chunking Instruction

Units are collections of lessons that have similar goals leading to broad understandings. Understandings can be defined in a number of ways. Wiggins and McTighe (2005) identified six aspects of understanding—explanation, interpretation, application, perspective-taking, empathy, and self-knowledge. Unit goals for understanding may include one, some, or all of these facets. All of these demonstrations of understanding are based on particular information that can be organized into conceptual knowledge that has been organized around supporting facts. Units help teachers plan for large pieces of content and skills and they help students make connections between individual teaching episodes. Units contain lessons that hang together and form an entity. Because understandings are organized in chunks, unit planning is critical for instruction focused on student success. Both units and lessons contain objectives addressing what students should understand, know, and be able to do (see Chapter 3). The unit objectives will be more general; the lesson objectives more specific. Individual lessons that comprise the unit will help students reach the detailed unit objectives. Laura Massey, a classroom teacher, has written a unit on understanding and predicting weather that is an example of the aligned relationship between unit and lesson goals. The complete unit can be found in *Differentiation in Practice: A Resource Guide for Differentiating Curriculum, Grades 5–9*, by Tomlinson and Eidson (2003). Table 2.2 demonstrates the relationships between factual and conceptual knowledge in unit and lesson planning in relation to a lesson on clouds included in Laura's unit on weather prediction.

The specificity of facts, concepts, and generalizations in the lesson is greater than that of the same type of knowledge specified in the unit. This weather unit has other lessons that cover air experiments, air pressure, air masses and fronts, the water cycle, storms, and global patterns. Clouds are only one lesson in the 12-lesson unit on weather as a system.

A different content analysis example comes from a unit on punctuation. The instructional objective of the unit states "students will understand that punctuation conveys meaning." This is the generalization toward which instruction is aimed. Another instructional objective is that "students will know the rules regarding periods, question marks, exclamation points, apostrophes, quotation

Table 2.2 Content: Unit and Lesson Alignment

	Unit: Weather's a System	**Lesson: Clouds**
Facts (factual knowledge)	Teacher presents examples of extreme weather brought in by clouds—The worst hurricanes ever in the U.S. were Camille (1969), Andrew (1992), and Katrina (2005). The worst tornadoes in this century were the Veterans' Day Weekend of 2002 (36 dead) and May 2003 (48 dead).	Teacher presents a list of the types of clouds observed by students on a particular day.
Concepts (conceptual knowledge)	Cause-and-effect Water cycle Water vapor Condensation Evaporation Properties of air Weather symbols	Water cycle Water vapor Condensation Evaporation Cirrus Cumulus Stratus Nimbus
Generalizations (conceptual knowledge)	Patterns repeat. We can make predictions based on patterns. Patterns give order to our world.	Clouds are classified according to specific characteristics. Clouds can help us predict the weather.

marks, commas, semicolons, colons, and hyphens." All of these punctuation marks are concepts. The facts that the teacher presents may be the individual errors made in the stories that her third grade students wrote. For example, Emily's story had no periods. Or Jeremy confused an exclamation point and a question mark. In a specific lesson on periods, exclamation points, and question marks, the teacher uses the same set of facts and works on the concepts "declarative sentence," "interrogative sentence," and "exclamatory sentence." He or she is still helping students understand that specific punctuation can change the meaning and emphasis of a sentence. The lesson is more specific in the content that the unit covers.

Developing Lesson Plans

Lesson plans are the component parts of a unit design. Just as a course is divided into units, units are divided into lessons. A lesson may span several days or it may take only one day. In deciding how many lessons are necessary to accomplish the unit objectives, it is necessary to be flexible. You may need to rethink and modify the unit objectives because they may prove too ambitious or too limited. The design process is always circular in that prior decisions may be modified as the teaching progresses. Each lesson should be a logical part of the unit plan. With a clear chart of the main factual, conceptual, procedural, and metacognitive knowledge to be studied, lesson planning flows easily.

Here are four guidelines to the development of effective lessons:

1. Limit the concepts and content to be covered in a lesson to allow time for the students to review, practice, and get feedback on what they have learned.
2. Be sure that new material is connected to what has been learned previously and that the connections are clear.
3. Check frequently to ensure that the students are acquiring the intended knowledge, attitudes, and skills; be prepared to alter your plans or to reteach if the learning is not taking place or if the students seem to be disengaged.
4. Never accept students' failure to learn as inevitable or unavoidable.

Remember that good lesson plans have common emphases—appropriate objectives, opportunity for practice and feedback, and flexibility.

Lesson Plan Elements

Lesson plans must have sufficient specificity for teachers to have a road to follow, but the flexibility to avoid mechanical and lifeless instruction that is unresponsive to student needs. Good lesson plans can help teachers find an appropriate balance of specificity and flexibility. There are common elements that must be considered before any instruction occurs.

- *Objectives.* Objectives detail what students should know, understand, and be able to do by the end of the instructional period. Chapter 3 explains instructional objectives in detail.
- *Rationale/standards.* The rationale explains the standard on which the lesson is based and why this particular content or procedure is being taught to these students at this time.
- *Assessment procedures.* Assessment decisions must be clearly aligned with the instructional objectives and the rationale. Formative assessment opportunities must be identified before instruction occurs. How will students be assessed and provided feedback during the lesson so that they can see if they are reaching the objectives? What are the opportunities for reteaching the material or skill? Summative assessments provide information about the attainment of instructional objectives after the instruction is complete. These also should be specified before instruction begins so that all instruction is aimed at helping students accomplish all of the goals of the assessment.

- *Instructional procedures.* There are many components of instruction. Some of the questions that should be answered in this section include
  - What, if any, instructional model will be used in the lesson?
  - How will students be engaged in the lesson? What hooks will be used?
  - How will the prior knowledge of individual students be tapped? What advance organizers can be used?
  - What support will be provided to students as they work toward the instructional objectives?
  - How will the instructional needs of individual students be met?

Deductive and Inductive Organization

In a deductive model of instruction, the lesson usually begins with the presentation of a generalization, a rule, or a concept definition. Students are then given specific examples along with facts associated with the generalization, concept, or rule. In moving from the general to the specific, students are encouraged to draw inferences and make predictions based on the examples.

In inductive lesson designs, students are first presented with specific data and facts, and gradually, through the process of investigating and reasoning, they form the generalization, rule, or concept definition. Most of the models presented in Part Two are inductive, because induction is more conducive to stimulating students' thinking. Deductive models, particularly the lecture, however, can be very effective when used judiciously and sparingly to deliver information.

Kim has been thinking about deductive and inductive approaches to her instruction. She feels that she spent too much time in her first year of teaching lecturing to her students. Although she was well prepared for her lectures and they didn't last more than 15 minutes, she is ready to try some inductive approaches to her lessons. Although Kim is nervous about not having a tight hold on her sixth graders, she believes that if she is organized and her instruction is aligned, she will be successful in trying some new ways to convey information.

Summary

This chapter has examined the content of lessons. The types of content that are taught (factual, conceptual, procedural, and metacognitive) form the foundation of the decisions made about a lesson. The instructional models (procedures) that are chosen must be aligned with the type of content that is to be learned. Lesson plans help make certain that teaching decisions are transparent and address the most important elements of teaching, including objectives, standards, reasons for teaching particular content to specific students, formative and summative assessment, and detailed instructional procedures. Effective teachers plan their lessons and deliver their instruction with flexibility.

Extensions

ACTIVITIES

1. Ask a variety of people who should determine what is taught in schools. Probe by asking who should determine what knowledge is worthy of being taught. Think about the answers you receive. Did any of the responses clarify your thinking?
2. Look at a textbook you might be using in the near future. Identify examples of factual, conceptual, procedural, and metacognitive knowledge.
3. Look carefully at a state standard in a content area that you will be teaching. What are the transferable big ideas in the standard? How are these big ideas related to other disciplines? Did you uncover any personal misconceptions as you read the standard and thought about your own thinking? Are there common misconceptions associated with this standard? How might you help students become more interested and excited about learning the knowledge presented in the standard?

REFLECTIVE QUESTIONS

1. With what ideas presented in this chapter did you disagree? Why?
2. How will the idea of metacognition affect you as a learner and as a teacher?
3. With what content that you will be teaching are you most unfamiliar? How will you go about becoming more familiar with the content? How will the lack of knowledge affect your teaching?

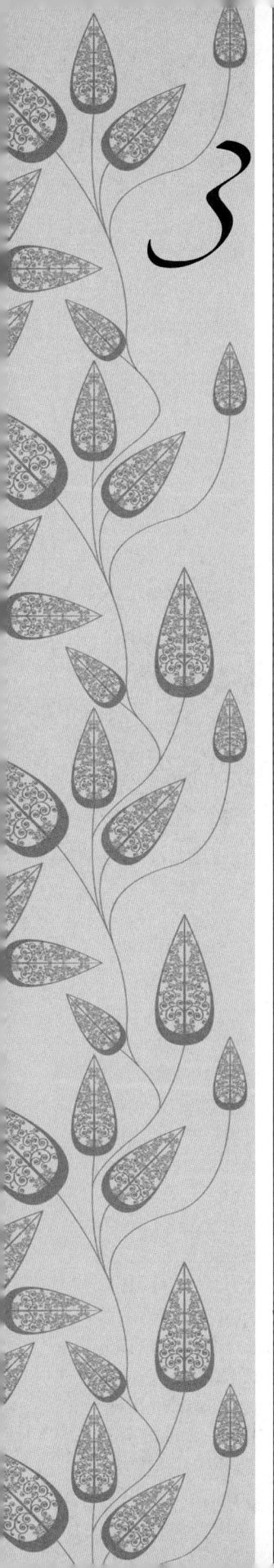

3
Instructional Objectives, Assessment, and Instruction

chapter OBJECTIVES

You Will Understand
- Good teaching requires clear instructional objectives that are aligned with assessments and instruction

You Will Know
- The purpose and forms of instructional objectives
- The role of formative and summative assessments
- How to choose appropriate strategies to help students achieve instructional objectives

You Will Be Able To
- Write clear instructional objectives that will allow you to choose appropriate assessments and instructional strategies

A few years ago we visited a third grade classroom in Appalachia. Of the 33 children in the crowded classroom, many had come to school hungry and without adequate clothing. The room was poorly heated, and materials were scarce. An elaborate chart of educational instructional objectives, printed on expensive, shiny paper, covered part of one wall. Every skill conceivable (so it seemed) was broken into minuscule parts. The chart's presence in the room had been mandated by the school district. When asked how the chart could be useful to her, the weary teacher smiled, and said, "At least it adds a little color to the walls."

Many teachers have been disillusioned with educational instructional objectives that seem to have little or nothing to do with the reality of their classrooms. They have been asked to spend precious time mechanically developing instructional objectives to fit a prescribed formula that has little connection to what they really teach.

Chapter 2 discussed global goals (societal) and educational standards (state or district). This chapter addresses instructional objectives (classroom). Instructional objectives are vibrant, living goals that are required for good teaching and student learning. Without clearly articulated targets, teachers and students will have difficulty traversing the road to student learning. The trick here is that the instructional objectives must represent the culmination of a process for the teacher—a process that includes prioritizing subject matter content and skills. Good instructional objectives cannot be legislated. Although they can and should be derived and adapted from state curriculum standards, they must be determined through careful consideration of disciplinary content, student prior knowledge, knowledge about how people learn, and available materials and resources. Good instructional objectives are not decoration; they are the illustration of an understanding of pedagogy. Instructional objectives allow teachers to purposefully adhere to the principles of learning that all good teaching must reflect.

Purpose of Instructional Objectives

Instructional objectives represent key decision points in teaching in which goals are articulated and shared. Clearly defined intentions allow lessons to be focused and challenging rather than serendipitous and shallow. Teachers and students alike require targets toward which to progress. Without a clearly defined end, a person can be swimming toward any number of beaches. Why are we learning about the Civil War? Do I just need to learn what interests me? Are there any ideas about the Civil War that will help me understand other conflicts? What is it my teacher wants me to learn? What do historians know and understand about the Civil War? What will be on the test? All of these questions should be reflected on to form a foundation for good teaching.

Instructional objectives can be stated as what students will *know, understand,* and be able to *do* (KUD), a format that provides a foundation for all curricular, instructional, and assessment decisions made in classrooms. This approach to designing instructional objectives helps ensure the alignment of instructional objectives with assessment and teaching strategies. Clearly articulated instructional objectives are easier to assess, and they provide boundaries for what will occur in a lesson or unit. Thus, instructional objectives imply what will happen in classrooms. A list of instructional objectives also gives teachers, students, and parents a preview of the assessments and instruction, whose content will follow directly from the objectives. This approach to curriculum is called backward design (Wiggins & McTighe, 2005). Beginning with the end in mind, instructional objectives detail what we want students to know, understand, and be able to do at the end of an instructional period.

Backward design is not a new concept. As early as 1962, Gilbert suggested that instruction should begin with the end in mind (Cohen, 1987). Mastery learning, an educational reform popular in the early 1970s, supports instructional alignment and backward design in that the assessments are planned before the instruction occurs, allowing teachers and students to focus on specific goals—rather than face uncertainty about tests or quizzes. The importance of this approach to instructional planning is supported by recent research on learning and by the current accountability movement that mandates end-of-course high-stakes testing (Bloom, 1983; National Research Council, 2000).

Teaching comprises many decisions made in the complex, multidimensional, fast-paced world of the classroom. Teachers may not even be consciously aware of the decisions that are made and the impact that these decisions have on teaching and student learning. Careful planning helps to control the happenstance found in schools. Successful teaching implies student learning. Research on teaching and learning indicates that there are clear paths to better instruction—a road to follow to increase student learning. Thus, not all decisions are equal. Those based on the knowledge of how students learn and how education can be organized to promote learning will result in greater student achievement. Writing good instructional objectives and aligning assessments and instruction with these objectives can increase the likelihood of successful student learning.

Clear targets improve the chances of student learning. It is known that different targets require aligned and coherent instructional approaches. There is no one "correct" way of organizing educational experiences, but the clarity of instructional objectives is critical. It is important to delineate the big ideas that are represented in *students will understand* instructional objectives; the discrete information that is represented in *students will know* instructional objectives; and skills and performances that are represented in *students will be able to* instructional objectives. This instructional frame guarantees that students have the best possible circumstances in which to succeed. In addition, research shows that students need learning experiences that are well organized, related to prior knowledge, and assessment focused. Because instructional objectives guide teacher and student behaviors, they allow teachers to present information in ways that are congruent with student needs while simultaneously meeting state curriculum standards.

Figure 3.1 shows the relationship between the three different forms of instructional objectives or learning targets. The broad understanding target is the most abstract, the *able to do* objectives are the most concrete. Figures 3.2 and 3.3 show the relationships between the three types of objectives in two different content areas.

Instruction can be designed to address the learner needs discussed in Chapter 1 if teachers are purposeful in constructing instructional objectives. For example, in considering the learner need of meaningful engagement, teachers can identify the knowledge, big ideas, and skills that will be meaningful and motivating to a particular group of students. Intentional planning helps teachers organize student experiences. Knowing what students should know, understand, and be able to do at the end of instruction means that teachers can continually monitor a student's progress toward specific objectives.

Lucid instructional objectives provide targets for scaffolding instruction. Figure 3.4 (on p. 42) shows teacher behaviors that can scaffold student learning. Unambiguous instructional targets also provide a framework for remediating student learning. Instructional objectives will help in the selection of different, sup-

Figure 3.1 Instructional Objectives

Students Will Understand
These objectives detail the big, abstract, transferable ideas of a discipline that help students and teachers organize facts, concepts, and skills into manageable chunks. *Understand* objectives allow for school content to be related to the real world.

Students Will Know
These objectives detail the content and skills that students must master to successfully complete the lesson or unit. They are the "stuff" of the lesson and cover the factual, conceptual, procedural, and metacognitive knowledge required to understand the big ideas in the *understand* objective.

Students Will Be Able To
These objectives detail what students will be able to do at the end of instruction and are focused on observable behavior and products.

Figure 3.2   KUD Objectives for a Lesson on Changes in Painting during the Renaissance

> Students will understand the effects of cultural movements on how different disciplines view the world and accomplish their work.
>
> ↕
>
> Students will know the paint mixing techniques of early and later Renaissance artists, the differences between egg tempera and oil paints, and the meanings of *egg tempera, oil paint, opaque, pigments,* and *translucent*.
>
> ↕
>
> Student will be able to reproduce egg tempera paint and distinguish between egg tempera and oil paint in specific Renaissance paintings.

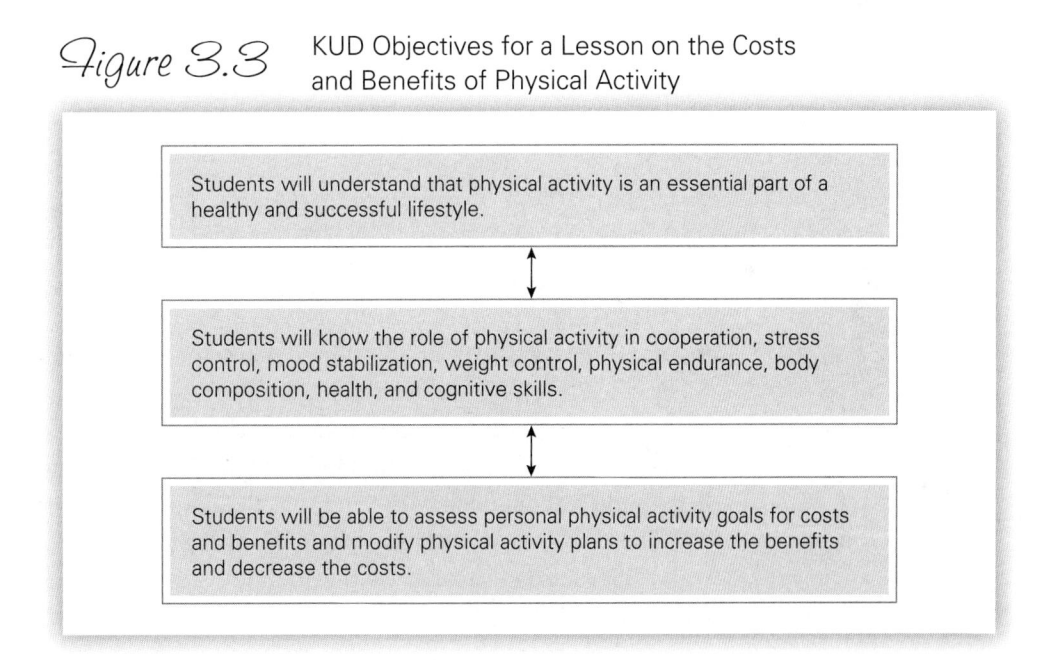

Figure 3.3   KUD Objectives for a Lesson on the Costs and Benefits of Physical Activity

> Students will understand that physical activity is an essential part of a healthy and successful lifestyle.
>
> ↕
>
> Students will know the role of physical activity in cooperation, stress control, mood stabilization, weight control, physical endurance, body composition, health, and cognitive skills.
>
> ↕
>
> Students will be able to assess personal physical activity goals for costs and benefits and modify physical activity plans to increase the benefits and decrease the costs.

porting instructional models for reteaching. Without these predetermined ends, student progress is difficult to ascertain, explain, and support, and opportunity is wasted. Remember that instructional objectives provide a focus for teaching and learning. Assessments and instructional strategies follow from clearly defined objectives. The alignment of objectives, assessments, and instruction improves the chances for successful student learning.

Figure 3.4 Scaffolding

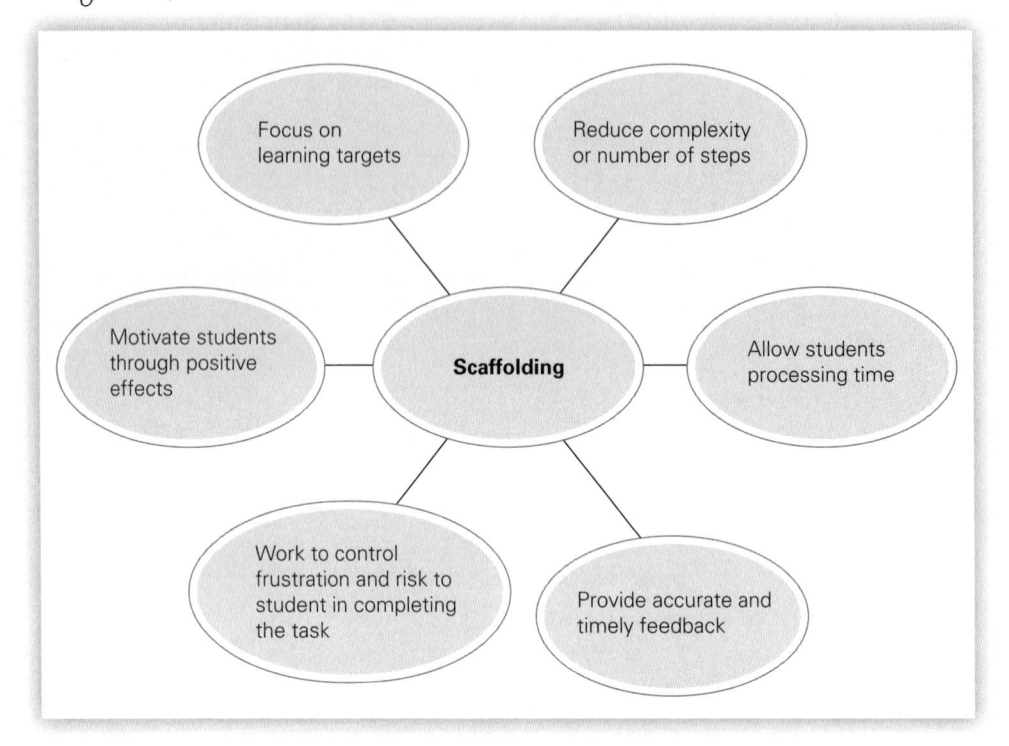

- Focus on learning targets
- Reduce complexity or number of steps
- Motivate students through positive effects
- Allow students processing time
- Work to control frustration and risk to student in completing the task
- Provide accurate and timely feedback

Formats for Instructional Objectives

Students Will Know Instructional Objectives

Instructional objectives are written in many forms (Gronlund & Brookhart, 2008; Marzano, 2001). We prefer the KUD format—*students will know; students will understand;* and *students will be able to do* design. This format allows for the articulation of specific understandings, knowledge, skills, and performances that can help guide teaching behaviors and make teaching transparent and equitable.

The decision of where to begin planning for instruction is somewhat arbitrary. Instructional objectives that define what teachers want students to know *(students will know)* is as good a place as any to start. However, in other circumstances, there may be reasons to begin with an *understand* or an *able to do* objective. It depends on the teacher, the context, the standards, and the pupils with whom a teacher is working. Writing instructional objectives is not a linear process; it is possible to begin anywhere and move among the different forms as the exact targets of a unit or a lesson emerge.

Students will know instructional objectives detail the content and skills a student must master to successfully complete the lesson or unit. The "stuff" of the lesson is listed in the *know* instructional objectives. With the glut of information available to everyone, teachers must be careful to prioritize and organize what is taught. With an approach that prioritizes and chunks information, students can learn the most worthy knowledge and skills and will be able to transfer this critical knowledge to novel situations both in and outside of school. The *students will know* objective forces teachers to choose and focus on particular types of knowledge during instruction.

Factual and conceptual knowledge may be defined as the basic elements of a discipline. Factual knowledge comprises knowledge of the terminology used within a content area and can be thought of as the basic building blocks of any content area, the foundation on which all other knowledge is built. Conceptual knowledge, being more general, subsumes and organizes discrete bits of information as they are related to one another and function together. For conceptual knowledge, students must have bits of factual information to categorize and classify. In order to understand the concept of war, for example, it is necessary to have been exposed to specific facts about a number of wars.

But not all knowledge is factual or conceptual. Procedural and metacognitive knowledge also form the substance of *students will know* instructional objectives. Procedural knowledge is the knowledge that is accumulated about how to do something and knowing when to use specific strategies and procedures; metacognitive knowledge encompasses information about learning, in general, and awareness of one's own learning, in particular.

Each of these four knowledge types is critical in learning a discipline. Each offers the "stuff" of what we teach—the focus of *students will know* instructional objectives. Table 3.1 demonstrates the different types of knowledge that are taught in school. It also demonstrates related *students will know* examples.

Table 3.1 Examples of Knowledge for Use in Geologic Time

Type of Knowledge	Example of *Students Will Know* Instructional Objective
Factual Geologic time is the age of Earth according to the record of rock strata.	Students will know the definition of geologic time.
Conceptual Geologists have divided Earth's history into eras—spans of time that are based on the general characteristics of living things during that time.	Students will know the critical attributes of fossils.
Procedural Geologists are able to determine the age of a rock through the natural radioactivity of chemical elements.	Students will know the procedures used for determining the age of rocks.
Metacognitive Students studying geologic time must remember the various divisions of relative geologic time in chronological order.	Students will know a variety of mnemonics for relative geologic time.

Students will know instructional objectives remind teachers of the essential disciplinary information worthy of teaching. These instructional objectives insure against digressions and help keep a healthy flow to classroom discourse. If the teaching target is for students to remember the characteristics of each of the geologic time eras, the lesson will focus on this information but not on, for example, the accuracy of the movie *Jurassic Park*. *Students will know* instructional objectives can be seen as the foundation of lesson and unit content. *Students will understand* instructional objectives, on the other hand, move beyond bits of "stuff." *Understand* objectives are the pinnacle toward which all information and tasks in school are aimed—abstract, big ideas that we will remember over a long period of time.

Students Will Understand Instructional Objectives

The *students will understand* instructional objectives help teachers and students make sense of the knowledge on which lessons are based. The big ideas represented in *students will understand* instructional objectives are critical in getting the meaning of the discrete pieces of information represented in the *students will know* instructional objectives. Because there are simply too many bits of material to learn, *understand* instructional objectives help teachers to organize facts, concepts, and skills into manageable chunks. The developmental level of the learner, available resources, and the teacher's background dictate the level of content specificity in lessons. Knowing the "stuff" of a discipline is not enough. Stuff needs to be interwoven into abstract, transferable ideas. Global goals for schooling demand that school content translate into real-world ideas and skills. Wiggins and McTighe (2005) call these transferable ideas "big ideas." Helping us prioritize and frame important knowledge, big ideas are the linchpins or central, cohesive elements of a discipline and are essential for understanding a subject area. Big ideas answer the important questions in a field of study. Lynn Erickson (2007) defines big ideas as statements that are broad and abstract, universally applied, and represented by different examples that share common characteristics. Because knowledge is constantly accumulating and changing, big ideas must be continually validated by contemporary factual examples. New information may change the emphasis of a strong generalization. Thus, the relationship between *students will know* instructional objectives and *students will understand* instructional objectives takes on importance. Without the demarcation of the broad, abstract understanding, teachers and curriculum developers may choose less important, insignificant bits of information to support the big idea; without an interrelated set of factual, conceptual, procedural, and metacognitive information, it is difficult to understand the abstractions toward which teaching is directed.

Wiggins and McTighe's (2005) definitions of big ideas are presented in Table 3.2. The critical characteristic of a big idea is that it has "pedagogical power"—it

Table 3.2 Wiggins and McTighe's Formulation of the Characteristics of Big Ideas

- Provide a focusing conceptual lens for any study
- Encompass breadth of meaning by connecting and organizing many facts, skills, and experiences, serving as the linchpin of understanding
- Point to ideas at the heart of expert understanding of a subject
- Require "uncoverage," because its meaning or value is rarely obvious to the learner, is counterintuitive, or is prone to misunderstanding
- Have greater transfer value, applying to many other inquiries and issues over time—horizontally (across subjects) and vertically (through the years in later courses) in the curriculum and out of school

Source: Adapted from Wiggins, G., & McTighe, J. (2005). *Understanding by design* (Expanded 2nd ed.). Alexandria, VA: Association for Supervision and Curriculum Development.

provides for understanding the core foundation of a discipline by making sense of the discrete facts and skills that are important to those who practice the discipline. These are the facts and skills that form the lesson and unit material—the *students will know* instructional objectives. But students need to move beyond pieces of information to understand the important ideas of a discipline. Content knowledge is a means to an end. Deep understanding of the discipline is the goal, and big understandings help to get there. With deep understanding, students are more likely to apply knowledge to new problems and situations.

Students will understand instructional objectives are broad and abstract; they work to tie together a number of conceptually linked lessons. Consider an instructional objective like the following:

> Students will understand that individual decisions and behaviors contribute to a healthy life.

Several lessons may need to be taught using this *understand* goal to help students gain information and skills necessary for demonstrating understanding of this big idea.

Students will understand instructional objectives aid in the articulation of what teachers and curriculum designers mean when they say they want students to "understand." What does it mean to understand?

Students will understand can mean that students are able to

- Explain
- Interpret
- Apply
- Identify critical perspectives
- Empathize
- Assess individual knowledge around a specific target (Wiggins & McTighe, 2005)

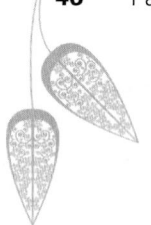

A *student will understand* instructional objective can also indicate, more generally, that students are able to construct meaning from instruction. In any case, understanding objectives are assessed through student performance. So, the *students will understand* objective is clearly associated with what we want students to *know* (the *understand* instructional objective is an abstraction of the *know* instructional objectives) and what we want students to be *able to do* (the performance aspect).

The relationship between *know, understand,* and *able to do* instructional objectives is critical. They are closely linked, and a change to one may shift emphasis on one of the other instructional objectives. This connection allows teachers to organize instruction for individual classes while still teaching to the important and transferable ideas in each discipline.

Examples of *students will understand* instructional objectives and the *students will know* instructional objectives to which they are related can be found in Table 3.3. Notice that *understand* instructional objectives are written in the form "*Students will understand that.*" By using this sentence stem, a generalization rather than a topic will follow. The statement will be a better signpost than one or two words. "*Students will understand that* all organisms need energy and matter to live and grow" provides more guidance to teachers as they plan

Table 3.3 Examples of *Students Will Understand* and *Students Will Know* Instructional Objectives

Students Will Understand	Students Will Know
Students will understand that numbers represent the quantity of objects.	Students will know the common language for comparing the quantity of objects (e.g., "more than," "less than," "same as").
Students will understand that human communities learned to overcome environmental conditions.	Students will know the social and cultural characteristics of hunter–gatherer communities.
Students will understand that substances can be classified by their physical and chemical properties.	Students will know that matter has different states.
Students will understand that messages must be adapted to the audience.	Students will know how to adjust messages for different audiences.
Students will understand that different languages use different patterns to communicate.	Students will know linguistic elements of the target language (e.g., time, tense, gender, syntax, style).

Source: Copyright 2009. Adapted with permission from *Content knowledge: A compendium of standards and benchmarks for K–12 education* (4th ed.). www.mcrel.org/standards-benchmarks. All rights reserved.

instruction than "*students will understand* basic principles of life science." Of course, as Wiggins and McTighe (2005) point out, not every generalization is worth teaching toward. The highlighted understanding should be timeless, cross-cultural, and something students will remember. *Understand* objectives constitute what students remember years after the discrete facts and skills have been forgotten. The *students will understand* instructional objective makes sense of the articulated content in the *students will know* instructional objective. The *understand* statement opens the file drawer of facts and skills that are needed to make sense of the big ideas. In summary, understandings or big ideas are abstract generalizations that are critical for grasping the essence of a discipline. *Students will understand* instructional objectives list these broad statements associated with *students will know* instructional objectives.

Students Will Be Able to Instructional Objectives

Instructional objectives written in the *able to* form are also statements of the learning that will occur as the result of instruction. This learning is observable and measurable and can involve cognitive, affective, and psychomotor instructional objectives (Airasian, 2005; Anderson & Krathwohl, 2001). This text focuses on the cognitive skills that are the foundation of classroom instruction. Discussions of the relationship between affective (social and emotional) and psychomotor objectives and academic achievement can be found in other resources (Elias, 2005). *Students will be able to* instructional strategies have also been called "behavioral objectives" because they focus on student behaviors. Some instructional objective strategies only use *students will be able to* formats. Bloom's taxonomy focused on the cognitive skills students should be able to demonstrate at the end of a teaching episode (Bloom, 1956). In fact, the taxonomy was written to provide a framework for developing common test items to be used across several universities. The focus on objectives has seen several iterations in the last 50 years, always with a focus on clearly articulated targets for student learning.

Students will be able to instructional objectives are written at different levels of specificity. Instructional objectives for a course are stated in more general terms than instructional objectives for a unit of study, which are more general than instructional objectives for a lesson to be completed in a class period. But whatever the level of generality, *students will be able to* instructional objectives must be in agreement with *students will know* and *students will understand* instructional objectives, and together all of the instructional objectives must allow for the congruence of objectives, assessment, and instruction. This textbook is devoted to cognitive instructional strategies—instructional models that are based on what is known about how people learn—so we will focus on the cognitive *students will be able to* instructional objectives. Other instructional or behavioral objective formats list affective (feelings, attitudes, and emotions) and psychomotor (physical and manipulative skills) descriptions. These are important classroom considerations. For example, a positive learning climate is associated with increased student learning. Our focus, however, is on good instruction, which we believe can contribute to a positive classroom climate.

The cognitive processes identified in *A Taxonomy for Learning, Teaching, and Assessing* (Anderson & Krathwohl, 2001) allow for careful construction of instructional objectives that target specific student behaviors. A common misconception is to confuse objectives with activities. Instructional objectives are not activities. They do not describe how students will spend their time. It is necessary to clearly identify the behaviors that students will demonstrate after successful instruction and not to confuse these performances with classroom pursuits. The construction *"students will be able to"* is important for the distinction between activities and instructional objectives because the objectives detail the behaviors that are expected as a result of the lesson. Instructional objectives define the purposes of instruction and help to limit the kinds of assessments and instructional strategies that will be used to help students reach the instructional targets.

Six categories of student behavior have been identified that describe student learning. These distinct cognitive processes form the basis for developing *students will be able to* instructional objectives.

- Remember
- Understand
- Apply
- Analyze
- Evaluate
- Create (Anderson & Krathwohl, 2001)

Note that *understand* in this list is synonymous with comprehension, not with understanding big ideas.

Learners need repetition and elaboration in lessons so that information can be readily stored in permanent memory. *Students will be able to* instructional objectives allow teachers to specify the knowledge and skills that must compose instruction. Specifically articulating the types of cognition students will be developing and practicing ensures opportunities for student learning. Each of these six categories is described using specific verbs to aid in the development of *students will be able to* instructional objectives. Table 3.4 describes each of the student cognitive behaviors as defined and adapted from Anderson and Krathwohl's "revised taxonomy" (2001).

Students will be able to instructional objectives should incorporate core disciplinary tasks, which are the realistic tasks accomplished in a subject area—experiments in science, analysis of historical documents in social studies, critique of peer work in language arts, and the like. It is important that learning outcomes, the lesson's instructional objectives, be worthwhile and representative of important disciplinary knowledge and skills. Time in school is short. It must be used wisely. It is important to remember that *students will be able to* instructional objectives are a common construction with which many teachers are familiar.

Table 3.4 Cognitive Behaviors

Behavior	Definition	Verbs
Remember	Retrieve relevant knowledge from long-term memory.	Identify Recognize Recall Retrieve
Understand	Construct meaning from instructional materials.	Interpret Paraphrase Illustrate Classify Categorize Summarize Generalize Infer Conclude Predict Compare Explain
Apply	Carry out or use a procedure in a novel situation.	Execute Implement
Analyze	Break material into parts and determine how parts relate to one another and to whole.	Discriminate Select Organize Integrate Outline Structure Attribute
Evaluate	Make judgments based on criteria and standards.	Check Critique Judge
Create	Put elements together to form a coherent whole or new structure.	Hypothesize Design Construct

Moving from Standards to Objectives

Standards are written in many different levels of specificity and clarity. Once you become familiar with the standards in your state, you will need to mold the standards for which you are responsible to align with instructional objectives. Standards are the mandated curriculum. They can not, however, be swallowed whole in the classroom. Nor can textbook objectives be used whole cloth. It is a teacher's professional responsibility to design objectives specific to each class based on state standards. Each classroom context brings different background information, achievement levels, resources, and interests to bear on the standards.

Excellent classroom teachers take all of these into consideration when developing instructional objectives—KUDs. Two skills are required for designing good instructional objectives from standards. First, you will need to be able to construct *understand, know,* and *do* objectives from the standards. Sometimes the standards are written as an *understand* objective. They are abstract and broad. From the standard, you will need to identify the aligned *knows* and *able to dos*. If the standard is written as a student behavior, you will need to construct an aligned *understand* objective and a list of items students will need to know in order to successfully do what the standard asks. The second required skill is to write the standard into student-friendly language—language that reflects the developmental level of the students with whom you are working. This allows students to take responsibility for their progression toward the targets you have set. Table 3.5 shows aligned *understand, know,* and *able to do* objectives that are derived from standards. For standards written to align more closely to one of the three forms of objectives, teachers must be able to move from one form to another in order to provide quality instruction.

Instructional Alignment

Instructional alignment represents more than the congruence among the three types of instructional objectives; it also reflects the congruence among the lesson or unit objectives, assessments, and instruction. This alignment allows for efficient and effective student learning.

Instruction is the teaching of knowledge and skills. Teachers instruct in the classroom—they teach. They make instructional decisions about what and how they teach. Interestingly, these decisions are also defined as instruction. To complicate matters, instruction is often linked with the word *curriculum*. Curriculum is what is taught, and what is taught is associated with standardized testing. If a high-stakes test is curricularly aligned, it tests what students have had the opportunity to learn. The opportunity to learn involves more than presenting information to pupils. It implies that students have had the scaffolding and extensions necessary to process the knowledge and skills they are acquiring.

Instructional alignment in the classroom is similar to curricular alignment, but it does not focus on high-stakes decisions. Instead, the emphasis centers on the opportunity for student learning on a day-to-day basis. Decisions at the classroom level focus on how to translate state standards into instructional objectives and in this manner describe what students need to know, understand, and be able to do. This alignment of the three elements of teaching—objectives, assessments, and instructional strategies—increases student learning. When instruction is not representative of the established targets or the assessments on which the targets will be demonstrated, the likelihood of success will diminish.

Table 3.5 Examples of Aligned *Students Will Understand, Students Will Know,* and *Students Will Be Able to* Instructional Objectives

Students Will Understand	Students Will Know	Students Will Be Able To
Students will understand that numbers represent the quantity of objects.	Students will know the common language for comparing the quantity of objects (e.g., "more than," "less than," "same as").	Students will be able to count objects and show one-to-one correspondence.
Students will understand that human communities learned to overcome environmental conditions.	Students will know the social and cultural characteristics of hunter–gatherer communities.	Students will be able to list three similarities and three differences between hunter–gatherer communities in Africa and the Americas.
Students will understand that substances can be classified by their physical and chemical properties.	Students will know that matter has different states.	Students will be able to explain how the state of water can be changed.
Students will understand that messages must be adapted to the audience.	Students will know how to adjust messages for different audiences.	Students will be able to defend a position to two different audiences by adjusting two aspects of the message or presentation.
Students will understand that different languages use different patterns to communicate.	Students will know linguistic elements of the target language (e.g., time, tense, gender, syntax, style).	Given a text in a target language and its English translation, students will be able to compare the linguistic elements of time, tense, and gender.

Source: Copyright 2009. Adapted with permission from *Content knowledge: A compendium of standards and benchmarks for K–12 education* (4th ed.). www.mcrel.org/standards-benchmarks. All rights reserved.

Let's look at a world history standard.

Understands how Aegean civilization emerged and how interrelations developed among peoples of the Eastern Mediterranean and Southwest Asia from 600 to 200 BCE (Marzano & Kendall, 2009).

The standard is the mandated curriculum and, consequently, instruction in world history must include the knowledge and skills that support the standard. The curriculum must be supported with the following knowledge:

1. The cultural diffusion of Greek, Egyptian, Persian, and Indian art and architecture through assimilation, conquest, migration, and trade

2. The benefits and costs of Alexander's conquests on numerous cultures
3. The extent to which Alexander's conquests brought about cultural mixing and exchange

An *understand* objective associated with this standard may read: "Students will understand that cultural diffusion is a consequence of assimilation, conquest, migration, and trade." Supporting *know* objectives would provide specific details about Alexander's conquests, their impact on other cultures, and the consequences that followed. Taking students' interest, achievement levels, and prior knowledge into consideration, *students will be able to* objectives can be written for a particular class. For this standard, there are many options for *do* objectives. For example, students will be able to draw a map of Alexander's conquest and subsequent trade routes. Or students will be able to write a journal of an immigrant to Greece from Egypt during this time. *Instructional objectives form the intersection between the curriculum (the state standards) and what happens in classrooms.*

Teachers look at the curriculum standards; the knowledge, understandings, and skills that compose the standard; the prior experience of their students; the way people learn; and the available resources in the school and the community. From this mix of content knowledge, pedagogical knowledge, and knowledge of student learning, classroom assessments are determined. The big idea of instructional alignment is the congruence among objectives, assessment, and instruction. This strategy promotes effective and efficient student learning.

Assessing Instructional Objectives

As you can see in Figure 3.5, once the instructional objectives have been written, but before instructional procedures have been considered, assessments that will provide information about the attainment of the instructional objectives must be planned. This is the key to backward design. Making certain that your instructional objectives and assessments clearly align provides an equitable way to prepare students for both formative and summative assessments. Instead of deciding on assessments during and after instruction, assessments are planned as soon as the instructional objectives are identified. Instruction is targeted toward helping students gain feedback and success to show they have reached the stated instructional objectives. Knowing the instructional targets and how these targets will be assessed focuses teacher and student behaviors during instruction. A clear path makes the ride more comfortable and successful.

Assessments are the basis for making judgments. Most decisions teachers make in the classroom reflect judgments, and many of these judgments are based on assessments. Some assessments make judgments about student learning in the form of grades. Other assessments provide information to students and teachers about what has been learned and what knowledge and skills still need to be addressed and practiced so that learning targets can be achieved.

Figure 3.5 Backward Design

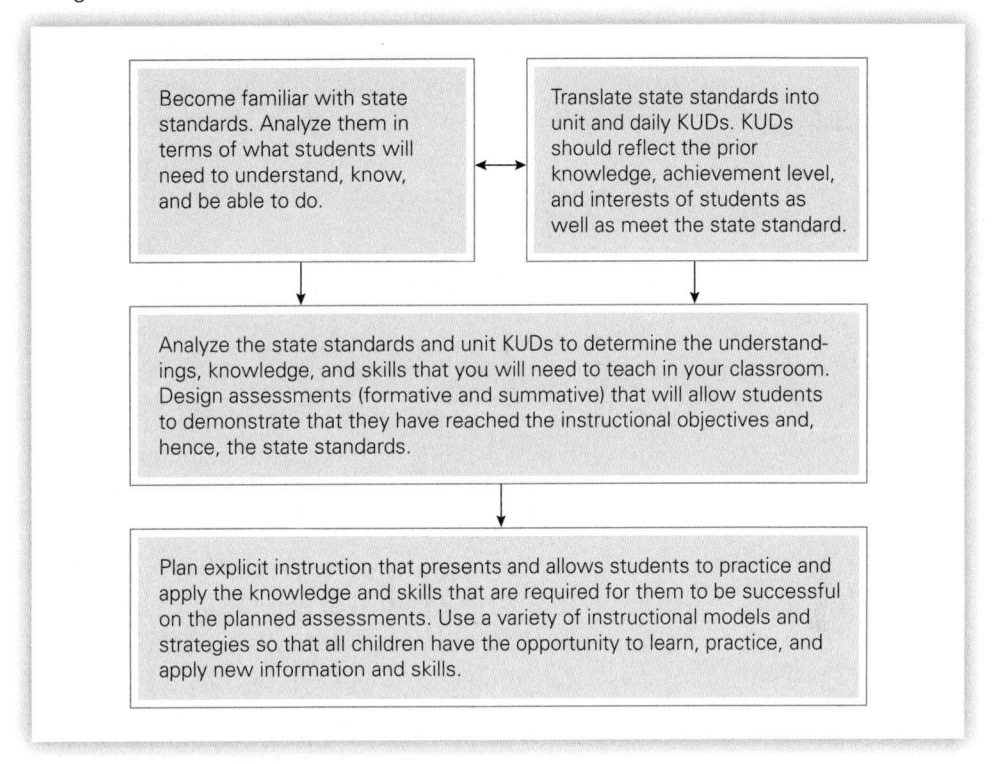

```
┌─────────────────────────────┐      ┌─────────────────────────────┐
│ Become familiar with state  │      │ Translate state standards   │
│ standards. Analyze them in  │◄────►│ into unit and daily KUDs.   │
│ terms of what students will │      │ KUDs should reflect the     │
│ need to understand, know,   │      │ prior knowledge, achievement│
│ and be able to do.          │      │ level, and interests of     │
│                             │      │ students as well as meet    │
│                             │      │ the state standard.         │
└──────────────┬──────────────┘      └──────────────┬──────────────┘
               │                                    │
               ▼                                    ▼
┌───────────────────────────────────────────────────────────────────┐
│ Analyze the state standards and unit KUDs to determine the        │
│ understandings, knowledge, and skills that you will need to teach │
│ in your classroom. Design assessments (formative and summative)   │
│ that will allow students to demonstrate that they have reached    │
│ the instructional objectives and, hence, the state standards.     │
└───────────────────────────────┬───────────────────────────────────┘
                                │
                                ▼
┌───────────────────────────────────────────────────────────────────┐
│ Plan explicit instruction that presents and allows students to    │
│ practice and apply the knowledge and skills that are required for │
│ them to be successful on the planned assessments. Use a variety   │
│ of instructional models and strategies so that all children have  │
│ the opportunity to learn, practice, and apply new information     │
│ and skills.                                                       │
└───────────────────────────────────────────────────────────────────┘
```

Formative Assessments

Assessments are designed in relation to instructional objectives that have been planned by the classroom teacher, the curriculum developer, the school district, and/or the state. Assessments can be either formative or summative. Both types of assessments should be used to support student learning. Formative assessments provide students and teachers with information about how students are progressing toward stated goals and are typically not evaluated for a grade. They allow students and teachers to think about student misconceptions or mistakes and to devise a plan for reaching the stated instructional objectives. Formative assessments use instructional objectives to provide feedback that is clear, accurate, and aimed at informing students of their progress. Boston defines formative assessment as "the diagnostic use of assessment to provide feedback to teachers and students over the course of instruction" (Boston, 2002).

The feedback that students receive on formative assessments allows the teacher and student to close the gap between the instructional objectives and the understandings and performances that the student has demonstrated. Black and colleagues (2003) have shown that formative assessment information increases achievement for all students, with the largest gains for lower-achieving students and students with learning disabilities. Formative assessments work best when teachers and students act on the information provided to adjust teaching and learning—to help students move closer to the targets. A formative assessment quiz helps students only if the items are clearly related to the instructional goals, if the feedback on student performance is clear and timely, and if both students and teachers have the opportunity to change instruction and learning opportunities in ways that help ensure future success in meeting the instructional targets. Formative assessments, because of the power they give students over their own learning, have been shown to increase student motivation and efficacy (Stiggins, 2005).

Summative Assessments

Summative assessments are designed to occur at the end of a chunk of instruction in which students have had the opportunity for formative assessment. Summative assessments provide information about student learning that is frequently translated into a grade. Formative and summative assessments must be clearly coupled. Assigning practice tasks during class that are substantially different from the upcoming summative assessment is unfair to students. All students should have the opportunity to practice and receive feedback (formative assessment) before they are tested and graded (summative assessment). This does not mean that the summative assessment and the instructional activities leading to the assessment must be identical, but the instruction preceding the assessment should be similar and contain all the important elements of the assessment. How similar will depend on the instructional objectives. If the goal is for students to recognize and identify specific bits of content, the assessment will be very familiar. If the assessment is designed to evaluate understanding, there will be some novelty in the assigned task to ensure practice in knowledge transfer.

Each of the instructional models in Part Two of this text incorporates assessment strategies and instructional objectives that are a "good fit"—they are congruent and form a coherent whole. For example, constructed response assessments (short answer, essay) work well with instructional objectives that ask students to apply, analyze, and evaluate knowledge. The cause-and-effect instructional model is congruent with these instructional objectives. Part Two will describe several instructional models in terms of objectives, procedures, assessments, and ways to personalize instruction.

Summary

This chapter has examined instructional objectives and instructional alignment. Good teaching is built on clearly articulated instructional objectives that provide a clear road to student success. Formative assessments furnish information to students and teachers during instruction while there is time to adapt and scaffold student learning. Summative assessments evaluate student learning at the end of an instructional episode, frequently for a grade. Instructional objectives and assessments determine the kinds of instructional strategies a teacher will use to help students reach learning targets.

Extensions

ACTIVITIES

1. Read the following health standard and the associated benchmarks carefully and list as many factual, conceptual, procedural, and metacognitive pieces of knowledge as you can using the matrix that follows.

    Standard: The student knows how to maintain and promote personal health.

    Benchmarks: The student

    - Understands the influence of rest, food choices, exercise, sleep, and recreation on a person's well-being
    - Knows common health problems that should be detected and treated early
    - Knows behaviors that are safe, risky, or harmful to self and others
    - Sets a personal health goal and makes progress toward its achievement
    - Knows that making health-related decisions and setting health goals sometimes requires asking for assistance
    - Knows the basic structure and functions of the human body systems (e.g., how they are interrelated; how they function to fight disease) (McRel, 2009)

    What types of knowledge are represented in the standard and benchmarks? Fill in at least two examples for each knowledge type.

Factual Knowledge	
Conceptual Knowledge	
Procedural Knowledge	
Metacognitive Knowledge	

2. Write a *student will be able to* objective for each of the provided *know* and *understand* objectives.

    Students will understand that political, economic, and religious interests contributed to the resistance of colonials to English rule.

    Students will know the significance of the first and second Continental Congresses.

    Students will know the moral and political ideas of the Great Awakening and how these ideas are associated with the American Revolution.

    Students will know the views and impact of key revolutionary individuals.

3. Read the following short case and determine whether the instructional objectives, assessment, and instructional strategies are aligned.

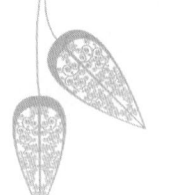

Case: Mrs. Jones teaches sixth grade world history. She has just finished a unit on ancient Mesopotamia, Egypt, and Kush based on the following instructional objectives:

- *Students will understand* that civilizations develop in a particular place to meet the physical needs of a society and that there is a strong relationship between religion and social and political order in Ancient Egypt and Mesopotamia.
- *Students will know* the geography of the early civilizations in the Near East and Africa, Hammurabi's Code, features of Egyptian art and architecture, Egyptian trade routes, and the political, commercial, and cultural ties between Kush and Egypt.
- *Students will be able to* analyze the geographic, political, economic, religious, and social structures of the early civilizations of Mesopotamia, Egypt, and Kush.

Mrs. Jones used cooperative learning, lecture, and discussion as her primary instructional strategies.

Her formative assessment was individual student conferences in which one question was asked: In which civilization would you have liked to live? Why?

Her summative assessment required students to make a diorama for each of the three civilizations.

Is Mrs. Jones's instruction aligned? Explain.

REFLECTIVE QUESTIONS

1. How would you explain the purpose of instructional objectives to someone interested in becoming a teacher?
2. What role do factual, procedural, conceptual, and metacognitive knowledge play in the construction and implementation of instructional objectives?
3. What are the difficulties in implementing formative assessments into instruction?

Summary for Part One

Planning for Instruction

In Part One, we have discussed how the needs of society and the learner are translated into educational goals, standards, and instructional objectives. Content analysis through examination of different kinds of knowledge and the order and sequence of content have been considered. In addition, lesson plan elements were described and a system for writing instructional objectives presented. These instructional objectives are designed to be congruent both with how learning happens as well as specific educational standards and assessments.

In the following chapters, we describe a series of instructional models that can be incorporated into the design process. A repertoire of instructional models allows the teacher to select the appropriate teaching strategies for each set of goals and objectives and each group of students in a particular setting. We have selected models in a variety of categories that we believe form a solid base of instructional approaches.

part 2

Matching Objectives to Instruction

A Models Approach

Remember what it was like to make something from a pattern for the first time, such as a model airplane or a cake? The task seemed difficult, if not impossible, in the beginning. You made some mistakes and needed some advice and coaching from more experienced hands. Gradually, you acquired the skills and techniques necessary for making many model airplanes and cakes even without following a pattern. In fact, you could even design models or special recipes of your own that others could follow.

Instructional models, like recipes or blueprints, present very specific and detailed steps necessary for a desired outcome. The selection of a particular instructional model also depends on a desired outcome. The chosen instructional methods should be congruent with what students are expected to learn as a result of the instruction.

When planning to make a chocolate cake, it is necessary to select a recipe for a chocolate cake, not lasagna or a burrito. A blueprint for a birdhouse will not produce a model airplane. Likewise, a model of teaching designed to bring about the recall of facts will not produce creative thinking or problem-solving skills. A model for teaching generalizations is not effective in teaching the skills necessary for learning to drive a car. *An instructional model is a step-by-step procedure that leads to specific learning outcomes.* The best models are based on what we know about students and how people learn; they have been used extensively and found to be effective in achieving specific instructional objectives. Effective instructional models do the following:

- They reflect research about how people learn.
- They are congruent with objectives and planned assessments.
- They allow students to become active participants in the learning process.

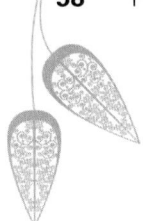

- They take students through specific, sequential steps.
- They are adaptable for all grade levels and a wide diversity of students.
- They provide the opportunity to develop critical thinking skills as well as learning concepts and skills.

Instructional models can be gathered from a variety of sources, including classrooms, educational research laboratories, and training institutions, as well as from the techniques and ideas of those professionals in many disciplines who work to educate and train others.

Why Models of Teaching?

The models-of-teaching approach emphasizes the need for variety in the classroom, which can only be accomplished by developing the teacher's repertoire of instructional approaches to meet a range of objectives. Today's classrooms are increasingly culturally diverse, and instructional models can help teachers meet the needs of many different students. These children and adolescents also come to school with a variety of learning orientations. Some students learn better in a highly structured environment; others need a more open setting with many choices. Some learn best through inductive thinking; others favor a deductive approach. Some students learn better by themselves; some work better in groups.

If a teacher creates a single environment in the classroom or repeatedly uses the same instructional approach, only those students who learn well in that environment or with that type of instruction will succeed. The teacher who appropriately uses a variety of instructional models and strategies is more likely to reach all students in the classroom; moreover, students will be able to expand a preferred mode of learning by being encouraged to learn in a variety of ways.

There is no one correct manner in which to instruct all the students all the time. Even special populations such as those learners with severe learning challenges can benefit from a variety of approaches. No group or stratum of society needs to be relegated to one approach for all school learning, although it may be reasonable to use certain approaches more than others.

In Part One, we discussed the design of aligned instruction and identified the types of objectives that should be represented in an instructional plan. Some objectives focus on broad understandings and generalizations, some on content knowledge, and some on facts and skills. It is only logical that instruction to bring about this variety of learning in the classroom needs to be varied.

A careful instructional design takes into account the age and interests of the learners, the knowledge that they bring with them to instruction, and the conditions under which instruction will occur. Additionally, the design must be grounded in the content standards and the knowledge we have about the classroom environments that promote learning.

Contents of Part Two

In Part Two, we present instructional models, selected from an array of sources, that provide a solid repertoire for the beginning teacher. We provide a research basis for each model, describe the steps, and discuss instructional situations in which the model might be used. The discussion of each model opens with two classroom scenarios, one in an elementary classroom and the other in a middle or secondary school classroom. Thus, before the model is described and its steps detailed, you will see what it looks like via a brief glance at student–teacher interactions around a topic that might be taught in any school at the particular level you are looking in on. Steps of the model are detailed to make it easy to adapt the model to your teaching. At several points, you will also encounter what are called Strategy Alerts, descriptions of instructional strategies that would easily find a place nested within the model. To close each chapter, we look again at the scenarios that opened the chapter, this time looking at the lesson plans that underlay the instruction which formed the basis of the scenarios.

Our experience in promoting models of instruction reminds us how difficult it is to "own" a model. It takes many hours of teaching and reflection about the teaching to feel that we truly understand and can adapt the model in many situations and with a variety of students.

Following the steps in the instructional models is essential in the beginning, but as the teacher gains experience and confidence, the possibilities for designing new approaches and for personalizing the models are endless. When teachers have multiple instructional procedures available, they no longer have to rely on one technique to gain the interest of the class and to teach students the essential as well as the advanced content. When one process is ineffective, they can switch to others. The teacher becomes a professional problem solver and decision maker.

The models presented here meet a wide range of instructional objectives. Each can be used to teach individual objectives; when combined in an instructional design, they can meet a variety of student needs, interests, and learning styles. We live in an age of educational accountability, and these models are designed to increase student learning. The models are designed to be used with all learners; no student is excluded from the process. The models covered in this part include the following:

- *Chapter 4: The Direct Instruction Model.* Direct instruction is a highly structured model that is helpful in teaching skills and discrete bits of information that can be broken down into small, distinct segments. This model is presented first because its steps provide a basic foundation for good instruction. In fact, the presentation step of this model can contain many of the other instructional models.
- *Chapter 5: The Concept Attainment Model.* This model helps students comprehend and analyze the meaning of a particular concept. Through a series of

positive and negative examples of the concept, students define the concept and determine its essential attributes. The concept attainment model is particularly effective in meeting objectives related to comprehension, comparison, discrimination, and recall.

- *Chapter 6: The Concept Development Model.* Originated by Hilda Taba, the concept development model teaches students to group data based on perceived similarities and differences and then to form categories and labels for the data, effectively producing a conceptual system. In the process, students learn to think about the conceptual relationships they are manipulating, the ideas that these concepts represent, and their own thinking. This model helps students understand how concepts originate and is effective with objectives related to contrasting, applying, categorizing, and analyzing data.

- *Chapter 7: Problem-Centered Inquiry Models.* In the inquiry model, learners take a puzzling situation and follow a scientific process that leads to the generation of a hypothesis. The emphasis here is on the need for careful, logical procedures in problem solving, on understanding the tentative nature of knowledge, and on the need for group endeavor in solving problems. Learners are encouraged to seek more than one answer to a question. The inquiry model is effective in meeting objectives related to problem solving, analysis, hypothesizing, and evaluation. Group process, cooperation, and communication are also emphasized.

- *Chapter 8: The Synectics Model.* The three versions of the synectics model presented here use group interaction to stimulate creative thought through metaphorical analogies. Creative thinking and expression become group activities in which each individual can participate. Through the model, students are able to use analogies and metaphors to extend ideas. The synectics model is particularly effective for those objectives related to exploration, comparison, identification, insight, and analogy.

- *Chapter 9: The Cause-and-Effect Model.* This model leads students through an investigation of a significant action, situation, condition, or conflict. Through inference, students hypothesize about causes and effects, consider prior causes and subsequent effects, and generalize about human behavior in similar situations. The cause-and-effect model is particularly effective for those objectives related to analysis, generating hypotheses, and making generalizations.

- *Chapter 10: The Socratic Seminar Model.* The Socratic seminar model guides the planning and selection of questions to be used in Socratic seminars. Both students and teachers are able to critically examine a text using sophisticated questions and supporting information. This model helps the teacher direct the process of classroom interactions for effective discussions. The Socratic seminar model is particularly effective for those objectives related to analysis, evaluation, and synthesis.

- *Chapter 11: The Vocabulary Acquisition Model.* The vocabulary model was developed for this text by one of the authors, Tom Estes, a recognized expert in the teaching of reading and vocabulary acquisition. This model presents the exciting possibility of teaching vocabulary through the history of language and word derivation rather than through the memorization of lists.

- *Chapter 12: The Integrative Model.* This model helps students and teachers make generalizations from organized bodies of knowledge in all curriculum areas. Together students observe, describe, explain, generalize, and hypothesize from data sets. (Each of these behaviors is related to specific objectives.) Many types of data can be used in this model—maps, matrices, charts, graphs, and photographs, for example.

- *Chapter 13: Cooperative Learning Models.* Cooperative learning models describe ways in which the teacher can encourage students to work with and help other students in the classroom. These models are effective for creating a positive environment in the classroom and for meeting cognitive objectives. These models are useful in all content areas and with students of different ages and varying achievement.

These models are appropriate for any age, with all achievement levels, and with any subject matter. It is up to the teacher to apply the appropriate objectives for the age and interests of the learner. We have used these models with learners from kindergarten to postgraduate, with students with special needs, with classes for the gifted, and with teachers and school administrators. The more we use these models for instruction, the more we are convinced of their effectiveness.

Chapter Format

Each of the chapters in Part Two has the same format and includes

- Chapter objectives
- Elementary and middle/secondary grades scenarios of teachers using the model
- The empirical and theoretical basis for the model
- The steps of the model
- Strategy Alerts describing specific instructional strategies that can be used with the model
- Evaluating learning using the model
- Meeting individual needs using the model
- Benefits of the model
- Extension activities and reflective questions
- Summary of the chapter
- Elementary and middle/secondary grade lesson plans aligned with the scenarios that open the chapter

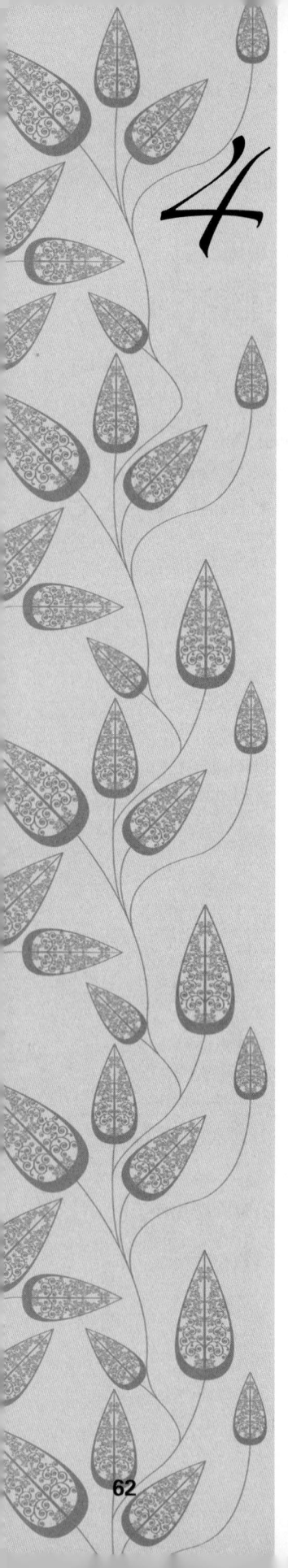

4 The Direct Instruction Model

Teaching Skills, Facts, and Knowledge

chapter OBJECTIVES

You Will Understand
- The direct instruction model provides an effective and efficient framework for instruction

You Will Know
- What the direct instruction model looks like in both elementary and secondary classrooms
- The basis in research and theory for using direct instruction in the classroom
- The steps of the direct instruction model
- How to use the guided practice step of direct instruction as a formative evaluation tool
- How to adapt the direct instruction model to meet individual needs

You Will Be Able To
- Identify the direct instruction model in K–12 classrooms
- Design, implement, and reflect on a direct instruction lesson

In the **ELEMENTARY** *classroom*

Ms. Davis is using nursery rhymes to help her kindergarten students identify and generate rhyming words. She begins the lesson by reading some of the rhymes from a Mother Goose book.

Ms. Davis: Why do you like me to read Mother Goose to you?

Anika: They are funny.

Micah: I like the sound.

Ms. Davis: What do you like about the sound?

Sophia: It has rhyming words.

Ms. Davis points out the rhyming words in several of the Mother Goose rhymes. Students enthusiastically point out rhyming words.

Ms. Davis: Today we are going to look at and hear rhymes and point out the rhyming words. We are also going to try to think of rhyming words. Let's begin by looking at this poster.

She directs the students' attention to a big poster with the nursery rhyme "Tom, Tom, the Piper's Son" written on it. Ms. Davis reads the poem, pointing to each word.

Anika: What is a piper?

Ms. Davis: Does anyone know what a piper is?

Macy: I think it's someone who plays a pipe.

Ms. Davis also defines the word *beat* and tells students that rhyming words are words that ends with the same sounds, giving them some examples (*cow* and *wow*, *hat* and *rat*, *ham* and *ram*, *man* and *pan*). Some of the students share rhyming words. Ms. Davis reads "Tom, Tom" again and asks students to raise their hands when they hear two rhyming words. She puts colored circles around the words that rhyme.

Ms. Davis: You've done a good job of identifying rhyming words. Are these words rhyming words? *Son* and *eat*? *Stole* and *piper*? *Crying* and *street*?

The students know that the words are not rhyming words because they do not sound alike. Together the class makes a list of rhyming words in Tom, Tom. For guided practice, Ms. Davis reads a poster of the nursery rhyme "Little Miss Muffet." She defines the unfamiliar words and asks individual students to come up to the poster and show her the rhyming words. Ms. Davis circles the rhyming words in matching colors.

Ms. Davis: Here are some rhyming words that we found today. Let's see if we can add to the list. What other words can you think of that rhyme with *beat* and *eat*?

Daniel: Heat.

Ava: Seat.

Anika: Meat.

Ms. Davis provides students with more rhyming words and asks students to explain why they rhyme. After several rounds, she takes out a felt bag that is labeled "Rhyming Words." Inside are small cards with a variety of words. Students are given the opportunity to pull out a card and say a rhyming word. Each student has a chance to play the game while the rest of the class gives a thumbs up when the word rhymes or a thumbs down when it doesn't.

Ms. Davis: You each have a big sheet of paper. On the paper, you will draw a picture of three things that rhyme with the word *hat*. Ms. Smith and I will come around to help you write the correct rhyming word under each picture. When you finish, you can draw three pictures of words that do not rhyme with the word *hat*.

On the **SECONDARY** *classroom*

The eighth graders were just settling into their fourth period English class. Mr. Bennett, their teacher, began the lesson by discussing some of the nature poems that they had read earlier in the school year.

Mr. Bennett: Is anyone familiar with the term *haiku*?

Emma: Hey guys, do you remember, we wrote haikus in sixth grade with Ms. Figgins?

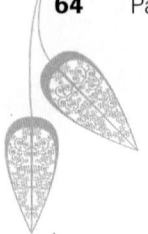

Chris: I remember. They're short.

Mr. Bennett: Yes, they are short. Let me show you some examples of haiku and you might remember the specific rules for writing them. Today's big idea is that poetic forms vary. We are going to look at one form of poetry—haiku. By the end of class you will be able to compare haiku with other poetry, learn the rules for writing haiku, and compose your own haiku. That's a lot to cover in a one class period, but I believe each one of you will walk out of class with a perfect haiku!

Mr. Bennett proceeds to share several examples of haiku with the class. He projects the poems and reads them orally. Through discussion, he helps students recognize that haiku are (1) very short—only three lines; (2) descriptive—usually about nature; (3) personal; and (4) are divided into two parts. In addition, Mr. Bennett points out the 5 syllable–7 syllable–5 syllable pattern.

Mr. Bennett: Now we will work in our base groups. The recorder for each group will be the person whose birthday is closest to today. Raise your hand when you know you are a recorder. I am giving each group a sheet with four poems that are about nature. Choose which of the poems are haiku and write a short explanation of why you have classified it as a haiku poem. You have five minutes to complete the sheet.

Five minutes pass, and Mr. Bennett has group five report out. He then asks if the other groups agree or disagree with their findings and asks students to put the list of rules for constructing a haiku in their English notebook. The class continues.

Mr. Bennett: You can see that haiku use descriptive language about something that is important to the poet. Let's brainstorm some ideas for a haiku. First, we can think about something that happens during a particular season and then come up with a list of words to describe the event. Let's think about winter. What might happen in the winter and what words would describe this best? We'll keep track of our word bank on the chalkboard. What might happen in the winter?

Barbara: A blizzard.

Eileen: When I think of a blizzard, I think of white.

Mr. Bennett: What other descriptive words remind you of a winter blizzard?

Sandi: Icy, snow piles, snowballs!

Etan: Cold, cozy, still.

Mr. Bennett: Cozy?

Etan: Cozy in my house with a fire in the fireplace!

Paul: Frozen and quiet.

After several more students share their ideas, Mr. Bennett follows the same format for spring, summer, and then fall. With four lists on the board, students are asked to vote on a season on which to focus for their first class haiku. After the vote, the whole class writes a haiku about a blizzard in winter. Mr. Bennett then asks the base groups to choose a different season on which to focus and to write a haiku about something that you can see or do during that season. Mr. Bennett circulates to each group providing feedback based on the rules for constructing a haiku.

> **Mr. Bennett:** Your groups have done a good job of writing haiku. Now, I would like you to write your own haiku. You can choose to write about any season or any other aspect of nature. Try to use at least one of the words on the board. Once you have written your haiku, share it with your partner and, using the rules we have discussed and that are in your notebook, critique each other's haiku.

Basis for the Direct Instruction Model

The theoretical and research foundation of the direct instruction model is varied. Behavioral psychology, social learning theory, and cognitive learning theory all contribute to an understanding of the model. Behavioral psychology contributes the principles of conditioning behavior: (1) clear targets; (2) diagnostic testing to see how much of the target behavior the learner already possesses; (3) realistic goals; (4) the task broken into small, interrelated segments that are introduced a single step at a time; (5) use of positive reinforcement principles; (6) good records to ensure a reasonable reinforcement schedule.

Social learning theory purports that people learn by observing others and that learning may or may not result in a change of observable behavior. In contrast to behavioral psychologists, social learning theorists posit that reinforcement and punishment have indirect effects on learning. Teacher modeling is an essential component of the direct instruction model, and students are encouraged to attend to the teacher's behavior. Students will learn the modeled behavior when they pay attention to the model, remember the behavior, replicate the behavior, and demonstrate what they have learned—all aspects of the direct instruction model.

Cognitive learning theory also contributes to the research base of the direct instruction model. As students construct their own knowledge from previous experiences, direct instruction carefully relates new knowledge and skills to the background knowledge students bring to the classroom. The model also allows students to develop proficiency by providing specific, timely feedback—a necessary requirement for students to accurately construct new capacities. There is ample evidence that this model is associated with increased student achievement (Rosenshine, 1986).

Steps in the Direct Instructional Model

The six steps of the direct instruction model identified by Barak Rosenshine are described in detail in this section.

Step 1: Review Previously Learned Material

In direct instruction, the students must clearly understand what they are expected to learn, the steps they will follow in that learning, and how the new learning connects to what has been learned previously. Read how the following teachers conduct a review:

1. Mrs. Benito is preparing to teach a lesson on alphabetizing. She begins by reviewing with the class what they learned the day before: "Yesterday we grouped words according to their first letters. On the table are the word stacks we made, each beginning with the same letter. Today we are going to order these stacks by the second letter's place in the alphabet, starting with the A stack. First, let us review the names of the first letters in each of the stacks we made yesterday."

2. In the gym, Mr. Terry instructs his swimming class: "Let's talk about what we did last week. How did you feel when you were in the water? Last week you learned how to float. First, get in the water and practice floating for about five minutes, so I can see if everyone remembers that skill. Then you will learn how to move your hands to propel yourself in the water."

3. In math class, Miss Tomlin says, "Yesterday we learned about using X to represent an unknown. Sara, will you please put the first homework problem on the board; Jesse, will you put up the second; and, Frank, will you please put up the third? Let's all look at these problems and determine their accuracy. I will ask you to explain why the problems are or are not correct. When we are sure that we understand how to use the unknown X, which you practiced for homework, we will learn how to use the X in an equation."

Each of these teachers is practicing an essential technique of the direct instruction model as described by Rosenshine: Begin with a short review of previous learning that is necessary for the new learning. Homework assigned for the previous lesson should be checked before proceeding. It is important to put problems on the board or examine the material learned the day before through questioning or testing before proceeding to a new skill level. If necessary, the previous lesson should be retaught before going on, particularly when the new skill is dependent on mastery of the preceding one.

Pretesting the class to determine skill levels is essential before teaching a new skill. Analyzing students' abilities to learn the skill helps the teacher determine the pace at which to proceed and allows the teacher to prepare for individual differences in the class. In earlier chapters, formative and summative assessments were discussed. Good instruction also demands diagnostic assessment—determining where students are in relation to the goals of the lesson or unit. Diagnostic assessments can be informal, as in the case of discussions, recitations, or individual interviews, or formal, as when a teacher utilizes a paper-and-pencil pretest.

Step 2: State Objectives for the Lesson

Lesson objectives should be stated clearly and written on the board in language the students can understand. We visited one second grade classroom during a writing lesson and saw this objective written on the board: *The students will practice holding the pencil in the proper position to form the letters for cursive writing.*

Do you see the problem here? The language is not appropriate for the age of the students or even for the instructional objective, that is, practice in forming cursive letters. The objective describes an activity—practice—that the students will do, not what students will be able to do at the end of an instructional period. The more appropriate objective would be: *Students will be able to form standard cursive letters.* The purpose of stating objectives is to tell the learners clearly and simply what the purpose of the instruction is and what outcomes they should expect. Lesson objectives should be connected to previous learning and within the reach of all the students.

[Handwritten note: Objectives need to be age appropriate]

Strategy Alert
Advance Organizers

An advance organizer can link prior knowledge and lesson objectives to propel students into learning new information and skills. Ausubel (1960) argues that teachers can promote student learning by making explicit connections between what they know and what they will be learning. Generally, the teacher prepares a brief talk before the lesson begins; graphic organizers or outlines can also be used. The key is to make explicit connections between old and new knowledge that will help the learner transfer and apply what is known to what will be learned. This is called "connecting the new to the known." Advance organizers are not summaries; they are constructed at a high level of generality. For example, the concept of independence could serve as an organizer for a lesson on the Revolutionary War, nutrition for a lesson on the basic food groups, and punctuation for a lesson on the comma. Teachers must do more than explain the meaning of something. Good teaching compares things by connecting new learning to previously learned material or to experiences that are familiar to students via analogy and comparison. For instance, a lesson on the Industrial Revolution could begin with a discussion of the transformation from manual to mechanical production, a transformation that continues to the present day.

In constructing advance organizers, keep the following in mind:

1. Review the lesson objectives and present the objectives in student-friendly language to the class.
2. Organize the content. Present general information first with specific examples and more detail later.
3. Remind students of the bigger picture—where the information or procedures fit in an organized body of knowledge.
4. You might include a variety of viewpoints or a critical approach to the subject matter.
5. Clarify important points by rephrasing previous information as you add new information.

Step 3: Present New Material

Teachers must prepare to present new material to students. It is not sufficient to know the content or the procedure; you must also be able to teach it. Many subject experts are unable to convey their expertise to others. They have become so familiar with the content that they do not remember what it feels like to be a novice learner in their area or the kinds of support that a novice learner might need. In fact, teachers need a variety of knowledge to be successful in classrooms. Pedagogical content knowledge is made up of the specialized skills that are required to teach effectively the specialized content and procedures of a discipline. Along with content knowledge and pedagogical content knowledge, teachers also must know general principles and methods of instruction and classroom management that are essential for pupil learning. Instructional models are an example of general pedagogical knowledge. They can be used across any content area and age level. So, both pedagogical content knowledge and general pedagogical knowledge must be tapped as teachers prepare to present new material.

Good presentations

- Are clear and detailed
- Include instructions and explanations
- Are punctuated with questions and corrective feedback
- Focus learners on the material
- Allow for the systematic evaluation of student understanding

To develop successful presentations, the classroom teacher should combine effective verbal techniques with media, questions, demonstrations, and student participation. The information that is presented should be interesting, highly structured, well organized, and limited in scope. The content to be learned must be selected and then analyzed according to the learners' needs. Presenting material that is too difficult or presenting too much material at one time hinders learning and defeats the purpose of the presentation. Presenting a few significant points accompanied by many illustrations and questions is generally more effective than covering many points. When introducing a new skill, the procedures should be broken into small segments that can be introduced in a sequence.

New information and skills can be presented to students in many ways. Each of the instructional models discussed in the second part of this text may be used to present new material to students. The presentation step of direct instruction can be either inductive or deductive, a lecture or group work, or a demonstration. An inductive lesson begins with many examples of a generalization and a principle, and by induction, students are guided to the principle. Most of the instructional models in this text are inductive. Common deductive forms of presenting new information and skills are lectures and demonstrations.

Lecture Presentations

Lectures are often an essential part of classroom instruction and one way in which new material is delivered to students. Lectures can be inserted into step 3 of the direct instruction model.

Steps in the Lecture Presentation Model

1. *Identify the main points to be covered.* After the material for the lesson has been carefully organized, the main points to be covered in a lecture should be selected. Most adults can listen to a lecture for only about 20 minutes without becoming inattentive. Children have an even shorter attention span. Many speakers adhere to a rule of no more than five and no fewer than three points to be covered in a single lecture. For younger children, three points may be too many. Depending on the amount of material to be covered in the lesson and the background knowledge of the learner, several lectures over a period of days may be desirable.

2. *Select an advance organizer.* After the content of the lesson has been carefully diagrammed and the main points to be covered identified, an advance organizer should be selected. Keep in mind the importance of selecting an idea that is more general than the new material and that can provide the learner with a context within which to relate the new learning. For instance, a lecture on baking a cake might begin with an advance organizer tracing the development of cakes from simple patties prepared by native tribes to the complex confections available in bakeries.

3. *Use examples to illustrate each point.* Examples serve as memory hooks for the listener. Many speakers do not use visual aids; they rely on stories and anecdotes to illustrate the main points. The same technique is effective in the classroom in helping the students remember the main points. Anecdotes, such as the following, remain in memory and assist in the recall of the points made in the lecture:

> When I was a child, we made ice cream on Sundays in a freezer with a hand crank.
>
> During the war, many things were rationed. You needed stamps to buy gasoline.
>
> When the apple bopped Newton, he got more than a lump on the brow.

In the classroom, the teacher can also use many audio or visual materials to illustrate the points made in the lecture.

4. *Use repetition to reinforce the main points.* Repeat all the points made previously when each new point is introduced. And ask questions when appropriate to determine the level of interest and understanding.

5. *Summarize the points and refer to the organizer.* At the end of the lecture, summarize the main points and conclude with a reference to the organizer. This helps to wrap up the presentation for the students.

Demonstrations

If the lesson is to include a demonstration, the teacher prepares the material to be learned in small segments and checks for understanding at the end of each segment. One of the most difficult tasks of the expert is to anticipate the learning steps of the beginner, particularly one who may not have the same aptitude or enthusiasm for the skill that the teacher has.

Visual and real examples work particularly well in the presentation stage of direct instruction. Too often, teachers depend on telling when showing, through either pictures or live demonstration, can be more effective and can provide learners with a memory hook for new information. Imagine a lesson on baking a cake without a demonstration phase; yet many teachers forget that one picture (activity, experiment, or demonstration) can be worth a thousand words.

In summary, the steps of using a demonstration to present information are as follows:

1. Analyze the content to be presented according to the needs of the learners.
2. Chart the content from the most general to the most specific material to be presented.
3. Break all skills into small segments to be presented in a logical order.
4. Develop an advance organizer for the lesson that will provide a reference point for the new material.
5. Select the main points or steps to be presented and limit these to a reasonable number, depending on the learners.
6. Select examples to illustrate each main point and connect each point or step to the one preceding and to the advance organizer.
7. Ask questions to check for understanding and watch for signals from the class that indicate lack of attention.
8. Summarize the main points and connect them to the next phase of the lesson.

Step 4: Guide Practice, Assess Performance, and Provide Corrective Feedback

Practice, both guided and independent, is an essential part of direct instruction. New material is presented in small steps, with ample opportunity for practice following each step of the process. In the following examples, the teacher controls the process and monitors the practice of both the group and individuals within the group.

- To tie our shoes we start with holding a lace in each hand. Now take the lace on the model shoe in front of you and hold a lace in each hand. Good. The next step is to cross the lace in the right hand over the one in the left hand [be sure to plan for children who are left-handed]. Let us all practice putting the right lace over the left lace like this. Tommy, hold up your right hand.

Good. Now cross the lace in that hand over the one in your left hand, like this. Very good.
- To operate a computer, we must first turn it on. Please locate the on/off button and push it to the *on* position.
- We have just seen a presentation on the four chambers of the heart. Let us review each of these four chambers as we fill in this diagram on the board together. Who can name one of the chambers?

Using Questions in Guided Practice

Teacher questions are an important part of guided practice. These questions should be prepared ahead of time. Teachers frequently err in feeling that the class will become bored if too many questions are asked during instruction; in learning new material, repetition and review are essential. Guided practice questions are diagnostic; they are used to see where students are in relation to the lesson's objectives. When direct instruction is used to teach basic skills, questions should ask students to recall specific information and demonstrate comprehension of the lesson's objectives. These questions are typically convergent, requiring a short one- or two-word answer. Wait time, the time a teacher allows for a student to answer a question, is also an essential component of the process. A wait of approximately three seconds seems to produce the best results, along with following up with students who do not respond (Slavin, 2000). To monitor participation during guided practice, the teacher can maintain a checklist of students responding to questions. If the same students answer most of the questions, the teacher should evaluate the questions asked and determine if the rest of the class is comprehending the material.

Effective teachers set up situations in which those who need further explanation or help can get it. They ask students to repeat the directions or the information. They ask students to summarize for each other and share those summaries. They call on students for additional examples and applications of information.

Rosenshine (1986) identifies four types of student responses to guided practice questions:

1. *Correct, quick, and firm.* The teacher's response to this type of answer is to ask a new question to keep the pace of the lesson moving, avoiding overemphasis on success.
2. *Correct but hesitant.* This type of response usually occurs during the initial stages of learning, and the teacher should provide some encouragement, such as saying, "That's good because you . . ."
3. *Incorrect but careless.* Simply correct and move on. The student knows the process but made a careless mistake.
4. *Incorrect and lacking knowledge of facts or process.* The teacher may provide hints, ask a simpler question, or reteach.

Using Feedback in Guided Practice

For efficient and effective learning, students must have correct and adequate information about their performance. The feedback must be clear and be related to detailed objectives or targets. Feedback is value neutral and tells students what happened, the result of their actions, and information about distance between their performance and the target goal. Good instruction allows students to self-assess by providing detailed feedback. Guided practice allows both teachers and students to see how close they are to the lesson's objectives.

If the students have not learned the material, don't blame them and don't go on. A swimming coach does not allow students to drown if they are in the deep end of the pool and cannot tread water. He or she goes back to a more basic step. The same approach is needed in learning any skill or new content. If students do not meet the instructional objectives, the teacher should evaluate and analyze the original presentation, determine the problem, and then find a way to reach the entire class. The success rate for the learning of directly taught skills should be as close to 100% as possible. Students who understand the first presentation will benefit from any reteaching, particularly if the later presentation is different from the first. Better yet is to have early learners help others by putting their understandings into their own words for others to follow. The guided practice step allows for reteaching.

Providing feedback during guided practice is an important teacher behavior. We know that achievement is enhanced by asking students to work until accuracy is achieved. To achieve success, feedback must be timely, specific to the task, and detailed. A student teacher using the direct instruction model for the first time might hear the following feedback:

- "Your presentation included an analogy that helped students make sense of the new material."
- "You did not provide feedback to students during guided practice."
- "The presentation did not have any audio or visual displays and continued for most of the period. There was little time for your students to practice the skill in either guided or independent practice."

Step 5: Assign Independent Practice, Assess Performance, and Provide Corrective Feedback

Independent practice requires careful monitoring of students practicing a new skill on their own or in small groups. Before students are assigned independent work, however, sufficient time must be spent in guided practice to ensure that they are prepared to work on their own. Observations during guided practice will indicate when students are ready to move to independent practice.

The teacher should circulate during independent practice, checking that no student is repeating a mistake or is actually practicing error. In addition, there should be some way for students to check their results as they proceed independently. Sometimes, the answers in the back of the textbook are an excellent resource. Some teachers provide checkpoints, or stations, in the classroom where students can go periodically to check their work.

Independent practice provides students the opportunity to process and rehearse the new information or skills that were presented in the earlier steps of the direct instruction model. The goal of this step is to help students "own" the new information or skill by moving from the guided practice phase—where slow and deliberate effort results in only a few errors—to automaticity when they are able to work quickly and respond automatically without having to think through each step of the process. Think about learning a new computer program or application for your cell phone. At first we are somewhat tentative as we learn the new procedures, but eventually our use becomes automatic and we spend more time thinking about why we are using the tool rather than how we are using the tool. Effective independent practice occurs when students are making only a few errors in the guided practice phase and before they get to the automaticity stage.

Types of Independent Practice

Most independent practice results in a product such as a worksheet or a set of end-of-chapter questions. Of course, teachers use many other ways for students to practice new information and skills that students find more engaging. They may embed the practice into a meaningful context, motivating students to complete the work. Possible independent practice products include

- Creating and solving problems or situations
- Designing a game, poster, or demonstration
- Writing a poem, story, book, or brochure
- Doing a role play or puppet show
- Drawing a map, picture, cartoon, or diagram

These products can be assigned as classroom independent seatwork, in learning centers, or as homework. In all cases, the task objectives must be congruent with those rehearsed in guided practice. The evaluation of independent practice

Strategy Alert

Scaffolding

The direct instruction model is designed to scaffold student learning by breaking knowledge and skills into small steps, modeling, and practice. By following the steps of the model, you are scaffolding student learning. In scaffolding, the teacher models what students are to learn just as in the direct instruction approach. The goal of scaffolding, as in direct instruction, is for students to gradually assume the responsibility of demonstrating the target behavior. This is accomplished through guided and independent practice. (See Figure 3.4 on p. 42.) ∎

products in the direct instruction model is discussed in the Evaluating Learning in the Direct Instruction Model section later in this chapter.

Step 6: Review Periodically, Offering Corrective Feedback If Necessary

Periodic review of the material should be built into every instructional plan. Overlearning is essential to mastering a new skill, particularly when each skill is necessary to learning the next. While students are in the process of learning a new skill, review of skills learned previously is essential for automaticity.

Homework should be checked as part of the review before proceeding. If homework is worth assigning, it is worth checking, yet many teachers neglect this important part of the review process. If the students have not understood the assignment, do not go on to the next step. Reteach the material and analyze the reasons for failure to learn.

If a weekly review indicates that a skill has not been retained, then reteaching is necessary. Students often forget skills and information during the summer, so it is particularly important to test for retention at the beginning of a new school year or semester.

Teachers should demand a high success rate for their students. If students are not learning, there must be a reason. Answers to the following questions can help teachers understand any lack of success.

- Did the students have the required background to learn the new set of skills or material?
- Were the steps in the learning process broken into sufficiently small steps?
- Was each step learned before a new step was introduced?
- Were the learning objectives and the directions stated clearly?
- Was the content organized logically, and were the examples, lectures, and demonstrations effective?
- Were sufficient questions asked to determine if the class understood what was being taught?
- Was there enough guided practice? Were all the students involved in the practice, and were errors corrected quickly?
- Was there independent practice of the skill or learning? Was this independent practice checked carefully to determine if the students were performing without error?
- Were there periodic review and opportunities for practice of the new learning?

Summary of Steps in the Direct Instruction Model

1. *Review previously learned material.* Make certain that students have mastered the material taught previously and that they understand the connections to the new learning.

> Go to the Assignments and Activities section of Topic 8: Explicit Instruction in the MyEducationLab for your course and complete the activity entitled "Using Explicit Instruction Elements."

2. *State objectives for the lesson.* The objectives should be presented to the students at the beginning of the lesson in student-friendly language.
3. *Present new material.* New material should be well organized and presented in an interesting manner. Frequent checks should be used to determine if the students are comprehending the information.
4. *Guide practice, assess performance, and provide corrective feedback.* Guide the students through practice sessions, making certain they are performing correctly.
5. *Assign independent practice, assess performance, and provide corrective feedback.* Continue to supervise the students as they work independently, checking for error. Homework should be assigned for independent practice only when the teacher feels certain that the students can perform the work correctly.
6. *Review periodically with corrective feedback if necessary.* Homework is checked before new instruction is given, and reteaching is conducted if necessary. The teacher conducts periodic checks to make certain that the new learning has been retained.

Evaluating Learning in the Direct Instruction Model

The purpose of the direct instruction model is to teach knowledge and skills that are readily definable, easily illustrated, and reliably improved with practice. Evaluating student learning occurs throughout the model in each one of the steps. For example, guided practice can serve as a formative assessment because it provides students and teachers with information about prior knowledge and skill acquisition. Formative assessments collect information to inform instructional decisions and student behavior. Teachers can use checklists or notes during guided practice to document the problems and accomplishments students exhibit so that, if necessary, reteaching can occur, ensuring that independent practice will produce automaticity. Guided practice tasks must be designed to provide meaningful clues to student knowledge and understanding and should be as identical to the task in the presentation step as possible. Students should be able to practice what they have seen modeled.

Assessment Alignment

Independent practice can also provide data about student learning. If paper-and-pencil tasks (worksheets, question responses, graphic organizers, problem sets, etc.) have been used throughout the lesson, they can also be used for the independent practice step. Assessment tasks must be congruent with the objectives and the instruction of the lesson. Instructional models offer an aligned blueprint, but the tasks that are used within the steps of the model must have internal alignment. This becomes particularly important if grades are being assigned to independent practice products. The replication of tasks can be less similar in independent practice than that in guided practice as you prepare students to transfer the skills to unfamiliar settings. But all assessments, especially graded assessments, must contain only the elements students had have the opportunity to practice during previous instruction.

Rubrics

Independent practice products can be evaluated using rubrics, which are guides for assessing student learning. They make scoring criteria clear and focus feedback for students, peers, and teachers. Good rubrics specify the characteristics of an outstanding assignment. These characteristics are developed by analyzing the assigned task, the purpose of the task, and the evaluation criteria embedded in the task. Differentiating among excellent, good, adequate, and poor examples of an assignment allows for the articulation of criteria. Independent practice product rubrics should be task specific. Although there are many examples of rubrics on the Internet, be sure that you are capturing the essential elements of quality for the direct instruction (or other model) lesson that you have taught. An example of a rubric for a haiku writing assignment is shown in Figure 4.1. This rubric would be helpful to Mr. Bennett as he evaluates the student work described in the scenario at the beginning of this chapter.

Figure 4.1 A Rubric for Evaluating Haiku

	Excellent	Satisfactory	Poor
Focus	Clear focus on nature; words support focus in an original way	Clear focus on nature; words used are commonly associated with topic	Focus on nature doesn't exist or is not clear
Voice	Strong personal voice; appeals to reader	Clear personal voice; only somewhat engaging	Personal voice is not apparent to reader
Word choice	Vivid words leave picture in reader's mind	Words used that communicate clearly, but lack variety	Limited vocabulary that does not capture reader
Structure	5 syllable–7 syllable–5 syllable format followed; no spelling errors	5 syllable–7 syllable–5 syllable format followed; a few spelling errors	Format incorrectly applied; includes some spelling errors

Meeting Individual Needs in Direct Instruction

By using a variety of instructional models and strategies, teachers differentiate instruction. Differentiation strategies are responsive to individuals and groups of students; using a variety of processes is one way of differentiating instruction. All instructional models provide opportunities for differentiation. It is not possible to describe all of these opportunities in this text. However, there are strategies that are a "good fit" for specific models. In the case of the direct instruction model, there are two important differentiation techniques that are closely tied to the purpose, basis, and processes of the model—flexible grouping and varying questions.

Flexible Grouping

All differentiation opportunities are based on clear objectives and an understanding of student background knowledge and achievements in relation to these targets. Both of these requirements (clear objectives and acknowledgment of students' prior knowledge) are met by the structure of the direct instruction model.

Practice is also a critical attribute of direct instruction. Flexible grouping allows students to practice new knowledge and skills with a group of peers of similar interests, skills, or background knowledge or with a mixed-achievement group so that peers can share insights and skills. Students learn in a social context, and groups need to be fluid to provide many opportunities to learn. The key here is flexibility—groups should never be stagnant during guided practice; they shift to meet the needs of individual students. Although much direct instruction is done with the whole class, continued guided practice can be completed in groups. It is important, however, that before group work is implemented, clear guidelines are taught and practiced.

Varying Questions

Variations in questions can be used as a differentiation technique within all of the steps of direct instruction. In fact, varying or adjusting questions is an important strategy within all of the models presented in this text. Questions can be adjusted based on learner readiness, experiences, interests, and preferred approaches to learning. By knowing where your students are in relation to your goals and their individual learning profiles, you can target questions to specific learners during the review, presentation, and guided practice steps of the direct instruction model. There are many ways to categorize questions. One way is to use the "revised taxonomy" discussed in Chapter 3 to vary the cognitive demand on your students. For those students with a low readiness level in relation to your specific objectives, you can focus your questioning on "remember" and "understand" levels. "Apply" questions can be used with learners who have demonstrated some foundational skill in the content with which you are working; for those students with high readiness levels you can focus on the "analyze," "evaluate," and "create" categories. Student background knowledge can also be used. For example, during a lesson on Gothic architecture the teacher might ask a student who has traveled in Europe and is interested in architecture a question about the gargoyles she saw. Other students may be asked questions about how they might decorate a building and why. The purpose of varying questions is to help individual learners make connections with the content and develop the understandings, knowledge, and skills of the lesson. All students are held accountable for learning the lesson's objectives, but their road to the objectives through teacher questioning may vary.

Benefits of the Direct Instruction Model

The direct instruction model has been clearly related to student achievement (Rosenshine, 1986) and provides the opportunity for students to learn clearly defined skills and knowledge. The model is a generative model that can be used as a frame or template for a number of instructional models, strategies, and approaches. Once the teacher has provided the lesson objectives and reviewed the necessary background knowledge, the next step is the presentation of content or skills. This step can be carried out with an inductive approach (examples are presented first, and then students inductively derive the broad principle or rule from the examples) or a deductive approach (teacher provides the broad principle or rule, and then students deduce examples that illustrate the principle or rule). The presentation phase could also use one of the instructional models found in this text. How the material is presented is not a critical attribute of the direct instruction model. What is critical in this model and what is essential in all good teaching are the links to background knowledge, the small chunks of information, and guided and independent practice, all with corrective feedback. These should be part of every instructional approach. The direct instruction model is inherently aligned—another important characteristic for instructional models. The goals of the model allow lesson objectives to be clearly articulated and all steps of the model are geared toward helping students be successful at demonstrating lesson objectives.

Elementary Grades Lesson

DIRECT INSTRUCTION: Rhyming with Mother Goose

OBJECTIVES

Students Will Understand
- We can hear rhymes when people talk, sing, or recite

Students Will Know
- Rhymes are heard when two or more words have similar ending sounds
- How to identify rhyming words in a Mother Goose rhyme (by listening for similar sounds)

Students Will Be Able To
- Identify rhyming and nonrhyming words in a Mother Goose rhyme
- Generate a rhyming word when given a spoken word

ASSESSMENTS
- *Diagnostic.* Ask students to define a rhyme. Ask students if a set of words rhyme or not.
- *Formative.* During guided and independent practice, students identify and generate rhyming words.

PROCEDURES
1. *Review previously learned material.* Show students the Mother Goose book that you have read before. Talk to the students about why we like Mother Goose rhymes. Highlight rhyming words and how they sound.
2. *State objectives of the lesson.* Tell the children that we frequently see and hear rhymes and that today we will identify rhyming words.
3. *Present new material.*

   Tom, Tom, the piper's son,
   Stole a pig, and away he run,
   The pig was eat,
   And Tom was beat,
   And Tom ran crying down the street

   Read "Tom, Tom the Piper's Son" from the prepared poster. Point to each word as you read. Define the words *piper* and *beat*. Read the poem again with one of the students tracking the words. Explain that rhyming words are words that end with the same sound and give examples—*cow* and *wow*, *hat* and *rat*, *ham* and *ram*, *man* and *pan*. Read "Tom, Tom" slowly and ask students to raise their hands when they hear two rhyming words. Then ask volunteers to identify the rhyming words in the text. Circle the rhyming words on the poster in the same color. Ask students if the following words are rhymes: *son* and *eat*, *stole* and *piper*, *crying* and *street*. Ask how we can tell that they are not rhyming words. Make a list on the board of rhyming and nonrhyming words in "Tom, Tom."
4. *Guided practice.* Show poster of "Little Miss Muffet." Define unfamiliar words. Ask students to circle the rhyming words in the same color. Provide corrective feedback. Continue with additional Mother Goose rhymes, if necessary.

   Little Miss Muffet sat on a tuffet
   Eating her curds and whey.
   There came a big spider,
   He sat down beside her.
   And frightened Miss Muffet away.

5. *Presentation II.* Give students two rhyming words and ask them to provide a different rhyming word. Begin with the rhymes identified in "Tom, Tom" and "Little Miss Muffet."

6. *Guided practice.* Have students reach into the rhyming word bag (a bag filled with index cards on which simple rhyming words are written) and pull out a word. The teacher reads the word and asks students to provide a rhyming word.
7. *Independent practice.* Students are asked to list three words that rhyme with a given word and three words that do not rhyme.

Middle/Secondary Grades Lesson

DIRECT INSTRUCTION: Writing Haiku

OBJECTIVES

Students Will Understand

- Poetic forms vary and serve different purposes

Students Will Know

- Haiku is a simple and sophisticated poetic form that sharpens language, observation, and expression
- The defining characteristics of haiku (very short, descriptive, personal, and divided into two parts)
- The rules for constructing haiku:
  - 5–7–5 form
  - Two parts; break after 1st or 2nd line
  - Clue to season in one word *(kigo)*
  - Snapshot of everyday experience in nature or human life

Students Will Be Able To

- Use the list of rules and conventions of haiku to distinguish between haiku and other forms of poetry
- Develop a list of words that might be used in writing a haiku
- Compose a haiku poem based on personal experience

ASSESSMENT

Students may choose to do one of the following:

- Submit their haiku to the school literary magazine
- Make a poster with haiku and illustrations
- Create their own haiku anthology
- Teach haiku writing to other classes or groups of students

PROCEDURES

1. Review previously learned material related to the study of haiku. Ask students what they know about haiku.
2. State lesson objectives.

3. Provide examples of haiku. Include both classic and contemporary examples. Have students read each poem aloud and ask students to comment on the similarities they see among the poems. Through this discussion, help students recognize that haiku are very short, descriptive, personal, and divided into two parts.
4. Based on reported similarities, provide an outline of the main rules for writing haiku.
5. Have students distinguish among several short poems dealing with nature by choosing the haiku and defending their choice by using the list of rules.
6. Have students brainstorm a glossary of words they might use, based on the rules and conventions of this form of poetry. Then, for each season, have students choose an occurrence that might be the subject of a haiku and brainstorm descriptive language that would help a reader visualize that scene. List their suggestions on the chalkboard and use the list to have students generate ideas for a haiku, encouraging them to see the range of possibilities beyond a description of nature. Write two or three haiku with the class. This may be done as a whole group or small-group activity.
7. Have students write a haiku based on a personal experience, using at least one of the words they have brainstormed in class. Pair students to edit and suggest improvements to one another's work.
8. For independent practice, students may choose one of the assessment options.

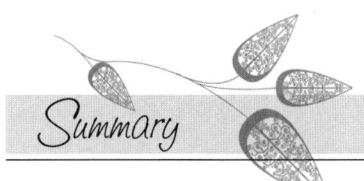

Summary

Go to the Building Teaching Skills and Dispositions section of Topic 8: Explicit Instruction in the MyEducationLab for your course and complete the activity entitled "Providing Useful Feedback."

It is important to repeat a statement made in the beginning of this chapter: The direct instruction model is a necessary, but not a sufficient, instructional tool. To be without this effective tool is a handicap because the steps in this model provide a framework for instructional design, but to use this model exclusively is deadening.

In a general sense, the other models presented in this text can be incorporated into the presentation of material phase of the direct instruction model. More specifically, this model can also be used to teach many knowledge-level objectives and skills.

The direct instruction model begins with a review of previously learned material, often in the form of an advance organizer. After connections to what is known are made explicit, the teacher presents clear objectives for the lesson. Presentations of new material may come in many forms and employ a variety of materials. Once the teacher has modeled the new information or skills, students practice while receiving corrective feedback. Ideally, once students can demonstrate that the task can be completed with only a few errors, independent practice can be assigned to develop automaticity. Feedback and periodic review ensures that students have reached and continue to maintain the lesson's objectives.

Extensions

ACTIVITIES

1. Interview a teacher about the types of instructional models that are used in his or her classroom and the reasons why instructional models are or are not helpful.
2. Design a direct instruction lesson for a foundational skill in a content area you are or will be teaching. Be sure to include KUD objectives, all of the steps of the lesson, and a formative assessment.
3. Prepare a one-page handout summarizing the direct instruction model.

REFLECTIVE QUESTIONS

1. Learning centers can be used for independent practice in the direct instruction model. What questions do you have about setting up learning centers in a classroom? How will you find the answers?
2. Rubrics are helpful to both teachers and students. What are the problems with using rubrics? How can teachers overcome these problems?
3. What knowledge or skills do you or will you be teaching that could be used successfully in a direct instruction lesson? Why do you believe this knowledge or skill is congruent with the direct instruction model?

5

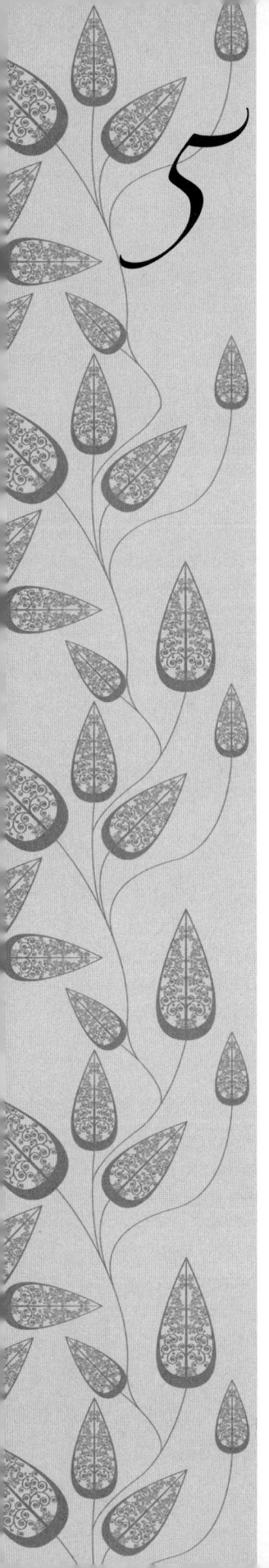

The Concept Attainment Model

Defining Concepts Inductively

chapter OBJECTIVES

You Will Understand
- Instruction can facilitate the attainment of a variety of important concepts

You Will Know
- How we learn concepts
- The definition of a concept
- What the concept attainment model looks like in both elementary and secondary classrooms
- The basis in research and theory for using concept attainment in the classroom
- The steps of the concept attainment model
- Variations of the concept attainment model

You Will Be Able To
- Design, implement, and reflect on a concept attainment lesson

In the **ELEMENTARY** *classroom*

During a unit on animal adaptations, Ms. Sarembock teaches the concept of hibernation. She wants her students to understand that hibernation is an animal behavior in which the animal appears to be sleeping while its bodily functions are dormant. At the beginning of class, Ms. Sarembock reminds her students of the rules of the concept attainment "game" that they have played before.

"Class, now that we have reviewed the way you will raise your hand and work together to solve the concept attainment mystery, let me tell you that our mystery has something to do with animal behaviors. Here are pictures of our first two examples." Ms. Sarembock shows pictures of a groundhog and a gopher and puts the pictures on the board under "Examples." "Is anyone ready to hypothesize as to what animal behavior the gopher and the groundhog have in common?"

The children begin to share ideas and the teacher writes each on the board under the "Hypotheses" column.

They hunt for food.
They stand watch.
They burrow.

83

They make tunnels.
They live underground.
They use their teeth.

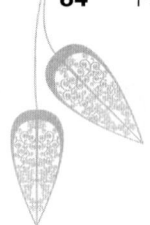

Ms. Sarembock tells the children that they have a good list. She reminds them what to do with the list as she shows them a nonexample of the animal behavior they are looking for. "Look at the picture of the animal that does not have behavior we are looking for." She shows them a picture of a dog and puts the picture on the board under "Nonexamples."

"What are the things that a dog has in common with our examples? Because the dog is not an example, whatever they have in common is not our mystery behavior." The discussion that follows results in a new hypothesis list as Ms. Sarembock crosses out the behaviors that don't fit. Only one behavior is left.

They make burrows.

After several more rounds of examples (frogs, garter snakes, bears, fish, salamanders, insects, and bats) and nonexamples (house cat, parrot, rats, kangaroos, camels, elephants), the class has this hypothesis list.

~~They hunt for food.~~
~~They stand watch.~~
~~They burrow.~~
~~They make tunnels.~~
~~They live underground.~~
~~They use their teeth to kill their enemies.~~
~~They have feet to run with.~~
~~They have fur.~~
We don't see them in the cold weather.

Ms. Sarembock asks the students to hypothesize what animal behavior occurs that would mean that we would not see the animals in the winter and, with the help of her class, defines the word *hibernate*. She then presents the students with some test examples, discusses the process with the students, and asks them to write a paragraph about why animals hibernate.

On the SECONDARY classroom

Mrs. Gonzales is teaching the concept of metaphor to her eighth grade class. She explains that they are going to learn the meaning of a new concept, and that the name of the concept will be a mystery until they have identified what makes the concept different from other ideas or concepts. She adds, "We will find the concept by looking at examples and contrasting nonexamples. The examples will have all of the essential parts of the concept; they will represent the essence of the concept. I will show you some negative examples, that may contain some of, but not all, the essential qualities of this concept. You will solve the mystery by comparing the examples and identifying the criterial elements of the positive examples." She puts three columns on the board—"Examples," "Nonexamples," and "Hypotheses."

The first example is put on the board under "Examples": "The moon is a silver ship sailing in the night sky." The students come up with the following hypotheses, which Mrs. Gonzales writes in the appropriate column on the board.

Descriptions of ships
Sentence
Poetry
Quotation
Comparison of different things

Mrs. Gonzales provides another example: "Superman—the Man of Steel." She asks students to review their list of hypotheses and asks them to remove any that do not fit with this new example. The students are able to eliminate (with explanations) all but the *comparison* entry.

With student input, the hypothesis list looks like this:

~~Descriptions of ships~~
~~Sentence~~
~~Poetry~~
~~Quotation~~
Comparison of different things

Next, the students are provided a negative example: "He had a heart like a lion."

Mrs. Gonzales: What about this example is different from the others?

Kanye: Not much, there is still a comparison of different things, but the word *like* is there.

Mrs. Gonzales: Would you like a positive or a negative example?

Class: A negative example.

The teacher writes "frightened as a mouse" under the appropriate column.

Kanye: It's still a comparison, but instead of *like* the word *as* is there.

Chad: Can we see another positive example?

The teacher writes "a recipe for disaster."

Ben (yelling from the back of the room): All of the examples are comparisons that don't use *like* or *as*.

Mrs. Gonzales: Here is a sentence. Tell me if it is an example or nonexample. "The father was a tower of strength."

Helen: That is an example because it is a comparison without using *like* or *as*.

Mrs. Gonzales: Is there anything you can add about the things that are compared?

Helen: Well, they are very different—comparing ships to moons and people and steel.

Mrs. Gonzales: Here is another example. "The ship plows the sea." What is being compared here?

Yolanda: The ship is being compared to a plow that is used in the ground at a farm.

Savanna: The ship is the plow in the example.

Mrs. Gonzales: Are you ready to label and state the definition of this concept?

Rebecca: I don't know the name, but the definition is a comparison of things that are different.

Tommy: A comparison of things that doesn't use *like* or *as*.

Ben: One object in the comparison actually becomes another, like the ship plowing the ocean. The ship becomes a plow.

Brian: How about putting together some of what you are saying—a comparison that joins two different things to make a new image or idea without using *like* or *as*?

Mrs. Gonzales: That is an excellent definition. We call this a metaphor. How did you figure out what the main attributes of a metaphor are?

Rebecca: By comparing what was similar in the different examples and what was different between the examples and nonexamples.

Mrs. Gonzales: Here is a selection of figurative language examples. Identify the metaphors.

Basis for the Concept Attainment Model

The concept attainment model is based on the research of Jerome Bruner, Jacqueline Goodnow, and George Austin, which was reported in the landmark work *A Study of Thinking* (1986). Bruner and associates were concerned primarily with the process through which individuals categorize data and attain concepts. Educators have been particularly interested in the use of this research in teaching concepts to learners. According to Bruner and his associates, categorizing reduces the world's complexity, allowing us to label the objects of the world. Because we establish categories or concepts based on defining characteristics, there is reduced demand for constant learning. Knowing the broad category *dog*, for example, helps us to identify a wide variety of dogs. We do not have to relearn the essential qualities of dogs each time we see one.

The common features that define a concept may be concrete or abstract. It is easier to learn tangible concepts that have only a few criterial characteristics than it is to learn a more abstract concept that has numerous fuzzy essential attributes. So it is easier to learn the concepts *maps* or *bicycles* than it is to understand the idea concepts of *freedom, justice,* or *honesty*. All concepts have (1) a name and definition, (2) examples of items that are included in the concept class, and (3) critical attributes that define the concept. We teach concepts to ease the cognitive pressure of learning too many discrete bits of information or facts.

Teaching concepts is congruent with the ways in which we process new information (see Chapter 2). Concepts help us to develop patterns and schemas to make sense of the world. Concepts are both a summary of what we already know and an organizing device to help us make sense of the new information with which we are bombarded.

Chapter 5 • The Concept Attainment Model 87

Concepts are different from facts and generalizations. Facts are discrete bits of information that typically are an outcome of observation and have no predictive value without other facts. Knowing that Hurricane Katrina hit the Gulf Coast on August 29, 2005, doesn't predict when or if another devastating hurricane will hit the area in the next few years. "Hurricanes frequently hit the Gulf Coast" is a generalization. Generalizations are statements that show a relationship between two or more concepts. In our example, the concepts are *hurricanes* and *Gulf Coast*.

To summarize, concepts are the ideas or abstractions that are formed as a result of categorizing data from a number of observations. To make sense of all the various stimuli in the world, learners of all ages form concepts and give them names. Imagine the cognitive overload if every single thing in the world were seen as a separate and unrelated entity. To form concepts, learners pay attention to likenesses rather than differences and place similar objects in the same category. Apples come in many sizes, shapes, and colors, but by attending to their similarities and ignoring their differences, we form an initial concept of *apple*.

Many concepts used in the classroom are abstract and have many interpretations; they frequently are used, however, as though every student shared the same definition. Consider the concept *democracy*. If you asked a class of university students to write their own definition of the term, you would get many different answers. Yet we often expect that learners in elementary school have a shared definition of conceptions like democracy in their vocabulary.

Teaching students to understand the meaning of the concepts taught in the classroom is one of the most important challenges of teaching. Concepts have names as well as definitions that contain essential attributes that place them in a particular category. For instance, for the concept *table*, one definition is "a piece of furniture consisting of a smooth, flat slab fixed on legs." The essential attributes of *table* are (1) piece of furniture; (2) smooth, flat slab; and (3) fixed on legs. The students are more apt to understand the meaning of the concept and be able to recognize the essential attributes if they arrive at a definition through numerous examples instead of through memorizing the concept name and definition.

In the concept attainment model, the emphasis is on the learners' determining the essential attributes of the concept that have been preselected by the teacher. The final step of this model encourages learners to explore how concepts are formed through a process of attending to similarities and ignoring differences. The model serves both to teach a meaning of a particular concept and to teach students how the thinking process occurs.

In preparing to use the concept attainment model, one must determine ahead of time the following basic elements of the concept to be learned:

1. The name of the concept
2. The concept definition or rule
3. Conceptual attributes
4. Examples of the concept
5. Relationship of the concept to other concepts (concept hierarchy)

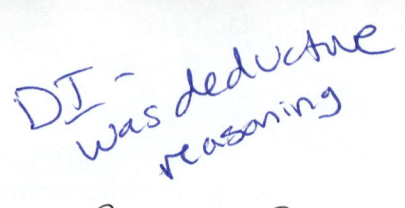

Steps in the Concept Attainment Model

Step 1: Select and Define a Concept through the Concept's Essential Characteristics

The concept attainment model is an inductive model. Using inductive reasoning, students move from observations to hypotheses to a general theory. In a deductive approach to teaching the teacher presents the broad generalizations and students move to specific examples. The direct instruction model is a deductive teaching model because it relies on deductive reasoning. The concept attainment process is most appropriate for teaching concepts that have clear criterial attributes so that students can observe what all of the concept examples have in common and think logically about a definition. For example, the parts of speech can be taught as concepts with clear attributes. The classification system in biology is very suitable for concept attainment as are the concepts of maps and types of government, triangles and other shapes in geometry, different artistic styles in fine arts, and each of the types of sentences (simple, compound, etc.). When using concept attainment choose concepts that can be defined by features that clearly distinguish them from other similar concepts.

Concept Hierarchies

The relationship between concepts is important. Figure 5.1 depicts a concept hierarchy for apples. The hierarchy helps teachers choose examples and nonexamples and helps students check their concept definition at the end of the concept attainment process. In teaching the concept *apple* students can see that the superordinate concept, the larger category, is defined as *fruit*. The age and readiness of students determines how you will relate the concepts. The concept hierarchy in Figure 5.1 works well for young children, whereas a botany class may divide fruit into true berry, pepo, hesperidium, epignous, aggregate, multiple, and accessory fruits. The simple fruit hierarchy shows the relationships between the superordinate, coordinate, and subordinate concepts. Fruit is the superordinate concept to apples; apples fit into the fruit category as do the coordinate concepts of pears and oranges. Coordinate concepts, such as pears and oranges, supply the nonexamples of a concept attainment lesson. They are fruit, but do not have the essential characteristics of an apple—they are a different kind of fruit. The types of apples—McIntosh, Gala, and Winesap—are the positive examples of the lesson. They are all apples and have all of the critical attributes that make an apple an apple. They have appleness!

Once you have identified a concept that is teachable by the concept attainment model, you need to construct a defini-

Figure 5.1 Concept Hierarchy of the Concept *Apple*

```
          Fruit
    ┌───────┼───────┐
   Pear   Apple   Orange
           │
        McIntosh
  Winesap       Gala
```

Chapter 5 • The Concept Attainment Model   89

tion that includes the superordinate concept and all of the essential features of the concept. From our knowledge of apples and through observation, we know that apples are colorful (red, green, yellow), tasty (sweet to tart), crispy, and grow on trees. The definition of an apple could be a tasty, crispy fruit that is red, green, or yellow and grows on trees. The students may define the word *apple* somewhat differently by the end of the lesson, but you will need a working definition to help you choose positive and negative examples. Rectangles may be the focus of a concept attainment lesson. Their essential defining attributes are clear—four sides, all right angles, and the opposite sides are parallel and equal. So, the definition of *rectangle* is a geometric figure (superordinate concept) that is four-sided, contains all right angles, and has opposite sides that are parallel and equal. A clear concept definition follows the form concept name, superordinate concept, and criterial attributes.

The point is not merely to find a definition that will, in turn, be given to the students. Instead, it is important that the teacher formulate the definitions to be used in the design of the concept attainment lesson and select the appropriate examples. The major purpose of the lesson is to allow students the chance to author their own definition, to create their own understanding. In any event, the outstanding function of the concept attainment model is to provide an alternative to telling learners what to understand and instead allowing them, literally, to participate in their understandings.

Step 2: Develop Positive and Negative Examples

Create as many examples of the concept as possible. Each positive example must contain *all* the essential attributes. For the rectangle, some examples can be drawn on the chalkboard, some can be made of cardboard, some can be projected with an overhead projector, and others can be cut out of construction paper; however, each example must contain all the essential attributes: four sides that meet at four right angles, each pair of sides parallel and of equal length (see Figure 5.2).

Prepare some negative examples that do not contain all the attributes. For instance, a triangle is a geometric figure, but it does not contain all the attributes of a rectangle. These negative examples will help students focus on the essential attributes.

Positive examples of apples—fruits that contain all of the essential attributes of apples—include McIntosh, Granny Smith, and Stayman. All of the positive examples come from subordinate concepts of apple. Subordinate concepts are concepts that "fill" the apple category. The negative examples come from the coordinate concepts—those concepts that

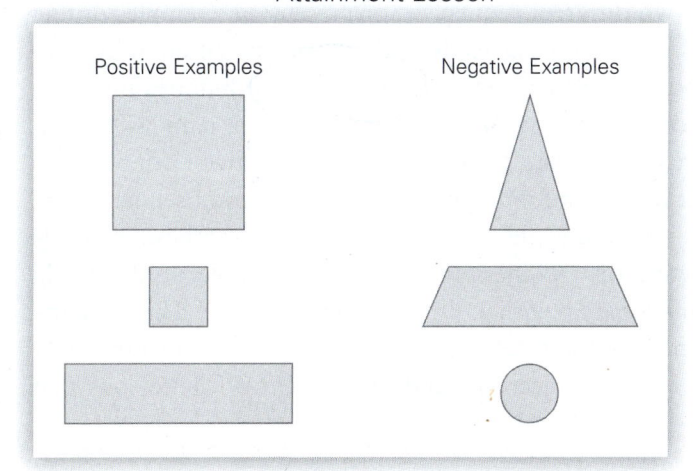

Figure 5.2 Positive and Negative Examples of Rectangles for a Concept Attainment Lesson

come from the same superordinate concept pool but do not contain all of the criterial attributes. There are many swimmers in the fruit pool, but not all of them are wearing the same bathing suit!

Step 3: Review the Concept Attainment Process with the Class

Explain carefully to the students that the goal of the activity is to define the mystery concept by finding out what all of the examples have in common that the nonexamples do not have. You may want to practice the process of identifying similarities and differences between examples and nonexamples of a concept as you describe the steps of the model. By helping students gradually construct an understanding of the concept, they will be able to define the concept in their own words.

Put three columns on the board. The first two, "Yes" and "No," are to keep track of the examples and nonexamples that you will present to the class. Even if you use pictures, realia (real-life objects), or posters for your examples, use words to describe the examples and nonexamples on these lists so that students can continue to refer to what has been presented as they are hypothesizing the concept label and characteristics. The third column, "Hypotheses," is where they will list, defend, and eliminate their suppositions. Keep a running list of all of the hypotheses that students generate. As new examples or nonexamples eliminate the categories or concept names, cross them out, rather than erase them, so that the list can be examined throughout the process and reviewed once a definition has been determined.

Step 4: Present the Examples

The way in which you sequence the examples and nonexamples during the concept attainment lesson controls the difficulty of generating an accurate hypothesis. Table 5.1 demonstrates two different sequences for presenting examples during a lesson on whole grains. Each sequence leads students toward different hypotheses. In sequence one, the teacher first presents two example (y)–nonexample (n) pairs, gently guiding students to the hypothesis that the concept name is "breakfast food." When students realize that "corn flakes" is a negative example, they will need to change their breakfast food hypothesis. In the second sequence, the teacher presents four yes examples, leading the class to a hypothesis of "side dishes." By the time "white rice" comes along as a nonexample, students will have to revisit the list and come up with a different concept name. The difficulty of the lesson is determined by the teacher and is based on the students' background knowledge, the lesson's objectives, and the content of the lessons that will follow.

Table 5.1 Whole Grain Examples

Sequence One	Sequence Two
oatmeal (y)	brown rice (y)
spaghetti (n)	quinoa (y)
muesli (y)	bulghur (y)
macaroni (n)	buckwheat (y)
popcorn (y)	white rice (n)
corn flakes (n)	noodles (n)
bulghur (y)	grits (n)
grits (n)	white bread (n)
wild rice (y)	whole wheat bread (y)

Step 5: Generate Hypotheses and Continue Example/Hypothesis Cycle

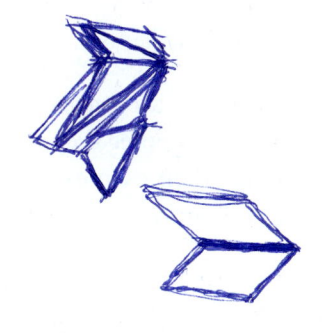

As examples and nonexamples are presented and students contrast the positive and negative examples, hypotheses will be generated. The hypotheses are categories that include all of the positive examples. Remind students that a hypothesis is a decision that is based on information. The examples and nonexamples are the information from which hypotheses are developed. And for a hypothesis to be viable, all of the positive examples must fit.

All student hypotheses should be recorded and crossed out if it is found that the evidence does not support the supposition. By crossing out the hypothesis rather than erasing it, students can return to the list to check and extend their own thinking. During this step, teachers must explicitly ask students to explain why the hypothesis is still supported given new information or examples or why it needs to be crossed out. The cycle of presenting positive and negative examples

Strategy Alert
Generating and Testing Hypotheses

As a function of listing the possible concept labels, students are generating and testing hypotheses. Student discussion is based on observing the examples and nonexamples and generating a theory or rule to explain what all of the examples have in common with each other and not with the nonexamples. Once a possible theory or hypothesis is formulated, it can be tested by reviewing the attribute list. Students must explain why or why not their hypotheses and earlier theories are viable. Generating and testing hypotheses is an important instructional strategy that has been shown to increase student learning. ■

and checking the hypothesis list may continue for several rounds depending on the specificity of student responses and the timeliness of the convergence on a hypothesis.

Step 6: Develop a Concept Label and Definition

Once a reasonable list of hypotheses has been generated, the teacher can ask the students to try to develop a label and definition of their new concept that incorporates all of the remaining hypotheses. At times, students will be able to come up with a definition and not a label. In other situations, they will be able to articulate a label or word describing a category quickly. Be patient with this part of the process; students are not accustomed to stating definitions in their own words. You may need to encourage one student to make an initial effort so that others can add to or change the definition. With experience, the class will gradually become more adept at this part of the process. A concept hierarchy can be shared with the students to aid in their definition construction and to show the relationships among the broader categories in which the concept fits. It is important to remember that the objective of a concept attainment lesson is not only that the students derive the definition. The major objective is to engage students in the process of defining and forming concepts.

Step 7: Provide Test Examples to Solidify the Definition

Once students have developed an initial definition of the concept they are learning, show them a few more positive and negative examples to test whether they can identify examples of the concept. Ask the students to provide their own examples and then to explain why their examples fit the concept definition.

Step 8: Discuss the Process with the Class

The discussion step is essential to ensure that the students understand how they reached the definition and are able to link this process to the natural process of their own thinking. Attention to likenesses and differences is essential to any type of research or analysis, in both formal and informal thinking; the more conscious a learner is of his or her own thinking process, the sharper that thinking will be. Identifying similarities and differences is associated with increased student achievement (Marzano, Pickering, & Pollock, 2001). Therefore, as you use concept attainment in teaching, have students identify the point at which they understood the essential attributes and tell which examples were the most helpful.

Summary of Steps in the Concept Attainment Model

Steps 1 and 2 are done prior to instruction.

1. *Select and define a concept through the concept's essential characteristics.* Determine if the concept is appropriate and teachable according to this

model. The definition should be clear, and the attributes should be identifiable. Determine those qualities that are essential to the concept.

2. *Develop positive and negative examples.* This is the key step, because the positive examples must contain all the essential attributes, yet they may contain some nonessential attributes that are gradually eliminated. Negative examples may have some of, but not all, the essential attributes.

3. *Review the concept attainment process with the class.* It is important to take the time to explain clearly what you will be doing and what each step will entail.

4. *Present the examples.* Think about the order in which positive and negative examples will be introduced. Keep a list of both positive and negative examples.

5. *Generate hypotheses and continue example/hypothesis cycle.* Be certain to ask why hypotheses are retained or eliminated.

6. *Develop a concept label and definition.* Focusing on the positive examples, students articulate a definition of the concept. Students may need help in producing a concept label.

7. *Provide test examples to solidify the definition.* Test examples will help you ascertain if the class understands the concept. Some of the students will arrive at the definition more quickly than others. Test examples will both provide more time to students who are still working on the concept meaning and provide reinforcement for those who know the label and definition.

8. *Discuss the process with the class.* Help students understand how they arrived at the definition. This shows students how we form concepts.

Variations on the Concept Attainment Model

The concept attainment model is flexible and can be adapted in a variety of ways and with a variety of materials, as shown by the following suggestions.

1. Present all of the positive and negative examples, labeled accordingly, to the students at one time and have them look for the essential attributes of the positive examples so that hypotheses about the concept label can be made.

2. Present all of the positive and negative examples without labeling any as positive or negative. The students group the examples into positive and negative categories and then hypothesize a concept label for those they determine to be positive.

3. Students develop positive and negative examples for a concept already studied in class. The object of the lesson would be to define the concept succinctly, to identify the essential characteristics of examples of the concept, and then choose examples and nonexamples. This can be done by individuals or groups and can be used as a formative assessment.

Figure 5.3 shows pictures given to groups with the instructions to determine the essential attributes and then to define the concept *chair*. In each of the positive examples in Figure 5.3—A, B, C, and D—all three essential attributes implied by the illustrations are present:

1. They are seats.
2. They were designed by someone.
3. They hold one person.

In the negative examples, a person could sit on E, F, and H, but those were not *designed* for seating. Example G was designed for seating, but for more than one person. Other negative examples are a bed and a low table; those were not designed for our specific purpose. A negative example from nature, such as a flat rock or a log on which a person might sit, emphasizes that chairs are intentionally designed.

Figure 5.3 Positive and Negative Examples of Chairs for a Group Concept Attainment Lesson

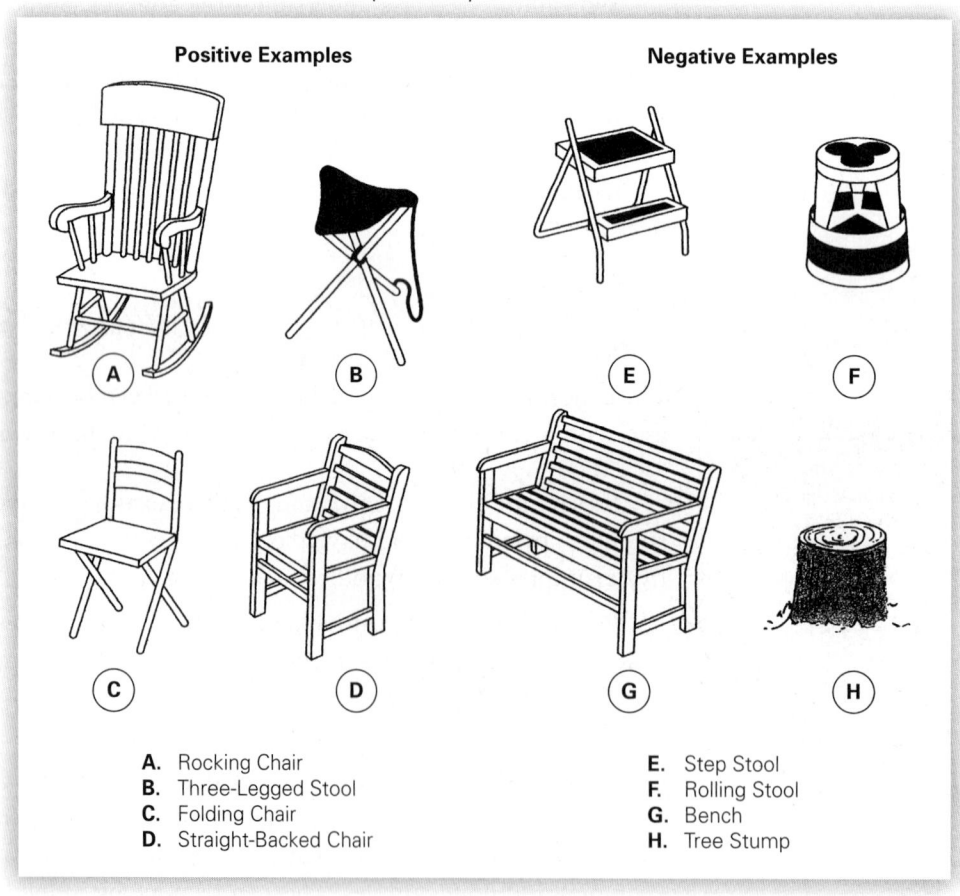

Positive Examples

A. Rocking Chair
B. Three-Legged Stool
C. Folding Chair
D. Straight-Backed Chair

Negative Examples

E. Step Stool
F. Rolling Stool
G. Bench
H. Tree Stump

When these examples have been presented to a class, students produced a variety of definitions, such as the following:

- An object that is manufactured for the purpose of providing a seat for one person
- A piece of furniture intended for the seating of one person
- A seat designed to hold one person in an upright position

All three of these definitions contain the essential attributes, even though they are stated in slightly different terms. The class may decide to vote on the definition that most clearly states the essential attributes.

Evaluating Learning in the Concept Attainment Model

Concept attainment is designed for students to learn the definition of a concept by identifying the concept's name, the larger category or superordinate concept, and the essential characteristics of the concept that make it what it is. Formative assessments can take place at several points in this process. Can students identify the concept label? Can they explain how the concept is related to "larger" concepts? Can they list the criterial attributes of the concepts—the collection of characteristics that make the concept unique? You might also challenge students to expand the definition of the concept and then provide positive and negative examples that would support the expanded definition.

Short-answer questions can ask students to supply an accurate definition or draw a concept hierarchy. Students can write short paragraphs identifying the similarities and differences between the examples and nonexamples. They can illustrate the concept on paper or in a model and label each of the critical characteristics. Once students are comfortable with the concept attainment process, they can generate examples and nonexamples of related concepts, explaining why they were chosen and in what order they would be presented.

Students can evaluate their own participation in the process after the lesson or they may complete a flow chart of their thinking during the lesson. If students are asked to track their thinking the pace of the lesson will need to be adapted. Metacognitive thinking can also be encouraged through journaling.

The concept attainment model itself can serve as a review at the beginning and end of units of instruction. The targeted concept can be something that students have been exposed to that needs additional practice or the concept attainment process can be used to link instructional units. Students can be asked to sort examples and nonexamples individually, in small groups, or as a large class. Students can identify which is the nonexample in a set of examples or identify the example in a set of nonexamples. In all cases, the student is practicing important skills. Concept attainment can be sliced, diced, and marinated in a variety of combinations to assess student learning both after a concept attainment model lesson or after a lesson using a different instructional approach.

Meeting Individual Needs in the Concept Attainment Model

All differentiation decisions must begin with knowledge about the learners' readiness, interests, and learning profiles. For the concept attainment model, differentiation opportunities occur before, during, and after the implementation of the model. As decisions are made about the concept to be used, attention should be paid to the level of complexity of the concept and the readiness level of students to both the method and the content.

Early exposures to concept attainment require experience with concrete concepts—concepts with limited attribute descriptions that use familiar vocabulary. Once students become knowledgeable about the method (after several experiences), teachers can scaffold student hypothesis generation by linking to previous concept attainment lessons. "Yes, Jamie, you are using the same observation skills that the class used when we learned the concept *rhythm*." For the students who need this scaffolding, you provide a specific reminder of how to be successful. Students can also relate the new concept to previously learned concepts through concept hierarchies and other graphic organizers. There will be students in each concept attainment lesson who will be able to intuit criterial elements of the concept readily. Others will need cues and support. Teachers can manipulate the complexity, abstraction, and accessibility of examples and non-examples to meet the individual needs of students. In some cases, students can provide their own positive and negative illustrations of the concept and develop detailed concept hierarchies to show concept relationships.

Participation rules and the role of competition in the classroom can be designed to meet student needs. Some students are more comfortable with a competitive approach to concept attainment, although the model promotes collaborative construction of concept definitions. Differentiation opportunities are abundant once the model of instruction is complete and students are applying the new conceptual knowledge they have acquired.

Learning or interest centers can be developed that allow for student choice and the activities at these centers can be tiered to help all students use their knowledge in sophisticated ways. Tiered activities are designed around common objectives—all students are expected to reach the same objectives. The activities themselves may vary in terms of complexity, amount of structure provided, pacing, number of steps, form of expression, and so on. Some teachers try to have three different ways of meeting the same objectives and allow students to choose the challenge—either a gentle walk, an uphill climb, or mountainous terrain. Readiness can also be used as a guide. One activity can be focused on supporting students struggling with a particular concept; another can be designed for students who appear to have learned the concept, but need extra reinforcement; and the last can challenge those students who have already mastered the concept. Tiered groups should be specific to a lesson and the groups should be flexible.

Benefits of the Concept Attainment Model

The concept attainment model mirrors the way that we learn concepts in the real world, allowing students to develop even greater concept analysis tools. The model is structured around two important academic skills—identifying similarities and differences and generating and testing hypotheses, both of which have been associated with increased student learning. Since hypothesis testing is not often seen outside of science classes, concept attainment gives students the opportunity to practice this skill in different settings.

In addition, the concept attainment model requires clear definitions with identified essential attributes that help students construct a personal understanding of a concept. Students are active participants in the lesson and are encouraged to develop conceptual flexibility, inductive reasoning skills, and a tolerance for ambiguity (Joyce, Weil, & Calhoun, 2009).

Elementary Grades Lesson

CONCEPT ATTAINMENT: Hibernation

OBJECTIVES

Students Will Understand
- There are cycles of change that affect all of earth's living creatures

Students Will Know
- The definition and essential characteristics of hibernation

Students Will Be Able To
- Generate and evaluate hypotheses
- Identify the essential characteristics of hibernation
- Define the concept of hibernation

ASSESSMENT

Ask students to draw a six-slide storyboard that shows a bear hibernating and explains why the bear hibernates.

PROCEDURES

1. *Select and define a concept by its essential characteristics.* Select examples of the concept that contain all essential and critical attributes and nonexamples that do not contain all of the essential attributes. The

development of a hierarchy is also helpful. Here is a possible hierarchy for this lesson:

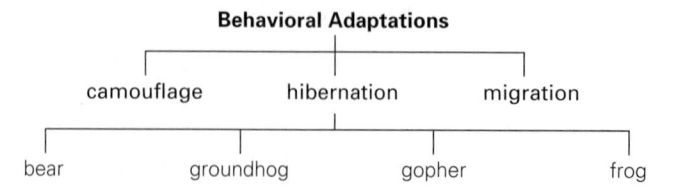

Behavioral Adaptations

```
        camouflage      hibernation      migration
           |          /     |     \         |
          bear   groundhog     gopher      frog
```

2. *Develop a list of positive and negative examples.*

Examples	**Nonexamples**
groundhogs	house cats
gophers	parrots
frogs	rats
garter snakes	kangaroos
fish	camels
salamanders	elephants
insects	monarch butterflies
bats	swallows

3. *Review the concept attainment process with the class.* Explain to students that they are going to explore an important concept by comparing some examples of the concept with some nonexamples. Students will share observations and compare the attributes in positive and negative examples while generating hypotheses about the concept label and definition.
4. *Present the positive and negative examples.* Choose an appropriate order for presenting the examples and nonexamples. This will vary for different groups of students.
5. *Generate hypotheses and continue example/hypothesis cycle.* Ask students to examine the positive examples and to ascertain the essential characteristics that are evident in all of the positive examples, but are not collectively evident in the negative examples. Students are asked to hypothesize possible categories that would include the positive examples. The whole group works together to infer hypothesis from their observations. You can provide cues for student observations. Cycle through example/hypothesis phases until students eliminate all but one hypothesis.
6. *Develop a concept label and definition.* Ask students to identify the critical characteristics of the concept (these characteristics will be part of the definition) and determine the category name and definition.
7. *Provide test examples to solidify the definition.* Ask students to classify additional examples as positive or negative or generate additional unique examples of their own. The teacher can confirm the hypothesis, name the concept, and restate the concept definition. A concept hierarchy may be shared at this point.
8. *Evaluate the process with the class.* Students are asked their thoughts during the concept attainment process. Where did you have difficulty? When did you "attain" the concept? What helped you figure out the concept label and definition? In what order would you have put the positive and negative examples?

Middle/Secondary Grades Lesson

CONCEPT ATTAINMENT: Metaphors

OBJECTIVES

Students Will Understand
- Figurative language enhances the power of texts

Students Will Know
- The definition and essential characteristics of metaphors

Students Will Be Able To
- Generate and evaluate hypotheses
- Identify the essential characteristics of metaphors
- Define the concept of metaphor

ASSESSMENT Provide students with examples of metaphors, personification, hyperbole, and similes and ask students to identify metaphors and explain why each example is a metaphor.

PROCEDURES

1. *Select and define a concept by its essential characteristics.* Select examples of the concept that contain all essential and critical attributes and nonexamples that do not contain all of the essential attributes. The development of a hierarchy is also helpful. Here is a possible hierarchy:

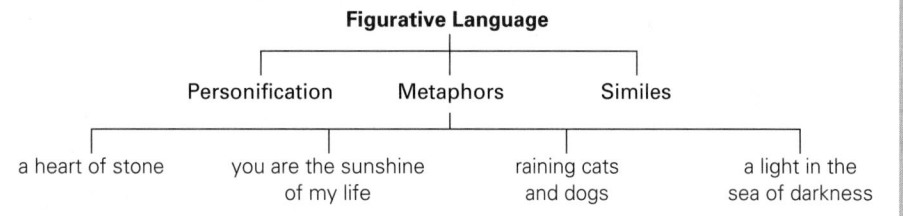

   Figurative Language

Personification	Metaphors	Similes
a heart of stone	you are the sunshine of my life	raining cats and dogs
		a light in the sea of darkness

2. *Develop a list of positive and negative examples.*

Examples	Nonexamples
The moon is a silver ship sailing in the night sky.	She is as cold as ice.
Superman—the man of steel	The stars smiled down on us.
A recipe for disaster	He had a heart like a lion.
The father was a tower of strength.	Frightened as a mouse
The ship plows the sea.	Jill is blind as a bat.
Jumping for joy	An angry wind is blowing.
It is raining cats and dogs.	Lend me your ears.
Heart of stone	His heart is as hard as stone.
A light in the sea of darkness	He's a thousand years old.

3. *Review the concept attainment process with the class.* Explain to students that they are going to explore an important concept by comparing some

examples of the concept with some nonexamples. Students will share observations and compare the attributes in positive and negative examples while generating hypotheses about the concept label and definition.

4. *Present the positive and negative examples.* Choose an appropriate order for presenting the examples and nonexamples. This will vary for different groups of students.
5. *Generate hypotheses and continue example/hypothesis cycle.* Ask students to examine the positive examples and to ascertain the essential characteristics that are evident in all of the positive examples, but are not collectively evident in the negative examples. Students are asked to hypothesize possible categories that would include the positive examples. The whole group works together to infer hypotheses from their observations. You can provide cues for student observations. Cycle through example/hypothesis phases until students eliminate all but one hypothesis.
6. *Develop a concept label and definition.* Ask students to identify the critical characteristics of the concept (these characteristics will be part of the definition) and determine the category name and definition.
7. *Provide test examples to solidify the definition.* Ask students to classify additional examples as positive or negative or generate additional unique examples of their own. The teacher can confirm the hypothesis, name concept, and restate concept definition. A concept hierarchy may be shared at this point.
8. *Evaluate the process with the class.* Students are asked their thoughts during the concept attainment process. Where did you have difficulty? When did you "attain" the concept? What helped you figure out the concept label and definition? In what order would you have put the positive and negative examples?

Summary

The concept attainment model describes the steps in teaching the meaning of a concept by presenting positive and negative examples of the concept to the class until the students can identify the essential attributes and state a concept definition. In addition, this model helps students understand the process through which concepts are defined. The teacher may present a new concept to the class or focus on one particular aspect of a familiar concept. Because the understanding of concepts is so essential to learning in the classroom, the time taken to identify and clarify these concepts is time well spent. In addition, teachers find that in preparing to teach this model they clarify their own understanding of essential concepts.

The concept attainment model is described as a series of steps.

1. Select and define an important concept.
2. Develop positive and negative examples.
3. Review the process.

4. Present positive and negative illustrations of the concept and identify essential attributes.
5. Develop hypotheses and converge on a definition through the example/hypothesis cycle.
6. Develop a concept label and definition.
7. Provide additional test examples.
8. Reflect on the process with the class.

Extensions

ACTIVITIES

1. Review a current textbook that you are or might be using in your teaching. Look for clear, understandable concept definitions that have explicit essential attributes identified. How many can you find? Is there a pattern of clear definitions? What is the pattern in the text for helping students learn concept definitions?
2. Interview a classroom teacher about the concepts they usually teach and the methods they use to convey the concepts.
3. Design a concept attainment model lesson for the students you are or plan on teaching. Keep a list of the questions you have about designing this lesson. What do you notice about these questions? What problems do you anticipate in implementing the lesson?

REFLECTIVE QUESTIONS

1. Concept attainment lessons take time and imagination to plan. Is it worth using our limited time to teach with this model? How can we maximize the time that we spend organizing a concept attainment lesson?
2. What kinds of behavior management problems will you need to plan for as you think about implementing the concept attainment model? Does the model always have to be used with the whole class? How can you adapt the model to ensure that there will be few or no behavior problems?
3. How can you use the concept attainment process to help prepare your students for standardized tests?

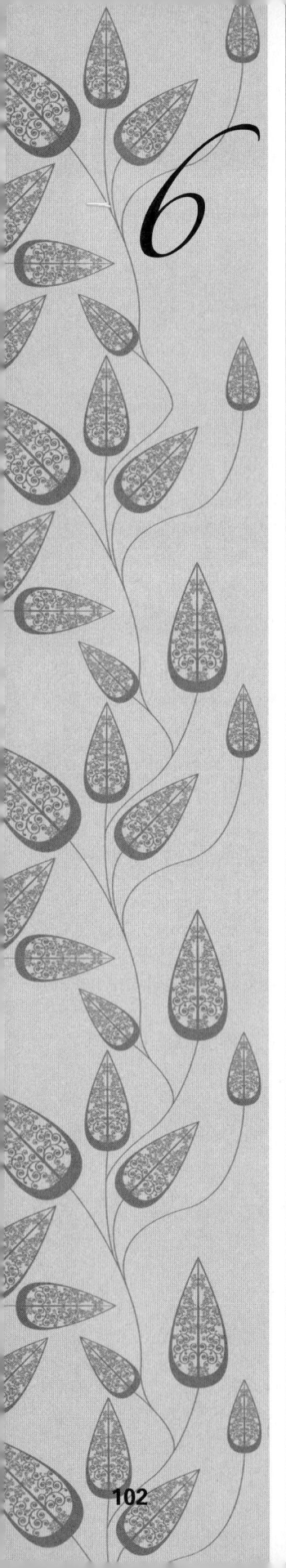

The Concept Development Model

Analyzing the Relationships between Parts of a Concept

chapter OBJECTIVES

You Will Understand
- Thinking is dependent upon the process of attaining and developing concepts

You Will Know
- The relationship between concept development and our mental processes
- The definition of concept development
- What the concept development model looks like in the K–12 classroom
- The steps of the concept development model
- Variations and extensions of using the concept development model in your classroom

You Will Be Able To
- Identify the concept development model in K–12 classrooms
- Design, implement, and reflect on a concept development lesson and on the concept development model

In the ELEMENTARY classroom

Ms. Fowler's second graders made a list of all of the items they saw on a walk around the school's courtyard. This is the list that they put together:

Coke can	basketball net	mushrooms
stones	cars	flowers
snail	school bus	doors
trading card	people	grass
candy wrappers	spider	coffee cup
worm	baseball cap	pine cones
leaves	cigarette butts	birds
plastic bag	bleachers	insects
sticks	frog	book
tennis ball	playground equipment	pencil

Ms. Fowler put each word on a card and made five sets of cards. After putting the students into five groups, she handed each group a set of cards and the lesson continued:

Ms. Fowler: We made a list of all of the things we saw on our walk. I made a card set of our list. Each group has a set of cards with all of the words. We are going to group words that have something in common. There are many ways that the words can be grouped. For example, we could put books, bleachers, birds, baseball cap, and basketball net together. Can you tell me what they have in common?

Charquea: They all begin with the letter *b*.

Ms. Fowler: Yes, they do. That is one way that we could organize the cards. In your groups, see if you can find other ways to group the words. Think of characteristics that the things have in common. Make certain that each card has a group.

The students worked together for a few minutes.

Ms. Fowler: Give each of your groups a name. You can use one of the blank cards to write down the name of the group. Put the name of the group at the top of the pile.

The students work for several more minutes.

Sarah: Ms. Fowler, my group is finished. When we did a lesson like this before, we mixed up the cards again and made a new set of groups. Should we do that?

Ms. Fowler: Yes we'll do that later. Let's let the others finish up.

The other groups finish.

Ms. Fowler: Let's make a list on the board of all of the category names that you made.

The second graders enthusiastically responded and produced the following list:

litter	things that move	useful things
dead things	outside things	things that grow
sports things	happy things	scary things

Ms. Fowler looks at the list and points out two of the categories: Things That Move and Things That Grow.

Ms. Fowler: I notice that these two categories apply to living things. Living things grow and living things can move or change.

Students are then asked if they can put groups together or put different cards into more than one group. By asking students for examples and combining both groups and different cards, the list of two category names becomes Things That Move and Things That Are Useful. Ms. Fowler continues by helping her students see that we can also divide the list into two categories and call the categories Living Things and Nonliving Things. Once the students have agreed that the two category names are acceptable, they check to make certain that each item on the original list fits into one of the categories.

The list of living and nonliving things is put on the board.

Ms. Fowler: When you look at this list, what do you notice?

Wendy: Some living things are insects and some are plants.

Rodney: The nonliving things don't grow.

Janine: Some living things are very small like a spider and some are very big like a tree.

Students continue to provide generalizations and Ms. Fowler points out the characteristics of living things as they share their ideas. Once everyone has had a chance to share, Ms. Fowler shows the class some pictures and asks them to tell her if each picture represents something that is living or nonliving.

In the **SECONDARY** *classroom*

A ninth grade class is exploring the concept *grudge* before they read a story in which a grudge is the cause of the conflict. The teacher, Mr. Hallahan, has reviewed the important ideas that the class has already covered in their characterization unit, highlighting the ways in which readers make inferences from a character's speech, actions, and responses from other characters. Today they are going to discuss how a specific feeling can communicate information about a character.

Mr. Hallahan: What sort of things does the word *grudge* bring to mind?

The class produces the following list:

hurt	binge	friends
mean	evil eye	enemies
fight	stare	stiff
cruel	hold	hard
fudge	hate	cold
yell	deep	whisper
stomach	dark	secrets
empty	not talking	argue
silent	talk behind back	faces
silly	eyes	childish
cloud	mist	embarrassed
burden	anger	feelings
cut off	people	heavy
ground	children	black
gossip	fat	misunderstandings

Mr. Hallahan: Which of these items are alike in some way? Which of these items do you think belong together? Once you have figured out which go together, think about why they go together and give the group a name. Try not to use a name to group the words; come up with a name after you have made the groups.

After several minutes, students begin to share some of their examples.

PAUL: We have a group and a name!

Feelings Caused by a Grudge

hurt	hate	hard	black
mean	empty	cold	heavy
cruel	silly	cut off	burden

SANDI: Our group had something similar. We also had the word *embarrassed* in our group.

MR. HALLAHAN: Let's have another example from your group work.

MARISA: OK, we had a category called things people do when they hold a grudge.

MR. HALLAHAN: What words did your group contain, Marisa?

MARISA: Whisper, not talking, embarrassed, secrets, fight, hold, cut off, evil eye, yell, hate, hurt, stare, argue, childish, mean, talking, talk behind back, cold, binge.

MR. HALLAHAN: What other categories did you find?

Students share other category labels and Mr. Hallahan repeatedly asks for examples of words that fit into that category. Complimenting the class on their grouping and labeling, Mr. Hallahan asks the class to go back to the original list and regroup the items.

MR. HALLAHAN: Are there other groups that could be made? Any ways that we can mix up the words and make new categories that are not listed on the board?

MARISA: I'm always confused at this part.

MR. HALLAHAN: Look at the list of categories on the board and try not to use any of them. Rely on your base group to help you and I'll come by to offer support. Are there other groups having trouble with this step? [There is no response.] Any new categories?

SANDI: We made a list of things that cause a grudge—anger, friends, gossip, enemies, fights, misunderstandings.

MARISA: We came up with one! Things associated with food: binge, people, fudge, stomach, heavy, silly, fat.

Mr. Hallahan encourages other groups to share their new categories and a few new ones are shared. The students in this class have used the concept development model before so as soon as all of the new categories are shared, they quickly move into synthesizing the activity by summarizing their discussion. Here are some of the students' statements about grudges.

MADISON: Holding a grudge is not good for you.

ARNOLD: Holding a grudge can make you do things you will be sorry for later.

> **Stu:** A grudge can grow from something little to something very destructive.
>
> **Marisa:** Fighting is just another way of acting when you feel bad because someone has hurt you. You hold a grudge. I eat. Some people fight. None of these helps to solve the problem.
>
> **Mr. Hallahan:** You have made some important observations about holding a grudge. How might a character who is holding a grudge in a story behave? What might we see the character saying or doing?

The discussion continues with examples and predictions conveyed by students. At the conclusion of the lesson, Mr. Hallahan reflects on the positive aspects of the experience.

> **Mr. Hallahan:** One benefit of using this model is the growing trust among class members as they share the contents of their "mental files." As this trust grows, their constraints about revealing thoughts and feelings diminish. These ninth grade students were more open and frank in this discussion about grudges than they had been in the past. As one student's idea triggered another student's idea, they became excited. They showed a growth in creativity that they had not exhibited before. I think that as I get more comfortable using the model, so do the students.

Basis for the Concept Development Model

The concept development model was developed by Hilda Taba (Joyce, Weil, & Calhoun, 2009). Much of Taba's work is out of print, but her ideas have had a major impact on inductive teaching strategies. She developed specific teaching moves that shift students toward inductive thought (see Table 6.1). The seminal *A Study of Thinking* by Bruner, Goodnow, and Austin (1986) is congruent with Taba's teaching ideas. In the introduction, the authors provide the reason for examining thinking at a time when behavioral psychology was the popular approach.

> We begin with what seems a paradox. The world of experience of any normal man is composed of a tremendous array of discriminably different objects, events, people, impressions. There are estimated to be more than 7 million discriminable colors alone, and in the course of a week or two we come in contact with a fair proportion of them. No two people we see have an identical appearance and even objects that we judge to be the same object over a period of time change appearance from moment to moment with alterations in light or in the position of the viewer. All of these differences we are capable of seeing, for human beings have an exquisite capacity for making distinctions. (p. 1)

The authors believed that by examining how we acquire and develop particular categories we gain insight into "one of the most elementary and general forms of cognition by which man adjusts to his environment" (p. 2). The goal of this

Table 6.1   Taba's Concept Development Sequence

Purpose of Question	Teacher Questions	Student Response
To list items	What do you see here? What did you notice when . . . ?	Makes a list of items that are observed from prompt
To find basis for grouping similar items and to show students that there are as many ways to group items as there are item characteristics	Do any of these items seem to belong together?	Finds similarities on which to base like groups
To identify common characteristics of items in a group and to form a label for the group	Why did you group these things together? What would you call these groups you have formed?	Identifies and verbalizes the common characteristics of items in a group
To flexibly group items in more than one place	Could some of these items belong in more than one group?	States a new relationship
To group and relabel items	Can we put these same items in different groups? Why would you regroup the items?	States additional relationships
To summarize information into one or two sentences	Can someone say in one sentence something about all of the groups? What did we learn?	Summarizes what they know about all of the groups

Source: Adapted from Taba, H., Durkin, M. C., Fraenkel, J. R., & McNaughton, A. H. (1971). *Teachers' handbook to elementary school social studies* (2nd ed.). Reading, MA: Addison-Wesley.

series of studies was to find out how we learn concepts and, in the end, resulted in both the concept attainment and concept development models.

The constructivist theory of learning is congruent with both concept attainment and concept development. We know that learning is an active process and students must make connections between prior knowledge and new information. A model of instruction can help students make those links more readily and with richer associations. Both concept attainment and concept development help students develop rich conceptual schemata—the organizational structure of the human mind.

Concept development goes beyond concept attainment. Simply put, the early research described in *A Study of Thinking* indicates that we attain concepts by identifying their criterial attributes. In extension, more recent theories demonstrate that ideas can also be represented by a prototype (a typical instance of a class) or an exemplar (a typical prototype) and that these are also useful in learning concepts (Klausmeier, 1990). In all cases, it is necessary to see the concepts to be taught in terms of their relation to other concepts and to possible misconceptions. Concept attainment (Chapter 5) helps students label and identify a class of things (e.g., a banana is a fruit that is long and slightly curved, has skin that goes from green to yellow, and has an edible, creamy inside). Concept development moves beyond the definition to inferences that are not observable. So you may accurately identify a banana and its criterial attributes in a concept attainment lesson. In a concept development lesson, you can then "develop" the concept of banana further by inferring other things (e.g., bananas rot quickly when the skin turns yellow, they are often used in muffins, etc.). Bruner and colleagues (1986) state that the "working definition of a concept is the network of inferences that are or may be set into play by an act of categorization." We categorize, we infer, we develop a concept. Thus, concept development is a strategy that extends and refines our knowledge by providing an opportunity to extend and refine our personal concepts—concrete or abstract. We need both concept attainment and concept development to learn and be able to transfer our knowledge of concepts.

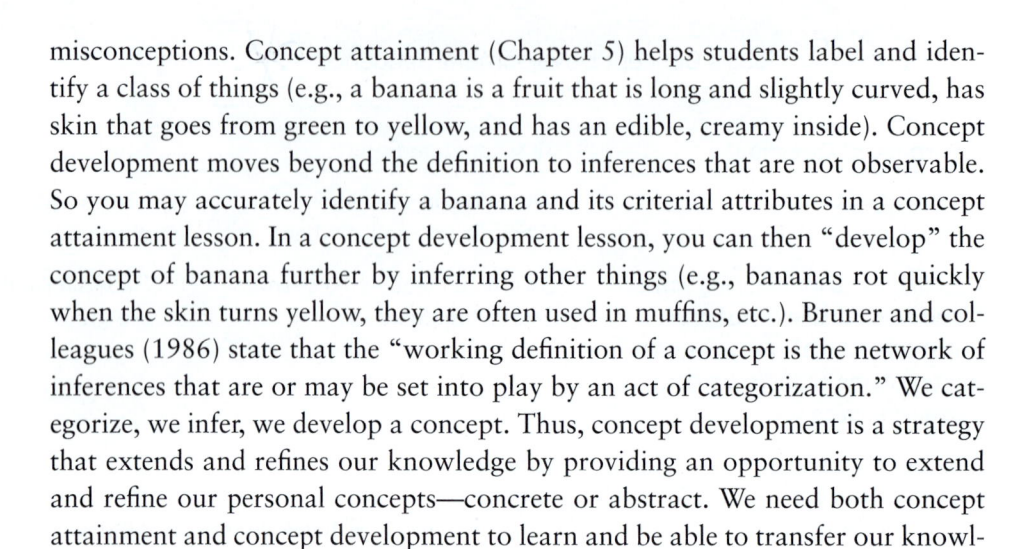

Conceptual Thinking Is Learned

A child will not approach his or her intellectual potential without guidance and practice in the process of thinking. And much possible critical thinking will never take place if a curriculum is so strongly content oriented that processes of learning and thinking are left to chance. On the other hand, we know that a strong content foundation is necessary for the application of learning skills (Willingham, 2009). In essence, we need content to teach thinking skills and we need thinking skills to use content well. To develop thinking skills is to develop an increasingly complex mental organization with which to view the world and to solve problems. Cognitive skills are seen as products of a dynamic interaction between the individual and the stimulation he or she receives.

Lev Vygotsky, founder of modern constructivist theories of developmental psychology, Bruner, and others assert that concept development and deep understanding are the essential goals of instruction. The students are learning to integrate new ideas and approaches to learning with prior views and experience, thus constructing new knowledge from within. The teacher acts as a guide and facilitator who provides the opportunity for students to link main concepts throughout the learning process.

Concepts Are Creative Ways of Structuring Reality

Concepts provide easy access as learners classify and thus simplify incoming information in a meaningful and retrievable form. Concepts make it possible for humans to process data mentally. Scientists tell us that our senses are constantly being bombarded by thousands of stimuli simultaneously. Our ability to simplify, as much as our ability to absorb complexity, allows us to act on our environment. Driving is an activity that would be impossible if we were attuned to every sign, tree, house, vehicle, or person we passed. Safety and the dictates of driving demand that we screen data and assimilate only certain relevant noises, landmarks, and conditions. Subconsciously, as we drive, we put incoming data into categories marked relevant or irrelevant.

As young children we learn to pick and choose, to assimilate only stimuli that we determine have meaning or, more accurately, to which we can assign meaning. When children come to school, the process does not change; what they can learn is what they can accommodate. Teaching is literally helping children in their natural process of learning new information and assigning meaning to that information.

Concepts Are the Building Blocks of Patterns

The process of creating conceptual frameworks is quite natural and forms the basis of our understanding of the world. Touching a hot stove leads to an understanding of heat. Hot becomes a category into which we place many things (see Figure 6.1), including the idea of caution. Experiments with falling objects (including one's own self) lead to an understanding of gravity. We impose order

Figure 6.1   Building a Concept

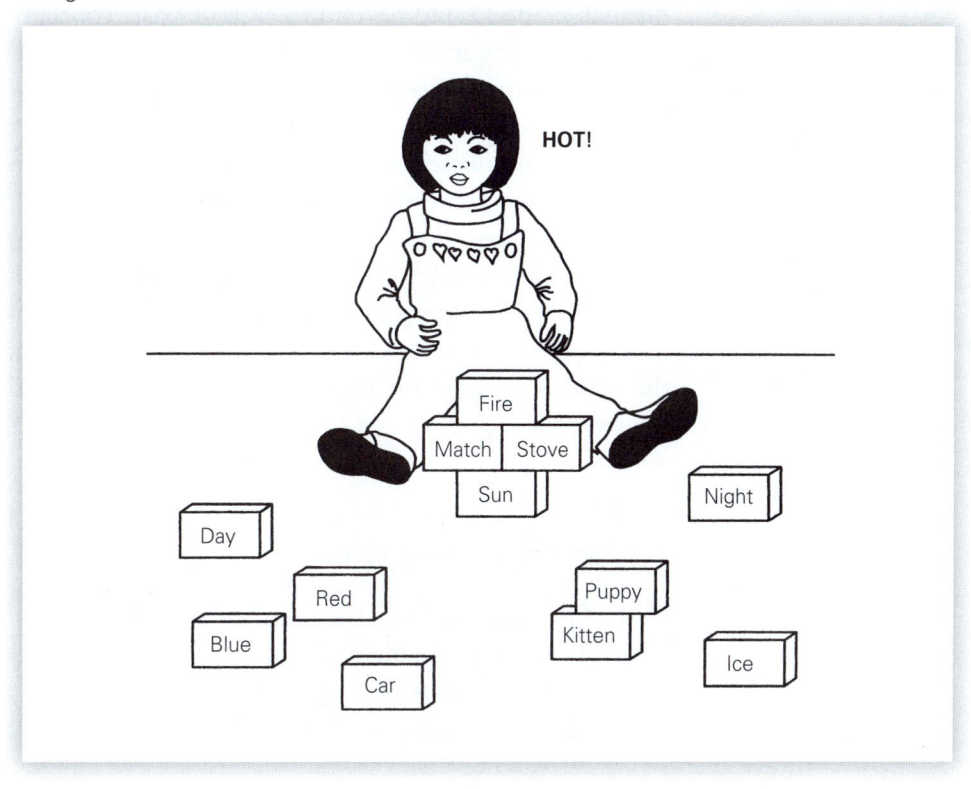

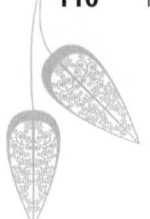

in our world by observing and creating patterns. We divide time into hours, minutes, and seconds. We divide space into miles, feet, inches, all manageable, bite-sized pieces. We attempt to predict the future by observing patterns in the present and recalling patterns from the past.

Concepts are the building blocks from which generalizations spring. By opening the contents of our personal mental files to others and by hearing about the contents of theirs, we refine and extend our understanding of concepts, and we refine and extend the precision of our generalizations about life. In the concept development model, a ministructure that mirrors how the human mind works is created. The focusing question produces data, not miscellaneous, indiscriminate data but data relevant to an idea contained in the focusing question. From the data come comparisons, contrasts, and finally a theory that makes sense of myriad data. This theory constitutes one's present view of the concept under scrutiny.

Steps in the Concept Development Model

When performed consecutively, the steps of the concept development model mirror a process humans employ individually as they marshal their thoughts on a particular subject, as they organize and reorganize these thoughts, as they seek out new relationships and new meanings, and as they make their way through the uncharted terrains of cognition. This model may be used in kindergarten through grade 12 and beyond to explore basic concepts in different disciplines. In social studies, it may be used to explore concepts such as *capitalism, imperialism,* and *expansionism;* in mathematics, to explore concepts such as *velocity, expansion,* and *relativity;* in science, to explore concepts such as *adaptation, evolution,* and *interdependence;* in English, to explore concepts such as *character, theme,* and *point of view.* These same concepts may be expressed in simpler terms for younger students.

Using this model to explore a central idea from any discipline allows teachers to assess students' prior understandings, enables students to broaden and enrich their previous understandings, and serves as an excellent review. Students enjoy the process, because the ingredients are their contributions and the product is their product.

Step 1: List as Many Items as Possible That Are Associated with the Subject

In the first step, students are asked to enumerate items related to a subject. In some cases, the teacher may provide a data set. The data may be drawn from students' own experience or from material that has been studied in the classroom. Before the class begins a study of space, a teacher might say, "Tell me everything you know about astronauts. Look carefully at the word. The first part of the word refers to star, as in the word *astrology,* the study of stars; the second part of the word refers to sailing ships and sailors, as in the word *nautical.* Thus the word *astronaut* refers to 'star sailor.'" Or after viewing a movie on outer space, the teacher might say, "Let's name everything that you just learned about existing in outer space."

Taba was very precise in the way she ordered and worded the questions guiding concept development. She believed that helping students develop concepts required specific strategies that are widely applicable, but which maintain a particular form. Her ideas for concept development are summarized in Table 6.1.

The items in step 1 should be written on a chalkboard or somewhere visibly accessible to all participants. *Items listed must be specific, or else the next step, grouping, will be confusing.* If you are asking the class to enumerate items about Halloween, for example, and a student says "scary things," ask the student to be more specific. If he has trouble you might ask, "What sort of things are scary?" You hope that he will name some scary things, such as a beckoning finger or a rattling skeleton. The problem with writing down *scary things* is that it does not name, it groups, and that gets you one step ahead in the process.

It is important to have a comprehensive list from which student generalizations can emerge, because generalizations have far more validity when they are based on a variety of data. Encourage students to continue listing, even after they appear to have run out of information. The ideas that follow the first pause are the less obvious ones, frequently derived from greater insight and more thought.

When the subject under scrutiny is already familiar to the participants, such as *football* or *grudge* or *school,* step 1 is similar to brainstorming. Here are a few items generated by a high school class that had performed the model several times. They were exploring the topic *football:*

> school colors, jostling, ball, pom-poms, muscle, strutting, blitz, striped shirts, hot dogs, whistles

They generated more than 140 items in 5 minutes.

Strategy Alert

Brainstorming

Brainstorming is the rapid, noncritical, noncensored listing of any and all ideas or associations on a given topic. Brainstorming focuses student attention on generating a number of ideas and encourages sharing and building on the ideas of others. Brainstorming taps into our emotions, imaginations, memories, in short, our whole creative selves. Students list everything they can think of about a particular subject and the leader lists each item—a word or a phrase. Connections may be obvious to all or personal to the contributor. All contributions are accepted. In brainstorming, students share their individual files with others. Be sure to encourage full participation by calling on students, if necessary. ■

Step 2: Group the Items Because They Are Alike in Some Way

When the teacher believes that sufficient items have been listed, it is time to move to the other half of the chalkboard and ask, "Which of the items we have listed go together because they are alike in some way?" In this step, students begin to examine the relationships among items. Try to elicit several groups. The first groups may be put together for the most obvious reasons. The groups mentioned after some thought are usually put together for more unusual reasons.

An example of one group is *helmets cracking, flying tackles, collisions, bone crunching,* and *injuries.* The teacher had assumed that all the items related to injuries, until a student added injuries to the group. The students later labeled the group the *might makes right* aspect of football.

By using individual cards or sticky notes, steps 2 and 3 can be completed in small groups.

Step 3: Label the Groups by Defining the Reasons for Grouping

In this step, students give labels to the newly formed groups. In a discussion of Halloween, for example, the items *beckoning fingers* and *rattling skeletons* and *leering pumpkins* might be labeled *scary things.* The sophistication of the labels depends on the age and background of the group. Older students, for instance, might use a label such as *habitat,* whereas younger students might label the group *places where animals live.*

It is important in this step to ask students to explain the reasons for their choices. Their explanations are often surprising! Even if the reasons for grouping seem obvious, ask students to articulate their reasons. Having to explain the label they gave a particular group of items forces them to articulate and defend their reasoning processes, frequently expressing connections they have sensed but have not precisely verbalized.

The teacher's role at this stage is basically that of recorder. The teacher may ask what other students think, but the students need to feel that their judgments are valued by the teacher and the rest of the class. It is important to develop the students' skills in drawing inferences and in making generalizations. The students should question one another and decide among themselves. The teacher may also insert particular inferences or generalizations that are found in the curriculum, but which students have not acknowledged. Teachers should explain their thinking about why they made these statements.

Examples of labels from the high school group analyzing football were *stadium, parking lot, commercialism, rules, might makes right, emotions, microcosm, costumes, food,* and *atmosphere.* This step helps students learn to generalize.

Step 4: Regroup or Subsume Individual Items or Whole Groups under Other Groups

Step 4 centers on the questions "Are there items now in one group that you could put in another group?" and later, "Are there whole groups that could be placed under one of the other labels?" Again, ask for the learner's reasoning here: "Why do you think _____ belongs under _____?"

For example, when regrouping on the topic *Halloween,* a student might want to add *witches on broomsticks,* which had been under *decorations,* to the group of scary things. If you believe the groupings were done for rather shallow or superficial reasons and that the students can go further, erase the second half of the board, leaving the initial items clearly visible, and ask the students if they can generate some new groups. Obvious groups such as *treats* or *decorations* are fine, but perhaps students will begin to see more obscure connections such as *feelings* or *masks* or *facades.* Also, no list of items is final; new items may be added at any time.

In step 3, the more obvious items come first; with grouping, the more obvious relationships are pointed out first. Also, the connections seen when the model is first used are much less complex than those recognized after practice. As time goes on, students will find out for themselves that every person, object, or idea has many characteristics and may be grouped in many different ways. For example, when a ninth grade student observed that the item *leering pumpkin* could be labeled *decorations* or *food* or *scary things,* depending on how you thought about it, she showed her understanding that the same object may be viewed from different perspectives. We all tend to put constraints on our thinking. If A is B, it cannot be C. In this model, students discover that one item can be viewed from several vantage points and can, therefore, appear in several groups.

Whole groups may be included with other groups. One group under *football* included *strutting, pushing, shoving, beefy, cocky,* and *butting heads.* One student had commented that these types of behaviors reminded him of bulls, so they had labeled the group *bulls.* In step 4, the students put this entire group under another group labeled *macho.*

Step 5: Synthesize the Information by Summarizing the Data and Forming Generalizations

In step 5, the teacher asks the class to look over the entire chalkboard, consider all the groups and labels, and try to make a general statement about the topic in one sentence. Students must try to pick out trends. Young children tend to think in terms of either/or. Either Halloween is a "good" holiday or a "bad" one. They do not see that Halloween can have two faces. Scary situations need not be dangerous if controlled, and they can even be fun. A private Halloween party can offer some thrilling and terrifying moments that pose no danger. If not supervised, however, trick-or-treaters can be in danger from traffic, overzealous pranksters, or the occasional sick mind. By looking at all the conflicting data at once, students begin to realize that Halloween is complex, fraught with pleasures and dangers. Even older students tend to think in terms of either/or. Football is either "good" or "bad," usually depending on whether they enjoy playing or watching it. They need to realize that football is an exciting and popular sport that can also be dangerous. This step offers an opportunity for students to begin to appreciate the richness and complexity of ideas.

Teachers will need to give students several examples of generalizations the first few times this model is used. Examples of generalizations from the analysis of football are as follows:

- The game of football is fun but dangerous.
- Many boys and men define themselves by their degree of success in football, which can be both helpful and harmful to their self-images.
- A football game is a microcosm of the major elements in our society, both good and bad.

Summary of Steps in the Concept Development Model

1. *List as many items as possible that are associated with the subject.* Ask the students to name as many ideas, objects, associations, memories, concepts, or attributes related to the subject under scrutiny as possible. Thus what the learners already know is identified. The information may be based on general knowledge that students have of a subject or on what they know or think they know already. It may come from a personal experience they have had, such as school-related field trips, a preparatory reading, or a film.

2. *Group the items because they are alike in some way.* Ask the students to group the items by finding ways in which they are similar or related. Thus what learners know is qualified. Similar ideas, or ideas related to a common concept, bear similar qualities. An important part of learning consists of identifying these qualities.

3. *Label the groups by defining the reasons for grouping.* Ask the students to articulate the relationships between the items. Thus what learners know is defined. Qualities that are borne in common by ideas form the basis of the categories into which those ideas fit. Often, different labels are possible.

4. *Regroup or subsume individual items or whole groups under other groups.* Ask the students to look at the board and see if they can find items or whole groups that they could put somewhere else. This step involves looking at a single item from different perspectives. It also involves analyzing through regrouping and subsuming additional items under already established labels or subsuming labels under other labels according to relative inclusiveness. For example, under

---

Go to the Building Teaching Skills and Dispositions section of Topic 10: Inductive Models in the MyEducationLab for your course and complete the activity entitled "Questioning."

the heading *democracy,* the category *campaign* containing items such as *shaking hands* and *making speeches* might be subsumed under another category, *elections.* The most creative connections occur in this step.

5. *Synthesize the information by summarizing the data and forming generalizations.* Ask the students to look over the board and see if they can make a general statement or generalization about the subject under scrutiny that summarizes the information in the briefest terms possible. To generalize, the students must put the parts together or synthesize the information. For example, if they were studying Halloween, they might say that Halloween is both fun and dangerous.

Evaluating Learning in the Concept Development Model

One of the purposes of the concept development model is to help students generate original ideas. Practice in brainstorming helps students become more creative and willing to share. Using a kitchen or Internet timer during step 1, students can try to generate as many items as possible in a short period of time. Both teachers and students can keep track of the number of ideas shared over several concept development lessons.

Along with the number of items shared, teachers and students can evaluate the originality of the group labels. There will be an increase in the number and the originality of the connections over time and experience with this model. Teachers can evaluate individual student thinking by asking each student to come up with a different group and asking him or her to write a paragraph about why the items in the group belong together. In addition, students can be asked to add new items or ideas to the groups that evolved from the class discussion.

The concept development process itself can be used as an evaluation tool. Teachers can design paper-and-pencil tasks that provide data sets and ask students to group, label, regroup, relabel, and make generalizations. This work can be assessed for accuracy, originality, and the number of groups generated. In addition, students can be asked to create short essays explaining how and why items were grouped as they were and how these groups support specific generalizations.

Meeting Individual Needs in the Concept Development Model

The concept development model is inherently differentiated—it meets a variety of student needs in the way it is structured and implemented. For example, student interests can be met by allowing students to generate data sets. Student readiness can be addressed by dividing students into groups and varying the information data base or prompts. In the lesson on Halloween, for example, the teacher can provide different data sets to particular groups of students. If one group is challenged by abstract concepts, the teacher might provide a data set that includes such words as *terrifying, horrifying, apprehension, anticipation, greed, profit, creativity, partners,* and *darkness*. These words represent less tangible and more symbolic concepts related to Halloween. Learning styles can be addressed by modifying the directions of the concept development task. Students who need more structure will receive detailed, specific directions that are clearly modeled and offer little choice, while students who are comfortable with a more open approach will receive directions that are somewhat vague, have no modeling, and include more choice.

Data sets can be lists of words, realia, pictures, or symbols so that student learning styles can be addressed. Some students will find grouping and regrouping an easier task if they hold the items in their hands and actually place the items in groups. Teachers can also vary the pace of the lesson and provide more time and practice to students as necessary.

Each of the steps in the concept development model is an opportunity to meet individual needs. Step 1 can cater to students' interests and misconceptions as teachers manipulate data sets to reach specific objectives. The scaffolding provided to students as they group like items together allows step 2 to work as a differentiation tool. Students can also be supported when they provide the reasons for grouping. Probing questions and a think–pair–share strategy can be helpful here. The questions and prompts can vary by readiness or interest. Regrouping and relabeling can be a difficult task for students. It should be modeled by the teacher. In fact, in some cases, it might make sense to eliminate this step, especially if students are new to the model. The last step, summarizing, can occur as discussion or recitation or can be a structured activity. For example, you can pair students and ask one of the pair to talk about the lesson for 30 seconds while the other student listens carefully. Roles are reversed and the first student listens while the second student reflects on the lesson for 30 seconds, but cannot repeat anything that the first student said. After the activity, students share a one-sentence summary.

Benefits of Using the Concept Development Model

The academic purpose of concept development is to extend and refine students' knowledge. Because we look at the world through the lens of our own personal experiences, recognizing our limitations and sharing our knowledge increase our grasp of the complexities of perception and open us to additional points of view. The concept development process also encourages the generation of original ideas because all subjects can be analyzed through listing, brainstorming, grouping, labeling, and generalizing—all of which promote creative thinking. In fact, the concept development process also promotes new avenues for extracting meaning from reading, methods for problem solving, and development of writing skills (it particularly helps with paragraph unity). While participating in a concept development lesson, students have the opportunity to summarize and examine the accuracy of their ideas.

The concept development approach also supports affective skills. Brainstorming requires seeking and listening to the ideas of others and describing personal feelings when appropriate. Students must also exhibit self-regulation as they listen to the ideas of peers without comment. They must be able to acknowledge the saliency of the ideas of peers. It is obvious that there are strong academic and social benefits for students when the concept development model is used in the classroom.

Elementary Grades Lesson

CONCEPT DEVELOPMENT: Living and Nonliving Things

OBJECTIVES

Students Will Understand
- Living things have particular characteristics that make them different from nonliving things

Students Will Know
- Living things need food, air, and water, and produce young

Students Will Be Able To
- Sort living and nonliving things and provide reasons for the choices

ASSESSMENT

Given a set of pictures, children will accurately distinguish between living and nonliving things and give reasons for categorizing a picture as a living thing.

PROCEDURES

1. If possible, take the children for a walk around the school and have them make a list of what they see.
2. Return to class and make a list that includes everyone's observations.
3. Ask students which things on the list belong together. Using a piece of colored chalk, circle the items that the children identify as belonging together. Use a different color for each group. Have students explain each grouping. Keep in mind your objectives (especially your *know* objective) and try to infuse the characteristics of living things into the discussion as much as possible.
4. Once the groups have been identified, ask students to label or name each group. Put the names on the board in the same color chalk as the group's circles.

> 5. Ask students if some of the items in the groups might fit into more than one group. Which items should go into which groups? Record the responses.
> 6. Ask if there are any other ways that the original list of items can be organized into a group. (This can be an optional step and will depend on the teacher's determination of student engagement at this point.)
> 7. Ask the students to tell you something about the groups and the discussion that the class had about the groups. Repeat each statement and ask students why or how they came up with their conclusion. Add any statements that promote the objectives. Provide cues and scaffolding for helping students summarize and synthesize.

Middle/Secondary Grades Lesson

CONCEPT DEVELOPMENT: Grudge

OBJECTIVES

Students Will Understand
- Characterization is the basis for reality in a story

Students Will Know
- How we can infer the feelings of a character

Students Will Be Able To
- Examine and expand on the concept of *grudge*

ASSESSMENT

After reading the assigned text, students will identify the speech, actions, and responses from others to the character holding a grudge. The product in which students make the identifications can be written, drawn, or performed and may be accomplished in pairs or individually.

PROCEDURES

(For this lesson, students are divided into reading circle groups.)

1. Review previous lessons in the characterization unit.
2. List as many items as possible that are associated with the subject. After making certain that everyone knows the word *grudge*, ask students to generate a data set of words associated with holding a grudge.
3. List words on the chalkboard or a SmartBoard, or project them from a computer or a transparency.
4. Group the items because they are alike in some way. Students put together like words from the list.
5. Label the groups by defining the reasons for grouping. Students are asked to label the groups and to share the category names with the whole class. Students provide explanations for their groupings and category labels.
6. Regroup or subsume individual items or whole groups under other groups. Students are asked to look at the original list and make different groups with

new names. Students share the groupings, labels, and reasons for sorting in this way.
7. Synthesize the information by summarizing the data and forming generalizations. Students summarize what they have learned about the word *grudge* in the lesson by making a one-sentence statement.
8. Students identify actions and words of literary characters who are holding a grudge.

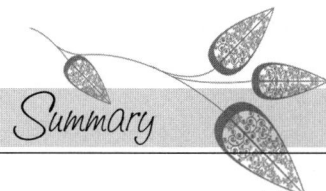

Summary

There are several benefits to using the concept development model approach regularly (once a month or more frequently). From this model, students learn much from one another about the concept, object, event, or person studied. They absorb a great deal of the accumulated knowledge and ideas of the whole group. They expand and refine their own concepts of the topic being studied; concomitantly, they expand and refine their ability to perform these mental processes.

Concepts are the building blocks of our intellectual activity. Knowledge is not static. Knowledge of even a simple object can grow and take on new dimensions, or it can recede and grow hazy with lack of exposure. It might be helpful to think of growth in knowledge as a series of overlays on an overhead projector. We add to and change an already existing impression, much as one makes an addition to a basic drawing. The concept development model is helpful to teachers, because it not only allows them to enrich the original impression but also affords a glimpse of that original impression on which to build.

The concept development model is organized as a series of steps.

1. List or present a list of items associated with a particular subject.
2. Group like items together.
3. Label the groups and provide a reason for the label.
4. Regroup or subsume individual items or whole groups under other groups.
5. Synthesize the information by summarizing and forming generalizations.

All of these steps encourage important cognitive and social skills and provide the opportunity for students to become more metacognitive about their learning.

Extensions

ACTIVITIES

1. Choose a concept that you teach or will be teaching. List as many items as you can that are related to the concept. Label each of the groups. Now, regroup the items and relabel. Remember to be flexible. You should only use an item once and you may omit items, if necessary. This exercise will remind you of what the

students will experience as they move through the steps of a concept development lesson.
2. All teaching is related to concept development. Choose a concept that you will teach in the future and review the steps in the concept development model. Script at least one question that you might ask your students at each step of the concept development process: listing, grouping, labeling, analyzing, and synthesizing.
3. Find a teacher's edition of a textbook that includes the concept you used for Activity 2. Compare your questions with those suggested in the text. How would you evaluate the text in supporting the acquisition and development of the concept? Do the authors assist students in the concept development process?

REFLECTIVE QUESTIONS

1. Are there concepts that you will be teaching that are not a good fit with the concept development model?
2. How might the use of concept development in your classroom contribute to your classroom management concerns?
3. How might you distinguish the concept attainment model from the concept development model?

# 7

Problem-Centered Inquiry Models

Teaching Problem Solving through Discovery and Questioning

chapter OBJECTIVES

You Will Understand
- Inquiry is a life skill

You Will Know
- What problem-centered inquiry models look like in both elementary and secondary classrooms
- The basis in research and theory for using several problem-centered inquiry models in the classroom
- The steps of the three problem-centered inquiry models
- How to adapt the inquiry models to meet individual needs
- Ways to assess inquiry model lessons

You will be able to
- Identify problem-centered inquiry models in K–12 classrooms
- Design, implement, and reflect on an inquiry lesson

In the ELEMENTARY classroom

The students in Ms. Levy's class are fascinated by butterflies. She decides to capitalize on this interest by asking students to help solve the problem of the declining population of monarch butterflies.

Ms. Levy: Let's take our science period today to talk about butterflies. Can you remember the stages of the life cycle of a butterfly?

Micah: Egg, caterpillar, chrysalis, and butterfly.

Ms. Levy: Is there another word for caterpillar?

Ivy: Larva.

Ms. Levy: Do monarch butterflies have the same life cycle?

Micah: Of course, it's a butterfly!

121

Ms. Levy continues to share information about the monarch butterfly—its migration and why the number of monarch butterflies is declining. The presentation also includes ideas about stewardship and the ways in which we can help to protect the earth. She asks students to get with a partner and think about how they might help the monarch butterfly. Allowing the students to work together for 3 or 4 minutes, Ms. Levy opens up the discussion for sharing.

> **Ms. Levy:** What suggestions do you have for helping monarch butterflies?
>
> **Perla:** We think we should raise money and give it to the Wildlife Center.
>
> **Alex:** We want to tell the community about the butterflies.
>
> **Madison:** We want to help protect the places that the butterflies live.
>
> **Charles:** That was my idea!
>
> **Ivy:** We want to build a butterfly garden like they have at the middle school. My brother worked on it and told us all about it.

Ms. Levy writes down all of these and other suggestions. She returns to each suggestion and asks students to tell her the questions that must be answered before a solution can be found and what resources will be necessary to answer the questions. She involves the students in determining a reasonable suggestion on which to focus and narrows the list to raising money for the Wildlife Center or planting a butterfly garden.

> **Ms. Levy:** Over the next couple of days, we will decide on how we can best help the monarch butterfly. In the meantime, talk to your family and friends about our plans and see if they have any questions or recommendations. Remember that our goal is to help the monarch butterfly. Now, are there any more questions before we begin to write our storyboard?
>
> **Perla:** I think we are going to need to get money to help the monarch butterfly no matter what way we decide.
>
> **Ivy:** How will we get money?
>
> **Ms. Levy:** That will be part of our problem solving. Let's think about that tonight and discuss more about ways to raise money tomorrow.

In the SECONDARY classroom

In her environmental science class, Ms. Whitaker introduces the unit on toxins using the inquiry process. She begins by asking the students if they have heard the expression "mad as a hatter." One girl raises her hand and says that she remembers a character called the Mad Hatter in the movie *Alice in Wonderland*. Another says that the movie was made from a book by Lewis Carroll in which the Mad Hatter had a tea party. Another student recalls having read a book in which someone was described as being mad as a hatter. "I thought it meant the character was really angry about his hat," the student says.

Ms. Whitaker tells the class that she is going to present them with a problem for which they will try to find an acceptable solution. They will ask her questions that can

Table 7.1 Fact Sheet Used by Teacher in Responding to Questions

1. Working conditions in 19th-century England were bad, and many people developed work-related illnesses without realizing the cause.
2. Workplaces were not well ventilated, and few safety precautions were taken. Workers did not wear protective clothing.
3. Most men's hats were made from felt, which was processed from the underhair of beavers imported from Canada.
4. Mercury was one of the chemicals used in the manufacture of felt hats.
5. As we now know, mercury is highly poisonous and, if allowed to build up in a person's body, can cause an illness resembling insanity.
6. Today, this illness is named Minamata disease after a small factory town in Japan where thousands of people were poisoned after eating fish taken from a bay into which tons of mercury had been dumped by a local industry from 1932 to 1968.

---

be answered yes or no. She explains the rules for the inquiry procedure, which she has posted at the front of the room, and then assigns the students to their caucus groups. She encourages the students to ask questions as though they were actually doing research. She also gives them examples of the type of questions they might ask her, ranging from simple fact questions to more complex questions, such as "If I did _____, could I expect _____ to happen?" Because she will be the source of the information, she has prepared a fact sheet for her own use (see Table 7.1).

Ms. Whitaker reads aloud the following problem statement:

> In England during the 18th and 19th centuries, a very large number of workers who made men's hats went "mad" and behaved as though they were insane. In fact, many of them were committed to the lunatic asylums of that time. Why did this group of people have such a high incidence of insanity, thus giving rise to the saying "mad as a hatter"?

She then asks the students to begin the questioning process.

Student: What about the people who made women's hats—did a lot of them go mad too?
Ms. Whitaker: No.
Student: Did men wear some particular kind of hat in those days?
Ms. Whitaker: Yes. Ask another question.
Student: Was it those stovepipe-looking hats like Abe Lincoln wore?
Ms. Whitaker: Be more specific.
Student: Those black hats with the high tops—they called them top hats, I think.
Ms. Whitaker: Yes, most were like that.
Student: Did it have something to do with what the hats were made of?
Ms. Whitaker: Yes.

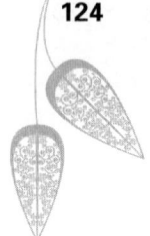

STUDENT: Can we caucus?

MS. WHITAKER: Yes.

STUDENT: [After the caucus] Didn't they also call those hats "beavers"?

MS. WHITAKER: Yes.

STUDENT: Were they made out of beaver pelts?

MS. WHITAKER: Yes. Ask another question. You may keep asking questions as long as you get a positive response.

STUDENT: If we went into one of those factories, could we see what was making the people go mad?

MS. WHITAKER: Be more specific, please.

STUDENT: Well, could we see the workers being beaten, for instance?

MS. WHITAKER: No. Let's review what you have found already. Pay attention to those facts that you already know. [She points to the board, where a student has been summarizing the responses to their questions.]

STUDENT: Did they have to treat the beaver pelts in some way?

MS. WHITAKER: Yes, they did.

STUDENT: Did they use high heat, which made the people go crazy?

MS. WHITAKER: They may have used heat, but it was not the primary cause of the problem.

STUDENT: Did they use a chemical?

MS. WHITAKER: Yes.

STUDENT: Was it poisonous?

MS. WHITAKER: Yes.

STUDENT: Did they inhale the fumes?

MS. WHITAKER: That might be a part of it. Do you wish to pose a theory?

STUDENT: The hatters were poisoned by handling a toxic substance used in the making of felt for the hats.

MS. WHITAKER: Now, let us ask questions to test this theory or to make it more complete.

STUDENT: Was it arsenic?

MS. WHITAKER: No.

STUDENT: Is this poison still in use today?

MS. WHITAKER: Yes.

STUDENT: Do they still use it to make hats?

MS. WHITAKER: Not to my knowledge.

STUDENT: Do people know that this substance is poisonous?

MS. WHITAKER: Yes.

STUDENT: Can we caucus?

MS. WHITAKER: Certainly. Remember we are now testing the theory that is written on the board.

STUDENT: [After the caucus] Was the substance mercury?

Ms. Whitaker: Yes, it was. So now you can restate your theory to make it more complete. [The students add the word *mercury*.]

The teacher asks the class to state some rules they could draw from the theory they postulated. They say that (1) people may be harmed by a substance when they are unaware of its dangers, and (2) when they do not know all the facts, people may ridicule a group for being different.

The students also discuss how they arrived at their theory and what steps were most helpful in deciding. They note that recording the data during the process was helpful.

Basis for the Inquiry Approach to Instruction

> Go to the Assignments and Activities section of Topic 11: Inquiry Models in the MyEducationLab for your course and complete the activity entitled "Choosing Discrepant Events."

Why are caterpillars fuzzy? What causes snakes to slither and bears to growl? Why do cats always land right side up? What happens to the lightning bug's light during the day? Is a baby fish afraid of the water? Did something take a bite out of the moon? Who ever thought up the name *brussels sprouts,* and why does ketchup stick in the bottle? Was the red color in the leaves hiding under the green? Is my skin brown because I was toasted? Will the rain melt the flowers?

Remember when the world was full of questions to ask rather than answers to learn? Somewhere on the way to adulthood, children inevitably get the idea that becoming a grown-up means leaving the world of questioning for the world of knowing. Schools institutionalize the departure from questions to answers as success becomes measured by putting the right answer into the blank or circling the correct response, knowing positively what is true and what is false. Almost all questions in school have one right answer, and questions for which there are no answers do not often arise.

True wisdom, however, might better be defined as the realization of how little one knows in contrast to how much one knows. The real excitement of learning is daring to challenge ignorance with unbridled curiosity. *Homo sapiens,* meaning quite literally "humankind who taste of knowledge," have aptly named themselves. If knowing how to learn is more important than knowing all the answers, then the greatest realization of a person's intellectual life must be that good questions are more important than right answers. Thus the quality of the questions one can ask, rather than the correctness of the answers one can give, shows one's wisdom. Scientist and philosopher Lewis Thomas has described this intellectual journey:

> Science, especially twentieth-century science, has provided us with a glimpse of something we never really knew before, the revelation of human ignorance. We have been accustomed to the belief, from one century to another, that except for one or two mysteries, we more or less comprehend everything on earth. Every age, not just the eighteenth century, regarded itself as the Age of Reason, and we have never lacked for explanations of the world and its ways. Now, we are being

brought up short. We do not understand much of anything, from the episode we rather dismissively (and, I think, defensively) choose to call the "big bang," all the way down to the particles in the atoms of a bacterial cell. We have a wilderness of mystery to make our way through in the centuries ahead. (Thomas, 1984)

The idea of inquiry learning is based on the premise that there is indeed a "wilderness of mystery" to be explored in all fields and that every school subject represents a discipline of inquiry in which all students, regardless of their past school achievement, can participate.

Too often children are taught in school as though the answers to all the important questions were in their textbooks. In reality, most of the problems faced by individuals have no easy answers. There are no reference books in which one can find the solution to life's perplexing problems. Although it is true that those who succeed in school are often those who can remember the "correct" answer, those who succeed in life are usually those who are willing to ask questions and search for solutions.

Robert Sternberg has made a persuasive argument that the problems presented by real life and those that children are taught to deal with in school are alarmingly different, so different that the training for thinking one receives in schools may be irrelevant to the thinking required in life. Sternberg's discussion of the differences between problems posed in school and the problems posed by life helps us to understand the importance of inquiry models of instruction. The following summary (with parenthetical statements inserted for transition) is meant to convey the essence of Sternberg's argument:

> In the everyday world, the first and sometimes most difficult step in problem solving is the recognition that a problem exists. . . . [Especially as] in everyday problem solving, it is often harder to figure out just what the problem is than to figure out how to solve it. . . . [Often the difficulty in solving everyday problems is that] everyday problems tend to be ill-structured. . . . In everyday problem solving, it is not usually clear just what information will be needed to solve a given problem, nor is it always clear where the requisite information can be found. . . . The solutions to everyday problems depend on and interact with the contexts in which the problems are presented. . . . Everyday problems generally have no one right solution, and even the criteria for what constitutes a test solution are often not clear. . . . [To further aggravate the matter] the solutions to everyday problems depend at least as much on informal knowledge as on formal knowledge. . . . [One of the biggest differences between problems encountered in school and those encountered in real life is that] solutions to important everyday problems have consequences that matter. . . . [Unlike in school where individuality is prized and competition rewarded] everyday problem solving often occurs in groups. . . . Everyday problems can be complicated, messy, and stubbornly persistent. (Sternberg, 1985a, pp. 195–198)

In a subsequent article, Sternberg points out that one might take a number of approaches in trying to create a more satisfactory congruence between problems children learn to solve in school and those they must solve in real life (Sternberg,

1985b). He notes that the basis of inquiry teaching is derived from fundamentals of problem solving.

The inquiry model is grounded in the theory of problem-based learning. In problem-based learning, the teacher serves as subject matter expert, resource guide, and task group consultant, but not as information transmitter or sole source of knowledge. The major role of the teacher is to encourage student participation, provide appropriate information to keep students on track, avoid negative feedback, and assume the role of fellow learner.

The idea of anchoring instruction in authentic problems is not especially new. It formed the basis of much of what John Dewey advocated at the beginning of the 20th century. It has been used in medical education for many years. The constructivist movement in education derives from a problem-centered perspective.

Jerome Bruner described four benefits to be gained from the experience of learning through the process of discovering answers to problems (Bruner, 1961).

1. *An increase in intellectual potency.* Bruner hypothesizes that in the process of discovery, the learner learns how to problem solve and learns the fundamentals of "the task of learning." He suggests that learners who engage in discovering possible answers for themselves learn to recognize constraints in hypothesizing solutions, which reduces what he calls potshotting or stringing out random hypotheses one after the other. These learners also learn to connect previously obtained information to new information and to develop persistence in sticking to a problem until it is satisfactorily resolved.

2. *The shift from extrinsic to intrinsic rewards.* Rather than striving for rewards gained primarily from giving back the right answer, students achieve rewards from the satisfaction of manipulating the environment and from solving problems. The learner develops an ability to delay gratification in seeking the solution to a problem rather than depending on the immediate reward of giving back to the teacher what was expected.

3. *Learning the heuristics of discovery.* Bruner points out that the process of inquiry involves learning how to pose a problem in such a form that it can be worked on and solved. He believes that only by practice and by being involved in the process of inquiry can one learn how best to go about solving problems. The more experienced the learner, the more the inquiry process can be generalized to other tasks and problems to be solved.

4. *Aid to memory processing.* The primary problem in the memory process is the retrieval of what is to be remembered, according to Bruner. He believes that material that is figured out by the learner is more readily available to memory than that stored on demand. In addition, the learner who is a good problem solver also discovers techniques for remembering information.

In the inquiry model, strategies used by scientists for solving problems are presented as a systematic mode for processing data and learning to approach puzzling situations in all fields of study. In teaching with any variety of the inquiry model, be aware that there are both convergent and divergent ways of conducting the process. If the teacher already knows the answer to a problem and wants the students to discover it, then the process is convergent. If the information presented to the students might lead to a number of legitimate responses, then the process is more divergent. The initial problems one chooses may be primarily convergent in that the answer is known and the teacher leads the students toward the right answer through the information given. But students should gradually be introduced to more divergent situations in which one right answer is not known or agreed to. Confronted with ill-structured and open-ended problems, students practice a heuristic process in learning to solve problems and deal with ambiguity such as that presented in the "everyday world" problems that Sternberg distinguishes.

Problem-Centered Model One: The Suchman Inquiry Model

Richard Suchman, who believed that the intellectual strategies used by scientists could be taught to young learners, developed one widely accepted approach to inquiry-based instruction. The natural curiosity of children and adolescents can be trained and disciplined in procedures of inquiry. When students ask *why* out of genuine interest, they are likely to grasp the information and to retain it as their own understanding. They will also come to understand the value of working within a discipline—that is, of participating in the way of knowing and thinking that is at the core of every discipline (Suchman, 1962).

Step 1: Select a Problem and Conduct Research

The Suchman model begins with the teacher selecting a puzzling situation or problem that is genuinely interesting and stimulating to the learner—a discrepant event. It may be a scientific problem, such as why moisture sometimes accumulates on the outside of a glass or why sugar disappears in water. It may be a puzzling event, such as the mystery of the Lost Colony or of the Bermuda Triangle. It may be a scene from a play or a story that requires the students to formulate an outcome. It may be a problem requiring mathematical skills, a problem in health, or a situation to be resolved in the athletic program. Here are some examples of potential problems for students to begin the inquiry process. The answers are not provided. Most of the problems have several possible answers:

1. In 1692, there was a surge in the number of witches put to death, marking the worst outbreak of the persecution of witches in America. Strangely, this outbreak occurred 47 years after the previous epidemic of witch persecution.

No one has been able to prove why this happened in 1692 in Essex County, Massachusetts, and Fairfield County, Connecticut, and not in other counties; however, there are several theories regarding this phenomenon, and one in particular that seems very plausible.

2. Jefferson Davis, the president of the Confederacy, was considered to be an outstanding leader and more capable than Abraham Lincoln at the beginning of the Civil War. Yet, by the end of the war, Davis was totally ineffectual. What might account for a leader becoming ineffectual?
3. Two plants growing in the classroom receive the same amount of water and are planted in the same soil, yet one of the plants is much larger than the other. The plants were replanted from seedlings that were exactly the same size. What might cause this difference in plant growth?
4. Rock strata in the eastern United States are very similar. In Florida, however, the rock strata are entirely different from any other area. What might account for this dramatic difference?

Any subject lends itself to inquiry. All that is required is a puzzling situation for which the students can find a logical and reasonable solution. For many students, especially those accustomed to the process of inquiry, the best and most realistic problem situations are those for which there may be more than one answer or for which no final answers have been determined.

Once a problem has been selected, the teacher completes the necessary research on the problem and prepares a data sheet for quick reference during the questioning periods. The teacher also determines how much information should be provided to the students at the beginning of the inquiry process and what additional information could be supplied if the class has difficulty.

Step 2: Introduce the Process and Present the Problem

Before beginning the inquiry lesson, the teacher explains the process to the class; in the Suchman model, the entire class can participate—both as a whole group and in caucuses. The teacher is the main source of data and will respond only to questions that can be answered with a yes or a no, thus placing the burden of framing the question on the learner. The teacher may choose to add additional information or guide the questioning, but the responsibility for hypothesizing must remain with the students; the teacher is in control of the process but not in control of the outcome or of student thinking. The students are presented with the following rules:

1. A student may ask a question only when called on.
2. Students may talk with one another only during caucus periods, times given to group discussion and cooperative work among students.
3. Questions must be phrased so that the teacher can answer with a yes or no response. (The teacher may choose to give additional information if needed.)

4. A student may continue to ask questions as long as the questions are receiving a positive response from the teacher.

The teacher reads the problem aloud or distributes problem statement sheets to the class. If the students are nonreaders, the teacher provides them with the problem orally and uses pictures to illustrate the problem if possible. Students are encouraged to ask for explanations if a term is unclear.

Step 3: Gather Data

In most classrooms, students ask questions that require the teacher to do the thinking. In this step of the model, each question must be asked as a tentative hypothesis that allows for the gathering of data. The student cannot ask, "What makes the plant lean toward the sun?" because that would require the teacher to give the information. Rather, the question must be phrased so that the teacher can respond with a yes or no answer: "Does the plant lean toward the sun because of a magnetic force?"

The teacher may decide to add information or expand on the problem at any time; it is important, however, to let the students experience some frustration as they question. There is a temptation for the teacher to rephrase the question and say, "Is this what you mean?" It is better to say, "Can you restate that question?" or "Can you state the question more clearly?" or "Can you state the question so that I can answer it either yes or no?" A teacher might also say "Yes, that is a part of the answer, but why don't you consider this additional piece of information in light of what you already have discovered?" The data gathered through the questioning process should be recorded on the board or on data sheets kept by each student.

Step 4: Develop a Theory and Verify

When a student poses a theoretical question that seems to be an answer to the problem, the question is stated as a theory and written on the board in a special area reserved for this purpose. After a theory has been identified, all data gathering relates directly to proving or disproving this one theory. In the problem regarding the different rates of plant growth, once the students have posed a theory that the amount of light received by plants affected the rate of growth, all questions are now focused on either accepting or rejecting this theory.

Students may ask to caucus to discuss the information and frame hypothetical questions they will ask the teacher. (Some teachers assign caucus groups and leaders prior to instruction, thus saving time and reducing confusion.) Depending on the nature of the problem, the teacher directs the students to other sources of information or to actual laboratory experiments. Students are encouraged to ask hypothetical questions at this point, such as, "If both plants are positioned in the same part of the room, will their growth be the same?" As before, the teacher's response is either yes or no.

If the students reach a point where the theory they have posed seems to be verified, then the class accepts the theory as a solution and moves to the next step of the model. If the theory is not acceptable and does not satisfy the class as plausible, it is rejected and the general data gathering begins again. The class may be allowed to caucus at any point but only with the teacher's permission.

Step 5: Explain the Theory and State the Rules Associated with It

In this step, students are asked to explain the theory accepted as a tentative solution and state the rules associated with that theory. In addition, they must determine how the theory could be tested to see if the rules can be generalized to other situations. Students will sometimes discover essential flaws in their theory at this stage, forcing them to return to data gathering and experimentation.

In terms of the problem of plant growth and sunlight, for instance, the teacher would have the students, in their own words, state the rule based on their theory that the sun was the factor, such as, "Plants need sunlight to grow strong and healthy." The class would then discuss whether all plants need the same amount of sun and decide how to test for that generalization.

Step 6: Analyze the Process

Students are asked to review the process they have just used to arrive at acceptance of the theory. At this step, it is important that the students consider how they could have expedited the process. Students should analyze the types of questions they asked to see how they could have formed more effective questioning techniques. As students become more efficient in using the steps of inquiry, the teacher may relinquish some control and allow the students to set up their own inquiry processes.

Step 7: Evaluate

Ask the students to locate and research their own puzzling situations. Conduct a survey of the class to select the most interesting problems.

Test to determine if the students understand the theory and if they can generalize the rules related to the theory to other situations.

For a theory that has no "right" answer, ask the students to identify another probable theory. The two theories could then be the basis for a debate in the class.

Summary of Steps in the Suchman Inquiry Model

1. *Select a problem and conduct research.* Choose a puzzling situation or an event that will entice the students to discover the answer and then research the problem for possible solutions.

2. *Introduce the process and present the problem.* Carefully explain and post the rules that the students will follow for the inquiry. Present the puzzling situation to the students in writing and provide them with a means for recording data.

3. *Gather data.* Respond to questions posed by the students for the purpose of gathering and verifying data. Guide the students to ask questions more clearly or more completely but avoid restating the questions for them. Encourage the students to call for a caucus when they need to talk with one another but do not permit students to talk to each other during the questioning periods. Reinforce the idea that this is a group process; the attention and participation of the entire class are needed.

4. *Develop a theory and verify.* When a student poses a theory, stop the questioning and write the theory on the chalkboard. The class decides to accept or reject it. Emphasize that at this stage the questioning is directed toward experimenting with one particular theory. If other theories are posed, write them on the board and tell the class that they will be explored later if the theory under examination does not prove adequate. Encourage the students to consider all possible types of questions. For example, if they are focusing on an event, encourage them to consider conditions that might cause it. Questions are valuable tools at this point in the model. Students may be encouraged to do further research or to experiment in the laboratory as they try to verify a particular theory. The Suchman model can be used over a variety of time frames. In the case of gathering data from sources outside of the teacher, the model may be used over a number of classroom periods.

5. *Explain the theory and state the rules associated with it.* Once a theory or a theoretical answer has been verified by the students, lead them into an explanation and application of the theory. Discuss the rules or effects of the theory as well as the predictive value the theory may have for other events.

6. *Analyze the process.* Finally, discuss the inquiry process with the class. Examine how they arrived at an acceptable theory to explain the problem and determine how the process could be improved. As the class gains confidence in the inquiry process, they may assume more responsibility for the process.

7. *Evaluate.* Test to determine if the students have understood the theory derived from the process and determine if they are able to generalize the rules to other situations. Also, encourage the students to look for other puzzling situations and to develop a habit of asking questions and looking for answers. Because this model is based on a scientific method, determine if the students are solving problems more effectively with this technique.

Problem-Centered Model Two: The WebQuest Model of Inquiry

Once students are familiar with the basic steps of the inquiry model, they may be ready for a more adventurous, less teacher-directed experience. The WebQuest model is a special form of inquiry teaching that takes advantage of the Web as a primary source of information. Originated by Bernie Dodge of San Diego State University, WebQuests are thematic units that incorporate information available on the Web with a variety of other resources. Though a WebQuest is presented to students as a Web page, sources of study include much more than the Web. Students also conduct textbook reading, supplemental reading and study in other sources, and independent activities related to the topic of the unit. In addition, the resources and activities embedded in a WebQuest include interviewing and reporting, observation and note taking, survey research, and many other "real-life" experiences that students write about.

The major difference between standard thematic units and WebQuests is that the former are focused on topics that students are to learn about and the latter are focused on problems that students are to solve. The "problem" is generated from the topic under study in the classroom. The distinguishing feature of a WebQuest lies in the instructional approach it requires. Is the students' learning to be guided by the topic and related materials or by their own investigation and inquiry? WebQuests create open-ended learning opportunities for students and teachers. The underlying purpose of a WebQuest is to pose a problem for students to solve with the resources put at their disposal to help them learn the content required in the curriculum. WebQuests provide an organizational scheme for student-centered, teacher-facilitated learning.

Before deciding you could not possibly create a unit of study based on Web resources, suspend your disbelief for a moment and think this through, step-by-step. You already know the basic steps of inquiry. With a little tweaking of those steps, a WebQuest will take no longer to build than any other well-thought-out unit of study. In fact, the steps for the teacher are reduced in preparing a WebQuest, because much of the responsibility for the learning that occurs in the context of a WebQuest falls on the shoulders of the students.

Step 1: The Teacher Selects a Problem and Conducts Preliminary Research

The WebQuest model begins with an open-ended problem or a puzzling situation that the students are going to explore with Web and text resources put at their disposal. The problem is based in the content of the curriculum, but its solution is based in the quest that the students will undertake. For example, if the curricular area is ecology, the problem might concern the reintroduction of wolves into Yellowstone Park. If the curricular area centers on the basic operations in mathematics, the problem might concern when, where, how, and why humans invented numbers, including the question of whether the base-ten system is ideal. If the curricular area is Columbus's "discovery" of America, the issue of the WebQuest might be whether Europeans were justified in claiming the Western Hemisphere as their own.

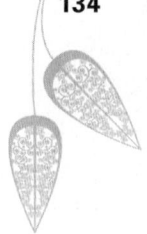

The first step in creating the quest is for the teacher to search for appropriate Web pages and other sources that address the issue or problem. Much of what is on the Web may not be accessible for English language learners, young readers, or students with less prior knowledge or experience with the topic, so the bulk of the work for the teacher will be to find links that will be the most helpful to the students for whom the WebQuest is being created.

The easiest way to illustrate this is by an example. For the purpose of illustrating how a WebQuest is built, consider the topic *weather*. Weather is in the curriculum at several grades, and it certainly encompasses many open-ended problems. We will look at the question, "What causes the weather to change, and would we want to change it if we could?"

The teacher's research is straightforward, and the resources are clear. Can the local meteorologist come talk to the class? Does the school library have books on the topic of weather? What does the students' science textbook have to say on the topic? Is there mention of weather in the students' other textbooks, such as the geography text? And, of course, what websites contain helpful information related to weather?

Answering the last question requires the use of a good search engine—an Internet tool that will automatically list all the websites it can find related to the topic of your search. The trick is to word the search topic in a way that keeps the number of "hits" reasonable. Because even the narrowest search may yield a thousand or more sites, your job is to sift and sort them, saving only those that will be the most useful to your students. Most search engines use ranking criteria that cause the most relevant sites to appear at the top of the list, typically based on the number of times the words in the search topic match words on a Web page.

The current favorite search tool, or engine, among Web enthusiasts is Google, because it is fast and accurate. There are many other choices available, however, and most searchers will use more than one tool. Because the engines differ somewhat in the criteria they use to choose and list their findings, using at least two search engines is usually worth the time and effort.

To make our weather example come to life, log on to the Web, open up Google at the address www.google.com, and conduct a search for the following: weather + change + snow + rain + wind. (The plus signs will restrict the findings to sites that contain all of these words.) Review the Google search tips and try out the various options to narrow the search. One of the values of a thorough search of the Web is that the sites you find will suggest ideas you might never have thought of otherwise. For example, the Web site www.cmos.ca/weatherlore.html contains a very readable discussion of the expressions and sayings related to the weather, such as, "Red sky at night, sailor's delight; Red sky in morning, sailor take warning." Students could be asked to find the source of all these weather expressions and how many have any basis in fact. The WebQuest would involve students in studying the scientific basis of many things "everyone knows" about the weather.

It is important to save the most relevant Web addresses that appear on the search results page. Most Web browsers make this very easy. You can simply put any address that seems particularly promising into the "Favorites" or "Bookmarks" folder, or you can create a subfolder called "Weather Sites" in your "Favorites" or "Bookmarks" folder and put the addresses there. Saving these Web addresses will make subsequent steps in constructing the WebQuest very easy.

Step 2: Present the Problem in the WebQuest Template

A convenient template is available that can be used to create and present a WebQuest to students. Go to the address http://webquest.sdsu.edu/LessonTemplate.html and download the "traditional no-frame version" of the template for the PC or Mac. If you are not comfortable with HTML or Web editors, there are several online authoring systems that are available for designing WebQuests—Quest Garden, Filamentality, 2WebQuest, PHPWebQuest, and TeacherWeb. Some of these are free; others require subscriptions. These and instructional videos can be found on WebQuest.org and other sites that promote the design of online quests.

Any computer server in your school would be a good place to store and access your Web page, and any school technical resources person can help you with this. Storing your Web page on such a server will make your Web page available to students from any computer at school or at home. Creating a Web page is no more complicated than the steps followed in creating a word processing document on a computer, but it is a new process, and thus an intimidating one for many people. If you are among this group, be patient and take your time. A whole world will be opened to you!

The WebQuest template is practically a fill-in-the-blank recipe that is organized into the following sections, which you merely elaborate to suit the context of instruction:

1. *Introduction.* A short paragraph is written to introduce the activity or lesson to the students. The introduction sets the stage and offers a teaser to grab the students' attention. For a WebQuest on the question "Why can't we do any-

thing about the weather?" the introduction might begin, "No newscaster gets more criticism than the meteorologists. Why are meteorologists so often wrong? What's so hard about predicting the weather? And for that matter, have you ever wondered why we really can't do anything about the weather?"

2. *The task.* The task section provides a crisp and clear description of what the end result of the learners' activities will be. Learners should see that they will need to gather information and then transform that information into something novel. The end point, for example, may be writing and sending a letter to the editor of the local newspaper or to the National Weather Service, or it might be creating a display illustrating the forces that cause weather to change.

3. *The process.* This section enumerates the steps the learners should go through to accomplish the task. If possible, these steps should be enumerated as a numbered list. This section of the WebQuest contains the Web links and names of other resources the students will need to complete the task. It also discusses how the students will organize and use the information they gather and how they will organize themselves. In the inquiry on weather, for example, students might work in groups to explore different aspects of weather such as precipitation, wind, heat and cold, hurricanes and tornadoes, or weather lore.

4. *Evaluation.* This section describes how the students' performance will be evaluated. Include the characteristics of the product you expect and what different levels of quality would look like.

5. *Conclusion.* Briefly summarize what students will have accomplished or learned by completing this inquiry activity or lesson.

6. *Credits and references.* This section lists the sources of any images, music, or text used in creating the WebQuest.

Step 3: Students Gather Data and Information to Solve the Problem

In the WebQuest form of inquiry, the students, not the teacher, gather the information and solve the problem. It is the students' inquiry that drives the learning. Through the structure of the WebQuest, all the resources, Web and other, are listed in the context of an open-ended problem that the students must solve by working alone or in groups. The teacher's role is to answer technical and other questions and to guide the students to the tools they will need to create a unique and reasonable product. The variety of these products is practically limitless, as a quick survey of WebQuest examples will demonstrate.

Step 4: Students Develop and Verify Their Solutions

Responsibility for developing, testing, and verifying solutions to the problem rests with the students. As they present the products of their work to the rest of the class or to other groups, they will "test" their findings. Because a problem posed by a WebQuest is open ended, there is not a single solution, and every solution is subject to revision. The greatest value of WebQuests and other forms of inquiry rests in their potential for teaching students that the nature of true scholarship lies in the search for plausible answers to the complex questions that humankind faces. WebQuests help students realize that researchers often do not understand much that must be learned, but they have the courage to face the "wilderness of mystery" that constitutes every discipline. Inquiry learning invites students to participate in this great adventure.

Summary of Steps in the WebQuest Model of Inquiry

1. *Select an open-ended problem that students can readily explore by searching the World Wide Web.* In this first step, the teacher narrows the problem to ensure that the solutions students arrive at are grounded in Web resources at an appropriate level of difficulty.

2. *Present the problem to students in the form of a WebQuest template.* The structure of this fill-in-the-blank format, organized into sections that logically reflect the steps of problem solution, makes it easy for students to see what they are to do in attacking the problem.

3. *Students gather data and information to solve the problem.* Now the students work on their own as much as possible, the teacher serving as technical adviser and answering questions related to the mechanics of the WebQuest. The result will be a product that lays out a logical solution to the problem.

4. *Students develop and verify their solution.* By sharing the product of their WebQuest with other students and adults, students get feedback that helps them refine their answers to the complex questions surrounding the problem. There are likely many solutions to the problems posed by a WebQuest, and the final step of the process is to test the plausibility of the solution students have decided on.

Problem-Centered Model Three: Problem-Based Inquiry Model

In one sense, all three problem-centered inquiry models might be called "problem-based learning," or PBL. The steps of the problem-based inquiry model and the use of an Inquiry Chart set this particular PBL model apart, however, as a distinct model of instruction. In all problem-based learning, the teacher serves as subject matter expert, resource guide, and task group consultant but not as information transmitter or sole source. The major role of the teacher is to encourage student participation, provide appropriate information to keep students on track, avoid negative feedback, and assume the role of fellow learner.

An ancient Chinese proverb provides the most succinct basis for problem-based learning: "Tell me, I forget. Show me, I remember. Involve me, I understand." When students are involved in a search for the solution to an open-ended problem whose solution they are committed to finding, they learn and retain more than if what they were studying were merely given to them in lecture or text. The difference between traditional schooling, in which the attempt is to transmit knowledge to the learner in digested form, and the transformational schooling of inquiry learning centers on who gets to make meaning of information. Where students are allowed to make their own meanings in attempts to solve ill-structured problems, they come to understand the topics of the curriculum at a deeper level and in more meaningful and memorable ways.

Here are some generalizations about problem-based learning, points that can serve as guidelines for thinking about issues and approaches to the design of problem-based learning opportunities for students. While there are many possible formats for presenting problem-based learning units, the following principles remain consistent:

- In a PBL unit, the ill-structured problem is presented first and serves as the organizing center and context for learning. In problem-based inquiry, the Inquiry Chart helps to organize the pursuit of a problem solution.
- The problem on which learning centers
  - Is ill-structured in nature
  - Is met as a messy situation
  - Often changes with the addition of new information
  - Is not solved easily or formulaically
  - Does not always result in a right answer
- In all PBL classrooms, students assume the role of problem-solvers; teachers assume the role of tutors and coaches.
- In the teaching and learning process, information is shared, but knowledge is a personal construction of the learner.
- Thinking is fully articulated and held to strict benchmarks.
- Assessment is an authentic companion to the problem and process.
- The PBL unit is not necessarily interdisciplinary in nature, but it is always integrative. Ideas and skills from other disciplines may be used.

Step 1: Explore the Problem

Problem-based learning does not happen in a curricular vacuum. Look at the curriculum you have to teach and ask yourself what problem or problems are embedded in the objectives of the curriculum. One way to do this is to look at the standards to which you are teaching or the test you will hold students accountable to, asking yourself, what problem does this information solve? Try to define that problem in a way that ensures students will become engaged with the issues.

Strategy Alert

Identifying Similarities and Differences

Identifying similarities and differences is a strong strategy that is a natural approach to learning and solving problems in and out of school. As students examine a problem, they need to ground their problem analysis in comparing what they know about this problem with what they know about how other problems have been solved. Students need to identify the commonalities and distinctions between the knowledge needed to solve the problem and the useful information that they already have.

Venn diagrams are a useful tool for this purpose. The structure of the diagram, intersecting circles with overlapping space, allows clear display of features of things that make them different and features that make them similar. Metaphors and analogies are also useful in identifying similarities and differences. Metaphors are used to describe something in a way that is descriptive and interesting. They rely on how two things are not alike in most concrete ways but similar in an abstract way. For example, we can compare schools and roads, and teachers and bus drivers with this metaphor: Schools are busy multilane highways, and teachers are the bus drivers that help students to their destinations. Analogies are comparisons that express the relation A is to B as C is to D—horse is to carriage as engine is to _____. Or rhombus is to square as oval is to _____. Or Sudan is to Africa as Brazil is to _____. ■

In teaching about the Constitution of the United States, the Bill of Rights is always a good source of problems to explore. Amendment One to the Constitution states: "Congress sha ll make no law respecting an establishment of religion, or prohibiting the free exercise thereof; or abridging the freedom of speech, or of the press; or the right of the people peaceably to assemble, and to petition the Government for a redress of grievances." Who can count the number of problems this simple statement has given rise to! For example, does freedom of speech include the right to speak out against one's supervisors in the workplace, as did several employees at the now infamous Enron company? Does the right to assembly mean that any group of students on school property can assemble for worship before or after classes are in session if they are not required to be elsewhere? How far can schools go in prohibiting student access to the Internet in the interest of protecting them from harm? One does not have to look far to see how many issues citizens face every day that relate to the 45 words of the simple statement that is the First Amendment.

Step 2: Use the Inquiry Chart to Map Learning

The idea of an Inquiry Chart (or I-Chart) stems from an article by James Hoffman (1992) in which he proposed a structure for guiding students' critical thinking in a way that supports the development and refinement of higher-order thinking skills demanded by mature literacy. We have adapted the idea of the Inquiry Chart only slightly to make it fit the purposes of problem-based learning. Examine Figure 7.1 as we describe the steps of its use.

Make a copy of the Inquiry Chart for each student. In the upper-left-hand corner of the chart, in place of Problem Statement, and with input from students, place a summary of the problem that was explored in step 1. Next, brainstorm with the students to formulate some questions that the problem suggests. Enter a few of these in the spaces to the right of the problem statement. Next, ask students to draw on their prior knowledge to create hypotheses of answers to the questions they have posed. These will be best guesses, subject to correction as the inquiry process continues. Now look to resources that might be useful in answering the questions and pursuing solutions to the problem. These resources may be text based, including selections from the textbook in use in the class; they may include primary documents (such as the Constitution itself or letters written and shared among the founders) or any number of other kinds of resources, such as websites and experts in the community who can be brought in.

Figure 7.1   Inquiry Chart

Problem Statement	Question	Question	Question	New Question
Hypotheses				
Text Source 1				
Text Source 2				
Primary Sources				
Other Sources				
Summary				

Source: Adapted from Hoffman, J. (1992). Critical reading/thinking across the curriculum: Using I-charts to support learning. *Language Arts, 69,* 121–127.

These steps complete the planning phase of the I-Chart. The next steps involve using a variety of resources in answer to the questions prompted by the problem statement. In general, students work in groups to answer questions and come up with potential solutions to the problem. This may lead to additional questions, and these can be entered in the far right column of the chart. As students fill in their own copies of the I-Chart, many teachers construct a large, butcher-paper-sized copy onto which the entire class can make entries. This serves to illustrate the cooperative, whole-class nature of the problem-based learning experience while at the same time allowing individuals and small groups to pursue different lines of inquiry.

Step 3: Share Different Solutions

Once the I-Chart is complete, students begin to formulate potential solutions to the problem. These are drawn in part from the summary of answers to each question on the chart, answers that are based in different resources. The idea here is to dramatize the fact that different resources may provide different answers to the same question; but, where several resources confirm one another in their answers, the student can be all the more certain that he or she is on the track of a justifiable solution to the problem. This is what constitutes critical inquiry and is the basis of critical literacy that problem-based study rests on.

Step 4: Take Action

The final step in the problem-based inquiry model of instruction is to decide on actions. Depending on how "local" the problem is, students may decide on poster sessions they can hold in public places. A panel of experts in the problem may be invited to hear the solutions the students have conceived. Letters to the editor of the local or national press may be appropriate. A spot on the community service television or a presentation to a local governing authority may be the perfect venue for sharing. If the problem that students have spent so much time investigating and "solving" is real to them, they will want to take appropriate action with what they have created in response to the problem. The possibilities for this are limited only by the imagination, and students who are committed to solving real-world problems are usually very creative in deciding what actions to take.

Summary of Steps in the Problem-Based Inquiry Model

1. *Explore the problem.* Virtually every part of the curriculum provides an answer to some problem or another. Science and history particularly are composed of answers to problems, and there is always a problem at the core of literature. The history of mathematics is replete with problems that demanded solutions.

World languages present opportunities for the study of problems of communication and culture. Survey the standards that you are teaching to, asking yourself "To what problem is this the solution?"

2. *Use the Inquiry Chart to map learning.* This chart maps the questions surrounding the problem to sources that students can use in finding answers to the questions.

3. *Share different solutions.* Different sources may provide at least slightly different answers to the questions or solutions to the problem. The I-Chart allows students to map different perspectives on the same questions.

4. *Take action.* The solutions to the real-world problem at the heart of the inquiry can now be put into action—through letters to the editor, communication with state or congressional representatives, presentations to relevant boards, or by whatever means the students' imaginations can conjure. The point is to take learning seriously enough to lead to action of some kind.

Evaluating Learning in the Problem-Centered Inquiry Models

In some schools, there is enough technological support so that each student could design a WebQuest as a culminating assessment. This assessment would allow students to follow their own interests in a structured and detailed manner. WebQuests can be designed by groups, individuals, or teachers. Teacher-designed WebQuests can serve as both instruction and assessments. WebQuests would need to be carefully evaluated with a rubric or checklist. The rubric or checklist should consider the visual appeal and ease of navigation of the quest; the efficacy, accuracy, and clarity of the task; and the quality of the resources.

Traditional paper-and-pencil tasks can also be incorporated in inquiry methods to help students and teachers see progress toward the clearly stated objectives. Essays can be used to hold students individually accountable for their part in a group inquiry project. Multiple-choice and short-answer items can demonstrate foundational knowledge and scaffold students to higher-level thinking. For example, if students are working on an inquiry about swine flu, it would be a good idea to make certain that they understand the mechanisms of influenza and something about the transmission of disease before solving the problem of the spread of this feared disease.

Assessment can also be part of the inquiry instruction. I-Searches, questions, and research plans can detail student knowledge and understanding. Teachers can determine student success by looking at the number and accuracy of questions and answers that are being explored and being used to build understanding. Longer inquiry projects can have a number of stop-and-share time checks so that the teacher can assess the probable success of the process and whether misconceptions are being constructed. Inquiry models offer a wealth of opportunity for assessment.

Meeting Individual Needs in the Problem-Centered Inquiry Models

> Go to the Building Teaching Skills and Dispositions section of Topic 11: Inquiry Models in the MyEducationLab for your course and complete the activity entitled "Planning for Inquiry Lessons."

Inquiry is built on asking questions and finding solutions. Teachers who use problem-centered inquiry instructional models have a great opportunity for responsive teaching. Students can ask questions and research hypotheses providing time for personal discovery using individual interests and skills. These individual searches are motivating for students of all ages. Teachers can help students link personal searches and quests to prior knowledge and clearly stated objectives so that students are readily able to incorporate new information and skills. This guided teaching allows students to become more metacognitive and self-regulatory.

Teacher-selected problems for group inquiry can also represent student interests and cultural background. And, when appropriate, students can be challenged to inquire about unfamiliar problems that help to extend and enrich their current knowledge. By guiding students to new resources and information, teachers can extend and enrich the knowledge that students bring to an important question. By understanding individual student needs, teachers will be able to make certain that there is a "good fit" between the kinds of inquiry used with students and the instructional goals.

Each inquiry requires data collection, and the data collection process allows for several differentiation approaches. For students who enjoy working with and talking to people, interviews and focus groups can be used. Library research will work well for those students who enjoy analytic tasks, while other students might prefer getting out into the "real world" and collecting information and data that can be used to answer the important questions being pursued. The important connection between differentiation and inquiry methods provides a multitude of differentiation opportunities. The trick is to find ways to personalize the approach while helping all students learn.

Benefits of Problem-Centered Inquiry Models

Problem-centered inquiry models have many benefits, the most obvious that the focus of learning is on questions rather than answers, on problems rather than solutions. Too often, instruction is about answers to questions that the learner is not even aware of, let alone curious about or interested in. Problem-based models, by contrast, are organized to generate the interest that provides a place for solutions and answers, giving ownership of the learning to the learner. Problems can also be identified that link to students' learning needs, interests, and readiness levels. Students may study different aspects of a problem, allowing for the differentiation of skills and knowledge. A major benefit of problem-centered inquiry is the flexibility afforded to teachers in adapting the curriculum to the needs of the students with whom they are working.

Elementary Grades Lesson

PROBLEM-CENTERED INQUIRY: Monarch Butterflies and Stewardship

OBJECTIVES

Students Will Understand
- We are all responsible for protecting the earth

Students Will Know
- The definition of the word *stewardship*
- The reasons for the decline in the population of monarch butterflies
- Places that monarch butterflies thrive

Students Will Be Able To
- Explore the question "How can we help the monarch butterfly repopulate?" and generate responses
- Translate responses into researchable questions
- Make a plan for collecting information and resources

ASSESSMENT

Students will draw a three-cell storyboard showing how they would like to solve the problem of the loss of population of the monarch butterfly.

PROCEDURES

1. Review with students the life cycle of a butterfly studied earlier.
2. Share information about the monarch butterfly, the long migration of the butterflies, and why the numbers of monarch butterflies are falling.
3. Use the think–pair strategy. Ask students to think with a partner about possible solutions to the problem of helping monarch butterflies repopulate. Focus on the questions What can we do? and Why should we do it?
4. Share possible solutions in a whole class discussion. Keep a list of suggestions of what we can do. Always go back to why we should help the monarch butterfly and the idea of stewardship.
5. Once there are five to ten suggestions on the list, return to each suggestion and determine what the class would need to know to implement the

suggestion. In this way, eliminate complicated or inappropriate suggestions. The list should include questions that need to be answered and resources needed to answer the questions.

6. Narrow the list to two or three solutions.
7. Ask students to discuss these solutions with friends and family as they begin their work on helping the monarch butterfly.
8. Students draw storyboard.

Middle/Secondary Grades Lesson

PROBLEM-CENTERED INQUIRY: Toxins

OBJECTIVES

Students Will Understand
- A structured inquiry approach can help resolve puzzling situations

Students Will Know
- The definition of *toxin*
- Working conditions in 18th- and 19th-century England
- The puzzle of the mad hatters
- How felt hats were made

Students Will Be Able To
- Work with the class to construct a reasonable theory that explains why so many hatters behaved as though they were insane

ASSESSMENT

Students will write a five-paragraph essay (1) explaining the puzzle of the mad hatters, (2) the conclusions that were reached in the class discussion about this puzzle, and (3) how this puzzling situation can be related to something in the world today.

PROCEDURES

1. Review the information surrounding the case of the mad hatters in 18th- and 19th-century England.
2. Remind students of the Suchman inquiry model. Explain the roles of students and teacher. Review the rules. (1) Students may only ask a question when called on, (2) Students may talk to each other only during caucus times, (3) Questions must be those that require only a yes/no answer, and (4) A student can continue to ask questions as long as a positive response is received from the teacher.
3. Students gather data by asking questions. Data should be recorded.
4. Students may ask to caucus.

5. Students pose a theory; class determines validity of theory.
6. Once the class accepts a theory, students are asked to explain the theory and the rules associated with it.
7. Analyze the Suchman inquiry process with the class.

Summary

The first inquiry model presented in this chapter is primarily based on the work of Richard Suchman. The model uses the steps employed in scientific inquiry to approach problems in general. The second utilizes the Web as a primary source of information as students solve problems through their own investigation.

The inquiry model is appropriate whenever the learning that is to take place requires students to be involved with information actively while challenging and questioning solutions to determine if they are acceptable. Used in conjunction with other models in a design process, the inquiry model provides a stimulating option for solving problems and teaching thinking skills.

Problem-based learning characterizes all the models in this chapter, but the problem-based inquiry model itself is built around a structure called the Inquiry Chart. The PBL model thus provides a structure for authentic student-generated questions. These questions provide a roadmap for learning, a map whose destination is action in consequence of learning.

Extensions

ACTIVITIES

1. Look through a current textbook. Are there any inquiry opportunities for students in the text? Can any of the lessons suggested by the text or in your district's pacing guides be adapted for an inquiry lesson? Make a list of at least five possible inquiry lessons.
2. Explore the www.webquest.org website. There is information about setting up WebQuests and sample WebQuests. Complete one WebQuest and find two that might be useful in your classroom.
3. Read the local newspaper for a week and keep track of all of the possible problems that your students may be able to address in a Suchman Inquiry lesson.

REFLECTIVE QUESTIONS

1. Which of the following would be appropriate problems for an inquiry lesson?
   a. What is the answer to 3×8?
   b. Who was president of the United States during the Civil War? Who was president of the Confederate States?

c. The changes of the tides on earth seem to be related to earth's position relative to the moon. What factors might explain this relationship?
d. We have learned how plants make food through photosynthesis. Here are pictures of certain plants that can grow in the dark. How are these plants able to survive?
e. Shakespeare did not leave a shred of paper that can be verified as his own writing, aside from a possible signature. Did he himself write all those plays and sonnets, or is it possible that someone else did the work and put Shakespeare's name on it to preserve his or her anonymity? Explore the Shakespeare mystery and find an answer to one of literature's most enduring questions.

8

The Synectics Model

Developing Creative Thinking and Problem Solving

chapter OBJECTIVES

You Will Understand
- Metaphorical thinking supports student academic learning, problem solving, and creative thinking

You Will Know
- The synectics process
- The ways in which synectics can be used within the K–12 curriculum
- How synectics can contribute to creative writing skills and problem solving by broadening perspectives

You Will Be Able To
- Identify, design, and implement a synectics model lesson

In the ELEMENTARY classroom

In his fifth grade social studies class, Mr. Broome is about to begin a synectics "Making the Strange Familiar" lesson. This variation of the synectics process involves leading students through the use of analogies to see relationships between new and unfamiliar material and information they already know. The class has been studying the Civil War for the last few days. Mr. Broome reads the picture book *Cecil's Story* by George Ella Lyon to the class. When he finished reading the book about the departure and return of a father during war, Mr. Broome asks the students to think about the similarities between the Civil War and an earthquake. He provides the following comparisons:

- In an earthquake, the land often splits open. The North and South were one country and then they split open.
- In an earthquake many people are killed by strong forces. In war, this is also true.
- Before an earthquake there are warning tremors. Before the Civil War, there were some warning signs that trouble was coming.
- After an earthquake, there are usually aftershocks; following the Civil War there were many aftershocks.

Mr. Broome asks the students to identify any of the aftershocks from yesterday's discussion and they share "Lincoln's assassination," "increase of racial prejudice," and "cotton became a less important crop."

Mr. Broome asks students to imagine what it feels like to be an earthquake. He writes on the chalkboard each of the feelings the students mention. Mr. Broome also asks students to explain why an earthquake would feel these things. Students share the following list:

powerful	angry	like a leader
natural	predictable	strong
noisy	stressed	embarrassed
forceful	frightening	sad
omnipotent	energetic	violent
ashamed	apologetic	unstoppable

Mr. Broome asks the students to find words on the list that fight with each other or don't fit well together—compressed conflicts. The conflicts are also listed on the board: *angry* and *natural, sad* and *energetic, stressed* and *powerful, predictable* and *powerful*, and *omnipotent* and *ashamed*.

The class then discusses how the Civil War was both powerful and predictable or how the participants might feel both omnipotent and ashamed. Students may role play some of these ideas, write about the ideas, or find specific examples of the ideas in the work they have done in class. This step of the synectics model allows for a differentiated product. After examining the ways that the Civil War was similar to an earthquake, Mr. Broome asks the class to consider how the Civil War and earthquakes differ. Daniel responds, "Earthquakes don't last as long."

Jeremy explains, "War is not a natural event the way an earthquake is." Other ideas that students share include that wars are caused by people and earthquakes are caused by shifting plates. Wars can be prevented; earthquakes cannot be prevented. When earthquakes are over, the government goes back to what it was. After a war, there are big changes, especially for those who lost.

Mr. Broome is pleased with the good thinking of his fifth grade class and asks students to write a paragraph about the Civil War using some of the words and images discussed in class. This paragraph is a good formative assessment for Mr. Broome as he is planning the rest of the unit's lessons, but he still wants students to use metaphorical thinking to help them understand the reasons for and consequences of the Civil War. He asks students to create their own analogies. "To what can you compare the Civil War that would help us learn about its impact? I would like you to think of as many things as you can to which you might compare the Civil War. Tomorrow, I'll ask you each to share your list with us all."

On the SECONDARY classroom

Ms. Amato's seventh grade students have been studying the early colonists in New England and they are about to begin a unit on the Salem witch trials. Ms. Amato asks the class to write a paragraph describing witches, a subject that they seem to know a lot about from a variety of media. Ms. Amato writes *Witches* on the board.

Ms. Amato: What words or phrases did you use to describe witches in your paragraph?

Rob: They are spooky.

Ms. Amato: Why do you think they are spooky?

Rob: Well, you never know what they are going to do, and people are afraid of them.

Ms. Amato: Would you say that they are unpredictable?

Rob: I suppose.

Jeremy: I think they are powerful because they can cast spells and make things change without our permission.

Emily: Some people believe that witches are evil and do the work of the devil.

Isabella: There are good witches too. Remember in *The Wizard of Oz,* it was a good witch who saved Dorothy. Witches are like people, some good, some bad.

Shenice: I wrote that witches are not real. They are based on superstition and ignorance.

Ayla: When I was little, I dressed up like a witch for Halloween. I wore a long, black dress and a pointed hat.

Jennell: Me, too. I put a big wart on my nose with clay and used an old mop to make stringy hair.

Deven: And they fly around on broomsticks.

The class continues to share and Ms. Amato writes the words on the board.

spooky	unpredictable
powerful	cast spells
some good/some bad	imaginary
based on superstition	based on ignorance
wear funny clothes	fly on brooms
make brew	can disappear

Ms. Amato: This is quite a list of descriptors. Look at the list closely for a few minutes and then tell me what plant comes into your mind when you look at some of these words. I'll list the plants on the board.

Jeremy: I think of a Venus flytrap because they can be beautiful but they trap insects.

Rob: How about an old oak tree in a swamp with moss hanging from the branches? I saw one like that on a trip, and it made me feel really spooky.

Isabella: How about a dead tree standing all alone in the field?

Emily: I think of those trees in the swamps with the big roots that grow down to the water.

Jeremy: Are you thinking of a cypress tree?

Emily: Yes. They seem to be powerful, but they are frightening, too. They aren't really evil, but they make me feel uncomfortable not knowing what is down below those roots.

Jennell: It makes me think of a weeping willow blowing in the wind. They always seem to be flying, and they make me feel sorry for them.

DEVEN: Well, I think of a potato. They usually have warts on them, and they have rough, ugly skin.

MS. AMATO: Look at the list and vote on which of the images you would like the class to pursue.

Venus flytrap plant	old oak tree with moss
weeping willow tree	cypress tree in swamp
potato	witch hazel

[A vote is taken.] It looks like the oak tree with moss has been selected. Close your eyes and imagine what it would be like to be a tree like this.

JEREMY: It feels lonely. There aren't any other trees around that are like me. I am old and different.

ROB: It feels like I am being used, with all this moss hanging on me. I can't get away, and this moss is taking advantage of me.

ISABELLA: I feel strong and powerful. I am bigger than everyone else, and this moss needs me.

JENNELL: I feel peaceful. It is very quiet here, and the wind is stirring in my branches.

DEVEN: I feel trapped because I can't get away. I just have to stay in this place forever.

PAUL: I feel independent. There is no one around and I am free.

lonely	needed
old	trapped
powerful	independent
different	used
taken advantage of	strong
peaceful	free

MS. AMATO: Look at the list and pick out pairs of words that seem to fight each other and have very different meanings.

The students come up with a list of compressed conflicts.

powerful and trapped	lonely and peaceful
trapped and free	powerful and taken advantage of
needed and taken advantage of	trapped and independent [class choice]

MS. AMATO: Let's try an animal for the direct analogy step. What animal seems to be both trapped and independent?

DEVEN: A horse in a corral. It is trapped, but is still very independent in the way in moves in the corral.

SHENICE: It reminds me of an animal—a leopard—in one of those zoos where the animals seem to be free but they really can't get away.

JENNELL: I've been at a zoo like that. You just walk around, and there aren't any cages or bars. The animals seem to be free, but you hope they really can't get away. There is always something that is stopping them. There was this beautiful big parrot that couldn't get away because its wings had been clipped.

ISABELLA: My grandmother has a parrot, and that bird is so independent. She won't talk or do anything unless she wants to, but she is still in that cage.

PAUL: I saw a film about trapping otters. The animals caught in the trap always seemed to be independent and fierce even with they were bleeding and in pain.

EMILY: My cat is like that. Even though she has to stay in the apartment and she can only sit in the window and look out, she is still independent.

MS. AMATO: Let us select one of these that seems to be the best example of something that is both independent and trapped. [A vote is taken.] It will be the otter caught in the trap that we will examine further. Now, here is the question. Suppose you lived back in the day when witches were condemned and put to death. How is a person who has been condemned as a witch like an otter who is caught in a trap?

ISABELLA: They would probably be fighting for their lives and would try anything to escape.

ROB: Trapping animals is illegal in most places now because it is so cruel to the animals. We don't believe that people should be called witches anymore either.

JEREMY: But there are people who want to be called witches today.

PAUL: Sometimes people hunt and trap animals because they are beautiful. Sometimes people were jealous of the witches because they were different and people wanted to destroy them.

SHENICE: People used to trap animals because they didn't know any better, and that was the way it was with witches. They just didn't know how wrong it was. There are still people today that think that it is OK to trap animals just like there are still people who believe in witchcraft.

MS. AMATO: We have discussed lots of images of witches. Now, think of a new description of witchcraft and think about how some of these images might have angered the people of Salem. Write a paragraph explaining why the people of Salem might have been afraid of the accused witches.

Basis for the Synectics Model

William Gordon is credited with the development of the process called synectics, which is derived from the Greek word *synecticos* meaning "understanding together that which is apparently different." Synectics uses group interaction to create new insights through this "understanding together" process. As an instructional model, synectics is specifically designed to enhance creativity in problem solving by having students consciously develop analogies that allow for an emotional as well as a rational approach to solutions.

Synectics has evolved over the years for both business and education. Specific techniques have been developed that are effective in teaching creative thinking and writing in all curriculum areas for problem-solving skills and new ways to use information. Synectics can teach students skills in making unique and creative connections between what they know and what they are to learn. Through the use of metaphor, connections develop or grow stronger during the synectics process. Metaphors and analogies highlight similarities and differences. These comparisons increase student understanding and the application of new skills and information (Prince, 1970).

Detached observation and analysis are essential to solving problems, but the ability to use empathy, imagination, and feelings is equally essential. The flashes of insight and creativity that come from our nonrational thinking create unique and extraordinary images and solutions. It is this irrational part of our thinking that synectics is designed to enhance.

The synectics process works most effectively when the objective is for students to look at reality in a different way and experiment with possibilities. Objectives calling for inductive thinking and seeing wholes in relation to parts require that students juxtapose seemingly disparate facts or occurrences. Because students seldom know how to do this, instruction that helps them recognize analogous relationships is very important. Synectics is the ideal means to this end. Experts have a more refined conceptual framework than do novices. To help our students develop more expertise in a content area we need to provide students opportunities to make their thinking public and to develop more intricate webs of knowledge and skills (National Research Council, 2000). Synectics allows students to share their prior knowledge and extend their understandings of the organized network of a specific discipline.

Originally, synectics was used in developing new products for industry by having groups play with metaphors in solving problems. In making the familiar strange, the mind is unlocked from the narrow confines that prevent creative insights and solutions. In making the strange familiar, the mind connects that which is already known to the unknown, thus facilitating the new learning.

Contrary to the common belief that creativity is an isolated activity that cannot really be understood or taught, Gordon maintains that it can be taught and that learners can understand how to use the process in solving problems or in developing more insight into descriptions and analyses. Using synectics in a group can actually enhance the creative process for many individuals. It provides an important kind of interaction: the sparking of ideas from one person to another.

Synectics also encourages interdisciplinary relationships. The act of combining seemingly unlike entities causes both students and teachers to search for relationships across the artificial boundaries of knowledge that can be so restrictive. How are volcanic eruptions and civil wars alike? Frost's poetry and Euclid's geometry? Paragraphs and biological classification? Grammar and diplomatic protocol? Maps and story plots?

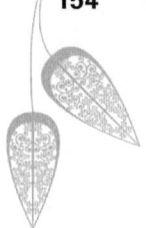

This ability to hold two very different concepts together in the mind has been described as Janusian thinking, after the Roman god with two faces, Janus. Janusian thinking consists of actively conceiving two or more opposite or antithetical concepts, ideas, or images simultaneously, as existing side by side, as equally operative or equally true, or as both. In apparent defiance of logic or matters of physical impossibility, the creative person formulates two or more opposites or antitheses coexisting and simultaneously operating, a formulation that leads to interrelated concepts, images, and creations (Rothenberg, 1979).

The ultimate goal of synectics is to find practical and realistic solutions to problems and more effective and powerful ways of communicating ideas. Yet the means used to achieve these goals is unique to the process. By insisting on the involvement of the irrational and emotional part of the brain before engaging the rational and the analytical, synectics seeks to open new dimensions of thought and new possibilities for problem solving.

There are three versions of synectics presented in this chapter. The first helps students see new patterns and relationships from previously learned knowledge and understandings. The second helps make new knowledge more meaningful by bridging new and familiar information. And the third approach to synectics uses analogies and metaphors to solve problems.

Version One: Making the Familiar Strange

In this version of the model, students are encouraged to see the ordinary and the familiar in a new and different way. Through this process, they can often see unexpected possibilities in what they may have thought to be routine and predictable. This is a good model for helping students look at familiar content in a new way. It extends information and helps to build new conceptual schema.

Step 1: Describe the Topic

The teacher begins by asking students to describe a topic with which they are familiar (e.g., a character of fiction, a concept, or an object), either in small-group discussions or by individually writing a paragraph. In the case of young children or students who cannot write, discuss the subject with them and write down their descriptive words and phrases. Or have them draw a picture or act out their interpretation of the subject. Use this step to frame an initial description of the topic.

When the students have completed their writing or discussion, ask them to share the words they have used to describe the topic. Write them on the chalkboard. (If there is no board space, use sheets of paper that can be torn from a chart and attached to the wall.) List the words or phrases without evaluating them; all student contributions are welcome.

Step 2: Create Direct Analogies

In the second phase of the model, the students form a direct analogy between the descriptive words on the board from step 1 and words from an apparently unrelated category. For instance, the teacher may ask them to examine the list and name a machine that reminds them of as many of those words as possible. Plants, foods, flowers, and animals are other possible categories.

Direct analogies are direct comparisons between two objects, ideas, or concepts. For instance, how is a classroom like an anthill? How are the veins of our bodies like a plumbing system? In each of these questions is an implied metaphor. With practice, students can increase the strangeness or abstraction of their metaphors.

Add each student's contribution to the board and encourage each person to explain why he or she chose a particular analogy. When the teacher feels that everyone has had an opportunity to participate and the class is ready, the students vote on one particular analogy that they would like to pursue in the next step of the synectics model.

In one class, students produced the following initial list of descriptive words while exploring the word *math*:

difficult	obscure
sometimes hard, sometimes easy	necessary
frightening	a key
rewarding	a mystery

When asked to name a machine that these words reminded them of, they listed the following:

- Computers, because they hold the key but they are hard to learn
- Pianos, because they have keys but they can be obscure and difficult
- A dentist's drill, because it is frightening but necessary

Step 3: Describe Personal Analogies

In the third phase of the synectics model, learners are asked to view reality from the perspective of the metaphorical object that they just selected. After giving students a short time to think, ask them to tell you how it feels to be this object and list their reactions on the board. Encourage each person to explain why he or she had a particular feeling. It takes older learners more time to accept this step in the model, but once they do, the response can be exhilarating.

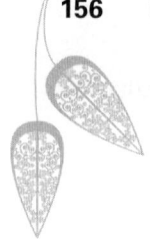

A group of teachers participating in a synectics lesson used student behavior in the lunchroom as their subject. The teachers were comparing the children to a swarm of bees; when asked to consider what it would feel like to be a bee inside a swarm, they expressed the following perceptions:

- *Helpless.* I have to do what the others are doing.
- *Powerful.* I am the queen and I can make the others follow me.
- *Frightened.* I don't know what will happen next.
- *Secure.* I don't have to make decisions for myself.
- *Dangerous.* I can harm people with my stinger.
- *Carefree.* I can fly, and I don't have to make decisions.
- *Armed.* I have my stinger.
- *Imprisoned.* I have to follow the swarm, and I am inside, and I can't escape.
- *Vulnerable.* I can be swatted if I get away from the group.
- *Independent.* I can fly away from trouble.

A group of third grade students described how it felt to be a rose blooming on a fence:

- It feels like I'm safe because I have thorns all around me.
- I feel fragile because I can't bloom very long and the heat makes me wilted.
- Beautiful and admired: People come by and see how nice I look.

Step 4: Identify Compressed Conflicts

The fourth step is the most exciting and important step in this model. Ask the students to examine the list of descriptive feelings they created in the last step and to put together pairs of words that seem to fight each other. For instance, our example of the teachers comparing the children to a swarm of bees might produce the following list:

Frightened and secure
Helpless and powerful
Armed and vulnerable
Carefree and frightened
Independent and imprisoned
Armed and carefree

These are all combinations of words that seem to be in conflict, yet each pair is in metaphoric tension. The conflict between such juxtaposed words causes a tension that is felt as each pair of disparate ideas is considered. This incompatibility invites the student to ignore the literal meaning of each word and to attend more closely to the abstract or figurative connections between the pair. Take all suggestions and encourage the students to explain why they think the words fight each other. Then have the students vote once again on which combination of words contains the best compressed conflict.

Step 5: Create a New Direct Analogy

Using the compressed conflict chosen by the class, ask the students to create another direct analogy. For instance, if the combination chosen was *independent and imprisoned,* ask the students to describe an animal that is both independent and imprisoned. Some possible analogies would be:

> A tiger in a cage
> A human being in society
> A powerful dog on a leash
> An astronaut in a space shuttle

Then, once again, have the students vote on the best direct analogy.

Another category for the compressed conflict could be that of food: Hot sauce in a bottle or seeds inside an orange are foods that are both independent and imprisoned. The more experience teachers and students have with the model, the more categories they will be able to use with confidence.

Step 6: Reexamine the Original Topic

In this step, return to the last direct analogy chosen by the class and compare it to the original topic. For instance, if the last analogy chosen was "a dog on a leash" and you had begun the process with "a character in a novel," you would ask the class to describe the characteristics of the leashed animal and then to consider the character in terms of those descriptors.

No mention is made of the original subject until this step. The purpose is to get away from the original topic, step by step, and then to return with all the rich imagery that has been developed during the process. An important part of this step is that each student hears the thoughts and relationships expressed by the others.

Asking the students to describe the original topic in writing again gives them the opportunity to use any of the images that were generated during the exercise, not only those of the last analogy. This works particularly well with older learners and with students who are experienced in working with this model. The list of analogies provides the students with a rich resource of words and images.

Summary of Steps in Making the Familiar Strange

  1. *Describe the topic.* Select a subject to explore with the class. It can be from any discipline: a character from a novel that has been read or a concept such as freedom or justice; a problem, such as behavior on the school bus; or a technique,

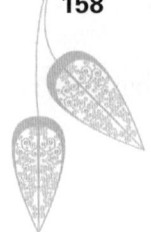

such as diving. Ask students to describe the topic. The descriptive words or phrases are written on the board.

2. *Create direct analogies.* Select a category, such as machine, plant, or food, and ask the students to examine the list of words generated in step 1 and describe how those words are like an item in the chosen category. Ask the students to explain the reasons for their choices.

3. *Describe personal analogies.* Have the students select one of the direct analogies and create personal analogies. Ask the students to become the object and describe how it feels and works. Write down the words used by the students to describe their feelings.

4. *Identify compressed conflicts.* Direct the students in creating a series of compressed conflicts using the words from the personal analogy stage. Ask the class to pair words that seem to conflict or fight with each other and that seem charged with tension.

5. *Create a new direct analogy.* For one of the pairs of words from the compressed conflict step, ask the students to create another direct analogy by selecting an object (animal, machine, fruit, or the like) that is described by the paired words.

6. *Reexamine the original topic.* Return to the original idea or task so that the students may produce a product or description that uses the ideas generated. They may concentrate on the final analogy or they may use ideas from the total experience.

Version Two: Making the Strange Familiar

In this variation of the synectics model, the teacher leads the students through the use of analogies to see relationships between new and unfamiliar material and information they already know.

Step 1: Provide Information

The teacher selects the new material to be learned, perhaps the study of reptiles, adjectives, fractions, or the periodic table. The teacher provides factual information for the topic.

Step 2: Present the Analogy

If the new subject is multiplication, the teacher might present the analogy by listing the similarities between multiplication and a factory.

- In a factory, the same objects are made over and over again. In multiplication, the same number is added over and over again.

- In a factory it is important to keep track of the numbers of things that are made. In multiplication, it is important to keep track of how many times you add a number.
- In a factory, there are machines to help the people make things. In multiplication, we can use manipulatives to help us find the answer to multiplication problems.
- In a factory, there is a boss who tells the workers what to do. In multiplication, the teacher tells us what problems to do.

Step 3: Use Personal Analogy to Create Compressed Conflicts

The teacher asks the students to imagine what it feels like to be a factory. The teacher writes these feelings on the board, and the students pair these words to create compressed conflicts. One pair is selected for further exploration. For instance the students might select *busy* and *lonely* or *productive* and *tired* as their compressed conflict.

Step 4: Compare the Compressed Conflict with the Subject

The class then discusses how multiplication is both productive and tired or busy and lonely. The teacher can ask students to explain how they feel on each side of the conflict.

Step 5: Identify Differences

Students explain where the analogy does not fit. The students might recognize that factories are buildings and multiplication is something we do. Factories are filled with people and multiplication is filled with numbers. They may also notice that factories can close, but multiplication will always be around.

Step 6: Reexamine the Original Subject

The teacher asks students to discuss or write about the original subject, multiplication in our example, using images and ideas that were discussed in the lesson.

Step 7: Create New Direct Analogies

The students are encouraged to create their own analogies for the original subject. The teacher instructs them to select analogies that are as far removed as possible from the subject. For instance, the idea of a calculator is quite close to multiplication. However, a track race seems very dissimilar and might therefore create some interesting comparisons.

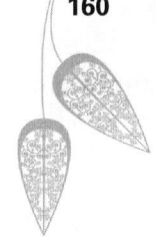

Summary of Steps in Making the Strange Familiar

1. *Provide information.* Students must understand basic facts and information related to the subject to be explored.

2. *Present the analogy.* Have a prepared analogy involving the subject that will be familiar to the students.

3. *Use personal analogy to create compressed conflicts.* Have students describe how it feels to become the subject; then have them create compressed conflicts.

4. *Compare the compressed conflict with the subject.* Students select one compressed conflict and then compare it to the original subject.

5. *Identify differences.* Students discuss the differences between the original subject and the compressed conflict.

6. *Reexamine the original subject.* Ask the students to write about or to discuss the original subject using the ideas, words, and images in the exercise.

7. *Create new direct analogies.* Encourage students to create new analogies different from the initial one.

Version Three: The Synectics Excursion

The synectics excursion process uses all three forms of analogy—direct, personal, and symbolic—to solve a problem. Ask students to design a particular product, such as a better mousetrap. Students may be asked to solve a problem that has surfaced in the school or community. Or ask them to develop procedures to accomplish a task more effectively, such as running a marathon or translating an ancient map to locate a buried treasure (Weaver, 1990; Wilson, Greer, & Johnson, 1963). They may even discuss issues of national and international importance!

Step 1: Present the Problem

The problem should be one that will excite the interest and the enthusiasm of the participants and should be stated in general terms by the teacher. For example, one problem is how to design a more efficient process for leaf removal.

Step 2: Provide Expert Information

Information about the situation and as much expert advice as possible are provided to the class. For instance, a catalog containing various rakes and leaf removal machines could be presented. A group of students could report on the current techniques for removing leaves, the problems faced by landfills, and the air pollution from burning leaves. A person from the city garbage collection department could be invited to discuss the problems of removing leaves and dealing with leaves once they arrive at a landfill.

Step 3: Question Obvious Solutions and Purge

The teacher encourages the students to brainstorm obvious solutions to the problem and the relative merits of these. Solutions identified by the group as unworkable are purged from consideration. The problem can be solved in this step if all the class agree to a particular solution; usually, however, the answers that come most readily are the least effective. The teacher should be prepared to assist the students in identifying the flaws. For instance, a student might suggest that the leaves be burned. The teacher might, in turn, question the problem of burning in relation to air pollution.

Step 4: Generate Individual Problem Statements

The students are asked to write and restate the problem individually as each understands it. They are instructed to break the problem down into the component parts and state one of these in their own words. For instance, an individual student might focus on the problem of overcrowded landfills. Another student might focus on the problem and the fire hazard of piles of leaves on the streets awaiting removal.

Step 5: Choose One Problem Statement for Focus

The students read their descriptions of the problem to the class, and the class selects one to pursue further. For instance, one student may have focused on developing a new technique for reducing leaves at the landfill, whereas another student may have focused on treating the leaves as a valuable natural resource. The class must choose to explore one possible approach to the problem.

Step 6: Question through the Use of Analogies

At this point, the teacher presents the students with a number of analogies. For instance:

Direct Analogies
1. A leaf on the ground is like what animal?
2. How is a leaf like an elderly person?
3. What do leaves and garbage have in common? How are they different?
4. How is a leaf like an orphan?

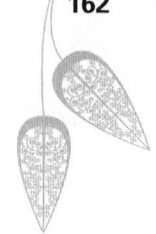

Personal Analogies
1. What would it feel like to be a leaf?
2. What does it feel like to be a machine that collects leaves?
3. What does it feel like to be abandoned?
4. What does it feel like to be a load of leaves in a landfill?

Symbolic Analogies
1. How can a leaf be both free and doomed?
2. How would you describe something that is both essential and a nuisance?
3. How would *useful* and *nuisance* apply to this problem? *Helpful* and *destructive*?

Fantasy Analogies
1. If you could suspend the laws of gravity, how could you prevent the leaves from falling off the tree?
2. If you could control the tree, how could you prevent the leaves from falling?
3. Create an animal that could help solve the problem.

Step 7: Force Analogies to Fit the Problem

The students are asked to return to the problem of designing a better system for leaf removal and to apply the analogies directly to this subject. For instance, the teacher might ask questions about the analogies.

1. If leaves are essential to life, why do we consider them a nuisance?
2. If leaves are like orphans, how can we provide more effective homes for them?
3. Allowing the leaves to remain where they fall is like allowing the elderly to remain productive.
4. Placing leaves in mulch piles and learning how to treat the mulch properly is like providing a home where the leaves can continue to be productive.

Step 8: Determine a Solution from a New Viewpoint

Using the force fit of one or more of the analogies, the teacher assists the group in looking at the problem from a new viewpoint. From this viewpoint, the group determines if they have discovered a solution to the problem. For instance, they may have decided that a special type of worm could be genetically engineered that would live in home mulch piles and reduce the leaves to mulch or that a mechanical "worm" could be designed to reduce leaves to mulch.

If students decide that there are still some situations in which leaves must be removed, the class can continue the cycle of exploring analogies leading to additional solutions.

Summary of Steps in the Synectics Excursion

1. *Present the problem.* Select and then present to the class an interesting and challenging problem.

2. *Provide expert information.* Provide the class with as much expert information as possible.

3. *Question obvious solutions and purge.* Lead the class in an exploration of the most obvious solutions and have the students purge those that are not feasible.

4. *Generate individual problem statements.* Have each student write a statement regarding the problem, giving his or her interpretation or focus.

5. *Choose one problem statement for focus.* The problem statements are read aloud, and one is selected by the class for focus.

6. *Question through the use of analogies.* Present analogies to the class stated in the form of evocative questions.

7. *Force analogies to fit the problem.* Return to the original problem and ask the students to force the analogies to fit the problem.

8. *Determine a solution from a new viewpoint.* Ask students to determine a solution by looking at the problem from a new viewpoint.

Evaluating Learning in the Synectics Model

Synectics requires students to construct analogies and to use the analogies to help find innovative solutions to problems. The model itself offers the opportunity for formative assessments. Teachers can monitor individual contributions to the discussion of personal and direct analogies and compressed conflicts during the implementation of the synectics process and during the subsequent discussion. Analogies can be assessed as to their construction and quality. While every contribution to the discussion is accepted, the teacher can take notice of the construction of the analogies and how prior knowledge is extended with the analogies.

A summative assessment might require a constructed response that examines the quality of the novel solution to the problem being examined and the accuracy of the concepts that have been used in analogies. So if students participated in a synectics lesson on homework, an essay question asking students to share what they learned about homework and how teachers and students can find a way to use homework to everyone's advantage may be asked. Students may also be asked to generate additional analogies and metaphors that are associated with the topics or problems under discussion. Rubrics can be developed to provide structure for feedback and student performance.

The synectics process itself can serve as an assessment. Asking students to develop direct analogies, personal analogies, and compressed conflicts can demonstrate student understanding of academic content. The steps of Making the Strange Familiar and Making the Familiar Strange can be used as the basis for a paper-and-pencil or Web-based assignment. Student work would be evaluated by the number and quality of the metaphors and the writing that accompanies the last step of the model.

Meeting Individual Needs in the Synectics Model

Providing support for students to learn specific skills, processes, and information results in increased student learning (Good & Brophy, 2003). When this support is also stretched to meet the needs of a variety of students, teachers differentiate. Scaffolding students through the different synectics processes allows a variety of opportunities for supporting student learning. In synectics, the goal is to help students develop a conscious creative process to find solutions to problems by examining relationships and patterns between new and unfamiliar things. Teachers can provide practice in constructing metaphors and analogies by using stretching exercises and graphic organizers.

Marzano (2001) defines creating metaphors as identifying a general pattern in one topic and finding another element that appears to be very different but follows the same abstract pattern. Teachers can use student interests as the foundation for building metaphors. Analogies identify relationships between pairs of concepts. Stretching exercises that ask students to develop direct and personal analogies and compressed conflicts before the complete instructional model is used can be helpful to students who are not comfortable with these comparisons or with students who need the opportunity to choose comparisons from an unlimited universe. The range of stretching exercises might extend from teachers providing the first element of the analogy and defining the abstract relationship, to providing the abstract relationship alone, to simply providing a broad topic in which analogies can be constructed. For example, students may be asked to compare a hurricane to food served at a restaurant, or to compare weather to food, or to make comparisons that include things that affect us with things that we need to survive. Below are some examples of sentence stretchers:

- How is a cat like a motorcycle?
- In what ways is taking a nap like taking a trip?
- How is bird migration like making dinner?
- What does it feel like to be a computer?
- How are maps like chocolate bars?
- What does it feel like to be the Declaration of Independence?

Strategy Alert
Graphic Organizers

Teachers can differentiate and scaffold students by providing a graphic organizer (see Figure 8.1) to practice building analogies. Graphic organizers play a powerful role in student learning by providing support for the development of new skills, such as generating analogies. A graphic organizer can help students see the connections between the two elements of an analogy. To differentiate, teachers can include more or less information on the organizer or ask students to develop their own graphic to demonstrate the comparisons.

Figure 8.1   Analogy Organizer

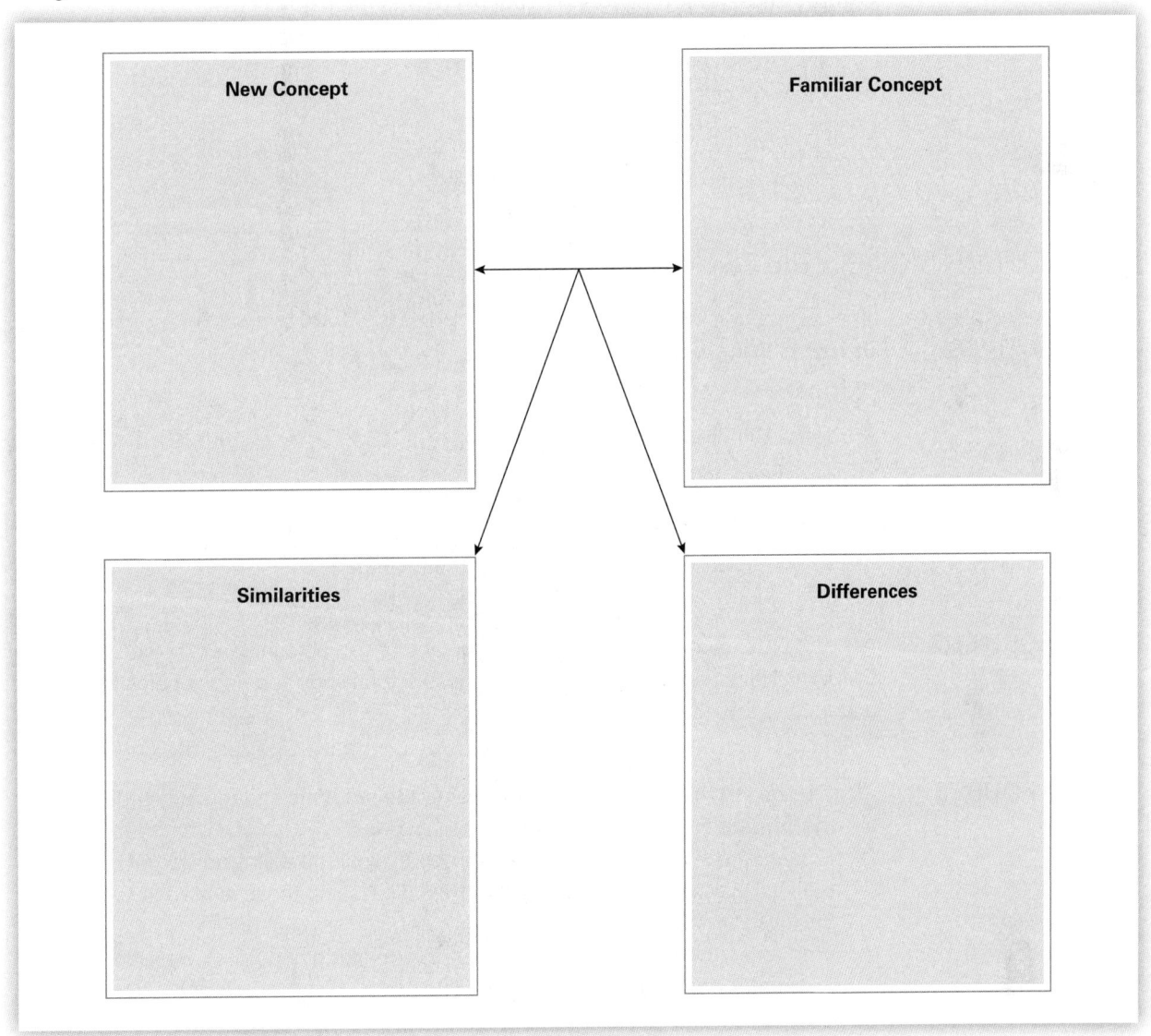

New Concept	Familiar Concept
Similarities	Differences

Benefits of the Synectics Model

Creativity is important in our everyday life. We need to be creative when we solve problems, express our feelings, demonstrate empathy, or move toward deep understanding of complex concepts. Synectics helps students find fresh ways of thinking about ideas and problems. Creativity is a learned behavior and the creative process is similar across all grades and curriculum subjects. Synectics is an adaptable and rewarding process. Since metaphors are the language of creativity and creativity allows for the development of new conceptual structures, synectics can play an important role in academic achievement and in the development of problem-solving and social skills. The use of direct and personal analogies and compressed conflicts invites all students to join into the discussion. And the model is very amenable to both differentiation and alternative assessment options.

Elementary Grades Lesson

SYNECTICS MODEL: The Civil War

OBJECTIVES

Students Will Understand
- The effects of war are long lasting

Students Will Know
- The short- and long-term effects of the Civil War

Students Will Be Able To
- Explore analogies and metaphors of the Civil War

ASSESSMENT

Ask students to construct a different analogy that can be compared to the Civil War. Have them explain why they chose the analogy and how it helps to understand the effects of war.

PROCEDURES

1. *Provide information.* Read *Cecil's War* to the students and remind students of the content of previous lessons.
2. *Present the analogy.* Present the analogy by listing the similarities between the Civil War and an earthquake and then discussing these similarities with the class.
   a. In an earthquake, the land often splits. The North and South were one country, and then they split apart violently.

b. In an earthquake, many people are killed by strong forces. In war, the same thing happens.
   c. Before an earthquake there are warning tremors. Before the Civil War there were warning signs that trouble was coming.
   d. After an earthquake, there are usually aftershocks; following the Civil War there were many aftershocks.
3. *Use personal analogy to create compressed conflicts.* Ask students what it feels like to be an earthquake and why they feel that way. Record the feelings that are shared by the students. Ask students to look over the list and find words that don't fit together, that fight. You may need to provide an example. Once there is a list of compressed conflicts ask students to choose one to pursue.
4. *Compare the compressed conflict with the subject.* Ask the class to discuss how the Civil War is like the chosen analogy. (You can ask the students to write about their feelings on each side of the conflict—the North and the South.)
5. *Identify differences.* Ask students to consider how the war and an earthquake are different.
6. *Reexamine the original subject.* Students reflect on the discussion and on what they know about the reasons for and consequences of the Civil War. Ask students to identify their own analogies to help demonstrate their understanding.

Middle/Secondary Grades Lesson

SYNECTICS MODEL: Witches

OBJECTIVES

Students Will Understand
- The political, religious, economic, and social stresses of life can lead to mob behavior

Students Will Know
- The images associated with witches

Students Will Be Able To
- Explore analogies and metaphors about witches and make connections between their ideas and those of the Salem, Massachusetts, community

ASSESSMENT Students will use the analogies discussed in class to explain why the people of Salem might have feared the witches.

PROCEDURES

1. *Describe the topic.* Ask student to write a short paragraph about witches that will be discussed in 10 minutes. Once students have completed writing, have them share some of their descriptive words. Write all contributions on the board.
2. *Create direct analogies.* Ask students to use the words in the list and name a plant that reminds them of as many of the words as possible. As students share their contributions, write them on the board. Encourage students to explain why they chose a particular analogy. When everyone has had an opportunity to participate and the class is ready, have the students vote on one particular analogy that will be pursued during the next steps.
3. *Describe personal analogies.* Ask students to "become" the analogy they selected in step 2. How does it feel to be this thing? Ask students to explain why they feel this way. Record all contributions on the board.
4. *Identify compressed conflicts.* Have students examine the list from step 3 and put together pairs of words that seem to fight or contradict each other. List all contributions and have students vote on the best compressed conflict.
5. *Create a new direct analogy.* Using the compressed conflict voted on in step 4, have students create another direct analogy comparing the compressed conflict to an animal. Have the class vote to choose their favorite direct analogy.
6. *Reexamine the original topic.* Return to the direct analogy identified in the previous step. Compare this direct analogy to witches. Have students share their observations. Make connections to Salem, Massachusetts.

Summary

Synectics is a process that uses the power of metaphor to expand imagination and creative thinking. Students are encouraged to look at problems in new and more dynamic ways and to express their ideas forcefully. The key to its success lies in getting learners to see relationships among ideas they might otherwise have never associated. The result alters the way the learner sees information and ideas to be learned.

Synectics can be used with learners of all ages. Students and teachers enjoy the process and are often astounded at the interesting and imaginative results. Although synectics is particularly effective in teaching writing, it is also effective in any type of learning where the objective is to develop new and creative insights into a problem. Participants—both teachers and students—are amazed at the power of metaphor to capture the imagination of learners.

Three synectics variations are discussed in this chapter. Making the Familiar Strange helps students view familiar knowledge from new perspectives. Making the Strange Familiar links new knowledge with what students already know. And the Synectics Excursion allows students to use metaphorical thinking to find solutions to problems.

9 The Cause-and-Effect Model
Influencing Events by Analyzing Causality

chapter OBJECTIVES

You Will Understand
- Cause-and-effect relationships are central to all disciplines

You Will Know
- What the cause-and-effect model looks like in elementary and secondary classrooms
- The basis in research and theory for using the cause-and-effect model
- The steps of the cause-and-effect model
- How to adapt the cause-and-effect model to meet individual student needs
- How to assess student learning with the cause-and-effect model

You Will Be Able To
- Design, implement, and evaluate a cause-and-effect lesson

In the **ELEMENTARY** *classroom*

Over the last several weeks, Mr. Fisher has noticed his fourth grade students had some difficulty with identifying causes and effects. As they review their science unit on the water cycle, Mr. Fisher sees an opportunity to practice cause-and-effect relationships and extend what students know about the water cycle.

Mr. Fisher begins the lesson by reading an excerpt from *The Long Winter*. The book tells the story of the difficult winter of 1800–1801 on the Dakota prairie.

Mr. Fisher: What do we know about the winter of 1800–1801?

Rebecca: There was a lot of snow and blizzards.

Laura: They didn't have the Internet to check the weather!

Mr. Fisher: What causes snowstorms and blizzards? How is what we learned about the water cycle involved in snowstorms and blizzards?

Julie: The water cycle explains how precipitation happens and snow is precipitation.

Randy: A blizzard is more than snow, though. It gets really windy and blows the snow around. Sometimes you can't see in a blizzard—everything is white.

Extensions

ACTIVITIES

1. The following words were developed by a class to describe the character of Tom Sawyer. What vehicle do the words in this list make you think of?

clever	naughty	young
headstrong	old-fashioned	original
brave	funny	smart

2. Select a topic and follow the steps of the Making the Familiar Strange model on your own. Then repeat the experience with several friends. Compare the richness of the images created both individually and when in a group.
3. Create an analogy to use with each of the following subjects: fractions, nutrition, bridges, nouns, Declaration of Independence, and poetry.
4. Select a problem about which you are concerned and go through the steps of the Synectics Excursion on our own. Determine if approaching the problem in this manner helps you explore possible solutions effectively. Then repeat the activity with a group of adults and see if the results are different.

REFLECTIVE QUESTIONS

1. How well do you need to know your content to develop analogies and guide your pupils in developing successful analogies?
2. What could a teacher do to help students who have difficulty working with synectics models?
3. In what ways can the synectics process improve your own teaching and learning?

Figure 9.1 Cause-and-Effect Organizer for *The Long Winter*

Prior Causes	Causes	The Long Winter of 1800–01	Effects	Later Effects
		• Cold • Lots of snow • Blizzards • Railway closed down trains • 7 months of bad weather		

Mr. Fisher discusses the role of warm and cold winds in winter storms and some of the characteristics of blizzards. He asks students in a think–pair–share exercise to compare rain, snowstorms, and blizzards and explain how precipitation occurs, making sure that they use the words *evaporation* and *condensation*. After the students share their comparisons, Mr. Fisher reviews the cause-and-effect organizer in Figure 9.1.

Beginning with the center of the organizer, Mr. Fisher asks students to share what they know about the long winter of 1800–1801. Several students volunteer information about the winter, which is listed on the organizer.

Mr. Fisher: What are the causes of blizzards?

Ruth: It's cold enough to make snow.

Tina: There is a lot of water in the air and clouds form.

Robert: Isn't there something about warm and cold are together in the air?

Mr. Fisher provides additional information on the warm and cold air interactions and helps students fill out the Causes section of the organizer.

Mr. Fisher: What was the immediate effect of the two-day blizzard in the story? What happened right after the storm stopped?

Ruth: Families had to go and find the children or other people who were missing.

Karen: They had to figure out whether to stay on their homestead or move into town.

Tina: They had to take care of the people who were sick or didn't have enough food.

Laura: They had to fix any damage.

After several other contributions, the class fills in the Effects section. Mr. Fisher leads a short discussion about prior causes and the class settles on the fact that although this was an unusually harsh winter, people did the best they could to survive.

ReNita: What do we put down in the last column?
Karen: Weather prediction got better.
Laura: People were better prepared.
Tina: Some people moved away.

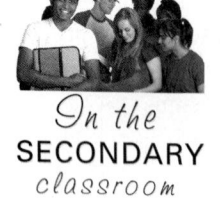

In the **SECONDARY** *classroom*

Mrs. Coffey's advanced senior class had just finished studying *Hamlet*. She felt there were certain issues they had not grappled with sufficiently. She decided to use the cause-and-effect model with one of the play's central issues: why Hamlet continued to hesitate to act against Claudius. This hesitation led to the death of all of the royalty at Elsinore Castle.

The emphasis would be on causes and prior causes, because the effects and subsequent effects were obvious. Mrs. Coffey wrote, "Hamlet continues to hesitate to take action against Claudius" under the heading *Topic* in the center of the chalkboard. She began by asking for causes:

Jerome: Hamlet was squeamish; he couldn't kill in cold blood. He couldn't even kill Claudius after the play, when he had proof.
Judy: But remember Hamlet's previous reputation for bravery and his military success against the older Fortinbras.
José: Hamlet wasn't sure about the ghost. It could have been a trick. People in those days believed ghosts could be real or could be messengers of the devil.
Maria: Hamlet was sort of in shock. Everyone at the castle was acting strangely—not like they had always acted. So he hesitated until he could figure out what was going on.
Phil: Like the suddenness of the queen's second marriage.
Jane: Hamlet didn't know whom to trust, except for Horatio.
Andy: He was afraid of death. That's what it says in his soliloquy.
Anne: But he seems more afraid of not setting his father's ghost free.
Phil: But if he takes action, everyone else might think he just wanted to be king.
Maria: No one else suspects the king. It's really odd.
Andy: Hamlet overanalyzes everything.
Maria: Well, what do you think he should have done?
Andy: He should have killed Claudius after the play.
Phil: And be thought of as a power-hungry murderer?
Andy: Couldn't Horatio have defended him?
Phil: But it's only Horatio, and he didn't even hear what the ghost said.
Caneka: He wants others to see what he sees: Claudius's guilt.
Maria: He hesitates because he hates Claudius so much.

EVERYBODY: But that's a reason to kill him.

MARIA: No, you don't understand. Hamlet has this sense of justice. If he's wrong, and he kills him, then he's worse than Claudius. That's why he has to expose him first.

[The others began to see Maria's point. Some agreed.]

MRS. COFFEY: Where should I put his sense of justice?

MARIA: I guess that's a prior cause.

[They moved to prior causes.]

PHIL: I guess the main prior cause is his father's death or murder.

RASHAD: The ghost's request for revenge.

CANEKA: He's got to be careful. These are all people who cared about him and he cared about: his mother, Ophelia, Horatio, Laertes, even Polonius.

JEROME: And Yorick, and Fortinbras admired him.

JANE: You know, I don't think all these people would have been fooled. I think Maria's right. If Hamlet had been evil or overly ambitious, they would not have cared for him quite so much. I think he does feel some princely responsibilities, and he does have a sense of justice. He isn't afraid for himself. He wants to be sure; he wants to do the right thing. It's ironic that people keep getting hurt because Hamlet is trying to do what is right. [They all began to agree with this perspective.]

Mrs. Coffey felt they had reached a depth of understanding of the play and of its main character that they might not have reached without this model.

Conclusions

1. Hamlet's hatred of Claudius caused him to be especially careful in trying to find proof of his guilt.
2. Hamlet understands that he must prove conclusively that Claudius is guilty or people will think Hamlet simply wanted to be king.
3. Hamlet realizes that if he takes action against Claudius, and Claudius is innocent, that he, Hamlet, is far more guilty than Claudius.

Generalizations

1. In trying to find proof of guilt, we must attempt to be objective, or the proof may be suspect.
2. Guilt must be proved convincingly, or justice will not have been served.
3. If we wrongly convict an innocent man, we are guilty of the injustice we have accused him of.

Basis for the Cause-and-Effect Model

The model presented in this chapter leads students through an investigation of a significant action, situation, condition, or conflict. Through a process of inference, students hypothesize about causes and effects, prior causes, and subsequent effects. Finally, they draw conclusions and arrive at generalizations about how people usually behave in similar situations. The teacher is a facilitator, asking set questions, not contributing to or commenting on the contributions except to ask follow-up questions.

In history, anything from a single action to a war to the passing of a bill to the election of a candidate can lead to fruitful discussion. Almost any experiment or condition in science will lend itself to this model, as will particular problem-solving strategies in mathematics. When a class has finished a piece of literature in English, a significant action or a climax or a pivotal moment makes a stimulating topic. Newspaper articles, particularly advice columns, can lead to exciting discussions, especially if the subject is important to the students. Using situations such as students coming late to class or disrupting class as the topic will enable students to understand the reasons behind certain rules.

Once an individual has performed this model in a group several times, he or she can perform it alone. It can become an extremely valuable metacognitive tool in that individual's repertoire of techniques for problem solving, generating ideas, making decisions, and analyzing data. The value of group explorations, however, cannot be overestimated. Hearing the ideas of others opens up many possibilities that students say would never have occurred to them on their own. They become more flexible thinkers and they can more readily construct individual knowledge from prior experience to newly shared information.

The cause-and-effect model begins by examining a specific situation and ends by generalizing about courses of action in similar situations. Students have an opportunity to study a situation in detail, to put names to mental activities they have used in their own thinking, and to hear the thinking of others. They also have an opportunity to speculate about different courses of action and their consequences. This is an inductive approach to teaching that also draws on an intellectual community to help students determine cause and effect.

Generalizations show the relationships among concepts. These relationships help direct student thinking in all discipline areas. Current theories of learning stress that students need to construct their own generalizations in a community of learners that provides for feedback and correction, if necessary. Retrieving and applying new knowledge is an indicator of learning and generalizations help students in transferring new knowledge. By definition, generalizations are approximations—gaining more factual and conceptual knowledge may change the focus or content of thinking. The practice of constructing generalizations through the use of making inferences and comparing similarities and differences is a critical thinking skill (National Research Council, 2000).

Identifying cause and effect allows students to anticipate future actions of both others and themselves. Most of us do anticipate the results of potential actions informally, but familiarity with this model gives us a tool that is more precise. We become more metacognitive by analyzing cause and effect. Cause and effect relationships are important in every content area and in disciplinary studies as well. In fact, examining cause and effect is a content reading strategy used in all content areas to help students comprehend informational text. Understanding why things happen is a basic human drive and this model provides a structure for examining these relationships and developing reasonable expectations.

Steps in the Cause-and-Effect Model

The discussion of the steps of the cause-and-effect model will center on two examples—one elementary and one secondary. Because much of our daily thinking is about cause and effect, it is important to have these specific examples from which to distinguish and construct knowledge about the models. It is important for you to read both examples regardless of what grade level or content area you will be teaching.

The secondary example is based on the book *A Separate Peace*, by John Knowles. The novel is about two friends in a boarding school who are deadly rivals in the eyes of one. Finny is a superb athlete. His roommate and best friend, Gene, is working hard to be class valedictorian. Finny keeps distracting Gene from studying by urging him to try various physical games and feats, and Gene begins to suspect that Finny is trying to sabotage his chance to be valedictorian. This is not true: Finny believes that Gene's academic ability comes with no effort, as Finny's athletic ability does. The topic to be analyzed is Gene's behavior on the jumping tree.

The elementary example is based on the book *The Little Engine That Could*, by Watty Piper. In this well-known story, a small engine carrying Christmas toys and food breaks down on the side of a mountain. The dolls and clowns and toys beg several large engines to pull them over the mountain so that the children can get their treats. The large engines refuse. Finally, a little blue engine comes along and, in spite of her size, says she will help. She pulls and strains and repeats "I think I can" over and over until she is successful. The topic for our sample discussion is why the little blue engine was willing to try something that the other engines had refused to do.

Figure 9.2 can be used to structure the discussion within each of the model's steps. The steps of the cause-and-effect model are listed by number on the organizer.

Step 1: Choose the Data or Topic, Action, or Problem to Be Analyzed

This may be a significant action, event, condition, or conflict. It may be fictional, hypothetical, or real. It may come from any discipline being taught. Write the data or topic in the center of the chalkboard or on a large tablet.

High school topic. Gene jounced the limb that Finny was on.

Elementary topic. The little blue engine was able to pull all the cars filled with dolls and toys and goodies over the mountain when bigger, stronger engines could not or would not.

Figure 9.2 Steps of the Cause-and-Effect Model

4 Prior Causes	2 Causes	1 Topic	3 Effects	5 Later Effects

6. Conclusions

7. Generalizations

Step 2: Ask for Causes and Support for Those Causes

In step 2, the students look for reasons for the situation.

High school questions. "What do you think are some of the causes of Gene's jouncing the limb?" "What else could have caused this action?" Ask the students to support their responses. For example, "Why did Gene's fear of falling make him lash out?" Write all responses on the chalkboard under Causes.

Elementary questions. "Why do you think the little blue engine was able to pull all those dolls and toys and presents over the mountain?" or "Why was such a little engine able to do something that bigger engines had said they could not do?" Ask for support: "What makes you think that?"

Strategy Alert
Flow Charts

A flow chart is a graphic organizer that shows the series of steps in a process. Flow charts can be linear, forked, or cyclical. A linear flow chart can be used to plot a chain of cause and effect by showing a logical ordering of information (see Figure 9.3, an example for the book used in the classroom scenario on pp. 170–172). Students can see that a chain of events is a process in which there are decision points that lead to different possibilities. Linear flow charts use arrows to show the order of events. Rectangles show the events and diamonds show important decision points. Students can plot events and see their relationships. Flow charts are frequently used in business and in computer programming. For classroom use, they can be streamlined to include the flow of events and one or two decision points allowing students to see the connections between events and decisions. Flow charts can be used as a summary before the cause-and-effect model begins and as a scaffold during the discussion of causes and effects. ■

Figure 9.3 Flow Chart Example for *The Long Winter*

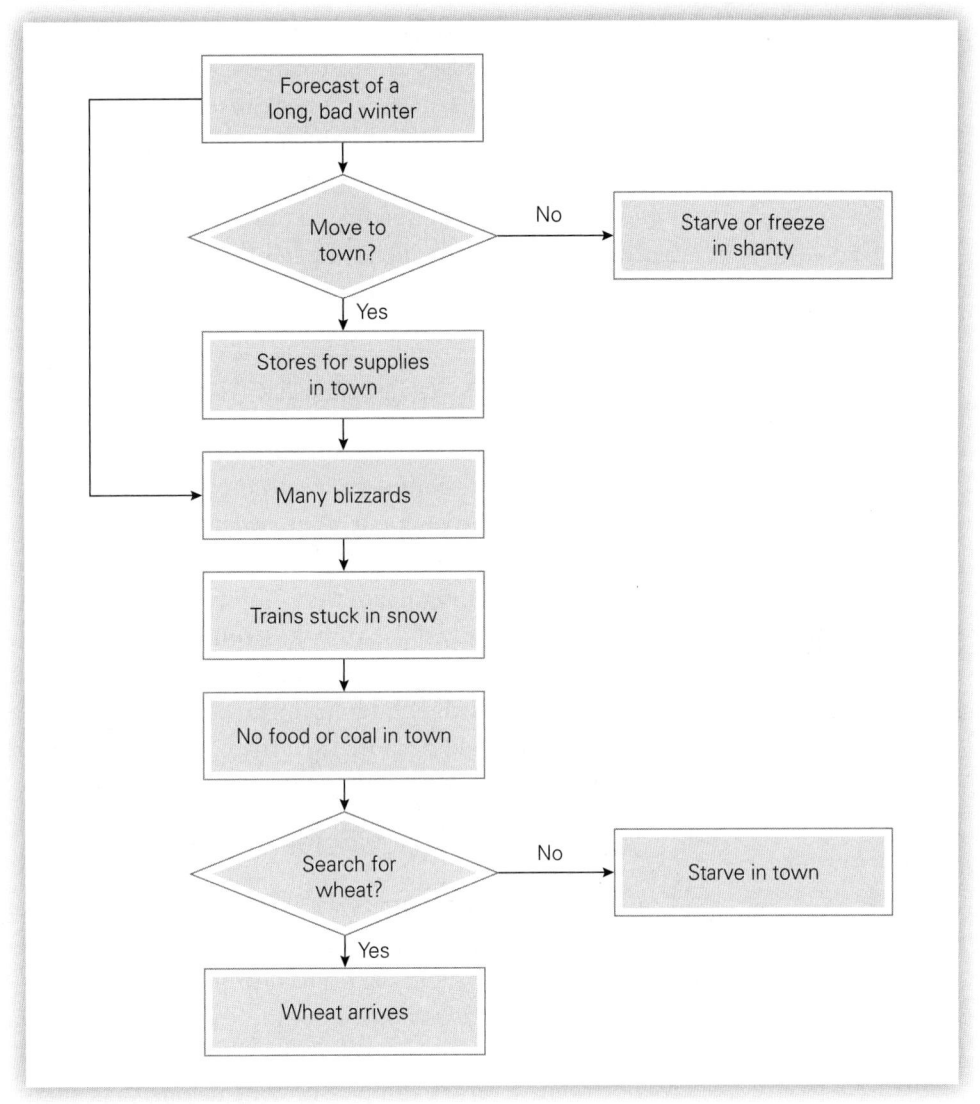

```
Forecast of a long, bad winter
   ↓
Move to town? —No→ Starve or freeze in shanty
   ↓ Yes
Stores for supplies in town
   ↓
Many blizzards
   ↓
Trains stuck in snow
   ↓
No food or coal in town
   ↓
Search for wheat? —No→ Starve in town
   ↓ Yes
Wheat arrives
```

Step 3: Ask for Effects and Support

Moving to the right side of the topic column, ask for effects.

High school questions. "What are some of the effects of Gene's jouncing the limb?" "What are some of the things that happened because Gene jounced the limb?" Ask for support: "Why do you think that?"

Elementary questions. "What are some of the things that happened because the little blue engine was able to pull all those presents over the mountain?" Ask for support: "What makes you think that?"

Step 4: Ask for Prior Causes and Support

Moving to the left side of the chalkboard, ask for prior causes. Take each cause and ask for the causes of those causes, the prior causes.

High school questions. "What caused Gene's low self-esteem?" Then ask for support: "How did Finny's athletic ability increase Gene's low self-esteem?"

Elementary questions. "Why did having done hard things before make it easier for the little blue engine to pull all those presents over the mountain?" Ask for support: "Why did believing in herself help the little blue engine?" Repeat the procedure, asking for the causes of each cause.

Step 5: Ask for Subsequent Effects and Support

After repeating the request for prior causes several times and students seem to be completely out of ideas, move to the far right of the board and ask for subsequent effects. Take each effect separately.

High school questions. "What were the effects of Gene's guilt?" Then ask for support for the subsequent effect: "Why was Gene's return to Devon a result of his guilt?" or simply, "What makes you think that?"

Elementary questions. "What were some of the things that you think happened because all the children in the city had happy Christmases?" "What do you think happened because the little engine felt wonderful?" Ask for support.

Step 6: Ask for Conclusions

Conclusions are statements we infer about the behavior of the persons in the situation under study. Conclusions can come from reading related items on the board from left to right or top to bottom.

High school question. "Looking over the whole chalkboard, what can we say about the way the people in this situation behaved?" Initially, you will have to give them several examples of conclusions. Ask the students to support their conclusions.

High School Conclusions
1. When Gene became convinced Finny was sabotaging his studies, he became suspicious of everything Finny did.
2. Discovering that Finny had not been competing with him made Gene lash out. This sounds contradictory, but discovering that Finny's plotting had existed only in Gene's mind made Gene feel even more inferior and increased his need to lash out.
3. Gene's fear of falling made him jounce the limb in self-defense.
4. Gene's own insecurity made him want to believe the worst of Finny.

Elementary question. "Thinking back about the story, what can we say about how the engines behaved when faced with a hard job?"

Elementary Conclusions
1. Proud engines can become mean.
2. Big engines think they're more important than little engines.
3. Engines with hearts are stronger.
4. Old, tired engines lose their belief in themselves.
5. Engines that believe in themselves can do lots of things.

Step 6 is the most difficult because it involves the most abstract thinking. As noted earlier, you will initially have to give the students several examples of conclusions drawn from the situation being discussed. Performing the model as a class and then in small groups will allow students to see numerous examples of conclusions, yours and those of other students, and, frequently, many catch on to how one thinks abstractly. Thinking abstractly seems to be one of those "lightbulb" experiences where examples suddenly clarify the necessary thought processes.

Step 7: Ask for Generalizations

Generalizations are conclusions expressed in general terms—that is, terms not specific to the topic or the people involved. Students should simply replace the specific names in the conclusions with general names such as *people* or *one*.

High school question. "What can we say about how people we know might behave when faced with a situation like that of Gene and Finny?"

High School Generalizations
1. Discovering that our suspicions about a friend are incorrect can make us angry at ourselves.
2. Being in physical danger can make us aggressive.
3. Feeling inferior makes us want to believe others share our shortcomings.
4. People who are very capable in one area sometimes assume others are also.

Elementary question. "If this were a story about people, would the people have behaved the way the engines did, or would they have behaved differently?"

Elementary Generalizations
1. When asked to do hard things, sometimes big, important people will not make the effort.
2. People who do not care about others will not make an effort to do hard things for others.
3. People who have self-confidence will try hard things.

Summary of Steps in the Cause-and-Effect Model

1. *Choose the data or topic, action, or problem to be analyzed.* When your students are familiar with the model, you may want to ask students to choose the critical action or situation to be analyzed in a chapter in history; a novel, short story, or poem in literature; or a situation in science.
2. *Ask for causes and support for those causes.* Try to elicit as many as possible. We tend to think simplistically in terms of a single cause as opposed to multiple causes.
3. *Ask for effects and support.* Again, elicit as many as possible.
4. *Ask for prior causes and support.*
5. *Ask for subsequent effects and support.* Comment occasionally on the connections between prior causes and subsequent effects. Seemingly unimportant actions can build into major effects.
6. *Ask for conclusions.* Conclusions are statements we infer about the behavior of the persons in the situation under study. Ask the students to support their conclusions.
7. *Ask for generalizations.* Generalizations are statements of inference about how people in general behave in situations similar to those under study.

Evaluating Learning in the Cause-and-Effect Model

The model allows students to infer causes and effects and any evaluation should focus on this relationship. Students may demonstrate their understanding of cause and effect by writing a story based on a single image and then expand the image through prior causes and subsequent effects. This allows students to move beyond chronology to the patterns of relationships found among characters.

The model's graphic organizer can serve as a blueprint for a persuasive essay. The conclusions are potential theses and the listed actions are supporting evidence. The evaluation metric can be how well the students can put these ideas together. The organizer is also useful as a way to establish whether students can generate a theme for a piece of writing. Abstract thinking about themes can be based on the cause-and-effect discussions that occur through the model. Essays can be evaluated in terms of the number of connections that were made between the identified causes and effects.

The ultimate goal of the cause-and-effect model is to help students predict future events in a systematic way. Students can be asked to predict future events and provide support for their predications in many ways. Written work, skits, diagrams, and case study analyses are a few of the ways an evaluation can be structured. Individual or small-group conferences can be held with the teacher asking for clarification of the relationships discussed in class. Students can also be assessed on the generalizations that were constructed at the end of the lesson. Or the assessment may ask students to make additional generalizations.

Meeting Individual Needs in the Cause-and-Effect Model

Although there are many opportunities for differentiation in the cause-and-effect model, the most important is the problem or situation under analysis and the text or situation from which the problem comes. Being responsive to student needs requires knowing the students in the class well enough to frame questions and experiences with individual students in mind. It is critical for teachers to choose a relevant problem to be analyzed and that explicit connections are made to students' prior knowledge and past experiences. Discussions can flex to individual students' needs through varying the complexity of questions and the teacher's attention to misconceptions. Teachers may also scaffold individual students by providing examples of conclusions and generalizations. This is especially important when the model is unfamiliar.

The graphic organizer presented in this chapter or other chronological or relational organizers support both visual learners and those students who are analytic. According to Sternberg and Grigorenko (2004), in order to meet the needs of all learners, teachers must focus their teaching on more than analytic skills. Creative and practical intelligences must also be addressed. The cause-and-effect model can be used to foster both of the approaches. For example, when constructing conclusions and generalizations students can be asked to apply those to real-life situations. In the discussion of *A Separate Peace,* the class might generalize that "being in physical danger can make us aggressive." Teachers can add a practical spin on the discussion by asking for examples of how this idea plays out in the real world and how it might apply to their school. In the elementary classroom, students might be asked to expand on what it means when big, important people will not make an effort to help. How can we help those people change their minds? What can we do to make it more likely that they will help? Even young children have a proclivity for analytic, creative, or practical approaches. Because we want to engage students in the area in which they are most comfortable and help them develop strength in all areas, it is important to use all three aspects of successful intelligence in our classrooms.

Creative intelligence tasks ask students to create, invent, discover, imagine, and predict. In the cause-and-effect model, students can create alternate problems to be analyzed, invent examples of conclusions and generalizations in other situations, discover new and different connections between the causes and the effect, imagine scenarios in which the generalizations play out, and predict what might happen if any of the causes or effects are changed. By using these three aspects of intelligence, teachers can widen the net so that all students have an increased chance to demonstrate what they have learned.

To assess the transfer of knowledge, students can be asked to analyze a new situation or problem. Students can complete a graphic organizer, develop a new organizer for demonstrating relationships, write a narrative that describes the cause and effect and the generalizations that can be made, or demonstrate these relationships in another way.

Performance assessments can be a useful tool. Tasks can be developed that ask students to apply their new cause-and-effect analysis skills. Students can be asked to provide an explanation for or a defense of a recent decision, their own or someone else's. A critique of a decision-making process can be made as a dramatic work, a letter to the editor, or a persuasive essay. Students may also create a display of the cause-and-effect relationships under study. In all cases, the performance task must be carefully constructed so that students are asked to share both content and critical thinking skills and not just performance abilities.

Student choice can be incorporated into the model as students develop familiarity and flexibility in its use. Once the phases of the model become routine, students can choose the problem or situation to which the steps should be applied. And they can choose how to present the information—through the graphic organizer, a narrative, a storyboard, or a multimedia presentation, for example.

Flexible grouping can become a way of differentiating instruction once students can use the model independently. Groups can be formed by choice, background knowledge and experience, readiness, and learning profile. For creative students, teachers can encourage students to vary the way the analysis is organized and presented. Students who are comfortable focusing on the practical applications of the problem can focus on the applications of the analysis.

Benefits of the Cause-and-Effect Model

The cause-and-effect model allows students to explore why things happened or are happening even if there is an unexpectedness about the effects. The model allows students to understand that causes are more than special occurrences that lead to specific events. Rather, causes may help to explain an effect and causes are usually complex and interrelated. Once students construct causal models, they can build patterns of explanation about a series of events. This model takes on one event or problem at a time, but its use over time with similar problems can allow for pattern recognition of similar causes or effects.

The model promotes student engagement and student construction of critical thinking skills as well as curriculum content. Cause and effect is part of everyday life and is represented in every discipline area. An understanding of how the cause-and-effect relationship works in varied settings with varied materials and knowledge helps to increase student learning and efficacy. Once the model is internalized by students, it becomes a metacognitive tool helping them analyze specific situations.

Elementary Grades Lesson

CAUSE AND EFFECT: Water Cycle, Blizzards, and *The Long Winter*

OBJECTIVES

Students Will Understand
- There is a relationship between the water cycle and weather

Students Will Know
- The three states of matter
- The definition of evaporation, condensation, and precipitation
- The causes and effects of blizzards

Students Will Be Able To
- Explain and diagram the water cycle
- Complete a cause-and-effect organizer about the long winter

ASSESSMENT

Students will complete the following cause-and-effect graphic organizer about the Ingalls living through the long winter.

Prior Causes	Causes	The Long Winter of 1800–1801	Effects	Later Effects

PROCEDURES

1. Read an excerpt from Laura Ingalls Wilder's *The Long Winter*.
2. Discuss the winter of 1800–1801 on the prairie.
3. Review the water cycle and how blizzards happen. Make certain that students can define evaporation, condensation, and precipitation.
4. Ask the following questions and guide students to the appropriate responses. Together fill out a sample cause-and-effect organizer.
   a. What do we know about that winter from our reading?
   b. What causes snowstorms and blizzards? (Highlight the water cycle and the role of cold and warm winds.) How do you know?

184 Part 2 • Matching Objectives to Instruction

      c. What was the immediate effect of the blizzards of 1800–1801? How do you know? What would the effects be of a blizzard today?

      d. We know that blizzards are caused by specific weather conditions. How does the earth's water cycle contribute to weather conditions? (Have students support their answers. Explain the term "prior causes.")

      e. What might the later effects of the long winter be? What might the later or subsequent effects be of a blizzard today?

5. What did we learn about the winter of 1800–1801 on the Dakota prairie?

6. What do you think that the people who survived the blizzard learned? How might their behavior have changed because of the experience?

7. If we had a blizzard today, how might our behavior differ from the behavior of those who survived the long winter of 1800–1801?

Secondary Grades Lesson

CAUSE AND EFFECT: Hamlet and Claudius

OBJECTIVES

Students Will Understand
- Guilt must be proven before action is taken

Students Will Know
- The plot and characters in *Hamlet*

Students Will Be Able To
- Discuss the causes and prior causes of Hamlet's hesitation to take action against Claudius

ASSESSMENT

Students will summarize the class discussion in two written paragraphs that focuses on the generalization: A civilized nation assumes that a person is innocent until proven guilty.

PROCEDURES

1. Provide students with the question for discussion: Why did Hamlet continue to hesitate to take action against Claudius?
2. Record all answers on the board.
3. Probe student responses, if necessary.
4. Monitor discussion to distinguish between causes and prior causes. For example, if someone says that Hamlet's sense of justice or lack of a need for revenge is a cause, explain why it is a prior cause.
5. Make certain that students support their statements.
6. Ask for conclusions. Remind students that conclusions are statements we infer about the behavior of the persons in the situation under study. Ask students to support their conclusions.

7. Ask for generalizations—statements that go beyond Hamlet's situation, but are instead about people in general. Ask students to support their generalizations.

Summary

The cause-and-effect model allows students to explore a problem situation to determine the relationships among actions and subsequent events. Active engagement is essential to the model as students identify prior causes and subsequent effects. The model can be used in both elementary and secondary classrooms and in all curriculum areas. The graphic organizer associated with the model helps students to visualize the chronology of the quandary (e.g., getting through a long winter or why a character behaved in a particular way) under discussion. Going from causes to effects and then from prior causes to subsequent effects may reveal the connections among these events more effectively. However, you may feel that establishing the cause to prior cause or effect to subsequent effect relationship is easier for students to grasp initially. In addition to the examples described in this chapter, the model can be used to review content. Using their textbooks or other informational sources, students can use critical events as their data source. This may be done as a whole class or with individual groups. Figure 9.4 shows a science example.

Figure 9.4 Cause and Effect as Content Review in Biology

Data	High blood glucose levels
Causes	Beta cells of pancreas undersecrete the hormone insulin; diabetes mellitus, body doesn't respond to insulin
Prior Causes	Heredity, age, obesity, destructive or infectious condition of pancreas
Effects	Glucose not absorbed into cells; glucose accumulates in plasma; excess sugar is excreted in urine; less water absorbed into blood by kidney tubules; because glucose not available, a shift in cellular metabolism to fats and proteins for energy production
Subsequent Effects	Extreme thirst; some fats may be deposited in blood vessels causing a variety of vascular problems (e.g., if retinal vessels are affected, blindness can result, or when limbs and feet are affected, gangrene can result); many fats completely oxidized producing acidosis which can result in diabetic coma
Conclusion	When glucose accumulates in plasma, excess sugar is excreted into urine
Generalization	What happens in one part of the body affects other parts of the body

Before class, decide on the topic or data to be analyzed. Just before the discussion, provide the organizer. The steps of the model include (1) choosing the topic, (2) asking for causes and support for the causes, (3) asking for effects and support for the effects, (4) asking for prior causes and support for the prior causes, (5) asking for subsequent effects and support for the subsequent effects, (6) asking for conclusions, and (7) asking for generalizations.

Extensions

ACTIVITIES

1. If you were appointed principal of a school where you had either studied or taught, think of a change of policy that you would initiate. Now list three effects and three subsequent effects that you think would occur after the policy was implemented.
2. Choose a piece of curriculum that you currently teach or will be teaching. Write a cause-and-effect content review for each of the steps of the model as in Figure 9.1.
3. Ask a practicing teacher what problems students have with identifying cause and effect. Explain the model to the teacher and explore the possibility that the steps of the model may help students understand these complex relationships. Probe the teacher for suggestions about implementing the model or making adjustments to the model.

REFLECTIVE QUESTIONS

1. Why do you think it is important to help students identify cause-and-effect relationships? Do you think this is a skill that will help students be successful in your classroom? Why or why not?
2. How does the cause-and-effect model relate to other instructional models in the text? In what ways is the model similar to concept attainment, concept development, and cooperative learning? In what ways is it different?
3. How might becoming proficient in using the cause-and-effect model contribute to your professional development?

10 The Socratic Seminar Model

Analyzing Text

chapter OBJECTIVES

You Will Understand
- Careful analysis of text can increase academic knowledge, cooperative skills, and the ability to think critically
- Discussions of open-ended problems can greatly enhance students' thinking

You Will Know
- How to choose text that raises issues worthy of discussion
- How to pose questions that leave open multiple possibilities for exploration
- How to encourage students to think carefully about their reading and study
- What the Socratic seminar model looks like in both elementary and secondary classrooms

You Will Be Able To
- Plan lessons that center on multiple reactions to the same text by different readers

In the ELEMENTARY classroom

The second graders in Alyssa Raskind's class were having trouble distinguishing between rights and responsibilities. Her students also needed practice in identifying problems and problem solutions in texts. She decided that a seminar on the book *Old Henry* might help her students figure out the differences. The book is about a man who moves into an old, vacant, run-down house and settles in without making the repairs that his neighbors feel should be accomplished. He prefers to read his books, paint his pictures, care for his birds, and live his more leisurely life. Eventually the conflict with his neighbors drives Henry away. But then the neighbors begin to miss Old Henry and his parrot, and in his new place, Henry begins to miss them.

Ms. Raskind spent some time thinking about the questions that would be used in the seminar and how she would remind the students of seminar rules and procedures. She determined that the seminar would have an entry ticket. Students would be asked to complete the sentence: A good neighbor is _____. Each student will need the completed sentence to participate in the seminar.

The seminar began once everyone was seated and had handed in their tickets.

Ms. Raskind: What are the responsibilities that neighbors have to each other?

Alex: They have to be nice to each other.

James: They have to help when your grandma is sick.

Annika: They bring you food when you are hungry.

Ms. Raskind: Neighbors can help you out and that is a nice thing to do, but is it a responsibility of being a neighbor to help out? Can you be a good neighbor without helping out? Think about what it means to have a responsibility. What kind of responsibilities do people who live in the same neighborhood have?

After some discussion, the class determines that neighbors have a responsibility to make certain that when neighbors have needs, they try to help them and that they have a responsibility to take care of the neighborhood. They also have a responsibility to not bother each other.

Ms. Raskind: Was Henry a good neighbor? Did he have the right to ignore the concerns of his neighbors?

Chloe: He was a good neighbor because he didn't bother anyone.

Sophia: But he wasn't a good neighbor because he didn't keep the neighborhood nice.

Chloe: He doesn't have to do everything his neighbors want him to do.

Ms. Raskind: Were Henry's neighbors good neighbors? Give me some examples of good neighbor behavior that you saw in the book.

The class continues to determine that Henry and his neighbors were not perfect and each learned something about being a good neighbor during the story.

Ms. Raskind: What is the problem in Henry's old neighborhood? How would you solve the problem?

Travis: Henry and his neighbors wanted different things.

Annika: Henry wanted to be left alone. The other people wanted a pretty neighborhood.

The conversation continues with a discussion of the rights and responsibilities of neighbors. Ms. Raskind reviews the discussion by helping her students summarize the big ideas that they covered.

Ms. Raskind: What did we decide a good neighbor's rights and responsibilities are?

The students reiterated their criteria for being a good neighbor in terms of rights and responsibilities and determined that Henry and his neighbors were all trying hard to be good neighbors. Ms. Raskind then asked the students if they had been good seminar participants. She called on Travis and asked him to tell her why he thought he had been a good participant.

Travis: I listened to everybody without interrupting. I asked Chloe a question. And I did not get mad when James kept talking.

Several other students shared their evaluations.

In the SECONDARY classroom

The students in the U.S. history class had participated in Socratic seminars before, but they were looking forward to today's lesson because it was a break from trying to memorize information about numerous Civil War battles. Last night Mr. Gupta asked them to read *The War Prayer* and "Sullivan Ballou's Letter to His Wife." He also asked them to find three similarities between the texts. This assignment would be used as an entrance ticket. Each student hands in the ticket in order to participate in the seminar.

> **MR. GUPTA:** Thank you for coming to class prepared. We have some difficult topics to discuss today as we continue our study of the Civil War. War has a profound impact on both the winners and the defeated. Today's seminar question examines the losers—What happens to the vanquished? We will begin by pointing out how Mark Twain and Sullivan Ballou describe the victors and the vanquished. Who would like to begin?
>
> **IVY:** Well, Twain seems to be really against war and makes a big deal out of the losers suffering. But isn't that what happens and doesn't that make countries work harder at trying to win?
>
> **DANIEL:** Where do you get the idea that Twain is against war?
>
> **IVY:** Twain wrote "If you pray for the blessing of rain upon your crop which needs it, by that act you are possibly praying for a curse upon some neighbor's crop which may not need rain and can be injured by it." I think that means that we shouldn't pray to win.
>
> **DANIEL:** So how does that show that Twain is against war?

Several other students join into the discussion and use the text to make the case that Twain was against war in general. Olivia, on the other hand, feels that the stranger wants everyone to know that war can be very bad, but doesn't say that all wars are bad.

> **MR. GUPTA:** How do the concerns of Sullivan Ballou and the stranger in the church compare? Would Sullivan Ballou have wanted Twain's *The War Prayer* to be published? How do you know?

Julio and Nolan jumped right into the conversation and Marisa followed. Here is a small part of what they said:

> **JULIO:** I don't think that Sullivan would have published *The War Prayer* because he believed that there were some ideals that were important enough to die for in war.
>
> **NOLAN:** I agree. He says, "And I am willing—perfectly willing—to lay down all my joys in this life, to help maintain this Government." He may have been afraid that if something like *The War Prayer* had been published, some people would not have supported the Union war effort.
>
> **MARISA:** But haven't there always been people against all wars?

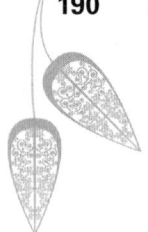

The discussion continues for a number of minutes when Mr. Gupta begins to question students about the Battle of Bull Run in which Sullivan Ballou is mortally injured.

MR. GUPTA: Do you think it is possible for the perceptions of a warrior to change in the course of battle?

Again, his students are anxious to share and show some consternation when Mr. Gupta interrupts and repeats the seminar question—What is the other side of victory? What happens to the vanquished?

FATMA: I don't know, but I wonder what Sullivan Ballou's family would have thought if their side had lost the war. They wouldn't have had a husband and father and their side still would have lost the war!

JULIO: Yes, but they did win and they still didn't have a husband and father.

Several students then comment on what the war brought both the Union and the Confederacy. Ten minutes before the end of class, Mr. Gupta asked the students to review the discussion and share some statements about what they had heard during the seminar.

IVY: War is bad for everyone.

NOLAN: There are some things that you have to fight for even if you know that people will suffer.

ANNIKA: Not everyone agrees with that. Some people feel all wars are bad.

Most of the class shares a statement or two to summarize the discussion and the seminar ends with students evaluating their own performance and the quality of the seminar question.

Basis for the Socratic Seminar Model

The idea of a Socratic seminar stems from one of the dialogues of Plato entitled *Meno*. In this dialogue, the character Meno asks whether virtue can be taught, and that leads Socrates to suggest that no idea can be taught directly. On the contrary, he suggests, all that we know must be extracted from us through a series of questions and a process of inquiry. This is the foundation of the Socratic seminar. The job of the teacher, according to Socrates, is to help the learner collect his or her thoughts from which to build new understandings from prior knowledge. This may well be the source of the etymology of the verb *to educate*, meaning "to lead out." As it has evolved to the present time, the Socratic seminar tends to focus on open-ended or controversial questions (for example, was U.S. isolationism justified in the 1930s?) that have no unequivocal resolution. That is not to say the topic of a seminar could never be a math problem, but if it were, the problem would have multiple solutions.

The purpose of this chapter is to present commentary about the instructional value of classroom discussions, in general, focusing particularly on Socratic seminars. Discussions play an important role in student learning because students are able to converse with knowledgeable peers and adults. Discussion allows for the acquisition and construction of information along with the linking of new information to personal prior experiences. Not all classroom talk is discussion oriented. There is a great deal of talk in the classroom that is not discussion. For instance, there are fast-paced teacher-to-student recitations that have a teacher question–student response–teacher feedback pattern. Discussions, on the other hand, provide the opportunity for sustained critical inquiry and student-to-student conversation and are an alternative to recitation-style teaching.

Discussions support student growth toward sophisticated cognitive, social, and emotional objectives. Socratic seminars boost students' content learning, develop students' cooperative social skills, and help students discover their competence as members of a productive learning community. In addition, the Socratic seminar provides a safe place for the discussion of values associated with the problems under deliberation.

The Socratic seminar model is designed to use the Socratic dialectic—the examination of ideas through a logical progression of questioning to help students reach a deep understanding of a controversial topic after considering a number of perspectives (Fischer, 2008). Socratic seminars are applicable in all content areas and at all grade levels. Every discipline has conflicting viewpoints that can be examined by identifying assumptions and various interpretations and by studying the construction of conclusions. Because Socratic seminars allow students to construct new knowledge by interacting with the ideas and understandings of others, it is congruent with what we know about how students learn and how they "own" their own understanding. Students are active learners during a Socratic seminar; they are not simply provided information by either the teacher or the text as in didactic instruction. Dialogical instruction requires that students consider a variety of perspectives. In a Socratic seminar, students are involved in discussions in which contradictory ideas are weighed logically with a view to the resolution of the inherent contradictions. The seminar is student centered rather than teacher centered, with the teacher playing the role of "guide on the side" instead of "sage on the stage." In fact, a visitor to a class where a Socratic seminar was in progress might need to look twice to find the teacher.

Versions of the Socratic Seminar

There are several current iterations of seminars structured around Socratic questioning. Each relies on a dialogue among students centered on a specific text or question. The Socratic seminar model is one that has evolved over time. Socratic questioning within a conversation that examines complex, rich questions stimulates student thinking. The premise of the Socratic seminar model is that student awareness of important questions plays a large role in intellectual development and that the exploration of a text allows for disciplined conversation or dialectic—a way to examine ideas logically. The Socratic seminar model asks students to think critically about a text (written, visual, or auditory) through a cooperative and respectful discussion based on personal reactions to the material. These personal responses reflect prior knowledge and experience. The model does not rely on memorizing discrete pieces of information, and it does not tolerate superficial coverage.

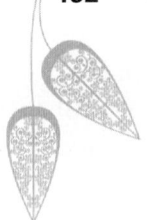

Seminars are congruent with what we know about how people learn and how classroom and school environments can be organized to promote learning. The Socratic seminar model allows for the development of a learner-centered, knowledge-centered, assessment-centered, and community-centered environment. In the words of Bransford, Brown, and Cocking (National Research Council, 2000), "If teaching is conceived as constructing a bridge between the subject matter and the student, learner-centered teachers keep a constant eye on both edges of the bridge." Seminars allow students to share insights and knowledge based on their own experiences and cultural lenses, enabling teachers to facilitate explanations, expose assumptions, and recognize misconceptions. In addition, there is a strong diagnostic component to Socratic seminars because thinking and learning are so transparent.

The public nature of these seminars requires a strong community focus in a knowledge-centered classroom. Students must use sophisticated academic skills as they discuss important topics—summarizing, paraphrasing, making explanations and interpretations, analyzing ideas and assumptions—all of which contribute to a milieu that promotes comfort and security in the sharing of important concepts and understandings. Students have the opportunity to become more knowledgeable in a safe environment as they make sense of these shared ideas.

In addition, the Socratic seminar model provides the chance for students to develop metacognitive skills as they receive feedback on their thoughts and the thoughts of their peers. Teachers and students are able to share their prior knowledge and experiences, cultural perspectives, and community orientations, allowing the teacher/facilitator the opportunity to make learner-centered decisions. Seminars are also aligned with what is known about good teaching because of the opportunities for self-evaluation and metacognition. As students participate in the discussion, there are norms against which they can evaluate their performance. And, inherently, a good seminar develops a community of learners engaged in inquiry—perhaps the most important characteristic of all learning environments.

Interestingly, Socratic seminars have been around for a lot longer than the research on how people learn. Certainly, dialogues are a natural way of communicating and have been used along with debate since the beginnings of civilization. Unlike debates, however, dialogues are collaborative. Every participant works at making meaning from the text and finding common ground. Dialogues have the potential to change a point of view by examining assumptions, leading to an open-minded approach to problem solving. The respect inherent in a Socratic seminar helps develop an active citizenry in a democracy that is continually engaged in searching many positions for a common solution.

Questioning

The caliber and success of all classroom discussions depends on the kinds of questions that are prepared by the teacher. Questions should help students learn. Good questions are educative—they provide the opportunity for deeper thought. There are several ways to distinguish among the types of questions that teachers can ask and the effect different kinds of questions can have on student learning. For the purposes of this chapter we will be examining the questions based on Bloom's revised taxonomy and Paul's Taxonomy of Socratic Questions (Anderson & Krathwohl, 2001; Paul, 1993). The Revised Taxonomy of Educational Objectives is useful for evaluating all of the components of instructional alignment—objectives, instruction, and assessment. Questioning is just one aspect of instruction. By delineating the range of cognitive processes and types of knowledge used in classrooms, the taxonomy provides guidance for planning, implementing, and evaluating instruction.

The revised taxonomy has six cognitive levels at which questions can be asked. Examples of questions at each of the following levels will be provided in the next section:

1. *Remembering questions* ask students to recall information.
2. *Understanding questions* ask students to explain ideas or concepts.
3. *Applying questions* ask students to use information in another familiar situation.
4. *Analyzing questions* ask students to break information into parts in order to explore the relationships among the parts.
5. *Evaluating questions* ask students to justify a decision or a course of action.
6. *Creating questions* ask students to generate new ways of thinking about things.

Richard Paul has categorized the types of questions that a teacher/facilitator can use in a Socratic seminar. These categories include:

- Questions of clarification
- Questions of assumptions
- Questions that probe reasons and evidence
- Questions about viewpoints or perspectives
- Questions that probe implications and consequences
- Questions about the question

Examples of Paul's questions are provided in the discussion of evaluating the Socratic seminar (step 6 of the model) later in this chapter.

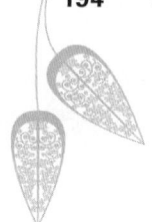

Examples of Question Types

Do you remember the story of "The Ugly Duckling" by Hans Christian Andersen? We will use this story as the text to help illustrate the different kinds of questions that can be used during a Socratic seminar. The story describes a mother duck waiting what seems like a very long time for her eggs to hatch. Finally, all but one egg hatches. While sitting on the last large egg, an old duck pays a visit and tells Mother Duck to leave the egg. But Mother Duck waits until the egg hatches and a very large and very ugly bird emerges. This duck is never accepted by the barnyard, the Queen Duck, or even his mother, who tries. After being harassed by his own siblings, the young duckling leaves to fend for himself, determined to find his place in the world. He wanders away and meets a trio of boisterous wild ducks, an old woman and her pets—a hen and a cat—and some beautiful swans flying south for the winter. Soon after, the pond freezes over, and the duckling becomes trapped in the ice. A kind woodsman rescues him and brings him home. The duckling is teased by the woodsman's children, and he again runs away. Somehow the duckling survives the winter on his own, and in the early spring he comes upon a pond where beautiful white swans are swimming. As he comes closer, the beautiful creatures welcome and accept him. Surprised, the duckling gazes in the water and realizes that he, too, is a swan.

Remembering

Remembering questions ask students to recall, restate, or remember learned information:

- What advice did the old duck give to Mother Duck as she waited for her large egg to hatch?
- Describe what happened to the duckling during the harsh winter.

Understanding

Understanding questions ask students to make sense of the information by interpreting and translating what is learned:

- How would you explain why the large egg took so long to hatch?
- What happened after the duckling left the farmyard?
- Can you illustrate the unfair treatment of the duckling?

Applying

Applying questions asks students to use information in a context different from the one in which it was learned:

- Can you think of another time when someone was treated poorly because of the way he or she looked?
- What would you have told Mother Duck as the duckling hatched?
- In the story, the swans left the cold winter for warmer climates. Do you know of any others who leave the cold weather and go to a warmer environment for the winter?

Analyzing

Analyzing questions ask students to break down the learned information into its parts:

- Which of the adventures that the duckling had could have been left out of the story?
- If the duckling hadn't found the small house with the old woman, what might have happened?
- Can you explain what must have happened to the duckling's brothers and sisters?
- Can you explain why the animals in the farmyard were mean to the duckling?
- What would have happened if the Queen Duck had accepted the duckling?

Evaluating

Evaluating questions ask students to make decisions based on reflection and assessment:

- How would you have treated the duckling if you lived in the farmyard?
- What do you think of how Mother Duck treated the duckling?
- Do you think it was a good idea to let the duckling leave the farmyard?
- How would you feel if you were the duckling as he first saw the beautiful swans?

Creating

Creating questions ask students to develop new ideas and information:

- Can you figure out what might have had to happen for the duckling to live in the farmyard happily?
- What would have happened if there had been two swan eggs in the nest?
- Can you tell a story about people who are treated poorly because of the way that they look?

Bloom's Revised Taxonomy of Educational Objectives is helpful in asking students a variety of questions with varying cognitive demands. Socratic seminars, however, also demand an analysis of a different kind of question. Seminars are fast-paced and require a number of unscripted follow-up questions as the students examine an issue in conversation with one another, guided by the teacher. These follow-up questions can benefit from Paul's Taxonomy of Socratic Questions because the perspective provided by the taxonomy reminds teachers to prompt students to clarify, examine assumptions, probe evidence, explain perspectives, and investigate implications and consequences (see Table 10.1 later in the chapter).

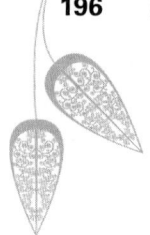

Steps in the Socratic Seminar Model

Step 1: Choose the Text—Written, Visual, or Audio

The text you choose should be related to the big ideas that are listed in your state curriculum standards and the *understand* objectives that you have designed for the unit of instruction being planned. The Socratic seminar model is appropriate for objectives that ask students to articulate ideas, use higher-level thinking, and problem solve in a community of learners. The text must be at an appropriate reading level so that students can read or examine it independently. If the text is art, music, or a video clip, age appropriateness is an important consideration. Students should feel comfortable reading and reflecting on the text and should not feel confused and frustrated when they enter the seminar.

The opening seminar question should be broad, abstract, and engaging—something that encapsulates the essence of the text, as in the following examples:

- How has the American Dream changed in the last 75 years? *(The Great Gatsby)*
- Is there such a thing as a good war? *(The Declaration of Independence)*
- Can important music sound bad? (musical excerpt)
- Does art have to be representational to be good? (piece of modern art)

Opening questions may transcend the text; that is, the question might be larger than the issues that are obvious in the text and transferable to other works, but the discussion should help students answer the broad question and should engage them in a way that elicits a personal response.

Step 2: Plan and Cluster Several Questions of Varying Cognitive Demand

Group the questions by topic. Identify basic questions and begin to cluster the questions. A basic question is an "umbrella" question—a higher-level question, fairly broad in scope, that raises an issue. Cluster questions are both lower- and higher-order questions that develop an issue. A cluster, as illustrated in Figure 10.1,

Figure 10.1 Sample Cluster on Genghis Khan

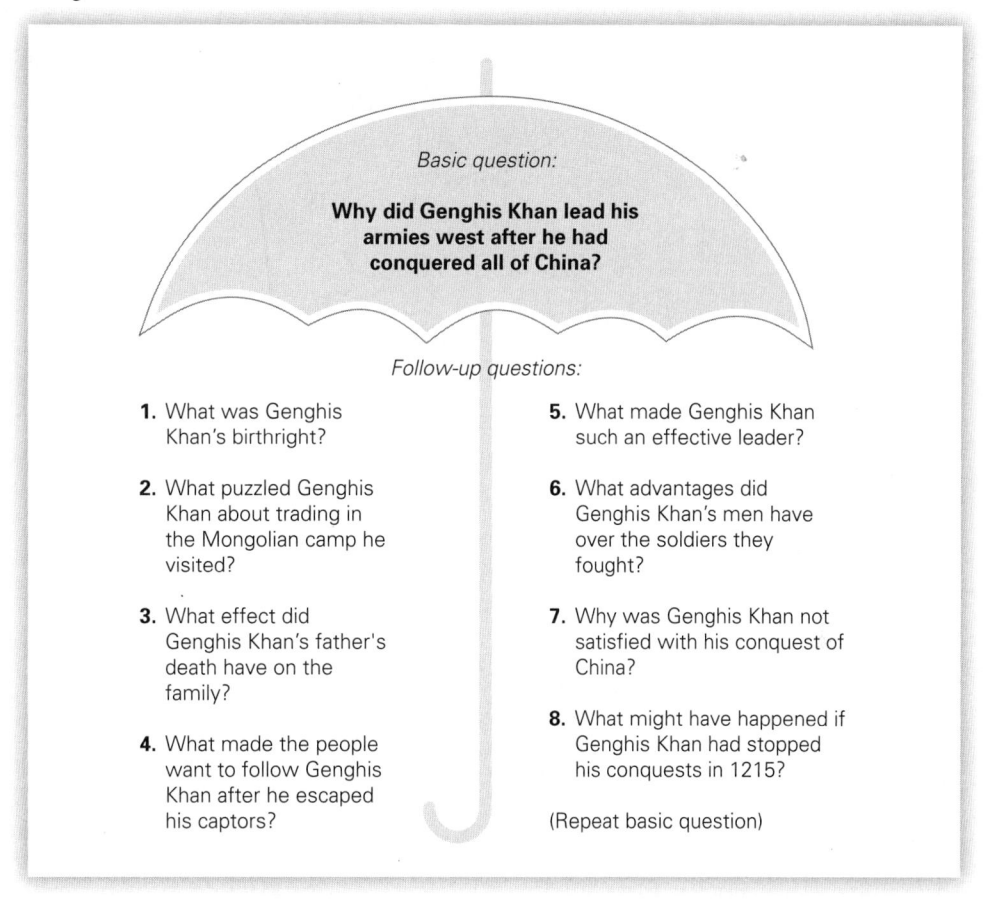

Basic question:

Why did Genghis Khan lead his armies west after he had conquered all of China?

Follow-up questions:

1. What was Genghis Khan's birthright?

2. What puzzled Genghis Khan about trading in the Mongolian camp he visited?

3. What effect did Genghis Khan's father's death have on the family?

4. What made the people want to follow Genghis Khan after he escaped his captors?

5. What made Genghis Khan such an effective leader?

6. What advantages did Genghis Khan's men have over the soldiers they fought?

7. Why was Genghis Khan not satisfied with his conquest of China?

8. What might have happened if Genghis Khan had stopped his conquests in 1215?

(Repeat basic question)

consists of one broad question and six to eight focused questions. Having several different clusters affords different entrances to the issue under discussion. This allows students to move beyond initial responses to the "big" question and toward a wide spectrum of information before settling on a personal perspective.

Clustering provides flexibility to the seminar leader as the discussion unfolds. Different clusters can be tapped depending on the answers to previous questions. It must be remembered that basic cluster questions may be answered in several different ways; the strength of supporting data from the text determines the validity of individual answers. If a question points to only one answer, it is not a basic question. The essence of the Socratic seminar is that there are valid justifications for all sides of an issue.

Step 3: Introduce the Model to the Students

Let students know that a major purpose of the Socratic seminar is to help them learn to think for themselves as they engage in intellectual interaction with others.

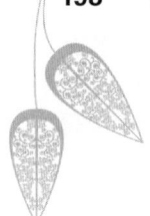

Seminars are designed to allow teachers and students to practice dialogue with certain characteristics:

- Openness to ideas from the text that disconfirm previously held beliefs
- Suspended judgment while dissecting the text with others
- Lack of defensiveness in communicating beliefs and reasoning with others
- Acceptance of other viewpoints as valid and as a way to discover a common ground

These behaviors are critical for citizens in our democracy—an important goal in the United States of America.

With your students, review the criteria for fruitful seminar participation. An excellent seminar member demonstrates respect for the learning of all participants by (1) showing patience with a variety of ideas and contributions, (2) asking for clarification, (3) moving the conversation forward, (4) addressing comments to all or most of the other participants, and (5) not speaking too much. The last characteristic is often the most difficult to get across to students. A number of factors can lead a single or small group of students to dominate a discussion. This is not a norm of Socratic seminars and must be addressed by the group and the group leader. Often, just reminding the offending students of the seminar's purpose is enough to remedy the situation.

Excellent seminar members also demonstrate reasoning skills by waiting to answer a question until evidence can be cited from the text and thoughts can be expressed clearly, thoughtfully, and logically. Outstanding group members make connections among several of the presented ideas and consider the viewpoints of others along with their own.

Figuring out what other people mean is an important part of getting along in the real world. This is not easy, because sometimes people do not want to say what they really mean or they have trouble expressing their thoughts and feelings precisely. People tend to think of the written word as more definitive than conversation. In conversation, body language, facial expression, and tone help communicate meaning. It is not unusual to have to think long and carefully in figuring out what a piece of writing means. Writers strive to say what they mean in clear terms, but there are always gaps between a writer's and reader's personal experiences and the meanings they give to words and phrases. Different people can read the same piece of writing and come up with different ideas about what it means. But if several readers discuss their ideas together, they will all come to a clearer understanding of the text. Socratic seminars are designed to help a community of learners make sense of a text together.

Before the discussion, the classroom should be prepared by putting desks or chairs in a circle so that everyone can see other participants. Each student should have a copy of the text with personal annotations highlighting interesting ideas or questions. Remind students of the ground rules of the seminar—the most important probably being that participants must not talk or contribute until they have been recognized.

Step 4: Conduct the Discussion

When leading the discussion, frequently ask follow-up questions that force students to reason aloud and air their thoughts. The tone of the probing should be encouraging as you ask students what they think and if they can support their ideas.

After asking a question, allow sufficient wait time before eliciting an answer. Wait until many hands are up and do not always call on the same people or on those whose hands went up first. The students will begin to understand that you prefer them to take time to consider a response. Again, ask for several students' opinions before asking another question. For each idea, ask follow-up questions about why the student thinks that and what evidence he or she can cite in the text to support the thoughts. Others' insights help students develop their own ideas. It is the richness of varying perspectives that makes the insights so penetrating.

If you feel that a student's comment is not valid, ask the student to support it from the text. If, however, the students fail to see that the inference is unsupported, you should not point it out; you should only ask further questions. Most students have very little confidence in their own abilities to solve problems or make decisions. If you step in and provide answers when they are floundering, they may learn more about the specific point you are discussing, but does that knowledge outweigh the imperceptible loss of confidence in themselves? The need for a pattern of supporting evidence for an idea will become clear through repeated discussions.

Remember that the questions you ask should be open-ended questions, not questions to which you have specific answers. Also remember that you must guard against less stringent probing related to those answers with which you agree. Guard against this by requesting supporting evidence for comments that seem true to you but that have not been adequately supported.

Because the stress in this model is on the process of developing critical thinking skills rather than the achievement of one specific conclusion, there is no closure in the sense of reaching a stated conclusion. The idea that there is no one right conclusion is difficult for students to grasp, but it is good if they come to grips with this concept. It is also good if they see that disagreements can be healthy and can lead to greater insights.

Step 5: Review and Summarize the Discussion

Once the seminar is complete, students need to share what they heard or observed during the session. In a short discussion of how they felt about the process and their own thinking, it is important that students practice metacognition so that the benefits of the seminar are not lost. In the same vein, the facilitator and students should make generalizations about the themes and images discussed, allowing students to continue to process the information and insights that were shared. Without this opportunity, many of the most salient ideas can be left unattached to the essential curriculum content of which the seminar was a part. Students must be reminded that the process of the seminar was important—critical thinking is a useful and important skill, and the ideas that were pursued together are representative of the knowledge for which the class is responsible.

Step 6: Evaluate the Discussion with the Students Based on Previously Stated Criteria

The Socratic seminar model is an excellent tool for students to use when thinking independently, when solving problems of interpretation, and when thinking in concert with or in opposition to their peers. But how does one evaluate this activity?

To evaluate the leader's performance, review the questions that were asked in the seminar. Did you deviate from your plan? When? Where? Why? How did you return to the questions again? Did you follow the leads of students? Did you feel you missed some opportunities to clarify comments, probe assumptions, ask for specific reasons and evidence, and question viewpoints, implications, and consequences? The six types of Socratic seminar questions identified by Paul and Elder (2006) in their taxonomy (Figure 10.2) provide a good evaluation checklist for discussion leaders.

Socratic seminars provide an opportunity for students to practice metacognitive thought. During the first few sessions of the seminar, students can use the following questions to evaluate their participation in the discussion:

- Did I speak clearly so everyone could hear?
- Did I cite reasons and evidence for each of my comments?
- Did I use the text as a source of my evidence?
- Did I listen to others respectfully?
- Did I impede the flow of the conversation?
- Did I speak with other discussants besides the leader?
- Did I paraphrase when appropriate?
- Did I ask for help when I was confused?
- Was I supportive of my classmates?
- Did I avoid hostile exchanges?
- Was I prepared for the seminar?

There are several ways of grading student participation in the seminar. A number of websites offer holistic rubrics evaluating overall performance using

Figure 10.2   Taxonomy of Socratic Questions

Clarification Questions
- What do you mean by . . . ?
- How does this relate to your first point?
- What exactly are you saying here?
- Can you tell me more about what you are thinking?
- What is an example of this?
- How does this relate to the previous point?

Assumption Questions
- What is your basic assumption?
- You are basing all of your comments on one assumption. Is this what you want?
- What other assumptions could we make?
- Why would someone make this assumption?
- Is that always true?
- How can you justify this assumption?

Reason and Evidence Questions
- How do you know that?
- Can you give us an example?
- Are these reasons enough to make that assumption or to generate that conclusion?
- What are your reasons for saying that?
- How does this apply to this case?
- What would change your mind?
- Why do you think that is true?
- Is there reason to doubt that evidence?

Viewpoint Questions
- What are you implying?
- What do you believe about . . . ?
- How would other types of people respond to this?
- What would someone who disagrees with this idea say?
- What are alternatives to the point of view?
- What effect would that have?

Implication and Consequence Questions
- How can we find out?
- If that happened, what else might happen?
- What effect might that have if this happens first?
- Is it likely that this will happen?
- What are you implying?
- If this is the case, then what else must be true?

Initial Questions
- Why are we examining this question?
- Is the question clear? Do we understand the question?
- To answer the question, what will first have to be answered?
- Is this the same issue as . . . ?
- Is this question easy or hard to answer? Why?
- How could someone settle this question?

Source: Adapted with permission from Paul, R., & Elder, L. (2006). *The art of Socratic questioning.* The Foundation for Critical Thinking. www.criticalthinking.org

categories congruent with those discussed here. Students can be evaluated on participation and preparation for the seminar using the following indicators:

- Participation
  - Demonstrates listening skills by paying attention to the details of the discussion
  - Utilizes the contributions of others in response
  - Keeps up with conversation flow by offering clarifications that extend previously shared ideas
  - Politely points out gaps of understanding, evidence, or logic
  - Ignores distractions
- Preparation
  - Demonstrates careful reading and thought through familiarity with the text—identifying main ideas, contradictions, and accurate use of vocabulary
  - Has annotated personal copy of the text that allows the participant frequently to refer to specific parts of the text

These attributes of participation and preparation can form the basis of an evaluation of all seminar participants. There are other assessment possibilities addressed in the evaluation section of this chapter.

Strategy Alert
Reciprocal Teaching

Reciprocal teaching is sometimes called a structured dialogue, the structure coming from the four activities that make it up: predicting, questioning, clarifying, and summarizing. The idea is that, as they read, students should constantly be predicting (and modifying those predictions), asking questions that arise, clarifying any confusion that occurs, and summarizing at successive points in the reading. The teacher and students model these activities by taking turns as a text is read.

Distribute to students a set of index cards, each labeled with one of the activities. Open the textbook or other reading material and ask if anyone with a "prediction" card would like to venture a guess as to what we might expect to learn from the reading. Write these predictions on the board. Next ask whether anyone with a "question" card can offer a question about the topic we are about to study.

Write these questions on the board also. Now ask that everyone read a page or two of the text, down to a logical breakpoint. Ask those students with "clarify" cards if they have seen any answers to questions that were raised before. Record these possible answers. Ask also if any part of the text seemed confusing or unclear, and, if so, whether the "clarify" students can clear anything up. This might mean looking something up in another resource. Next comes the "summarizing" cards. What could be said to summarize what we have read thus far? Put brief summaries on the board.

Now have students exchange cards with another person who has a different card. Repeat the process several times as the text is read through, or until you are certain that students are empowered to complete the activities on their own. ∎

> **myeducationlab**
> The Power of Classroom Practice
> www.myeducationlab.com
>
> Go to the Assignments and Activities section of Topic 9: Group Interaction Models in the MyEducationLab for your course and complete the activity entitled "Social and Emotional Skills in Group Interaction Models."

Summary of Steps in the Socratic Seminar Model

1. *Choose the text—written or visual or audio.* Read the material (or provide access to supporting material if it is in visual or audio form). Relate the text to curriculum standards and choose a basic, powerful, essential question.

2. *Plan and cluster several questions of varying cognitive demand.* Questions should allow students to take a position and also reflect what you know about the students and their readiness and interests.

3. *Introduce the model to the students.* Through a series of questions about what students think they should learn, explain the benefits of the Socratic seminar model. Next, introduce expectations of student behavior and how behavior during seminars will be assessed. Assign the reading and remind students of how to prepare for the discussion.

4. *Conduct the discussion.* During the discussion, try to maintain a nondirective role as much as possible. Encourage interactions among the students. Use your cluster questions and show flexibility as you probe student positions and understandings.

5. *Review and summarize the discussion.* Review the major points made during the discussion or encourage the students to jot down ideas that impressed them. Ask for their contributions. You might also ask if any students changed their minds during the discussion about the answers to the basic questions. How did their ideas change, and why?

6. *Evaluate the discussion with students based on previously stated criteria.* The seminar leader and students should evaluate personal behavior during the discussion. Grading should be assigned through the use of rubrics and checklists.

Evaluating Learning in the Socratic Seminar Model

This chapter discussed some of the metacognitive approaches to assessment available to teachers as they implement the Socratic seminar model. These checklists and rubrics may also be used to evaluate students for a grade. There are several considerations to bear in mind as assessment tools are chosen for classroom use:

- Tools must be clearly aligned with curriculum standards and class objectives.
- Tools must be developmentally appropriate.
- Tools must be clearly written and understood by both the teacher and the students.
- Common tools must be used for all students involved in a particular discussion.
- Clear indicators of which behaviors result in which grades should be made public.

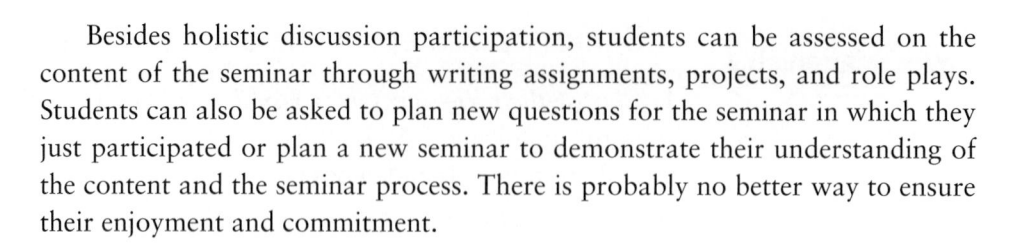

Besides holistic discussion participation, students can be assessed on the content of the seminar through writing assignments, projects, and role plays. Students can also be asked to plan new questions for the seminar in which they just participated or plan a new seminar to demonstrate their understanding of the content and the seminar process. There is probably no better way to ensure their enjoyment and commitment.

Meeting Individual Needs in the Socratic Seminar Model

The Socratic seminar, as do most models, offers a host of possibilities for personalizing instruction. The choice of the text is one critical chance to differentiate. By choosing audio and visual text, on occasion, teachers can meet the learning preferences of a variety of students and provide the chance to build new strengths for others. Texts can also be chosen to respond to students' cultural background and interests.

Planning specific questions offers another chance to personalize instruction. Clusters of questions can be planned to meet the specific learning needs of particular students, to extend cultural understandings, and to pique student interests. All of these goals can be reached while also helping students demonstrate the achievement of standards and objectives.

Students can participate at varying levels during a seminar. Assigned opportunities or student choices could include observing a seminar and providing feedback to participants, charting discussions, preparing seminar questions, and keeping track of personal participation. The key is to use the information that you have collected through close observations of your students to make significant instructional decisions. Decisions about these options will be based on teacher observations and evidence of student interests, readiness, and learning preferences.

Benefits of the Socratic Seminar Model

The main argument in favor of the Socratic seminar model is that it is always based on an open-ended question designed to lead students to active discussion in which multiple ideas can be proposed. The seminar is based not on "right" answers but on "thoughtful engagement" with a question and information related to it. Students in a seminar have the opportunity to make sense of difficult ideas within a supportive learning community. They are asked to support these ideas clearly and with evidence. In addition, students become more comfortable listening to peers and to ideas with which they may disagree. Thoughtful engagement is the seed for critical thinking and for creating new relationships and ideas.

Elementary Grades Lesson

SOCRATIC SEMINAR: *Old Henry,* by Joan W. Blos	
OBJECTIVES	**Students Will Understand** • Citizens have a responsibility to protect the rights of others and this might cause problems **Students Will Know** • The rights and responsibilities of neighbors • How to identify the main idea, the problem, and a solution in a text **Students Will Be Able To** • Cooperatively participate in active and thoughtful discussion of the text • Identify the feelings and beliefs of Old Henry and his neighbors and what responsibilities each had to the other • Explain the conflict between Old Henry and his neighbors • Identify how the conflict was resolved and in what additional ways the conflict might have been resolved • Consider and build on a variety of perspectives
SEMINAR TEXT SUMMARY	*Old Henry* is the story of a man who moves into an old, vacant, run-down house in a neighborhood of houses that are in good shape—lawns are mowed, houses are painted, and repairs are made. But Old Henry likes his house just like it is when he buys it and prefers to read his books, paint his pictures, care for his birds, and live his more leisurely life. The neighbors were astounded that Henry did not sweep his walks or cut his grass or fix things up. No, things suited him just fine. Eventually the conflict with the neighbors drove Henry away. But then the neighbors began to miss Old Henry and his parrot, and in his new place, Henry began to miss them.
ASSESSMENT	Students will make a six-frame storyboard of the book *Old Henry* that has a different ending. The storyboard should identify the problem, show how the characters feel, and propose a solution.
PROCEDURES	(The first three steps may take place prior to the lesson.) 1. Choose the text. Read the material. Relate the text to curriculum standards and choose a basic, powerful, and essential question. This lesson asks the question, Does Henry have a right to ignore the concerns of his neighbors? 2. Develop question clusters similar to the following examples. a. Cluster 1: What is a neighborhood? How does a neighborhood get made? Do the citizens of a neighborhood have any responsibilities? What are these responsibilities? What responsibilities did the citizens in Old Henry's neighborhood have? Did Old Henry have any responsibilities? How do you

know what their responsibilities are? Did either the neighbors or Old Henry have any rights addressing how they could live in the neighborhood? How does the neighbors' behavior tell you about what they see as their rights and responsibilities?

   b. Cluster 2: What is the problem in the book? What does Old Henry think the problem is? What do the neighbors think the problem is? What does Old Henry want? What do the neighbors want? What did Old Henry decide to do? Is this a solution to the problem? How did Old Henry and the neighbors feel after Old Henry left? What was the next problem? How did Henry solve the problem? How would you solve the problem? Were the neighbors and Old Henry good citizens? How do you know?

3. Introduce the model to the students. Ask the students what they think they should learn and how they might benefit from the Socratic seminar model. Next, introduce expectations of student behavior and how student behavior will be assessed. Remind students that good seminar participants (1) are patient with the ideas of classmates, (2) ask a question when something is confusing, (3) move the conversation forward—don't let the discussion focus on only one idea, (4) address comments to the teacher and classmates, and (5) make sure everyone has a chance to speak. Read the text to the students.
4. Conduct the discussion.
5. Review and summarize the discussion.
6. Evaluate the discussion with the students. Ask students to consider if they were good seminar discussants. Did they speak clearly? Give reasons for their answers? Listen respectfully? Use the ideas of other students well? Keep the conversation moving? Offer support and encouragement to their peers?

Middle/Secondary Grades Lesson

SOCRATIC SEMINAR: *The War Prayer* and "Sullivan Ballou's Letter to His Wife"

OBJECTIVES

Students Will Understand
- The impact of war is beyond the battlefield

Students Will Know
- The details about the battle of Bull Run and why it is considered a turning point in the Civil War

Students Will Be Able To
- Cooperatively participate in active and thoughtful discussion of the text
- Identify Twain's and Ballou's assumptions and interpretations of the consequences of war
- Consider and build on a variety of perspectives

SEMINAR TEXTS Each of these short pieces is available on the Internet.

ASSESSMENT Students will write a short essay contrasting Twain's and Ballou's positions on the benefits and costs of war using excerpts from the texts to support their conclusions.

PROCEDURES (The first three steps may take place prior to the lesson.)

1. Choose the text. Read the material. Relate the text to curriculum standards and choose a basic, powerful, and essential question. This lesson asks, What is the other side of victory? What happens to the vanquished?
2. Develop question clusters similar to the following possibilities.
   a. Cluster 1: How were the concerns of Sullivan Ballou and the stranger in the church different? How were they similar? What concerns about war have you noticed in our country? If Sullivan Ballou had not died of his wounds, would his letter have been as powerful? Would you have published Twain's *The War Prayer?* Would you republish it now? Can you share your beliefs about war, in general, and the Civil War, specifically?
   b. Cluster 2: The Battle of Bull Run was considered a pivotal battle of the Civil War because the perceptions of both sides concerning quick victory and the costs of war had to change. What did Sullivan Ballou think would happen in the battle? How might the perceptions of warriors change the course of the battle? What might Mark Twain have written about the Battle of Bull Run? If you could speak with either Twain or Ballou, what would you say? Why?
3. Introduce the model to the students. Ask the students what they think they should learn and how they might benefit from the Socratic seminar model. Next, introduce expectations of student behavior and how student behavior will be assessed. Remind students that good seminar participants (1) exhibit patience with the ideas of others, (2) ask for clarifications, (3) move the conversation forward, (4) address comments to all, and (5) do not monopolize the conversation. Prepare an entry ticket to ensure that students have read or viewed the text. The ticket may be a question or series of questions, a journal entry, a document analysis worksheet, or other work sample.
4. Conduct the discussion.
5. Review and summarize the discussion.

6. Evaluate the discussion with the students. Ask students to consider if they were prepared for the seminar, spoke clearly, gave reasons from the text for their comments, listened respectfully, paraphrased when appropriate, kept the conversation flowing, asked for help when confused, or offered support for others.

Summary

This chapter examines a specific discussion strategy—Socratic seminars based on dialectic conversations among students about particular texts. The chapter discusses how to prepare for, conduct, and evaluate a Socratic seminar and provides information about classroom questioning that helps to structure both the seminar and other classroom discussions. The Socratic seminar provides opportunities for differentiating content to meet student needs and allows for variations in assessments.

Extensions

ACTIVITIES

1. Choose a favorite nursery rhyme. Construct a series of questions using all the levels of questions in Bloom's revised taxonomy—remembering, understanding, applying, analyzing, evaluating, and creating.
2. One of the challenges in engaging in a Socratic seminar is that people are inclined to debate rather than to dialogue. What do you think are the differences in these two forms of interaction? Prepare a table with two columns and a number of rows. Label the columns "Dialogue" and "Debate." Label the rows, as a start, with features such as "interactions," "beliefs," "questions," or "purposes." The goal of this activity is to create a list of features that distinguish these two kinds of verbal give-and-take.

REFLECTIVE QUESTIONS

1. Students in your class may be accustomed to discussions driven by right answers, and surely there are many settings where this is appropriate. But the Socratic seminar is a context in which multiple answers to open-ended questions compete for dominance and all may be winners. Do you think this approach will be difficult or easy to adopt? What can you do to ensure that every opinion and perspective is honored in the seminar setting?
2. It is important that at the onset of a Socratic seminar each participant has read the targeted text. What are some ways to ensure this is the case?
3. Aside from deepening skills of reading comprehension, what other skills do you see the seminar as fostering? Might it be a good idea to ask the students to help with this skills list?

11

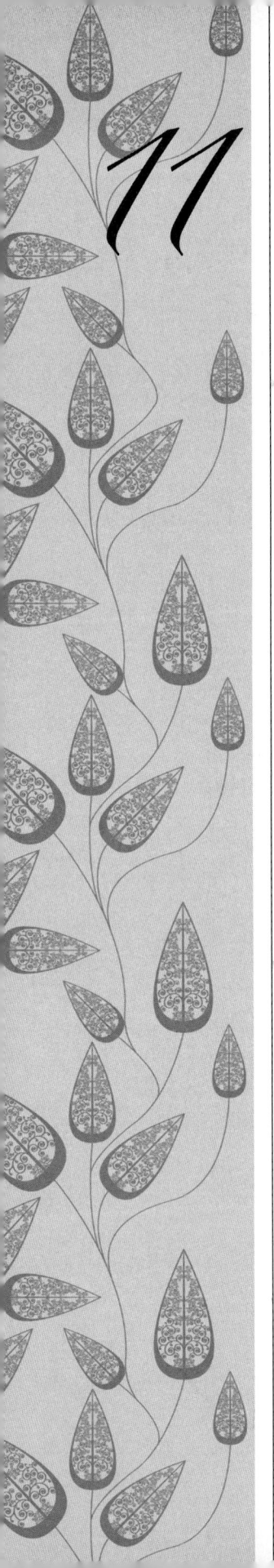

The Vocabulary Acquisition Model

Learning the Spellings and Meanings of Words

chapter OBJECTIVES

You Will Understand
- The spellings and meanings of words reflect the concepts underlying the study of all subjects of the curriculum

You Will Know
- How to diagnose students' understanding of critical vocabulary
- How to initiate vocabulary instruction by beginning with what students already understand
- How to plan instruction in vocabulary so as to tie language study to concept development
- What the vocabulary acquisition model looks like in K–12 classrooms

You Will Be Able To
- Plan lessons around major concepts of the curriculum tied to the vocabulary in which those concepts are expressed

In the **ELEMENTARY** *classroom*

Mrs. Schafer designed an introductory lesson to teach her third grade class the basic units of measure—volume, mass, and length. Her goal was that students would learn to measure volume to the nearest milliliter, mass to the nearest kilogram, and length to the nearest millimeter. The prefixes associated with these units, milli- (one thousandth), kilo- (thousand), and centi- (one hundredth) were particularly important for the students to learn in association with these measures.

To put these measures in concrete form that the students could understand, Mrs. Schafer brought a bag of wooden blocks, scraps of wood of various sizes from her home for students in groups of three to manipulate. As a pretest, she asked the students to define in their own words the ideas of volume, mass, and length, and to match each with its typical unit of measurement: cubic millimeter, kilogram, and millimeter. The students' answers varied, but the class decided that volume means "the amount of space" occupied by something, mass means "how much of something," and length means "how long" something is.

209

These definitions were written on the chalkboard. Next to *volume* was written *milliliter,* next to *mass* was written *kilogram,* and next to *length* was written *millimeter.*

Mrs. Schafer: We are going to study the basic units of measure today by measuring some things. Using the wooden blocks you have at your desks, your task will be to make measures of volume, mass, and length of each one.

Baker: How are we going to measure these things?

Mrs. Schafer: You have a ruler at your desk and I have a scale here that will give you mass in metric terms. You should also check the values in the Table of Metric System Units (Table 11.1) I have provided. Remember, the metric system is simple because it is a system of units of ten, or tens, hundreds, and thousands.

Marcia: But we don't measure that way. We use feet and inches.

Mrs. Schafer: That is generally true, but around the world and in all the sciences, the metric system is the choice. Think of it as learning two languages, one that you use in some places, the other in other places. You might find you like your new language of measure, once you get the hang of it. Many rulers have both scales so you can have a choice.

Preston: Wow. I never noticed that on my ruler.

Mrs. Schafer: Here are three hints to make it easy for you. I've also written these on the board:

1. To measure length, find the number in millimeters with the rulers you have at your desks. Be sure to use the scale labeled *mm*.
2. To measure mass, assign a number in fractions of a kilogram, which you get by weighing the blocks on the metric scale.
3. To measure volume, give a number in cubic centimeters. To get this, measure the height, length, and width of a block in centimeters and multiply these three values together.

Table 11.1   Table of Metric System Units

Quantity Measured	Unit	Symbol	Relationship
Length	millimeter	mm	10 mm = 1 cm
	centimeter	cm	100 cm = 1 m
	meter	m	
	kilometer	km	1 km = 1000 m
Mass	milligram	mg	1000 mg = 1 g
	gram	g	
	kilogram	kg	1 kg = 1000 g
	metric ton	t	1 t = 1000 kg
Volume	milliliter	mL	1000 mL = 1 L
	cubic centimeter	cm^3	$1\ cm^3 = 1\ mL$
	liter	L	$1000\ L = 1\ m^3$
	cubic meter	m^3	

You may discuss these procedures as you complete your measures. If you run into difficulty, raise your hand and I will come help you.

In the **SECONDARY** *classroom*

The eighth grade social studies class is just beginning a unit on the Middle Ages. Their teacher, Mr. Torres, is concerned about the sophisticated vocabulary in the text and decides to begin the unit with a vocabulary acquisition process. The standards on which Mr. Torres is basing his unit indicate that students should know the sequence of events and the influence of the Catholic Church throughout Europe during A.D. 500 to about 1000. Since the Crusades occurred just after this period, Mr. Torres decided to begin with these words. He asks the students to write down anything they associate with the words *Middle Ages* and *Crusades*.

He notices that most of the students spell *middle* correctly, but the associations vary. The most common idea that comes up in the ensuing discussion is the concept of "between." The word *crusade* was spelled in several different ways and defined in reference to war, religion, and Robin Hood.

MR. TORRES: Look first at the word *middle* in the phrase Middle Ages. Middle of what? What does it mean to say of anything that it's in the middle?

KAREN: It's between two other things. Between two ages.

MR. TORRES: Like middle school is between elementary and high school and a middle child is between an older and younger sibling.

MARCUS: But is Middle Ages between old age and young age? Like some people are middle-aged.

KAREN: Sort of. It's more between ancient times and modern times, right?

OMAR: But we are only supposed to be studying A.D. 500 to 1000 and there is nothing modern about the year 1000.

MR. TORRES: Karen is correct and so is Omar. The Middle Ages occurred between the end of the Roman Empire and the beginning of the Crusades—it was the middle of these two historical periods when the Church served the social, political, and religious needs of the people. Let's look more closely at the idea of middle. Sometimes in English, it gets spelled *med*. Like in medium. How are middle and medium related?

IVY: Medium is in between two extremes—big and little, hot and cold, and things like that.

MR. TORRES: Yes, can you think of other words in which *med* occurs? We can see if they have anything to do with middle.

JASON: Median, like in a road.

DOMINIQUE: Mediate, but what does mediate have to do with anything in the middle?

JASON: It's like finding the middle of an argument so both sides will be happy.

SUSAN: I've heard of medieval. Is that the same thing?

Mr. Torres: That's an adjective describing something from the Middle Ages. "Chivalry was a medieval custom," for example. You could say that instead of saying "Middle Age custom." But you see how the idea of middle is in all of these words?

Marcus: How about Mediterranean?

Rachel: Or medical?

Mr. Torres: Let's look at the map and see where the Mediterranean Sea is.

Jason: Like between Africa and Europe?

Marcus: But in the middle of what?

Susan: All that land. It's almost all surrounded by land.

Mr. Torres: Now, I'm not certain about medical. I do know that *med* can also be related to the basic idea of measure. Medical can be related to *med* words because doctors take measure—they take your temperature and weight. Let's look at the word *crusade*. Remember what we know about the Crusades—they had a profound impact on social, political, and economic factors in Western Europe.

The conversation about *crusade* begins with *ade*, which Mr. Torres points out means "furnished with." The students think of lemonade, Kool-Aid, and orangeade. All are flavored drinks "furnished" with sweeteners. Mr. Torres provides the information that the word element *crus* means "cross." Those who marched on the Crusades were furnished with a cross and sent to the Middle East to furnish the cross to the "barbarians" who were occupying the territory after the fall of the Roman Empire.

Basis for the Vocabulary Acquisition Model

The Spelling–Meaning Connection

Unfortunately, the connection between spelling and meaning is ignored in most spelling and vocabulary instruction. This is one of a number of peculiarities about how words are taught in school. The expressions "vocabulary words" and "spelling words" would be redundant anywhere but in school, where "vocabulary words" are typically assigned in grade levels beyond the primary grades, with "spelling words" reserved for the early grade levels of school. But virtually anyone, in school or out, would recognize that these expressions refer to words studied in school, usually in lists, *as* vocabulary words or spelling words, with focus on their definitions, spellings, or both. Furthermore, there is probably nothing more universal in education than the way those words are studied, usually beginning with a list of words more or less arbitrarily grouped together and assigned weekly. The accompanying instructions generally require activities such as "Look the words up in a dictionary, use each one in a sentence, and learn their correct spellings and definitions for a test on Friday."

Sometimes, of course, students are required merely to memorize the spellings and definitions of the words by looking at each word to get an image of its spelling, copying the word in their own handwriting, and writing the word and its definition 10 times without looking at the correct spelling. Endless hours are spent in activities like this every week of the school year! One has to wonder how many Thursday nights find parents "calling words" to their children, not just for language arts or English class but for every subject in school at one time or another.

Despite all this effort, the cost-effectiveness of this approach is extremely meager because of two major problems with trying to learn lists of words: (1) Whatever the students learn from the experience of memorizing words is mostly lost within a few hours or days of the test, and (2) the students learn practically nothing about the *system* of English spelling and word meaning. The experience of many people who have studied words in the traditional ways just described illustrates each of these two shortcomings.

The first shortcoming can be tested any time a teacher wants to quiz the students. Imagine a teacher saying, first thing one Monday morning, that Friday's test was lost in a flood and that the students will have to retake the test now. To require that students spell or define words on Monday that they learned for Friday would loudly be met with cries of "Unfair! We need time to study! Let us have at least 10 minutes."

The second shortcoming is easiest to illustrate by listing a few words that many people have difficulty spelling because they have little knowledge of how meaning and spelling are connected. Here's a simple example. What do all the following words have in common?

adequate
advent
accustom
accommodate
arrange
affirm
aggravate
acknowledge
allocate
appall
acquire
assist
attain

These words are difficult to spell, even for some adults. It's the rare speller who realizes that each of these words begins with a form of the prefix ad- meaning "at, or toward." Thus *adequate* means "to move toward equal" (the root of the word can be seen in *equate*), and *advent* means "toward the coming." *Vent* is from the Latin word for "come," as in the familiar quote from Julius Caesar, "Veni, vidi, vici," or "I came, I saw, I conquered." Likewise, and despite the spelling changes, *accustom* means "to move toward custom"; *accommodate* means "to move toward common"; *arrange* means "to move into line" (*range* being a word for *line,* as in "range of colors"); and so on down this list of words and many others that begin either with ad- or with a- followed by a double consonant. The double consonant following the initial letter *a* is likely to be the prefix ad- assimilated to the root word. Incidentally, the word *assimilate* is an example of assimilation. The root of the word is *similar,* and *assimilate* means "to move toward similar." At some point it must have been spelled and pronounced something like *adsimilate.* But precisely because such a spelling was difficult to articulate, English speakers gradually began to pronounce the *d* as if it were similar to the letter following, and so the *d* in ad- is frequently assimilated to the initial consonant of the root word to which it is attached. (Two words on the above list have double assimilated letters. In *acknowledge* and *acquire,* the *k* sound of the *c* is assimilated to the sound of *k* or *q*.) This example is not a minilesson in linguistics, but it illustrates a crucial feature of the system of the English language: The spelling of words in English is based on meaning, not just on sound, and the connection between meaning and sound is an important part of the basis for spelling. But that is generally *not* the way spelling and meaning are taught in school.

Each of these two shortcomings of vocabulary and spelling instruction—the great loss of memory for what is memorized and the failure of instruction to acknowledge the system governing the connection of spoken and written language—is predictable in light of what has been learned recently about characteristics of the brain, the organ of learning. It would be no exaggeration to say that requirements to "look the words up in a dictionary, use each one in a sentence, and memorize their correct spellings and definitions for a test on Friday" are contrary to the way the human brain works.

The brain is a pattern-seeking machine, an organ designed specifically to look for pattern and meaning and to ignore what it judges to be random or meaningless information. Fortunately, the vocabulary of English is neither random nor meaningless. In fact, it is systematic and meaningful. This can guide the study of the spellings and definitions of words *precisely because the human brain thrives on pattern and meaning.* The vocabulary acquisition model described here honors this insight.

Principles Underlying the Vocabulary Acquisition Model

The model for vocabulary acquisition described here rests on the following three principles:

- *Principle 1: The principle of system.* Language is nonarbitrary and metaphoric; it is fundamentally a tool for communicating about unfamiliar things in terms related to familiar things.

The study of any subject, in school or otherwise, is an exploration of a way of knowing and thinking about the topics that constitute the subject as well as the language in which that knowing and thinking are expressed. Much successful teaching hinges on the relationship between concepts and vocabulary, between ideas and the language in which those ideas are expressed. Words do not arbitrarily label ideas, concepts, or things. To the contrary, words in English make up a system that mirrors the connections among ideas, concepts, and things.

- *Principle 2: The principle of incidence.* Vocabulary is naturally and incidentally acquired as a means for expression of understandings.

People generally acquire only those words that are important and necessary to the expression of ideas they understand and care about. They usually do this incidentally, as in conversation with someone else who cares about the same thing or in reading about something in which they are interested.

- *Principle 3: The principle of conceptualization.* Teaching vocabulary is a matter of helping learners move simultaneously to greater sophistication in their understanding of concepts and their understanding of language.

What would these principles look like in teaching? How might these principles change the way teachers interact with students regarding the various topics of the curriculum? Certainly the instructional conversation should include discussion *about* the language in which ideas and information are expressed as well as discussion of ideas and information *in* the language of the topic. The plan for teaching that honors the principles of system, incidence, and conceptualization would include plans for teaching the vocabulary in which ideas and information are expressed.

Part of the answer to the oft-repeated question "What should schools teach?" is to say, "Teach students to participate in the great conversations that have defined what it means to be educated." Teach them the joy of language in which distinctions of thought are reflected. Conduct their way into the particular conversations that have contributed to humankind's knowledge. Use the language of the discipline, and, more important, invite the students to adopt the language as their own as they come to see how the language they are acquiring ties together the concepts they are studying.

It seems impossible that someone could understand a subject such as geometry or a topic such as right triangles within that subject and lack the language with which to express that understanding. Likewise, it is difficult to imagine how one might understand social studies or a topic such as forms of government within social studies and yet have no technical language to discuss those forms. Every subject and every topic in the curriculum is couched in a language peculiar to its expression. Think, for example, of the words and phrases associated with the topic of right triangles: *right angle, hypotenuse, square,* and *square root,* just to name the basics. Likewise, the terms associated with forms of government are essential to expression of what one understands about governments. Among these terms are the words *represent, govern,* and the root *archy* in its many forms. Also in that group is *polis* with the meaning "city," the common root of words such as *politic, police, polish, cosmopolitan,* and *polite.*

Think of teaching as a conversation, a special conversation in which comments of the teacher and texts lead students toward inquiry and curiosity about the concepts under study and about the language in which those concepts are expressed. (The root of the word *educate* means "to lead." Teachers and textbooks alike must, if they are to achieve their purpose, lead learners toward new ideas and concepts by drawing from them the connections between what they know and what they are trying to learn.) This conversation, teaching, is extraordinary in several ways. One conversational participant usually knows a great deal more than the others about the point of the conversation, and that same one, the teacher or author, usually talks more than the others. The purpose of that talk, though, is to engage the other participants in thinking that leads to insights and understandings. Such conversation might accurately be seen as a shared inquiry. The major goal of education is to introduce learners to the conversation that has created the concepts they are trying to learn, extending to them an invitation to contribute to the creation itself.

The special conversation that is teaching is conducted in language particular to the topic under discussion. Concepts and ideas new to the learners are initially framed in language familiar to them. As understandings emerge in the learner, the teacher and text may introduce language that expands the thinking and the range of such understandings. Students participate in that conversation to become conversant with the curriculum topics.

The success of students' learning requires that they learn two things simultaneously. First, learners must understand what they are taught well enough to put their understandings in their "own" words. Second, they must "own" the language in which the understandings they have acquired are typically expressed by experts. Learners need to see experts' vocabulary as both a way of labeling concepts and a way of tying those concepts into the structure of human knowledge.

There is no shortcut to knowledge, yet obviously there are more ways to be expert in a topic than firsthand experience. Much that we know, that we claim to be expert in, we gain from conversation. In instructional conversation, ideas and experiences are gained vicariously, and the learner is free to take risks, to be wrong, or to be right in unique ways. Imagine classroom conversations marked by the qualities associated with expertise, and you begin to get an idea of an aim that is possible in teaching: learners who are virtual experts in their studies.

This aim will be realized when teachers see themselves as more than conveyors of information, when they define themselves as conductors of and participants in a conversation to which students are invited to participate. This conversation is about more than the topic under study, however. It is a conversation simultaneously about a topic and about the language in which the topic has come to be expressed. The guide to that conversation is as follows:

1. Teach the topics of the curriculum as bodies of knowledge, information, and concepts that are born in language, live in language, and expand in language.

2. Teach as if everything to be taught and everything to be learned existed and was understandable in language created precisely for its expression.
3. Teach the topics of the curriculum *as* language.

How Vocabulary Is Acquired

Learners young and old all acquire vocabulary in fundamentally the same way: from the conversations they engage in, first with intimate caretakers, later with teachers and with authors of texts removed in space and time. *Vocabulary* shares a common root with *vocation: voc,* meaning "to call." So vocabulary is the lexicon, or glossary, of a calling and the means by which experts express their callings. In formal study, vocabulary is the language particular to a subject, created as a means of expression for understandings and ideas gained from experience. When learners acquire understandings and words to express those understandings, they replicate, in microcosm, the evolution of the information they are gaining. Put another way, as learners become experts, their understandings evolve through the stages in which those understandings originally evolved. The differences lie in efficiency and timeliness. The teacher saves the learner the trouble of re-creating knowledge, all the while realizing that creating their "own" knowledge is precisely what learners must do in the context of the conversation they are invited into. Seen as conversation, teaching requires of the teacher two kinds of expertise, expertise in the subject to be taught and expertise in the language of the subject.

Steps in the Vocabulary Acquisition Model

Step 1: Pretest Knowledge of Words Critical to Content

At the beginning of any unit of study or new topic, students can profit from a pretest of knowledge of words critical to the content under study. The *unannounced* pretest (a diagnostic assessment) is an opportunity for students to show what they know and can be a place to begin learning more. As you call each word out, ask students to spell and define the words the best they can. Emphasize that this is a test not to find out what they *do not* know but a test to find out what they *do* know. Teaching and learning has to proceed from the known to the new, so the first step in learning is often to identify the known.

To generate the list of words to be pretested, carefully examine the information to be taught—the textbook or other source(s) of information—and identify the basic vocabulary in which that information is expressed. These need not be technical words, but they must be words that express the basic concepts underlying the information. Keep the list short, as the goal is to teach a few words so well that the understandings will generalize to many other words. As an example, consider parts of a science lesson at the fifth grade level on the topic Changing Forms of Energy. Perusing the textbook chapter carefully, we identified and pretested the following five words: *energy, potential, kinetic, conservation,* and *transformation.* As we expected, our fifth grade students gave us quite a number of spellings and a great variety of definitions for each word. This particular pretest and the conversation that followed are used in the following sections to illustrate the steps in this model.

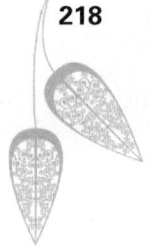

Step 2: Elaborate On and Discuss Invented Spellings and Hypothesized Meanings

Students usually come to believe that school is a place that honors being right, without error. The basic idea of the pretest is to acknowledge that "error" is a judgment of what is more or less conventional, such as whether a spelling attempt matches its correct form. This right or wrong evaluation, however, is only one possible judgment. "State of knowledge" is an alternative, potentially more useful, judgment. It opens up a greater range of possibilities for the teacher and admits a greater range of thought on the part of the learner. Certainly it is more respectful in conveying to the learner that every person's knowledge is incomplete. Knowledge of language in any aspect (spelling and word meaning in speaking, listening, reading, and writing) is never an all-or-nothing affair.

If possible, display the various spellings and meanings given for each word for all to see, with the names of the students deleted. Emphasize that each attempted spelling and each meaning given reflects some knowledge of the ideas and words that represent them. Many misspellings are phonetically derived; they are attempts to represent sound with print. But English spelling is based on meaning as well as sound. (Thus "spelling demons" such as words like *debt, sign, hasten,* and *mortgage,* with their confusing silent letters, are easy to spell once one sees the connection to *debit, signal, haste,* and *mortality*.) Students recognize this on an intuitive level when they misspell a word by spelling another word whose sound pattern is similar and with whose meaning they are familiar or when they assign a definition to a word that is actually the definition of a word that merely sounds like the word given them to define.

The Example Pretest

Examine each of the words on the pretest and discuss the relationships of their sound, their meaning, and their spelling. In our Changing Forms of Energy pretest, 28 of 37 students spelled *energy* correctly. The other 9 students offered a total of 8 different spellings such as *energey* and *inergi* and *entergy.* But half of the students who produced the alternative spellings did, however unknowingly, preserve the root of the word, *erg,* from the Greek *ergon,* meaning "work." Although this root is not something these fifth grade students know, it is something they are ready to learn. Definitions of *energy* offered by the students fell into two categories, and each definition related to one or the other meaning. Thus the students defined the word in relation to the idea of work or in relation solely to a human quality, as in "full of energy." But here, as in the spellings, the connections are in place for an excellent lesson in why the word *energy* means what it does and is spelled as it is.

The word *potential* presented more challenge to these students, as might be expected. Only 7 of the 37 students spelled the word correctly. Most of the misspellings occurred in the -tial ending of the word, a phonetically strange construction in which the ending of the base word, *potent,* is attached to the suffix -ial, and the sound of *t* changes to *sh*. This is another example of assimilation, where the pronunciation of a letter is changed when it occurs immediately before or after another sound that makes it difficult to enunciate. (Try saying *potent* and then adding *ial*.) Thus *potent* shifts in its pronunciation when the suffix -ial is added, creating *po/ten/tial*. Yet -ial is a key to the meaning and the spelling of this word: These letters form a suffix with the meaning "of, or related to," as seen in words such as *residential, presidential, tutorial,* and *special*. (Even the word *special* follows this rule. The literal meaning of *special* is "of, or related to, a particular species, kind, or form.") With an understanding of the suffix -ial, students can see that the base of *potential* is a word that they may have seen or heard before: *potent,* meaning "powerful," from a Latin word meaning "to be able." Potential energy, then, is energy that can be used when called on but that is not at the moment being used.

The word *kinetic* was spelled correctly by only 3 of the 37 students, although 18 students did show that the word was somehow related to the concept of energy (12 students) or electricity (5 students). Mainly the students tried to spell the word as a word they did know whose sound was similar and whose meaning was familiar: *connect* or *Connecticut* or *conversation*. As it happens, there is one other familiar word that they did not associate with *kinetic: cinema*. The key to teaching the word *kinetic* lies in the concepts associated with the movies. Movie is a synonym for *cinema,* short for cinematograph, a picture of motion, or motion picture. *Cinema* derives from the Greek word *kinema,* meaning "motion," from the idea of movement, a concept expressed in science as *kinesis* and *kinetic*. Kinetic energy, then, is energy achieved by motion. This is key to understanding the idea of inertia when this concept arises later in the curriculum.

Conservation fared little better with these students than did kinetic. Although 19 of the 37 spelled it correctly, no student defined the word in relation to energy. Eleven students connected the word to science in one way, in the concept of ecology. But most of the students spelled and defined the word in relation to some other word they knew, such as *conversation, convention, observation, concentration,* or *concern*. The bright spot, and the initial instructional handle, was that 26 students spelled the *ser* part of the word correctly. Although unknown to

> ## Strategy Alert
> **Think–Pair–Share**
>
> The think–pair–share strategy can apply as a follow-up to the invented spellings and hypothesized meanings of vocabulary study. Ask students to work in pairs to discuss the various spellings of the pretested words, all the while assuming that no misspelling is random. For each word, students will individually think of reasons for the various spellings offered, followed by paired discussion of reasons for the spellings and hypothesized meanings, and concluding with an opportunity to share ideas with the whole class. Keep the pace lively by allowing only a couple of minutes for each step in the process and quickly moving on to the next word to be discussed. ■

these students, like the root *erg* of *energy, ser* is a root that means "to protect." It occurs in words like *preserve, reserve, reservoir,* and, oddly, in the word *hero,* which in its Greek form is the source of this root. Perhaps a hero is one who protects, as to conserve is to protect.

The last of the five words, *transformation,* was spelled correctly by 20 of the 37 students and defined in relation to the idea of "change" by 24 students. Although a few students confused the word with *transportation,* for the most part they all had some idea of the word's meaning. One student at least vaguely connected the word to the concept of energy. What all the students revealed in their spellings and their definitions of this last word was a readiness to learn the concept of changing forms. The first step in their instruction might be to connect *transformation* to *transformer,* a kind of toy many of them have played with.

Words like these five that students are asked to spell on a pretest are not likely to be easy for them. After all, these are words labeling the concepts they are going to be taught, not things they necessarily already know. But by examining the knowledge they do have, as revealed in their best attempts at spelling and definition, a conversation arises that forms the basis of teaching what we want students to learn on the basis of what they already know.

Step 3: Explore Patterns of Meaning

The Teacher's Guide for the *Iowa Tests of Basic Skills* (ITBS), a widely used benchmark of educational attainment, offers an interesting list of suggestions for improving vocabulary. We do not want to imply that improved Iowa scores are the point of vocabulary instruction, but if a test like the vocabulary subtest of ITBS has any validity (as we think it does), then improvements in vocabulary will show up in the test scores of students. This is what the authors of the ITBS manual have to say about vocabulary improvement:

> Understanding the meanings of words is essential to all communication and learning. In general, the school can contribute to vocabulary power through a) planned, systematic instruction; b) informal instruction whenever the opportunity arises;

c) wide reading of a variety of materials; and d) activities and experience, field trips, etc. One of the most important responsibilities of teachers in each subject area is to provide pupils with an understanding of the specialized vocabulary and concepts of the subject. (p. 47)

There are no known shortcuts to vocabulary instruction; vocabulary development is a continuous program. The following suggestions may prove helpful:

1. Keep the emphasis on meaning rather than mere recognition or mechanical pronunciation of words.
2. Teach words in context, not in isolation.
3. Teach children to ask about any new, confusing, or unusual words as they encounter them.
4. Put such words on the board, and encourage their frequent use.
5. Make definite provision for word study and word building: explain origins of words, roots, affixes, compound words, and so on.
6. Have frequent oral tests covering new words, using them in sentences, and discussing their meanings.
7. Give practice in synonyms and antonyms, both for words and for phrases.
8. Conduct discussions of differences in meaning of words that are similar but not identical. (Most dictionaries have "usage notes" and cross references that provide excellent materials for this purpose.)
9. Give pupils, particularly in the upper grades, experience using a thesaurus.
10. Encourage children of different language backgrounds to share interesting words, concepts, and idioms (Iowa Tests of Basic Skills, 1986).

A test manual may be an unlikely place to find a prescription for success in vocabulary instruction, but one group of teachers we know at Louisa Middle School in Mineral, Virginia, took this page of the ITBS manual as exactly that. The following suggestions are distilled from those teachers' experiences with

Strategy Alert

Link

The Link instructional strategy is a powerful tool for vocabulary recall. Information that can be linked to or associated with already familiar data and ideas is most likely to be recalled. For example, think of helping students to understand and remember lines of longitude and latitude. Longitude is marked by the "long" up and down lines on the globe; latitude is marked by the "lateral" lines that run across the globe. Think of the lines of longitude as running longwise between the north and south poles; think of the lines of latitude as being similar in direction to a lateral to another player in football. For another example of using Link in instruction, the continents "contain" countries or vast sections of land, as a box of puzzle pieces might contain pieces that are the shape of the countries "contained" by Africa, Europe, Asia, and North and South America. This linking from larger to smaller pieces of land will help students make distinctions among these five continents and the countries they include. ■

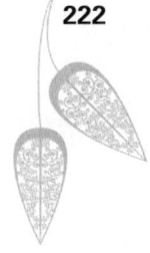

this model of vocabulary development interpreted through the lens of the ITBS suggestions.

I: Involve the students. Invite them to share *their* ideas about how a target word is spelled and defined.

T: Tell them about the word. Show correct spelling, meaning, and derivation; reinforce elements of their ideas that relate to the correct information; tell the story of the word's origin if it is known.

B: Brainstorm with the students. Accept the words they believe to be synonymous with the target word as well as words that they think are related in meaning to the target word. Using your knowledge and various reference sources, model for and lead the students in an analysis of the words on the brainstormed list by having them compare meanings of those words to the definition of the target word.

S: Create sentences: Have each student select one of the words from the list they generated or select the target word and use the selected word in a sentence; discuss parts of speech and word usage within the sentences they share.

Each teacher in the school chooses the words he or she will teach in a particular week. It may be a single word per week or several words. In general, the words chosen for teaching are core concept words in the content area—words like *energy* in science, *fraction* in math, *federal* in social studies, *participle* in grammar, and *descriptive* in literature.

To begin, the teacher asks the students to spell and define the target word as best they can. Next, they share their spellings and definitions with a partner or in a small group. To conclude this first step, the pair or group composes one spelling and definition and writes it on the chalkboard.

Each student receives or draws, in a personal vocabulary journal, a copy of the graphic organizer for vocabulary acquisition shown in Figure 11.1. The target word, correctly spelled, is written in the center of the graphic by the teacher and copied by the students. They compare their spellings and begin to discuss differences. Then the teacher writes the prime dictionary definition in the appropriate space on the graphic. Again, the students compare their definitions. They discuss similarities between spellings and definitions, with emphasis on why the word is spelled as it is and why it means what it means. Often, the students are very close in their spellings and definitions; and, because learning what a thing is *not* can be very helpful in understanding what it *is*, the discussion of differences between the conventional and unconventional spellings and definitions helps everyone get closer to actually knowing the word.

Next, the students' proposed sentences are examined in the same spirit as the spellings and definitions. The teacher and students create an exemplary sentence using the target word, based on what they have found together to that point. The

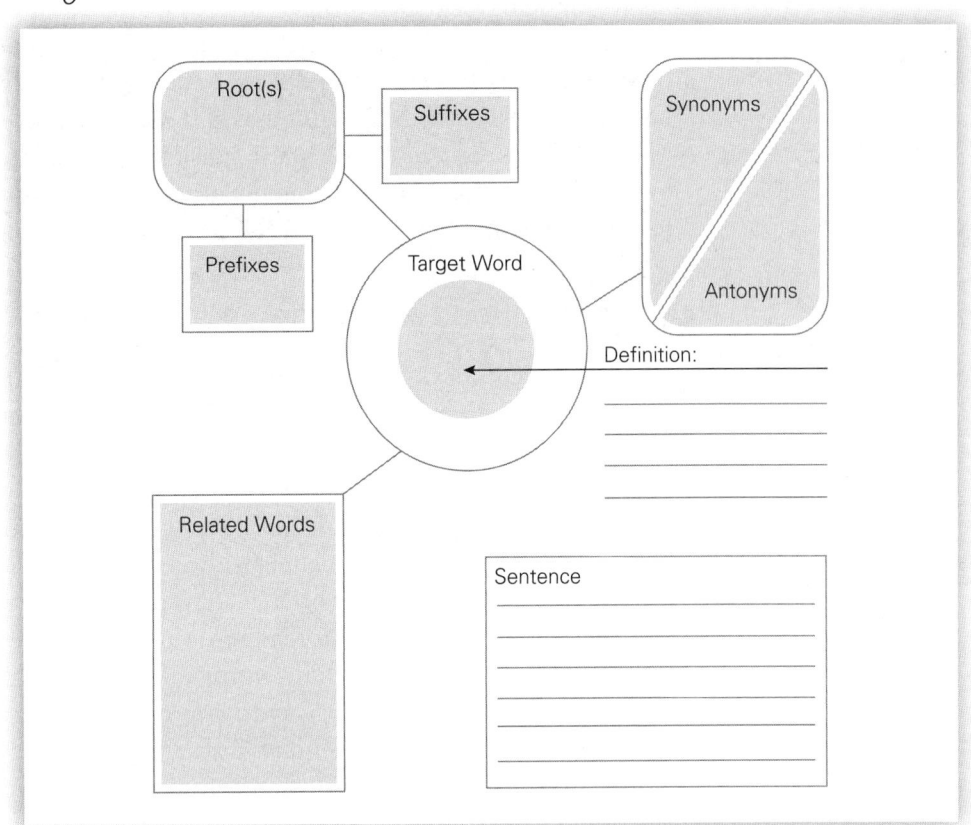

Figure 11.1 Graphic Organizer for Vocabulary Acquisition

teacher refers the students to the actual spelling and definition as the context of the discussion requires. This keeps the focus on the actual target of the lesson.

Next, the brainstormed words are examined to see which are related words, which are synonyms, and which are antonyms. At this point students can offer additional words to be included on the chart. Related words are words with the same root, words that form a "meaning" family. Synonyms are words of similar meaning, and antonyms are words of opposite meaning. Knowing a word often means knowing words it is like and words it is not like; acquiring this knowledge is, of course, the point of the exercise.

At the same time that the class is discussing related words, synonyms, and antonyms, possible prefixes, roots, and suffixes can be brought to light. English is a system of combinations. Young readers need to learn to combine, or blend, sounds into words as they decode print to speech. But beyond the basic phonics patterns, readers need to see the patterns of meaning that are also encoded in print. Why is there a silent *g* in *sign*, for example? The answer is that the *g* is needed to maintain the meaning connection between *sign* and *signal* and any number of other words of the same meaning family. Why do we say *rented*, *walked*, and *roused*, in each case spelling the "-ed" part the same but pronouncing it differently? We spell this part of each word the same to maintain the similar function of the word part in each word. We pronounce the endings differently because we gravitate, over time, to the easiest way to say words, a fact that often has led to a mismatch between sound and spelling. There are thousands of similar examples. Bearing in mind that English is a combinatorial system that works to encode both meaning and sound can help readers enormously in their quest for understanding, which is, after all, the point of reading.

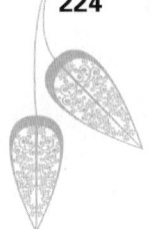

Step 4: Read and Study

Once the target ideas and vocabulary are introduced and discussed in the vocabulary acquisition model, reading and study may be guided by any companion model such as concept development, classroom discussion, or cooperative learning. Encourage the students to observe carefully how the words they have studied are used in the text(s) they will read. Seeing a new word used in an appropriate context is another step in vocabulary acquisition. In addition, the students can listen for uses of any of the words in conversation, on radio, or on television or watch for uses of the word in readings other than their textbook. Fiction and nonfiction alike will use all these words in many ways. It is likely, in fact, that wide reading is the single best way to improve one's vocabulary, but only if one is sensitive to the subtle distinctions that writers achieve by their careful choice of words. Conversation and discussion before reading and study in the vocabulary acquisition model will heighten this sensitivity for many learners.

Step 5: Evaluate and Posttest

The effects of the vocabulary acquisition model are relatively easy to assess. The model begins with a pretest and ends with a posttest of the spellings and meanings of the same words. One can expect very large differences in the scores on these two tests, considering the intensity of vocabulary study. In this model, mastery is the goal and near perfect scores the intent.

The posttest can include more than spellings and definitions of words, although those might be the basis of grading the posttest. It is critical that learners see beyond words and their definitions, that they understand the ideas of synonymity, usage, and etymology. Use the posttest, then, as an opportunity to probe beyond mere spelling and definition. Ask for synonyms, examples of use, and explanations of etymology. Vocabulary instruction is not merely about the words that are taught. The point is the insight into language and ideas that students gain from their discussion and study, insights that will generalize across many different words because of the ways in which all language is connected at the level of roots, base words, and affixes. When these connections are emphasized, students can be fairly tested with the expectation that they will excel.

Part of the evaluation of language is always informal. We all commonly make judgments about a person when we hear the person speak or see the person's writing. The conversation about the vocabulary that has been taught with the vocabulary acquisition model will continue across time, and in that conversation, evaluation and encouragement to use more precise language will be inevitable. Keep an informal tally of how often the words taught in past lessons are used. Draw the students' attention to places where a recently discussed word may say more precisely what they mean. Such informal diagnostic attention to the words students own and use might be the best part of evaluation for the vocabulary acquisition model.

When testing learners about what they have been expected to learn from their study, include a spelling and meaning test covering the words and concepts targeted in the vocabulary acquisition lesson. The results will show marked improvement of understandings of spellings and meanings of words. The effect will be significantly higher grades, with the added benefit of reinforcing vocabulary study. Furthermore, teaching using this model will greatly enhance the chances that if last Friday's test is washed away in a weekend flood, the students will do just fine on Monday's retest.

Summary of Steps in the Vocabulary Acquisition Model

1. *Pretest knowledge of words critical to content.* This test will establish baseline information for the teacher and students alike, information on what students already know about the fundamental concepts of a topic to be taught. By how they spell and define words, students provide a window on their understandings and a starting point for the instruction.

2. *Elaborate on and discuss invented spellings and hypothesized meanings.* Invention and hypothesis form the basis of instruction and growth in understanding. New understandings are built on prior knowledge, and whatever students attempt in spelling and defining words can become the basis for growth in understanding.

3. *Explore patterns of meaning.* Discuss how words fit together with their synonyms, how words are used in the language, and how words came into existence in modern English. Spelling is more than speech represented in print. English is a morphophonemic system, which means that a word in print gives clues to its pronunciation and to its meaning. Thus how a word is spelled often has as much to do with what the word means as with how it sounds in speech.

4. *Read and study.* Exploring basic concepts before reading and study creates a context in which students can confirm what they already know while they elaborate and refine their understandings.

5. *Evaluate and posttest.* The evaluation of learning makes best sense when the teacher and students can examine an outcome measure, a test following

instruction, against a preinstructional measure of the same information. The steps of the vocabulary acquisition model are set up to ensure marked growth in understandings and knowledge of words and their associated concepts.

Evaluating Learning in the Vocabulary Acquisition Model

There are many creative alternative, and perhaps better, ways to assess students' understanding of vocabulary aside from asking them to spell and define words they have studied.

- Call out different words of the same meaning family with different suffixes and have students identify the part of speech of each word.
- Ask students to identify synonyms and antonyms for words that they have studied.
- See whether students can identify the meanings of new words that they haven't studied, using their knowledge of the meaning parts of words.
- Give students a fill-in-the-blank exercise with sentences (accompanied by a bank of words at the bottom of the page) in which they must change or add prefixes or suffixes to words to make them fit the context.
- Set students the task to identify root parts of boldfaced words in sentences and then define the roots and the words.
- Give students a set of incomplete sentences or a story that they must complete by using words that have a certain root.
- Rather than simply spell words on a test, ask students to break them into their meaning parts.
- Occasionally ask students to define nonsense words based on their knowledge of the meanings of word parts.

Meeting Individual Needs in the Vocabulary Acquisition Model

The relationship between reading comprehension and vocabulary knowledge is strong and unequivocal. The problem with teaching vocabulary is that, although the finding may be intuitively contradictory, research has repeatedly demonstrated that the least effective way to teach vocabulary is through direct instruction on word meanings—for example, by having students look up the meanings of words in a list and use the words in a sentence. Instead, the vocabulary of a reader will improve as he or she acquires strategies for learning word meanings independently and as he or she reads widely. Here, in one sentence, is a summary of what years of research into vocabulary development has taught us: *All vocabulary instruction should aim at skills and strategies that help students become independent word learners, able to figure out the meanings of unfamiliar words they encounter in frequent, wide reading.*

The key to independence in word learning and the ability to figure out the meaning of an unfamiliar word lies in a simple precept of language: Just as sentences and phrases are built out of words combined by the rules of syntax, words themselves are built out of smaller bits, called morphemes, combined by another set of rules, the rules of morphology (Pinker, 1994). Language users are hardly aware of these latter rules and procedures, since at the simplest level such as the formation of a plural noun, the processes are virtually automatic. But at some point, language becomes much more complex, and the similarity of morphemes becomes obscured by variations in spelling and pronunciation. Consider words like con*grat*ulate, *grat*eful, and in*grat*iate, all of which are built from the same root with slightly different spellings. Students as well as most of their teachers are unable to see most of the morphemic building blocks that compose words in English. But as they become explicitly conscious of what was before only implicit about how words encode their meanings, they begin to recognize meanings of words they have never seen before. Maturing readers become increasingly aware of the meanings of the parts from which words are built.

Building Vocabulary through Classroom Conversation

The most important feature of vocabulary development in the classroom lies in daily conversation about words. The essential facts, concepts, and generalizations of every content area of study live in the core vocabulary of those subjects. What builds vocabulary is curiosity and fascination with language. The basic goal of vocabulary instruction is to engage students throughout the day in figuring out how words have come to mean what they mean. Focus not so much on *what* words mean as on *how* they mean. The answer to that question will lie in the etymology of the word. It is noteworthy that 65% of English words are made up partly or entirely of prefixes, roots, and suffixes derived from Latin and Greek. There is a morphological formula that students need to learn to look for and use: (prefix)(es) + Root(s) + (suffix)(es) = WORD. (The parentheticals are optional. All a word absolutely requires is a root.) This formula means that every word in English is a combination of one or more roots plus, usually, one or more prefixes and suffixes. Understanding how words are built from these units of meaning is the foundation of reading for meaning. Many words are simply roots that stand alone as words without an affix. For example, "act" is a root that can stand alone as a word. Most words, however, are built out of several morphemes, each of which contributes to part of the meaning of the word—for example, *acts, acting, active, action, actively, react, reactor,* and so on. A root such as "anim," by contrast, is not a word; it must combine with at least one prefix or suffix to make a word. For example, *animal, unanimous,* and *inanimate* all share the same root, meaning "mind" or "spirit." Understanding that words are built of units of meaning, as a house is built of bricks and pieces of wood or a computer is built of its various components, opens up a whole new perspective on language. For younger students, this can be illustrated with pop beads of various colors that snap together in the same way that units of meaning go together to form words. As students move from sounding out words to understanding what words mean, they will be able to see meaning in words that are completely new to them. Why? Because they are not really completely new if the reader already understands the parts from which words are built. English is composed of over a million words, built of a few hundred meaningful parts. Once a core of these parts is mastered, there remain relatively few truly "unfamiliar" words one is likely to encounter in reading.

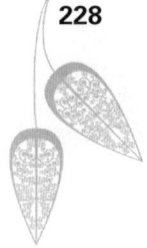

Using Vocabulary to Tie the Curriculum Together

Vocabulary has the power to tie together many pieces of the curriculum. Encourage students to hunt for words in content area textbooks, newspapers, fiction, and other texts, looking for words that are in the family of the root they are studying this week or have studied previously. Once students begin to explore the cross-curricular connections that lie in language, what they will discover is that many words of a single root family can be found in multiple subject areas of the curriculum. To take one example: The root "fract," referring to "break," can be seen in math *(fractions),* in science *(refraction),* in social studies *(fractious),* in health *(fracture),* and even in English, where its spelling changes slightly but the meaning connection remains *(fragment).* There are dozens of these cross-curricular connections that can serve to expand and deepen understandings of essential concepts.

Instruction in the Most Basic Meaningful Parts of Words

Do not automatically assume that students know much about prefixes and suffixes. Begin with simple affixes, those that attach to roots without changing their own spelling or the spelling of the root. A good starting point for teaching prefixes is to teach the prefixes that are the most common in English; 58% of all prefixed words have one of the following three prefixes: un-, meaning "not," as in *unfair* or *unequal*; in- (also spelled ig-, il-, im-, or ir-), meaning "not," as in *insane, illegal, irregular,* or *immortal*; and dis- (also spelled di- or dif-), meaning "apart" or "not," as in *disrupt, disgrace, divert,* or *diffuse*.

The common suffixes are also easy to identify and teach, since -s, -es, -ing, and -ed account for 65% of all suffixed words in English. Concentrate initially on suffixes that alter the grammatical form but do not alter the meaning of a root. The most elementary suffixes are -s, -ing, -ed, and -ly. You will teach more than these few, certainly, but do not assume students necessarily know these basics. The suffix -s changes a noun from its singular form to its plural form *or* marks a verb as third-person singular. Thus "act" + "s" = *acts*, more than one act. But *acts* is also the third person of the verb *to act:* "She acts." The syntax of a sentence will determine the difference between these two forms. The suffix -ing indicates the present participle (progressive or adjectival form) of a verb or its gerund form. This is how we distinguish "I run" from constructions like "I am running," "Running deer are dangerous to traffic," or "Running is good exercise." The suffix -ed marks the past tense of a regular verb, as in "act" + "ed" = *acted*. The suffix -ly changes an adjective into an adverb, as in "act" + "ive" + "ly" = *actively*, meaning "done in an active manner."

Model Curiosity

During class, model for students your own curiosity about the meaning elements of language by frequently calling attention to word elements that you come across in print. You might also hold a spelling bee in which students get one point for the correct spelling of a word and additional points for identifying the prefixes, roots, and suffixes of the word. Additional strategies include the following, offering a variety of opportunities for meeting individual needs.

- Display words on walls and bulletin boards. Use color coding to differentiate prefixes, roots, and suffixes so that these meaning parts are visible. This is particularly helpful for younger students and students with special needs who respond to aids such as color coding.
- Using index cards, write a word part on one side of each card and a key word illustrating the element on the other side. Allow students to play games such as Memory or Go Fish in which they must put these elements together to form real words.
- Define words in ways that ensure the definition is in students' own words and contains the meaning of the root in the definition to illustrate the connection between the word and the root.
- Complete a word hunt for words with the same root, using students' textbooks. For example, have students look in the American history textbook chapter on civil rights to locate words with the roots "leg, legis," meaning law, or "judic, judg, jud," meaning fairness or rightness, or "greg," meaning group or flock.
- Represent the meanings of roots or words through pictures. For example, have students find, cut, and paste pictures from magazines or draw pictures representing a root such as "gener," meaning family, creation, birth, or sort.
- Create exercises in which students add on and take away prefixes and suffixes to make a variety of words in the same root family with different meanings or parts of speech.

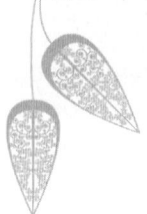

Especially for students whose reading skills are low, it will be very helpful to have them look for and build lists of words that begin or end with one of the common prefixes and suffixes. Many students are not aware of prefixes or suffixes and do not see the meaning connections among words that share these beginnings and endings.

Students whose first language is Spanish may have an advantage over students who know only English. This advantage can be shared with English-only students and can certainly work in favor of students who are struggling to learn English. Many times the spelling of prefixes or suffixes in Spanish is close enough to spellings in English words as to make the meaning connections transparent and easy to grasp. Table 11.2 illustrates a few of these transparencies that can be of help to English learners with Spanish as a first language.

Table 11.2 Illustrations of Equivalencies of Affixes in Spanish and English

Affix Meaning	English Form	Spanish Form	English Examples	Spanish Examples
genus, condition	-y	-ia/-ía	complacency anatomy	complacencia anatomía
state or quality	-ity	-idad	civility fidelity	civilidad fidelidad
state or process	-(t)ion	-(c)ión	information composition	información composición
agent	-or	-or	doctor actor	doctor actor
act or function	-ure	-ura	censure curvature	censura curvatura
down	cata-	cata-	(to) catalogue catastrophe	catalogar catástrofe
upon	epi-	epi-	epitaph epidemic	epitafio epidemia
below	hypo-	hipo-	hypothesis hypothermia	hipótesio hipotermia
together (Greek)	sym-	sim-	symmetry sympathy	simetría simpatía
together (Latin)	con-	con-	confection contiguous	confección contiguo
out	ex-	ex-	exclusive (to) expatriate	exclusivo expatriar

Benefits of the Vocabulary Acquisition Model

The vocabulary acquisition model benefits from being built on what we know about how students learn and how new concepts are learned. Fundamentally, the new is always tied to the known when learning is successful. The elements of the model provide scaffolding for students as they interact with new ideas and the words that accurately express them. This model also opens the door to disciplinary conversations in which students make cross-curricular connections.

Elementary Grades Lesson

VOCABULARY ACQUISITION: Units of Measurement

OBJECTIVES

Students Will Understand
- Prefixes are the key to change in the scale of units of measurement

Students Will Know
- The prefixes used in units of measurement, and the measurements used for volume, mass, and length

Students Will Be Able To
- Measure objects using the correct units and prefixes

ASSESSMENTS
- *Diagnostic.* Pretest
- *Formative.* Students will measure different objects using the correct units and prefixes.

PROCEDURES
1. Give students a pretest on relevant units of measurement.
2. Elaborate and discuss invented meanings. The teacher will ask students what they think each of the beginnings and endings of these words means on the diagnostic test. Teacher should make certain that the following prefixes are mentioned: deci-, deca-, centi-, milli-, and kilo-. The teacher should also make sure that the following base words are mentioned: liter, gram, and meter. The teacher will ask students to justify their responses on the pretest.
3. Explore patterns of meaning.
    a. Provide definitions of prefixes.
    b. Explain what liters, meters, and grams are used to measure.
    c. Ask students for examples of use of these units.
    d. Explain the distinction between the Standard International (SI) and U.S. systems of measurement.
    e. Explain the focus on the SI system in science class.

4. Read and study. Have students measure a variety of objects in terms of volume, mass, and length. Put the units of measurement on the class matrix.
5. Evaluate and posttest. In groups of three, students will measure and record three different objects using the correct prefix and unit.

Middle/Secondary Grades Lesson

VOCABULARY ACQUISITION: The Middle Ages

OBJECTIVES

Students Will Understand
- The Catholic Church shaped the Middle Ages

Students Will Know
- The origin and historical development of the words *Middle Ages* and *Crusades*

Students Will Be Able To
- Apply their knowledge of word origins to historical themes
- Identify their current knowledge of the Middle Ages
- Generate personal questions about the Middle Ages

ASSESSMENT

Students will be asked to read a short text about the Middle Ages and define unfamiliar words by using the strategies identified in the model.

PROCEDURES

1. Pretest knowledge of words. Ask students to define *medieval* and *crusade*.
2. Have students share their responses in class.
3. Elaborate on and discuss invented spellings and hypothesized meanings. Tell students about the word(s) and brainstorm synonyms. Have students create sentences from the list they generated.
4. Have students use the word(s) as often as possible as you review the major content understandings to follow in the next lessons:
   a. The Roman Catholic Church grew in importance after Roman authority declined and during the medieval period the Church served the social, political, and religious needs of the people.
   b. The Crusades were expeditions to the Holy Land to demonstrate piety. They had a profound impact on social, political, and economic factors in Western Europe.
5. Have students read the text on the Middle Ages and identify unfamiliar words.
6. Choose two or three words for study and with students use the Graphic Organizer for Vocabulary Acquisition to analyze one word together and one word individually.

Summary

Vocabulary is notoriously badly taught in schools, with endless memorization and consequent forgetting. We have provided an alternative that fills in some of the missing pieces. Adoption of this model can result in lasting acquisition of the vocabulary learned in school.

Three principles underlie this model: (1) There is a system governing vocabulary, such that words are related to each other in ways reflected in their spellings and meanings; (2) words are acquired by learners as they acquire precise ways of expressing what they have come to understand; and (3) the learning of concepts and the vocabulary that labels those concepts happen in support of one another.

Every subject taught in school is more than a body of arbitrary facts. We can think of everything taught in school as the result of a conversation that has been going on for a long time. The words of this conversation do not merely label things or ideas but are the ways we distinguish things and ideas one from another. Thus each subject area of the curriculum represents a particular way of viewing, interpreting, and describing the world with words that reflect the distinctions that constitute the subject under study.

The model is intended to create a conversation that begins with what students know about words essential to their study, the words that carry the brunt of the conceptual load of their school topics. Beginning with an unannounced pretest, this conversation would turn next to the place of these words in the English language: the synonyms of the words, various uses of the words, and the origin and historical development of the words. Following this part of the discussion, students turn to their reading and study, which should now be much more successful than they might have been otherwise. After all, students should be fairly familiar with the basic concepts of their study before reading begins. The model ends with a posttest. Scores on this test of spellings and definitions should be much higher than the pretest scores.

Implementation of the vocabulary acquisition model is described as a sequence of steps.

1. Pretest knowledge of words critical to the content to be taught with an *unannounced* test. Assure students that this is not a test to see what they don't know but a test to see what they do know already about how these words are spelled and what they mean.
2. Discuss the invented spellings and hypothesized meanings of the words revealed by the pretest.
3. Explore the patterns of meaning in the words, using strategies like think–pair–share or Link.
4. Assign readings on the topic under study, not only from the textbook in use but a variety of texts selected from the library and other sources. This will ensure that more students get to see the concepts and vocabulary in contexts they can apprehend without frustration.

Evaluate student learning with a posttest that is identical to the pretest.

The intent of the model is to have students achieve mastery of the topics of their study; thus their grades in school might soar. If that happens, we think the vocabulary development model is well worth the time and effort. If students catch a glimpse of the joy of language that can live with them from that point forward, they will leave school with a gift for language that will distinguish them from others.

Extensions

ACTIVITIES

1. In most textbooks, a list of words appears at the beginning of each chapter. These are sometimes called the key words for the chapter. Students also encounter boldfaced or otherwise highlighted words in their reading, words that are important to the topic under study and likely included in the glossary at the end of the text. Examine a textbook, perhaps the one you are using in teaching, to see how words' meanings are conveyed. Can you find any discussion of why the words mean what they do or why they are spelled as they are? Are the etymologies of the words mentioned?

2. Take a close look at the next lesson you are going to teach or a lesson you have taught. Pick out the key concepts—the three or four really big ideas—in that lesson. Now look at the words in which those ideas are expressed. Examine the words carefully to figure out why they mean what they mean. Look them up in a good dictionary to ascertain their etymology. How could you use this information to better teach these concepts?

REFLECTIVE QUESTIONS

1. Textbook chapters often begin with key vocabulary. Would it be helpful to use these words as the basis of vocabulary instruction, or should you look for additional words that are key to the major concepts being taught? Should students be invited to participate in this word search?

2. Too often, spelling "counts" only in English class, and sometimes not there. However, once you can link spelling and meaning, would it be of value to students to know that at some point across the grades, words are spelled at least as much by how they mean as by how they sound?

3. Words are built of meaningful parts called prefixes, roots, and suffixes. Think seriously about the common word parts that frequently occur in the subject area you teach, whether it is one of the sciences, a branch of social studies, or an area of mathematics. Could your students build lists of these word parts and words in which they occur in their reading?

12

The Integrative Model
Generalizing from Data

chapter OBJECTIVES

You Will Understand
- The amount of information presented in school is overwhelming and disjointed

You Will Know
- What the integrative model looks like in both elementary and secondary classrooms
- The basis in research and theory for using the integrative model in the classroom
- The steps of the integrative model
- How to organize data for use in integrative lessons
- How to adapt the model to meet individual needs
- Ways to assess integrative lessons

You Will Be Able To
- Identify the integrative model in K–12 classrooms
- Design, implement, and reflect on an integrative lesson

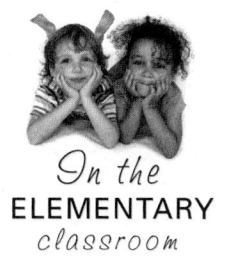

In the ELEMENTARY classroom

As Tom Baran works with his third graders on fractions, he decides that his students will benefit from using fraction strips as they practice comparing the numerical values of fractions with the same numerator but different denominators. The standard guiding Tom's teaching focuses on understanding that the denominator tells the number of equal parts in a whole and the numerator tells how many equal-size parts are being considered. Tom has thought about his students' skill sets and has determined that they need to review how to compare fractions. He decides that the integrative model will allow him not only to review information about fractions, but will help his students in identifying patterns, hypothesizing, and generalizing. Using Table 12.1, Tom scripts his integrative fraction lesson.

MR. BARAN: Look at the comparing fractions table. What do you notice? What is the table about?

RIKO: There are a bunch of fractions with greater than or less than symbols.

MR. BARAN: Yes, can you read each box on the matrix? Is the pair in each box correct?

235

Table 12.1 Comparing Fractions

1/2 > 1/5	1/4 > 1/6	1/8 > 1/10
1/5 < 1/3	1/10 < 1/5	1/10 < 1/3
1/5 > 1/8	1/6 > 1/10	1/5 = 1/5

Once Mr. Baran is comfortable that students can accurately and completely describe relationships between the pairs, he moves on to the second step of the model—the causal step. In this step, he reminds students that they can use their fraction bars (Figure 12.1) to help answer any of the questions.

> **Mr. Baran:** Let's look at the first pair in the top row. It says that 1/2 is larger than 1/5. Explain to me why.
>
> **Marisa:** If you compare the fifths fraction bar and the half fraction bar, 1/2 is bigger.
>
> **Nolan:** And the bottom number, the denominator, is a smaller number.
>
> **Mr. Baran:** Now, let's move down the first column to the next pair. Which is the larger number? Explain how you know this.
>
> **Pedro:** The larger number is 1/3. The denominator is smaller so the pieces are larger.

Figure 12.1 Fraction Bars

Mr. Baran: Riko, pick one of the pairs and tell me which is the smaller number and how you know it is smaller.

Riko answers the question and Mr. Baran continues to ask students to describe and explain the comparisons in Table 12.1. Mr. Baran continues working with this table until he is certain that students can explain why one fractional number is smaller or larger than the other. If necessary, he may include additional examples.

Mr. Baran: What if we made some changes to our comparing fractions table? What would happen to the first pair if 1/2 were changed to 1/3? Would 1/3 also be larger than 1/5? Raise your hand if you think so.

Everyone in the class has a hand raised. Mr. Baran continues to make changes until he feels comfortable that students can substitute numbers and still identify which fraction in the pair is smaller or larger. He even asks students to hypothesize different combinations. For example, if we substitute 1/8 for 1/2 in the first pair, would the relationship be the same or would you need to change the symbol? As students become facile at predicting the effects of different combinations, Tom asks students to summarize their discussion by making a statement.

Riko: Like we learned last week, wholes can be broken into equal-sized parts.

Fatma: The bottom number tells how many equal parts there are in a whole.

Nolan: The smaller the number in the denominator, the fewer the parts of the whole.

Marisa: If the top number is one, small numbers are bigger than larger numbers in the denominator.

In the **SECONDARY** *classroom*

Using a family photograph taken in 1950, Iris Sterman leads a discussion in her middle school social studies class about chronology and changes over time—two critical social studies concepts. Mrs. Sterman's objectives are that students will understand that American society has changed in many ways during the last 60 years and these changes have had a major impact on American families. Students will know and explain differences in clothing, homes, technology, educational opportunities, and attitudes toward women from 1950 to the present. Her *able to do* objectives are that students will make generalizations by examining an old photograph and that they will be able to hypothesize changes to family life in the next 60 years.

Mrs. Sterman begins her class by asking students to work with their social studies partners and examine the photograph that she has distributed. She asks the pairs to make a list of the things that they notice about the picture. After five minutes, Mrs. Sterman begins the discussion:

Mrs. Sterman: What did you notice in the picture?

Marcy: The picture is old, and the people in the picture are wearing funny-looking clothes.

Kenny: Are they all part of the same family? They look like they are getting ready to go to church or something. They are all dressed up, and that little girl even has a hat on, but it isn't cold outside.

Mrs. Sterman: Let's talk about the clothes in the picture. This picture was taken in 1950—that's 60 years ago. Do you think that clothes are different now? In what ways?

Jordan: Girls don't wear those kinds of dresses anymore, and they look like they are too small. The collar on the boy's shirt is also way big.

Mrs. Sterman: What else do you notice about what these children are wearing?

Randi: The shoes? No one is wearing flip-flops, and the girls are all wearing white socks. This picture looks like the ones my Nana has in her house.

Mrs. Sterman: You have noticed three important things. The children in the picture, who are cousins, by the way, are dressed up. The dresses and shirt they are wearing are different from what you would find in stores today. Likewise, the shoes the children are wearing are different from shoes children would be wearing today. Think about a family picture that was taken this year—a family picture of five cousins. How would the 21st-century picture differ from this 1950 picture? Think about the clothes that the cousins would be wearing in a picture taken last week.

Randi: Flip-flops!

Arnold: Everyone would be in jeans and T-shirts with the names of sports teams.

Brett: No one would be standing so still.

Mrs. Sterman: That is an interesting observation, Brett. Why do you think the children in the picture were standing "so still"?

Alyssa: Maybe it's because they didn't usually get their picture taken. We have an exchange student in our house, and he said that in his village picture taking happens only on holidays and at graduations.

Mrs. Sterman: Do you think that there were a lot of family pictures taken in 1950?

Randi: My Nana has boxes and boxes of photographs that she always wants me to look at with her. It gets really boring, but she has pictures of my great-great-grandparents, and that was way before 1950.

Mrs. Sterman: So there have been family photographs for a long time. Do you remember the Civil War photographs we saw at the museum? How long before this photograph of the cousins was taken were those pictures taken?

The discussion continues with students bringing up points about the changes in the technology of cameras and the differences in houses. Mrs. Sterman also asks her students what changes have occurred in society since their grandparents took family pictures of children. We return to the discussion as she is asking about some of these societal differences.

Mrs. Sterman: You mention that some of the differences between your grandparents' America and today is that there is more divorce, more mothers work, and I said that more people graduate from high school and go to college than they did 60 years ago. You also noticed that cameras and clothes have changed over the last 60 or so years. Can you tell me why some of these changes have happened?

Marcy: Did they have jeans in 1950?

Brett: Yeah, a Levi commercial I saw said that jeans were invented during the California Gold Rush, and that was before the 1900s!

Randi: So, how come kids didn't wear jeans?

Barbara: I think people in the old days dressed up more. When I look at pictures of my grandparents when they were little, they are always dressed up.

Nancy: My father says that clothes have changed a lot. He tells us that we are lucky that we don't have to iron our clothes the way he did. Maybe the clothes have changed because of what they are made of.

Mrs. Sterman: That's a really good point, Nancy. The way clothes are made has also changed.

RANDI: Oh, oh. I know—there are better machines now and the machines can make more clothes faster. Maybe that's why we can buy so many clothes. Maybe the people in the picture didn't have as many choices. Maybe that's why those dresses look so small—they had to keep them a long time or they were handed down from somebody else.

Mrs. Sterman asks for other explanations and then moves the discussion to the hypothesis phase of the model. Notice that this has already begun when the children start to speak with the hypothetical "maybe."

MRS. STERMAN: The cousins in the picture look like they are taking care of the little girl. The older girl is looking at the baby in the picture and one of the other cousins has her hand on the baby's shoulder. I'd like you to think about how the picture might have changed if the littlest cousin were not in the picture.

The students comment on how everyone might be looking at the camera and that we might, then, be able to see more details of the clothes. Mrs. Sterman continues asking students to hypothesize by asking what might have happened to the cousins in the last 60 years.

MRS. STERMAN: If the boy cousin in the picture was 10 in 1950, what might have happened to him in terms of military service? When can a young man enter the military? Were we at war during the time that this young man was between the ages of 18 and 35? What do you think might have happened to this young man if he did serve in the military?

Many students responded to these questions, and there was some discussion about whether or not the young man could have been killed in the Vietnam War. Perhaps because he was older than the average infantry soldier, he might have been an officer. Mrs. Sterman then points the students to the young girls in the picture. She asks the students to choose one girl and, with their partners, write a story about what might have happened to her during the 60 years that followed the taking of the photograph. Mrs. Sterman told them that their stories had to reflect some of the themes that were previously discussed—technology, divorce, opportunity for education, and working mothers. Students then shared their stories with the class.

MRS. STERMAN: What interesting stories! What can we say about the changes that have occurred in our society since this picture was taken?

Here are some examples of the generalizations that students produced:

- The Vietnam War made a difference to families.
- Family pictures would look different today because we have better cameras and technology than they did in 1950.
- Children in 1950 had fewer choices than we do when it comes to getting dressed in the morning.
- Machines and different fabrics have made cheaper clothes available to families.
- More children finish high school today than in 1950. Finishing high school can make a difference to families because people can get better-paying jobs.

Basis for the Integrative Model

The integrative model is rooted in the inductive strategies of Hilda Taba (Taba et al., 1971) as interpreted and developed by Eggen and Kauchak (2006). Basically, the model is a controlled discussion—a structured conversation that allows teachers to focus on helping students learn academic information while practicing complex reasoning skills. In an integrative discussion, students have the opportunity to construct personal understandings of organized bodies of knowledge—information that includes intricate relationships among facts, concepts, and generalizations.

The integrative model is designed to help students see relationships among the components of a complex topic (for example, migration, animal classification, or branches of government). As students try to make sense of complicated webs of association, they build or revise the schemata that they have previously constructed to make sense of similar information. Schema theory supports the integrative model in that the instruction helps participants arrange information so that it is easily assimilated and subsequently retrieved. A schema is a structure that organizes large amounts of information into a retrievable system (Schunk, 2004). People's brains are active in storing information and making new connections as they are exposed to novel experiences and information. Schemata are the configurations that organize these experiences by connecting prior and new knowledge. The integrative model presents content to students in an organized way, allowing connections to be built smoothly and effectively.

In addition, the integrative model allows for increased knowledge. Brain capacity benefits from experience, and experience that is well organized provides the best advantage. Through structured bodies of knowledge, students are able to prioritize information and link new data to existing schemas, increasing the opportunity for school success. Bransford and his colleagues (National Research Council, 2000) acknowledge that not all instruction is equal, noting that:

> it is clear that there are qualitative differences among kinds of learning opportunities. In addition, the brain "creates" informational experiences through mental activities such as inferencing, category formation, and so forth. These are the types of learning opportunities that can be facilitated. (p. 127)

The structure of the model allows students to use important critical thinking skills. The expectation underlying the model is that students will make logical inferences, identify similarities and differences, generate explanations and hypotheses, and synthesize information while they are learning academic content. These strategies are associated with school achievement. When teachers identify similarities and differences or ask students independently to identify similarities and differences, students' understandings are enhanced. These identifications can be made through comparisons, classification, and the development of metaphors and analogies.

Patterns are crucial components of the integrative model. Schemata are the means by which learners impose patterns on complex information, the tools with which students deal with content and procedures. Schools cannot cover all of the bits of information that are available for curriculum development and instructional design. There is too much information to incorporate into long-term memory. The integrative model helps teachers and students organize discrete pieces of information into a more manageable whole so that deep understanding of topics and the relationships among topical elements can be developed. In fact, "the more complex and interconnected a schema is, the more places learners have to connect new knowledge and understanding"(Eggen & Kauchak, 2006, p. 212).

Steps in the Integrative Model

Step 1: Planning for the Integrative Model

Organized bodies of knowledge are just that—organized. Integrative lessons are developed around data sets—bits and pieces of information that are ordered in matrices, graphs, maps, pictures, or other displays. First a topic must be identified. Content standards, curriculum materials, and district scope and sequences are replete with topics that are rich in complexity and relationships. Second, teachers decide on the target generalizations toward which a lesson is built—the *understand* objectives and the knowledge that supports the big ideas. As objectives are being determined, it is helpful to construct a concept map showing the relationships among the focal elements under study. A corresponding matrix may then be developed by the teacher, by students independently or in small groups, or as part of a class discussion. Teachers or curriculum materials will determine the relationships that are highlighted—the categories that will organize the information. In fact, curriculum materials, newspapers, and magazines, as well as electronic resources such as the Web, can offer a range of data sources that can serve as the basis for an integrative lesson. In the end, the teacher decides the sources by which students will have the opportunity to learn about a topic.

Debbie Moss is planning a new geography unit on regions in the United States. Regions constitute a rich topic for information and connections. There are economic, cultural, and physical aspects of regions, connections that students need to understand. Checking the state standards, Debbie finds that students must be able to explain how regional landscapes reflect the cultural and economic characteristics of their inhabitants and how cultural differences can link or divide regions. By looking through the state's curriculum framework, reflecting on the prior knowledge and needs of her students, and examining the available resources, Debbie highlights the big ideas and essential knowledge and skills that will compose her unit, planning behaviors that are similar across all of the models in this text.

The big idea of Debbie's unit is that regions have unifying characteristics that are both physical and cultural and that the characteristics of regions may change as people interact with their physical, cultural, and economic environment. Debbie believes that her students will need to know that the concept of regions is used to simplify a complex world and that physical and cultural regions can change over time. Students will also need to know that regional landscapes include specific cultural characteristics (architecture, language, history, and religion). *Able to do* goals of this integrative instruction include being able to locate regions on maps, interpret regional patterns, compare and contrast information, draw conclusions and make generalizations about data, and explain cause-and-effect relationships. Based on a unit described in the text *Differentiation in Practice* (Tomlinson & Edison, 2003), Debbie has decided that the culminating assessment will be an independent project that asks students to view the course material through the lens of a physical, cultural, or economic geographer (see Table 12.2).

Feeling a sense of accomplishment as her planning continues, Debbie is now ready to think about the kinds of instruction that will help her students reach the unit objectives. Debbie considers lecturing as an instructional possibility, but she doesn't believe that she can help students see the connections among the different aspects of regions through a short lecture. She also thinks about a cooperative learning jigsaw (see Chapter 13) but determines that this, too, will not highlight the interconnections among the physical, cultural, and economic aspects of the regions. Finally, Debbie considers the benefits of the integrative model, an instructional model that uses rich, complexly organized bodies of knowledge, or, in the words of the designers of the model, "topics that combine facts, concepts, generalizations, and the relationships among them" (Eggen & Kauchak, 2006, p. 213). Debbie determines that the model examined in this chapter is a good match for her objectives because regional differences and the historic, economic, and cultural consequences of these differences constitute an example of such a complex topic.

Effective data displays help in the development of generalizations; they include facts that are not too narrow to make connections. Also, effective data displays have enough information so that students have the chance to provide explanations for the relationships that they identify. As the following description of the steps of the model illustrates, the matrix in Table 12.2 meets both of these requirements—opportunity for generalization and opportunity for explanation of relationships.

Table 12.2   U.S. Geographic Regions

Four Geographic Regions	Physical Characteristics	Cultural Characteristics	Economic Characteristics
Northeast States included: Connecticut, New Jersey, Maine, Massachusetts, New Hampshire, New York, Pennsylvania, Rhode Island, and Vermont	• Bordered by Canada, Midwest, South, and the Atlantic Ocean • Rocky coast to fertile farmland • Four major rivers: Delaware, Hudson, Connecticut, Kennebec • Berkshires, Adirondack, Green, White Mountains • Lake Champlain, Great Lakes of Ontario and Erie, Niagara Falls	• Education legacy (top-rated colleges) • Dominant in American history • Religiously diverse—Protestant beginnings, Catholics and Jews • Ethnic diversity of African American, Hispanic, Asian American, Italian, Irish, German, and Franco American	• Wealthiest part of the United States • Urban—medium to large manufacturing cities; now looking for new economic base • Wide disparities between rich and poor in cities • Major cities—New York, Boston, and others offer financial and governmental services that are not reliant on unskilled labor • Mass transit within and between cities
Midwest States included: Ohio, Indiana, Michigan, Illinois, Wisconsin, Iowa, Kansas, Minnesota, Missouri, Nebraska, North Dakota, and South Dakota	• U.S. Census Bureau regions: East North Central States and West North Central States • Great Lakes and Ohio and Mississippi Rivers • Foothills of the Appalachians and Porcupine Mountains	• Cultural crossroads • European immigrants • German Catholics/Calvinist/Protestantism—"Bible Belt" • Slavery was not allowed in this area • Land-grant colleges • Rural heritage-pioneer • Strong support for Democratic party	• Chicago largest city • Other cities: Cleveland, Columbus, Indianapolis, Detroit, St. Louis, Kansas City, Minneapolis • Fertile soil—nation's breadbasket—corn, oats, and wheat • Abandonment by many industries of Midwest—"Rust Belt"
South States included: Delaware, Florida, Georgia, Maryland, North Carolina, South Carolina, Virginia, West Virginia, District of Columbia, Alabama, Kentucky, Mississippi, Tennessee, Arkansas, Louisiana, Oklahoma, and Texas	• U.S. Census Bureau Regions: East South Central, South Atlantic, and West South Central • Mississippi River, Chesapeake Bay, Florida Everglades, southern Appalachian Mountains (Blue Ridge and Great Smoky Mountains), and South Carolina's Sea Islands	• European Celtic immigrants • Slavery was allowed • Switch from solidly Democrat to now more Republican • More conservative than the North • "Bible Belt"—Protestantism predominates • Also Jews, Muslims, and Catholics • Southern cuisine, music, and sports	• Houston largest city • Other cities: Dallas/Fort Worth, Miami, Atlanta, Baltimore, and Tampa • Rural areas • Crops/trees easily grown—oaks, magnolias, dogwoods
West States included: Alaska, Arizona, California, Colorado, Hawaii, Idaho, Montana, New Mexico, Nevada, Oregon, Utah, Washington, and Wyoming	• U.S. Census Bureau Regions: Mountain and Pacific • Most geographically diverse: Pacific Coast, temperate rainforests of Northwest, Rocky Mountains, Great Plains, and deserts • Missouri, Colorado, Columbia, and Snake Rivers	• Wyoming least-populated state while California is the most-populated • Sparsely settled • Asian, Mexican, and Native American populations • Mormons • Cowboy image and westward expansion • West not unified politically; urban and Pacific coast Democratic, interior states more Republican	• Los Angeles largest city • Other cities: San Diego, San Jose, San Francisco, Seattle, Portland, Denver, Phoenix, Las Vegas, and Salt Lake City • Beef cattle industry • Apples in Washington and potatoes in Idaho • Los Angeles—aerospace industry since World War II

Step 2: Describe, Compare, and Search for Patterns in a Data Set

The integrative model allows teachers to level the classroom playing field. All students have the opportunity to engage in the discussion because the data is organized and available to students as the conversation occurs. The teacher begins the lesson by providing background information on the data set and focuses the students' attention by asking them to describe what they notice. Debbie begins using Table 12.2 by asking her students to look at the matrix carefully. She calls on students by name to describe how many columns and rows there are and what the columns and rows present. She then asks students to consider the following questions:

- What are the physical characteristics of the West region? How do these characteristics differ from the South or Northeast regions?
- Which region has the greatest physical diversity?
- Which region has the least-populated state and which has the most-populated state? What determines the population of a state?
- What types of businesses support the economies of these four regions? How are these businesses similar to one another? Different? Why do these regions have different economic characteristics?
- What similarities and differences do you notice on this matrix?

Other questions can be generated. Many other similarities and differences could be noticed by either the teacher or the students. Instructional options include directing attention to a particular attribute of the data display, directing students to look for and describe specific similarities and differences, and asking students to identify the comparisons they notice. During this phase of the model, teachers and students control the pace of the discussion, and clear and simple questions are used to facilitate the construction of basic information about the topic.

Step 3: Explain the Identified Similarities and Differences

Once students have identified the rich similarities and differences displayed in the matrix, they should be asked to explain the identified comparisons. Explaining the reasons for similarities and differences engages students in deep analysis of the data set. For example, Debbie might follow up on some of the identified comparisons with the following questions:

- How can you explain the differences in economic characteristics between the Northeast and West?
- Why might you expect to see some similarities between major cities of all four regions of the United States?

- What political similarities and differences did you notice among the regions? Do any of these differences have something to do with immigration patterns to the region?
- What might account for differences in population across regions?

Although some relationships cannot be explained, there will be many relationships in the data set that invite explanation. Since explanation is a higher level of reasoning than description, providing this opportunity helps to increase the complexity of the schemas that students develop about the topic. Explanations tie bits of information together, weaving a variety of threads into developing schemas that will become more intricate as the lesson progresses and more explanations are shared, much as a handwoven rug becomes more colorful and detailed as workers weave in individual threads. The role of the teacher in this phase of the model is to look at the list of identified comparisons and ask for elucidation, making certain that students document their explanations with information from the data source.

Step 4: Hypothesize What Would Happen under Different Conditions

During this stage of the model, students are asked to hypothesize an outcome if conditions change, allowing an opportunity to apply recently acquired knowledge and link it to prior knowledge and skills. Students should be asked to explain their hypotheses and conclusions. Marzano (2001) discusses the use of organized bodies of knowledge, or systems of knowledge, as a method for practicing hypothesis testing and increasing student understanding. Debbie might ask students to imagine what would have happened if the United States had not developed the atom bomb to drop on Hiroshima and Nagasaki, which forced Japan to surrender, or to think about what would happen if there were a major revitalization of "Rust Belt" cities of the Midwest.

Designing experiences that provide students with guidance in testing hypotheses is inherent to the integrative model. In addition, teachers can provide templates for explanations, provide sentence stems to help students articulate their reasoning, develop rubrics that identify and describe the quality of explanations, and set up numerous opportunities for students to share their explanations.

Step 5: Make Broad Generalizations about the Topic and the Discussion

In this phase of the model, students summarize and synthesize the discussion and make broad generalizations about the topic under study. The primary-recency effect (students remember best what they first heard in a lesson and remember second best the last thing they experienced in a lesson) plays a role in this phase

Strategy Alert

Summarizing

Teaching summarization skills gives students agency to process and remember new information. Summarization will be a benefit in all of the instructional models in this text, but it is particularly appropriate for the integrative model because of the amount of academic content in play. Students can summarize in any medium, either individually or in groups. Students can learn to follow a series of steps to form a summary: (1) Delete the material that is not important and does not contribute to understanding, (2) remove redundancies, (3) substitute category names for lists of things, (4) identify or supply a topic sentence. Teachers can help students practice summarization through a series of specific questions, through the use of graphic organizers (e.g., Venn diagrams, cause and effect, chronological series), or by using metaphors and analogies. Different kinds of questions are appropriate for different kinds of texts, which indicates that teachers must take the time to discuss the kinds of information found in a text with students. Content area teachers should point out common text structures and graphic representations in their discipline. Other strategies can also be used in the quest for accurate and powerful summarizations, such as memory models and graphic organizers. ■

(Wormeli, 2004). Teachers can use the integrative model to develop a questioning plan that builds on this effect. In step 5, it is important that students share their synthesis of the lesson—the broad generalizations that help to describe the complexity of the topic.

Generalizing is a sophisticated skill that is enhanced when good summaries of a discussion are provided. Once they have captured the robust information that was shared, students can synthesize that information and create broad statements to represent the deep understandings that they have developed. Debbie might ask students to summarize the conversations that occurred in class. She might also ask students to make broad statements about some of the relationships discovered among the physical, cultural, and economic characteristics of the regions under study.

Summary of Steps in the Integrative Model

Table 12.3 shows examples of objections to literature texts students may have been assigned. The steps of the integrative model are summarized for a lesson based on this table, with examples of specific questions a teacher might ask in each of the steps.

1. *Planning for the integrative model.* Identify the topic. Target generalizations. Prepare a data display such as the matrix on objections to books.
2. *Describe, compare, and search for patterns in a data set.*
    - Describe: What do you notice about the types of objections that were made about *The Catcher in the Rye*?
    - Describe: What types of concerns are expressed in these objections?

Table 12.3 Objections to Books Commonly Used in School

Title	Objections
The Adventures of Huckleberry Finn	Characterization and language offensive to African Americans; use of word "orgy"; taking name of Lord in vain; promotes discrimination
The Catcher in the Rye	Not proper for teenagers; dirty words; negative impact; too sophisticated; lack of plot; profuse vulgarity; sacrilegious, pornographic; objectionable references to homosexuality; not a positive example for youth; no redeeming social value; hero has loose morals and lack of direction
Deliverance	Unacceptable language; sexual references; sex scenes; antireligious matters; promotes homosexuality
The Good Earth	Content includes sex lives of old men with concubines and prostitutes; killing of children
The Grapes of Wrath	Immoral; obscene; objectionable political ideas; sexual activity; antichurch; depressing story; bad language; demeaning to Southerners
I Know Why the Caged Bird Sings	Sections not suitable for young people; pornographic; demeaning to African Americans; too realistic
The Learning Tree	Adult language; sexually explicit; too mature for teenagers; Christ portrayed as white man who loves only white people; teaches secular humanism
1984	Immoral; depressing; obscene; study of communism; communism portrayed in positive light; disliked treatment of marriage and family; drug-oriented; sordid
To Kill a Mockingbird	Immoral; obscene; indecent; vulgar; includes reference to rapes; racist themes; not suitable for adolescents
The Scarlet Letter	Degrades Christian ministry; vulgarity; immorality; adultery; too frank

Source: Information from Burress, L. (1989). *Battle of the books: Literacy censorship in the public schools, 1950–1985.* Metuchen, NJ: Scarecrow Press.

- Compare: How would you characterize the objections to *Huckleberry Finn*? To *1984*?
- Compare: What are the similarities between the objections to *The Grapes of Wrath* and *1984*?
- Search for patterns: What differences do you notice between the objections to *The Scarlet Letter* and the other books?

3. *Explain identified similarities and differences.*
   - What information is provided on this chart to help explain why these books were the most objected to at the end of the 20th century?
   - Can you explain why the attempts of groups to have these books taken out of public schools have been successful in some situations and unsuccessful in others?
   - What types of books might not receive any objections by parents, teachers, school boards, or community members?
4. *Hypothesize what would happen under different conditions.*
   - Suppose a school curriculum included Homer's *The Odyssey*. Do you think any objections would be made regarding this book? Support your answer from the matrix.
   - What would you do if a parent came to your class asking that you not teach a particular book to your class? What would you say?
   - You are assigned to teach one of these books. Would you make any special preparations?
5. *Make broad generalizations about the topic and the discussion.* Think about the target generalizations you want students to reach about this topic, such as the following:
   - Many community members object to sexual references in adolescent novels.
   - Community members do not believe children in school should be exposed to adult themes.
   - Teachers need to be sensitive to these beliefs and should be prepared for objections.

Evaluating Learning in the Integrative Model

Like most of the models presented in this text, each step of the integrative model can serve as an assessment—process as well as content can be evaluated in this way. After some experience with the integrative approach, an assessment could provide students with a similar data set such as a matrix, map, picture, or other visual organizer. They would then be asked to follow each or some of the steps of the model: (1) identifying similarities and differences, (2) explaining the reasons for these similarities and differences, (3) hypothesizing as to different outcomes if the data set changes, and (4) making generalizations about the relationships represented in the data set. Evaluation criteria may include the number and quality of the comparison identifications and the logic, knowledge, and quality of explanations. For example, the family picture lesson described earlier in this chapter may have been part of an immigration unit. The integrative process may have been the basis for the quiz in Figure 12.2.

Figure 12.2 Sample Integrative Assessment for Immigration Unit

Immigration Unit

Quiz 1

Directions: On your desk are two pictures, one of the family that we discussed in class and one of a family of recent legal immigrants. Answer the following questions on a separate sheet of paper.

1. What do you notice in the new picture? List four things that you see.
2. How do the two pictures compare? List two similarities and two differences.
3. Why do you think the pictures are different? Give two reasons.
4. Think about the family in the second picture moving into your neighborhood. What might happen? Why do you think that would happen?
5. Some of our neighbors don't want legal immigrants coming into our city. What would need to happen to change that attitude?

More traditional assessments can also be used with the integrative model. The rich data sets that are the foundation of the model (see Table 12.2) are a source for selected response items. When developing multiple-choice questions, matching items, and essay questions from data sets, remember to use best practice guidelines. Multiple-choice questions should be clear, have only one correct or best answer, have similar option lengths, and so forth. A number of assessment texts and Internet sites discuss writing test items (Stiggins, 2008).

Meeting Individual Needs in the Integrative Model

The key to an aligned integrative lesson is the data set. Whatever is used to help students learn the target content and thinking skills must be appropriate to the interests, readiness levels, and learning approaches of students. Data sets can come from textbooks, trade books, newspapers, Internet sources, reference books, or from the teacher's or students' thinking. They can be a collection of real-life objects, a piece of art, a map, a table of relevant information, a photograph, or any other item or collection that shows a relationship in information. Thus, data sets can be manipulated to meet the needs of students by varying the type of media for levels of complexity and abstraction and by highlighting specific bits of information to play to student interests.

Teachers can prepare the data set specifically for the objectives of the lesson and the specific students in the class or adaptations can be made from published materials. Students can be part of developing the data set in small or large groups by putting together matrices or graphs of information that will be explored with

> ### Strategy Alert
> **Cubing**
>
> As students complete the integrative process by making generalizations, cubing can help to complete and extend the discussion. Cubes have six sides with a different task on each side. Tasks are designed for specific groups of students and can vary on a number of attributes. Students roll the cube to find a task. Tasks can vary on the level of cognitive complexity, student interests, or specific remediation needs. Different groups can have different cubes. Cubes to extend thinking on a specific topic may use the following prompts:
>
> - Describe it: Include all aspects of the topic.
> - Compare it: Find similarities and differences.
> - Associate it: Tell how it fits with other things we have studied.
> - Apply it: Tell how it is used.
> - Analyze it: Tell how you can break it into smaller parts.
> - Argue it: Argue for or against a position related to the topic. ■

the integrative process. The integrative model is useful for the whole class, flexible small groups, and individuals at interest centers—another way to meet specific student needs.

Questions are also a powerful differentiation tool and become even more powerful with the integrative model. Building on what is known about classrooms and students, questions can be personalized. Although the template has an order of questions, the teacher can make connections for specific students by providing more or less background information. For example, in Debbie's geography class, she could highlight the travels of individual students, their background knowledge, or interests. She may provide cues to finding patterns for students having less experience with the model or use other visual clues on the data set to help some students distinguish patterns.

Benefits of the Integrative Model

All of the instructional models in this text help to develop students' critical thinking skills. The integrative model, however, also helps students navigate through organized bodies of information—webs of information that have rich and varied connections about which students must make sense. The integrative model is efficient and congruent with the way we learn. Since a great deal of curriculum content is detailed and layered, having a method by which students can access this information is important. The integrative model also allows students to make connections between what they know and what is being presented by helping them to build personal schemata. These personal schemata also become increasingly intricate because of the steps of the model itself. By participating in the model, students develop generalizations that explore relationships within a specific organized body of knowledge. The questioning helps students move from conclusions to inferences—and beyond the presented information.

In addition, the integrative model extends the power of textbooks and curriculum materials. Many textbooks are not friendly to the needs of students. They are written in unfamiliar language, the organization can be confusing, and the amount of information is astounding. The integrative model provides a structure for making sense of the contents of textbooks. Teachers can use visual materials from texts and provide scaffolding for divergent and higher-level thinking. The integrative model is also congruent with new classroom technologies. Data sets can be projected from computers, brought up on a SmartBoard, or found on a laptop. Most important, the integrative model permits the teacher to control the amount of information presented to students because data sets can be borrowed, constructed by teachers, or developed by students. The complexity of the information and the sophistication of the questions can flex readily to the teacher's instructional decisions.

Elementary Grades Lesson

INTEGRATIVE MODEL: Fractions

OBJECTIVES

Students Will Understand
- All parts of a set must be equal to one another and total the whole

Students Will Know
- The meaning of numerator and denominator
- How to compare the size of fractions
- Similarities and differences among a set of fractions

Students Will Be Able To
- Compare fractions
- Explain the relationships between fractions
- Hypothesize new relationships between fractions
- Summarize the information in the lesson and form a generalization to describe the patterns that were noticed in the class

ASSESSMENT

Students will design a worksheet (with answers) that helps students practice comparing fractions.

PROCEDURES

1. *Describe, compare, and search for patterns.* Ask the following questions:
   - What do you notice?
   - What is this table about?

- What do the symbols mean?
- Can you read each box in the matrix?
- Do you notice any patterns in the boxes?

2. *Explain similarities and differences.* Project the following table.

1/2 > 1/5	1/4 > 1/6	1/8 > 1/10
1/5 < 1/3	1/10 < 1/5	1/10 < 1/3
1/5 > 1/8	1/6 > 1/10	1/5 = 1/5

Ask these questions:
- Let's look at the first pair in the top row. It says that 1/2 is larger than 1/5. Explain to me why this is true.
- Move down the first column to the next pair. Which is the larger number? How do you know?
- (Ask an individual student) Pick one of the pairs and tell me which is the smaller number and how you know that it is smaller.
- (Ask an individual student) Pick one of the pairs and tell me which is the larger number and how you know that it is larger.
- Continue to ask similar questions.

3. *Hypothesize outcomes for different conditions.* Ask these questions about the table:
- What would happen to the first pair if 1/2 were changed to 1/3?
- Is 1/3 larger than 1/5?
- What would happen to the first pair if 1/8 were substituted for 1/2? Would we need to change the symbol?

Continue with similar questions.

4. *Generalize to form broad relationships.*
- Ask students to summarize the information in the lesson by providing a statement that captures the discussion.
- Ask students to discuss the patterns that they noticed in the lesson.

Middle/Secondary Grades Lesson

INTEGRATIVE MODEL: Societal Changes Affecting Families

OBJECTIVES

Students Will Understand
- American society has changed in many ways during the last 60 years and that these changes have had a major impact on American families

Students Will Know
- Differences in clothing, photography, homes, technology, educational opportunities, and attitudes toward women from 1950 to the present

Students Will Be Able To
- Make generalizations from an old photograph
- Hypothesize changes to family life in the next 60 years

ASSESSMENT Have students prepare 10 interview questions for someone the same age as those in the picture that will provide information about the important trends of the last 60 years.

PROCEDURES
1. *Describe, compare, and search for patterns.*
   - Review with students the broad changes in our society over the last 60 years and how these changes might affect families.
   - List these societal changes on the board.
   - Share the photograph with students.
   - What do you notice about the photograph? Describe what you see.
   - How would you compare this photograph to what you would expect a contemporary photograph of five cousins to look like?
   - What societal changes might these cousins have been affected by during the last 60 years?
   - Add any additional information to the board.
2. *Explain similarities and differences.*
   - Explain the similarities and differences noted between this photograph and one taken today.
   - Explain the similarities and differences between the social issues affecting men and women in the photograph during the last 60 years.
3. *Hypothesize outcomes for different conditions.*
   - Reflect on the changes of the last 60 years and invent a likely scenario for someone in the picture.
   - Reflect on the changes in the next 60 years and invent a likely scenario for people in your family.
4. *Generalize to form a broad relationship.*
   - Make statements about the changes in the United States over the last 60 years that might have had an effect on the children in the picture and on their families.

Summary

The purpose of the integrative model is to help students make sense of complex and rich relationships found in most disciplinary knowledge. The integrative model supports critical thinking strategies while helping students learn specific content concepts, facts, and generalizations. Students do not always have the opportunity to

> Go to the Assignments and Activities section of Topic 10: Inductive Models in the MyEducationLab for your course and complete the activity entitled "Using Inductive Models."

examine relationships among the components of disciplinary knowledge. The model allows examination of these relationships by providing guidelines for the types of questions teachers ask, the social structure of the classroom, and the data source of the discussion.

The model begins with careful planning by the teacher to choose a topic and select the essential understandings to be attained by students during the lesson. It is important that these understandings guide both the questioning and construction of the data set. Once the (1) planning is completed, (2) students describe, compare, and search for patterns in the provided information; (3) explain identified similarities and differences; (4) hypothesize as to what would happen under different conditions; and (5) make broad generalizations about the topic and the discussion.

Extensions

ACTIVITIES

1. Find an organized body of knowledge or a rich set of interrelated concepts, facts, and generalizations in the state standards with which you currently work or will be working. Design a concept map to show the relationships among the information that you will be teaching.
2. Revisit the scenarios at the beginning of the chapter. Do you think the objectives of these lessons were met? What evidence do you have to support your conclusion? List what you see as the best features of the lessons and the features that you think might be changed if you were to try to replicate the lesson.
3. Make a two-page handout explaining the integrative model that could be used with in-service teachers in the area you would like to teach. Try to anticipate the questions that teachers would have about the model and include at least one graphic.

REFLECTIVE QUESTIONS

1. What do you think about textbooks in your field? Will you be relying on textbooks? Why? Why not? With what caveats?
2. What are the most important generalizations in the discipline that you will be teaching? How do you know that these are the important generalizations?
3. What problems do you anticipate as you attempt to implement the integrative model? What aspects of the model will you find beneficial?

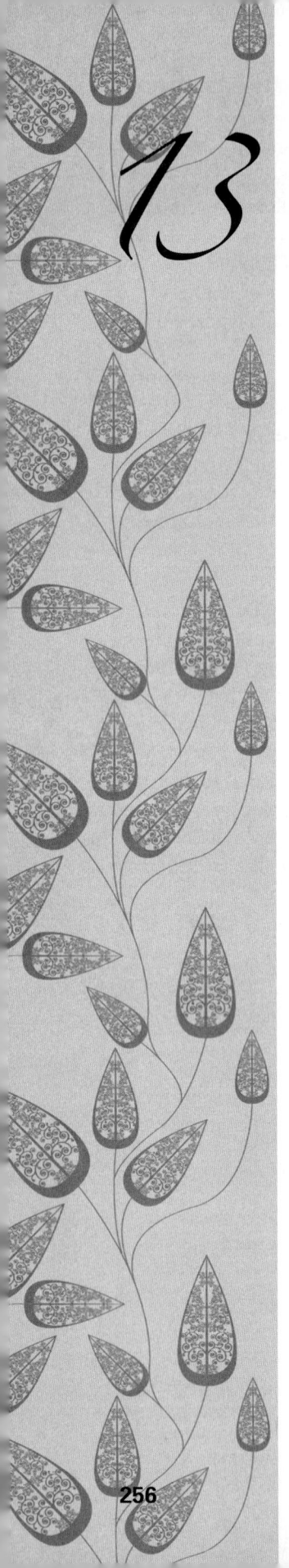

13 Cooperative Learning Models
Improving Student Learning Using Small Groups

chapter OBJECTIVES

You Will Understand
- Cooperative learning offers the opportunity to develop social, academic, and cognitive skills effectively and efficiently

You Will Know
- There is a profit from learning to work with others
- Problems can be solved together
- Conflicting ideas can be resolved in group settings
- What cooperative learning models look like in K–12 classrooms

You Will Be Able To
- Design, implement, and reflect on cooperative learning models in your planning and teaching
- Explain to students, parents, and peers the value of cooperative learning

In the **ELEMENTARY** *classroom*

In Ms. Wright's fourth grade science class the new unit is on clouds and weather. Ms. Wright's team has been working with the fourth graders on basic cooperative skills. Now they move into groups well and speak quietly when they are working, taking turns and listening carefully. Polite behavior has become the norm, although this was not always true at the beginning of the school year. With this in mind, Ms. Wright has decided on a jigsaw lesson to begin the new unit.

She introduces the jigsaw model to the students carefully. She shares the learning objectives and composition of the groups and explains the jigsaw process.

Ms. Wright: Today we are going to work on learning new information about clouds. People have been interested in clouds and their relation to weather as long as there have been people on earth. Why do you think people were interested in clouds?

Cookie: They are always changing.

Larry: Yes, but we can tell what kind of weather is coming if you look at the clouds, so there must be a pattern.

Ms. Wright: We learn a lot about our world by observing it and trying to make sense of what we see. Watching clouds is one way of trying to figure out some kind of order in our world. Today, we are going to begin a unit on clouds and weather. You will learn about five different kinds of clouds, the ways in which clouds form, and the kind of weather that is associated with specific kinds of clouds. First, we are going to get into our expert groups. Together you are going to learn about your cloud type.

Ms. Wright projects the groups and tells the students they have 2 minutes to settle into their groups and read the directions for the activity.

Ms. Wright: Elizabeth, please remind us of what we do when we work in jigsaw groups.

Elizabeth: We stay with our group until all work is completed, we follow our class rules, we make certain that everyone in our group understands the material before we ask you for help. The directions say that you are going to assign our cloud types. Can we choose?

Ms. Wright: You are going to choose your cloud type out of a hat. The questions that you are to answer are on the direction sheet. You can use Internet sources, our class library, and our textbook. Remember that before the end of our expert groups today, you will make a brochure that describes your cloud type with six different pieces of information, tells the way that your cloud is formed, and explains the type of weather associated with your cloud. The brochure will be the basis of your presentation to your learning groups tomorrow. Be certain that everyone in your group is ready to present to their learning groups before the end of class. I will make copies of your brochure for you so that there are enough for everyone in the class.

The expert groups get to work and Ms. Wright circulates around the room, helping groups figure out how to divide the task so that they can finish in the allotted time. At the end of the period, all of the groups are ready for the next day's learning groups.

In the **SECONDARY** *classroom*

Madame Bonigiraud's overarching objective is to have her students understand that communication is about sending and receiving messages. Today's lesson will focus on communicating using appropriate formal and informal phrases in different settings. Madame has chosen the graffiti model because of the feedback the model will provide her about student understanding and for the review it will provide the students.

Madame: We are going to do a graffiti exercise today. We've done this once before. Do you remember how to do this poster activity?

Denis: Yes, we had too much time to work on our posters and it got too loud!

Madame: I remember. Today, we will only have three minutes with each poster and that should help. Let me remind you of the expectations of this activity.

Madame Bonigiraud reviews the process and behavioral expectations for the students. She asks students to explain the process again to make certain that everyone will know what to do.

MADAME: I believe that many of you have accounts on Facebook and know about wall posts and commenting on other people's posts, right?

MARGUERITE: Oh, yeah! You can also just click "like it" if you agree with what someone has posted.

NICOLAS: Some posts are private though, so there's no point in commenting—you just write your own note back. It's just between your wall and theirs.

MADAME: Right, you are both describing communication. Sometimes, it goes back and forth a little until both people have talked through a whole idea. In either case, the original post should be as clear as possible, if the writer wants to communicate. Today, we will discuss formal and informal language. Clear communication demands that we know when to use formal or informal language

ADRIEN: Do you mean we talk in one way in one setting and a different way in another setting?

MATHILDE: Well, I don't use the same words with my grandmother as I do with my friends at the movies.

MADAME: That is exactly right. Let's see what phrases you would use in the settings on these posters. I will use this timer to keep us on track.

The group activity begins and continues over the next 15 minutes. Madame Bonigiraud circulates, responding to questions, correcting misconceptions and inaccuracies, and offering suggestions. The students are working well together and following the cooperative rules that have been discussed throughout the school year. The timer keeps the students on track throughout the activity. They are enthusiastic when they share their group findings with the whole class.

MADAME: Can we make any broad generalizations from the group presentations?

GUSTAVE: There are times when it is appropriate to use formal phrases.

ADRIEN: It is easier to come up with formal than informal phrases.

MATHILDE: I think that's because we used a lot of the phrases from our textbook.

MADAME: How do people learn informal expressions?

ADRIEN: I think we learn the informal expressions by living in the place, from hearing, and by using the expressions.

The discussion continues until the bell rings.

Basis of Cooperative Learning Models

Go to the Building Teaching Skills and Dispositions section of Topic 9: Group Interaction Models in the MyEducationLab for your course and complete the activity entitled "Infusing Social and Emotional Skills into Instruction."

The age of accountability has many advantages and some disadvantages for teachers—especially novice teachers. Standards provide guidance for the development of objectives (what students need to understand, know, and be able to do), but standards often explicate so much content that, taken at face value, teaching becomes coverage. In addition, there have been continuous calls that our society and workplace demand more than academic content as the goal of schooling. Schooling is meant to socialize our children into adult society, demanding attention to character development and social skills. These pressures can make a teacher's daily planning an overwhelming process. The models of instruction presented in this text are designed to help with everyday instructional decisions. The models allow for the organization of the learning environment so that students can both reach content goals and have the opportunity to develop higher-level thinking. Cooperative learning models also allow pupils the chance to develop personal and social skills.

Cooperative learning models have been used at all educational levels, including professional development in business, education, law, and medicine. The concept of group learning is not new in education. Reading groups, team sports, group science projects, student drama productions, and school newspapers are a few examples of activities that permeate the American school experience.

People are used to working in groups both in and out of school—some of these groups are cooperative, and some of them are not. What makes a group cooperative? Group dynamics was a much examined topic between the two world wars and into the mid-20th century when a shift to the study of individuals occurred. Most researchers agree that groups are cooperative when there is a common or closely related set of goals, equal distribution of labor in meeting the goals, and close contact as the goals are being pursued. Face-to-face interdependence and individual accountability are such as the hallmarks of cooperative learning.

Not all groups are cooperative, and not all school tasks should be completed cooperatively. Cooperative learning models are instructional sequences—a series of processes that structure pupil interactions in order to accomplish a specific, usually teacher-assigned goal. There is not a single approach to cooperative learning. In fact, there have been several interpretations of how the power of groups can be used to help pupils succeed academically and socially. Specific academic and social skills enhanced by cooperative learning approaches are identified in Figure 13.1. This chapter will examine the support for cooperative learning models and will present a general template of cooperative learning along with four specific cooperative learning models—jigsaw, graffiti, academic controversy, and student teams-achievement division (STAD).

Cooperative learning is supported by information processing theories and cognitive theories of learning. Information processing highlights the encoding process of learners, which is the act of relating new information to the ideas and concepts stored in long-term memory. Encoding strategies can be taught directly, but not everyone benefits from the encoding strategies chosen by a teacher, so more elaborative forms of connection-making can be useful. Teaching students to self-question as they integrate new information is helpful, as is listening to other students as they are involved in the same academic task. Learning with others can increase knowledge through modeling and coaching.

Cognitive theories of learning also support the use of cooperative groups in classrooms. According to theorists, activity is the center of human learning,

Figure 13.1 Cooperative Skills

Basic Cooperative Skills: Foundational Skills for Groups to Work in a Classroom Setting

- Moving into groups responsibly
- Speaking quietly
- Taking turns
- Addressing group members by name
- Eliminating put-downs
- Remaining with the group
- Encouraging everyone to participate
- Paying attention to materials
- Looking at the person speaking

Functioning Skills: Managing Group Efforts to Complete the Task and Maintain Productive Relationships

- Being able to restate the assignment limits
- Offering procedural ideas
- Seeking ideas of others
- Paraphrasing contributions of others in the group
- Describing personal feelings when appropriate
- Setting and calling attention to time
- Supporting peers through eye contact
- Asking or providing help or clarification
- Using humor, enthusiasm to energize

Formulating Skills: Intellectual Skills Needed for Deep Understanding

- Summarizing document or discussion completely without reference to the original document
- Seeking accuracy of processed information
- Seeking elaboration of information by relating it to past knowledge shared by the group
- Developing mnemonics to remember ideas and facts
- Checking for understanding by articulating reasons behind behavior and products
- Providing feedback as to procedures and progress to task completion

Fermenting Skills: Highest Intellectual and Social Skills

- Criticizing ideas, not people
- Integrating a number of different ideas into a single position
- Asking for justification of a peer's position
- Extending another's conclusion by adding further information or implications
- Going beyond first, apparent, or simple answers
- Testing conclusions against reality and group process constraints

Source: Based on information from Johnson, D. W., Johnson, R. T., and Holubec, E. J. (1994). *The new circles of learning: Cooperation in the classroom and school.* Alexandria, VA: Association for Supervision and Curriculum Development.

and interactions with peers are a springboard for cognitive development. Cooperative learning models are based on both of these ideas and provide carefully structured activities in a social environment. Cooperative learning groups allow students to share cultural experiences and examples that provide an opportunity for increased learning by all group members. Because most higher-level mental processes are social, the cooperative group is fertile learning ground. As students act within a group, the group changes and evolves, leaving a dynamic and opportunistic learning environment. It is natural that children learn in a social environment in cooperation with peers.

Cooperative Learning Model: The Template

> **myeducationlab**
> Go to the Assignments and Activities section of Topic 9: Group Interaction Models in the MyEducationLab for your course and complete the activity entitled "Positive Interdependence and Individual Accountability."

All lessons, curricula, and courses can be designed to include cooperative learning by tailoring existing materials to include the five key elements of cooperative learning.

These skills are critically important in almost all work settings. Their value to students beyond the years of formal schooling can hardly be overestimated.

1. Positive interdependence to ensure that work is equally distributed among all participating students and no one takes on a disproportionate share of the work
2. Individual accountability, meaning that each student is responsible for his or her own learning
3. Face-to-face interaction in which students explain to one another how to solve problems, share information, and connect information to prior knowledge
4. The explicit teaching of social skills
5. Group processing when a discussion ensues about whether the activity met cooperative learning goals

In addition, consideration must be given to the curriculum, the physical setting, and a diagnosis of and remediation for problems that pupils might have in working cooperatively. This template model was adapted from Patricia Blosser's (1991) list of steps that are required to plan for and implement a cooperative learning lesson. It is a template because it provides guidance to teachers at any developmental level in any content area and can be adapted by the teacher from previously existing curriculum materials or lesson activities and units found on the Internet. The teacher is required in the model to design the cooperative structure of the task and setting. The other models found in the chapter have the key elements of cooperative learning within their organizational structure. The general model requires that teachers build that structure—providing both opportunity and challenge. There are three planning steps and seven implementation steps in the template model.

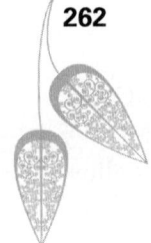

Planning Steps

1. *Develop clear instructional goals* in the know, understand, and able to do format.

2. *Consider and plan the size and composition of groups.* Try to keep groups to four. Groups should be heterogeneous in ways that are *applicable to the goals of the lesson* (gender, achievement, ethnicity, prior experiences, and the like). For example, if you want students to examine a science problem from a variety of perspectives, you want to vary the groups as much as possible. If, on the other hand, your objective is to provide the opportunity for students to practice new math skills, you want to group students on the same achievement level but with different genders and ethnicities.

3. *Make certain that the cooperative activity has all of the key elements of cooperative learning*—face-to-face communication for positive interaction, materials and roles that support interdependence, necessary social skills, positive goal interdependence, and individual accountability.

Implementation Steps

1. *Explain the task.* Explain the academic task clearly and succinctly. Remember that clarity is an important need of learners.

2. *Identify the social skills that are critical for the success of the group.* Remind students of the attributes of the skills and the criteria employed to determine if students used the skills appropriately. Review a T-chart that shows what the skill sounds like and looks like. For example, in a lesson on the Vietnam War, the objective is to identify the positions of the North and South Vietnamese. Your pupils have been assigned to study the position of each of the groups by looking at newspapers from around the globe. This is a complex task for your students, and you want to remind them of the importance of supporting each other during this difficult task. You can ask students what behaviors they will see when a person is being supportive. Pupils may identify such supportive behaviors as eye contact, praise, leaning forward, and the like. You also want to ask students what supportive behaviors sound like. What do your peers say when they are being supportive of your efforts in completing a difficult task? Specify these desired behaviors and the criteria that will be used to evaluate whether or not students have been supportive in their groups.

3. *Monitor and provide feedback to individual groups as they are working.* Use the rules of providing good feedback. Make certain that feedback is focused on specific pupil behaviors, that it is descriptive, and that it is provided while the groups are working on the cooperative task.

4. *Ask each group to summarize.* Provide closure for the lesson by asking each group to summarize its work. Summaries can be provided by a student given that role at the outset of the lesson or by asking students in each group to count off and choosing one of the students to summarize, allowing for another individual accountability opportunity.

5. *Evaluate.* Evaluate student work from established criteria. This can be done either during the lesson or soon after. Students should be involved in the evaluation process, helping to create the evaluation rubric.

6. *Assess group process.* Assess group cooperation by evaluating the way in which the groups performed. Each group member should have the opportunity to comment on the positive and negative aspects of the group process.

Summary of Cooperative Learning Template Model Steps

Planning
1. Design *Know, Understand, Able to Do* (KUD) objectives.
2. Plan size and composition of groups.
3. Plan for all key elements of cooperative learning.

Implementation
1. Explain the task.
2. Identify critical social skills.
3. Monitor and provide feedback during group work.
4. Ask each group to summarize.
5. Evaluate.
6. Assess group processes.

Specific Cooperative Models

Becoming familiar with specific cooperative models helps teachers and students incorporate the best attributes of cooperative learning into the classroom. Some cooperative structures can be categorized as strategies and are frequently used in all classroom settings. The graffiti model, the jigsaw model, the academic controversy model, and student teams-achievement division are lesson arrangements that can be used in any content area and at any grade level. They vary from strategies because they have a blueprint for teacher and student behavior that is much more detailed than teaching strategies that may be used and adapted in many ways.

The Graffiti Model

Graffiti is a cooperative brainstorming process that can be used at any point in a unit of instruction to check for understanding, to evaluate progress toward objectives, and to do an informal needs assessment. Pupils work in groups on previously identified questions or topics and simultaneously record responses on large sheets of paper during a specified period of time. After the time period has elapsed, either groups or sheets of paper move until each group has answered each available question. When a group returns to the original question, they read and summarize all of the class's responses and make several generalizations representing the comments. As in all cooperative models, preparation should begin with the planning steps of the template model—identifying objectives and organizing group size and composition.

The graffiti structure ensures positive interdependence and face-to-face interaction. Group skills should be taught or reviewed prior to the graffiti activity. Individual accountability can be assured through several means. Students can initial their responses and generalizations. Numbered heads or letters may be used. And an individual assessment can be administered to students at the end of the lesson.

Step 1: Prepare the Graffiti Questions and Group Number and Composition

The teacher prepares a series of questions aligned with the instructional objectives of the lesson. There should be as many questions as groups. Each question should be written on a large sheet of paper. A topic or prompt may also be used. Questions can be diagnostic—asking students to share prior knowledge on a new topic or a review of material previously covered in class.

Step 2: Distribute Materials

Depending on the objectives, students may use text materials as they respond to questions. If it is important to identify which responses are from a particular group, distribute colored markers so that each team has a different color. This will provide an easy way for each team to keep track of its own answers.

Step 3: Groups Answer Questions

Each team receives a sheet of paper with a question or topic, and groups are asked to read the question and spend 30 seconds thinking about a response. (If appropriate, you can give students more time as they examine text to find or solidify an answer.) Cue the students after 30 seconds and give them a set amount of time for writing responses on the sheet of paper. This time period should be delineated at the beginning of the lesson and should be the same throughout each question-answering phase. Three- to five-minute periods are usually appropriate.

Step 4: Exchange Questions

At the end of the timed interval, question sheets are exchanged. Or groups can physically move to the next question. The process continues until all of the groups have had the opportunity to respond to the prompts or questions on each sheet.

Step 5: Return to the Original Question, Summarize, and Make Generalizations

Each team returns to its original question. Team members review all of the responses on the graffiti sheet and arrange the responses into categories. Categories are listed on the back of the sheet. Once all of the possible categories have been listed, students produce generalizations that encompass all of the categories.

Step 6: Share Information

Each group has the opportunity to share the information from its graffiti sheet with the full class. To ensure individual accountability, have students number off and call one number to share information. Students can also be given a quiz at the end of the lesson.

Step 7: Evaluate the Group Process

A teacher-led discussion is held in which the robustness and accuracy of generalizations are discussed and the graffiti process itself is evaluated.

Summary of Graffiti Model Steps

1. Prepare the graffiti questions and decide on group number and composition.
2. Distribute materials.
3. Groups answer questions.
4. Exchange questions.
5. Return to the original question, summarize, and make generalizations.
6. Share information.
7. Evaluate the group process.

The Jigsaw Model

The jigsaw model by Elliot Aronson and colleagues was developed in the early 1970s as a way to help students and teachers successfully navigate newly desegregated schools (Aronson et al., 1978). Instead of providing each student with all of the necessary materials to study independently, Aronson assigned students to teams and gave each team member one piece of information. To reach all of the lesson's objectives, students were forced to fit their individual pieces together as if they were working on a jigsaw puzzle. The puzzle could not be completed unless each team member shared his or her piece. Three decades of research support this specific cooperative learning model. The model presented in this chapter is based on the original jigsaw as developed by Aronson and his team, with some of the adaptations of later researchers such as Robert Slavin (1996).

A jigsaw lesson divides the class up into two different kinds of groups, expert groups and learning groups. The expert groups all read and study the same materials—they become expert on the topic and prepare an outline or graphic that summarizes the critical information of their unit. As a group, they determine how this information will be shared with their peers. After the expert groups have completed their study, they meet with their learning group composed of a member of each expert group. Each expert teaches his or her topic to the members of the learning group. Students may be given a quiz, a graphic organizer, or an exit card to complete at the end of the learning group to ensure individual accountability.

Step 1: Introduce the Jigsaw

In the first few encounters with the jigsaw model, students should be carefully supported. With students who have less experience in cooperative learning models, a graphic representation like the one shown in Figure 13.2 may be helpful. Explain the cooperative process by highlighting the following points of the lesson in which students will be involved:

- The learning objectives for this lesson
- The composition and size of each group
- The differences between the expert and learning group
- How much time students will have to work in each group
- Access to the required materials
- The expert group task goal
- The learning group task goal
- The method of determining individual accountability

Step 2: Assign Heterogeneously Grouped Students to Expert and Learning Groups

Whenever the lesson objectives and materials warrant, students should be grouped heterogeneously for cooperative lessons. By controlling team assignments, the teacher may ensure that teams are balanced in terms of achievement, motiva-

Figure 13.2 Jigsaw Expert and Learning Groups

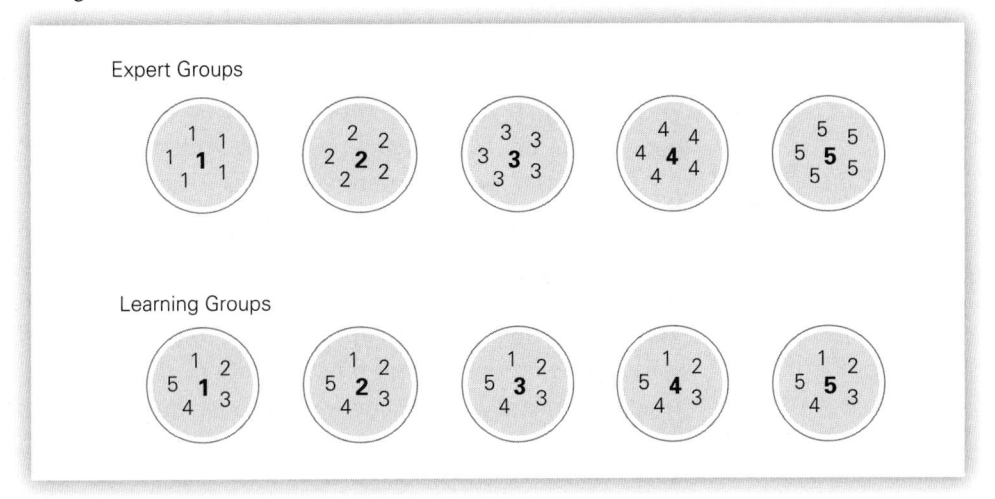

tion, gender, ethnicity, and other factors deemed important. When students are allowed to choose teammates, friendships tend to determine team membership, and many of the advantages of cooperative learning, especially achievement and social skills, are lost. Groups can also be formed randomly by pulling names from a hat, lining up students by height, birth date, number of siblings, or the like, and having students count off. One of the important principles of group composition is that unless you are using semester- or year-long cooperative groups, cooperative learning groups should vary across lessons. And even when base groups are used in classrooms, there should be times when students are assigned to different groups for particular lessons. This alleviates the concern students have about not working with their friends. Students should have the expectation that over time they will have the opportunity to work with all class members.

After the teacher assigns students to expert teams, each team will meet to begin the process. If this is a jigsaw that will be used over a significant number of class periods or with a new group of students, allow pupils to choose a group name and make certain that they are familiar with each member of the group.

Once expert groups have been listed, review the rules that will be in effect while groups are working. These rules will be specific to the class and the behavioral norms that have been established but might include the following:

1. No student may leave his or her team area until all students have completed the assigned work.
2. Each team member is responsible for learning the material and making certain that every member of the team also has learned the material.
3. If an individual group member is having difficulty understanding any part of the assignment, all members of the team respond with attempts to assist before the teacher is asked for help.

Step 3: Explain the Task and Assemble Expert Groups

Students assemble into expert groups. The teacher introduces the lesson objectives and how the jigsaw will help the students reach these objectives. Students are provided the materials they will rely on as they become experts and are given the opportunity to have any procedural questions answered.

The jigsaw task is structured so that a topic is subdivided among the groups. For example, if pupils were expected to understand the interdependence of community, groups may be assigned to become experts on different members of that community. Or if pupils were expected to understand that an ordinary individual can have an impact on history, groups may be assigned to become experts on some of the individuals who have had a profound effect on important events in American history. In a general methods education class, a jigsaw on different models of classroom management can be used.

Step 4: Allow Expert Groups to Process Information

Expert groups should be provided sufficient time to process the new information. Expert team members can assist one another with the reading material and making sense of the ideas that are being studied. These teams can be given guiding questions to help make connections between new information and background knowledge. Members of expert groups should complete the questions individually before discussing them as a group. Expert group members should then decide on what is most important about their topic and how they will convey this information to their peers in learning groups.

Step 5: Experts Teach in Their Learning Group

When all students master their expert topics, learning teams are assembled, and the experts teach their topics in turn. A time limit should be given for each presentation, and the time periods should be monitored. Each expert is responsible for teaching his or her topic, checking for understanding, and assisting teammates in learning the material. A graphic organizer (such as a matrix, Venn diagram, or concept map) can be provided to all learning group members so that the most important ideas can be recorded and retrieved.

Step 6: Hold Individuals Accountable

Individual students are held accountable for their learning though a quiz, participation checklist, essay, discussion, or other assessment method aligned with the learning objectives for the lesson or unit.

Step 7: Evaluate the Jigsaw Process

Students are asked to debrief the jigsaw process and their own learning in relation to the lesson or unit objectives. This can occur in a full-class discussion, within the expert groups, on an exit card, or in an individual conference with the teacher.

Summary of Jigsaw Model Steps

1. Introduce the jigsaw.
2. Assign heterogeneously grouped students to expert and learning groups.
3. Explain the task and assemble expert groups.
4. Allow expert groups to process information.
5. Experts teach in their learning group.
6. Hold individuals accountable.
7. Evaluate the jigsaw process.

The Academic Controversy Model

An academic controversy is a sophisticated, intellectual cooperative learning structure. Designed by Johnson and Johnson (1995) to harness the power of conflicts in classrooms, this approach is based on the belief that intellectual conflict is healthy and that students need to be trained in how to discuss controversial topics.

Johnson and Johnson have proposed a theory to explain how controversies can promote academic learning, productivity, and positive relationships. They believe that individuals at first categorize and organize information based on prior experiences and knowledge. As their conclusions are presented to others in the position-building and position-sharing steps of the model, students deepen their understanding and use higher-level thinking strategies. When confronted with different viewpoints and conclusions, conceptual conflict and disequilibrium are aroused. This leads to an active search for more information, more connections, and a path for resolving this uncertainty. Uncertainty is associated with increased attention and higher-level thinking—a strong motivator in classrooms. At the end of the process, students accommodate multiple viewpoints.

Before the academic controversy can begin, a topic must be identified and materials supporting each side of the issue gathered. Teachers are responsible for deciding on the topic of the academic controversy and the materials that will be used to provide background. The topic must be developmentally appropriate for students and should have identifiable pro and con sides. Materials should be organized into pro and con packets and may include primary source documents, summaries, graphic organizers, pictures, and the like. Older students may find their own source materials. Academic controversies can be adapted for younger students by structuring and adapting the information required for understanding each position. These controversies may come from community, school, or classroom experiences: Should cookies be served in the cafeteria? Should there be more time for physical education classes? Should report cards be abolished? Regardless of the sophistication of the topic, it is important that students be exposed to the sophisticated process. They also should have the opportunity to practice the individual skills before they are used in the academic controversy.

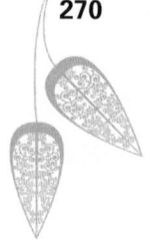

It is not only the ideas and understandings that are complex; the process itself requires some high-level social skills, many of them fermenting skills (see Figure 13.1). Students should be reminded of what the critical social skills are for this instructional event and have a discussion about what those skills look like and sound like in the classroom.

Teachers are also, as in all cooperative learning, responsible for determining group composition and size. Ideally, there should be four students in a cooperative group—two students assigned to each position. Students are provided with their pro or con packets and given class time to do the readings on their position or assigned the readings for homework. Younger students can brainstorm their position with the teacher. Directions for the controversy must be clear and should be provided orally and in writing. Once these preparations are made, the academic controversy model begins.

Step 1: Students Prepare Their Positions

Students meet with their same position partner and review their position materials. Together they determine the theses of their position and arrange the supporting evidence (facts, information, and experiences) to support their claims. Students need to develop a presentation that leads their peers to understand and support their argument.

Step 2: Students Present and Advocate Their Positions

Once the pair has worked out a strong position, they return to the original foursome, and each pair presents its arguments. It is important that both members of the pair are involved in presenting their position. The positions should be organized around several points of evidence that are supported by examples, stories, and personal experiences. As presentations are given, the opposing pair listens so that a list of arguments can be made and each argument can be evaluated as weak or strong. If there are particularly muddy points in the presentation, the opposing group should ask for clarification.

There is no arguing or debating during this step of the model. Students should be learning the opposing position on which they will better craft their own position and be able to share what they have learned on an individual accountability measure.

Step 3: Open Discussion and Rebuttals

Once both positions have been argued, the group of four discusses both positions by listing the arguments and discussing the strength of each. Pairs continue to advocate for their position and attempt to refute the position of the opposition. Rebuttals should be based on counterarguments, clarifications, and extensions. Students should ask each other for supporting information, clarification, and about how reasonable the claims are. In this phase of the model, uncertainty is building, and students need to be comfortable expressing opinions and being challenged. In turn, they must be comfortable challenging opinions in a polite and reasonable manner.

Step 4: Reverse Positions

Students reverse positions and present each other's perspectives by first discussing the new presentation with their partner. It is important that new positions are presented forcefully and persuasively and, if possible, new facts, information, or evidence is presented. The pro team gives the argument for the con position, and the con position is presented by the pro team.

Step 5: Synthesize and Integrate the Best Evidence into a Joint Position

Once each member of the team has participated in presenting both sides of the issue, the four group members drop their advocacy and synthesize in order to integrate what is known into a joint position on which both sides can agree. To do this, students will need to step back and revisit the question from a variety of perspectives. Students need to look at the different positions, summarize them, and then create a new unifying position—a synthesis.

Step 6: Present the Group Synthesis

Students can present their positions to the class by having a single group member present that position. Students can be asked to describe the new position in a written paragraph or two, or students can be asked to share their new position in an outline or using presentation software. Individual accountability can also be ensured by giving each student a test on the information that was embedded in each of the position packets.

Step 7: Group Processing of the Controversy and Participation of Members

The class has a discussion about the positive and negative aspects of the experience and what were the most successful and least successful aspects of the group experience.

Summary of Academic Controversy Steps

1. Students prepare their positions.
2. Students present and advocate their positions.
3. Open discussion and rebuttals.
4. Reverse positions.
5. Synthesize and integrate the best evidence into a joint position.
6. Present the group synthesis.
7. Group processing of the controversy and participation of members.

The Student Teams-Achievement Division (STAD) Model

The student teams-achievement division (STAD) model was developed at Johns Hopkins University in the context of research on cooperative learning. STAD is a model used for meeting well-defined instructional objectives. Students study in four- or five-member learning teams that are representative of the characteristics of the class as a whole, heterogeneous with respect to students' ability, race, gender, ethnicity, and so on. The team study typically follows a succinct presentation of the basic material and objectives by the teacher. The material to be learned centers on specific information (capitals of the major countries of Europe, data on the major rivers of Africa, spelling and grammar rules, basic mathematics, biological classification, properties of the planets in our solar system—anything in the curriculum grounded in single right answers that must be learned). Students study the material in whatever way makes the best sense to them, using whatever approach to study and learning they choose. They may take turns quizzing each other, discuss problems as a group, check Web resources and other texts, and generally use whatever means they wish to master the material. The participants should also be clear that their task is to learn the concepts, not simply to fill out worksheets. The goal of every member of the group is to master the material and do whatever possible to help every member of the team to achieve the same goal.

Step 1: Present a New Concept

STAD is not a model to be used as the basis of all instruction, but is designed for meeting well-defined instructional objectives. Because of the nature of the content for which STAD is appropriate, many teachers use a direct instruction model for step 1, the presentation of the new material. The teacher plays the role of facilitator and coach, a resource that the students can call on as needed. In the example that follows, the objective is to teach students to apply four rules for the formation of plural nouns.

1. Most nouns form their plural by simply adding *s* to the singular form:
   girl, girls   tiger, tigers   toy, toys
   shirt, shirts   angel, angels   willow, willows
2. Some nouns ending in *f* or *fe* form their plural by changing their ending to *ve* before adding *s*.
   wife, wives   leaf, leaves
   life, lives   self, selves
3. Nouns ending in *s, sh, ch,* or *x* form their plural by adding *es*.
   fox, foxes   kiss, kisses
   wish, wishes   church, churches
4. Nouns ending in *o* preceded by a vowel usually form their plural by adding *s,* but nouns ending in *o* preceded by a consonant usually form their plural by adding *es*.
   radio, radios   rodeo, rodeos
   zoo, zoos   zero, zeroes
   hero, heroes   tomato, tomatoes
   potato, potatoes   memento, mementoes,
   ratio, ratios   or momentos

Step 2: Form Teams for Study and Practice

Divide students into heterogeneously grouped study teams. Each team should have one member from the high achievement, high average achievement, low average achievement, and low achievement groups. Teams should also be heterogeneous with respect to characteristics like race and gender. Once the study teams are formed, resources like worksheets and study guides are provided for team study. Participants know that their job is not complete until all team members are convinced that everyone fully understands the material being studied.

Step 3: Test Students on Newly Learned Materials

In the third step, individuals composing the teams are given quizzes to complete independently for individual scoring and team scoring. Individual scores are totaled for the team score, and teams are rewarded for improvement over past performance (for example, on pretests).

Step 4: Recognize Winning Teams

Possible means of student recognition include posting the names of top-scoring team members on the bulletin board, awarding certificates, and sending home notes to parents. Extra recess time, first in lines, extra time on preferred tasks, or no weekend homework are other ways that academic accomplishments may be rewarded.

Summary of STAD Steps

1. Present a new concept.
2. Forms teams for study and practice.
3. Test students on newly learned material and provide scores for individuals and for teams.
4. Recognize winning teams.

Evaluating Learning in the Cooperative Learning Models

> **myeducationlab**
> The Power of Classroom Practice
> www.myeducationlab.com
>
> Go to the Assignments and Activities section of Topic 9: Group Interaction Models in the MyEducationLab for your course and complete the activity entitled "Anticipating Problems."

Groups are powerful and occur naturally in the classroom and in the school hallways and playgrounds. In fact, groups are ubiquitous and influential and enhance achievement, relationships, psychological health, and social skills. It makes sense to incorporate group work into classroom instruction, and, because instruction and assessments should be aligned and integrated, it makes sense to occasionally use groups to help with evaluation. Because time for providing feedback, grading tests, and developing evaluations is always at a premium, student help with evaluation tasks can be invaluable. Peer review and student grading can take place in cooperative groups and still be reliable and valid. The key is that the groups must be cooperative and adhere to the five basic elements of cooperative learning.

Teachers decide when cooperative learning is to be used, with what content, in what structure, and how the outcomes will be assessed. As the cooperative group works on the teacher-designed instructional task, students can provide "immediate remediation and enrichment" to each other as they work together. Practice in how to provide neutral feedback can be provided to students. As indicated, individual accountability is essential for each group product and can be determined through the use of multiple-choice, matching, and essay test items and projects. But the group product should also be evaluated. Students can be involved in establishing criteria and building a rubric for these products, and they can practice using the rubrics on draft or model products—helping students as they are developing their own work. The important rule of thumb with both individual and group assessments is that they are aligned and reasonable for the identified objectives of the lesson or unit.

Meeting Individual Needs in the Cooperative Learning Models

Cooperative group work easily translates into differentiation opportunities if the key elements of cooperative learning are in place. Cooperative learning goals and differentiation are both responsive teaching strategies. Objectives are the key to all differentiation and cooperative learning decisions. Once the *know, understand,* and *able to do* objectives are in place, the teacher can determine how best to help all students reach the goals. Differentiation can be achieved with the content or with the task. Jigsaws, for example, are a natural content-differentiation activity and can be organized by interest or need. Group tasks can also be determined by student learning profiles—different groups can be formed around intelligence preferences (practical, analytic, or creative tasks), student interests, or academic, social, or emotional skill needs. It is important to remember, however, that cooperative learning models have goals that go beyond academic achievement and that learning from others with a different constellation of characteristics is an important cooperative learning attribute. Individual students have a unique set of strengths and weaknesses and cooperative groups can build on strengths and shore up weaknesses. To do this, teachers must know a great deal about their students.

For example, Debbie Moss differentiates the regions unit (see Chapter 12) in a number of ways. As previously discussed, she differentiates through questioning in an integrative lesson. She also differentiates through student interest in a jigsaw lesson. She provides students the choice of researching the history of the different regions—Northeast, Midwest, South, and West—and organizes cooperative groups around these choices. Within the groups, students are also assigned roles based on Debbie's understanding of her students. Students who are comfortable with text are assigned the role of summarizer; students who are more analytic may be assigned the role of researcher; creative students may organize the presentation to the jigsaw learning group, and so on. Debbie keeps careful records so that students are not always assigned to the same role.

Benefits of the Cooperative Learning Models

In traditional classes, most of students' experience with content is limited to listening and taking notes. In classrooms organized for cooperative learning, students listen, write, tell, paraphrase, read, assist others, and interact. When students work cooperatively, they process information by discussing subject matter with peers rather than acting as passive recipients of information. Because they are working in small groups, even reticent students tend to enter discussions and ask clarifying questions.

Many studies have shown that when correctly implemented, cooperative learning improves information acquisition and retention, higher-level thinking skills, interpersonal and communication skills, and self-confidence. Beyond the classroom, there are as yet unimagined advantages to learning in groups. Most of the jobs that today's students will need to fill at graduation do not even exist today, and almost all of them will require skills of learning and working with others. Kevin Faughnan, director of IBM's Academic Initiative, has this to say to students in U.S. classrooms today: "Getting smart about your skills today, which must include a balance of deep technical skill and an interdisciplinary approach to business, will help you find that dream job tomorrow" (Faughnan, 2009). Ideas such as these point to the benefits of cooperative learning models.

Elementary Grades Lesson

COOPERATIVE LEARNING JIGSAW: Clouds

OBJECTIVES

Students Will Understand

- Clouds provide pleasure and information

Students Will Know

- The characteristics of five cloud types (stratus, cirrus, cumulus, cumulonimbus, and fog)
- The ways in which clouds form
- The types of weather associated with specific clouds

Students Will Be Able To

- Summarize information about clouds
- Work together in a cooperative group
- Design and execute a pamphlet about a type of cloud

ASSESSMENTS

- Students will develop a pamphlet describing an assigned cloud type that includes six pieces of information about the cloud, how the cloud is formed, and the types of weather associated with the cloud type. The pamphlet will be evaluated on whether the information is accurate.
- Students will complete self-evaluations on their team work on this project including specific contributions made to the project

PROCEDURES	1. Introduce the jigsaw model. Tell students the lesson's objectives, the composition of expert and learning groups and specific directions for the task, the resources available for completing the task, and the method for determining individual accountability.
2. Assign groups to expert and learning groups and review behavioral norms.
3. Assemble expert groups and review the task.
4. Give students the time to complete the task. Circulate to provide assistance and support to students.
5. Remind students that they will be working in learning groups tomorrow, but will have time to review with their expert group at the beginning of the class. Students will take a short quiz about clouds after the learning group presentations and question/answer sessions are complete.

Middle/Secondary Grades Lesson

COOPERATIVE LEARNING GRAFFITI: Formal and Informal Speech

OBJECTIVES	**Students Will Understand**
- How we speak in different settings demonstrates our cultural awareness and language fluency

Students Will Know
- When to use formal and informal expressions
- Forms of formal and informal expressions

Students Will Be Able To
- Explain the difference between formal and informal speech
- Distinguish between settings in which formal and informal speech is used
- List a minimum of five phrases that might be used in an assigned setting |
| **ASSESSMENT** | Students will be randomly assigned to pictures and asked to create a brief dialogue (five exchanges) that would be likely in the context of the picture. Students will also write a description or narration of the episode. |
| **PROCEDURES** | 1. Prepare questions or posters and groups.
2. Introduce the graffiti model. Share the following directions with the class:
   - Once you are in your groups, look at your poster and note the location about which you will write (e.g., home/family, school/friends, shopping/business, hospital/patient, sporting event/friends). |

- In your group, think about the setting and with whom you would interact. Are you expected to use formal or informal language when speaking with these people? Why? What kinds of phrases are you likely to say?
- On your poster board, write at least three phrases or expressions that you would commonly say or hear in the setting listed on the poster.
- Posters will be exchanged in a clockwise pattern and you will add three additional phrases.
- When your original poster returns, read all of the phrases and see if you notice patterns or inaccuracies. Is the language appropriate for the setting? What did you notice about the kinds of phrases that were shared? Summarize your findings and make generalizations that will be shared with the class.

3. Distribute materials—posters, markers.
4. Groups answer questions. Allow 3 minutes for each poster until the last round and then provide 5 minutes.
5. Exchange posters in a clockwise pattern.
6. Summarize and make generalizations about the original poster.
7. Share information.
8. Discuss the process.

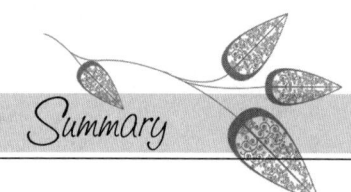

Summary

The cooperative learning models discussed in this chapter each promote interdependence of learners, individual accountability, positive face-to-face interactions, and social skills that foster group processing. These are the key elements of all cooperative learning. The graffiti model allows pupils to work in groups to respond to prepared questions and to share answers that lead to generalizations. The jigsaw model places initial responsibility for learning on groups that each become "experts" on a topic before splitting into separate groups composed of "experts" on the various topics, now with the secondary responsibility to teach one another what they have learned as members of the initial groups. The academic controversy model asks students to research and prepare a position on a controversial issue, organize and persuasively present that position, refute the persuasive presentation given by peers on the opposite side of the issue, view the issue from multiple perspectives, and collectively create a position integrating the opposing views. The student teams-achievement division (STAD) model is initiated with a direct instruction lesson on a concept to be studied cooperatively. Following the direct instruction, typically delivered by the teacher, students form heterogeneous study teams for practice. They then test one another on the new material, with rewards for high scores, most improved from pretests, and highest group scores total. Winning teams are acknowledged in various ways.

Extensions

ACTIVITIES

1. Select a chapter from a content area textbook. Choose a specific topic from the chapter. List four or five important subtopics presented and develop expert question sheets for each subtopic. Select an appropriate instructional model that can be combined with jigsaw to provide an introduction to the chapter.
2. Brainstorm with students a list of jobs they might aspire to. Expect these to range from professional sports to military enlistment. Once you have compiled a list of a dozen or so professions, ask students to list all the ways they might expect a person in that profession to engage in cooperative learning and work.
3. Interview two or three practicing teachers about their use of cooperative learning. Do they use cooperative models? If not, why? If so, what do they see as the benefits of cooperative learning? What problems have they encountered? What recommendations do they have for you as you implement cooperative learning in your classroom?

REFLECTIVE QUESTIONS

1. What do you anticipate will be the biggest threat to classroom management as you implement cooperative learning?
2. What long-term benefits do you feel are associated with cooperative learning? On what are you basing your hypothesis?
3. How will you teach the different levels of cooperative skills to your students? In what ways are cooperative skills related to academic skills?

Summary for Part Two

Matching Objectives to Instruction: A Models Approach

Part Two describes more than ten instructional models that can be used in K–12 classrooms for particular learning outcomes. All of the models help students learn knowledge and skills. In addition, they focus on specific higher-order thinking skills. For example, direct instruction develops skills and discrete bits of information through guided independent practice, increasing student metacognition. Concept attainment and concept development support contrasting, categorizing, applying, and analyzing. Three problem-centered inquiry models are presented that align with objectives related to problem solving, analysis, hypothesizing, and evaluation. Synectics provides opportunities for exploration, comparison, and creating analogies. The cause-and-effect model is effective for objectives related to analysis, evaluation, and synthesis. Learning vocabulary through the history of language and word derivation is the focus of the vocabulary acquisition model. The integrative model provides practice in observation, description, explanation, and constructing generalizations and hypotheses with large bodies of related information. The cooperative learning chapter details the skills and knowledge necessary for developing a positive learning environment while meeting cognitive objectives. Steps, benefits, and classroom applications are presented for each model.

Classrooms are diverse settings. Students differ on many characteristics. Instructional models provide a way to vary access to the required knowledge and skills. The needs of many different students are served with the use of different instructional models. Variety widens the net and helps meet the preferred learning style of some students while stretching the ability to use different ways of learning for others.

part 3

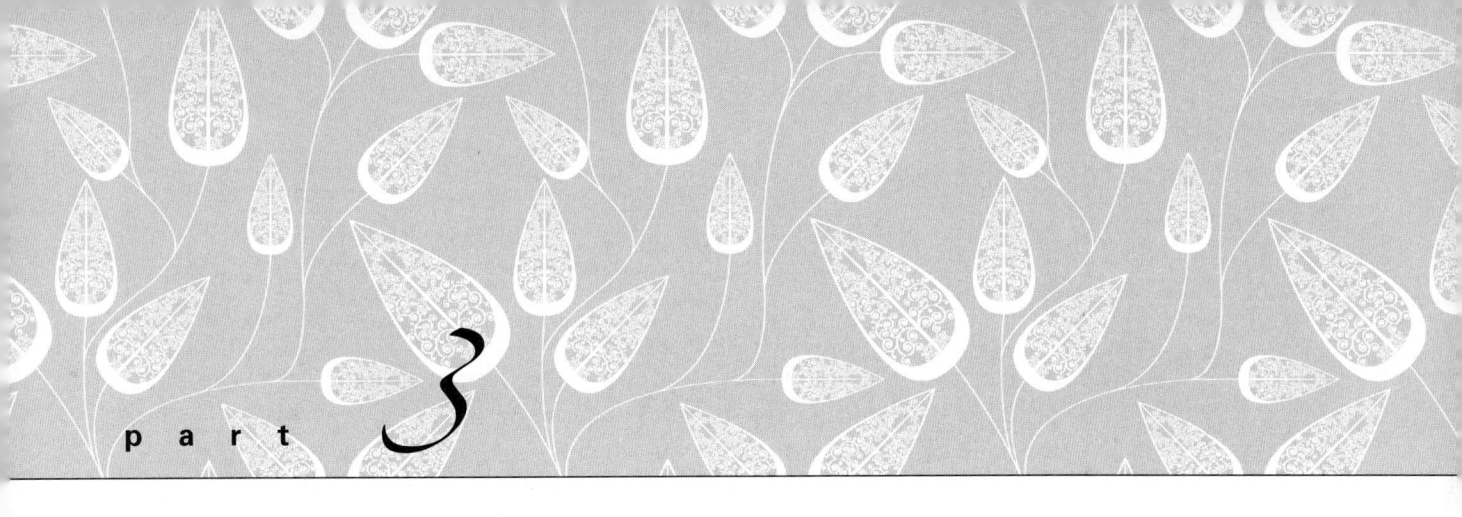

Putting It All Together
Matching Objectives to Instructional Models

An essential activity of the professional instructor, as emphasized in the preface to this book, is the process of designing or structuring (the root of *instruct*) that which is to be taught. We have emphasized the process of setting goals and objectives and designing the units and lessons so that they are aligned with the goals.

In Part Three, we describe the integration of planning, instruction, assessment, and management that takes place in an effective classroom environment. Each teacher, however, must develop his or her own way of achieving this integration. There is no one way to approach the process of putting it all together in the classroom. Classroom decisions are dependent on the individual school content. But every good teacher attends to certain essential components of this process: (1) planning, (2) instruction, (3) assessment, and (4) classroom management.

In Parts One and Two, we discussed the first three components. In Part Three, we describe how teachers in classrooms use the ideas presented in Parts One and Two, and we give some general suggestions for managing the classroom. Of the four chapters in this section, Chapter 14 is a case study of a kindergarten class plan, Chapter 15 is a middle school case study, and Chapter 16 is a high school case study. Evident in these three examples are individual approaches to instructional planning, which use some of the processes and strategies described earlier. The teachers in these examples do not arrive at their plans by the same route nor do they incorporate exactly the same instructional steps in their individual plans. All the teachers do, however, attend to the needs of their students, and they systematically determine objectives and match those objectives to instruction and assessment.

Chapter 17 describes techniques for dealing with classroom management. Most of the material presented in this last chapter is drawn from our personal experience; we have attempted, however, to connect this experience with research regarding effective classroom practice.

It is our belief that teachers are essentially instructional experts, not therapists or counselors. Like all good managers, they must have very keen interpersonal skills and be able to think quickly on their feet. Anyone responsible for managing groups of people and for the welfare of individuals under their direction should have the personality and skills to manage the group and to give direction. But we should not ask of teachers what we do not ask of other professionals. Teachers should not be expected to prescribe and treat seriously challenged individuals without help from other professionals, such as psychologists, social workers, and guidance counselors, nor should they be expected to teach in life-threatening situations.

Having said this, it is our belief that many students who are considered to be serious discipline problems and are sent out of the classroom, often labeled as hyperactive or emotionally disturbed, are in fact suffering because of the way they are being taught. Youngsters who are bored, whose learning style is different from the teaching style, or who are asked to learn material that is too difficult or too easy can become discipline problems. Too often, teachers diagnose instructional problems as emotional, physical, or mental problems, thus failing to meet the challenge of finding an instructional solution. In this part of the text we reemphasize the need for careful instructional planning and design and for creating a classroom environment in which students can and will learn (Noguera, 2008).

14 A Kindergarten Case Study

chapter OBJECTIVES

You Will Understand
- Effective instructional planning requires knowledge of content, students, and pedagogy

You Will Know
- Some instructional planning steps
- The construction of objectives written in student-friendly language
- The instructional decision making of a specific teacher

You Will Be Able To
- Reflect and comment on the instructional planning of a teacher
- Develop a detailed plan for one lesson in a unit
- Determine if the teacher described in this chapter uses backward design

Gloria Abbott, kindergarten teacher at Central Elementary School, relaxed one warm summer afternoon with a pad and a pencil and wrote down some thoughts on her chosen profession, on the role of education, and on what she wants for her students. She realized that some rethinking of her approach to teaching would help her to begin the new school year with a renewed energy and commitment. Miss Abbott made these notes:

> I went into teaching because I enjoy being with children and because I think that teaching is the most important profession. It has always seemed to me to have the greatest potential to make the most lasting positive difference to the largest number of people. The fate of our democracy, our very way of life, depends on the political and economic participation of all its citizens. But despite these lofty ideals and aspirations, my frustration is that I may not be able to do my part. Although I want all the students to

learn, I know that many of them leave my classroom without the skills they need to succeed at the next level. Some of the children are bored because they already know what I am trying to teach. Others are frustrated because they have difficulty in learning what I am teaching.

What I love most are the times when I read to the children and we talk about the characters and the story. Some of the so-called at-risk children have the best insights. I want them all to love ideas and to exercise their imaginations in creative use of language. I also want these students to gain respect for one another; too often I see that some children are left out of activities and ignored by the rest. I want the students to work together and to learn to cooperate with one another in the classroom. Most of all, I want them to leave kindergarten with more curiosity about learning than when they walked into school in September.

In reading what she had written, Miss Abbott circled the key words and phrases that indicated her primary concerns for the children in her classroom. Then she wrote the following goals:

The Children Will Know
- How to read and how to read to learn

The Children Will Understand
- Ideas and language that stimulate their imaginations

The Children Will Be Able To
- Do what is required of them for success in first grade
- Perform at an appropriately challenging skill level
- Learn with confidence in their abilities
- Apply basic properties of numbers

"Fine," she thought to herself. "Now, how do I make this happen?"

The first step was to find out as much as possible about the children who would be coming next fall, a habit she had neglected in recent years. Her school is located in a small southern city, in a neighborhood close to a university. Some of her students are the children of university faculty, and others are the sons and daughters of the hourly employees, such as secretaries who run the offices, janitors who clean the buildings, and cooks who prepare the meals. Most of the children of the faculty are white; many of the children of the support staff are black. Some of the children have traveled around the world; some have never been out of the city.

Frequently, she had walked around the neighborhoods where students in her class lived. There were some streets where maids were carefully sweeping the porches and gardeners were mowing the verdant lawns. On other streets, houses stood on lots where no grass grew in the hard-packed dirt in front of sagging stoops.

She knew that regardless of the neighborhood, some children would suffer from abuse and neglect and others would be nurtured and cared for. She realized how important it was for her to bring together these children from different neighborhoods and family environments and to provide a classroom atmosphere where all could succeed. Could she make each child feel important, safe, and competent with her and with one another? Could each of them feel that school was a place of happiness where they were glad to be? Could she feel that way as well?

Readiness tests had been given to each child when he or she had enrolled in the system. Miss Abbott spent the next day going through the results. One of the children who would be in her classroom could have entered the second grade based on the tests. More than one-third of the children, however, were more than one year below the norm. Over two-thirds of the children would be eligible for the after-school child-care program because of working parents. Most of the children showed some potential for problems in their readiness to learn. In the past, she would have focused on the number of children with potential learning problems and wished that they were in some other class. This time, she told herself that these children must be a part of the challenge of teaching. In the planning process, she would attend to their special needs.

The old school building was not air-conditioned, so she would again have to get the children outdoors as much as possible during the early fall months.

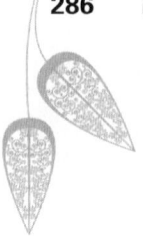

These ventures would have to be tied to learning, however, and not just for cooling off. There was no money in the school budget for trips, so when they went outside it would need to be in the neighborhood of the school or on the playground. Also, if she were going to move the group around, they would need to understand the rules and to cooperate with her and with one another.

She checked the state standards that listed the important skills children should master in kindergarten. The visual art standards address the concept of lines and the characteristics of lines (they can be straight/curved, thick/thin, long/short, vertical/horizontal, and diagonal). Kindergarten students should also be able to identify and use a variety of shapes—circles, squares, triangles, and ovals.

The word *line* caused her to remember that during the first weeks of school the students would learn to line up before leaving the room and stay in line as they moved through the halls. This was important when she took the children on walking trips in the neighborhood. On the playground they were to develop gross motor skills by bouncing a ball across a line.

As she reviewed the standards, it occurred to her that the concept of *line* arose frequently and might be an excellent focus for the first unit; she could introduce a number of ideas about lines that could be expanded on throughout the year. For instance, the concept of *lines* can represent a drawing within, as well as an acceptance of, limits. Lines are used to form boundaries and to represent infinity. Two ends of a curved line can be joined to form a circle. Straight lines can be assembled to form a square. Miss Abbott smiled as she realized that in her enthusiasm she could go off in many directions at once. There was a limit to what she could include in one unit and how much these children could absorb. "Keep in mind how many times the same concept has to be experienced before it can be understood," she reminded herself. It was time to order her own thoughts in developing the unit on lines.

Miss Abbott's Plan

Typically, Miss Abbott planned a unit to last for 2 to 6 weeks, depending on the time of year and the content to be covered. Miss Abbott usually divided each unit into four to six lessons, with each lesson lasting 3 to 5 days. There was an organizing theme for each unit (for example, the unit on community helpers that every kindergarten teacher taught) and an organizing subtheme or idea for each lesson (for example, nurses and doctors, police and fire officers). The unit objectives were explained to the students at the beginning of the unit; lesson objectives were explained at the beginning of each week and cumulatively reviewed each day in oral and written form. A space on the chalkboard was reserved solely for this purpose; if the students were to learn to read, they needed to see important information in print, and this was one way to effect that. And she had always thought it important to keep the kindergartners informed about what led to what in their study.

Her experience had taught her much about teaching. In the past, Miss Abbott had often developed daily lesson plans that were unrelated to one another and were not part of any design. Over the years, she became convinced that students did better when they could see connections in what they were learning each day. Unit planning helped her to decide what to include and in what order.

After again consulting the state standards, she decided that the general objectives for this first unit on lines would be as follows:

Students Will Know
- How to work cooperatively in groups and to express enthusiasm about the process of their own and others' learning
- A line is something that has two ends connected by something that looks like a string or a rope
- Lines can be straight or curved and vertical, horizontal, or diagonal
- A row of words or numbers on a page is a line
- A row of people or things is a line

Students Will Understand
- Lines together form many shapes

Students Will Be Able To
- Distinguish between a straight line and a curved line
- Identify a circle
- Identify a square

Then she preliminarily organized the content for the unit in the following arrangement:

Learning about Lines

Straight lines	Lines that curve
Lines of people/Lines on a page	Faces and flowers
Squares	Circles

As she moved parts around and decided what the children could learn and what would be appropriate, she realized that there was probably more content here than she could cover in one unit. Why not limit this introductory unit to 2 weeks and reserve major study of the concepts of geometric shapes—the square and the circle—for a separate, but related, unit to follow? There would then be less chance of confusion at the critical stage when the young learners would need to be clear on the fundamental notion of *line* as distinct from two- and three-dimensional shapes. Besides, by separating this first unit into two related units, she could do more with the second part on geometric shapes.

Thus the initial unit on lines would be planned in anticipation of a follow-up unit. Now her diagram of the content included squares and circles, but these would each be the focus of a future unit of study. In other words, she could make lines the organizing concept of the unit and that would tie several units of study together. Her revised list looked like this:

Learning about Lines

Straight lines	Lines that curve
Lines of people/Lines on a page	~~Faces and flowers~~
~~Squares~~	~~Circles~~
~~Angles and sides~~	Inside and outside of lines

As she prepared the first lesson in the unit on lines for the opening day of school, Miss Abbott was plagued again by second thoughts. After all, this was a difficult concept, and these were very young children. Yet, she thought, they hear this word *line* all the time. Adults are always talking to them about lines: "Wait in line to get on the bus," "Neatly line up your shoes," and "Draw a line." Even so, she wondered how to make this abstract concept more concrete.

It occurred to her that the children might need to have a line to hold in their hands to touch and to feel. The kind of line that might be familiar to them would be a fishing line, but nylon fishing line might cut. The line she needed would have to be something strong that would not break and still would not hurt the children's hands. She visualized bright lines of yarn extending out the door of the classroom on the first morning to draw in the children. Now she felt more confident about planning the details for the unit on lines. She calculated that each lesson in the unit would occupy less than an hour each day.

Unit: Lines That Draw Us Together

Teaching time. Ten days, 1 hour or less per day.

Unit objectives.

Students Will Understand
- Not all lines are alike and lines can be made in many ways

Students Will Know
- We all need to work together so that everyone can learn
- A line is something that has two ends connected by something that looks like a rope
- A row of words, numbers, things, or people is a line

Students Will Be Able To
- Line up efficiently
- Select examples of lines and explain reasons for their choices
- Group different kinds of lines together
- Go inside and outside of a line when provided specific directions

Table 14.1 shows the unit objectives in student-friendly language. When objectives are shared with students, they should be in language that is developmentally appropriate and connected with prior school experiences.

Table 14.1 Objectives in Student-Friendly Language

Understand	Lines can be different and made in many ways.
Know	We help each other learn.
	A line has two ends that are connected with something like string or rope.
	Rows of words, numbers, people, and things are a line.
Able to do	Line up quickly and quietly.
	Point to lines.
	Describe a line.
	Put pictures of different kinds of lines together.
	Stay inside and outside of a line.

Opening Activity—Drawing in the Students

Objective. The children will understand that this classroom is a safe and productive environment in which they can successfully learn important ideas.

Just outside the classroom will be a table. Lines of yarn will extend from the classroom and will be draped across the table. Attached at the end of each line will be a cardboard fish with a child's name on it. A parent volunteer will stand at the door, and as the children arrive they will line up. One at a time, the children will come forward, and the volunteer will give each child the string with his or her name on it and call out the name. The teacher will pull in the yarn and welcome each child. When all the children are assembled in the room, and throughout the first week, stories emphasizing lines will be read aloud to the class (for example, *The Line Up Book* by Marisabina Russo and *Lines and Shapes* by Solvig Russell).

Estimated time. Day One of unit; 30 minutes.

Materials. 12-foot lengths of heavy, brightly colored yarn; cardboard name tags in the shape of fish; and appropriate books.

Assessment. Ask the parent volunteer to observe the children's reactions, particularly those children who display fear or frustration with the activity. Make notes following the activity.

Lesson One: Practicing the "Line-Up"

Instructional model. Direct instruction.

Estimated time. On appropriate occasions each day of first 2 weeks, 2 to 7 minutes (or faster) per occasion, depending on skill level.

Objective. Students will know that a row of people is a *line*. Students will be able to form a *line* in an orderly and expeditious manner.

Rationale for choice of model. "People moving" is one of the fundamental routines that teachers must establish at the beginning of each year. Going to lunch, to recess, to other classrooms, to the bathroom are all part of the typical day of the elementary student and his or her teacher. Precisely because lining up to move is such a basic routine, direct instruction is most suitable for its mastery. Sometimes the model is called the training model, a terminology we have rejected as having a negative connotation, although it does get the point across. Kindergarten-age children do have to be trained to get in line with minimum confusion; in a week of short practice sessions, the students will be so accustomed to lining up on command that the procedure will be second nature to them. Such behavioral habits lend themselves perfectly to a direct instruction approach.

Application of the model. Lines will be taped to the floor with a place for each child marked on each line. Each child will practice taking his or her place on the different lines, on command, as appropriate to the purpose of the line-up. The children will be called to their places: by name at first, then by rows, and then by boys/girls. As each student takes a place on the line, he or she will establish a direction and a path from desk to line, depending on where the line-up is and how it is arranged. Short practice periods each day will establish the necessary behavioral patterns.

Assessment. The activity of lining up will be timed repeatedly, and a daily record will be kept of the increasing efficiency of the class in taking their places on the line.

Lesson Two: Defining a Line

Instructional model. Concept attainment.

Estimated time. Day Two of unit; 20 minutes.

Objective. Students will be able to describe the critical attributes of examples of *lines.*

Rationale for choice of model. A concept is a general idea derived from encounters with specific instances. Before this lesson and the lessons and units that will build on it can proceed, it is crucial that students have a working definition of lines. There will be many opportunities for them to refine their concept of line in the lessons and learning activities to follow. The intent of this concept attainment activity is to establish the general idea of line so that students have the groundwork on which to build successively sophisticated understandings. For example, these children eventually will learn that although two points define a line, every line extends in two directions to infinity. An infinite number of lines in a plane define that plane, which is also infinite in its single dimension. But these and many other very sophisticated concepts will be built on the initial understanding of what a line is and is not. Thus the choice of concept attainment as the instructional model to introduce the general idea of line is appropriate.

Application of the model. The children will sit in a circle on the floor. They will then be presented with a number of positive and negative examples of the concept.

> **Positive Examples**
> A clothesline
> A fishing line
> A line drawn on the board
> A line taped to the floor
> The cracks between the ceiling tiles and between the floor tiles
> A picture of the crosswalk on the back-to-school safety poster

Negative Examples
A bowl
A fork
A shoe
A picture of a fish

Assessment. A variety of items like those used in the lesson will be placed on a table. At different times of the day, ask each child individually to select something that can be used as a line or to represent a line and ask the child to explain the selection. Those children who did not understand the concept can receive individual attention at this stage.

Lesson Three: Refining the Concept of Line

Instructional model. Concept development.

Estimated time. Day Three of unit; 30 minutes.

Objective. Students will be able to distinguish between those items that are *lines* and those that are not.

Rationale for choice of model. Having acquired the basic idea of line, the students will now need practice in applying their idea to a variety of circumstances. It is not enough to know, conceptually, what a line is unless the learners can categorize things they encounter as lines or not lines. Although this skill was alluded to in the previous day's lesson, the question now is: Can the children think with their new ideas? The development of concepts rests only superficially on definition. To think *with* definitions, the learners will need practice in categorization. Categorization is the essence of concept development; thus that is this lesson's model of choice.

Application of the model. Pictures of different items will be selected and prepared for the flannel board; some items will be lines, and some will not. Of the lines, some will be curved, and some will be straight. The group will decide which items can be grouped together and will talk about what these items all have in common and why they are alike in some way.

Materials. Pictures of lines and pictures of other items; a flannel board and material to prepare the pictures.

Assessment. The teacher will observe the group and note those children who are not participating or who do not seem to understand the concept of line well enough to apply it to the task of discrimination. In addition, students will be asked to look for lines on their way to and from school, and they will discuss the examples they find in class.

Activity: The Line Game

Objective. The children will be able to describe staying inside and outside of a *line*.

Description of activity. Two lines will be drawn on the playground. The students will line up just outside the lines, on each side, to begin the hokey pokey song. The first time they will practice just "I put my body in, I put my body out" and so on. The emphasis will be on going inside and outside the line as they dance. The related concepts of inside and outside, however, will not be stressed at first. The activity will be repeated several days for fun and then used as an organizer in teaching students about "staying inside the line" (for example, "When we do the hokey pokey on the playground, what do we say we are doing with the line?").

Assessment. See if the children can follow the directions. Make a clipboard list of those children who cannot remember the words or who have coordination problems.

Notes on Lessons One, Two, and Three

The following is an anecdotal record of what happened when Miss Abbott taught her unit on lines.

The opening activity went very well except for the awkward moment when several of the children arrived at the same time and the lines got tangled. Miss Abbott decided that the next time she used this activity she would use soft clothesline rope.

Preparing the concept attainment lesson had taken more time than Miss Abbott had anticipated. Her first task was to define for herself the meaning of *line*. She wrote down that a line was something that had a beginning and an end and was connected. Then she realized that she could not tell what was the beginning and what was the end and just what was it that connected the two. The definition of a line was not as simple as she had thought. The dictionary had 30 different definitions of the word, but the root of the word was from the Latin *linea* for "linen thread." The definition she finally settled on was two ends connected by something that looks like a string or a rope.

After each child had been seated in a circle on the floor, Miss Abbott held up the word *line* and said, "This is a word we are going to learn all about today. This word is line."

Tommy said, "I can read that word."

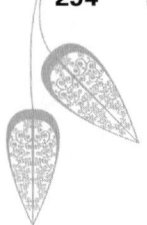

Miss Abbott remembered the high test results for Tommy. "Good, Tommy," she said and continued. "Look at the line you followed into the room today. Tell me what it looks like."

The children said that it was made of yarn, that it went from one place to the other, and that you could follow it. "Let's look at another line and see if it is like the line you followed."

This time she held up a clothesline. "Is this one made of yarn?"

"No," came a chorus of answers.

"Then a line doesn't have to be made out of yarn. How is this line like the one you followed?"

"Well, it has two ends like a snake. But it doesn't have a head and a tail," said one of the children. Several of the children began to talk about snakes, and Miss Abbott had to bring them back.

"Tommy, point to the two ends of the line you followed in and to the two ends of the clothesline. That's right, Tommy. Now, everybody find the two ends of your line. Can we say that a line has two ends? What is between the two ends?" Miss Abbott asked as she held up the line of yarn and the clothesline. The children were puzzled, and several began to creep away from the group. Miss Abbott realized that for most of them this was too hard, but Tommy came to the rescue.

"Something that's skinny and bends," he said. This response caught the attention of the children, and they got back in the circle.

Miss Abbott held up a fishing line. "Does this have two ends?"

"Yes," they chorused. "And you can catch fish on it," one of the little boys said.

"Are the two ends connected by something that is—can I use the word *thin*, Tommy?—that is thin and can bend?"

Shanice said that she liked the word *skinny*, and so did the rest of the class. Miss Abbott decided that for the time being she would accept their word.

Next she pointed to a line that had been taped to the floor. "This is a line, too," she said. "Does it have two ends?"

"Yes," they chorused.

"Is it skinny?"

"Yeeess!" They were really into the action now.

"But," she asked, "will this line bend?"

Tommy did not want to lose his definition. "You could draw another line that would be bent," he said.

"Yes, Tommy, you are right. But this line will not bend. So, in your definition, a line doesn't have to bend. Tommy, you hold up the clothesline. Shanice, you hold up the fishing line, and all of you look at your yarn lines. What can we see that is the same about them all?"

"Well, they have two ends, and they have a skinny thing in between and they are floppy," said Maria.

"Don't forget the line taped to the floor," said Miss Abbott. "Is that line floppy?"

Maria liked the word *floppy,* but she agreed that the line taped to the floor was not. "Our lines have two ends with something skinny in between."

Miss Abbott thought about how "skinny" seemed to please the children. It had not occurred to her when she planned the lesson, but it was a word that seemed to fit. She held up a cup. "Is this a line?" she asked.

"No," they said in unison. "Because it doesn't have two ends and it isn't skinny."

"It isn't floppy either," said Maria, attempting to get her word back in.

Tommy said, "It doesn't have to be floppy, stupid."

Miss Abbott put her hand on Tommy's shoulder and said, "No one in this class is stupid. We all work together." She made a mental note to think through why Tommy needed to say what he did and to plan for a lesson soon in which they could discuss name calling.

Miss Abbott held up a long piece of string. "Is this a line?" she asked.

"Well, it has two ends with something skinny between. Yes."

A fork got a quick rejection, as did a plate and a hat.

The next day they had lesson three, using the concept development model, in which she asked the children to put together all the things that were lines and those things that were not. So far, so good, she thought. And then she realized that she was really excited about what was happening in the class. Exciting and stimulating were two words that had been missing from her classroom for some time.

Epilogue

As the weeks progressed, Miss Abbott became more enthusiastic about the abilities of all her students. Tommy, who was often the catalyst for ideas and a source of information, gradually developed a respect for the rights and abilities of the other students. As concepts grew one upon the other, the children responded to the logic behind what they were being asked to learn. One memorable moment came during the lesson on squares when they were discussing the relationship between lines and squares. Shanice said, "You know, Miss Abbott, *skinny* isn't a very good word to describe a line." And all the class agreed.

In the months that followed, Miss Abbott introduced the related concepts of circle and square building on the concept definition of a line as two ends connected by something that looks like a string or rope. A clothesline was used to show how simple geometric figures could be formed from a line.

Summary

Knowledge of the backgrounds and abilities of the students in a class is essential to planning, if that knowledge is coupled with a determination to see each child's needs as a welcome challenge. Young children can be presented with content that is challenging and interesting to them as long as appropriate instructional techniques are used.

Teachers need to adapt state standards into clear objectives, design developmentally appropriate assessments to evaluate whether or not students have reached the objectives, and then decide on which instructional models and strategies would best help students develop the skills necessary for success on the assessment.

Extensions

ACTIVITIES

1. Construct a flow chart that shows the steps Miss Abbott used in planning the unit described in this chapter.
2. Outline a unit on geometric shapes that might follow Miss Abbott's unit on "learning about lines."
3. Write a detailed lesson plan for one of the lessons described in the chapter. Include KUD objectives, formative assessments, and instructional procedures.

REFLECTIVE QUESTIONS

1. Miss Abbott checks the readiness test scores of her future students. How much influence should readiness tests have on instructional decision making?
2. Is Miss Abbott using backward design in her planning? Explain your position.
3. What advice would you give Miss Abbott as she plans her next unit?

15 A Middle School Case Study

chapter OBJECTIVES

You Will Understand
- Effective instructional planning requires knowledge of content, students, and pedagogy

You Will Know
- The components and thinking behind an interdisciplinary unit
- How a common theme can be used to connect disparate pieces of content
- Examples for selecting instructional models to meet a wide variety of goals

You Will Be Able To
- Reflect and comment on the instructional planning of a group of teachers
- Develop a detailed plan for one lesson in a unit
- Determine if the teachers described in this chapter used the principles of backward design

The interdisciplinary teaching team for the seventh grade at Mumford Middle School had a problem. Some of the teachers on the team, which covered the subjects of math, social studies, language arts, and science, were concerned that the students were fixed in their opinions. As Alice Brown, the science teacher, said one morning in frustration, "Narrow-minded, that's what they are! These kids just won't entertain a new thought about a fact or idea in the courses they take or about each other. Sometimes teaching them feels more like plowing rock than planting seeds."

So began a conversation that would extend over several days and result in one of the most exciting teaching experiences any of these teachers had known. Like many teachers, the team had fallen into a rut, but they were about to find a way out of it.

Sam Lopez, the math teacher, who was a native of the small midwestern farming community in which the school was located, came to the defense of the local community. "This may not be cosmopolitan Madison Avenue, Alice, but in place of refinement, there is good, solid common sense in this community and in these kids. Their behavior is generally very good, and you know it is. They do what they are told and what their parents expect them to do."

"Yes," replied Alice, "but they also think the way they are told, and they can be cruel to those who are different in any way. In science, it is very important to be willing to look at ideas with an open and inquiring mind."

Mary Teague, the social studies teacher, took her usual role of conciliator. "I appreciate that they are dependable and that they are motivated to do well. I, too, however, am concerned that we challenge their intellects and encourage them to play with ideas instead of being so concerned that they get a good grade."

Henry Martin, the English and language arts teacher and the usual bemused observer, said, "If we decide to challenge their intellects, we'd better be sure that the school board doesn't decide to challenge us. Those board members may not be very enthusiastic about the kids playing around with ideas."

"I'm not thinking of turning them into radical revolutionaries," said Alice. "I just want them to have some perspective, a point of view broader than that shared by the members of this community."

"Sounds radical enough to me," Henry rejoined. "Oh, well, it might break the boredom for a while."

Alice ignored the cynicism. "It just so happens that lately I've been thinking of a unit of study based on the concept of *perspective*. My hope is that I can get our students to consider the various ways in which a problem may be approached, whether it is a problem in science or in any other subject."

"It's funny you should mention the word *perspective* this morning, Alice," said Sam. "I have been working on a unit in geometry, where perspective is all-important. My thought was that because the kids are fascinated with the design capabilities of computers, I might introduce them to linear perspective in a way that would teach them both about a new design program we have and about lines in three-dimensional space."

Alice responded with renewed enthusiasm, momentarily forgetting her frustration with the students. "You know, understanding the use of perspective marked the Renaissance. It literally changed forever the way we would describe and know the universe. I have always wanted to know more about the mathematical principles involved in the great paradigm shift of the Renaissance. I'd also like to teach the impact of perspective on our understanding of the physical world, particularly in regard to mapmaking. Could we plan this unit together?" she asked Sam.

"The concept of perspective certainly fits into the unit I am preparing to teach on the westward movement," Mary interjected. "I've been trying to think how to get across the idea that historians have their own perspectives that influence the way in which they recount events. No doubt, any historical perspective differs from that of the people who were involved in the events of history. Think how much difference it makes if one looks at the westward movement from the perspective of a settler or from the perspective of a Native American. I've heard it said that those who win the wars win the right to write the histories."

"You know, we haven't taught an interdisciplinary unit in a long time. Why don't we design a unit with a focus on the concept *perspective?*" said Alice, her excitement evident to all.

Henry abandoned his role of detached observer and enthusiastically joined in. "I have been planning a unit in literature on point of view, but perspective is really the basis for understanding the meaning of point of view. As I recall, the viewpoint—or point of view—is the point where parallel lines converge in a painting to convey a sense of depth." Turning to Alice, he said, "It was the Renaissance painters who rediscovered this technique from Greek writings and who were able to create perspective in their painting just as the mapmakers learned to do. Perspective is a much better concept to use for the focus of my unit. And I can choose material that will fit into your time frame of the westward movement," he continued, as he turned toward Mary. "That way we can look at historical perspective through the eyes of fictional characters as well as the historian. And each of the connections to perspective that we have discussed is addressed in our state standards."

As usual, the other team members were astonished at the wealth of information Henry could bring to a discussion when he chose. Everyone was ready, without actually putting the matter to any sort of vote, to try an interdisciplinary unit based on the concept of *perspective*.

The four team members shared a common planning time and were able to schedule the students for blocks of time each day. The rooms in which they taught were traditional classrooms except for one movable wall that allowed them to create a larger classroom for special purposes. In the past, their attempts at team teaching had been only partially successful, but this time they seemed to have ignited one another's interest.

At the next team meeting, Mary suggested that they brainstorm objectives for the unit. "For instance," she said, "I want the students to compare and contrast the perspectives of various groups regarding the westward movement. I want them to evaluate the perspective of the historian who is writing as well as to identify other possible perspectives of those who were involved in the events."

"I am concerned that they be able to define the term *perspective* in a general sense and then to see how perspective relates to writing," said Henry. "In their writing, I want them to use various perspectives to describe an event as well as develop more dynamic ways to describe how others feel and act."

"I want them to be able to accept the possibility that there are various ways to look at the same phenomenon," said Alice, "and I want them to recognize and value the importance of looking beyond and questioning what appears to be obvious. I also want them to use the scientific approach in solving problems that require inquiry, particularly problems in which perspective affects how we interpret the physical world."

"I want them to use parallel lines and viewpoint to create perspective in simple designs with the use of the computer," said Sam. "Some of these kids are way ahead of me already on the computer, and I am really going to have to do my homework to keep up. That's part of the great fun we have teaching in a field that is developing faster than any of us can imagine, let alone keep up with. But in all the excitement of computers, I want the students to develop respect for the capabilities of this tool in describing three-dimensional phenomena on a two-dimensional screen."

Henry rolled his eyes as he sensed just how enthusiastic everyone was becoming, but he did so very slightly, not wishing to offend as much as to poke a little fun. But Alice wasn't going to let the seriousness of the moment pass. "And all of us are concerned that the students develop more understanding for others and increase their willingness to consider another point of view in solving problems in human relations," she said.

"We have our objectives for the unit right in front of us," said Mary. "There is *so much* content that we could incorporate into this unit! I think we should each bring to our next meeting an outline of the most important concepts that need to be covered in each discipline. The state standards can help with this and we can develop a common big idea."

When they met again, each of them had diagrammed the main concepts that they thought should be included in the unit on *perspective* based on their understanding of the content and the requirements of the state standards (see Table 15.1).

Table 15.1 Interdisciplinary Unit on Perspective: Concepts and Skills

Students will understand that the study of perspective—how we look at things—allows for rich connections among a variety of topics.	
Geometry	point, line, plane, parallel, convergent, design, linear perspective
Science	exploration, mapmaking, scientific inquiry, nature of science
Literature	point of view, characters, plot, narrator
History	point of view, participants, events, document analysis, historiography
Art	viewpoint, convergence, parallel, lines, illusion

It was obvious that *viewpoint,* so important in creating perspective, had become an essential concept as it applied to understanding events and ideas relating to perspective. The teachers then realized that the meaning of *viewpoint* was one that the art teacher, Mrs. Fisk, could best explain to the students. She agreed that a discussion on the point at which parallel lines converge in a painting, or in a design, to create the illusion of space would serve as an excellent advance organizer for the study of perspective. It was exciting to think that a fundamental concept of the art curriculum would be the focal point for study in many different disciplines simultaneously. This single concept would bring everything together, just as it had during the Renaissance! After their discussion with Mrs. Fisk, she agreed to do the keynote lesson twice—each time in the double classroom with two of the teachers and their classes present.

The Mumford Plan

When designing the unit, the team members at Mumford Middle School decided to emphasize the geometry and earth science portions during the first part of the unit, followed by the literature and history sections. The art teacher's introductory lesson would extend across two days, at which time the main concepts related to perspective would be introduced. *Viewpoint,* or physical point of view, would be tied to visual perspective and to ideas and attitudes.

Mrs. Fisk planned to teach the definition of *viewpoint* by using the concept attainment model, allowing the definition to serve as an organizer and point of reference for all the team teachers throughout the unit. Her idea was to spend one day helping the students to capture elementary perspective in their own drawings. The next day she would bring in prints of pre-Renaissance and Renaissance art to use as positive and negative examples of perspective in art. A collection of M. C. Escher's pen-and-ink drawings, in which the mathematician/artist plays with perspective in a variety of ways, would serve as material for a culminating reinforcement activity. She would close with a brief lesson on how the students could achieve such play and deliberate ambiguity in their own drawings.

Following this lesson, all the teachers would explain the plans for the unit as it pertained to their classes; provide an outline of assignments, assessments, and activities; and answer any questions the students might have about the unit.

A diagnostic test of the students' understanding of the content to be covered, to provide valuable information to the teachers regarding any changes or modification that might need to be made in the unit's design, would be given at this point. The test was particularly important to Sam in setting up the teams for instruction in computer skills.

The geometry and science lessons would be taught for approximately 3 weeks. After the students had a basic introduction to computer-aided design (CAD), they would learn to create simple three-dimensional designs with the use of the computer. Sam decided that a form of the jigsaw model used in conjunction with direct instruction would be an excellent way to teach the principles of CAD. Students would first work through a tutorial on the basics of computer design individually. Then, pairs of students would be given elementary problems to solve with immediate feedback on their success. Next, teams of students with a range of achievement related to the computer would be formed, making it possible for students with more advanced computer skills to work with those having less skill. Each team would be charged with solving a different problem set while acquiring a different set of computer skills associated with computer-aided design. Individual team members would be expert in a particular aspect of design, and they would have the responsibility of teaching other students in their study group.

Following the computer lessons, the science teacher would introduce the relationship of perspective to an understanding of the physical world, particularly in recording what is observed through the design of maps. Alice would present puzzling but relatively common problem situations involving perspective. The students would solve these problems with an inquiry approach using the Suchman model (see Chapter 7). For instance, one problem would be to describe the appearance of a ship on the horizon and explain why it seems to grow larger as it draws near. Another problem would be to explain why the moon seems to be very large on the horizon but appears to grow smaller as it rises in the sky. The third and most difficult problem the students would be asked to solve by inquiry would be that of how to transfer the surface of a sphere (like a globe of Earth) onto a flat surface without distorting the relative sizes of land masses.

With these introductions to the concept of *perspective* as a foundation, Mary and Henry would work with the students toward an understanding of the way in which individuals interpret events in literature and in history, stressing that interpretation often depends on the individual's point of view. They decided that concept development, direct instruction, and jigsaw models would be effective in meeting their objectives. (This part of the unit is described in more detail in the next section.)

To illustrate how the models approach to teaching would work in this unit, we present the detailed lesson design from the portion that focused on the concept of *perspective* in history and literature, which is described in Table 15.2.

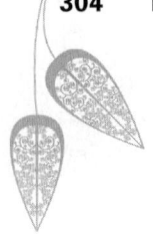

Table 15.2 Perspective in History and Literature, Middle School Plan

Lesson	Time	Objectives	Models and Activities
1. Point of view (4 days)	4 hours	1. Students will know that a variety of points of view can exist on a given subject. 2. Students will understand that personal attitudes and beliefs have an impact on the meaning of *point of view* and *perspective* in art, science, and mathematics. 3. Students will know the meanings of *bias* and *preconception*.	Concept development Vocabulary acquisition
2. Perceptions (3 days)	3 hours	Students will be able to describe how preconceptions and experience can sometimes override perceptions.	Direct instruction Role play
3. Relating perceptions to perspective (3 days)	3 hours	1. Students will understand that the way individuals perceive events is related to the concept of *perspective* in literature and history. 2. Students will be able to identify various perspectives in writing.	Jigsaw Classroom discussion

Unit: Perspective—It All Depends on Where You Were When

Teaching time. 2 weeks.

Objectives.

Students Will Understand

- The meaning of perspective in geometry and science is parallel to the same concepts in literature and history

Students Will Know

- The definition of perspective as it is defined in literature and history

Students Will Be Able To

- Relate the concept *perspective* to literature and history by recognizing how individuals perceive both real and fictional events

- Identify various perspectives in a situation, represent the point of view of each participant, and explain how the point of view determines the perspective
- Describe how previous experiences and preconceptions affect the perception of events
- Characterize a perspective other than their own in relation to a situation

Advance organizer. Relate the meaning of *viewpoint* as it has been discussed in art, geometry, and science to the application of the term in literature, history, and human relations. Introduce the idea that it is the point of view that determines perspective.

Lesson One: Toward a Perspective on Point of View

Instructional models. Concept development and vocabulary acquisition.

Estimated time. 2 hours.

Objectives.

Students Will Understand
- A variety of points of view can exist on a single subject

Students Will Be Able To
- Relate attitudes and beliefs to the meaning of *point of view* and *perspective* in art, science, and math

Students Will Know
- The meanings of *bias* and *preconception* and will be able to relate these terms to their own experience

Rationale for choice of models. It has been said that there are three kinds of thinkers: those who believe that what they think is the only way to think, those who consider others who think like they do to be the best thinkers, and those who can think in several ways about the same thing. The psychologist Jean Piaget termed the first thinker *egocentric*, the second thinker *concrete*, the last and best thinker *formal*. But Piaget's great contribution to psychology was in proving that the child learns from experience by constructing a model of how the world is. Concept development will provide the students the opportunity to see that different points of view (of possibly equal validity) can be held by reasonable thinkers on the same topic. As they have the chance to discriminate between different points of view on a similar topic, they will see that each thinker is at once a concrete thinker, who sees the world through one set of eyes, and a formal thinker, who can recognize the reasonableness of alternative views of the same facts and ideas. Vocabulary acquisition will provide a definition for the terms *bias* and *preconception*.

Application of the models. After the students have clearly identified the terms, they will be given a series of quotations representing points of view that are both alike and different in various ways. For instance, some will represent the same bias, some will be about the same event, some will be spoken by the same person. The students will be asked to group and categorize these quotations and then to explain the reason for their decisions. The students will work in pairs and then come together as a large group to discuss their decisions and the reasons for their decisions.

Assessment. At the conclusion of this lesson, the students will discuss what they learned earlier in the unit during the math and science portions and how that material relates to the new learning of this lesson. Students will be asked to make two explicit connections on a card to be given to the teacher as they exit the class. This discussion will also serve as a midpoint evaluation of the students' progress.

Lesson Two: Perception—It Depends on Where You Are Coming From

Instructional models. Direct instruction and role play.

Estimated time. 3 hours.

Objective. The students will be able to describe how preconceptions and experience affect the perception of an event.

Rationale for choice of model. Instruction will be both indirect and direct as the teachers will set up a circumstance that gives rise to questions to be answered by direct instruction followed by a role play that will provide the material for a class discussion. (As this example demonstrates, direct instruction does not equal passive learning.) Basically, the questions the teachers will pose and the activities in which the students will engage center on the issue of perception: what one is predisposed to see versus what one sees. But predisposition is always governed by three factors, and those factors are the point of this instruction. By setting up a series of experiences for the students whereby they see that the relation between where they are (figuratively and literally) and what they are observing determines what they see, the stage is set for presenting the three factors that define "where the observer is coming from."

Application of the models. The lesson will begin with the reading of a description of a house. The description includes the setting of the house; the number of windows, doors, and rooms; the present furnishings and decorations; where the occupants keep their valuables; and so on. Half the class will be asked to read the account as if they were a professional burglar, and the other half will read the account as if they were a prospective buyer of the house. (Because directions to the students will be written, rather than given orally, each half of the class will be unaware of the alternative perspective taken by the other half.) Following a silent reading of the passage, students will retell what they recall. (Research has shown that readers will focus their attention on the aspects of the information that bear on their interest [Goetz et al., 1983].) This initial experience will provide dramatic proof that the same experience for different people is a different experience. When perception is different, experience is different.

Next the teachers will have one group of students role play an armed robbery and have the observers write what they perceive to have happened. A second group will then enact the robbery after having been given additional information by the teacher. The observers will be asked to reevaluate their original perspectives based on perceptions they now have and with different information. This activity can be continued until all groups have an opportunity to participate in the role play. Following the role plays will be a discussion of the effect of the change of perspective on their reactions.

Using this activity as an organizer, the teachers will present the three factors that influence the perspective of those who witness events:

1. The viewpoint of the perceiver
2. Previous experience of the observer
3. Preconceptions

After these have been explained, with many examples, students will be questioned and will be asked to give examples themselves to check for understanding. More guided practice will occur when students view a video of an accident and then identify the various perspectives of the witnesses as these relate to point of view, possible previous experiences, and preconceptions. For independent practice, the students will be given an assignment to describe an event depicted on a television sitcom from the point of view, previous experience, and preconceptions of the different characters involved. They will then be asked to retell the event using another point of view, experience, and preconception.

Assessment. Students will be given a worksheet to take home that will ask them to answer specific questions relating to the television program. Those students who choose to write their own essay may do so, but those who have more difficulty in writing may follow the format of the worksheet. These worksheets and essays will be evaluated to determine if the class understood the assignment.

Lesson Three: Relating Perception and Perspective

Instructional model. Jigsaw.

Estimated time. 3 hours class time plus outside work in preparation.

Objectives.

Students Will Be Able To
- Relate the concept of *perspective* to literature and history by identifying how individuals, both real and fictional, perceive events from their particular points of view
- Identify various perspectives in selections of writing, and explain the point of view of each author
- Explain how perception determines perspective

Rationale for choice of models. Jigsaw is both an instructional model and an instructional activity, with the great virtues of accommodating a wide range of student achievement in a single classroom and allowing for great efficiency of effort on the part of the group. In this instance, the students can collectively read many selections and thus encounter many historical and fictional perspectives and points of view. By cooperating in their learning and sharing in their understandings, they will cover much ground quickly, reading literally hundreds of pages of material and experiencing the same ideas through many different eyes. Jigsaw thus allows each learner to come to the insights of many different learners merely by sharing his or her own insights.

Application of the models. The students will be assigned to teams of four, with a range of achievement in each group. Each individual in the team will be given a reading assignment related to the westward movement; assignments will be selected to match the reading readiness of different team members. The teams will be given different sets of readings: some short stories, some selections from novels, some from original source documents, and some from textbook chapters on the westward expansion. The students have 3 days to study the material and will be directed to discuss their selections with members of a study group who have been assigned readings similar to their own. They are to identify the perspective of the author and of the major characters or persons in the story or essay and then to explain this perspective to the other members of their team. Following team discussions, the class as a whole will discuss the selections and the various perspectives presented in the material using the classroom discussion model.

Assessment. Students will be provided a short excerpt about a family making the trip West. They will write an essay that demonstrates their attainment of the lesson's objectives.

Epilogue

At the end of the actual unit of study, the interdisciplinary teaching team had dinner together to discuss and evaluate their experience in teaching the unit. Although some activities had been unsuccessful, everyone wholeheartedly agreed that the unit had been a success. The assessments of how well the students had met the cognitive objectives indicated a high rate of achievement, and attitudinal surveys, designed to ensure anonymity, indicated that most of the students had enjoyed the unit and had an increased awareness of different perspectives.

The team remembered the final discussions with particular pleasure. The students had been presented with a situation that involved a person from another country with an entirely different culture enrolling at the school. The discussion centered on the various problems the student would encounter and how that individual's perspective would differ from that of others. The teachers had taped and compared the various discussions. All agreed that the students had gained insights into how others might feel about a particular situation. The teachers had also learned that these young people had the capacity to deal with complicated ideas and to respond to material that challenged their preconceptions. "My perception is that these really are a great bunch of kids," said Henry. And to that, there was agreement all around.

Summary

Cooperative planning by teachers across disciplines can provide a rewarding professional experience. In addition, such cooperation enriches the learning experience for students, particularly young adolescents, who enjoy seeing the way in which a concept threads meaning through a variety of disciplines, increasing the understanding of each.

Interdisciplinary study provides the opportunity to scaffold student learning. Comprehension is increased when students can contrast many examples within and across disciplinary areas that provide a deep comparison pool (Willingham, 2009). In addition, student interest and motivation in one area may spill over to another.

It takes time to organize and prepare interdisciplinary units, and teachers must be willing to take the time to plan cooperatively. The rewards for both teachers and students are high and the use of instructional models can help to support the effort.

Extensions

ACTIVITIES

1. Discuss interdisciplinary teaching with a group of teachers. What do they see as the costs and benefits? Do the same with a group of students at the age level in which you are teaching or hope to teach. What are the difficulties and benefits they identify?
2. Think about the big ideas, concepts, and skills that you are or will be teaching. Can you identify skills or ideas that would be a good fit for an interdisciplinary approach? Develop an overarching understanding and some disciplinary

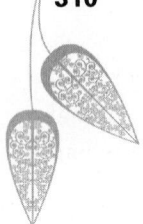

concepts and skills that can be linked together and molded into an interdisciplinary unit.
3. Write a detailed lesson plan for one of the lessons described in the chapter. Include KUD objectives, formative assessments, and instructional procedures.

REFLECTIVE QUESTIONS

1. What are the arguments against asking first-year teachers to participate in interdisciplinary work? What are the arguments for first-year teachers participating in such an effort?
2. How would you evaluate the role of the art teacher in the unit on perspective described in this chapter? Would you have increased her involvement? How? Why? Why not?
3. How would you evaluate the use of backward design by the teachers in this chapter? Was it used? How? How might backward design support interdisciplinary efforts?

16 A High School Case Study

chapter OBJECTIVES

You Will Understand
- Effective instructional planning requires knowledge of content, students, and pedagogy

You Will Know
- The opportunities for using diverse instructional models in a high school classroom
- The relationship between desired objectives and instructional models
- The role of student past achievement and experiences in choosing content and instruction

You Will Be Able To
- Reflect and comment on the instructional planning of a high school English teacher
- Develop a detailed plan for one lesson in a unit
- Determine if the teacher described in this chapter used the principles of backward design

As the pungent scent of Rudy's Dry Cleaners greeted Jake Samuels, an unfamiliar voice said, "Hi, Mr. Samuels."

"Hi," responded Mr. Samuels, trying to place the friendly face.

"I'm Chris Pezzoli. I go to Madison High School. May I help you?"

"My cleaning, please," Mr. Samuels answered, as he handed Chris the laundry ticket, still curious about where he had seen this young man. He was just a face in a sea of faces in the halls at Madison.

"Yes, sir. Coming right up." Chris started the line of clothes moving around. As Mr. Samuels's suit appeared, Chris handed it to him, saying, "I always wanted to have you for English, but I'm in a general class. I've heard what a good teacher you are, but you teach only the advanced classes." He hesitated, feeling a little embarrassed at his own boldness.

311

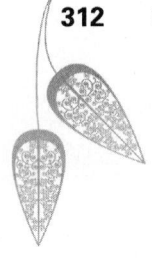

"Thanks for the vote of confidence. I'm sorry I'm not teaching you, Chris. I'd like to."

"So long." Chris shrugged and smiled. "See you around."

As he left the cleaners, Mr. Samuels thought about Chris. He thought about his own schedule. Now that he was chairperson of the department, he taught only three classes. And Chris was right, they were all top-track classes. The encounter reminded him, though, that he missed the general classes he used to teach. Those students struck a special chord for him, possibly because his was the last English class they might take. He remembered how he always wanted to give it all to them—everything he loved about English—served up on a silver platter so invitingly that they would surely seek more.

He began to think aloud. "Instead we water it down, trying to make it more palatable. But there's a contradiction in that. Shouldn't it be just the reverse? Shouldn't we enrich the content of classes for general students?"

As he turned onto Madison Avenue, he was deep in thought. Sure, there had been problems when he taught general education and remedial classes. His teaching style of lecture and discussion did not work for students who had difficulty taking notes or paying attention for long periods. But he had learned so much in the past few years as department chairperson, observing other teachers and attending workshops and in-service sessions on instructional strategies. He had learned to use a variety of instructional models in his advanced classes, and he was certain that these would work well with all students. The idea he was contemplating would give him an opportunity to put his theory to the test. He wanted to try it.

At 4 o'clock the following Monday afternoon, Mr. Samuels poked his head into the classroom next to his. His colleague, Ms. O'Brien, was correcting papers.

"Liz, do you have a minute?"

"Sure, come on in. I'm always too drained to get anything accomplished this time of day. Good to see you, Jake. How do you manage to look so chipper at the end of a long day?"

"Thanks, I don't always feel chipper. It's just a facade I put on. I need to talk to you, though. I met a student of yours the other day, Chris Pezzoli. Tell me about him."

"Well, Chris is a very nice young man, imaginative and hard working, very likable. He's in my fourth-period class. I see his parents around town now and again. His dad was laid off when the woolen mill closed. He does odd jobs, forced self-employment, he calls it, but he hasn't been able to pick up anything steady. Chris's mother works, but they really need what Chris brings in from his job at a dry cleaner's. I know he's going to work there full time after graduation. I'm trying to talk him into taking community college courses at night, but I think it's futile. Of course, if his dad does find something steady. . . ." Her words trailed off without much hope in her voice.

Mr. Samuels interrupted, "I've been thinking about these kids in the general classes and about how much I miss teaching them. I had an idea. How would you like to try switching classes fourth period for about 4 weeks as a kind of experiment? I have some ideas I'd like to try with the kids. I thought I'd try to teach them *Macbeth*." After a pause, he grinned. "Think I'm crazy? You'd be teaching the poetry of the romantics, not one of my favorite units, but just your cup of tea, I know."

Ms. O'Brien looked at him for a minute as his suggestion took shape in her mind. "Do I think you're crazy? Yes. Do I think it's a good idea? It just might be an excellent idea. I'd love to see how they would respond . . . and I'd love to have a crack at your kids. Nineteenth-century poetry is my first love."

Mr. Samuels's Plan

That night Mr. Samuels put aside the papers he was planning to grade. He thought about Chris and the large, probably slightly jaded group he would face. But the challenge of it was energizing; he was more excited than he had been for some time. He began making notes on what he wanted to accomplish.

First, he wanted them to enjoy the play. He pondered a minute, then crossed out *enjoy* and replaced it with an overworked word he seldom used in such a context, *love*. Yes, he wanted them to *love* this play, maybe the finest piece of literature ever written. He starred that goal. It would guide everything he did those 4 weeks. Next, he wanted them to know how shrewd Shakespeare was and how relevant his thinking remains today.

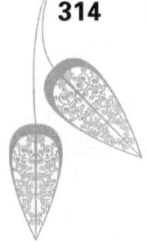

Mr. Samuels wanted them to examine the concept *ambition* and how it can be a constructive force in moderation and a dangerous force in excess. To do this, they must understand the complexity of Macbeth's and Lady Macbeth's characters. If these characters are seen as all bad, the students would miss a great deal of the play's wisdom. He wanted them to grasp the power of suggestion and of what it could mean to plant an idea in an all-too-fertile mind. Further, he wanted them to be stirred by the beauty, subtlety, and bawdiness of the language. He hoped to draw them into this Elizabethan world, much as Shakespeare had drawn his audiences into his plays.

Where did these goals come from? Mr. Samuels was an expert teacher with years of experience, and because of that he was willing to rely intuitively on his judgment as a teacher, his expertise in *Macbeth*, his convictions about these students' needs, and his knowledge of his state standards. Thus, with some confidence, he translated his vaguely defined goals into a specific list.

The students would do the following:

Students Will Know
- The poetic rhythm of iambic pentameter
- The major distinguishing characteristics of Elizabethan England
- The meaning of the phrase *power of suggestion*
- The complex qualities of the major characters in *Macbeth*
- *Macbeth* is a play that often evokes strong feelings in readers—many readers love the play and believe it is the best play ever written in English literature
- The themes in the story of *Macbeth* are as powerful and relevant as when it was first written

Students Will Understand
- Ambition is constructive in moderation and harmful in excess

Students Will Be Able To
- Master difficult material and as a consequence gain confidence in their own intellect

In the not-so-distant past, he might have stopped his general planning at this point and begun to think in terms of daily lessons. He had recently realized, however, that he needed to be far more precise in his planning. This meant listing specific student needs after researching the students' backgrounds. It meant selecting specific objectives and models that would help him reach those objectives. It also meant devising means of evaluating how well he had achieved those objectives. It sounded complicated, but it was becoming second nature and saved time and effort in the end. Most of all, it increased his sense of satisfaction.

During the next week he gathered a lot of data: He talked to Ms. O'Brien; he reviewed records and test scores; he casually and unobtrusively observed the class he was to teach; and he carefully reread the play and outlined the content for essential understandings. He remembered Chris's shrug. It had been eloquent; it had said, "We don't deserve the best."

Mr. Samuels believed that the students needed to be given challenging material, and implicit in his choice of *Macbeth* was the statement, "You can do it; I will not teach down to you." But that in turn implied a commitment to give the students the support they needed to become independent. Although the thought seemed almost contradictory, it implied that he must not fail them or allow them to fail themselves. He knew they would not, but if the unit were to build their confidence, they would first have to commit themselves to the challenge, to like what they were doing well enough not to fail in it. He listed what the students would need:

1. To be presented with challenging material
2. To know that someone thought they could grasp difficult material
3. To be taken seriously and have their opinions sought and valued
4. To gain confidence in their own abilities
5. To talk about important issues and real feelings
6. To gain a sense of accomplishment because they had mastered difficult material successfully

Based on the combination of goals and needs that he had listed, Mr. Samuels wrote general objectives for the unit on *Macbeth* and considered how he might evaluate the unit's success. After all, if he could not demonstrate to himself that the students had learned and profited from this unit, then he should stay with the advanced classes. Mr. Samuels wrote his objectives, including methods to evaluate each objective:

1. Students will understand that *Macbeth* is a compelling piece of literature and be interested in learning more about it. This will be evaluated by using a pre- and post-unit survey in which students can react to items without fear of being identified.

2. Students will be able to relate themes in the play, *Macbeth,* to their daily lives. This will be evaluated through the skits that students design to place scenes from *Macbeth* into contemporary settings.

3. Students will understand how the sound of words can augment meaning and humor. They will know the poetic rhythm of iambic pentameter. This will be evaluated by having them present a piece of their favorite music and explain how beat and lyrics work together.

4. Students will be able to analyze the main characters and identify the elements in those characters that create complexity. This objective can be evaluated through either or both words and images. Pictures can be drawn or a collage constructed or an essay written about one or more of the characters and their varied and conflicting characteristics. (He knew that not all students are successful in communicating their knowledge through words. The students could, however, sometimes express concepts through a different medium. Although there are a number of written assignments in the unit, Mr. Samuels also wanted to be sure that he measured what he was teaching and not just the students' reading and writing skills.)

5. Students will know the major distinguishing characteristics of Elizabethan England, and they will convey their knowledge by teaching some aspect of Elizabethan society to a small group of peers. Evaluation will be based on student preparation and performance in teaching the material.

6. Students will know the meaning of the phrase *power of suggestion* and the idea of self-fulfilling prophecy. Students will be asked to give examples of each from their everyday life. Examples will be evaluated based on relevance and quality.

With these objectives in mind, Mr. Samuels contemplated the possible models he would use to achieve them, in what sequence he would use them, and how much time he would allot for each part of the unit plan:

1. He would start with a concept attainment lesson on classics . . . no, he would use the term *best sellers,* because that had more drawing power and was much more appropriate. Shakespeare, after all, was very conscious of box-office appeal. (Later, they would talk about the distinction between a classic and a best seller and about how some works of art are both.) He would use positive examples of best sellers, such as the Bible, *The Kite Runner* (the movie and book), and hip-hop music. His negative examples would consist of a lesser-known short story from their text, a poem he had written, a record called *Comin' Home* that a friend had cut, a favorite painting by a little-known artist from his hometown. Once they could define the concept of *best seller,* he would ask what elements they would include if they were trying to write a play that would be a *best seller*. He would make a list of their ideas (he predicted that they would mention things like suspense, violence, and a little romance), and then as a group they would try to derive a set of standards of excellence from this list.

Later they would apply their standards to *Macbeth*, considered in the time of its first appearance in the Globe Theatre. How many of the same standards did Shakespeare seem to apply? What standards did he employ that they did not? What ingredients did they think of that Shakespeare did not cover (for example, the medium of delivery)? How would the passage of 400 years alter the standards of literature? These questions and others that arose would cast a new light on the play for these young readers.

2. Next, he would use direct instruction with lectures, monologues, videos, and artwork to give them background information on Shakespeare's life and times.

He would emphasize the tricks Shakespeare used to capture the attention of the audience in the opening scenes. He would show the ghost in the opening scene of *Hamlet* and the fight in the opening scene of *Romeo and Juliet* and would make the students guess what ploy would be used to open *Macbeth*.

3. He would also use a cooperative learning model, jigsaw, for background information. He would divide the class into five groups. The groups would research in preparation for teaching one another, in a variety of ways, about Elizabethan daily life (food, fashion, sports, sanitation, and so on), government, art and architecture, social class structure, education, and agriculture and industry.

4. He would open the play with the movie version of the first two acts of *Macbeth,* allowing the students to track the play in their books as they watched it. With a basic understanding of the plot firmly established, they would read Act 3 together, dramatizing various scenes and speeches and closely examining words, connotations, and concepts.

5. He would have the students perform the concept development model on the word *ambition.*

6. If the reading of Act 3 went well, they would read Act 4 together rather than view the film. He would use cooperative learning again for Act 5. In groups, they would role play various possible scenarios to present to the class.

7. While they were working on their scenes, he would interject a lesson on Lady Macbeth, using the synectics model. This would be a powerful and effective tool for showing them the contradictions and opposing forces within a character.

8. When they had finished the play, he would conduct a Socratic seminar. To gain a more sympathetic view of the main characters, they would examine the text through the eyes of specific characters and try to hypothesize particular feelings and motivations.

9. Finally, he would build on these insights by using an inquiry model to explore how the tragedy came about. At the beginning of the play, Macbeth is not such a villain. He had many good qualities, but in a very brief time he had caused the downfall of most of his country's leadership. How had this happened? Was so much violence plausible? This was the puzzle he hoped to get them to consider. He suspected that they would see the cause of the tragedy purely in terms of too much ambition, and he wanted them to look further, to delve into other causes. To understand the answer to the questions posed, they would have to go outside the play and inquire about conditions in 11th-century Scotland. What about the isolation of life then, near the height of the Middle Ages? Perhaps it is easier to plot against someone you seldom see. It was a violent time, with frequent attacks from unknown sources, and a street-gang mentality had developed in response to the constant threat against the territory. Macbeth had gained his reputation by warring successfully. Mr. Samuels wanted the students to search for these explanations themselves; he did not want to spoon-feed them.

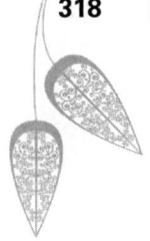

Table 16.1   Macbeth—A Study in Ambition Turned to Avarice

The Stage of Anticipation (before the Play)	The Stage of Realization (during the Play)	The Stage of Contemplation (after the Play)
Concept attainment on best sellers	Synectics on Lady Macbeth	Socratic seminar days
Direct instruction on background	Concept development and cause and effect on ambition/power of suggestion	Inquiry
Jigsaw—research and student presentations on background	Role plays of scenarios for Act 5	

Mr. Samuels charted the sequence of lessons within the unit that he had developed (see Table 16.1). He felt that one detailed lesson—using concept development and classroom discussion—held an important key for understanding the play. Initially, he had focused solely in this lesson on the concept *ambition*, but the more he thought about this, the more he felt two primary concepts—*ambition* and *the power of suggestion*—were inextricably woven in the play. This lesson is described in the next section.

Unit: Macbeth—A Study in Ambition Turned to Avarice

Description of Six Lessons on Ambition and the Power of Suggestion

Teaching time. 6 to 8 days, on approximately the following schedule:

Monday and Tuesday. Concept development lesson on the witches, culminating with a paragraph by each student on one group of items in the concept development lesson. The group's label will be the topic sentence, and the categorized items will be the supporting evidence.

Wednesday. Cause-and-effect lesson on the dual concepts of ambition and power of suggestion in *Macbeth*.

Thursday. Classroom discussion to continue, with emphasis on contemporary examples and how these concepts are connected in time and behaviors.

Friday. Students to find expression (such as a formal paper, collage, audio recording, drawing, or dialogue) for the single idea from the discussion that they found most interesting.

Monday. Students share their work in groups of three to get feedback, reactions, and suggestions.

Tuesday. Students share their final products with the class.

Common lesson objectives.

Students Will Be Able To

- Express in one of several artistic media their comprehension of the meaning of the word *ambition* in its best sense
- State orally their understanding of the danger of a trait possessed in excess
- Demonstrate in writing how the concept of *ambition* relates to their daily lives
- Infer, from discussions of events in the play, the causes of Macbeth's and Lady Macbeth's excessive ambition
- Describe in writing the power of suggestion by using examples from their daily lives
- Give examples of connections between the power of suggestion and ambition
- Generate hypotheses about the form witches might take in contemporary life

Rationale for Instructional Models: Concept Development and Cause and Effect. The students in this class will be likely to see things in rather concrete terms and to cast things in black and white. By verbalizing all the impressions they have of the witches in this play, they should see collectively what they may not see individually—namely, that the witches are symbolic of the fate that plays in every person's life. The students also need to see that the witches are Shakespeare's ploy for speaking directly to his audience about what is going on in Macbeth's mind and how strong the power of suggestion is. The cause-and-effect model will extend the ideas generated by the class in the concept development activity by looking at the relationship of the actions of a number of characters.

Application of the Concept Development Model. In effect, these two sophisticated concepts, the power of suggestion leading to unbridled ambition, will be approached through the witches.

Specific learning activities will have the students do the following:

1. List everything they remember about the witches (including inferences about their purpose).
2. Group these details.

3. Label these groups, showing their understanding and agreement on the reason for connecting the items.
4. Rethink these connections and new ones by forming new groups
5. Demonstrate their grasp of the witches' role by synthesizing the items and forming generalizations.

The following are some of the question that will direct this concept development lesson. The parenthetic instructions are reminders Mr. Samuels made to himself:

1. What specific things does the word *witches* bring to mind in the play *Macbeth*? Or name everything you can think of that is connected with the witches. (Do not stop until you have a comprehensive list.)
2. Look carefully at this list. Are there items that belong together or that are alike in some way?
3. Why do you think *cauldron* and *smoke* go together? (Do not label the group until the students have agreed on the reason for the grouping.)
4. Look at the original list again. Are there other groups we could put together? (Move slowly here. Give them time to rethink. List groups.)
5. Looking over the entire chalkboard, what can we say in general about witches?

Assessment of the concept development model. The students will express their enriched understanding of the witches' role by developing one of the groups into a paragraph in which the label becomes the topic sentence and the items become supporting evidence.

Application of the cause-and-effect model. A follow-up discussion to the concept development activity.

Estimated time. 2 days.

Stated Problem 1: Duncan's Murder
1. Discuss the problem—Duncan's murder.
2. Discuss causes and support. Ask students to discuss the reasons for King Duncan's murder with specific supporting examples.
3. Discuss effects and support. What are some of the effects of Duncan's murder? How do you know that these are effects?
4. Discuss prior causes and support. What caused Macbeth to believe the prophecies of the witches? What makes you think so?
5. Discuss subsequent effects and support. What were the effects of Macbeth's killing spree? Explain why you believe these effects were important.
6. What conclusions can you make about Macbeth and Duncan's murder?
7. What general statements can you make about our discussion?

Stated Problem 2: The Power of Suggestion and Ambition

1. Discuss the problem—the power of suggestion and ambition.
2. Discuss causes and support. What caused or contributed to Macbeth's ambition to become king? What makes you say so?
3. Discuss effects and support. What effect did this ambition have? Based on what evidence?
4. Discuss prior causes and support. What caused Macbeth and his wife to plot and murder? Explain your answers.
5. Discuss subsequent effects and support. What were the effects of Macbeth believing the prophecies? How do you know that the connections between the prophecies and your beliefs about subsequent effects are reasonable?
6. What conclusions can you make about ambition and the power of suggestion?
7. What general statements can you make about our discussion?

Assessment of the cause-and-effect model. The discussions would give Mr. Samuels an excellent idea of how well the students were grasping these concepts. But their knowledge would be taken one step further. They needed practice in writing, because this was a weak area, and it was necessary to know how well each student had grasped these understandings. He would ask them to do one of the following:

1. Choose one of the concepts (ambition or power of suggestion) and, in a one-page paper, give an example of how that concept has affected you in your daily life.
2. Write a one- to two-page paper on your goals in life and what forces have shaped them.
3. Write about the most ambitious person you know. Compare that person with King and Lady Macbeth.

The students were to write a first draft of their papers, share them with small groups of students to get *positive* suggestions, and then write a final draft.

Epilogue

When the four weeks ended, Mr. Samuels was pleased with the outcome of his experiment. By and large the students had responded to his vote of confidence in their ability; and, as he had suspected, they had been capable of talking about far more sophisticated ideas than they had been able to get on paper. He was disappointed that they had not been able to read more of the text together. As he had anticipated, it had been very difficult for them, and they had gotten discouraged and a bit defensive. The reading would have gone much better if they had seen the entire movie version first so that they would have known what to expect.

The instructional models had allowed the students to be active participants in the learning process. As a result, they had fidgeted less than normally and had seemed to take pride in participating. One highlight of the unit had been the synectics lesson. The following is an abbreviated description of that lesson.

Step 1. Students worked in groups of three to discuss Lady Macbeth and to brainstorm ideas and impressions of her. As follow-up, each student wrote a short paragraph about her. From these paragraphs, the students compiled a list of their strongest specific descriptive words: *shrill, shrew, iceberg, obsessed, conspirator, vixen, acid-tongued, murderous, two-faced, treacherous, sly, wily, conniving.*

Step 2. The students were asked to look at what they had written, to see if those words suggested an animal or a machine. Here are some examples of their answers:

tiger (stalks its prey secretly)
spider (lures its prey within its clutches)
stiletto (looks delicate, is deadly)

Step 3. Next, the students were asked to pick one item from the list, to pretend they were that object, and to describe how that object felt. They picked the stiletto. Here are some of the feelings individual students described:

I feel *dainty:* I am slender, small, tapering, fancy, swift (and deadly).
I feel *proud:* I am slim and fancy and quite beautiful.
I feel *sly:* I can be easily hidden, and I fly quickly, silently.
I feel *powerful:* I can hurt enemies before they even know it.
I feel *sneaky:* I can be concealed and used on someone unsuspecting.
I feel *lonely:* I have no friends; I sit alone in my case.
I feel *imprisoned:* I am kept covered and hidden.
I feel *helpless:* I have no control over when and how I am used.
I feel *deadly:* I am small and quiet but razor sharp.

Step 4. The students then were asked to look at their list of feelings and pick out words that seemed to contradict or fight with each other. They picked

proud and *sneaky*
dainty and *powerful*
imprisoned and *powerful*
dainty and *deadly*

Step 5. The class chose *imprisoned* and *powerful* to pursue. They were asked to name things that are both imprisoned and powerful. They named the following:

Nuclear power
A submarine captain

A boxer against the ropes
A wounded bear
A gladiator performing for an emperor
A tiger in a cage

Step 6. Returning to the subject of Lady Macbeth, Mr. Samuels asked the students to choose one of these images and compare it to her. Most chose "a gladiator performing for an emperor." They described her as powerful and deadly but a puppet of her ambition as a gladiator is a puppet of his emperor.

Summary

Teaching strategies that work for advanced classes are generally effective in all classes. The combination of careful planning and instructional variety allows students to become engaged in learning challenging material that is often withheld because it is thought too difficult. Students who may not go on to college have a particular need to encounter such content in primary and secondary school, for if not here, they may never have the chance.

The teachers described in this chapter and the two preceding are all individuals with different backgrounds, interests, and teaching experiences. Like those of you reading this text, they have a variety of concerns, and they approach instruction in different ways. They all share, however, a respect for their profession and a desire to improve, to find better ways to reach students, and to be successful in the classroom. They are all seeking answers.

None of these professionals is willing to follow prescriptive formulas in a mindless fashion, but all attend to essential concerns in their planning. The focus of these teachers is on the learners. They give careful thought to the outcome of instruction and assume the responsibility of evaluating to determine if what was taught was also learned.

It is our hope that these chapters raise more questions than answers in the minds of our readers. We believe that teaching is an adventure for life and that no day is like another. No one can tell you exactly how to teach. We have suggested directions; you must chart the course.

Extensions

ACTIVITIES

1. Visit a high school classroom that has been designated a lower-track class. Ask the students what they are learning and what they wish they were learning. Listen carefully to what the students are saying about school and the curriculum. Once your conversations are over, think about what the school can do to help each student have the opportunity to interact with challenging content.

2. Construct a unit blueprint or outline in your content area that would expose lower-achieving students to challenging content. What issues influence your instructional decisions? What role does background knowledge play? Must students be able to demonstrate all prerequisite skills to interact with this content?
3. Draw a graphic organizer for the instructional decisions made in this chapter's unit or for a unit that you will be teaching. Was the process of organizing the information graphically helpful? In what ways?

REFLECTIVE QUESTIONS

1. The chapter case study is focused on *Macbeth*. What challenging content might you teach in your content area to a group of students who have not had the opportunity for rich content and varied instruction? Why? How would you make the case to your peers that this content is reasonable for lower-achieving students?
2. Mr. Samuels used a variety of instructional models. Were they used appropriately? How might you determine the answer to this question? Were there other models that would have been effective in this unit? Which models? Why?
3. What elements of backward design were obvious in Mr. Samuel's planning? Which elements were missing?

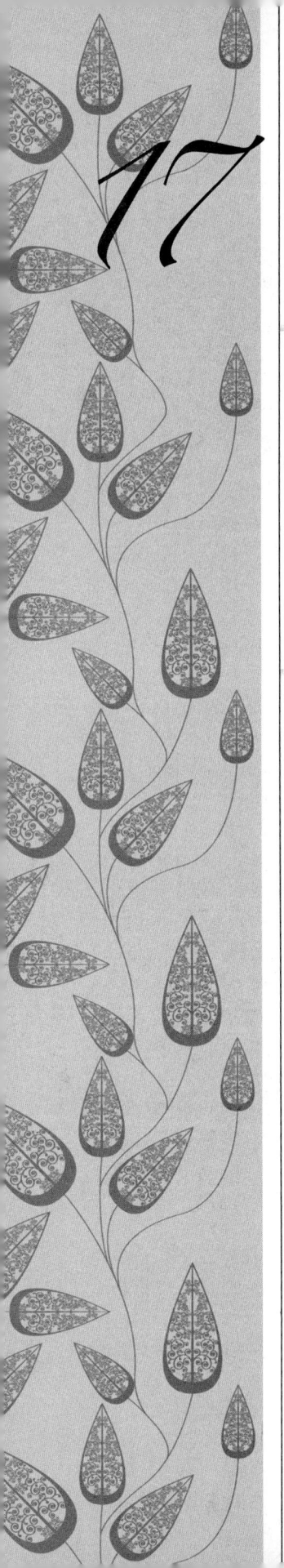

17 The Wisdom of Practice
Creating a Positive Learning Environment

chapter OBJECTIVES

You Will Understand
- Novice teachers can swim in a pool of knowledge of teaching

You Will Know
- Specific teaching practices that support student and teacher learning

You Will Be Able To
- Apply new information to the context in which you find yourself

The difference between the expert and the novice in any profession is something more than years of service. There are professionals with 20-year service pins that should read "one year's service 20 times." Teaching is not exempt from this paradox. Some teachers are novices forever, and some are experts when they put their foot in the door. But what are the differences between ordinary and expert teachers? Are gifted teachers born with their gifts, or can those gifts be learned? By examining the nature of expertise, the first question can be answered. It will then be apparent that the second question is moot: These gifts are not really gifts at all. What are seen as gifts in others are actually the result of deliberative, reflective efforts to become expert. The expert will always relish the challenge and delight in the work of confronting a new circumstance or problem, armed with knowledge gained from previous experience.

Gladwell (2008) summarizes research in support of "the 10,000 hour rule." The rule posits that it takes the opportunity to practice about 10,000 hours to become an expert in anything. Gifted teachers attend to the nuances and lessons of classroom experience. They accumulate hours and hours of reflective professional practice.

One big difference between the expert and the novice teacher is that the expert has a greater repertoire of instructional strategies to fall back on when things do not go exactly as expected. The corollary to this difference between novice and expert is that the expert knows how to arrange matters in advance so as to improve the chances of success. The expert teachers, or those who are called gifted, are the ones who most often beat the odds of failure. How does this happen? What does the expert teacher know that all good teachers should know?

Before we try to answer that question, remember that there is no formula for becoming a good teacher. Models of instruction are not formulas such as "one part oxygen plus two parts hydrogen equals water." Rather, models of instruction are more akin to recipes that have to be adapted to the needs and tastes of the cook and to the available ingredients. Teaching, like cooking, is a purposeful activity in the sense that through conscious reflection or deliberation the process can always be improved. Its quality and its outcome always depend on the judgment of the teacher. Part of that judgment centers on the students and their changing needs, and part centers on the process of teaching.

To say that there is no formula for good teaching is not to deny that an accumulated wisdom about the practice of teaching does exist. Judgments are always grounded in knowledge, and the expert knows things the novice does not. Fortunately, there is a large body of recorded experience and research on effective schools and instructional practices that provides the basis for many generalizations about teaching. In this chapter, we share some of those generalizations under the rubric "The Wisdom of Practice." The basis of these generalizations lies in a corpus of research and in our own experience and that of countless other teachers whom we have asked, "What makes you a good teacher?" But research and the experience of others are never quite enough to define someone else's choices. We invite you to test each generalization in your own practice.

David Berliner (1986) has pointed out that "two large domains of knowledge must be readily accessed [by the expert teacher]. Those two domains of knowledge [are] subject matter knowledge and knowledge of organization and management of classrooms" (p. 7). It was of particular interest to us, then, to note that of the 25 different characteristics and behaviors one group of teachers mentioned in answer to our question ("What makes you a good teacher?"), only one teacher mentioned knowledge of subject matter. That gave us pause at first; certainly teachers must be expert in the content they wish to teach. When we stopped to reflect, though, we realized that good teachers likely take knowledge of their subject matter as a given, a necessary but not sufficient condition for good teaching. In other words, most teachers would probably say that knowing what you are trying to teach is essential to good teaching, but knowing how to teach it is what distinguishes good teachers from mere content experts. Perhaps the real earmark of expertise in teaching lies in understanding how to blend two different domains of knowledge—knowledge of what to teach and knowledge of how to teach—in a way that compromises neither domain. We have condensed that understanding into 11 insights that good teachers have.

Good Teachers Are the Leaders of Their Classrooms

We have asked students of elementary and high school age the same question: "What changes would you make in the instruction you have received thus far in school?" We prefaced the question by explaining that the administration had asked us to make recommendations on how to improve instruction in the school, but that we did not feel capable of framing those recommendations without trying to see the present instructional program from the eyes of those learners who had experienced it.

In general, the learners had only three things to say, although they said them in many different ways. Notice that in every case, their proposed changes were under the teacher's control.

- I'd like teachers to stick to the point.
- I'd like a classroom in which kids didn't get away with fooling around.
- I'd like to know that whatever I'm to be tested on, I have been taught.

Whether teaching 6-year-old or 60-year-old students, the teacher is the person in charge of the classroom, and everyone will feel better if that is clearly established from the start. The teacher is not a buddy or a chum, but neither is the teacher a warden or a tyrant. The teacher is the professional responsible for keeping the class focused on what is being taught, for developing a learning community, for maintaining discipline in a fair and consistent manner, and for ensuring the alignment and reliability and validity of evaluation (Weinstein, 2006). Although much of that responsibility can and should be shared with learners, the teacher must retain the right of ultimate authority in the interest of the safety and physical, emotional, personal, and intellectual well-being of the students.

The teacher's bearing, voice, appearance, and approach to the class should emphasize professionalism and careful preparation for the job. We all are reassured when we feel that persons responsible in controlled situations know what they are doing and will do it responsibly. Students of all ages depend on their teachers for that reassurance.

There is a fine line between being controlling and nurturing that all teachers need to address. Walker (2009) parses the dilemma into when to lighten up and when to tighten up. Expert teachers walk that fine line with an authoritative teaching style. This style is defined as the "use of positive instructional practices within a highly controlling and nurturing context" (p. 126). Expert teachers have high expectations for student behavior and demand compliance and self-regulation toward transparent, relevant, and fair goals. At the same time these teachers are nurturing and build a community in which the norm is positive emotional connections (Pianta et al., 2007; Walker, 2009).

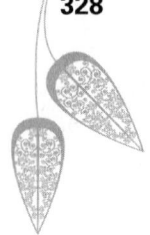

"Crisp," "businesslike," and "to the point" describe a classroom under a teacher's control. Research on classroom management quite clearly shows that good teachers establish a system of management as soon as possible in organizing each new class of students. Expert teachers agree that the first few days of school are critical in establishing and practicing instructional and managerial routines for the smooth operation of the classroom. A substantial line of research supports this insight (Weinstein, 2006). To make these routines automatic, good teachers tell their students what they expect, they demonstrate it for the students, they guide the students in practicing expected moves, and they accept no less than mastery execution of the routines necessary for successful learning and instruction. It is important to note that demonstration and guidance aimed at correct routine are more effective than later correction of errors in routine. "An ounce of prevention" is the watchword in classroom management.

Good Teachers Create a Productive Physical Environment for Learning

Schools vary in many ways, including the physical environment. Some classrooms have natural light, numerous resources, furniture in good shape, and other attributes that make the classroom a pleasant place to be. Classrooms in schools with few economic resources are less pleasant and may send a negative message to children. Regardless of the condition of the classroom, it is imperative that we try to make the physical space in which children are learning as pleasant and productive as possible. A good learning environment is enhanced by good facilities, but good facilities do not guarantee the development of a strong learning community. A strong learning community can be developed in even poor facilities, but this requires creativity, time, and effort in schools that already have difficult demands.

Relationship to Student Learning

The physical environment of the classroom has an influence on student learning and teacher satisfaction (Brophy, 2006). It matters that a teacher mediates the space so that students can work productively in the classroom. Teachers must ensure that the physical environment allows students to feel safe and secure—worrying about whether the ceiling is going to fall on you is not conducive to working hard at learning. Students are also more productive in rooms that allow for interactions among students and between students and the teachers. It is helpful if classrooms reflect the school aspects—students, curriculum, teachers. Comfort is more than physical; psychological comfort is associated with learning. The classroom should be pleasant and aesthetically pleasing while still providing intellectual stimulation (Weinstein, 2006).

Furniture Arrangement/Seating

Ideally, classroom arrangements should be flexible so that the furniture arrangement will not impede student success. It is difficult to work cooperatively in rows, and tables of four can leave some students unable to see a presentation. The need for personal physical space is critical for both instructional and management success. Chairs, tables, or desks should not be too close together. There should be clear paths for unimpeded student movement—a routine can be established for what to do with full backpacks, for example.

Seating arrangements can do a great deal to enhance the success of instruction, and it is essential to plan for the orderly rearrangement of seating as the class activities change. Rows can be used in crowded or difficult to manage classrooms or when all students need to be looking forward, but they are not appropriate for all instruction. Circles and semicircles are generally more effective for sharing information and discussion. Clusters of two, three, or four desks create a setting for small-group cooperative work among students.

Students need instruction in how to change seating patterns in the classroom efficiently. For instance, if after a presentation the students are to work in small groups, it is necessary to explain carefully in advance how the seats will be arranged and where each group is to be located. Classrooms can also be set up in such a way that individual and group work can go on at the same time. Plan in advance for the type of seating arrangement you will need so that sound and sight disturbances can be minimized. Procedures for furniture arrangement should be routine.

Climate Control

It is essential to attend to lighting, air, and temperature. Many excellent lessons have been ruined because the temperature in the classroom was too hot or too cold for students to concentrate.

If the room in which you teach is too crowded, if it is too hot or too cold, or if the air is stale, try to find another space. Talk with the principal about the physical conditions that are creating a problem. As an instructional specialist, you will be the person most aware of the effects of the physical environment on the learners.

Equipment and Displays

Classrooms are cluttered places—books, papers, writing tools, computers, overhead projectors, a large desk for the teacher, tables or desks, chairs, plants, pictures, chalkboard, and many small items that are used to personalize the space. Insofar as possible, the classroom should be an attractive, organized, and inviting place to be. Teachers and students need to be able quickly to find and retrieve the materials and equipment used in lessons. Materials and tools should be in working order and stored in an accessible area. Too much transition time takes away from the momentum of the lesson and provides too great an opportunity for distractions and disruptions.

Displays can consist of student work, motivational and informational posters or bulletin boards, and artifacts. Displays can be used to reinforce the essential concepts of the lesson or unit under study. Put students' work up for all to see, in a manner that reinforces all the students and just not a few. Be certain to ask the students for their permission before you display their work. Pictures of class members and examples of student hobbies or collections can make the classroom reflect positively on individual students and groups and help both the students and teacher feel attachment to the space in which they work.

Good Teachers Manage Human Relations Effectively

Teaching is very complex, and classroom management is one of the more intricate of a teacher's responsibilities. There is no lack of advice about the best methods for managing classrooms and student behavior. By demonstrating respect for students and their learning and organizing the classroom and instruction for successful academic encounters, many behavior management problems can be avoided. Creating classroom learning communities means that classroom norms encourage intellectual development within a caring and supportive environment (Weinstein, 2002).

Steven Wolk (2002) offers several management suggestions that have been adapted for sharing in this text:

1. Get to know your students—their achievements, potential, interests, cultural background, and learning preferences.
2. Manage the class schedule to enhance student engagement.
3. Give students responsibility for helping the classroom run smoothly.
4. Use the physical environment of the room to promote your instructional objectives.
5. Keep the classroom organized, free of clutter, and responsive to the developmental needs of students.

6. Develop a reasonable set of rules and explicitly teach students the rules.
7. First, do no harm. Monitor student behavior. Ignore trivial, annoying behaviors. Try to diffuse disciplinary problems by using proximity, humor, or a private discussion with a student.
8. Identify and work with students with chronic behavior problems.
9. Use good instructional strategies to keep students engaged and academically motivated.
10. Provide clear expectations and directions and an avenue for students to seek help if they are confused.
11. Help students develop self-assessment skills.
12. Be cognizant of cultural influences on learning and behavior.
13. Always be respectful to students. Be just. Provide specific, positive feedback concerning behavior and academic skills.
14. Don't use schoolwork as punishment.

Remember the close connection between instruction and behavior management in classrooms.

Thomas Lasley (1981) has suggested four generalizations about classroom and behavior management that have held up over the decades regardless of the classroom context. According to his extensive review of the literature on the issue of classroom management, the effective teacher does the following:

1. Develops and implements a workable set of classroom rules
2. Structures and monitors the classroom in a manner that minimizes disruptive behavior
3. Clearly defines and quickly and consistently responds to inappropriate behavior
4. Couches the response to inappropriate behavior in a tone that does not denigrate the students to whom the response is directed

Good Teachers Engage Learners in the Process of Their Own Learning

Eleanor Duckworth (2006) believes we must always put learners in as direct contact as possible with whatever we want them to learn. That is usually the purpose of field trips and other hands-on activities in schools. But there are many ways that students can be given direct contact with their learning. They can model the formation and movements of the solar system. They can keep diaries of their observations of animals that share their community. They can construct models, engage in mock and simulated experiences, and conduct interviews.

Second, and this is related to the first principle, Duckworth admonishes that we provide frequent opportunities for learners to explain what they understand, both to the teacher and to other students. Anytime teachers are tempted to tell students something they want them to know, they should start by asking the students to explain what they already know.

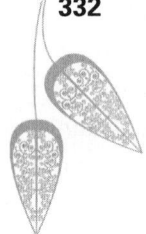

We agree that these guidelines are critical to a beginning teacher's instructional effectiveness. We know that learners will learn more in proportion to how engaged they are with what they are trying to learn. This is the *law of meaningful engagement,* although it is a law violated all too often.

Students learn best when they believe they can learn and are challenged. A competent, interested learner is more likely to be successful. This relaxed alertness allows students to become immersed in complex experiences that use their senses, make connections between prior and new information, and allow them to apply new skills and knowledge. Along with relaxed alertness and immersion in complex experiences, learners need active processing in which there is continuous reflection about what is being learned and constructed (Caine, Caine, McClintic, & Klimek, 2008). These three ingredients of successful learning experiences are similar to what we have referred to as meaningful engagement.

The learner's understanding and insight must be the goal of instruction. Metacognition—the ability to monitor one's learning so that further progress can be made—is a necessary component of student understanding. Teachers must develop activities so that students can receive authentic feedback about their progress toward established goals. One of the great paradoxes of education, which few laypersons but every good teacher will sooner or later discover, is that understanding cannot be given to the learner directly any more than a parent can teach a child to tie her shoes by merely telling her how. Give her a shoe to practice on (or, better, let her practice on her own shoe), and have her explain to you or to another person what she is doing as she practices. If that advice is good for learning to tie shoes, how much better is it for learning all the complicated things students are expected to know in school?

Good Teachers Teach Up

They Recognize the Pygmalion Effect

In Greek mythology, Pygmalion was the sculptor from Cyprus who carved and then fell in love with a statue of a woman whom the goddess Aphrodite later gave life. The Pygmalion theme repeats itself often in Western literature, in stories and verse. George Bernard Shaw made Henry Higgins, an aristocrat whose hobby is phonetics, and Eliza Doolittle, the Cockney flower-seller, immortal. Hollywood loves this romantic, fairy tale theme, centered on the power of education (particularly language) to elevate one's social class.

Maybe love does not conquer all, but it is a powerful ingredient of education, or so the Pygmalion story would imply. It is best not to forget, too, that, in each version of the story, the sculptor has much to learn from his creation. That important lesson is expressed by Eliza near the end of Shaw's play, where she is trying to explain to her friend and benefactor Colonel Pickering how she was transformed from flower girl to lady of refinement. Eliza explains that the difference between a flower girl and a lady is not how she behaves, but how she is treated.

From that speech we get the expression the *Pygmalion effect*. The Pygmalion effect in schools was made famous by Rosenthal and Jacobson (1968). Essentially, their research asserts that a teacher's expectation that the student *will* do well can have a positive effect on the academic success of that student. The opposite of the Pygmalion effect in schools, that teachers treat high- and low-achieving students differently to the detriment of the low-achieving student, has also been brought to light by research (Weinstein, 2002). Thomas Good (1981) lists several ways in which teachers most often discriminate in their treatment of the high and low achievers.

- By seating low-achieving students farther away from the teacher than other students
- By paying less attention to low-achieving students than to other students
- By calling on low-achieving students less frequently than other students to answer questions
- By giving low-achieving students less time to answer questions when they are called on than other students
- By not providing cues or asking follow-up questions to help low-achieving students answer questions
- By criticizing low-achieving students more frequently than other students for incorrect answers
- By giving low-achieving students less praise than other students for correct or marginal responses
- By giving low-achieving students less feedback and less detail in the feedback they are given than other students
- By interrupting the performance of low-achieving students more often than that of the high-achieving students
- By demanding less effort and less work from low-achieving students than from high-achieving students

Rhona Weinstein (2002), after an exhaustive study of the power of expectations in schools, made the following conclusions:

- Students know that teachers have different expectations for different students.
- How children are treated in schools and classrooms matters. For instance, if school policies are structured on the belief that IQ is stable, the opportunities available to some students will be limited.

- Expectations become part of the fabric of the institution and the processes by which expectations are communicated are similar at all levels of schooling.
- When teachers have low expectations for students and treat students differently because of those expectations, achievement gaps persist and grow.
- Expectations interact with other attributes that may put a student at risk for school difficulties—race, culture, language, socioeconomic status, gender, learning preferences, and prior knowledge.

"By our overemphasis on appraising achievement and sorting children, we fail to create conditions in classrooms and schools that substantially develop ability. We fail to meet all learners with a challenging curriculum accompanied by differentially appropriate, nonstigmatizing, and flexible educational supports" (Weinstein, 2002, pp. 291–292).

They Capitalize on What Students Know

What students know about the content determines how well they will learn new information. Teachers should find something in what students already know to establish a basis for new understandings. Students often feel as if they know nothing of what is taught in school and could not care less because it all seems so irrelevant. But good teachers help learners see that they already know much about what they are trying to learn, and they impress on students that *what they already know is the single most important factor influencing what they will learn.* Learners are crucially important to their own learning, and teaching should make them feel that way.

Gordon Wells (1986) calls children "meaning makers." He draws an irresistible analogy in discussing how adults must communicate with children, saying that it is very like playing ball with a young child:

> What the adult has to do for this game to be successful is, first, to ensure that the child is ready, with arms cupped, to catch the ball. Then the ball must be thrown gently and accurately so that it lands squarely in the child's arms. When it is the child's turn to throw, the adult must be prepared to run wherever it goes and bring it back to where the child really intended it to go. Such is the collaboration required in [teaching], the adult doing a great deal of supportive work to enable the ball to be kept in play. (p. 50)

Wells was talking about conversation with children. We think that the analogy is perfect for the requirements of teaching and so we substituted the word *teaching* for *conversation,* which also reminds us that teaching is very like a conversation.

They Celebrate Differences among Students

An old adage says "None of us is as smart as all of us." That statement is also true in a classroom. If teachers make it clear that what each one knows or learns is of value to everyone, then they make it safe for everyone to share whatever they know and thus to value their own understanding, no matter how meager. Half of this concept is polite behavior—respect—and the other half is intellectual honesty: No one knows everything about anything, not even the teacher, and that is acceptable. Simply put, two heads are always better than one.

They Realize That There Is More Than One Right Answer to Important Questions

Every teacher's manual includes suggestions about what to say to students and what to expect them to say in return. The manuals for teaching reading to elementary school students often go as far as to put what the teacher is to say in one color print and what the students are to say in another color print. But a lesson script can only be an approximation. In fact, the one certain truth found in all teacher's manuals is that answers will vary. Part of the art of teaching lies in knowing how to take advantage of the variance.

They Provide Appropriate, Quality Feedback

Remember learning to drive a car? If you were lucky, the person teaching you kept affirming that you could do it and praising you for all you were doing right. When difficulties arose, your instructor concentrated on helping you focus on what to do rather than berating you for your shortcomings. But if you were unlucky, the person teaching you continually harped on everything you were doing wrong. The effect of this was to shake your confidence, whether or not that was the intent. Feedback that is related to learning is neutral, focused on the task, and timely (Brookhart, 2008).

It is important for students to know where and why they made errors so that these errors can be corrected. Feedback should be focused on the task and not on the individual and should be based on publicly stated criteria (e.g., a rubric). A productive learning environment involves consistent and focused feedback, including attention to as many strengths of students as weaknesses. These practices encourage a safe and effective learning environment in which students can grow and learn (Brookhart, 2008).

Good Teachers Are Good Learners

They Serve as a Model for Learning

Although we are tempted to say that the teacher should be the best learner in the class, we know how stiff the competition for that honor will always be. Also, we would not want to set it up as a competition. Yet the teacher must be an eager learner and be willing to share the process of learning with other learners, the class. Good teachers learn from their own study and share that study with their students. Frequently, even daily, they bring a new idea to class from something they have read or seen. They are scholars, and they share the process and the product of their scholarship. Teachers learn from their students, both about teaching and about the content they are studying together. Having the chance to teach someone else is one of the best ways to learn, and it is always a favor to both the learner and the teacher to reverse their roles from time to time. Teachers learn from teaching, and not just about their teaching but about their students and what they are studying (Huebner, 2009).

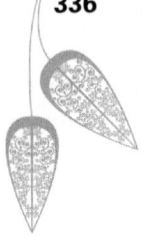

It is a serious mistake for any teacher to project the image of the person who knows it all and is here to tell everyone. First, such an attitude conveys an erroneous impression of the nature of knowledge, as if it were a once-and-for-all matter. The knowledge humans possess is expanding so rapidly that the infrastructure of knowledge has to be continually adapted to accommodate new insights and understandings. Thus teachers, like their students, are faced with needing to learn constantly just to keep abreast. The exciting result for the teacher who realizes this is that there is always a ready audience with which to share new insights and understandings. By contrast, a know-all, tell-all attitude treats knowledge as a fixed entity, excluding learners from the process of learning and dooming them to focus on the acquisition of information that may be obsolete even before their school days have passed. The more appropriate image of teacher as learner invites students to join with others (the teacher included) in the joy and thrill of coming to know. The long-term effect is that students will learn well, learn more, and be learners for life.

They Recognize the Importance of Professional Knowledge

There are professional organizations for every branch and subject of teaching and for the field of education in general. A major function of these groups is to provide a comprehensive literature to assist teachers and administrators in their mission to educate. This literature consists mainly of professional journals, books, audio and videorecordings, and research and technical reports. Each professional organization also hosts regional, state, national, and international meetings and forums in which teachers share and discuss common problems and ideas. Taken together, these sources form the basis of postgraduate professional study in education.

Disciplinary knowledge increases and changes quickly. It is not only in the sciences that new theories are constructed and tested; all academic fields have benefited from the proliferation of technological tools and communication channels. We have the tools to understand more about our world and we have the tools to share these discoveries rapidly. As new understandings are combined with prior learning, even more knowledge is generated. The cycle moves quickly.

For classroom teachers, there is a need to keep abreast of rich and tested theories of how we learn and what impact policies have on student development and achievement, along with advances in the content areas and in ways that content can be communicated to students.

A review of the literature identifies the following characteristics of effective professional development:

- Focus on enriching the teacher's content knowledge and how to teach this content to students
- Attention to how students learn specific content
- Opportunities provided for teachers to engage and process the new learning
- Application and reflection of new knowledge
- Collaborative, collegial, and occurs within the teaching context
- Sustained over time (Darling-Hammond & Richardson, 2009)

They Act as Researchers

In addition to attempting to keep abreast of the professional literature (as any professional must), teachers are in a position to be their own directors of research and development. Action research allows teachers to study their own practices alone or with others. A teacher who wants to learn more about what is happening in his or her own classroom may use action research procedures as may a group of teachers who collaborate to understand more about what is happening beyond a specific classroom (Brighton, 2009). Table 17.1 details the steps commonly used in action research.

Table 17.1 Steps in Action Research

Step 1	Identify a problem	Choose an area or focus that concerns you in your professional practice. Read about this area of teaching. Formulate a specific question(s) to be answered.
Step 2	Develop a plan	Decide how you will collect data to answer the question, what data will be collected and why, what you will do to support data collection, how you will analyze the information you collect, and what you will do with your conclusions.
Step 3	Collect data	Use a variety of data sources and data collection techniques—personal reflections, interviews, student work, audio and video, and so on.
Step 4	Analyze data	Use appropriate data analysis techniques. Collaborate with knowledgeable others to find patterns in the data that help you to answer your questions.
Step 5	Reflect on and share the results	Reflect on your findings and how they will affect your professional practice. Share the findings with other professionals.

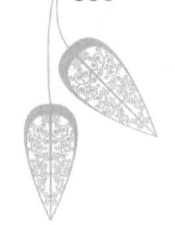

Good Teachers Develop Instructional Objectives with Learners

The quality of instruction in a classroom will be determined largely by whether the students have a vested interest in the instruction and in their own learning. In other words, they have to care about what happens in the class and be willing to cooperate to reach shared objectives. Instructional objectives, from the point of view of the learners, are learning objectives. Whether the objectives are achieved will depend on the learners' willingness to adopt the teacher's instructional objectives as their own learning objectives.

We are not advocating that teachers plan their instruction based on what students are willing to say they want to learn, even though that can often be taken into account. We do advocate that teachers share the process of their own planning for instruction with their students. One way to do this is to initiate a unit of study with an exploration of what the students have already studied on the topic, followed by a listing of what else they think they want to know. Many studies of effective instructional practices make clear that teaching that builds on what learners already know leads to higher achievement.

Good Teachers Find Out Why a Plan Is Not Working

L. W. Anderson (1982) has summarized the major conclusions to be drawn from the vast body of literature on effective teaching. His review was conducted many years ago and new research continues to support his conclusions. Effective teachers, he suggests,

- Know their students
- Assign appropriate tasks to their students
- Orient their students to the learning task
- Monitor the learning progress of their students
- Relate teaching and testing, testing what they teach
- Promote student involvement and engagement in the learning process
- Provide continuity for their students so that learning tasks and objectives build on one another
- Correct student errors and misunderstandings

If these effective teaching behaviors are to be a reality, it is important that the teacher be aware of options. If one approach or technique is not working with a class, analyze the problem and redesign the instructional plan. For instance, some classes are not ready for group work. Many times, teachers will attempt a group activity and, when chaos develops, decide that they will never try it again.

Students must be prepared for group activities, and the procedures for setting up those activities must be carefully planned and directed. The models described in the chapter on cooperative learning are only a few of many effective group-process models. With some instructional models, the students may need more preparation time. Perhaps certain steps in the model have not been adequately explained. Or sometimes the instructional plan is too ambitious, the content to be covered is too extensive, or the students do not have the necessary readiness and predisposition for learning. Evaluate the situation and consider what options you have to correct the difficulty. Treat problems as challenges rather than frustrations.

Good Teachers Strive to Make Their Teaching Engaging

The relationship between interest and curiosity is no accident; learners are interested in learning those things about which they feel the greatest curiosity. Therefore, if teachers can pique the curiosity of learners, they will make what they teach interesting to learners. Students are motivated to learn when they are engaged. Student engagement goes beyond interest. A National Research Council (2004) study on secondary school engagement found that when course structure and instruction reflect students' prior knowledge, interests, culture, and real-life experience and when it is varied and challenging, students are more motivated to persist in important tasks. We know that ongoing diagnostic and formative assessments contribute to making school more relevant and reflective of a student's outside-of-school life.

Interestingly, there is also evidence that high expectations for all students help keep students interested in school work. These high expectations and the types of instruction that result help students feel respected and valued. A challenging curriculum, varied tasks that are representative of past experience, and opportunities for scaffolded experiences contribute to student engagement. Student motivation and interest are also predicated on respect. As teachers communicate their respect to students through challenging and interesting classroom experiences, high expectations, engaging materials and tools, and a caring and helpful environment, schools will be filled with motivated and successful students.

Good Teachers Give Learners Access to Information and Opportunity to Practice

Research on effective schools unequivocally supports the idea that learning is likely to occur when learners have access to information and the opportunity to practice using that information. But what kind of information and practice are appropriate? Most obviously, students need whatever information is necessary to accomplish the learning objective at hand: accurate information presented in a palatable form. And students need practice in applying or recalling the new information as a means of solving problems that require it. In the case of a learning objective that called for students to compare and contrast the causes of the French and Indian War with the causes of the War of 1812, the students would need information about these two wars and guidance and feedback on their attempts to make appropriate comparisons and contrasts.

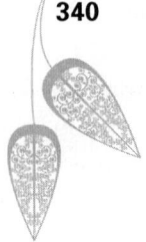

The information needed by students is more than facts, data, and algorithms, however. Paraphrasing from a research report by Robert Yinger (1987), we can identify these other kinds of information as (1) knowledge of what to do with information gained and how to use it in practice, (2) knowledge of when the information will apply and how to apply it, and (3) knowledge of whether the uses of the information have been successful.

Likewise, the practice students need is not solely of those behaviors implicit in the specific learning objective they have been given. In addition to learners applying or recalling information, D. N. Perkins and Gabriel Salomon (1988) state that learners need practice in "low-road" and "high-road" transfer.

When teachers introduce a literary classic with reference to the related experiences of their students, they are creating conditions for low-road transfer. When teachers point out parallels between the elements of content, such as the points of comparison between the civil rights movement in the United States and the breakdown of apartheid in South Africa, they are facilitating high-road transfer.

Low-road transfer is direct application of information to contexts and problems like those in which the information was first encountered. For example, students might practice applying the Pythagorean theorem by calculating the diagonals of their classroom and of a football field. High-road transfer is indirect application of information to contexts and problems unlike those in which the information was first encountered. For example, students might compare the events and political alignments of the French and Indian War with the alignments of loyalties in the play *Romeo and Juliet*. It is always important to keep in mind that long-term, meaningful learning depends on the access students have to good information and the opportunity to transfer and apply that information in ways that make it both meaningful and memorable.

Good Teachers Teach for Two Kinds of Knowledge

It is impossible for students to learn in school all they would ever need to know in their lives. They must, therefore, learn how to learn. In every course of study in school, students are given access to a portion of the accumulated knowledge and wisdom of humankind: the facts, ideas, algorithms, events, and implications of history, literature, science, math, health, and so on. But such "knowing that" will not stand the learner in good stead in the future if he or she does not also acquire a complementary kind of knowledge: the skills of reading, writing, study, and thinking necessary for continued growth and lifelong scholarship, or "knowing how."

Thus teaching in the classroom we envision would give students access to information to be learned and to a conscious knowledge of how to learn it. In this classroom, the teacher creates an environment in which students are responsible for knowing and for knowing how they know, for taking control of the processes of their own learning and thinking. The intended result is an improvement of the learning and thinking necessary for participation in the discipline under study. We would want teachers at all grade levels and in all content areas to believe that the most important thing they have to teach students is the process of learning. This thought reminds us of the old expression "Give a man a fish, and he'll eat for a day; teach a man to fish, and he'll eat for a lifetime." Consider the analogy: "Teach students only the information you want them to have, and they'll pass the test tomorrow; teach students how to learn, and they'll pass the test for the rest of their lives."

Summary

There is more to managing a classroom of learners than just containing the students. In fact, the need for most of that kind of management is preempted when the teacher takes control of the learning in the classroom and in effect turns the responsibility for learning over to the learners. Good teachers manage their instruction with that objective in mind. They are able to do so because they operate out of a knowledge base and because intuition feeds their good judgment. In this chapter and throughout this book, we have shared the idea that there are always options the good teacher can consider, even though most of the time good teaching, like any skilled performance, looks completely spontaneous. We hope that our suggestions will become part of your instructional repertoire.

Extensions

ACTIVITIES

1. Discuss professional development with some practicing teachers. What do they think of the professional development experiences they have had? What makes professional development good, helpful, or a waste of time? What do they suggest you do to get the most out of professional development?
2. Ask a group of students of the age that you are or will be teaching what makes a good classroom environment. Probe to find out what teachers and students can do to make an effective learning community.

3. Review your district (or a district in which you might work) policies with an eye toward high expectations for students. Which policies promote high expectations for students? Which policies assume that students will be low achievers? Ask teachers and administrators if these policies affect responses to student behavior in a particular school.

REFLECTIVE QUESTIONS

1. What do you still want to know about teaching? How will you find out what you want to know?
2. What do you believe about students and their capacity for learning? How will these beliefs affect your behaviors in the classroom?
3. Many people believe that teaching is sharing content expertise. How would you respond to this idea so that you convey the complexity of teaching?

Summary for Part Three

Putting It All Together: Matching Objectives to Instructional Models

In Part Three, we have exemplified the principles and practices advocated in Parts One and Two. Our examples came from various grade levels. We then presented a more general list of attitudes and practices that make a good teacher. Every teacher wishes to improve in the science and the art of instructional practice, and the case studies presented here, set against our general suggestions for creating a positive learning environment, are intended to assist in that improvement.

In our presentation of these three case studies, we intentionally varied the manner in which the steps were followed, precisely because there is no one prescribed formula to reach a successful instructional plan. One might rigidly follow a set of prescribed procedures and, without a spirit of creativity and enthusiasm, have a very negative teaching experience.

Our intentions through this book have been to suggest procedures for planning, selecting, and utilizing instructional models and to describe behaviors for interacting with learners in the classroom. In our many years of experience working with teachers and prospective teachers, we have found that the spirit of adventure, the intellectual excitement, and the creative innovations that they bring to the task are what make any set of procedures work in the classroom.

References

Airasian, P. W. (2005). *Classroom assessment: Concepts and applications* (5th ed.). Boston: McGraw-Hill.

Anderson, L. W. (1982). *Teachers, teaching, and educational effectiveness.* Columbia: University of South Carolina, College of Education.

Anderson, L. W., & Krathwohl, D. (Eds.). (2001). *A taxonomy for learning, teaching and assessing: A revision of Bloom's taxonomy of educational objectives.* New York: Longman.

Aronson, E., Blaney, N., Stephan, C., Sikes, J., & Snapes, M. (1978). *The jigsaw classroom.* Beverly Hills, CA: Sage Publications.

Ausubel, D. (1960). The use of advance organizers in the learning and retention of meaningful verbal material. *Journal of Educational Psychology, 51,* 267–272.

Ausubel, D. (1968). *The psychology of meaningful verbal learning: An introduction to school learning.* New York: Grune & Stratton.

Berliner, D. C. (1986). In pursuit of the expert pedagogue. *Educational Researcher, 15,* 7–9.

Black, P., Harrison, C., Lee, C., Marshall, B., & William, D. (2003). *Assessment for learning: Putting it into practice.* Maidenhead, UK: Open University Press.

Bloom, B. S. (Ed.). (1956). *Taxonomy of educational objectives: The classification of educational goals by a committee of college and university examiners.* New York: Longmans, Green.

Bloom, B. S. (1983). *Human characteristics and school learning.* New York: McGraw-Hill.

Blosser, P. E. (1991). Using cooperative learning in science education. *ERIC Clearinghouse for Science, Mathematics, and Environmental Education Bulletin.* Retrieved January 30, 2006, from www.stemworks.org/Bulletins/SEB92-1.html

Boston, C. (2002). The concept of formative assessment. *Practical Assessment, Research, & Evaluation, 8*(9), 1. Retrieved February 15, 2004, from http://pareonline.net/getvn.asp?v=8&n=9

Brighton, C. M. (2009). Embarking on action research. *Educational Leadership, 66*(5), 40–44.

Bronfenbrenner, U. (1979). *The ecology of human development: Experiments by nature and design.* Cambridge, MA: Harvard University Press.

Brookhart, S. M. (2008). *How to give effective feedback to your students.* Alexandria, VA: Association for Supervision and Curriculum Development.

Brophy, J. (2006). History of research on classroom management. In C. M. Evertson & C. S. Simon (Eds.), *Handbook of classroom management: Research, practice, and contemporary issues.* Mahwah, NJ: Erlbaum.

Bruner, J. S. (1961). Act of discovery. *Harvard Educational Review, 31*(1), 21–32.

Bruner, J. S., Goodnow, J. J., & Austin, G. A. (1986). *A study of thinking.* New Brunswick, NJ: Transaction Publishers.

Caine, R. N., & Caine, G. (1994). *Making connections: Teaching and the human brain.* Menlo Park, CA: Addison-Wesley.

Caine, R. N., Caine, G., McClintic, C., & Klimek, K. (2008). *12 brain/mind learning principles in action* (2nd ed.). Thousand Oaks, CA: Corwin Press.

Cohen, S. A. (1987). Instructional alignment: Searching for a magic bullet. *Educational Researcher, 16*(8), 16–20.

Darling-Hammond, L., & Richardson, N. (2009). Teacher learning. *Educational Leadership, 66*(5), 46–52.

Dinsmore, D. L., Alexander, P. A., & Loughlin, S. M. (2008). Focusing the conceptual lens on metacognition, self-regulation, and self-regulated learning. *Educational Psychology Review, 20,* 391–409.

Donovan, M. S., & Bransford, J. D. (Eds.). (2005). *How students learn history, mathematics, and science in the classroom.* Washington, DC: The National Academies Press.

Duckworth, E. (2006). *The having of wonderful ideas: And other essays on teaching and learning.* New York: Teachers College Press.

Eggen, P. D., & Kauchak, D. P. (2006). *Strategies and models for teachers: Teaching content and thinking skills* (5th ed.). Boston: Pearson/Allyn & Bacon.

Elias, M. J. (2005). *Social decision making/social problem solving for middle school students: Skills and activities for academic, social, and emotional success.* Champaign, IL: Research Press.

Erickson, L. H. (2007). *Stirring the head, heart, and soul: Redefining curriculum, instruction, and concept based learning* (3rd ed.). Thousand Oaks, CA: Corwin Press.

Faughnan, K. (2009). Get smart about skills for tomorrow's jobs. ZDNet News and Blogs. Retrieved January 12, 2010, from www.zdnet.com/2100-9595_22-258867.html

Fischer, C. (2008). *The Socratic method.* Great Neck, NY: Great Neck Publishing.

Fisher, D., & Frey, N. (2008). *Better learning through structured teaching: A framework for the gradual release of responsibility.* Alexandria, VA: Association for Supervision and Curriculum Development.

Fulghum, R. (1989). *It was on fire when I lay down on it.* New York: Villard Books.

Gardner, H. (2006). *Multiple intelligences: New horizons in theory and practice.* New York: Basic Books.

Gladwell, M. (2008). *Outliers: The story of success.* New York: Little, Brown.

Goetz, E. T., Schallert, D. L., Reynolds, R. E., & Radin, D. I. (1983). Reading in perspective: What real cops and pretend burglars look for in a story. *Journal of Educational Psychology, 75,* 500–510.

Good, T. L. (1981). Teacher expectations and student perceptions: A decade of research. *Educational Leadership, 38,* 415–422.

Good, T. L., & Brophy, J. E. (2003). *Looking in classrooms* (9th ed.). Reading, MA: Addison-Wesley.

Good, T. L., & Brophy, J. E. (2007). *Looking in classrooms* (10th ed.). Reading, MA: Addison-Wesley.

Gove, P. B. (Ed.) (2002). *Webster's third international dictionary* (Unabridged ed.). Springfield, MA: Merriam-Webster.

Gronlund, N. E., & Brookhart, S. M. (2008). *Gronlund's writing instructional objectives* (8th ed.). Upper Saddle River, NJ: Prentice Hall.

Hoffman, J. (1992). Critical reading/thinking across the curriculum: Using I-charts to support learning. *Language Arts, 69,* 121–127.

Huebner, T. (2009). What research says about the continuum of teacher learning. *Educational Leadership, 66*(5), 88–91.

Iowa tests of basic skills, multilevel battery, levels 9–12, teacher's guide. (1986). Chicago: Riverside.

Jensen, E. (2005). *Teaching with the brain in mind* (2nd ed.). Alexandria, VA: Association for Supervision and Curriculum Development.

Johnson, D. W., & Johnson, R. T. (1995). *Creative controversy: Intellectual challenge in the classroom.* Edina, MN: Interaction Book Company.

Joyce, B., Weil, M., & Calhoun, E. (2009) *Models of teaching* (8th ed.). Boston: Pearson.

Kilgore, A. M. (1984). Models of teaching and teacher evaluation. In R. L. Egbert & M. M. Kluender, *Using research to improve teacher education: Teacher education monograph no. 1* (pp. 108–126). Lincoln: The Nebraska Consortium.

Klausmeier, H. J. (1990). Conceptualizing. In B. F. Jones & L. Idol (Eds.), *Dimensions of thinking and cognitive instruction: Implications for educational reform* (pp. 93–138). Mahwah, NJ: Erlbaum.

Knowles, J. (1960). *A separate peace.* New York: Macmillan.

Kohn, A. (1999). *Punished by rewards: The trouble with gold stars, incentive plans, praise, and other bribes.* Boston: Houghton Mifflin.

Lasley, T. J. (1981). Research perspectives on classroom management. *Journal of Teacher Education, 32*(2), 14–17.

Marzano, R. J. (2001). *A handbook for classroom instruction that works.* Alexandria, VA: Association for Supervision and Curriculum Development.

Marzano, R. J. (2003). *What works in schools? Translating research into action.* Alexandria, VA: Association for Supervision and Curriculum Development.

Marzano, R. J., & Kendall, J. (2009). *Content knowledge: A compendium of standards and benchmarks for K–12 education* (4th ed.). Denver, CO: Mid-continent Research for Education and Learning. Retrieved from www.mcrel.org/standard-benchmarks

Marzano, R. J., Pickering, D. J., & Pollock, J. E. (2001). *Classroom instruction that works: Research based strategies for increasing student achievement.* Alexandria, VA: Association for Supervision and Curriculum Development.

McCaleb, J. L., & White, J. A. (1980). Critical dimensions in evaluating teacher clarity. *Journal of Classroom Instruction, 15*(2), 27–30.

National Commission on Excellence in Education. (1983, April). *A nation at risk.* Retrieved February 14, 2009, from www.edgov.pubs/NatAtRisk/index.html

National Research Council. (2000). *How people learn: Brain, mind, experience, and school.* Committee on Developments in the Science of Learning. J. D. Bransford, A. L. Brown, & R. R. Cocking (Eds.). Commission on Behavioral and Social Sciences and Education. Washington, DC: The National Academies Press.

National Research Council Institute of Medicine. (2004). *Engaging schools: Fostering high school students' motivation to learn.* Washington, DC: The National Academies Press.

Noguera, P. A. (2008). *The trouble with black boys: . . . And other reflections on race, equity, and the future of public education.* San Francisco: Jossey-Bass.

Ogle, D. M. (1986). K-W-L: A teaching model that develops active reading of expository text. *The Reading Teacher, 39,* 564–570.

Paul, R. (1993). *Critical thinking: How to prepare students for a rapidly changing world.* Santa Rosa, CA: Foundation for Critical Thinking.

Paul, R., & Elder, L. (2006). *The art of Socratic questioning.* Dillon Beach, CA: The Foundation for Critical Thinking.

Perkins, D. N., & Salomon, G. (1988). Teaching for transfer. *Educational Leadership, 46,* 22–31.

Pianta, R. C., Hamre, B. K., Haynes, N. J., Mintz, S. L., & LaParo, K. M. (2007). *CLASS: Classroom assessment scoring system manual, pilot.* Unpublished manuscript.

Pinker, S. (1994). *The language instinct: How the mind creates language.* New York: HarperCollins.

Piper, W. (1930, 1984). *The little engine that could.* New York: Platt & Munk (1930). New York: Putnam Publishing Group (1984).

Plato. (2000). *Meno* (B. Jowett, Trans.). (Original work written about 400 B.C.E.). Retrieved July 3, 2009, from www.classicallibrary.org/plato/dialogues/10_meno.htm

Prince, G. (1970). *The practice of creativity.* New York: Collier.

Rosenshine, B. (1983). Teaching functions in instructional programs. *Elementary School Journal, 83,* 338.

Rosenshine, B. (1986). Synthesis of research on explicit teaching. *Educational Leadership, 43,* 60–69.

Rosenthal, R., & Jacobson, L. (1968). *Pygmalion in the classroom: Teacher expectation and pupils' intellectual development.* New York: Holt, Rinehart & Winston.

Rothenberg, A. (1979). Einstein's creative thinking and the general theory of relativity: A documented report. *American Journal of Psychiatry, 136,* 39–40.

Schunk, D. H. (2004). *Learning theories: An educational perspective* (4th ed.). Upper Saddle River, NJ: Pearson Education.

Slavin, R. (1996). *Education for all.* Exton, PA: Swets & Zeitlinger Publishers.

Slavin, R. E. (2000). *Educational psychology: Theory and practice* (6th ed.). Boston: Allyn & Bacon.

Spillane, J. P. (2004). *Standards deviation: How schools misunderstood education policy.* Cambridge, MA: Harvard University Press.

Sternberg, R. J. (1985a). Teaching critical thinking, part I: Are we making critical mistakes? *Phi Delta Kappan, 67,* 194–198.

Sternberg, R. J. (1985b). Teaching critical thinking, part II: Possible solutions. *Phi Delta Kappan, 67,* 277–280.

Sternberg, R. J. (1998). *The triarchic mind: A new theory of human intelligence.* New York: Viking Penguin.

Sternberg, R. J., & Grigorenko, E. L. (2004). Successful intelligence in the classroom. *Theory into Practice, 43,* 274–280.

Stiggins, R. J. (2005). *Student-involved assessment for learning* (4th ed.). Upper Saddle River, NJ: Pearson/Merrill/Prentice Hall.

Stiggins, R. J. (2008). *An introduction to student-involved assessment FOR learning.* Upper Saddle River, NJ: Pearson.

Suchman, J. R. (1962). *The elementary school training program in scientific inquiry.* Report to the U.S. Office of Education, Project Title VII. Urbana: University of Illinois Press.

Taba, H., Durkin, M. C., Fraenkel, J. R., & McNaughton, A. H. (1971). *Teachers' handbook to elementary social studies* (2nd ed.). Reading, MA: Addison-Wesley.

Thomas, L. (1984). The art of teaching science. In N. R. Comley et al. (Eds.), *Fields of writing* (pp. 559–564). New York: St. Martin's Press.

Tomlinson, C. A. (2003). *Fulfilling the promise of the differentiated classroom: Strategies and tools for responsive teaching.* Alexandria, VA: Association for Supervision and Curriculum Development.

Tomlinson, C. A., & Eidson, C. C. (2003). *Differentiation in practice: A resource guide for differentiating curriculum, grades 5–9.* Alexandria, VA: Association for Supervision and Curriculum Development.

Walker, J. (2009). Authoritative classroom management: How control and nurturance work together. *Theory into Practice, 48,* 122–129.

Weaver, W. T., & Prince, G. M. (1990). Synectics: Its potential for education. *Phi Delta Kappan, 72,* 378–388.

Weinstein, C. S. (2006). *Secondary classroom management: Lessons from research and practice* (3rd ed.). New York: McGraw-Hill.

Weinstein, R. S. (2002). *Reaching higher: The power of expectations in schooling.* Cambridge, MA: Harvard University Press.

Wells, G. (1986). *The meaning makers.* Portsmouth, NH: Heinemann Educational Books.

Wiggins, G., & McTighe, J. (2005). *Understanding by design* (Expanded 2nd ed.). Alexandria, VA: Association for Supervision and Curriculum Development.

Wilder, L. I. (1940). *The long winter.* New York: Harper Collins.

Williams, R., & Tollett, J. (2005). *The non-designer's web book* (3rd ed.). Berkeley, CA: Peachpit Press.

Willingham, D. T. (2009). *Why don't students like school?: A cognitive scientist answers questions about how the mind works and what it means for the classroom.* San Francisco: Jossey-Bass.

Wilson, S. H., Greer, J. F., & Johnson, R. M. (1963). Synectics: A creative problem-solving technique for the gifted. *Gifted Child Quarterly, 17,* 260–266.

Wolk, S. (2002). *Being good: Rethinking classroom management and student discipline.* Portsmouth, NH: Heinemann.

Wormeli, R. (2004). *Summarization in any subject: 50 techniques to improve student learning.* Alexandria, VA: Association for Supervision and Curriculum Development.

Yinger, R. J. (1987). Learning the language of practice. *Curriculum Inquiry, 17,* 293–318.

Index

Academic controversy model, 269–272
Accountability, 14, 15, 39, 60, 258–259, 261–271, 274, 277–278
Achievement
    conceptual networks and, 16
    cooperative learning and, 262
    direct instruction model and, 65, 77–78
    feedback and, 72
    inquiry approach to learning and, 126
    instructional planning and, 30, 39, 338
    integrative model and, 241
    jigsaw model and, 266–267, 308–309
    as part of teacher knowledge of students, 330, 336
    Socratic seminar model and, 204
    student teams-achievement model and, 272–273, 278
    synectics model and, 166
    teacher expectations and, 7, 334
    thinking skills improvement and, 4
Active processing, 332
Advance organizers
    purpose of, 35, 69–70, 81, 302, 305
    selecting, 69
    Strategy Alert describing, 67
Alignment, 33
    assessment, 22, 38–39, 41, 75–76, 193, 327
    instructional, 22, 38–39, 41, 50–52, 193
Analogies, 11–12, 148–149, 279
    in integrative model, 242
    metaphorical, 60, 153
    organizer for, 165
    in synectics model, 152–155, 157–169
Analysis
    in cause-and-effect model, 181–182
    in concept attainment, 97
    content, 32, 48, 56, 207, 301
    in integrative model, 245
    in Socratic seminar model, 196
    in synectics model, 153
    in various instructional models, 60
    in vocabulary development model, 222
"Analyzing" questions, 193, 195
Anderson, L. W., 23–24, 38, 338
"Applying" questions, 193–194
Aronson, E., 265–266
Assessment, 1–2, 12, 35, 52, 80
    aligned, 75
    in cause-and-effect model, 181–182, 184, 321
    in concept attainment model, 95, 97, 99, 117
    in concept development lesson, 118, 320
    in cooperative learning models, 274–275
    diagnostic, 13, 66, 79, 339
    formative. *See* Formative assessment
    in graffiti model, 263–264, 277
    in guided practice and, 75
    informal, 11, 290–293, 296, 306–308
    inquiry and, 142–143
    in integrative model, 249–250, 252, 254
    in jigsaw model, 266, 276
    in problem-based learning, 138, 142
    self-assessment, 331
    in Socratic seminar model, 192, 195, 202–203, 205, 207–208
    summative. *See* Summative assessment
    in synectics model, 149, 163–164, 166–167
    in vocabulary acquisition model, 217, 231–232
    with WebQuests, 137
"Assumption" questions, 201
Austin, G. A., 86, 106, 108, 127
Ausubel, D., 27, 29, 67
Automaticity, 7, 73–74, 75, 81

Backward design, 283, 296–297, 310–311, 324
    defined, 39, 52
    procedure, 53
Berliner, D. C., 326
Bias, 19, 304–306
Black, P., 53
Bloom, B. S., 47, 193, 195
Bloom's taxonomy, 47
    revised, 193, 195, 208
Blosser, P. E., 261
Boston, C., 53
Brain
    development, 4–5
    emotions and, 154
    "fight or flight" reaction, 5
    individual differences in, 6
    in integrative model, 241
    learning and, 4
    organization and reorganization, 7
    in vocabulary development model, 213–214, 222–223

Brainstorming
  in academic controversy model, 270
  background knowledge and, 11
  in concept development model, 111, 115–117
  and cooperative learning, 279
  in direct instruction model, 81
  in graffiti model, 263
  haiku and, 80–81
  in high school instruction, 322
  and inquiry chart, 140
  KWL strategy and, 28
  in middle school instruction, 300
  procedural knowledge and, 26
  Strategy Alert describing, 111
  in synectics model, 161
Bruner, J. S., 86, 106, 108, 127

Caine, G., 5
Caine, R. N., 5
Case studies
  high school, 311–324
  kindergarten, 283–296
  middle school, 297–310
Cause-and-effect model, 170–176
  basis for, 173–174, 319
  benefits of, 182, 279
  compared to other models, 186
  concept development activity and, 320
  defined, 185
  described, 60
  differentiation opportunities in, 181
  evaluating learning in, 180, 321
  lesson plans, examples of
    elementary, 170–172, 177, 183–184
    middle/secondary, 172–173, 184–185
  steps in, 175–176
Choice, as learner need, 9–10
Chunking
  English language learners and, 8
  in instructional planning, 29, 32
Clarity
  of instructional objectives, 39
  as learner need, 8, 9, 12, 262
  punctuation and, 20
  of standards, 49
  of tasks, 142
Climate control, in the classroom, 329
Clustering, 11, 197
Cognitive behavior, 48–49
Cognitive learning theory, direct instruction model and, 65
Cognitive skills
  Bloom's taxonomy and, 47
  as foundation of classroom instruction, 47
  and KUD objectives, 41
  as product of interaction of an individual and stimulation, 108
Competition
  in concept attainment model, 96
  in contrast to cooperation, 126
Computer-aided design (CAD), 303
Concept attainment model, 83–104
  basis for, 86
  benefits of, 97
  and concept hierarchy, 86
  described, 59–60, 87–88, 100
  differentiation opportunities in, 96
  evaluating learning in, 95–96
  lesson plans, examples of
    elementary, 83–84, 97–98
    middle/secondary, 84–86, 99–100
  purpose of, 89, 95
  steps in, 88, 92, 100–101
  variations on, 93
Concept development model, 102–120
  basis for, 106–107
  benefits of, 116–117
  building blocks of patterns and, 109
  conceptual thinking and, 108
  constructivist theory of learning and, 107
  described, 60, 110
  differentiation opportunities in, 115–116
  evaluating learning in, 115
  facts, concepts, and generalizations and, 25
  lesson plans, examples of
    elementary, 102–104, 117–118
    secondary, 104–106, 118–119, 305–306, 319–320
  purposes of, 115
  steps in, 110–115, 119
Concepts
  abstract, 86, 87, 108, 116, 288
  concrete, 86, 96, 108, 288
Conceptual knowledge, 24
  as a basic element of a discipline, 43
  as basis for instruction, 25
  in cause-and-effect model, 174
  chunking instruction and, 32
  in concept attainment model, 96
  defined, 5, 7
  relationship to factual knowledge, 32–33
Congruence
  defined as alignment, 50, 52
  of objectives, assessment, and instruction, 47
  of problems in school and out, 126
Content, organization of, 18
  as basis of lessons and units, 21–22, 31, 33–34, 35, 40, 44

categories of knowledge and, 23, 27
chunking and, 29
clarity and, 12
core concept words and, 222, 225, 227
as goal of models of instruction, 9, 21, 35, 241
in a high school class, 301
in a kindergarten class, 288
learner needs and, 68
in a middle school class, 301
resources for, 19–20
scope of instruction and, 30, 32, 34
students will know objectives and, 40, 44–45
success with direct instruction model and, 74
summative assessments and, 54
thinking skills and, 108
and *understand* objectives, 40, 44–45
and WebQuests, 133
Cooperative learning models, 256–279
academic controversy model, 269–272
basis for, 258–261
benefits of, 275–276
defined, 61, 278
differentiation opportunities in, 275
evaluating learning in, 274–275
graffiti model, 263–265
jigsaw model, 265–269
lesson plans, examples of
elementary, 256–257, 276–277
middle/secondary, 257–258, 277–278, 307–308
planning and implementation, 262–263
student teams-achievement division (STAD) model, 272–274
template for, 261
Core disciplinary tasks, 48
"Creating" questions, 193, 195
Creative writing, and synectics model of instruction, 148
Creativity, in synectics model of instruction, 152–153, 166
Cubing, Strategy Alert describing, 251
Curriculum
backward design and, 39
defined, 19–20, 50
educational standards and, 49, 51, 196
instructional objectives and, 52
problem-based inquiry model and, 141, 144
vocabulary and, 215–217, 228, 233

Data gathering, in Suchman inquiry model, 130–131
Debates
vs. dialogues in Socratic seminars, 192
in regard to standards, 19
Deductive instruction, 10, 35, 58, 68
in direct instruction model, 78
Demonstrations, 68, 70

Diagnostic assessment, 13, 66, 79, 217, 339
Dialogues vs. debates in Socratic seminars, 192
Differentiation of instruction
in cause-and-effect model, 181
in concept development model, 116
in cooperative learning models, 275
data collection in problem-centered inquiry models and, 143–144
in integrative model, 251
as means of accommodating individual needs of students, 77, 96
in synectics model, 166
Direct analogies, in synectics model, 155, 158–161, 163–164, 168
Direct instruction model, 62–82
basis for, 65
benefits of, 78–80
cognitive learning theory and, 65
differentiation opportunities in, 77–78
defined, 59, 81, 279
demonstrations and, 70
evaluating learning in, 75–76
feedback, 72
in high school, 316, 318
in kindergarten, 290–291
lecture presentations, 69
flexible grouping, 77
steps in, 69
varying questions, 77
lesson plans, examples of
elementary, 62–63, 78–80
middle/secondary, 63–65, 80–81, 306–307
in middle school, 303–304, 306
periodic review and, 74
practice and, 70
guided, 70–72
independent, 73
questioning and, 71
scaffolding, Strategy Alert describing, 73
in the STAD model, 273, 278
steps in, 65–75
teacher modeling and, 65
vocabulary instruction and, 228
Disabilities, 8, 53
Discovery, in problem-centered inquiry models, 127, 143
Discrepant events, 128
Discussions
in cause-and-effect model, 174, 180–181, 319
in cooperative learning models, 276
in diagnostic evaluation, 66, 321
in jigsaw model, 308–309
in Socratic seminar model, 60, 187, 204, 208
based on teacher questions, 193
instructional value of, 190–191, 199

350 Index

Discussions *(continued)*
   in synectics model, 154
   in vocabulary acquisition model, 221
Displays, classroom, 330
   in direct instruction model, 72
   in integrative model, 242–243
Duckworth, E., 331

Education, purpose of, 20
Eggen, P. D., 241–243, 245
Elder, L., 200–201
Engagement, in learning, 332, 338–339
   as argument in favor of Socratic seminar model, 204
   as a benefit of cause-and-effect model, 182, 185
   KWL strategy and, 28
   as means of classroom management, 330
   as a need of learners, 9, 11–12, 40
Erickson, L. H., 44
Errors
   to be avoided in independent practice, 72–75, 81
   as basis of instruction, 33, 338
   related to feedback, 335
   in textbooks, 19
   in vocabulary acquisition model, 218
Essential attributes, of concepts, 60, 86–87, 89, 92–95, 97, 99–101
"Evaluating" questions, 193, 195
Evaluation. *See* Assessment
Expectations
   in cause-and-effect model, 175
   content standards and, 20–21
   in cooperative learning models, 257
   by the learner, 9
   in Socratic seminar model, 203, 206–207
   by the teacher, 7, 10, 328, 331, 333–334, 339, 342

Face-to-face interactions, in cooperative learning groups, 278
Facts
   in accumulated knowledge and wisdom, 340
   big ideas and, 45
   chunking for instructional planning and, 29, 40, 44
   in concept attainment model, 87
   conceptual knowledge and, 5, 7, 32, 43, 305
   in cooperative learning models, 260, 270–271
   in deductive teaching, 35, 183
   defined, 23, 87
   in direct instruction model, 71
   examples of, 25, 33
   as foundation for higher-level thinking, 24
   high-stakes tests and, 16
   in integrative model, 241, 243, 254
   standards of learning and, 21, 256
   in textbooks, 19

   "understand" instructional objectives and, 44–45
   in vocabulary acquisition model, 227, 233
Fantasy analogies, in synectics model, 162
Faughnan, K., 276
Feedback
   in cause-and-effect model, 174
   comparison/contrast and, 340
   in cooperative learning models, 260, 262–263, 274
   in direct instruction model, 65, 68, 70, 78, 81
      in guided practice, 72, 75, 79
      in independent practice, 72, 75
      in periodic review, 74, 75
   effective lessons and, 34, 335
   engaged learning and, 332
   formative assessments and, 53–54
   in graffiti model, 257
   instructional objectives and, 52
   in jigsaw model, 303
   in management of human relations, 331
   meaningful engagement and, 12
   metacognition and, 5
   in problem-centered inquiry models, 127, 137
   Pygmalion effect and, 333
   scaffolding and, 42
   on skills practice, 7, 13
   in Socratic seminar model, 192, 204
   standards measurement and, 16
   summative assessments and, 54
   using rubrics, 76, 163
Flow charts
   example, 177
   Strategy Alert describing, 176
Focus
   instructional objectives and, 38, 41, 336
   instructional planning and, 30–32, 58, 323, 327
Formative assessment, 7, 13, 34, 53–54, 66, 75, 79, 82, 93, 296, 310, 339
Fraction bars, 236
Fulghum, R., 6

Gardner, H., 11
Generalizations
   basis of, in facts, 23, 111
   in cause-and-effect model, 60, 173–174, 176, 179–182, 185–186
   about classroom and behavior management, 331
   in concept attainment model, 88, 104
   in concept development model, 110–115, 119
   concepts and, 24, 110
   in cooperative learning models, 264–265, 280
   as a critical thinking skill, 174
   defined, 17, 24, 47, 87, 174
   examples of, in contrast to facts and concepts, 25, 33, 114, 240

in graffiti model, 265, 278
in high school class, 320
in integrative model, 61, 237, 241–243, 246–247, 249, 251, 254–255
in problem-centered inquiry models, 138
related to teaching, 326
in Socratic seminar model, 200
in vocabulary development model, 227
Generating and testing hypotheses
in cause-and-effect model, 60
in concept attainment model, 83–85, 88, 90–93, 97
in elementary lesson, 98
in middle/secondary grades lesson, 100–101
in high school classroom, 319
in integrative model, 241, 246
in problem-centered inquiry model, 140, 143
Strategy Alert describing, 91
Gifted students, 6, 61
Gifted teachers, 325–326
Gladwell, M., 325
Global objective of education, 27
Goals, educational, 17, 56
Good, T. L., 333
Goodnow, J. J., 86, 106, 108, 127
Graffiti model, 263–265, 278
Graphic organizers
as advance organizers, 67
in cause-and-effect model, 180–183, 185
in concept attainment model, 96
flow charts, 176
in jigsaw model, 266, 268, 270
Strategy Alert describing, 165
as summarizing technique, 247
in synectics model, 164–165
in vocabulary acquisition model, 222–223, 232
Grigorenko, E. L., 181
Grouping students
in cause-and-effect model, 179, 182, 185
classroom arrangement and, 329
in concept attainment model, 94–95, 97
in concept development model, 103, 112, 116, 118
in cooperative learning models, 256–257, 259–269, 273–278
in direct instruction model, 64, 77
in high school, 317, 319–322
in integrative model, 242, 247, 250–251
in kindergarten, 287
in middle school, 307
in problem-centered inquiry models, 123, 126, 130, 136–137, 141, 143
in synectics model, 153
in vocabulary acquisition model, 209, 232
Guided practice, 13
in direct instruction model, 62–63, 71–77, 79–80

in elementary grades lesson, 79–80
in middle school, 307

Heuristics of discovery, 127
High school case study, 311–324
epilogue, 321–323
lessons, 318–321
plan, 313–318
High-stakes tests, 16, 21
Hoffman, J., 139
Homework, 66, 73–75
in synectics model, 163
Human relations management, 330–331

I-Chart (inquiry chart), in problem-centered inquiry models, 139–141, 142
Identifying similarities and differences
in cause-and-effect model, 174
in concept attainment model, 90, 92, 95, 97
in concept development model, 60
in integrative model, 241, 245–246, 249, 253–254
Strategy Alert describing, 139
in synectics model, 153
Independent practice
in direct instruction model, 72–76, 78–82, 279
in middle school, 307
Individual accountability, in cooperative learning groups, 259, 261–266, 271, 274, 278
Inductive instruction, 10, 35, 58, 68
in cause-and-effect model, 174
in concept attainment model, 88
in concept development model, 106
in direct instruction model, 78
in integrative model, 241
Instructional alignment, 39, 50
defined, 52
Revised Taxonomy of Educational Objectives and, 193
Instructional design
backward, 16
course design and, 21
defined, 58
direct instruction model and, 82
Instructional models
critical thinking skills and, 251
factual knowledge and, 23
instructional alignment and, 75
metacognitive knowledge and, 27
purposes of, 17, 57–58, 68, 77, 322
related to how people learn, 47, 280
standards and objectives and, 21, 342
Instructional objectives
assessing, 52–54
defined, 38
development of, with students, 338

352 Index

Instructional objectives *(continued)*
   forms of, 40
   KUD format and, 42–51
   purpose of, 38–41, 48, 52
Instructional procedures, for lesson plans, 35
Integrative model, 61, 235–255
   basis for, 241–242
   benefits of, 251–252
   differentiation opportunities in, 250–251
   evaluating learning in, 249–250
   lesson plans, examples of
      elementary, 235–237, 252–253
      middle/secondary, 237–240, 253–254
   steps in, 242–249
Intellectual potency, in problem-centered inquiry models, 127
Intelligence
   creative and practical, 181–182
   definitions, 10–11
   effects of learning on, 4
   intellectual preferences, 275
Interdisciplinary relationships, 153
Iowa Tests of Basis Skills (ITBS), vocabulary improvement and, 220–221

Jacobson, L., 333
Janusian thinking, 154
Jigsaw model, 265–269, 303
Johnson, D. W., 269
Johnson, R. T., 269
Judgments
   based on vocabulary, 225
   as cognitive behavior, 49
   related to assessments, 52
   student, 112

Kauchak, D. P., 241–243, 245
Kindergarten
   case study, 283–296
   direct instruction lesson on rhymes, 62–63
   unit on lines, 287–296
Knowledge
   advance organizers and 67
   aligned instruction and, 1, 13, 50
   assessment of, 7, 11
   background or prior, 58, 107, 139, 225
   backward design and, 53
   big ideas and, 44
   categories of, 23–27
   clarity and, 12
   in concept development model, 108, 116, 119
   in cooperative learning models, 259
   in direct instruction model, 65, 73, 75
   diversity and, 9
   integrative model and, 241, 243
   needed by students, 340–341
   new learning and, 11
   organization of the brain and, 4
   pedagogical, 68, 326–327, 336
   procedural and metacognitive, 43
   in Socratic seminar model, 190–192
   in synectics model, 153–154, 168
   transfer of, 5, 53
   in vocabulary development model, 216–218, 223, 226
Kohn, A., 6
Krathwohl, D., 23–24, 48
KUD format
   description of, 43
   for instructional objectives, 41, 42–47
KWL, Strategy Alert describing, 28

Lasley, T. J., 331
Law of meaningful engagement, 332
Learners
   access to information and opportunity to practice, 339
   emotional connections to knowledge, 328
   needs of, 9–13
   Pygmalion effect, 332–334
   teachers as, 335–337
Learning
   appropriate challenge and, 5, 10–11
   conceptual thinking, 108
   cooperative, 61. *See also* Cooperative learning models
   excitement of, 125
   how learning happens, 4–8
   metacognitive knowledge and, 27
   new, based on prior learning, 27–28, 32
   physical environment and, 328–329
   reflective, 12
   styles, 10, 116
   teachers as models of good learning, 335–336
   transfer of new, 5, 340
Learning environment, positive, 325–341
   celebration of student differences, 334–335
   developing instructional objectives with student input, 338
   human relations management and, 330–331
   importance of professional knowledge and, 336–337
   information access in, 339–340
   knowledge of how to learn and, 340–341
   physical aspects, 328–329
   practice opportunities in, 339–340
   quality feedback and, 335
   realization of more than one right answer, 335
   teachers' leadership of the classroom and, 327
Lecture presentations, in direct instruction model, 69
Lesson plans
   developing, 33–34, 35

elements in, 34–35
Library research, in problem-centered inquiry models, 143
Link, Strategy Alert describing, 221
Literature
　interpretation, and point of view, 303–305
　objections to, 248

Macbeth study unit
　goals for, 314–316
　instructional plan, 314–318
　lessons, 318–323
　objectives for, 315–316
Main points, identifying, in lecture presentations, 69
Making the familiar strange, 153, 154–158
Making the strange familiar, 153, 158–160
Marzano, R. J., 164, 246
Mastery learning, 39
Mathematics
　in problem-centered inquiry models, 134
　skills for pattern recognition, 21–22
McTighe, J., 30, 32, 44–45, 47
Meanings of words
　discussing, in vocabulary acquisition model, 221
　exploring patterns of, 220–224
　hypothesized, 218–220
Memory
　chunking and, 28
　cooperative learning and, 259
　facilitation of
　　by examples, 69
　　by process of discovery, 127
　　by repetition and elaboration, 48
　　by showing, 70
　factual knowledge and, 16
　functions, 5
　long-term, 49, 242, 259
　of word meanings, 214
　working, 5
Meno, as basis of Socratic seminar model, 190
Metacognition
　defined, 5, 12
　in Socratic seminars, 192, 200
　strategies, 6
　student understanding and, 332
Metacognitive knowledge, 26–27
Metaphors
　in concept attainment model, 99
　defined, 164
　in problem-centered inquiry models, Strategy Alert describing, 139
　in synectics model, 153–155, 164, 166, 168
Middle school case study, 297–310
　background, 297–302
　epilogue, 308

perspective, an interdisciplinary unit
　advance organizer for, 305
　lessons, 305–308
　plan for, 303–304
Misconceptions
　concept development and, 107–108, 116
　confronting, 11
　formative assessments and, 53
　related to scope of instruction, 30
　teaching standards and, 36
Misspellings, or invented spellings, 218–220
Models of teaching approach, reasons for, 58
Morphemes, defined, 227–228
Morphology, defined, 227
Multiple-choice questions, 250

A Nation at Risk (National Commission on Excellence in Education), 14
Newspaper articles, for stimulating discussion, 174
No Child Left Behind Act (NCLB), 13
Novice vs. expert teachers, 325–327

Objectives
　educational, 20
　instructional. *See* Instructional objectives
Opportunity
　to connect new to known, 11
　to learn, 10, 50, 53, 78
Organization, of content, 18–35

Paper-and-pencil tasks, 115, 142
Paragraphs, as assessment, 95, 184
Participation
　criteria, 198
　evaluating, 95, 200–202
　monitoring, 71, 204, 268
Patterns
　of development, 8
　in integrative model, 242, 245
　of meaning, 220–223, 225, 231, 233
　recognition, 22, 109–110
　in synectics model, 154, 164
Paul, R., 193, 196, 200–201
Perception, lesson examples, 306–307, 307–308
Performance assessment, 182
Perkins, D. N., 340
Personal analogies, in synectics model, 155–156, 162, 164
Perspective
　in cooperative learning models, 271
　in interdisciplinary units, 298–302, 303–304, 304–306, 307–308
　in Socratic seminar model, 187, 191–193
Planning, instructional, 29–35, 39
　case studies

Planning, instructional *(continued)*
  high school, 311–323
  kindergarten, 282–295
  middle school, 297–309
 steps in, 1–2
Posttest, in vocabulary acquisition model, 224–225
Practice
 guided, 63, 71–73, 75–80
 independent, 72–76, 80, 81, 307
Predictions, 33, 35, 202
Prefixes, 223, 227, 228–229, 230
Presentation
 attributes, 68
 demonstration, 70
 in direct instruction model, 78, 81
 lecture, 69
 in STAD model, 272–273
Problem-based inquiry model, 137–142
Problem-based learning
 in problem-based inquiry model, 137–142
 steps in, 138–142
 theory of, 127
Problem-centered inquiry models, 60, 121–147
 basis for, 125–128
 benefits of, 143–144
 differentiation opportunities in, 143
 evaluating learning in, 142–143
 lesson plans, examples of
  elementary, 121–122, 144–145
  middle/secondary, 122–125, 145–146
 problem-based inquiry model, 137–142
 Suchman inquiry model, 128–132
 WebQuest model of inquiry, 133–137
Problems
 in school vs. real life, 126–127
 in Socratic seminars, 192
 solving, 126. *See also* Solutions
 in synectics model, 152–154
Problem statements, for synectics excursion process, 161
Procedural knowledge, 25–26, 43
Professional development of teachers, characteristics of, 337
Pygmalion effect, 332–334

Questions
 in cause-and-effect model, 174–185
 cognitive levels of, 193
 in cooperative learning model, 264–265, 268
 clustering, 196–197
 decisions about instructional design and, 30, 31, 35, 38
 for diagnosis of student achievement, 74
 for evaluating participation in discussion, 200
 examples of, in integrative model, 245–246, 250, 252, 253–254
 in guided practice, 71

multiple-choice best practice guidelines, 250
 in problem-centered inquiry models, 121–125, 143
 quality of, 125–126
 related to standards, 15
 in Socratic seminar model, 187–193, 196–200
 in Suchman model, 129–132
 in Taba's Concept Development Sequence, 107
 taxonomy of Socratic, 201
 types of, 194–195
 varying, 77–78, 204, 250, 333

Rationale/standards, for lesson plan, 34
Reading comprehension, vocabulary knowledge and, 226
Reciprocal teaching, Strategy Alert describing, 202
Regrouping, in concept development model, 113, 114, 116
Reinforcement, 65, 93
Relationships
 in academic controversy model, 269
 in cause-and-effect model, 241, 242
 in concept development model, 110, 112–114
 in concept hierarchy, 88, 92, 96
 in integrative model, 241, 242
 in synectics model, 148, 153, 158, 164
Relaxed alertness, 5–6, 332
"Remembering" questions, 193, 194
Repetition, to reinforce main point of lecture, 69
Research
 action, 337
 in Suchman inquiry model, 128–131
 in WebQuest model of inquiry, 133–137
Researchers
 effective schools, 339
 teachers as, 337
Responses, to guided practice questions, 71
Responsive teaching, 142, 275
Review
 of content, in cause-and-effect model, 185
 of discussion, in Socratic seminar model, 199–200
 periodic, in direct instruction model, 74
 of previously learned material, in direct instruction model, 66
Revised taxonomy
 of cognitive behaviors (Anderson & Krathwohl), 49, 77
 of educational objectives (Bloom), 193, 195
Rewards
 extrinsic vs. intrinsic, 127
 punished by (Kohn), 6
Roots, 227, 229
Rosenshine, B., 65–66, 71
Rosenthal, R., 333
Rubrics, 76, 200, 203, 246

Safety, 9
Salomon, G., 340
Scaffolding
  Strategy Alert describing, 73
  teacher behaviors, 42
Schema theory, 107, 241–242, 251
Search engines, 134
Seating arrangements, for classrooms, 329
Sensory memory, 5
Sequence
  instructional decisions and, 31–32, 90–91
  of steps in vocabulary acquisition model, 233
  Taba's concept development, 107
Short-answer questions, 95
Similarities and differences
  analogy or metaphor and, 153, 165
  in concept attainment model, 87, 97
  in cubing, 251
  explaining, in integrative model, 245–246, 249
  identifying, 60, 92, 139, 241–242
  in vocabulary acquisition model, 222
Social learning theory, in direct instruction model, 65
Social skills, in cooperative learning model, 260, 262
Society, needs of, 13
Socratic dialectic, 191
Socratic seminar model
  basis for, 190–192
  benefits of, 204
  differentiation opportunities in, 204
  evaluating learning in, 203–204
  lesson plans, examples of
    elementary, 187–188, 205–206
    middle/secondary, 189–190, 206–208
  questioning in, 193
    examples of, 194–196
    types of questions, 193–195, 201
  steps in, 196–200
  versions of, 191–193
Solutions
  to everyday problems, 126
  formulating, 141
  resources for, 140
Spelling
  instructional shortcomings, 212–214
  invented, 218
  meaning connection and, 212–214
Standards
  determination of, 19
  important questions regarding, 15
  instructional design and, 16, 21–23, 27, 49–50, 53, 258
  learning, 13–14
  objectives and, 20
  positive effects of, 14
  questions and, 15
Sternberg, J. R., 11, 126–128, 181
Strategies
  associated with school achievement, 241
  for vocabulary acquisition, 229
Strategy Alerts
  advance organizers, 67
  brainstorming, 111
  cubing, 251
  flow charts, 176
  generating and testing hypotheses, 91
  graphic organizers, 165
  identifying similarities and differences, 139
  KWL, 28
  Link, 221
  reciprocal teaching, 202
  scaffolding, 73
  summarizing, 247
  think–pair–share, 220
Stretching exercises, 164
Student teams-achievement division (STAD), 272–274
Subject areas
  standards for, 15, 21
  and vocabulary, 228
Suchman inquiry model, 128–132
Suffixes, 223, 227, 228–229, 230
Summarizing
  in concept development model, 113, 116
  in Socratic seminar model, 192
  Strategy Alert describing, 247
Summative assessment, 13, 28, 34, 54, 56, 66, 243
Symbolic analogies, 162
Synectics excursion, 160–163
Synectics model, 148–168
  basis for, 152–154
  benefits of, 166
  differentiation opportunities in, 164
  evaluating learning in, 163–164
  excursion, 160–163
  lesson plans, examples of
    elementary, 148–149, 166–167
    middle/secondary, 149–152, 167–168, 322–323
  steps
    in making the familiar strange, 154–158
    in making the strange familiar, 158–160
    in the synectics excursion, 160–163
Synonyms, 223
Synthesizing, in concept development model, 113–114

Taba, Hilda
  concept development model, 60, 106, 107, 111
  integrative model, 241
A Taxonomy for Learning, Teaching, and Assessing (Anderson & Krathwohl), 48

356   Index

Taxonomy of Educational Objectives, revised (Bloom), 47, 193, 195
Taxonomy of Socratic Questions, (Paul), 193, 196, 201
Teachers
  and accountability, 13–16, 31
  characteristics, 282, 335–337
  and classroom management, 328
  and curricular decisions, 19–23, 29–30, 32, 39–40
  discrimination in treatment of high and low achievers, 333–334
  effective practice and, 332–335, 338–341
  expert vs. novice, 325–327
  physical environment and, 328–330
  Pygmalion effect and, 332–333
  students' prior knowledge and, 28–29, 110–111, 334
  teaching and, 68
Teaching, as a conversation, 216
Testing hypotheses, 91, 246
Tests
  instructional alignment and, 50
  types of thinking demanded, 15–16
Text selection, in Socratic seminar model, 196
Theory development and verification, in Suchman model, 130–131
Theory explanation and rules, in Suchman model, 131
Thinking
  in academic controversy model, 269
  in cause-and-effect model, 174
  conceptual, 24, 106
  in cooperative learning model, 259
  creative, in synectics model, 152–153
  critical, I-Chart for, 139–140
  in integrative model, 241, 250
  Janusian, 154
  metacognitive, 5, 12, 95
  similarities and differences and, 92
  in Socratic seminar model, 196–201
  types demanded on tests, 15–16
  in vocabulary acquisition model, 214–216
Think–pair–share strategy, 116
  Strategy Alert describing, 220
Transfer
  assessing, 182
  of information/learning/knowledge/skills, 5, 67

Understanding
  defined, 32–33
  as student cognitive process, 48–49
"Understanding" questions, 193
U.S. Constitution, 19

Venn diagrams, defined, 139
Viewpoint
  in academic controversy model, 269
  concept of perspective and, 302, 305
  questions, 201
  in Socratic seminar model, 191, 198
  in synectics model, 162–163
Vocabulary acquisition model, 60–61, 209–234
  basis for, 212–217
  benefits of, 231
  differentiation opportunities in, 226–230
  evaluating learning in, 226
  lesson plans, examples of
    elementary, 209–211, 231–232
    middle/secondary, 211–212, 232
  steps in, 212–217
Vocabulary journal, 222
Vygotsky, Lev, 108

Wait time, for answers to questions, 71, 199
WebQuest model of inquiry, 133–137
  basis for, 133
  benefits of, 133
  defined, 133
  evaluating learning in, 136, 142
  vs. standard thematic units, 133
  steps in, 133–137
  template for, 135–136
Weinstein, R. S., 333
Wells, G., 331
Wiggins, G., 30, 32, 44–45, 47
Willingham, D. T., 16
Wisdom of practice, 325–342
Wolk, S., 330
Words, displaying, 229

Yinger, R. J., 340
Young adult literature, objections to, 248–249